# Web Programming
# Step by Step

Marty Stepp        Jessica Miller        Victoria Kirst

University of Washington
authors@webstepbook.com

Janxiu Cai

independently self-published via Lulu.com

http://www.webstepbook.com/

Published independently through Lulu, Inc.
Cover Design: Victoria Kirst
Cover Photography: Bruno Sersocima
Chapter Artwork: Sylvia Tashev
Text and Layout Design: Victoria Kirst, Marty Stepp
Figures and Illustrations: Victoria Kirst
Copy Editing and Proofreading: Sylvia Tashev
Indexing: Marty Stepp
System Administrator and Server Resources Manager: Morgan Doocy

Access supplemental materials, errata, and other resources from our World Wide Web site:

- http://www.webstepbook.com/

The example programs and applications presented in this textbook have been included for their instructional value. They have been tested but are not offered nor guaranteed for any specific purpose other than educational value. The authors do not offer any warranty or representation for the correctness or usage of these examples, nor does it accept any liabilities with respect to these programs or applications.

ISBN 978-0-578-01239-1

# Dedications

To my parents, Larry and Vicki Stepp. The last book I dedicated to you didn't sell, so let's try this again. When you're little, you don't realize what a profound effect your parents have on you. They are your model for how to behave, how to think, how to act. They shape your view of the world. It's taken me many years to realize how fortunate I was growing up. Blindly following in your footsteps, I appear to have stumbled into a modestly successful life. Thank you for setting such a good example that even I couldn't screw it up too badly. I love you always.
-- Marty

To my family and friends for allowing me to borrow time from nurturing our relationships to work on this book. Thanks especially to Martin giving up your free time to work on this project; it is always a pleasure and great learning experience to work with you.
-- Jessica

Thanks to my family for being a constant source of kindness and support, thanks to my friends for putting up with my social negligence, and thanks to Marty and Jessica for letting me join them in making this book! It has been a wonderful, memorable experience.
-- Victoria

# Preface

Alongside the increasing importance of the web has come high demand for web-savvy developers. Computer science programs have been slow to react to this, but many are now offering web programming courses. In our own experience, we find that learning web programming is full of its own unique pitfalls. Students need a textbook that not only introduces the languages used on the web but also clarifies difficult concepts unique to web programming, techniques for design and debugging, and solving common errors.

This book comes into existence because of an introductory web programming course that was added to the University of Washington's computer science program a few years ago. We tried teaching this course using some of the existing web programming books, but we felt that they were inadequate. Despite the cutting-edge nature of the web, many existing web programming textbooks seem like they were written many years ago. Some show example programs that only work properly in Microsoft's Internet Explorer browser on Windows. We also felt that other web textbooks were too language-driven. Each chapter covers a web language (such as HTML or JavaScript) in its entirety, when it is neither practical nor advisable to try to do so. Lastly, most web books choose to cover too many server-side programming languages, and often provide incomplete coverage of each one. We were put off by this focus on breadth over depth.

This textbook focuses on the university classroom setting and on being the best textbook for college students. We have tried to maintain a pace, topic order, and writing style directed at students. We focus on depth and clear coverage of each topic instead of the brisk style in many web books. We use a problem-solving (rather than language-driven) approach, in which each chapter is designed to prepare students for a new programming assignment rather than just explaining details of syntax of web languages like HTML and JavaScript. We consider it extremely important to discuss design, debugging techniques, common errors that can occur during web programming, how to spot them, and how to fix them. We have also made it a point of emphasis to include well-conceived pedagogic resources such as self-check problems, sample exercises and assignments, and end-of-chapter case studies. This is also a heavily class-tested textbook with a large repository of supporting materials such as homework assignments, exams, lecture slides, web tutorials and links.

We also try to embrace the modern "Web 2.0" spirit that seems lacking in other web texts. This includes lengthy coverage of Ajax and dynamic web pages throughout several chapters; strict adherence to the latest W3C web standards, to ensure pages that work on all browsers and devices; and examples that encompass real web applications in a modern style. We present multi-tier web architectures and the separation of presentation, logic, and data. We also focus on W3C web standards, so that all code and pages shown will display properly in all web browsers.

The book is intended for university-level students who have completed a CS1 course in a modern object-oriented language such as Java. Apart from a basic knowledge of computer programming, the book will be written for a broad range of students, computer science majors and non-majors alike, and will not assume lengthy programming experience beyond basic fundamentals (loops, if/else, types, procedures, arrays, objects). The book could be used for the web development course like the University of Washington's, where less than half of the students go on to major in Computer Science or Computer Engineering, or in a more advanced majors-only course that explores web programming in greater detail.

## About the Authors

- Marty Stepp is a computer science instructor at the University of Washington and has created UW's new web programming course. Marty has co-authored introductory programming textbooks in C# (*Computing Fundamentals with C#*) and Java (*Building Java Programs*). Previously Marty worked as a web developer at Microsoft and received his master's degree in Computer Science at the University of Arizona.

- Jessica Miller is currently a software developer in Dublin, Ireland working for a leading Irish e-commerce company. Previously, she has developed web applications for companies such as Microsoft Research and Google. As a graduate student, she co-authored academic papers on a variety of topics including value-sensitive design, temporal databases, search, and algorithms. Jessica received her BS in Computer Science and BA in Spanish from University of Arizona and her MS in Computer Science from University of Washington.

- Victoria Kirst is a graduate student studying Computer Science at the University of Washington. She has been a TA for UW's introductory courses, including Marty's web programming course, and has written a variety of web applications for these courses. Victoria has also developed software for Cisco Systems and received her BS in Computer Science from the University of Washington.

## Software and Supplemental Resources

To write most of the programs in this textbook, one needs only a text editor and web browser. We do not insist on a particular editor, though the authors are fond of TextPad (Windows) and TextMate (Mac). We generally recommend the Firefox web browser, though any standard-compliant browser will suffice. For some chapters it is helpful to have access to a computer running web server software such as Apache or Microsoft IIS, along with add-ons such as PHP and MySQL.

We have several supplemental resources available on the web, such as additional exercises, answers to self-check problems, lecture slides, suggestions for homework assignments, weekly labs, and exams. These resources can be found on our textbook's web site:

- http://www.webstepbook.com/

## Chapters, Units, and Dependencies

The chapters of this textbook can be thought of as belonging to several "units" of material:

- Unit 1: Basic client-side web pages with HTML and CSS (Chapters 1-4)
- Unit 2: Server-side web programming with PHP (Chapters 5-6)
- Unit 3: Client-side web programming with JavaScript (Chapters 7-9)
- Unit 4: Accessing server-side data with Ajax and SQL (Chapters 10-11)
- Unit 5: Advanced topics (Chapters 12 and above; Appendices)

Chapter 1 consists of background material about the internet and WWW and may be considered optional to instructors. Chapters 2-3 (Basic HTML and CSS) and the first half of Chapter 4 (Page Layout) must be covered essentially in order. Then the reader or instructor can proceed directly to server-side PHP or jump ahead to client-side JavaScript. The JavaScript material uses HTML form control elements, covered at the beginning of Chapter 6. SQL and databases can be covered at any time after server-side programming basics have been introduced.

The following diagram summarizes the dependencies between the chapters:

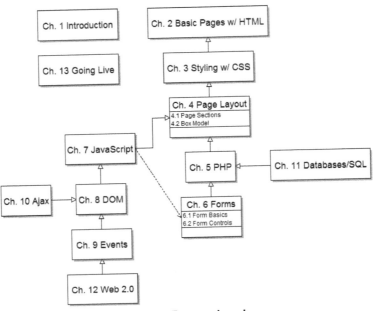

**Chapter Dependencies**

## Acknowledgments

We would like to thank the University of Washington undergraduates who served as teaching assistants for our web programming course over the last two years. Their hard work and input helped us to create our weekly lectures, labs, homework assignments, exams, and other resources. We thank Daniel Davenport, Morgan Doocy, Ian Gienger, Brian Harris, Stefanie Hatcher, Kenneth Kuan, Brian Le, Amit Levy, Hélène Martin, Jeff Prouty, Ryan Tucker, and Kevin Wallace.

Sylvia Tashev, a computer science undergraduate at the University of Washington, drew all of the sketches that adorn the title pages for each chapter. The creative sketches and the scenes depicted in them were all her creations. We thank Sylvia for lending her extraordinary talent to this book.

Several University of Washington undergraduates who had previously taken or TAed our course volunteered their time to create end-of-chapter exercises for this textbook. We thank Jehad Affoneh, Will Beebe, Brad Bicknell, Young Wahn (Solomon) Choe, Jon Connolly, Kelly Dunn, Matthew Fonda, Nathan Gaither, Stefanie Hatcher, Hoon Kwon, Justin Labak, Brian Le, Michael Mathews, Brent Sandona, Soyoung Shin, Khulpatr Sinteppadon, Min Sul, Sylvia Tashev, and Ryan Tucker.

We'd like to thank the students and instructors who have contacted us with errata and suggestions for improvement. We thank Herman Koppelman, Jeffrey Lehman, Benson Limketkai, Albert Lui, Sean McGuire, Kristi Nguyen, Steven Pell, Dale Skrien, Andy Simmons, Greg Stallings, and Sylvia Tashev for their contributions.

Though we ultimately chose to self-publish this textbook, representatives and editors from major publishers were very kind to us in discussing the possibility of publishing this textbook with them. We thank Denise Penrose of Morgan Kaufman, Laura Colantoni of Elsevier, and Matt Goldstein of Addison Wesley for their conversations with us about the web textbook market, the competition, reviews of preliminary content, and offering us lucrative opportunities for partnership.

Marty Stepp would like to thank Michelle Lee Pressman for helping him cope with all of the stress caused by the ambitious undertaking of writing this textbook. Marty would also like to thank Amanda Camp, without whose extensive support he probably would not have survived long enough to have a publishing career in the first place: "Amanda, I owe my last textbook to you; I'll have to settle for acknowledging you in this one! Sorry about the OBOB."

# Table of Contents

# Chapter 1  The Internet and World Wide Web

## Introduction

Before we dive into programming the web, we'll discuss the nature of the internet itself and the web we use today. A basic understanding of how the web works is important when web programming so that you can understand the messages shown to you by a web browser, the errors you receive when programming, and so on.

In this chapter we'll look briefly at the history of the internet, as well as the underlying hardware and software technologies that make it work. We'll talk about how web servers and web browsers communicate, the languages of the web, and common web error message codes.

## 1.1    What is the Internet?

Perhaps we should let Alaska senator Ted Stevens explain the internet. The following is an excerpt from a now-infamous statement he gave before the US Senate on July 28, 2006. Stevens led a committee attempting to regulate the internet (against the idea of network neutrality) and argued that internet service providers should be allowed to charge fees for high-priority access to their networks:

> *Ten movies streaming across that, that Internet, and what happens to your own personal Internet? I just the other day got... an Internet was sent by my staff at 10 o'clock in the morning on Friday, I got it yesterday [Tuesday]. Why? Because it got tangled up with all these things going on the Internet commercially.*
> *[...] They want to deliver vast amounts of information over the Internet. And again, the Internet is not something that you just dump something on. It's not a big truck.* **It's a series of tubes.** *And if you don't understand, those tubes can be filled and if they are filled, when you put your message in, it gets in line and it's going to be delayed by anyone that puts into that tube enormous amounts of material, enormous amounts of material.*

---

**Internet**

A worldwide series of connected computer networks.

---

Perhaps we can improve on Senator Stevens' description. The *Internet* is a worldwide set of computer networks that spans many technologies and uses for personal, commercial, academic, and government use. The internet is used for, among other things, e-mail, chat, audio/video, file transfer, and web pages. The *World Wide Web (WWW)* is the set of web pages and sites that represents a subset of the overall internet. Despite common confusion between the two, the WWW and the internet are not synonyms.

### 1.1.1    History

The internet was not born at any one time but evolved over a series of technological advances. The predecessor of the modern internet was a United States Department of Defense network called ARPANET which was used in the late 1960s and 1970s to send electronic mail and transfer files. There had been large computer networks before ARPANET, but it had some unique features that would prove important in the eventual internet. Examples of such features were:

- sending data between computers in "packet" chunks,
- the ability for network subsets to stand on their own,
- the ability to dynamically add and remove computers,
- open standards, so that anyone could create a new device or program to connect to it,
- and a lack of any centralized control over the network.

A key aspect of a network is that its computers must send and receive data in a standard way to be able to understand each other. Such a standard for information flow between computers is also called a *protocol*. ARPANET continued to grow through the 1970s and began using many of the modern internet technologies and protocols in the mid-1980s. The internet opened to commercial interests in 1988 when MCI and other companies were allowed to send electronic mail through it.

> **protocol**
> A standard format for communications between computers.

The most rapid growth in popularity of the internet came in 1991 when a European scientific group called CERN proposed a new project and set of standards collectively called the World Wide Web. The Web was largely created by English scientist Tim Berners-Lee in 1989.

You can read more about the creation of the internet at the Internet Society's A Brief History of the Internet site, linked in the References section of this chapter.

## 1.1.2    People and Organizations

Who's in charge of the internet? The simple answer is that nobody runs the whole show. This is one of the most appealing features of the internet: The lack of centralized control. However, we do want some level of standardization and consistency across the internet, and several organizational and standardization groups have been formed to aid in this process.

The Internet Engineering Task Force (IETF) creates specifications for internet protocol standards, governing the way information is exchanged on the internet. An IETF standardization document is often called a Request for Comments or *RFC* for short. The Internet Corporation for Assigned Names and Numbers (ICANN) controls web site names. The World Wide Web Consortium (or *W3C*), headed by the same Tim Berners-Lee who created the original Web, provides recommendations for web standards for the various web programming languages and how web pages should look in browsers.

## 1.1.3    Technologies

A key idea behind the internet is that it works in layers. A typical internet application such as a web browser or instant messenger sends data that goes through layers of hardware and software such as the following:

- a physical layer of devices such as Ethernet cables, fiber-optic lines, or modems
- a data link layer allowing those devices to talk directly to each other, such as Ethernet protocol, wireless ("wifi") protocols, or DSL's point-to-point protocol (PPP)
- a network or internet layer represented by the internet protocol (IP)
- a transport layer that adds reliability to the network layer, such as TCP or UDP
- an application layer that implements the specific communication for this kind of program, such as HTTP (web), POP3/IMAP (email), SSH, FTP, etc.

In this section we'll look briefly at the last three of these layers to understand how internet communication occurs.

## Internet Protocol (IP)

The internet protocol, or *IP* for short, is the underlying system of communication for all data sent across the internet. It is a simple protocol for one computer to send packets of data to another.

> **IP address**
>
> A 32-bit number identifying a computer on a network using the IP protocol.

A major aspect of any protocol is the issue of addressing. That is, how do I specify to whom I want to send my message? IP deals with addressing by giving every computer on the internet a unique 32-bit ID number called an *IP address*. To a computer, an IP address is just a large integer, but when written out for people to read, an IP address is often broken into four smaller integers between 0 and 255, such as 145.10.34.3. The 32 bits of the address are divided into 4 groups of 8 bits; 8 bits of binary data can represent $2^8 = 256$ different unique integers, so each of the four parts of an IP address is a number between 0 and 255.

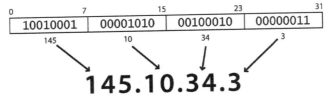

**Figure 1.1 IP address**

Every web server you visit has an IP address, and your own computer has one, too. You can find out your IP address by visiting a web site such as **whatismyip.com**, or by running a program on your computer such as **ipconfig** (Windows) or **ifconfig** (Mac/Linux). Most computers can connect to themselves using the special IP address 127.0.0.1 or by using the name **localhost**.

Two computers communicating with each other via the internet are almost never directly physically connected to each other. Instead, the computers are linked by a long chain of intermediate machines called routers. A *router* is a device that receives IP packets and hands them off to another computer on the network. Routers have several input and output connections and use tables of information to know where to send each packet of IP data by looking at the packet's destination IP address.

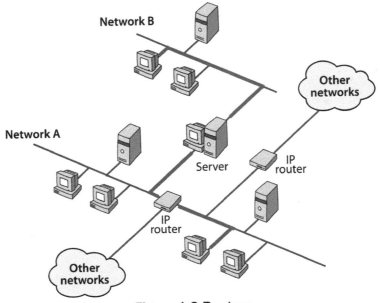

**Figure 1.2 Routers**

IP is a very minimal protocol; addressing and end-to-end routing are essentially all it provides. IP does not provide any functionality to prevent against problems such as:

- **Data loss**: Information might be lost in transit.
- **Corruption**: Information might arrive in a corrupted or altered state.
- **Duplication**: A single message might arrive twice.
- **Sequencing**: Information could arrive out of order. (Message A might be sent before B, but B might arrive at the destination before A.)

These issues are handled by protocols that work on top of IP.

### Transmission Control Protocol (TCP)

The Transmission Control Protocol (or *TCP* for short) is another communication standard implemented on top of IP. When one computer sends a packet to another using IP, once the packet arrives, the set of software rules that interpret and handle its data are called TCP.

> **TCP**
>
> A protocol that provides reliable, in-order delivery of information between computers.

TCP exists to solve the limitations of IP listed previously. TCP guarantees reliable, non-corrupt, in-order delivery from one computer to another. It does this by adding extra information to IP data such as validity-checking information and unique numbers for each packet of data, so that they can be placed in order when they arrive at their destination. Computers communicating with TCP send acknowledgements when data has arrived and re-send data when no acknowledgement comes back, to make sure every packet arrives at the destination.

TCP also adds the ability for multiple programs and services to share the same physical computer and internet connection. It does this by associating each program/service with a unique integer called a *port*. You may have seen TCP ports while using the web or other internet-enabled programs. Certain common internet services have been given standard ports, such as:

| TCP port | service |
|---|---|
| 21 | file transfer (FTP) |
| 22 | secure shell (SSH) |
| 25, 110 | email (SMTP, POP3) |
| 80 | web (HTTP) |
| 443 | secure web (HTTPS) |
| 993, 995 | secure email |

**Table 1.1 Common ports and services**

TCP is an important layer of the internet because it frees the author of an internet application from worrying about the reliability of the underlying network. When information is sent with TCP, you have reasonable assurance that it will arrive at its destination successfully. Since TCP is always run on top of the IP protocol, the combination of the two is frequently referred to as *TCP/IP*.

TCP is not the only protocol that runs on top of IP; others such as the UDP protocol are better suited to other types of applications such as streaming media and online games.

## Self-Check

1. What is the difference between the internet and the World Wide Web (WWW)?
2. What are some of the most important aspects or features of the internet?
3. What organization decides on standards for web pages and languages?
4. What features are provided by the Internet Protocol (IP), and what additional features are added by TCP?
5. Which of the following are legal IP addresses?
   a) www.google.com
   b) 150.135.1.150
   c) 123.456.789.10
   d) 241.259.17.127
   e) 10.0.0.1
6. What is your computer's public IP address? What are the IP addresses of the following sites?
   a) www.google.com
   b) www.facebook.com
   c) www.microsoft.com
   d) www.mozilla.org

## 1.2    The World Wide Web (WWW)

The World Wide Web (WWW for short) is a worldwide set of documents formatted in a language named Hypertext Markup Language (HTML). The web is built on top of TCP/IP and adds several concepts, languages, and technologies specific for retrieving and viewing rich text and multimedia content. As you know, a key aspect of the web is that the pages are connected to each other through text references called hyperlinks (or just links).

### 1.2.1    Clients and Servers

The web consists of many computers called *web servers* that are connected to the internet and waiting for connections, usually on TCP port 80. A web server can be just a normal computer or a much larger and more powerful machine, depending on the site and the amount of traffic and processing power it needs.

> **web server**
>
> A computer running software to accept web requests from clients and respond to them by sending web pages to the clients.

These servers run special web server software to serve their web pages. As of this writing the most popular server software is Apache web server, a free program that can run on Windows, Linux, or Mac. Another popular server software package is Microsoft's Internet Information Server (IIS), which is also free but runs only on Windows. Older versions of IIS were considered inferior to Apache because of security and performance problems, but nowadays both are mature web server applications that power large fractions of the servers on the web.

As you know, users connect to a web server using *web browser* software that retrieves and displays web pages. Currently popular web browsers include the following:

- Microsoft Internet Explorer (Windows only)
- Mozilla Firefox
- Apple Safari (Mac only)
- Google Chrome
- Opera

In general when you write web sites, you do not need to worry about what browser the user will be using to view your page. However, in certain cases the different browsers display the same content in different ways, and some browsers are unable to view certain kinds of content. So as we learn web programming in this textbook, at times we'll mention incompatibilities and differences between browsers that may affect your code.

> **web browser**
>
> Software to request and display web pages from web servers.

Internet Explorer is still the most widely used browser as of this writing, but it is an outdated piece of software that does not display all web pages correctly according to web standards. IE also has a long history of security problems that expose its users to viruses and other infections. Firefox and Safari are more modern browsers that display many more web pages correctly according to standards. Opera is perhaps the most sophisticated browser of all, able to display even the most complex web sites properly, but it has a small market share outside of mobile devices and other niche areas.

### 1.2.2    URLs and DNS

While IP addresses used by TCP/IP uniquely identify the computers on the internet, they're not easy for people to remember. To help with this problem, a layer called the *Domain Name System (DNS)* was created. DNS allows the user to type in a plain text name for a web server, and the system will look up the IP address for that web server and connect

> **DNS**
>
> A global mapping between human-readable names and IP addresses for web servers.

to it. Such a plain text name for a web server is called a *domain name*. Businesses and other users can purchase domain names for their own sites, so that users across the internet will be able to type the domain name into their browser and connect to the company's site. A known set of main servers act as the *root DNS servers* that provide name / IP address mapping for the rest of the internet.

A domain name becomes part of a larger string of text that the user types into their web browser to request a particular web site or document. This larger string is called a uniform resource locator or *URL*. A URL contains a complete description of a particular document on the Web. For example:

```
http://www.aw-bc.com/info/regesstepp/index.html
      ⇑            ⇑              ⇑
   protocol      host           path
```

A URL begins with a protocol such as `http`, `ftp`, or `mailto` (email). A URL also contains a host or domain name, followed by a path to a file or document on that web server.

Many domain names begin with `www`, but this is merely by convention and is not required nor part of any technical standard. The suffix that ends a domain name, such as `.com` or `.org`, is called a *top-level domain*. Top-level domains roughly organize web sites by geography, type of organization, and content, such as `.com` (commercial), `.edu` (educational), `.org` (charitable organization), `.gov` (governmental site), `.fr` (France), `.cn` (China), `.com.au` (Australia), and so on. (As a side note, ICANN recently rejected a proposal to add a `.xxx` top-level domain name for adult web sites.)

One problem with top-level domains is that the `.com` suffix has perhaps become too popular for its own good. Many web users believe that every site's name must end with `.com`. This is related to the rapid rise in popularity of the web in the late 1990s, often called the *dot-com boom*. During the boom, many sites purchased `.com` domain names even though they were not used for commercial purposes. This is when most people discovered and starting using the web, so most people assume `.com` is the only legal suffix.

URLs can optionally contain other information. For example, a URL can end with an *anchor* specifying to jump to a particular place within the document. A URL can also specify which TCP port to use to connect to the server. (If the port is omitted, the browser uses the standard web port of 80.) The following URLs demonstrate these features:

```
http://www.textpad.com/download/index.html#downloads
                                             ⇑
                                          anchor
```

```
http://www.cs.washington.edu:8080/secret/money.txt
                             ⇑
                           port
```

URLs can be more complex than this, including passing information called query string parameters, but we'll discuss this in a later chapter.

## 1.2.3  Hypertext Transfer Protocol (HTTP)

TCP is a powerful protocol, but the World Wide Web adds yet another layer on top of TCP to aid in the fetching and viewing of web pages. The Hypertext Transfer Protocol (or *HTTP* for short) is a set of commands that a computer can send to a server to request files. HTTP commands include:

- **GET**: Requests a specific file or resource from the server.
- **POST**: Submits form information to the server.
- **PUT**: Uploads a file to the server.
- **HEAD**: Requests information about a file from the server, but not the file's entire contents.

When you request a page in your web browser, the browser sends a GET message to the appropriate web server. The server sends back the page, and your browser displays it. To illustrate that web browsers are not all that magical, we can actually simulate the behavior of a web browser from a dumb terminal. If you open a Command Prompt (Windows) or Terminal (Mac or Linux), you can type commands such as those shown in Example 1.1 to fetch web pages; the terminal prompt is represented by $ ; the commands typed by the user appear in bold.

```
$ telnet www.cs.washington.edu 80
Trying 128.208.3.88...
Connected to 128.208.3.88 (128.208.3.88).
Escape character is '^]'.

GET /index.html

<!DOCTYPE HTML PUBLIC "-//W3C//DTD HTML 4.0 ...">
<html><title>University of Washington Computer Science</title>
...
</body></html>
Connection closed by foreign host.
```

**Example 1.1 Telnet session to fetch a web page**

The first command runs the primitive terminal program `telnet` and tells it to connect to the web server at URL www.cs.washington.edu on TCP port 80. Once the connection is made, we type an HTTP GET command to retrieve the document named /index.html. The text of this document (shortened by ... above) is sent back to our terminal, then the server disconnects us.

HTTP is called a *stateless protocol*; there is no persistent connection between the computer and the web server. A computer requests a document, and the server sends it back. If the computer and server want to engage in a more long-lived communication (such as logging in to an e-commerce site and purchasing items), this must be simulated through other advanced web technologies we'll learn about later in this book.

When you request a document from a web server, it sends this document back to you (if it exists), along with a number called an HTTP *status code*. The HTTP status code is an indication of whether your request was successful. You have probably seen some of these status codes while browsing the web. Several common HTTP status codes are shown in Table 1.2.

| Code | Meaning |
|---------|-----------------------------------------------------|
| 200 | OK |
| 301-303 | The page has moved (temporarily or permanently) |
| 403 | You are forbidden to access this page |
| 404 | Page not found |
| 500 | The server experienced an internal error |

**Table 1.2 Common HTTP status codes**

The error code doesn't show up on the screen in our telnet example above, but if an error code other than 200 (OK) comes back, your browser will display an error message, as shown in Figure 1.3.

**Figure 1.3 HTTP error 404 in browser**

Some web sites display elaborate or funny error messages on 404 Not Found errors, such as homestarrunner.com. Try going to that site and typing in a bogus page URL and see what happens.

### MIME Types

There are many types of data that are transmitted over the Internet, including text, images, audio, video, and more. Many web protocols categorize each type of data using a two-part identifier called a *MIME type* (or Internet media type). Every MIME type consists of a broad category type and a subtype separated by a slash / character. For example, the MIME type image/jpeg represents JPEG images, usually stored in .jpg files.

Table 1.3 lists several common MIME types. More complete lists of MIME types can be found in the References section of this chapter. You do not need to know much about MIME types to do basic web programming, but occasionally you will need to specify a resource's MIME type in order to access it. For example, when we link web pages to style information and script code, we will specify the MIME types for the CSS and JavaScript languages.

| MIME type | File extension(s) | Description |
|---|---|---|
| application/octet-stream | .exe | executable programs |
| audio/mpeg | .mp3, .mpg | MPEG or MP3 music |
| image/gif | .gif | GIF images |
| image/jpeg | .jpg | JPEG images |
| image/png | .png | PNG images |
| multipart/form-data | | web form data |
| text/css | .css | style sheets |
| text/html | .html, .htm, .php | web pages |
| text/javascript | .js | JavaScript programs |
| text/plain | .txt | plain text data |
| text/xml | .xml | XML formatted data |
| video/quicktime | .qt, .mov | Quicktime movie |

**Table 1.3 Common MIME types**

## 1.2.4    Languages of the Web

There are a large number of programming and document description languages used to describe and format the content on the Web. Among these are:

- Hypertext Markup Language (**HTML**): used for writing web pages
- Cascading Style Sheets (**CSS**): supplies stylistic info to web pages
- PHP Hypertext Processor (**PHP**): allows the web server to generate pages dynamically (one of many server-side languages including Java, Ruby on Rails, ASP.NET, Python, and others)
- **JavaScript**: allows interactive and programmable web pages
- Extensible Markup Language (**XML**): allows organizing and formatting data
- Structured Query Language (**SQL**): allows interaction with databases

The remainder of this textbook will be devoted to learning the preceding languages at an introductory level, so that we can create rich and interactive web sites and applications.

## Self-Check

7. Name three major web browsers and one major web server program used today. Why does a web site designer need to care about the different browsers used by visitors to the site?
8. What would be the correct URL to download the file coralize.js from the folder /bin/bookmark/ on the server www.coralcdn.org.nyud.net on port 8080?
9. What is the difference between an HTTP GET and POST request?
10. What does an HTTP error 403 mean? Why might you see an HTTP error 500?

## Chapter Summary

- The internet is a worldwide set of computer networks for personal, commercial, academic, and government use. The World Wide Web (WWW) is a subset of the internet containing a set of web pages and sites.
- The internet protocol (IP) is a simple underlying system of addressing for internet communication. Every computer on the internet has an IP address.
- TCP is a protocol layered on top of IP that guarantees reliable, in-order delivery from one computer to another. The combination of TCP and IP is called TCP/IP. Protocols for common services such as the web, email, and file transfer are layered on top of TCP.
- A URL is a string of text that the user types into their web browser to request a particular web site or document. URLs map to IP addresses through a service called DNS.
- HTTP is the protocol for the web, layered on top of TCP. HTTP allows a browser or program to request a web document. HTTP requests produce web pages or error codes.
- Web programming involves many languages: HTML, CSS, PHP, JavaScript, XML, and SQL.

## References

- Senator Ted Stevens explains internet: http://youtube.com/watch?v=f99PcP0aFNE
- A Brief History of the Internet: http://www.isoc.org/internet/history/brief.shtml
- Internet Engineering Task Force (IETF): http://www.ietf.org/
- IETF Requests for Comments (RFCs): http://www.ietf.org/rfc.html
- Internet Corporation for Assigned Names and Numbers (ICANN):
  - http://www.icann.org/
- World Wide Web Consortium (W3C): http://www.w3.org/
- HowStuffWorks: What is an IP address?
  - http://computer.howstuffworks.com/question549.htm
- What Is My IP address: http://www.whatismyip.com/
- List of all TCP and UDP port numbers:
  - http://en.wikipedia.org/wiki/List_of_TCP_and_UDP_port_numbers
- Apache web server project: http://www.apache.org/
- Mozilla Firefox web browser: http://www.getfirefox.com/
- Opera web browser: http://www.opera.com/
- List of top-level domains:
  - http://en.wikipedia.org/wiki/List_of_Internet_top-level_domains
- ICANN rejects proposal for .xxx top-level domain:
  - http://news.com.com/ICANN+rejects+.xxx+domain/2100-1047_3-6071124.html
- List of all HTTP error codes: http://en.wikipedia.org/wiki/Http_error_codes
- List of MIME types (alphabetical):
  - http://www.w3schools.com/media/media_mimeref.asp
- List of MIME types (by file extension):
  - http://www.webmaster-toolkit.com/mime-types.shtml
- Homestar Runner: http://www.homestarrunner.com/

# Chapter 2  HTML Basics

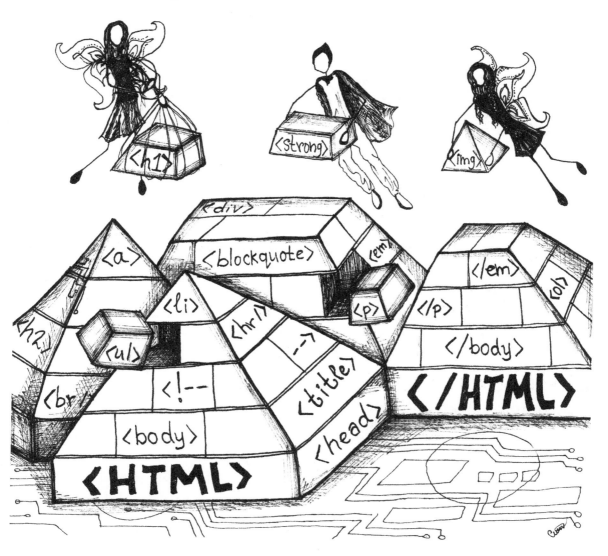

# Introduction

We'll begin our study of web programming by learning the core language for writing web pages: Hypertext Markup Language (HTML). HTML describes the contents of your page, such as headings, paragraphs, images, and lists.

The version of HTML we'll learn is the latest and most standard, called XHTML. The pages you'll write will work in any modern browser.

This chapter doesn't attempt to provide a complete list of HTML tags and attributes. Certain aspects of the language, such as forms and tables, are left for later chapters that focus on those elements.

Each of our chapters will include a larger example called a "case study" that we will develop throughout or at the end of the chapter. This chapter's case study will be a recurring example of a blog page about travels to various far-away lands. As we learn new concepts in this chapter, we'll apply many of them to improving this page.

## 2.1  Basic HTML

In this section we'll discuss the basics of HTML and web pages, as well as a brief history of the language and how it came to be the way it is today. In following sections we'll dive into the details of HTML syntax for creating complex web pages.

### 2.1.1  History

Since its creation in 1991 by Tim Berners-Lee, one of the founding fathers of the Internet, HTML has been the dominant language for creating web pages. HTML is a language consisting of text content surrounded by markings that specify the meaning of the content. As with many languages, HTML has gone through different versions and standardization processes over the years:

- 1993: Initial official proposed description of HTML submitted to the IETF standards group.
- 1995: HTML 2 becomes an official standard language by a publication called RFC 1866.
- 1996-97: HTML 3.2 standardizes various features including forms, tables, image maps, and internationalization.
- 1997: HTML 4 is proposed by W3C standards body, adding style sheets, scripting, frames, embedding objects, internationalization, and accessibility for disabilities.
- HTML 4.01, the last major version of the language, is published in 1999 by W3C. A majority of the pages on the web today still use HTML 4.01 as their stated language.
- 2000-01: XHTML, a more standardized offshoot of HTML based on a language named XML, is proposed by W3C.

The language has several major goals that are reflected in the evolution made to it over the years. Each new version has endeavored to: add new features; improve interoperability, make HTML compatible with all major browsers, platforms, and devices; and be accessible to all kinds of users, including those with disabilities affecting sight and hearing.

In these chapters we will focus on *XHTML*, a more recently created dialect of HTML. XHTML is a stricter language than HTML, and its syntax is more regular and standardized. XHTML has a more clearly refined set of goals than past versions of HTML. While older HTML was a mixed language used to describe a document's content, appearance, and behavior, XHTML chooses to focus solely on describing the document's content and structure. The tasks of describing exactly how the document should look and how it should behave are handled by other languages that interact with XHTML.

A well-written web page has the following division of responsibilities:

- HTML describes the content of the document.
- Style Sheets (written in a language named CSS) describe the appearance of the document.
- Scripts (written in languages such as JavaScript) describe the behavior of the document.

We will learn the HTML syntax in detail throughout this chapter and later chapters. Example 2.1 shows an initial example of a complete HTML document. Figure 2.1 shows the output when you save the above code into a file called wonderful_world.html and open it in the Firefox browser.

In general it does not matter what name you give to your HTML file, but one particular file name is worth mentioning. Most web servers consider the filename index.html (and similar names such as index.php, index.jsp, etc.) to represent the main page for a particular web site. So if you omit the file name from a URL, index.html is assumed to be the filename. This is useful because, for example, you can tell people your web site's URL is http://www.example.com/, and when they visit that URL, they'll actually be shown the contents of http://www.example.com/index.html.

```
<!DOCTYPE html PUBLIC "-//W3C//DTD XHTML 1.1//EN"
    "http://www.w3.org/TR/xhtml11/DTD/xhtml11.dtd">
<html xmlns="http://www.w3.org/1999/xhtml">
  <head>
    <title>What a Wonderful World</title>
  </head>

  <body>
    <h1>My first web page</h1>

    <p>
      A friend told me once that he thought the www
      in URLs stood for what a wonderful world
      (I think it does!).
    </p>
  </body>
</html>
```

**Example 2.1 Basic web page wonderful_world.html**

Figure 2.1 Basic web page appearance in Firefox browser

HTML is a rich and complex language that can describe not only standard text documents but also tables of data, forms for sending information to a server (such as for purchasing items from an online store), complex images and multimedia, interactive games, and more. Because the language is so rich, we will study it in layers, learning more of its features in several subsequent chapters. In this chapter, we'll learn the basics of structuring text content and images.

> **element**
>
> A piece of HTML markup that surrounds text content and describes its meaning in the page.

An HTML document is a text file named with an `.html` extension. It contains text content and HTML markup to tell the browser how that content should be structured. The *content* is information that you would like the user to see. The *markup* consists of *tags* that describe the content and tell the browser how to structure and display it.

Tags consist of a lowercase tag name surrounded by angle brackets. For example, a paragraph is represented by the `<p>` tag. Most tags come in pairs, with an opening tag (for example, `<p>`) followed by some text, followed by a closing tag (for example, `</p>`). A pair of HTML tags and their enclosed content are collectively called an *element*. Figure 2.2 summarizes the basic syntax of an HTML element.

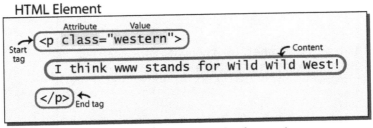

Figure 2.2 A paragraph element

## 2.1.2 Page Structure

The basic syntax of an XHTML page is shown in Example 2.2. Every page we write in this textbook will have this same basic structure. When we show code examples later in the chapter and elsewhere in the book, we will show just a subset of the page, only the relevant contents of the body.

```
<!DOCTYPE html PUBLIC "-//W3C//DTD XHTML 1.1//EN"
    "http://www.w3.org/TR/xhtml11/DTD/xhtml11.dtd">
<html xmlns="http://www.w3.org/1999/xhtml">
  <head>
    <title>page title</title>
    other resources or information about the page
  </head>

  <body>
    page content
  </body>
</html>
```

**Example 2.2 Syntax template for a basic XHTML page**

The first three lines are the document type definition and opening `html` tag. The document type definition is a declaration that our page is written using XHTML v1.1 syntax (along with the URL to the XHTML specification); the opening `html` tag specifies the beginning of the page. We aren't going to examine the contents of these lines in detail. The main thing you should know is that these lines are required if we want our page to comply with web standards. Therefore these exact 3 lines will appear at the top of every web page we write in this textbook, so you can copy them and paste them into the pages you write.

The rest of the page consists of two major sections, the header and body. The header, represented by the `head` tag, contains general information about the page. The body, represented by the `body` tag, holds the content to display.

Header information is used by the browser but not displayed on the page. The most common element in the header is `title`, which specifies the title text to be shown in the browser's top bar. The header also includes any CSS style sheets or JavaScript code to attach to the page. (We'll learn about those later.)

## 2.1.3 Block Elements

There are two types of elements: block elements and inline elements. A *block element*, such as a paragraph or bulleted list, generally represents a significant element of the page and can contain a large amount of content spanning many lines. A block element can contain other block and inline elements inside it, called nested elements; for example, a paragraph can contain a link. The browser displays each block element with a line break and vertical margins above and below it. In the following sections, we'll show several block elements you can place inside the page's `body` section.

> **block element**
>
> A significant item on a web page (paragraph, list, etc.) that occupies a rectangular block of space on the page.

### Paragraphs (p)

| Element | p |
|---|---|
| Description | Paragraph of text (block) |
| Syntax | `<p>content</p>` |

Much of the content of web pages is organized into paragraphs. Each paragraph begins with the `<p>` tag and ends with the `</p>` tag. Each `p` (like all block elements) is displayed on its own line with a vertical margin above and below it.

The web browser displays as many words of the paragraph content as will fit in the browser window and wraps the remaining content. The web browser collapses any whitespace between words in the paragraph down to a single space. It ignores spaces or line breaks you place between words and reformats the text so that there is exactly one space between words and sentences.  Example 2.3 demonstrates several paragraphs and the resulting output that would appear in the browser. Notice that the line breaks and spacing in the output are unrelated to those in the HTML source code.

```
<p>
  You wake up at Seatac, SFO, LAX. You wake up at O'Hare, Dallas-Fort
  Worth, BWI.  Pacific, Mountain, Central.  Lose an hour, gain an hour.
  This is your life, and it's ending one minute at a time.
</p>

<p>
  You wake up at Air Harbor International. If you wake up at a different
  time, in a different place, could you wake up as a different person?
</p>
```

You wake up at Seatac, SFO, LAX. You wake up at O'Hare, Dallas-Fort Worth, BWI. Pacific, Mountain, Central. Lose an hour, gain an hour. This is your life, and it's ending one minute at a time.

You wake up at Air Harbor International. If you wake up at a different time, in a different place, could you wake up as a different person?

**Example 2.3 Paragraphs**

We'll follow some stylistic conventions for spacing and indentation in our HTML code. We generally separate block elements by blank lines, unless their inner content is very short and fits on a single line. When the text of a paragraph spans multiple lines, we'll indent it to indicate the nesting. Since block elements can contain other block elements, we'll indicate this nesting with a line break and an increase in indentation.

## Headings (h1 - h6)

| | |
|---|---|
| **Elements** | h1, h2, h3, h4, h5, h6 |
| **Description** | Headings to label/separate sections of the page (block) |
| **Syntax** | `<h1>`**content**`</h1>`<br>`<h2>`**content**`</h2>`<br>...<br>`<h6>`**content**`</h6>` |

Headings are used to label major sections of your page's content. There are six levels of headings, from h1 to h6. Level 1 headings (h1) are usually for page titles, second degree headings (h2) are usually for major section headings, third degree headings (h3) are subsections of h2 elements, and so on. Lower level headings should only be used under headings of the next higher level; for example, you shouldn't use an h3 unless there is a preceding h2 and the h3 represents a subsection inside that h2's content. In this way, headings represent a hierarchy of the sections of a web page.

To reflect this hierarchy, by default the browser displays the six heading levels at different sizes. An h1 is the largest header, and h6 is the smallest. On most browsers h1 through h3 display with a size larger than normal text, h4 text is about the same size as normal, and h5 and h6 display heading text smaller than normal. (Later we'll learn how to change this if so desired.)

Example 2.4 demonstrates several headings.

```
<h1>Traveler Times Newspaper</h1>

<h2>Latin America</h2>

<h3>Puerto Escondido: Sun, Surf, and Sand</h3>

<p>
  Puerto Escondido is known for one of the world's
  best surfing beaches, Playa Zicatela. ...
</p>

<h3>Tikal: Mayan Ruins in the Guatemalan Jungle</h3>

<p>
  Tikal is the largest of the ancient ruined cities
  of the Mayan civilization. ...
</p>


<h2>Europe</h2>

<h3>Drunk in Dublin</h3>

<p>
  Throwin' back pints with the locals in Dublin this past
  summer made me really appreciate the pub culture. ...
</p>
```

# Traveler Times Newspaper

## Latin America

### Puerto Escondido: Sun, Surf, and Sand

Puerto Escondido is known for one of the world's best surfing beaches, Playa Zicatela. ...

### Tikal: Mayan Ruins in the Guatemalan Jungle

Tikal is the largest of the ancient ruined cities of the Mayan civilization. ...

## Europe

### Drunk in Dublin

Throwin' back pints with the locals in Dublin this past summer made me really appreciate the pub culture. ...

**Example 2.4 Headings (output)**

## Semantic HTML

A lot of new web developers make the mistake of choosing heading tags based on how each one looks in the browser. They'll make decisions like, "An h1 looks too large when I use it as the page's main header, so I'll use an h3 instead." This mistaken line of thinking causes other poor decisions, such as creating a blank p paragraph element to get a vertical spacing between two other elements on the page.

**semantic HTML**

A best practice of choosing tags based on the meaning of content, not the appearance you want on the page.

A savvy web developer instead chooses tags based on what the content is, not how it might look in the browser. You should choose a heading's level based on its content and what levels of headings precede it. The best practice is to give each top-level heading an h1 tag, and then if you create a subheading within that topic, use an h2 for it. A subheading of that h2 would be an h3, and so on.

The notion of choosing tags based on the meaning of the content rather than on its appearance is called *semantic HTML*. There are many important reasons for using semantic HTML. It's considered better style. It also makes the content easier for non-standard browsers to understand. Don't worry about your h1 being too large on the screen; the appearance of tags is completely customizable by the web developer using Cascading Style Sheets (CSS), which we'll discuss in the next chapter.

## Horizontal Rule (hr)

| Element | hr |
|---|---|
| Description | Horizontal rule, a line to separate sections (block) |
| Syntax | <hr /> |

A *horizontal rule* is a line that separates sections of a web page by placing a horizontal line between them. The tag used to create a horizontal rule is hr.

**empty element**

One that does not contain any text content.

Most HTML elements consist of an opening tag and a closing tag, but an hr does not contain any content. Such an element is called an *empty element*. XHTML has a different syntax for empty elements: they consist simply of one tag that closes itself. The syntax for such a tag is:

```
<tag />
```

The tag is opened and closed at once, so we write <hr />. Not every tag can be legally opened and closed at once in this way, but we'll try to point out the ones that can as we go along. Example 2.5 shows a horizontal rule and its output.

```
<h2>Latin America</h2>
<h3>Puerto Escondido: Sun, Surf, and Sand</h3>
<p>
  Puerto Escondido is known for one of the world's
  best surfing beaches, Playa Zicatela. ...
</p>
<hr />

<h2>Europe</h2>
```

## Latin America

### Puerto Escondido: Sun, Surf, and Sand

Puerto Escondido is known for one of the world's best surfing beaches, Playa Zicatela. ...

---

## Europe

**Example 2.5 Horizontal rules**

### Comments

| Description | Comments (to document or "comment out" text) |
|---|---|
| Syntax | `<!-- text -->` |

Any text between the `<!--` and `-->` tags is considered to be a comment. Comments are ignored by the browser and not displayed on the page. Comments can be used to document the page or to "comment out" (disable) a portion of its content. Example 2.6 demonstrates comments. Notice how the content inside each comment block does not appear in the output.

```
<!-- All article titles should be in h3 tags -->
<h3>Puerto Escondido: Sun, Surf, and Sand</h3>
<p>
  Puerto Escondido is known for one of the world's
  best surfing beaches, Playa Zicatela. ...
</p>

<!--
<h2>Europe</h2>
<h3>Drunk in Dublin</h3>
<p>
  Throwin' back pints with the locals in Dublin this past
  summer made me really appreciate the pub culture. ...
</p>
-->
```

**Puerto Escondido: Sun, Surf, and Sand**

Puerto Escondido is known for one of the world's best surfing beaches, Playa Zicatela. ...

**Example 2.6 XHTML comments**

One annoying note about comment syntax is that once a comment is opened with `<!--` tag there cannot be another pair of hyphens in the comment until the closing `-->` tag. The most common places we've found `--` sequences in our own pages are when we're writing a piece of computer code such as `i--;` or when the text uses `--` to represent a long dash. Be especially careful when commenting out text in either of these contexts. (Later in this chapter, we'll show a way to represent a long dash without using two hyphens.)

## 2.1.4 Inline Elements

**inline element**

A smaller item on a web page (link, image, etc.) that resides inside a block element.

An *inline element*, such as a link or image, represents a smaller item on the page. Every inline element must be nested inside a block element. An inline element can contain other inline elements, but cannot contain any block elements. The browser displays each inline element on the same line as any surrounding content. In the following sections we'll examine several useful inline elements that can be placed inside the block elements shown previously.

### Images (`img`)

| | |
|---|---|
| **Element** | img |
| **Description** | Image (inline) |
| **Syntax** | `<img src="URL" alt="description" />` |

They say a picture is worth 1000 words; most web pages use images to enhance their appearance and present useful information. You can add an image to a web page with the `img` tag, another example of an empty tag that can be closed immediately. Example 2.7's output shows an image; it is displayed right beside the neighboring text because `img` is an inline element.

```
<p>
  I wish I could snowboard as well as this guy:
  <img src="images/snowboarder.jpg" alt="snowboarder" />
</p>
```

I wish I could snowboard as well as this guy:

**Example 2.7 Image**

**attribute**

A piece of additional information about an HTML element, placed inside its opening tag.

The `img` tag introduces a new piece of HTML syntax. An *attribute* is a piece of additional information about an element, placed within that element's opening tag. The attribute has a name written in lower case and a value in quotation marks. The syntax for a tag with an attribute is shown in Example 2.8.

```
<tag attribute="value">content</tag>
```

**Example 2.8 Syntax template for element with attribute**

A single element can have many attributes, separated by spaces. In the case of an empty element such as `img`, the syntax is shown in Example 2.9.

```
<tag attribute="value" attribute="value" />
```

**Example 2.9 Syntax template for empty element with multiple attributes**

Some tags require certain attributes to work properly. For example, an `img` element is required to contain two attributes named `src` (the URL at which the image is located) and `alt` (an alternative text representation of the image's content for visually impaired users).

Images are not contained in the HTML document itself but are stored as separate files. The browser will first download your HTML file, then download any images used in the page.

The other required attribute is `alt`, whose value should be a short description of the image. If the browser is unable to fetch the image, it will show the `alt` text in its place. The attribute is required because it makes pages accessible to users with sight impairments who cannot see the images. Such users use *screen reader* software that reads the values of `alt` attributes out loud.

| Name | Value | Description |
|------|-------|-------------|
| src | URL | location of image file (required) |
| alt | text | alternative text to display if image cannot be loaded (required) |
| title | text | tooltip describing the image |
| width | # or % | width of the image (as pixels or percentage of window) |
| height | # or % | height of the image (as pixels or percentage of window) |

**Table 2.1 Common `img` Attributes**

There are two kinds of URLs. An *absolute URL* is one that is fully specified, including protocol such as http, the name of the host site, the directory on the host site in which the file resides, and the name of the file. An absolute URL is needed when the image is on a different web site than the web page. For example, the following URL refers to an image on the site named `i.imdb.com` in the directory called `images/nb15`:

> **absolute URL**
> A complete URL to a web resource.

```
<img src="http://i.imdb.com/images/nb15/logo2.gif" alt="IMDB logo" />
```

A *relative URL* is one that is specified with respect to where the referring web page resides. These URLs point to files that are a part of the same web site as the referring web page. The main difference between a relative URL and an absolute URL is that a relative URL leaves off the protocol, site name, and directory information up to the directory where the page resides.

> **relative URL**
> A partial URL specified in relation to some existing URL.

In the following example, the first URL points to a file in the same directory as the current page, and the second points to the same file in the **images** subdirectory of the current page's directory.

```
<img src="snowboarder.jpg" alt="snowboarder" />
<img src="images/snowboarder.jpg" alt="snowboarder" />
```

You can also write `..` (two dots) in a relative URL to represent the parent of the current directory. For example, suppose your web page resides in the directory:

```
http://www.example.com/pages/site/examples/index.html
```

If you specify an image with:

```
<img src="../../images/snowboarder.jpg" alt="snowboarder" />
```

The browser will look for the image in the directory:

```
http://www.example.com/pages/images/
```

The `img` tag can have other optional attributes. One is `title`, whose value is shown as a tooltip when the user hovers the mouse cursor over the image. The `title` attribute is not unique to images; many of the elements in this chapter can have a `title` attribute if you want tooltips on them. Some web programmers get `alt` and `title` mixed up, partly because Internet Explorer mistakenly displays `alt` values as tooltips. Just remember that a̲lt is for a̲ccessibility, and t̲itle is for t̲ooltips.

The `width` and `height` attributes can adjust the size of the image. Their values can be specified in pixels (such as `"240"`) or as a percentage of the browser window size (such as `"33%"`). By default, the image is shown at its actual size, so if this is how you want the image to appear, you don't need to specify a width or height. But specifying them can help the browser to display the web page more quickly, because it will know how much screen space to allocate to the image before it downloads the image file. Example 2.10 demonstrates an image with additional attributes set.

```
<p>
  I wish I could snowboard as well as this guy:
  <img src="images/snowboarder.jpg" alt="a snowboarder"
  title="snowboarding picture from sierrasnowboard.com"
  width="400" height="120" />
</p>
```

I wish I could snowboard as well as this guy:

**Example 2.10 Image with additional attributes**

**Common Error**

Leading / on URLs

Some new web programmers mistakenly place a leading / on a relative URL. For example, consider the following two URLs, the first to a web page called `index.html` and the second to an image called `smiley.gif` located in the `images` subfolder relative to the web page:

```
http://www.example.com/mysite/files/index.html
http://www.example.com/mysite/files/images/smiley.gif
```

If the author of `index.html` wants to display `smiley.gif`, the following is wrong:

```
<img src="/images/smiley.gif" alt="smiley face" />
```

The problem is with the leading / character. The browser looks for the file `smiley.gif` in the `images/` subdirectory of the web site's root directory. The path the browser tries to load is:

```
http://www.example.com/images/smiley.gif
```

If the browser fails to fetch an image file, it displays its `alt` text instead, or if there is no `alt` text, an X icon. When you see this, right-click it in your browser and select View Image or Properties, as shown in Figure 2.3. From there you can see the image's complete URL. Below is the code the developer intended:

```
<img src="images/smiley.gif" alt="smiley face" />
```

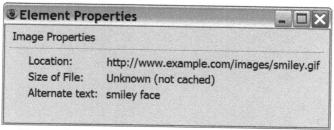

**Figure 2.3 Image element properties in Firefox**

## Links (a)

| Element | a |
|---|---|
| **Description** | Anchor or link (inline) |
| **Syntax** | `<a href="`**URL**`">`**content**`</a>` |

A *hyperlink* (or *link* for short) is a one-way connection from one web page to another. Links are one of the simplest yet most crucial aspects of the web, since links allow the user to travel between related pages. The **a** element (short for "anchor"), one of HTML's most important and frequently used elements, designates a link to another page. Example 2.11 shows the code for a link.

```
<p>
  <a href="http://www.imdb.com/">IMDB</a> is
  a great resource to find out information about movies.
</p>
```

IMDB is a great resource to find out information about movies.

**Example 2.11 Link**

The URL specified in the **href** attribute (in the above code, http://www.imdb.com/) is called the *target* of the link. If you click the link, the browser will navigate to this destination web page. While hovering the mouse over the link, the browser displays the link's destination URL in its bottom status bar. Like the **src** attribute of an image, the **href** value can be an absolute or relative URL.

| Name | Value | Description |
|---|---|---|
| `href` | URL | Destination URL of link |

**Table 2.2 Commonly Used a Attributes**

The content inside the **a** element ("IMDB" above) is what will be displayed on the page. By default the browser displays link text with an underline and a different color such as blue or purple. The browser also changes the mouse cursor to a hand when the user hovers over the link.

An image can also be used as a link. To do this, place an **img** element inside an **a** element. Example 2.12 demonstrates this.

```
<p>
  <a href="http://www.imdb.com/">
    <img src="http://i.imdb.com/images/nb15/logo2.gif" alt="IMDB logo" />
  </a>
  is a great resource to find information about movies.
</p>
```

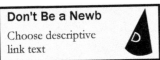 is a great resource to find information about movies.

**Example 2.12 Image as link**

To indicate a link on an image, many browsers (though not Apple's Safari) place a colored border around it and change the mouse cursor to a hand when hovered over it. If you don't like the border, we'll learn how to remove it in the next chapter.

**Don't Be a Newb**

Choose descriptive link text

Lots of web pages have links with non-descriptive text such as, "Click here to check your course schedule," where the word "here" is the link. This is poor web design. A better design is to use link text that describes the page being linked to, such as, "Please check your course schedules before March 15." Better yet would be putting the important link text first, such as, "Course schedules (please check yours before March 15!)"

Not only is this easier to read and easier for the user to know at a glance what the link targets, but it also makes the web page easier for search engines to understand. If a search engine such as Google examines your web site, it will see that the link goes to a page about course schedules. This will make Google's algorithms more likely to include your link higher in the search results for a query of "course schedules". And who doesn't want a higher Google ranking?

## Line Breaks (br)

| Element | br |
|---|---|
| Description | Line break (inline) |
| Syntax | <br /> |

As we saw in the **p** element section, browsers ignore line breaks in most elements. You can force a line break by placing a **br** tag in the element's content. This is another example of an empty tag, so it is written as **<br />**. Example 2.13 demonstrates the usage of the **br** element and the resulting output. Notice that a **br** tag ends a line even if more text appears later on that line of the source code, as in the second line inside the paragraph code.

```
<p>
  Remember compliments you receive. <br />
  Forget the insults. <br /> If you succeed

  in doing this, tell me how.
</p>
```

Remember compliments you receive.
Forget the insults.
If you succeed in doing this, tell me how.

**Example 2.13 Manual line breaks**

Some programmers overuse the **br** tag whenever they want to go to the next line in their page's text. This is a misuse of the **br** tag. Manual line breaks aren't needed to wrap lines of text in a paragraph; the browser will do this for you. Also, don't use a line break just because you want to create a vertical blank space between two pieces of content. Example 2.14 demonstrates the objectionable technique, and Example 2.15 shows a better version of the same code.

**Don't Be a Newb**

Line break ≠
paragraph break

```
<p>
  This is the first paragraph of my essay <br />
  <br />
  and this is the second paragraph,
  boy is it interesting <br />
  <br />
  and here is yet another paragraph,
  probably the 3rd but I lost count
</p>
```

**Example 2.14 Overuse of br tag**

```
<p>This is the first paragraph of my essay</p>

<p>and this is the second paragraph, boy is it interesting</p>

<p>
  and here is yet another paragraph,
  probably the 3rd but I lost count
</p>
```

**Example 2.15 Corrected text with p tags**

Here's a simple heuristic: If you ever place two **br** elements in a row, you're probably using bad style. Instead, separate the sections of text into separate block elements such as paragraphs. We'll learn how to set elements' margins in Chapter 4 to place arbitrary blank space between paragraphs.

**Emphasis (em, `strong`)**

| Element(s) | Em | strong |
|---|---|---|
| Description | Emphasis (inline) | Strong emphasis (in-line) |
| Syntax | `<em>`**content**`</em>` | `<strong>...</strong>` |

The em and `strong` elements specify content that should be emphasized. By default, browsers display em elements by italicizing the content and `strong` elements by bolding the content. Example 2.16 demonstrates both elements.

```
<p>
  XHTML is <em>really</em>, <strong>REALLY</strong> fun!
</p>
```

XHTML is *really*, **REALLY** fun!

**Example 2.16 Emphasis**

It may be tempting to think of em as the "italic" tag and `strong` as the "bold" tag because they are usually displayed that way. But it's important to emphasize that tags aren't just used to indicate formatting; they are used to specify the semantics (meaning) of content. The em and `strong` tags indicate that their content should be emphasized in some way by the browser. The browser might choose to emphasize them by changing their color, or by making the text size larger, rather than by using bold and italic styles. (Later in this chapter we'll learn how to tell the browser exactly how you want it to emphasize these elements.)

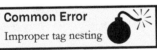 **Common Error**
Improper tag nesting

Tags must be properly nested. In other words, if a tag T1 contains a tag T2 as part of its content, the inner tag T2 must be closed before the outer tag T1 is closed. Example 2.17 shows improperly nested tags.

```
<p>
  HTML is <em>really, <strong>Really</em>,
  REALLY</strong> fun!
</p>
```

**Example 2.17 Common error: Improper XHTML element nesting**

The browser does render the text the way we intended: The word REALLY is shown with bold but not italic formatting. We'll encounter many cases like this where the browser tries its best to display a page even when its XHTML content is not valid. But being valid is a good thing, so a better way to get the same effect is shown in Example 2.18.

```
<p>
  HTML is <em>really, <strong>Really</strong></em>,
  <strong>REALLY</strong> fun!
</p>
```

**Example 2.18 Corrected element nesting**

## Self-Check

1.  How should (and shouldn't) HTML be used in a web page? What are some differences between HTML and XHTML?

2.  What's wrong with the tags the author has chosen for the following HTML content?

```
<body>
  <h2>Traveler Times</h2>
  <h4>Puerto Escondido: Sun, Surf, and Sand</h4>
  <h6>
    Known for one of the world's best beaches, Playa Zicatela. ...
    <br /> <br />
    I was there and had a blast!  It was a lot of fun.
  </h6>

  <h3>Europe</h3>
  <h5>Drunk in Dublin</h5>
  <h6>
    Throwin' back pints with the locals in Dublin this past <br />
    summer made me really appreciate the pub culture.
  </h6>
</body>
```

3.  What are the differences between block and inline elements? Give an example of each.

4.  What is the difference between an element and an attribute? Give an example of an element that requires attributes.

## 2.2  More HTML Elements

Let's continue our introduction to HTML with some new useful elements. The elements in this section will be used to create such things as lists and tables, quotations, computer source code, and pre-formatted text.

### 2.2.1  Lists

Many web pages contain lists of items, such as bulleted lists or numbered lists. HTML has three types of lists: unordered (bulleted) lists, ordered (numbered) lists, and definition lists. We'll talk about the first two types in the following sections.

**Unordered lists (`ul`, `li`)**

| Element | ul | li |
|---|---|---|
| Description | Unordered list (block) | List item (block) |
| Syntax | `<ul>`<br>    `<li>content</li>`<br>    ...<br>    `<li>content</li>`<br>`</ul>` | `<li>content</li>` |

An unordered list contains items whose ordering is not important, such as a to-do list or grocery list. To create unordered lists in HTML, use the `ul` and the `li` elements (both are block-level). A `ul` element represents an overall list of items, and an `li` element represents a single item within the list. Example 2.19 demonstrates an unordered list.

```
<p>Angelina J.'s To-Do List:</p>

<ul>
  <li>Adopt baby from third world country.</li>
  <li>Star in sci-fi adventure flick.</li>
  <li>Go on motorcycle ride with Bradipoo.</li>
  <li>Chill at mansion in Namibia.</li>
</ul>
```

Angelina J.'s To-Do List:

- Adopt baby from third world country.
- Star in sci-fi adventure flick.
- Go on motorcycle ride with Bradipoo.
- Chill at mansion in Namibia.

**Example 2.19 Unordered list**

Despite the claim that order shouldn't matter in an unordered list, the browser will faithfully display the list items in the order you specify from top to bottom. If a single item spans multiple lines, the text of subsequent lines will wrap at the same indentation level as the text of the first one.

**Common Error**
Not closing a list

When creating a list, it is easy to get so focused on creating the list elements that you forget to put a closing tag on the list. However, if you forget to close a list, all subsequent contents will be considered part of the list and therefore will be indented to the level of the text of the list items, as shown in Example 2.20.

```
<p>Angelina J.'s To-Do List:</p>
<ul>
  <li>Adopt baby from third world country.</li>
  <li>Star in sci-fi adventure flick.</li>
  <li>...</li>

<p>Brad P.'s To-Do List...</p>
```

Angelina J.'s To-Do List:

* Adopt baby from third world country.
* Star in sci-fi adventure flick.
* ...

    Brad P.'s To-Do List...

**Example 2.20 Common error: Forgetting to close a list**

If you see this strange behavior after a list, the reason is probably because you forgot to close the list. To fix it, trace up the page until you find the place where the odd indentation begins, or use the XHTML validator shown later in this chapter.

### Ordered lists (`ol`, `li`)

| Element | ol |
|---|---|
| **Description** | Ordered or numbered list (block) |
| **Syntax** | `<ol>`<br>    `<li>`**content**`</li>`<br>    `<li>`**content**`</li>`<br>    **...**<br>    `<li>`**content**`</li>`<br>`</ol>` |

An ordered list is one where the ordering of the items is important, such as a set of directions, steps of a recipe, or a top 10 list. Ordered lists are specified by the `ol` and `li` elements, where an `ol` represents the overall numbered list of items. Example 2.21 demonstrates an ordered list.

```
<p>Burbank Airport to Mulholland Drive:</p>

<ol>
  <li>Go west on Hollywood Way.</li>
  <li>Go north on US-101.</li>
  <li>Take I-405 South toward Santa Monica.</li>
  <li>
    Take exit for Skirball Center Drive
    towards Mulholland Dr.
  </li>
</ol>
```

Burbank Airport to Mulholland Drive:

1. Go west on Hollywood Way.
2. Go north on US-101.
3. Take I-405 South toward Santa Monica.
4. Take exit for Skirball Center Drive towards Mulholland Dr.

**Example 2.21 Ordered list**

Notice that, as with other block elements, the browser ignores our whitespace and line wrapping in the last `li` element and decides for itself how to separate words within each list item.

An unordered list's default appearance is to use solid filled round bullets before each list item. An ordered list's default gives numbers to each list item, such as 1, 2, 3, 4, etc. The amount a list will be indented is determined by its padding, which we'll discuss in the Layout chapter.

### Nested Lists

A list can contain other lists. To nest a list inside another, you define the sub-list inside a list item element (i.e. the `li` element). A list item can contain a sub-list of the same or different list type. Example 2.22 demonstrates a nested list.

```
<p>Categories of Eaters:</p>

<ol>
  <li>Omnivores: Eats both plants and animals
    <ul>
      <li>Most humans</li>
      <li>Pigs</li>
    </ul>
  </li>
  <li>Herbivores: Eats plants</li>
  <li>Carnivores: Eats animals</li>
</ol>
```

Categories of Eaters:

1. Omnivores: Eats both plants and animals
   - Most humans
   - Pigs
2. Herbivores: Eats plants
3. Carnivores: Eats animals

**Example 2.22 Nested list**

When nesting a list inside another list, the sub-list must be defined after the parent list item's opening tag and be closed before the parent item's closing tag. Two common errors in list nesting are closing the parent list's item element too early, and forgetting to close the enclosing list item completely. Both of these errors are demonstrated in order in the Example 2.23.

> **Common Error**
> Improper nested
> list placement

```
<ul>
  <li>Simpsons:</li>
    <ul>
      <li>Bart</li>
      <li>Lisa</li>
    </ul>
  </li>
  <li>Family Guy:
    <ul>
      <li>Peter</li>
      <li>Lois</li>
    </ul>
</ul>
```

**Example 2.23 Common error: Improper nested list placement**

Although some browsers are still able to display these lists correctly, it is still invalid XHTML.

## Definition lists (dl, dt, dd)

| Element | dl | dt | dd |
|---|---|---|---|
| Description | Definition list (block) | Term (block) | Description/definition (block) |
| Syntax | `<dl>`<br><br>　`<dt>`**content**`</dt>`<br><br>　`<dd>`**content**`</dd>`<br><br>　...<br><br>　`<dt>`**content**`</dt>`<br><br>　`<dd>`**content**`</dd>`<br><br>`</dl>` | `<dt>`**content**`</dt>` | `<dd>`**content**`</dd>` |

A *definition list* is one where each item has two parts: a name and a value associated with that name. Definition lists are good for representing items where two pieces of information are closely related to each other, such as a list of vocabulary words and their definitions, a list of topics and descriptions of those topics, or a list of people's names and phone numbers. If you're familiar with the concept of a map (sometimes called a dictionary, hash table, or associative array) in programming, a definition list is analogous to a map where the keys are the terms and the values are the definitions.

The overall definition list is represented by the **dl** element. A name is designated by the **dt** element (short for "definition term"), and a value is designated by the **dd** element (short for "definition description"). All three are block-level elements. Example 2.24 shows a definition list and its resulting appearance in the browser.

```
<p>Categories of Eaters:</p>
<dl>
  <dt>Carnivores</dt>
  <dd>Eats meat</dd>

  <dt>Vegetarian</dt>
  <dd>Does not eat meat</dd>

  <dt>Omnivores</dt>
  <dd>Eats both plants and animals</dd>

  <dt>Hamburgeretarian</dt>
  <dd>Eats only hamburgers</dd>
</dl>
```

Categories of Eaters:

Carnivores
     Eats meat
Vegetarian
     Does not eat meat
Omnivores
     Eats both plants and animals
Hamburgeretarian
     Eats only hamburgers

**Example 2.24 Definition list**

## 2.2.2 Tables

| Element | table | tr | td | th | caption |
|---------|-------|-----|-----------|---------|---------------|
| Description | Table (block) | Row | Cell (column) | Heading | Table caption |
| Syntax | `<table>`<br>  `<caption>`**content**`</caption>`<br>  `<tr><th>`**column title** `</th>`...`<th>`**column title**`</th></tr>`<br>  `<tr><td>`**content**`</td>`...`<td>`**content**`</td></tr>`<br>  `...`<br>  `<tr><td>`**content**`</td>`...`<td>`**content**`</td></tr>`<br>`</table>` | | | | |

**Table 2.3 Tags for HTML tables**

The **table**, **tr**, and **td** elements are used to display tabular information. For example, a student's class schedule, a table of facts about countries, results of a survey, or nutritional information about food are all sets of information likely best represented by a table. To create tables in HTML, we begin by declaring the table using the **table** element (a block-level element). Nested in the table element, there is a list of **tr** ("table row") elements representing the rows of the table. Within each **tr** element, there is a list of td ("table data") elements that wrap the actual data of each table cell. **td** elements that are all in the same place of each row's **td** list form a column. By default, the content of a **td** element is left-aligned. Example 2.25 shows an HTML table.

Frequently you want to give columns and/or rows in a table titles so that the reader knows what information is in each column and/or row. The th tag is used to create headers for either columns or rows or both. By default, cells created with the th tag are bolded and centered. Example 2.25 labels the columns of the table using the th tag. You also might want to label the table as a whole. To do this, you can use the caption element which goes just after the opening table tag. By default, the content of the caption element is centered above the table. Example 2.25 creates a table with the caption of "Nation Information". The table, tr, and td elements are necessary to create a table, but labeling elements (i.e. th and caption) are optional.

```
<table>
  <caption>Nation Information</caption>
  <tr>
    <th>Country</th>
    <th>Happiness Ranking</th>
    <th>Life Expectancy</th>
    <th>GDP per Capita</th>
  </tr>
  <tr><td>Denmark</td><td>1</td><td>77.8 years</td><td>$34,600</td></tr>
  <tr><td>Bahamas</td><td>5</td><td>65.6 years</td><td>$20,200</td></tr>
  <tr><td>Bhutan</td><td>8</td><td>55 years</td><td>$1,400</td></tr>
</table>
```

Nation Information

| Country | Happiness Ranking | Life Expectancy | GDP per Capita |
|---------|-------------------|-----------------|----------------|
| Denmark | 1 | 77.8 years | $34,600 |
| Bahamas | 5 | 65.6 years | $20,200 |
| Bhutan | 8 | 55 years | $1,400 |

**Example 2.25 Table**

Table cells can span across more than one column or row. The colspan attribute indicates how many columns the cell should occupy and the rowspan attribute indicates how many rows it should occupy. Table 2.4 gives the syntax for the colspan and rowspan attributes and Example 2.26 shows their use to classify countries in terms of continent and level of industrialization (i.e. developed or developing country). When you use a cell with a colspan or rowspan, you should place fewer tds in the affected other rows or columns to account for this. For example, the rows of information about developed countries have only four tds because the th heading above spans down into those rows.

| Element | td, th |
|---------|--------|
| Description | Table data cell or table header cell (can span multiple rows/columns) |
| Example | `<td rowspan="rows" colspan="columns">`<br>    **content**<br>`</td>` |

**Table 2.4 Table cell row/column spans**

```
<table border="1">
  <caption>Nation Information</caption>
  <tr>
    <th></th>
    <th>Country</th>
    <th>Happiness Ranking</th>
    <th>Life Expectancy</th>
    <th>GDP per Capita</th>
  </tr>
  <tr><th colspan="5">North America</th></tr>
  <tr>
    <th rowspan="1">Developing</th>
    <td>Bahamas</td><td>5</td><td>65.6 years</td><td>$20,200</td>
  </tr>
  <tr>
    <th rowspan="2">Developed</th>
    <td>Canada</td><td>8</td><td>80.4 years</td><td>$38,200</td>
  </tr>
  <tr>
    <td>United States</td><td>17</td><td>78.1 years</td><td>$45,800</td>
  </tr>
</table>
```

| Nation Information | | | | |
|---|---|---|---|---|
| | Country | Happiness Ranking | Life Expectancy | GDP per Capita |
| North America | | | | |
| Developing | Bahamas | 5 | 65.6 years | $20,200 |
| Developed | Canada | 8 | 80.4 years | $38,200 |
| | United States | 17 | 78.1 years | $45,800 |

**Example 2.26 colspan and rowspan Attributes**

Example 2.26 uses the **border** attribute on the **table** element to show borders around the table. We used the **border** attribute here to more clearly illustrate how **colspan** and **rowspan** work, however, in the next chapter we will explore better ways to style tables with borders, colors, and fonts.

**Don't Be A Newb**

Tables should not be used for layout

The web was originally born for academic purposes that did not demand beautifully laid out web page content. So in the '90s there was no better way to achieve a grid-like layout than tables. As the Internet grew, more web pages were written for the common person who appreciates good layout. In the late '90s the W3C created a language called CSS that is especially for styling and layout of web pages. Yet many poorly written pages still use tables to lay out their content.

Other than the fact that using tables for layout is woefully outdated, there are a number of other reasons to not use tables for layout including speed and inflexibility. Perhaps the most important reason not to use tables for layout is that the **table** tag comes with a semantic meaning: it means the content inside of it is a table of data. Clearly this is not the case if you are just using the **table** tag to place content in your web page in a certain visual way.

So rather than being stuck in the last century and laying out your web page using tables, wait until later in this textbook when we will teach you the more powerful way to lay out pages with CSS.

## 2.2.3 Quotations

There are two elements for representing quotations: **q** (for short inline quotations) and **blockquote** (for longer block quotations). We'll examine them in the following sections.

### Inline Quotations (q)

| | |
|---|---|
| **Element** | q |
| **Description** | Short quotation (inline) |
| **Syntax** | `<q>`**content**`</q>` |

The **q** element is an inline element used to denote short quotations that appear within a paragraph, sentence, or phrase. When using the **q** element, you don't need to put any quotation marks around the content; the browser should display the quotes automatically. Example 2.27 demonstrates the **q** element.

```
<p>
   Quoth the Raven, <q>Nevermore.</q>
</p>
```

Quoth the Raven, "Nevermore."

**Example 2.27 Inline quotation**

Internet Explorer does not abide by the web standard, and does not render the quotation marks automatically. To get the quotes, you must add them yourself.

### Block Quotations (blockquote)

| | |
|---|---|
| **Element** | blockquote |
| **Description** | Long quotation (block) |
| **Syntax** | `<blockquote>`<br>**content**<br>`</blockquote>` |

The **blockquote** element is a block-level element used to denote lengthy quotations that make up one or more complete paragraphs, or are otherwise not suitable to include inline. A **blockquote** element is not automatically rendered with quotation marks, but instead is normally rendered as indented text. Example 2.28 demonstrates the **blockquote** element.

Any content placed into a **blockquote** element must be nested inside a block-level element, such as a paragraph or heading. In other words, the following is not legal XHTML code:

```
<blockquote>
   hello
</blockquote>
```

```
<p>
  On June 12th, 1987 Ronald Reagan challenged
  Mikhail Gorbachev to tear down the Berlin Wall,
</p>

<blockquote>
  <p>
    General Secretary Gorbachev, if you seek peace, if
    you seek prosperity for the Soviet Union and Eastern
    Europe, if you seek liberalization: Come here to
    this gate! Mr. Gorbachev, open this gate!
    Mr. Gorbachev, tear down this wall!
  </p>
</blockquote>
```

On June 12th, 1987 Ronald Reagan challenged Mikhail Gorbachev to tear down the Berlin Wall,

General Secretary Gorbachev, if you seek peace, if you seek prosperity for the Soviet Union and Eastern Europe, if you seek liberalization: Come here to this gate! Mr. Gorbachev, open this gate! Mr. Gorbachev, tear down this wall!

**Example 2.28 Block quotation**

**Don't Be a Newb**

Don't use **blockquote** to indent text

Many newbie web programmers use the **blockquote** element as a means to indent text. But remember that XHTML tags should be chosen based on what their content actually is and not on how you want the content to appear (that is the job of CSS, which we'll learn soon). If you are using **blockquote** to indent text that is not a quotation, you're using the tag improperly. In the next chapter we will see how to use CSS margin properties to indent.

## 2.2.4 Pre-Formatted Text

You might have wondered, how would I write a web page about writing web pages? If your page mentions the **p** tag and you wrote **<p>** in your HTML document, it would start a new paragraph, rather than actually showing the text **<p>** on the page. Also, if you showed a long piece of source code that spans several lines, the browser would mangle its formatting, since the browser collapses all whitespace into a single space. In the following sections we'll talk about some elements and entities that are useful for displaying special characters and source code.

### Character Entity References

**entity reference**

A special sequence used to represent complex characters in a web page such as ™ or €.

Normally to display a character on your web page, you just have to type it on your keyboard. However there are many characters and symbols that may not be on your keyboard; you can use a special symbol called a *character entity reference* in your page to display one of these characters. Some characters displayed by character entity references include:

- Letters with accents or other decorations (e.g., ñ, ö, á)
- Punctuation characters (e.g., ¿, •, ©)
- Currency characters (e.g., €, £, ¥)
- Mathematical symbols (e.g., ∑, ƒ, ∞)
- Shapes and arrows (e.g., ↔, ↑, ♥)

Additionally there are several HTML characters that you must use character entities for in order for them to appear correctly on the webpage and not be interpreted by the browser. These include:

- blank spaces (groups of spaces are collapsed in HTML)
- less-than signs (begins an HTML tag)
- greater than signs (ends an HTML tag)
- ampersands (begins a character entity)

There are two ways to designate a character entity references: using an entity name or an entity number. Entity names use the following syntax:

```
&entityName;
```

Entity numbers use the following syntax:

```
&#UnicodeNumber;
```

Entity references are case-sensitive. Table 2.5 lists some of the most commonly used ones. On the Internet there are many complete lists of character entity references. The References section of this chapter links to one of them.

Example 2.29 shows an HTML fragment that uses several character entities to encode a segment of HTML code to be displayed in the page.

| Character | Description | Entity Name/# |
|-----------|-------------|---------------|
| & | Ampersand | &amp; |
| < | Less-than | &lt; |
| > | Greater-than | &gt; |
| " | Quotation mark | &quot; |
| © | Copyright mark | &copy; |
| ° | Degree | &deg; |
| | Non-breaking space |   |
| ‽ | Interrobang | &#8253; |

**Table 2.5 Common character entity references**

```
<p>
  To link to Google's most popular search, use this XHTML code: <br />
  &lt;a href=&quot;http://www.google.com/search?q=marty ↵
&amp;ie=utf-8&quot;&gt;Search for Marty&lt;/a&gt;
</p>

To link to Google's most popular search, use this XHTML code:
<a href="http://google.com/search?q=marty&ie=utf-8"> Search for Marty </a>
```

**Example 2.29 Character entity references**

## Computer Code (code)

| Element | code |
|---|---|
| Description | Computer code (inline) |
| Syntax | `<code>`**content**`</code>` |

The **code** element is an inline element that designates a short piece of text as being computer code, such as a piece of Java or C language code, an HTML element name, or a filename. By default the browser displays the content of code elements in a monospace font (one where all letters are the same width). The **code** element is inline, so it should be enclosed in a block-level element. Example 2.30 demonstrates the **code** element.

```
<p>
  The <code>System.out.println</code> method produces
  console output in a Java program.
</p>
```

The `System.out.println` method produces console output in a Java program.

**Example 2.30 Computer code**

As with other elements, whitespace inside a **code** element is collapsed into a single space. Therefore the **code** element is suitable only for short snippets of code text and not for long, multi-line pieces of source code where whitespace matters.

## Preformatted Text (pre)

| Element | pre |
|---|---|
| Description | Pre-formatted text (block) |
| Syntax | `<pre>` <br> **content** <br> `</pre>` |

We've seen several times now that the browser collapses any span of whitespace in an element's content down to a single space. Usually this helps the readability of the page, but pages with content about computer programming, poetry, ASCII art, and other topics often need to display *pre-formatted* text where the exact whitespace does matter. For an example, when the browser displays the poem in Example 2.31, the whitespace is flattened, which probably isn't what the poet intended.

```
<p>
  Roses are red
  Violets are blue
  All my base
  Are belong to you
</p>
```

Roses are red Violets are blue All my base Are belong to you

**Example 2.31 Flattened whitespace**

The **pre** element is a block-level element that, unlike the others, preserves all the whitespace in its content exactly as written. A **pre** block should be used for any content in which spacing between characters is meaningful. By default, when rendering contents of a **pre** element, the browser leaves all whitespace intact, renders the text in a fixed-width font, and disables automatic word wrapping. Text in a **pre** element can trail off the right edge of the page, requiring a horizontal scroll bar to appear.

```
<pre>
Check out this cool <em>ASCII peace sign</em>:
     .-|-.
    / | \
   ; /|\ ;
    \/ | \/
     '---'
</pre>
```

```
Check out this cool ASCII peace sign:
     .-|-.
    / | \
   ; /|\ ;
    \/ | \/
     '---'
```

**Example 2.32 Pre-formatted text**

Example 2.32 demonstrates the **pre** element. Notice that the text "ASCII peace sign" is italicized. Although the content of the **pre** element is rendered as written, the content is still interpreted as HTML. The **pre** block can contain inline elements such as anchors, emphasis, and images.

If you need to show large samples of source code in your web page, the **pre** element generally does what you want from an appearance perspective. The text in a **pre** element is shown in a monospace font with the whitespace left intact. But discerning web developers who display source code use not only a **pre** element but also a **code** element inside it, as shown in Example 2.33.

**Style Suggestion**
Using **pre** and **code** together

```
<pre><code>
    public static void main(String[] args) {
        System.out.println("Hello, world!");
    }
</code></pre>
```

**Example 2.33 Using pre and code together**

The **code** element is completely unnecessary from a visual standpoint and does nothing to alter the appearance of the source code in the **pre** block. However, putting the **code** tag there provides a more semantic meaning for the content: It is not just any preformatted text, it is source code.

One might argue, "Why should I use the **code** element inside the **pre** if it looks just fine without it?" One answer is, again, we don't choose our tags solely based on how they look in our browser. We choose them to give the proper semantic meaning to the content, and then we worry about appearance later. Another reason for the inner **code** element is that we can apply a style to all source code on the page, without that style affecting other **pre** blocks in the page that contain things other than source code.

## 2.2.5 A Few Miscellaneous Elements

| Element | sup, sub | abbr |
|---|---|---|
| Description | Superscript, subscript (inline) | Abbreviation (inline) |
| Syntax | `<sup>`**content**`</sup>` <br> `<sub>`**content**`</sub>` | `<abbr title="`**long**`">`**short**`</abbr>` |

There are a few last inline elements we'd like to show that don't fit well into any other section. The `sup` and `sub` elements specify that their text should be in superscript (raised) or subscript (lowered) respectively, which is useful for mathematical and scientific equations.

The `abbr` element specifies an abbreviation. The abbreviated form becomes the content between the `<abbr>` and `</abbr>` tags, and the full form is placed in the opening tag as a `title` attribute. The abbreviation will appear with a dashed underline by default, and its full form will appear as a tooltip when the user hovers the mouse over it.

Example 2.34 demonstrates the usage of all of these elements as well as their appearance in the browser when the user hovers the mouse over the abbreviation PEMDAS.

```
<p>
  Don't forget to use the helpful acronym
  <abbr title="Please Excuse My Dear Aunt Sally">PEMDAS</abbr>
  to remember Java operator precedence!
</p>

<p>
  The displacement of a body in motion is given by:
  x<sub>t</sub> = v<sub>0</sub>t + .5at<sup>2</sup>
</p>
```

Don't forget to use the helpful acronym PEMDAS to remember Java operator precedence!

Please Excuse My Dear Aunt Sally

The displacement of a body in motion is given by: $x_t = v_0t + .5at^2$

**Example 2.34 Abbreviations, subscript, and superscript**

## Self-Check

5. What is the difference between the `ul` and `ol` elements?
6. What tags can be directly nested in a `table` tag? What tags can be directly nested in a `tr` tag?
7. What HTML code would you use to make a page show the following:

```
Today's HTML lesson:
To place a < in your page, write &lt; in the HTML.
To show an &, put &amp; instead.
```

8. What element(s) can you use to respect the whitespace in a piece of text (e.g., a piece of programming code)?

## 2.3 Web Standards

The term *web standards* describes a general group of formal standards and technical specifications for various aspects of the World Wide Web. The term is often associated with designing and developing web sites in a way that endorses a set of standardized best practices.

Web standards include recommendations published by groups such as the World Wide Web Consortium (W3C), the Internet Engineering Task Force (IETF), the International Organization for Standardization (ISO), ECMA International, the Unicode Consortium, and other groups. These recommendations describe the standard syntax, semantics, and suggested usage of HTML, XHTML, SVG, CSS, the scripting language ECMAScript (a.k.a. JavaScript), Document Object Models, and several other languages and tools.

When a web page is compliant with web standards, it has valid content in all of its various languages such as HTML, CSS, and JavaScript. Standards-compliant code should also meet accessibility and semantic guidelines.

### 2.3.1 Why Follow Web Standards?

Like lots of other web developers, we believe it's very important to follow web standards. All of the documents in this textbook (except those created specifically to demonstrate errors) comply with web standards as much as possible.

But sadly, a lot of the pages out on the web don't follow web standards perfectly. They contain invalid syntax, non-standard tags that only work in certain browsers, missing tags or information that are required by the standards (such as the `alt` attribute on an `img` element). In fact, several *WYSIWYG* (What you see is what you get) HTML editors produce web pages that flagrantly disobey the standards.

In many cases, as we've already seen, the browser will happily render these invalid pages anyway. It can even be easier to write invalid pages, because it may save you from typing extra attributes or tags. So, you may ask, "Why should I bother to follow the web standards when the page already looks fine in my browser?"

Just because it looks right in your browser, doesn't mean it will look right for others. Compliant pages are much more likely to render correctly in a variety of browsers. And even if it does look right today, it might not tomorrow. The quirks that browsers currently use to try to display invalid pages aren't guaranteed to be around forever and shouldn't be relied upon. Standards-compliant pages are more future-proof and more likely to still look right many years in the future.

Compliant pages are often easier for search engines to examine, which increases the likelihood that your page will come up early in the search engine results for relevant keywords. Compliant pages are also more accessible to users with disabilities, which broadens your page's audience.

Pages can also be validated, meaning that their code can be checked to make sure it is standards-compliant. This provides a good sanity check to make sure that there are no major syntax mistakes in your web content.

### 2.3.2 The W3C XHTML Validator

Many computer programming languages have an application called a *compiler* or *interpreter* that can verify whether your program's syntax is valid. The browser serves as an interpreter for XHTML, but the browser does not provide much information about whether a page or its style is valid. As we have seen, some errors lead to an incorrect onscreen appearance of the page. But many do not, since many browsers try their best to accept and correct invalid XHTML code.

Luckily, the W3C provides validation services for XHTML and other languages that you can use to be sure your syntax is correct. The W3C XHTML *validator*, found at <u>http://validator.w3.org/</u>, is a web site that checks your XHTML code to be sure it meets the official W3C specifications. A validator is a great thing to run the documents and styles you create because it will allow you to quickly find and fix problems in your web pages. Common mistakes the validators can detect and give you hints on how to fix include malformed elements, unclosed tags, incorrectly nested elements, and deprecated elements and properties, among other things.

The validator allows you to submit your code for validation in three ways:

- Provide the validator a URL of an XHTML file on the Internet,
- Upload an XHTML file from your hard drive, or
- Copy and paste the XHTML code to be validated.

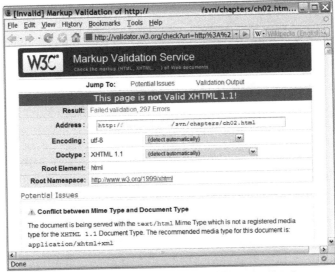

**Figure 2.4 W3C XHTML validator output**

The validator's output looks like that shown in Figure 2.4. One thing to note about the output is that a single mistake in your code often cascades into a listing of many errors in the validator. You should always take a look at the first error first, fix it, and then re-run the validator. For example, when we initially ran the validator on our own XHTML version of this chapter, it listed 297 errors! However, all of them were caused by around a dozen total mistakes, most of them minor errors such as missing `</p>` or `</li>` tags.

If your pages are accessible on the Internet, another way to send your code to the validator is to add a link on any page you create that, when clicked, will run the W3C validator on that page. This link should target the URL http://validator.w3.org/check/referer. Many documents use a standard image for such links, as demonstrated in Example 2.35.

```
<p>
  <a href="http://validator.w3.org/check/referer">
    <img src="http://www.w3.org/Icons/valid-xhtml11"
    alt="Validate XHTML" width="88" height="31" /></a>
</p>
```

W3C XHTML 1.1 ✔

**Example 2.35 W3C XHTML validator button**

We have placed such an image on each of our pages related to this textbook, to show our support for standards-compliant web sites. (Hopefully our files don't contain any errors!)

The validator is pickier than most browsers, which may render malformed XHTML correctly. But by adhering to the standards, you are assured your page will render correctly across any compliant browser. Therefore we recommend you run the validator on any page used in a professional or classroom setting.

### 2.3.3  Web Page Metadata

| Element | meta |
|---|---|
| **Description** | Metadata about your page (placed in **head** section) |
| **Syntax** | `<meta name="`**`name`**`" content="`**`value`**`" />` |
| | `<meta http-equiv="`**`name`**`" content="`**`value`**`" />` |

*Metadata* is data about data. In the case of web pages, sometimes it's useful to put some information inside your page that describes the page itself. For example, you may want to describe the page so that search engines can more easily learn how to catalog your page when they examine it. Or you may be providing additional information about the page to web editing software like Dreamweaver or FrontPage. Or you might want to inform the user's browser that the page has moved to a new location. All of these things are done by placing **meta** tags in the **head** section of a page.

```
<meta name="description" content="UW CSE 190 course web site." />
<meta name="keywords" content="web programming, HTML, CSS, PHP" />
```

A **meta** tag can carry one of a variety of different pieces of information based on its **name** or **http-equiv** attributes. Here are the most common values of those attributes and their meanings:

| Name | Value | Description |
|---|---|---|
| name | author | names of author(s) of the page |
| | description | describes the page's content; used as Google "snippet" |
| | keywords | suggestion to search engines about keywords for this site |
| | generator | what software was used to create this page |
| | revised | date when the page was last updated |
| http-equiv | content-type | MIME type of data held in this page |
| | expires | date when the page's content will become out of date |
| | refresh | time and/or URL to which the browser should redirect |

You don't strictly need any **meta** tags in your page for it to be valid XHTML, and **meta** tags have no appearance in the browser. But they are very useful when writing a professional and W3C-valid site. The **meta content-type** tag is used by the W3C validator to understand the character encoding of your page. Without this tag, you may get a "tentatively valid" warning from the validator.

Search engines like Google also use the content of your **meta description** tag as their short "snippet" of text to display in their search results, along with the page's **title** as the main search link text. Being able to impact how search engines display your page is very powerful if you want more hits! One of the authors of this textbook has previously published a Java book, and Example 2.36 shows the actual page header for his Java book's web site. Figure 2.5 shows how the **meta** tags have made it into the actual Google search results.

```
<!DOCTYPE html PUBLIC "-//W3C//DTD XHTML 1.1//EN"
"http://www.w3.org/TR/xhtml11/DTD/xhtml11.dtd">
<html xmlns="http://www.w3.org/1999/xhtml">
  <head>
    <title>Building Java Programs: A Back to Basics Approach,
      by Stuart Reges and Marty Stepp</title>
    <meta http-equiv="content-type" content="text/html; charset=utf-8" />
    <meta name="description"
      content="Authors' web site for Building Java Programs, a textbook
      designed for use in a first course in computer science." />
    <meta name="keywords" content="web programming, HTML, CSS, PHP" />
  </head>

  <body>
    ...
  </body>
</html>
```

**Example 2.36 Web page with meta tags**

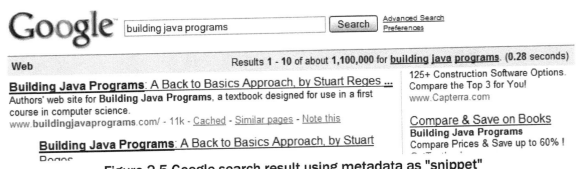

**Figure 2.5 Google search result using metadata as "snippet"**

Another handy use of **meta** tags is for redirecting the browser when a page moves. To do this, use a **meta** tag with a name of **refresh** and content of the number of seconds to delay before refreshing, followed by a semicolon, followed by **url=** and the new URL to which the browser should redirect. You can use a delay of 0 seconds for an immediate redirect. For example, if your page has moved to the URL of http://www.example.com/foo.html, you'd use the following tag:

```
<meta http-equiv="refresh" content="5;url=http://www.example.com/foo.html" />
```

## Self-Check

9.   What are web standards? Why should you follow them?

10.  Does the front page of Google use compliant HTML? If not, how many errors does it have?

11.  Pick three web sites and use the XHTML validator to see if they comply to W3C standards.

12.  What are three uses of **meta** tags? Which **meta** tag is used for a search engine "snippet"?

13.  Many HTML editing programs such as Dreamweaver or Microsoft FrontPage insert **meta generator** tags in documents you create with them, like this:

```
<meta name="generator" content="Microsoft FrontPage 6.0" />
```

Why do you suppose they do this, even though the **meta** tag cannot be seen on the page?

## 2.4 Case Study: Traveler Times

We'll end each chapter with a larger "case study" example that brings together many of the concepts taught in that chapter. In general we'll present a problem and go through the steps to create a web page to solve it. This chapter is an exception since our large example, Traveler Times, is a page we've been building in several examples as we've gone along. So this time we're going to just show the finished page as an example. A few things have been added that weren't seen before, such as `meta` tags, HTML entities for characters such as €, and few lists and links to other relevant pages. Figure 2.6 shows the page appearance in the browser, and Example 2.37 shows the HTML code.

# Traveler Times Newspaper

## Latin America

### Puerto Escondido: Sun, Surf, and Sand

Puerto Escondido is known for one of the world's best surfing beaches, Playa Zicatela. It has a beautiful yellow sand beach and huge world-class surfing waves (but be careful if you go swimming...the current is *very* strong!).

Here is a picture of a surfer at Puerto Escondido... ¡Qué onda!

### Tikal: Mayan Ruins in the Guatemalan Jungle

Tikal is the largest of the ancient ruined cities of the Mayan civilization. It is a really awesome, magical place. If you go to Tikal, you have three main lodging options:

- Tikal National Park: Fancier hotels.
- El Remate (~30km away): Hotels or hostels.
- Flores (~50km away): Hotels or hostels.

## Europe

### Drunk in Dublin

Throwin' back pints with the locals in Dublin this past summer made me really appreciate the pub culture. The top three bars in Dublin for good "craic" (i.e. good fun) in order of my preference are:

1. Davy Byrne's
2. Kehoe's
3. Long Hall

The price of a pint of beer is about €5. Although I would recommend the cider (around €8 a pint).

**Figure 2.6 Traveler Times page appearance in browser**

```
<!DOCTYPE html PUBLIC "-//W3C//DTD XHTML 1.1//EN"
    "http://www.w3.org/TR/xhtml11/DTD/xhtml11.dtd">
<html xmlns="http://www.w3.org/1999/xhtml">
  <head>
    <title>Traveler Times</title>
    <meta http-equiv="content-type" content="text/html; charset=utf-8" />
    <meta name="description" content="Page of Jessica's many travels." />

  </head>

  <body>
    <h1>Traveler Times Newspaper</h1>

    <h2>Latin America</h2>
    <h3>Puerto Escondido: Sun, Surf, and Sand</h3>
    <p>Puerto Escondido is known for one of the world's best surfing
      beaches, Playa Zicatela.  It has a beautiful yellow sand beach
      and huge world-class surfing waves (but be careful if you go
      swimming...the current is <em>very</em> strong!).</p>
    <p>Here is a picture of a surfer at Puerto Escondido...
      &iexcl;Qu&eacute; onda! <br /> <img src="images/surfer.jpg"
      width="292" height="193" alt="Surfer" /></p>

    <h3>Tikal: Mayan Ruins in the Guatemalan Jungle</h3>
    <p>Tikal is the largest of the ancient ruined cities of the Mayan
      civilization. It is a really awesome, magical place.
      If you go to Tikal, you have three main lodging options:</p>

    <ul>
      <li><a href="http://www.tikalpark.com/tikalhotels.htm">Tikal
        National Park</a>: Fancier hotels.</li>
      <li><a href="http://www.passplanet.com/Guatemala/el_remate.htm">
        El Remate</a> (~30km away): Hotels or hostels.</li>
      <li><a href="http://wikitravel.org/en/Flores_(Guatemala)">
        Flores</a> (~50km away): Hotels or hostels.</li>
    </ul>

    <h2>Europe</h2>
    <h3>Drunk in Dublin</h3>
    <p>Throwin' back pints with the locals in Dublin this past summer
      made me really appreciate the pub culture.  The top three bars in
      Dublin for good <q>craic</q> (i.e. good fun) in order of my
      preference are:</p>

    <ol>
      <li>Davy Byrne's</li>
      <li>Kehoe's</li>
      <li>Long Hall</li>
    </ol>

    <p>The price of a pint of beer is about &#8364;5.  Although I
      would recommend the cider (around &#8364;8 a pint).</p>
  </body>
</html>
```

Example 2.37 Traveler Times page code `traveler.html`

## Chapter Summary

- Hypertext Markup Language (HTML) is the language that describes web page content. XHTML is a newer version of HTML that is more standardized across web browsers.
- HTML consists of elements. An element consists of text, tags describing the text, and attributes. Some common HTML elements are for paragraphs, headings, links, images, and lists.
- Elements are classified as block or inline. Block elements appear differently in the browser; each is given its own horizontal and vertical space on the page.
- HTML elements should be chosen based on content rather than appearance in the browser.
- The W3C XHTML validator checks the syntax of your code.

## References

- List of all HTML tags:                  http://www.w3schools.com/tags/default.asp
- List of HTML character entities:        http://www.w3schools.com/tags/ref_entities.asp
- W3C XHTML 1.1 Specification:            http://www.w3.org/TR/xhtml11/
- W3C XHTML 1.1 Elements Reference:       http://www.w3.org/2007/07/xhtml-basic-ref.html
- Differences between HTML/XHTML:         http://www.w3.org/TR/xhtml1/#diffs
- HTML 4.01 specification:                http://www.w3.org/TR/html401
- Original HTML proposal:          http://www.w3.org/MarkUp/draft-ietf-iiir-html-01.txt
- W3C XHTML validator:                    http://validator.w3.org/
- Wikipedia - XHTML:                      http://en.wikipedia.org/wiki/Xhtml
- Wikipedia - Web standards:              http://en.wikipedia.org/wiki/Web_standards

# Chapter 3  CSS for Styling

# Introduction

We'll continue our study of basic web programming by learning the core language for styling web pages: Cascading Style Sheets (CSS). While HTML describes the contents of your page, such as headings, paragraphs, images, and lists, CSS describes the way those contents should look, such as colors, fonts, and alignment.

Originally web pages did not use CSS, and instead used HTML formatting tags to indicate that text should be bold, red, a different font, etc. But this blurred the intended purpose of the HTML language, which was to describe documents and their content, not to describe formatting and appearance. CSS lets you write a page with a clear separation between its content and the way that content should look in a web browser.

Read on! You'll be surprised at the professional-looking pages you'll already be able to create by the end of this chapter.

## 3.1  Basic CSS

Originally web pages supplied formatting information such as layout, fonts, and colors by using formatting elements and attributes. Example 3.1 illustrates this antiquated technique.

```
<p>
    <font face="Comic Sans MS">Welcome to Greasy Joe's!</font>
    <br />
    You will <b>never, <i>ever, <u>EVER</u></i></b> beat
    <font size="+1" color="red">OUR prices</font>.
</p>
```

Welcome to Greasy Joe's!
You will **never,** *ever,* ***EVER*** beat OUR prices.

**Example 3.1 Old-school formatting (don't do this!)**

**deprecated**

Officially labeled as out of date and discouraged from use.

The elements such as **b**, **i**, **u**, and **font** are legal in older HTML. But they are discouraged from use or *deprecated* in XHTML, because they describe appearance and formatting, rather than content.

Cascading style sheets ("CSS") describe the appearance, layout, and presentation of information on a web page (as opposed to HTML, which describes the content of the page). A style sheet describes how information is to be displayed, not what is being displayed.

Style sheet information can be added to a web page in three ways: Inline with an individual HTML element with a `style` attribute, embedded in the page's `head` section as a `style` element, or placed into an external .css file and applied to the page using the `link` element. We will use the third approach, placing our CSS information into its own file.

Placing CSS content into its own file has several advantages. For one, the CSS content is completely separated from the HTML this way, which emphasizes the separation of content from presentation. Also, if the style sheet is a separate file, it can be used by many HTML documents.

## 3.1.1 CSS Syntax

A CSS file contains one or more rules. A *rule* is the fundamental unit of CSS that specifies a set of page elements or tags, and a set of styles to apply to them.

> **rule**
>
> A CSS statement describing a set of page tags and a set of styles to apply to those tags.

Each rule consists of one or more *selectors* describing which content the style applies to. Following the selectors, a rule lists presentational *properties* and their values that should apply to the selected content. The syntax for CSS rules is shown in Example 3.2.

```
selector {
    property: value;
    property: value;
    ...
    property: value;
}
```

**Example 3.2 Syntax template for CSS selector**

The CSS rule in Example 3.3 sets all paragraphs in the page to be written in a red Trebuchet MS font. (In our CSS examples, assume that the CSS code shown is part of a .css stylesheet file that has been linked to the HTML document.)

> **selector**
>
> Specification of which element(s) a CSS rule applies to.

```
<p>20% off, this weekend only!</p>
```

```
p {
    font-family: "Trebuchet MS";
    color: red;
}
```

20% off, this weekend only!

**Example 3.3 HTML code and CSS rule**

Property names are always lowercase. Properties with multi-word names separate them with hyphens, such as `font-family` or `list-style-type`. It is legal for a CSS rule to contain multiple selectors, as shown in the syntax template in Example 3.4.

> **property**
>
> A stylistic aspect that can be set in a CSS rule.

```
selector1, selector2, ..., selectorN {
  property: value;
  property: value;
  ...
  property: value;
}
```

**Example 3.4 Syntax template for CSS rule with multiple selectors**

For example, the rule in Example 3.5 makes both level 1 headings and level 2 headings green.

```
h1, h2 {
  color: green;
}
```

**Example 3.5 CSS rule with multiple selectors**

## 3.1.2 Applying CSS to a Web Page

| Element | link |
|---|---|
| Description | Link to an external file, such as a style sheet |
| Syntax | `<link href="filename" type="text/css" rel="stylesheet" />` |

The clearest, most portable way of applying styles to web pages is by using an external stylesheet. This is done by including a `link` element in the HTML file's `head` section. Example 3.6 shows how to apply the styles in a CSS file named style.css to a page:

```
<link href="style.css" type="text/css" rel="stylesheet" />
```

**Example 3.6 Link to external stylesheet**

Style information can also be embedded in an HTML file by placing a `style` element in the page's header, as shown in Example 3.7, though we consider this poor style.

```
<!DOCTYPE html PUBLIC "-//W3C//DTD XHTML 1.1//EN"
    "http://www.w3.org/TR/xhtml11/DTD/xhtml11.dtd">
<html xmlns="http://www.w3.org/1999/xhtml">
  <head>
    <title>Chapter 1</title>
    <style type="text/css">
    h1 {
      color: red;
    }
    </style>
  </head>

  <body>
    <h1>This heading will be red now.</h1>
  </body>
</html>
```

**Example 3.7 Embedded styles (avoid!)**

Lastly, style information can be applied inline with a particular element on the page using the `style` attribute. Inline styles have the highest precedence and override any other styles applied elsewhere to the element. When applying inline styling, no selectors are designated, since the style rules implicitly apply to the element to which they've been attached.

```
<h1 style="color: blue;">
  This heading will be blue now.
</h1>
```

**Example 3.8 Inline styling (avoid!)**

It's legal to link to multiple stylesheets to the same page. All styles from each CSS file will be applied. If two sheets define conflicting styles with the same selector, the latter's properties will be used.

As stated previously, we recommend exclusively using the `link` tag to connect your HTML document to an external CSS style sheet file. As a slight tangent, the `link` tag can also be used to link to other kinds of resources, such as setting a favorites icon or *favicon* for a web page. A page's favicon is a small image that will show up when it is displayed in the browser or as a bookmark. The general syntax for setting a favicon is shown in Example 3.9.

```
<link href="filename" type="MIME type" rel="shortcut icon" />
```

**Example 3.9 Syntax template for favorites icon ("favicon")**

For example, if you have an image of a red "Y" icon stored in a file yahoo.gif in the same directory as your web page, you could use it as your page's favicon with the code shown in Example 3.10.

```
<link href="yahoo.gif" type="image/gif" rel="shortcut icon" />
```

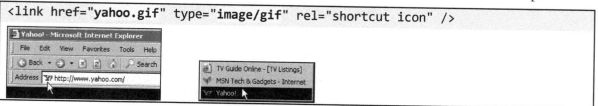

**Example 3.10 Favicon**

Though you can apply styles inline and embed them into the web page, elite web developers avoid applying styles in these ways if possible. Inline styles blur the separation between content and presentation. They can't be shared across multiple web pages. They also clutter your HTML

**Style Suggestion**

Don't mix CSS and HTML

code with CSS information. Keeping your CSS separate will keep your pages clean, easier to read, and more conceptually pure. While you're writing the HTML, focus on the content and the proper tags to represent that content, not on its appearance or styling.

In the following sections we will introduce CSS properties that will allow you to style the content of your web pages with different colors, fonts, and other text decorations.

### 3.1.3 Color Properties

| Property | color |
|---|---|
| Description | Element's foreground (text) color |
| Value | A color (specified as a name, RGB, or hex) |

| Property | `background-color` |
|---|---|
| Description | Element's background color |
| Value | A color (specified as a name, RGB, or hex) |

CSS specifies foreground colors for HTML elements with the `color` property. When a foreground color is specified, the color of the content's text and borders are set. To set the background color of content, use the `background-color` property. Example 3.11 shows code could be placed into an HTML document and a CSS stylesheet linked to that document.

```
<p>Whoa.  I know kung fu.</p>
```

```
p {
  color: green;
  background-color: yellow;
}
```

Whoa. I know kung fu.

**Example 3.11 Color styles**

Colors can be specified in three ways:

- predefined color names such as `orange`
- red-green-blue color codes such as `rgb(255, 165, 0)`
- hexadecimal color codes such as `#ffa500`

Table 3.1 lists the standard color names that are recognized by all modern browsers. Some browsers recognize more than these, but the ones in the table are guaranteed to work in all browsers.

| | | | |
|---|---|---|---|
| aqua | black | blue | fuchsia |
| gray | green | lime | maroon |
| navy | olive | purple | red |
| silver | teal | white | yellow |

**Table 3.1 Color names**

**Don't Be a Newb**

Avoid ugly color schemes

When it comes to color, keep it simple. A lot of inexperienced web developers want their web sites to look unique, so they choose outlandish color schemes. Usually this just makes the page unpleasant to read. Most standard text looks best in black with a white background. If you use other colors, make sure they have enough contrast to be readable. And no matter how much you like the Matrix, colored text with a black background usually looks bad. Avoid black backgrounds unless the page truly calls for it.

As you may know, computers use red, green, and blue as their primary colors. CSS lets you specify colors using a red-green-blue ("RGB") color code containing three values specifying 0 (none) to 255 (full) usage of those three colors. All 0s represents black and all 255s represents white. Example 3.12 specifies to draw all `h2` and `h3` elements with half red, no green, and full blue, resulting in a dark purple color:

```
h2, h3 {
  color: rgb(128, 0, 255);
}
```

**Example 3.12 RGB color**

You can also use hexadecimal ("hex") codes to specify the red, green, and blue values in base-16 format. In a hexadecimal number, each digit can have one of 16 possible values from 0-9 or A-F (representing 10-15). Each digit to the left has a value 16 times the digit on its right. For example, consider the hexadecimal number B7. B is 11 in hex, and the B is in the 16s place, so B7 represents the decimal number (16 * 11 + 7) or 183. Using two hexadecimal digits, you can represent a number from 00 through FF, in other words, a number from 0 through (16 * 15 + 15) = 255.

A CSS hexadecimal color code contains a # sign followed by six hexadecimal digits. The first two digits represent the red value from 0 to 255, the next two represent the green value from 0 to 255, and the last two the blue value from 0 to 255. The style shown in Example 3.13 represents the same dark purple color as the one shown in Example 3.12.

```
h2, h3 {
  color: #8000FF;
}
```

**Example 3.13 Hex color**

It may seem strange to represent colors in this way. One benefit of the hex format is its compactness: You can represent any color with exactly six hexadecimal digits. However, if you're using a color that has a name in CSS such as red or orange, we still recommend using the name rather than the equivalent hex code such as #FF0000 or #FFAA00.

---

### Did You Know: Keyword-Stuffing, White-on-White

Search engines crawl web pages, meaning that they download pages, look through their text for keywords and links, then crawl the pages in those links. Search engines use the words on the page to decide what results and in what order to display the results in later searches.

Web publishers know that their page can get a better ranking with search engines if they increase the number of copies of the keywords (e.g., "cheap home loans") in their pages. This practice is called *keyword stuffing*. For example:

```
cheap cheap cheap cheap cheap
home loans home loans home loans home loans
```

(I can only imagine what the above will do to our book's search ranking!)

The problem with keyword stuffing is that while it fools a search engine, it doesn't fool the user, who sees all the stray words as garbage or a sign of lack of professionalism. So the malicious page author uses white text on a white background. The search engine will see the text just fine, but you won't.

Thankfully, search engines have gotten smarter, and keyword stuffing largely doesn't fool them any more. But the practice still exists in some of the less savory corners of the web.

### 3.1.4 CSS Comments

Like all the languages in this textbook, CSS allows comments. As you'd expect, comments in CSS are ignored by the browser. Use them for documentation or to "comment out" styles or properties.

CSS uses the C-style /* and */ to surround comments, which can span one to many lines. Don't confuse this with <!-- and -->, the comment syntax for HTML. A quick mnemonic device: CSS uses "C-Style Syntax" for its comments. Example 3.14 shows an example of CSS commenting.

```
/* The following is patterned after
   cnn.com's design. */
p {
  font-weight: bold;
  font-style: italic;
  /* font-size: 200%; */
}
```

**Example 3.14 CSS comments**

Most web developers don't comment their code very much. Partly this is because HTML and CSS are more declarative and self-explanatory than many other computer languages. Excessive commenting can actually make your page less readable. We recommend comment headers on top of your .css files and on any style that merits additional explanation, such as the complex layout styles we'll see in the next chapter. Your instructor or workplace may have its own commenting policy.

### 3.1.5 Font Properties

In this section we will talk about a number of the most common font properties you can use to style fonts for text content. We will not cover all font properties, but if you would like to know more about how to style fonts, W3 Schools provides a complete list of font properties.

**Font Families (Names)**

| Property | `font-family` |
|---|---|
| Description | Font name to use |
| Value | A name such as `serif` or `"Courier New"` |

The `font-family` property specifies the font to use to render text for a given HTML element. Example 3.15 demonstrates setting fonts for various elements.

```
h2 {
    font-family: "Arial Narrow";
}
p {
    font-family: "Georgia";
}
```

### I am a level 2 heading.

I am a paragraph.

**Example 3.15 Setting fonts**

Multi-word font names must be enclosed in quotes, such as `"Times New Roman"`. Though not necessary, we also quote single-word font names for consistency, such as `"Arial"`.

There are lots of interesting details about fonts, but most of them are outside the scope of this textbook. A few useful things to know about are serifs and monospace fonts. A *serif* is a small protrusion on the edge of a letter. Some fonts such as Times New Roman place serifs on their letters for visual effect. A font that doesn't use serifs is usually called a sans-serif font ("sans" is French for "without"). Most books use serifed fonts, and serifed fonts are generally believed to be easier to read than sans-serif fonts on printed pages. But serifs are sometimes hard to read on computer screens, so many web sites use predominantly sans-serif fonts for a cleaner look.

A *monospace* font is one where every letter is drawn at exactly the same width on the screen. Courier is a common example of a monospace font. By contrast, variable-width fonts such as Times New Roman or Arial draw some letters such as "i" thinner than other letters such as "m". Variable-width fonts are widely considered to be more pleasant and easier to read than fixed-width fonts, except for certain special cases such as when displaying program source code.

| serif | sans-serif | variable width | monospace |
|-------|-----------|----------------|-----------|
| a | a | hello | `hello` |

**Table 3.2 Differences in fonts**

One problem is that fonts vary between operating systems and computers. You can never be certain which fonts will be installed by the user visiting your page. Therefore, you are encouraged to list more than one font family in your CSS. You can do this by separating them by commas. When the browser encounters the rule, it will check each font in order, using the first available on the system.

CSS also recognizes a set of generic font names, listed in Table 3.3. A generic font doesn't refer to a specific font by name, but rather refer to a general category of font such as `cursive` or `monospace`. Every browser and operating system is guaranteed to have a font in that category.

| cursive | fantasy | monospace | sans-serif | serif |
|---------|---------|-----------|------------|-------|

**Table 3.3 Generic font families**

If you want to be certain that your page will look roughly the way you intend regardless of what fonts the user has installed, you should list a generic font in your CSS rule after any specific fonts, as shown in Example 3.16.

```
p {
  font-family: "Garamond", "Times New Roman", serif;
}
```

**Example 3.16 Multiple and generic fonts**

The ideal setting for a `font-family` value is a list of fonts in the following order:

- the font you really want
- another one or two similar fonts that are usually installed on major operating systems
- the nearest generic font family name

The style in Example 3.17 should look pretty similar regardless of who visits the page.

```
p {
  font-family: "Helvetica", "Verdana", "Arial", sans-serif;
}
```

**Example 3.17 Well-chosen font family list**

## Font Sizes

| Property | `font-size` |
|---|---|
| Description | Size of text to display |
| Value | A unit value, percentage, or named value |

The `font-size` property specifies how large to make the element's text on the page. Example 3.18 sets all paragraphs to use a size 14pt font.

```
p {
  font-size: 14pt;
}
```

**Example 3.18 Font size**

Font sizes (and sizes of onscreen items in general) can be specified in several ways:

- Units such as pixels (`px`), points (`pt`), and m-sizes (`em`)
- Percentage font sizes such as `120%`
- Absolute font sizes such as `small`
- Relative font sizes such as `larger`

**pixel**

The smallest dot on a computer screen; a unit of measure of sizes of onscreen elements.

A pixel (`px`), short for "picture element," is a single dot on the computer's monitor. A point (`pt`) is supposed to represent 1/72 of an inch on the screen. An m-size (`em`) is roughly the size of the letter 'm' in the element's current font. `1em` represents 100% of the font's size.

In terms of their relative sizes, an `em` is much larger than a `pt`, and a `pt` is generally a bit larger than a `px`. Figure 3.1 compares several similar font sizes.

$$18\text{px}, 18\text{pt}, 1.8\text{em}$$

**Figure 3.1 Font size comparison**

You can also specify a font size as a percentage. This is relative to the standard font size for that element, which is considered to be 100%. Example 3.19 demonstrates this.

```
h6 {
  font-size: 125%;
}
```

**Example 3.19 Font size as percentage**

There are a number of pre-defined text values that can be used to designate the absolute size of a font, such as `small`. In order to convert these values to an actual size, the browser keeps a pre-defined table that maps each of these text values to a unit size, such as `10pt` for `small`.

In addition to named absolute font sizes there are two named relative font sizes: `smaller` and `larger`. These will bump the font size up or down to the closest named font size level of the element's parent. For example, if we had a `body` element whose font size was set to `small` and we wanted `p` elements inside the body to be a bit larger, by setting the `p` element's font size to `larger`, the `p` element would get rendered at whatever size the browser defined for `large`.

The downfall of using named font sizes is that each browser could potentially have different unit values corresponding to the value and so the same page might look different in different browsers. However, if you want a quick and dirty way to designate font size, Table 3.4 shows a full list of the pre-defined, named font size values.

| | | |
|---|---|---|
| xx-small | x-small | small |
| medium | large | x-large |
| xx-large | smaller | larger |

**Table 3.4 Font size names**

## Font Styles and Weights

| Property | font-style |
|---|---|
| **Description** | Whether or not to italicize text |
| **Value** | normal (default), italic |

The `font-style` property is used to specify whether a given element's text should be italic or not. Its relevant values are `italic` and `normal`; the default for most elements is `normal`.

| Property | font-weight |
|---|---|
| Description | Whether or not to bold text |
| Value | normal (default), bold |

The font-weight property is similar to font-style but represents boldness. Its relevant values are bold and normal; the default for most elements is normal (though some elements default to bold, such as headings h1 through h6). Example 3.20 demonstrates setting both properties.

```
p {
  font-weight: bold;
  font-style: italic;
}
```

*You want the truth? You can't handle the truth!*

**Example 3.20 Font weights and styles**

## The font Property

| Property | font |
|---|---|
| Description | Shortcut for setting all font properties |
| Value | **style  weight  size  family** |

There's a shortcut property named font that lets you set many aspects of the font in one step. To use the font property, list the values corresponding to the various font properties in the order listed above, separating each by one space. You do not need to list a value for all properties above, but you do need to list the values in the order defined above.  (Font style and weight must be first, in either order, followed by font size, and finally the list of font names.)

```
p {
  font: italic bold 14px "Comic Sans MS", cursive;
}
```

Hello...I love you,
Won't you tell me your name?

**Example 3.21 The font property**

## 3.1.6 Text Properties

| CSS property | Description | Values |
|---|---|---|
| `text-align` | alignment of inline content | `left`, `center`, `right`, `justify` |
| `text-indent` | indent first line | a size (**px, pt, %, em**) |
| `text-decoration` | underline, etc. | `underline`, `overline`, `line-through`, `blink`, `none` |
| `letter-spacing` | horizontal gap between letters | a size (**px, pt, %, em**) |
| `line-height` | vertical size of each line | a size (**px, pt, %, em**) |
| `word-spacing` | horizontal gap between words | a size (**px, pt, %, em**) |

CSS has other properties to affect the appearance of text. Example 3.22 shows a piece of code that sets several text properties (though unfortunately a printed textbook cannot display blinking text, so the word "complete" appears solid in the output shown). Notice that the first line is indented 5em and subsequent lines are not.

```
<p>
  Strike me down with all of your hatred and
  <br /> your journey towards the dark side
  will be <strong>complete</strong>.
</p>
```

```
p {
  text-align: justify;
  text-decoration: underline;
  text-indent: 5em;
}
strong {
  text-decoration: blink;
}
```

> Strike me down with all of your hatred and your journey towards the dark side will be **complete**.

**Example 3.22 Text properties**

The text decoration of **none** is useful for removing a decoration from an element that would otherwise have one. The most common example of this is to remove the underline from links. For example, the word "MySpace" in Example 3.23 isn't underlined, but it still links to myspace.com:

```
<p>
  OMG, check out my page on
  <a href="http://www.myspace.com/">MySpace</a>, bro!
</p>
```

```
a {
  text-decoration: none;
}
```

OMG, check out my page on MySpace, bro!

**Example 3.23 Link without decoration**

Example 3.24 demonstrates some other text properties for adjusting spacing and line height.

```
p {
  letter-spacing: 0.25em;
  line-height: 1.5em;
  word-spacing: 3em;
}
```

Strike     me     down     with     all     of     your     hatred

and     your     journey     towards     the     dark     side     will

be     complete.

**Example 3.24 More text properties**

**Don't Be a Newb**
Avoid blinking text

In the late '90s, a lot of web developers put blinking text into their web pages to emphasize certain text. (HTML even has a now-deprecated `blink` tag, perhaps the most shameful tag in the whole language.) The collective users of the internet have decided that blinking text is dreadful and annoying. It's like writing an email IN ALL UPPERCASE LETTERS: You just shouldn't do it.

The W3C isn't exactly enamored with blinking text themselves. Their web accessibility guidelines say, "If blinking content ... is used, provide a mechanism for stopping the blinking." So we recommend not using blinking text unless your page is reporting a natural disaster. Maybe not even then.

## Self-Check

1.  Why is it a good practice to put your CSS code in an external file using a link tag, rather than placing it directly inside your page's HTML?
2.  What are the three ways to specify a color in CSS? Suppose you want a brown background. How would you specify a brown color? (You may want to consult one of the HTML color table links given in the References section.)
3.  What's wrong with the following CSS code? Identify at least four syntax errors or mistakes.

```
p {
  background color: red;
  foreground-color: yellow;
  Font-Family: Times New Roman, serif;
}

h1, h2, h3, {
  font-style: bold;
  font-size: 24em;
}
```

## 3.2 More CSS

Now that we've learned introductory styling with CSS, let's learn additional CSS rules and learn about some properties that apply to particular elements.

### 3.2.1 Style Inheritance and Conflicts

Most style rules you apply to an element also apply to any other elements nested inside it. Such CSS properties, such as fonts and colors, are said to be *inherited* from the outer element to the inner one.

> **inheritance**
>
> A process where style rules on an element are also applied to elements inside it.

One common example of style inheritance is to apply a style to the entire body of the page. A style with **body** as its selector will apply to all content in the page body. Of course, you can add other styles to elements inside the body by creating style rules specific to those elements. Notice how all text in Example 3.25 is underlined because of the style rule applied to the page's body.

```
<body>
  <h4>Heading</h4>
  <p>Hello, how are you? I am fine, thanks.</p>
  <ul>
    <li>A list with one item</li>
  </ul>
</body>
```

```
body {
  text-decoration: underline;
}
p {
  background-color: yellow;
}
ul {
  font-style: italic;
}
```

**Heading**

Hello, how are you? I am fine, thanks.

- *A list with one item*

**Example 3.25 Styles with inheritance**

Sometimes when multiple style rules apply to the same element, they conflict. For example, in Example 3.26 the **body** style rule specifies a cyan background color, but the **p** rule specifies a yellow background. When two style rules conflict, CSS applies rules of precedence to decide which style will be used. The general rule of thumb for CSS precedence is that the more specific or closely matching selector "wins" for a given element. In the example, paragraphs will use the **p** style but other elements will use the default cyan background. We'll discuss conflicting styles and complex style rules more in the next chapter.

```
<body>
  <h4>Heading</h4>

  <p>
    Hello, how are you?
    I am fine, thanks.
  </p>
</body>
```

```
body {
  background-color: cyan;
  text-decoration: underline;
}
p {
  background-color: yellow;
  font-style: italic;
}
```

Heading

Hello, how are you? I am fine, thanks.

**Example 3.26 Styles that conflict**

It is possible to have two style rules with exactly the same selector. This can happen frequently if you are linking to more than one CSS file in your HTML document. In cases like this, the last rule wins. For example, if your HTML document links to a style1.css file that sets all h2 elements to be red, and your HTML document also links to a style2.css file that sets all h2 elements to be blue, the blue rule from style2.css will be used since it will be loaded last by the browser. The same is true if you have multiple rules in the same CSS file that target the same element; the last one wins.

```
h2 { color: red; }
h2 { color: blue; }    /* overrides the previous color setting */
```

## 3.2.2 IDs and ID Selectors

We've seen how to apply a CSS style to all occurrences of a particular element. To achieve complex layouts, we'll need to apply a style to a particular single element, such as an individual heading or paragraph. One way to do this that we mentioned in the last chapter is to attach a **style** attribute to the element. However, doing so is not recommended because it clutters your HTML code with style information that ought to be in a separate file. But there's a better way to get the same effect.

| ID selector |
| --- |
| A CSS rule that applies only to a particular element on the page with a given ID. |

Any HTML element can be given an attribute named **id** to uniquely identify it. The value you use for the **id** is up to you, but it must begin with a letter followed by letters, digits, hyphens, underscores, colons and periods (spaces are not allowed). Each **id** must be unique throughout the document; no two elements may use the same **id**.

It's possible to create a CSS rule that applies only to the single element on the page that has a particular id. Such a rule uses an *ID selector*, which contains a hash sign (#) followed by the id to select. The general syntax for ID selectors is shown in Example 3.27.

```
#id {
  property: value;
  ...
  property: value;
}
```

**Example 3.27 Syntax template for ID selector**

Example 3.28 demonstrates an h2 element that has been given an **id** of europe and a CSS rule that applies an italic font style to that particular heading.

```
<h2 id="europe">Europe</h2>
```

```
#europe {
  font-style: italic;
}
```

**Example 3.28 Italic ID selector**

### Links to Sections of a Page

Most links point from one page to another, but it's also legal to have a link that points from one part of a page to another part of that same page. You have probably seen this in long pages with links at the top that, when clicked, cause your browser to scroll down to a later section of the page.

To link to a section of your page, first label that section of the page by placing an **id** attribute on an element. Then create a link that points to that **id**. The syntax of such a link is to write the page's URL followed by a hash sign #, then the **id** of interest. If you're linking to an **id** within the current page, you can simply write the hash sign and the **id**. Example 3.29 demonstrates a link to an element with an **id** of europe. If the user clicks the link, the browser scrolls to that heading.

```
<p>
  Traveling to <a href="#europe">Europe</a> is fun... but it ain't cheap!
</p>
```

Traveling to <u>Europe</u> is fun... but it ain't cheap!

**Example 3.29 Linking to a target anchor**

## 3.2.3 Classes and Class Selectors

Imagine that you'd like to apply the same style to a dozen different paragraphs throughout your page, but not to every paragraph. The **id** attribute isn't a good choice here. An **id** must be a unique identifier; no two elements can have the same **id** value. We could give each of the dozen paragraphs its own **id** and apply the style to all of them separated by commas, but this would be cumbersome.

Luckily, there's another HTML attribute made for situations just like this. The **class** attribute is an identifier you can attach to any HTML element. Multiple elements can have the same **class** value. CSS rules can be created that target classes, which will apply the style to all elements with that class. Such rules use a *class selector*, which contains a dot followed by the class to select.

> **class selector**
>
> A CSS rule that applies only to particular element(s) on the page that have a given class.

Example 3.31's code declares classes so that corresponding styles can be applied to them. Notice that the first and third paragraphs without **class** attributes do not receive any styling in the output.

```
.class {
  property: value;
  property: value;
  ...
  property: value;
}
```

**Example 3.30 Syntax template for class selector**

```
<p>first paragraph</p>
<p class="urgent">second paragraph</p>
<p>third paragraph</p>
<p class="urgent">fourth paragraph</p>
<p class="new">fifth paragraph</p>
```

```
.urgent {
  color: red;
}
.new {
  background-color: yellow;
}
```

first paragraph

second paragraph

third paragraph

fourth paragraph

fifth paragraph

**Example 3.31 Class selectors**

An HTML element can specify multiple classes by separating them with spaces. All style rules that apply to any of the classes will be applied to the element. (If multiple rules define a value for the same property, the value from the rule written latest in the CSS file will be used.) Example 3.32 demonstrates this by adding a sixth paragraph to Example 3.31's code and applying two classes to it.

```
<p class="urgent new">sixth paragraph</p>
```

sixth paragraph

**Example 3.32 Multiple classes**

It's also legal for the CSS rule to state the tag name before the dot and class name. This will apply the style only to all elements with that tag name that have the given class. For example, the CSS rule in Example 3.34 would apply to all h2 headings that have class urgent, but not to any other elements, regardless of whether or not they have class urgent.

```
tagname.class {
  property: value;
  ...
}
```

**Example 3.33 Syntax template for tag/class selector**

```
h2.urgent {
  text-align: center;
}
```

**Example 3.34 Tag/class selector**

Some web programmers have trouble remembering which of `id` and `class` uses the hash sign `#` for its CSS selector and which uses the dot. We use a mnemonic device to help remember this. Our students have learned Java before learning CSS; compiling a Java program produces a `.class` ("dot-class") file. So we tell them to remember "dot-class" because the dot goes with `class` here as well.

The names you give for your IDs and classes are largely up to you, but some names are better than others. Many programmers name them poorly, choosing names based on how they want the content to look. Examples are `redtext`, `boldheading`, `centered`, and `bigfont`. These are poor names because they focus on appearance rather than on the meaning of content. If the web designer changes the appearance, such as making `redtext` items blue, the names won't make sense.

**Don't Be a Newb**
Give your IDs and classes semantic names

Instead, focus on the semantics and meaning of the content. Why is the text red? If the text is red to alert the user about an important warning, name the class warning instead. What text is being shown in the `biggerfont`? If the `biggerfont` is used for emphasis, maybe you should just use an `em` HTML tag instead and then style `em` tags to use a larger non-italic font. Semantic names are better for those designing the page and anyone reading it later to try to understand its content.

## 3.2.4 CSS for Lists

Each type of list has a default appearance: an unordered list uses solid filled round bullets on each list item, and an ordered list gives numbers to each list item. But you can change the style of numbering or bullets on a list by setting its `list-style-type` CSS property.

| Property | list-style-type |
|---|---|
| Description | Style of bullets or numbering in a list |
| Value | `none` — no marker<br>`disc` (default for a `ul`) — a filled circle<br>`circle`, `square` — a hollow circle or filled square<br>`decimal` (default for an `ol`) — 1, 2, 3, ...<br>`decimal-leading-zero` — 01, 02, 03, ...<br>`lower-roman` — i, ii, iii, iv, v, ...<br>`upper-roman` — I, II, III, IV, V, ...<br>`lower-alpha` — a, b, c, d, e, ...<br>`upper-alpha` — A, B, C, D, E, ...<br>`lower-greek` — alpha, beta, gamma, ...<br>`hebrew, armenian, georgian, hiragana, katakana, ...` |

Example 3.35 demonstrates an ordered list with lowercase Roman numerals. The amount a list will be indented is determined by its left padding, which we'll discuss in the next chapter.

```
<p>The worst prequel episodes ever:</p>
<ol>
  <li>The Phantom Menace</li>
  <li>Attack of the Clones</li>
  <li>Revenge of the Sith</li>
</ol>
```

```
ol {
  list-style-type: lower-roman;
}
```

The worst prequel episodes ever:

i. The Phantom Menace
ii. Attack of the Clones
iii. Revenge of the Sith

**Example 3.35 List type styling**

## 3.2.5 CSS for Tables

HTML tables can also be styled using CSS. In this section we use the CSS font and color properties in addition to table-specific CSS properties (e.g., `caption-side`) and two new HTML elements, `col` and `colgroup`, to alter the appearance of tables.

| Property | caption-side |
|---|---|
| Description | Sets the position of the table caption |
| Value | top (default), bottom, left, right |

To alter the appearance of all table content (captions, rows, and cells), we can add styling using the `table` selector. Example 3.36 uses the `table` selector to style all text in the "Beverage Caffeination" table to have a 14px Comic Sans MS font. You can add styles to specific elements within a table with CSS as well. By default, captions have a `font-weight` of `normal`, but in Example 3.36 we have given our `caption` a bold `font-weight`. The `tr` selector styles all elements within a row, headers and cells inclusive (as shown in Example 3.36 Table styling by using the `tr` selector to give row text a blue `color`). To style table headers and table cells you can use the `th` and `tr` selectors. In Example 3.36, the headers are italicized and underlined (headers have a `font-weight` of `bold` and a centered alignment by default) and regular table cell contents have a yellow `background-color` and are aligned to the right (the default text alignment of table cells is to the left). Example 3.36 has also used the `caption-side` property to move the caption "Beverage Caffeination" to the left of the table.

```
table {
  caption-side: left;
  font: 14px "Comic Sans MS";
}

caption {
  font-size: 18px;
  font-weight: bold;
}

tr {
  color: blue;
}

th {
  font-style: italic;
  text-decoration: underline;
}

td {
  background-color: yellow;
  text-align: right;
}
```

**Beverage Caffeination**

| Beverage | mg of Caffeine |
|---|---|
| Brewed Coffee | 80 - 135 |
| Brewed Tea | 60 |

**Example 3.36 Table styling**

Notice in Example 3.36 how the conflict between the font-size in the table and caption selector gets resolved: the style closest to the content (i.e. the caption selector's font) determines the size of the text in the caption.

It is easy to see how to style rows using the tr selector, but what happens if we want to style columns? One option is to create a class for the column and set the class attribute of each td and tr tag in the column to be that of the CSS class. This option is supported by all browsers. The second option is via the col and colgroup elements. The col tag can be used to define styles that apply to an entire column. The colgroup tag groups a number of col tags together to style a group of columns in one fell swoop. The best way to use the col and colgroup tags are to create a CSS class for the columns' styles and set the class attribute of these tags to the CSS class. The styles are applied to the columns in the order the col and colgroup tags are declared within the table tag. The col and colgroup tags are in the W3C Recommendation for HTML 4 and 5, but unfortunately are only fully supported by Opera and Internet Explorer. Hopefully we will see full support for col and colgroup from the other browsers in the future. Example 3.37 shows the usage of col and colgroup.

| Element | col | colgroup |
|---|---|---|
| Description | Column (for styling) | Column group (for styling) |
| Syntax | `<col attributes />` | `<colgroup attributes>`<br>  `<col attributes />`<br>  ...<br>  `<col attributes />`<br>`</colgroup>` |

```
<table border="1">
  <col class="product"/>
  <colgroup class="facts">
    <col /> <col /> <col class="fat" />
  </colgroup>
  <tr>
    <th>Product</th>
    <th>Size (oz)</th>
    <th>Caffeine (mg)</th>
    <th>Fat (g)</th>
  </tr>
  <tr><td>Green Tea</td><td>8</td><td>20</td><td>0</td></tr>
  <tr><td>Dark chocolate</td><td>2</td><td>20</td><td>19</td></tr>
</table>
```

```
.product {
  text-align: center;
  text-decoration: underline;
}

.facts {
  background-color: pink;
}

.fat {
  font-style: italic;
}
```

| Product | Size (oz) | Caffeine (mg) | Fat (g) |
|---|---|---|---|
| Green Tea | 8 | 20 | 0 |
| Dark chocolate | 2 | 20 | 19 |

**Example 3.37 col and colgroup elements**

Rather than specifying individual `col` tags inside a `colgroup`, it is also legal to give the group a `span` attribute indicating how many columns it applies to. For example, if we hadn't wanted to italicize the Fat column, the following would also have been a legal way to declare the last column group:

```
<colgroup class="facts" span="3"></colgroup>
```

## 3.2.6  W3C CSS Validator

Because browsers don't show any error messages when CSS is incorrect, it can be difficult to tell whether your CSS code is valid. Sometimes you'll see an unusual appearance on the page that will alert you to a problem in your styles, but other mistakes are more subtle.

The W3C provides a validation service for CSS that you can use to be sure your CSS syntax is correct. The W3C CSS validator, found at http://jigsaw.w3.org/css-validator/, is a web site that checks your CSS code to be sure it meets the official W3C specifications.

If your webpage is accessible on the Internet, another way to send your code to the validator is to add a link on any page you create that, when clicked, will run the W3C CSS validator on that page. This link should target http://jigsaw.w3.org/css-validator/check/referer. Many documents use the following standard W3C images for their XHTML and CSS validator links.

```
<p>
  <a href="http://validator.w3.org/check/referer">
    <img src="http://www.w3.org/Icons/valid-xhtml11"
    alt="Validate XHTML" width="88" height="31" /></a>

  <a href="http://jigsaw.w3.org/css-validator/check/referer">
    <img src="http://jigsaw.w3.org/css-validator/images/vcss"
    alt="Validate CSS" width="88" height="31" /></a>
</p>
```

**Example 3.38 W3C validator buttons**

We have placed validator links at the bottom of each of our textbook web pages to show support for standards-compliant web sites. (Hopefully our pages don't contain any errors!)

## Self-Check

4.  What CSS would cause unordered and ordered lists to have blue text and black background?
5.  How do you decide when to use a **class** and when to use an **id**? Which would you use for each of the following cases:
    a)  You want to style one paragraph representing your company's mission statement.
    b)  Several groups of list items are important, so they should appear in a red color.
    c)  All **h2** headings on the page should be underlined.
6.  What color (foreground and background) will be used for each element below?

```
<body>
  <p>I'm a paragraph; what color am I?</p>

  <div class="central">
    <p>I'm another paragraph; what color am I?</p>
    <ul><li id="item">I'm a list item; what color am I?</li></ul>
  </div>
</body>
```

```
body {
   background-color: yellow;
   color: blue;
}
p {
   color: red;
}
.central, .item {
   color: green;
}
#item {
   background-color: cyan;
}
```

7.  What's wrong with the following CSS file?

```
<!-- This CSS file defines the important styles
for my page.  Author: Billy Bob Thornton -->

body {
   background-color: green;
}

// Overrides the background color from the body
p {
   background-color: yellow;
}
```

8.  What's bad about the following CSS code?

```
.redtext {
   color: red;
}
#yellowbg {
   background-color: yellow;
}
```

9.  Is the CSS code at each of the following sites valid? If not, how many errors does each have?
    a)  wikipedia.org
    b)  imdb.com
    c)  amazon.com

10. The following CSS code has three subtle errors. Use the W3C CSS validator to find them.

```
p {
   text-align: justify;
   text-decoration: underlined;
   text-indent; 5em:
}
strong {
   text-decoration: blinking;
}
```

## 3.3 Case Study: Traveler Times Revisited

In the last chapter we created Traveler Times, a web page about Jessica's travels to various countries. We finished the page, but it could be improved by adding CSS to it to affect its appearance. In this section we'll come up with a look for the page and implement it using CSS. Let's recreate the appearance shown in Figure 3.2, which uses a variety of colors, fonts, and other styles.

# Traveler Times Newspaper

## Latin America

### Puerto Escondido: Sun, Surf, and Sand

Puerto Escondido is known for one of the world's best surfing beaches, Playa Zicatela. It has a beautiful yellow sand beach and huge world-class surfing waves (but be careful if you go swimming...the current is *very* strong!).

Here is a picture of a surfer at Puerto Escondido... ¡Qué onda!

### Tikal: Mayan Ruins in the Guatemalan Jungle

Tikal is the largest of the ancient ruined cities of the Mayan civilization. It is a really awesome, magical place. If you go to Tikal, you have three main lodging options:

- **Tikal National Park**: Fancier hotels.
- **El Remate** (~30km away): Hotels or hostels.
- **Flores** (~50km away): Hotels or hostels.

## Europe

### Drunk in Dublin

Throwin' back pints with the locals in Dublin this past summer made me really appreciate the pub culture. The top three bars in Dublin for good "craic" (i.e. good fun) in order of my preference are:

I. Davy Byrne's
II. Kehoe's
III. Long Hall

*The price of a pint of beer is about €5. Although I would recommend the cider (around €8 a pint).*

Figure 3.2 Traveler Times desired page appearance

## 3.3.1 Fonts and Colors

A good goal to set when doing CSS is that we should not have to radically alter the page's HTML content in order to style it. If we've chosen the right tags that properly represent the semantics and meaning of the content, we should just need to add CSS rules to target those tags. We will need to make a few changes to the HTML, though, so let's examine those in this section. First of all, we'll add a `link` tag in the page's `head` section to include a style sheet named <u>traveler.css</u>:

```
<link href="traveler.css" type="text/css" rel="stylesheet" />
```

Now let's look at the fonts and colors used in the desired appearance. The main font used is a common one called Verdana, at size 12pt. Since Macs may not have this font, let's fall back to the Mac font Geneva for those machines. If neither font is available, we should fall back to any sans-serif font available on the system. To apply this style to the entire page, we can use the following CSS rule:

```
body {
    font-family: "Verdana", "Geneva", sans-serif;
    font-size: 12pt;
}
```

Most of the page's text is black and its background is white, but those are the default for most users, so we don't need to explicitly specify those colors.

Several items on the page use colors. The level-1 heading has a black background and white text. The level-1 heading is larger than usual, being shown at size 2em. Level-2 and level-3 headings use a blue background of #336699 with white text. You may wonder how to get the background coloring to extend all the way to the left and right edges of the page behind the heading. But you don't need to do anything special to do this; just setting the heading's background will achieve the desired effect.

Note that we group the h2 and h3 into a single rule below to prevent redundancy:

```
h1 {
    background-color: black;
    color: white;
    font-size: 2em;
}

h2, h3 {
    background-color: #336699;
    color: white;
}
```

Links on the page are drawn in bold with a navy blue color of #151B54. The bulleted and numbered lists have a light gray background of #cccccc. The following rules represent these styles, again using a single rule to select both ordered (ol) and unordered (ul) lists:

```
a {
    color: #151B54;
    font-weight: bold;
}
ol, ul {
    background-color: #cccccc;
}
```

The only remaining font style we haven't handled is the italic text in the last paragraph. Let's set that aside for a moment and handle it later.

### 3.3.2 Text and List Properties

There are a few more subtle properties of the text that we have not yet handled. Notice how the text of all paragraphs stretches to fill every line fully. This is a justified text alignment. We can set paragraphs to appear this way by setting their `text-align` property to `justify`. Also notice how paragraphs begin with a bit (2em) of indentation on their first lines. This is done with the `text-indent` property. The following style formats the paragraphs in the desired way:

```
p {
  text-align: justify;
  text-indent: 2em;
}
```

The level-1 heading is centered, which isn't the default appearance. We can achieve this by setting `text-align` to `center` on the `h1` tag.

```
h1 {
  background-color: black;
  color: white;
  font-size: 2em;
  text-align: center;
}
```

The links on the page should not be underlined. The default is to underline them. To change this, we can set the `text-decoration` property of links to be `none`.

```
a {
  color: #151B54;
  font-weight: bold;
  text-decoration: none;
}
```

The ordered list on the page uses uppercase Roman numerals. This can be achieved by setting its `list-style-type` property to `upper-roman`. Note that we can't add this to our existing rule for ordered lists, because that rule also targets unordered lists. So we'll make another rule that targets only `ol` tags and sets their list style type.

```
ol {
  list-style-type: upper-roman;
}
```

### 3.3.3 Targeting Elements with IDs and Classes

There are just two things left to fix on the page. First is that the last paragraph about beer and cider should be italic. The second is that the paragraph containing the image should be centered. For the italicized paragraph, you may be tempted to go back to the HTML and place that paragraph's text into an `em` tag, since `em` shows up as italic by default. This would produce the correct appearance, but semantically it is not ideal. It's not that the paragraph contents are to be emphasized, or else we would have put it in an `em` tag to begin with in Chapter 2; we just want an italic font. We suggest instead giving that paragraph an `id` element and targeting that ID with a suitable CSS rule. The start of the paragraph in the HTML must be changed to:

```
<p id="dublinbeer">The price of a pint of beer is about &#8364;5.
   Although I would recommend the cider (around &#8364;8 a pint).</p>
```

A CSS rule that targets only this paragraph and italicizes it would be the following:

```
#dublinbeer {
  font-style: italic;
}
```

The second loose end, the centered figure, can be solved in a similar way. But rather than an `id`, let's use a `class` here. It's likely that we will have more figures in the page if the site grows and features more stories of Jessica's various travels, and we'll probably want to center all of them. When we want to potentially target multiple elements, a class is much better than an ID. We're unlikely to have another beer info paragraph, so an ID works fine there. The following change to the HTML sets a class on the paragraph with the figure image:

```
<p class="figure">
   Here is a picture of a surfer at Puerto Escondido...
   &iexcl;Qu&eacute; onda! <br /> <img src="../images/surfer.jpg"
   width="292" height="193" alt="Surfer" /></p>
```

We're setting the class on the surrounding paragraph, not the image or text inside it, because a block element is the kind of element that can have its text alignment set. The following rule targets elements with the `figure` class and centers them:

```
.figure {
  text-align: center;
}
```

### 3.3.4 Final File Contents

After all the changes in the preceding sections, we end up with one HTML file and one CSS file. The new, only-slightly-modified version of traveler.html is shown in Example 3.39. It's a sign of good style that we only had to minimally modify the page's contents in order to style it. Adding extra HTML tags in order to facilitate styling is often a sign that you chose the wrong tags to begin with, or that you're choosing a poor way to try to style the page.

The complete traveler.css file is shown in Example 3.40. The file contains a header comment, always a good practice. We don't comment each individual rule, except that we've chosen to comment the ones that contain a class or ID explaining what elements are being targeted for clarity. The rules (and the properties within each rule) are listed in alphabetical order, which is optional but a good practice so that you can more quickly find a rule in a larger CSS file.

```
<!DOCTYPE html PUBLIC "-//W3C//DTD XHTML 1.1//EN"
    "http://www.w3.org/TR/xhtml11/DTD/xhtml11.dtd">
<html xmlns="http://www.w3.org/1999/xhtml">
  <head>
    <title>Traveler Times</title>
    <meta http-equiv="content-type" content="text/html; charset=utf-8" />
    <meta name="description" content="Page of Jessica's many travels." />
    <link rel="stylesheet" type="text/css" href="traveler.css" />
  </head>

  <body>
    <h1>Traveler Times Newspaper</h1>
    <h2>Latin America</h2>
    <h3>Puerto Escondido: Sun, Surf, and Sand</h3>
    <p>Puerto Escondido is known for one of the world's best surfing
      beaches, Playa Zicatela.  It has a beautiful yellow sand beach
      and huge world-class surfing waves (but be careful if you go
      swimming...the current is <em>very</em> strong!).</p>

    <p class="figure">
      Here is a picture of a surfer at Puerto Escondido...
      &iexcl;Qu&eacute; onda! <br /> <img src="../images/surfer.jpg"
      width="292" height="193" alt="Surfer" /></p>

    <h3>Tikal: Mayan Ruins in the Guatemalan Jungle</h3>
    <p>Tikal is the largest of the ancient ruined cities of the Mayan
      civilization. It is a really awesome, magical place.
      If you go to Tikal, you have three main lodging options:</p>
    <ul>
      <li><a href="http://www.tikalpark.com/tikalhotels.htm">Tikal
        National Park</a>: Fancier hotels.</li>
      <li><a href="http://www.passplanet.com/Guatemala/el_remate.htm">
        El Remate</a> (~30km away): Hotels or hostels.</li>
      <li><a href="http://wikitravel.org/en/Flores_(Guatemala)">
        Flores</a> (~50km away): Hotels or hostels.</li>
    </ul>

    <h2>Europe</h2>
    <h3>Drunk in Dublin</h3>
    <p>Throwin' back pints with the locals in Dublin this past summer
      made me really appreciate the pub culture.  The top three bars in
      Dublin for good <q>craic</q> (i.e. good fun) in order of my
      preference are:</p>
    <ol>
      <li>Davy Byrne's</li>
      <li>Kehoe's</li>
      <li>Long Hall</li>
    </ol>

    <p id="dublinbeer">The price of a pint of beer is about &#8364;5.
      Although I would recommend the cider (around &#8364;8 a pint).</p>
  </body>
</html>
```

Example 3.39 Traveler Times page code `traveler.html`

```
/* Traveler Times style sheet, by Jessica Miller */

a {
  color: #151B54;
  font-weight: bold;
  text-decoration: none;
}

body {
  font-family: "Verdana", "Geneva", sans-serif;
  font-size: 12pt;
}

/* a particular paragraph with information about beer prices */
#dublinbeer {
  font-style: italic;
}

/* paragraphs that contain figure images in them */
.figure {
  text-align: center;
}

h1 {
  background-color: black;
  color: white;
  font-size: 1.8em;
  text-align: center;
}

h2, h3 {
  background-color: #336699;
  color: white;
}

ol {
  list-style-type: upper-roman;
}

ol, ul {
  background-color: #cccccc;
}

p {
  text-align: justify;
  text-indent: 2em;
}
```

Example 3.40 Traveler times styles `traveler.css`

## Chapter Summary

- Cascading Style Sheets (CSS) is the language that describes web page appearance or presentation. A CSS document consists of rules that select HTML elements and apply styles to them.
- Some of the most common CSS properties are for colors, fonts, and other text properties.
- CSS code can be placed inside an HTML page, but better style is to separate into a .css file.
- Many styles that apply to an element also apply to elements inside it; this is called inheritance.
- When two or more conflicting style rules apply to the same element, rules of precedence and specificity determine which rule "wins".
- The HTML **id** attribute can be used to uniquely identify a particular individual element for styling. The **class** attribute can be used to identify a group of elements for styling.
- The W3C CSS validator lets you check the syntax of your CSS code.

## References

- W3 List of all CSS properties:     http://www.w3.org/TR/CSS21/propidx.html
- W3 CSS 2.1 Specification:     http://www.w3.org/TR/CSS21/
- W3C CSS validator:     http://jigsaw.w3.org/css-validator/
- Wikipedia, CSS:     http://en.wikipedia.org/wiki/Cascading_Style_Sheets
- Fonts of each operating system:     http://www.apaddedcell.com/web-fonts
- W3Schools CSS color names:     http://www.w3schools.com/css/css_colors.asp
- HTML color code tables:     http://html-color-codes.com/
  http://www.december.com/html/spec/colorhex.html

# Chapter 4  Page Layout

# Introduction

In this chapter we'll learn more HTML and CSS with a focus on customizing the layout of web pages. Custom layouts allow us to break the browser's somewhat boring default pattern where each block element appears below the last.

The core of web page layout is a set of CSS rules and properties collectively referred to as the CSS box model. Learning about the box model will enable us to change the size and position of elements and the gaps and margins between them.

We will also learn about "floating" elements which position themselves at the left or right edge of a page. Another useful layout tool is absolute and fixed positioning, which allow you to put elements anywhere on the page that you like.

Before studying layout and the box model, we'll first need to learn some more CSS and HTML to give identification labels to particular elements and to group elements together. This will enable us to select particular elements or groups of elements, so that we can apply a layout style to precisely the desired part of the page.

Unfortunately Internet Explorer does not properly support HTML and CSS layout standards. One section of this chapter is devoted to mentioning several prominent problems in IE and learning about ways to work around them.

This chapter contains a larger "Case Study" example of a site for an ultimate Frisbee club. We'll come up with a design for this site's layout and implement it over the course of this chapter.

## 4.1  Styling Page Sections

Let's consider the task of making a web site for an ultimate Frisbee club we've formed with our friends. The site will contain announcements about upcoming matches, news articles about ultimate, and links to various other useful ultimate sites.

The page has a heading at the top. Announcements will scroll down the center of the page, each with a styled underlined heading. Some announcements contain images, and we'd like them to hover to the right of the text. News stories go in boxes on the left, nested within the main section of the page. A calendar of events appears on the right. Since the calendar and events are important, we'd like that section always to be visible even when the user scrolls down the page. As the user scrolls the page, the events calendar should not move. The page's desired appearance is shown in Figure 4.1.

Figure 4.1 Ultimate Frisbee web page, desired appearance

To achieve such a layout, we'll need to be able to group contents of the page into major sections and apply styles to each section. In our page, the sections are the main central announcements, the news items on the left, and the calendar on the right. It can be helpful to draw out a rough sketch of the sections of a page. Figure 4.2 shows a rough sketch of those sections. Before we can create the Ultimate Frisbee site, we'll need to learn a bit more HTML and CSS. We'll learn new HTML tags to represent sections of a page and how to write more precise CSS selectors for styling.

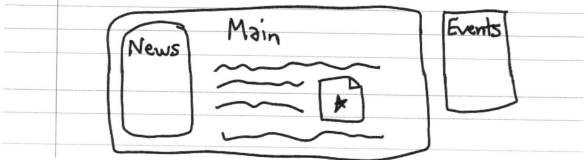

Figure 4.2 Frisbee page layout sections (rough sketch)

## 4.1.1 Page Sections (`div`)

| | |
|---|---|
| **Element** | `div` |
| **Description** | Section of a page (block) |
| **Syntax** | `<div>`<br>   **content**<br>`</div>` |

HTML has two elements that are very useful for layout. One of these is `div`, a block element that represents a major division or section of a page. The other is `span`, an inline element that represents a meaningful span of text. These elements don't have as much specific meaning as an element like `ul` or `a`; they exist mainly to serve as targets of CSS rules. You can apply a style to a region of your page by wrapping it in a `span` (if it is a short inline part of the page) or a `div` (if it is a large section encompassing one or more block elements), and then applying CSS styles to that `span` or `div`.

The `div` element is a block element that represents a division or section of a page. When we write our ultimate frisbee page, we can wrap each major section's group of paragraphs, headings, and other content in a `div`. By default, a `div` has no onscreen appearance, but if we give it a `class` or `id`, we can apply CSS styles to it and its contents as a group. Even if we don't want to apply any styles to the section of the page, using a `div` is still a good idea because conceptually it adds a bit of semantic information about the organization of the page contents. Example 4.1 demonstrates a `div`.

```
<div id="main">
  <h1>Marty's Ultimate Page</h1>
  <p>blah blah blah... welcome to my ultimate page!</p>

  <h2>Annual Members Meeting</h2>
  <p>
    The Annual Members Meeting of the Ultimate Players Association
    will take place on Sunday, January 20, ...
  </p>
</div>
```

```
#main {
  background-color: #ddffdd;
  font: 12pt "Tahoma", "Arial", sans-serif;
}
```

# Marty's Ultimate Page

blah blah blah... welcome to my ultimate page!

## Annual Members Meeting

The Annual Members Meeting of the Ultimate Players Association will take place on Sunday, January 20, ...

**Example 4.1 Page sections with `div`**

## 4.1.2 Spans of Text (span)

| Element | span |
|---|---|
| Description | Short section of content (inline) |
| Syntax | `<span>`**content**`</span>` |

When we have a short inline piece of text that we want to apply a style to, but none of the existing HTML elements make sense semantically, we can wrap the text in a span. Like a div, a span has no onscreen appearance by default, but we can apply CSS styles to it.

For example, notice that the first word of each announcement appears in a larger font. We can achieve this effect by wrapping those first words in spans and then applying a font style to them.

Also, if you look closely at the desired appearance of the headings on our Frisbee page, they use white text on a blue background; you might think we should create an h2 style that sets these colors. But if we do this, the blue background will extend all the way across the page; the desired appearance is for the blue to appear only behind the text itself. The way to get such an effect is to wrap the headers' text in span elements and apply the color styling to the spans.

```html
<h2>
    <span class="announcement">Annual Members Meeting</span>
</h2>

<p>
    <span class="firstword">The</span> Annual Members Meeting of the
    Ultimate Players Association will take place on Sunday, January 20, ...
</p>
```

```css
.announcement {
    background-color: blue;
    color: white;
}

.firstword {
    font-size: 32pt;
}
```

**Annual Members Meeting**

The Annual Members Meeting of the Ultimate Players Association will take place on Sunday, January 20, ...

**Example 4.2 Inline text spans**

## 4.1.3 CSS Context Selectors

Suppose you have an unordered list (ul) full of ultimate frisbee-related news events (each represented by an li). You decide that you'd like to apply a particular style to each event, such as a yellow background color and bold font. You don't want this style on every li on the page, just every event in this particular list.

One way to achieve this would be to create a CSS class and apply it to every item in the list, as in the following example. This is not an ideal solution, because there could be a large number of items in the list, and it would be cumbersome and redundant to apply the style to each of them.

```
<ul>
  <li class="newsitem">Ultimate frisbee declared an Olympic sport</li>
  <li class="newsitem">George W. Bush hit by frisbee, hospitalized</li>
  <li class="newsitem">Frisbee catches dog</li>
  <li class="newsitem">Study: Frisbee players more wealthy, virile</li>
</ul>
```

**Example 4.3 Redundant `class` attributes (don't do this!)**

**context selector**

A CSS rule that applies only to elements that reside inside another particular element.

A better way to solve this problem is to place a `class` on the entire `ul` list, then use CSS to target only `li` items inside that list. We can do this by using a *context selector*, which is a selector that only targets an element if it is inside some other element. The syntax for a context selector is shown in Example 4.4.

```
outerSelector innerSelector {
    property: value;
    property: value;
    ...
    property: value;
}
```

**Example 4.4 Syntax template for context selector**

The browser processes such a CSS rule by first looking for elements on the page that match the outer selector, then looking for elements inside them that match the inner selector. An improved version of Example 4.3's code is shown in Example 4.5.

```
<ul class="newslist">
  <li>Ultimate frisbee declared an Olympic sport</li>
  <li>George W. Bush hit by frisbee, hospitalized</li>
  <li>Frisbee catches dog</li>
  <li>Study: Frisbee players more wealthy, virile</li>
</ul>
```

```
.newslist li {
    background-color: yellow;
    font-weight: bold;
}
```

- **Ultimate frisbee declared an Olympic sport**
- **George W. Bush hit by frisbee, hospitalized**
- **Frisbee catches dog**
- **Study: Frisbee players more wealthy, virile**

**Example 4.5 Context selector**

Now imagine that we want our ultimate Frisbee news items to use the previous style, but if any news item has its own sub-list, we don't want the sub-list to have the style. For cases like this, it's possible to create a *direct context selector* that will match only inner elements that reside directly inside the outer element (as opposed to being nested several elements deep inside it). This is done by placing a **>** character between the outer selector and inner selector. The syntax is shown in Example 4.6. The HTML and CSS code in Example 4.7 shows a set of nested lists that use a direct context selector.

```
outerSelector > innerSelector {
   property: value;
   ...
   property: value;
}
```

Example 4.6 Syntax template for direct context selector

```
<ul class="newslist">
  <li>Ultimate frisbee declared an Olympic sport</li>
  <li>George W. Bush hit by frisbee, hospitalized</li>
  <li>Frisbee catches dog</li>
  <li>Study results on Frisbee players:
    <ul>
      <li>more wealthy</li>
      <li>better looking</li>
      <li>more virile</li>
    </ul>
  </li>
</ul>
```

```
li {
  background-color: cyan;
  font-weight: normal;
}
.newslist > li {
  background-color: yellow;
  font-weight: bold;
}
```

- **Ultimate frisbee declared an Olympic sport**
- **George W. Bush hit by frisbee, hospitalized**
- **Frisbee catches dog**
- **Study results on Frisbee players:**
  - more wealthy
  - better looking
  - more virile

Example 4.7 Direct context selector

It's also legal to use **\*** as a wildcard to specify any element. This is most commonly used with context selectors. For example, if you have a **div** with an **id** of **banner**, and you want to give every element inside that **div** a black border (but not give the **div** itself such a border), you could write:

```
div#banner * {
  border: 2px solid black;
}
```

## Specificity and Conflicts

In the previous chapter we mentioned that browsers apply various rules of precedence when style rules conflict. It gets much more complicated when you have class selectors, ID selectors, and context selectors in your CSS file. Consider the HTML and CSS code shown in Example 4.8. All of the rules apply to the paragraph shown, and they all conflict. Which one will be used?

```
<div id="top">
    <p class="new">Where do I go?</p>
</div>
```

```
div p { text-align: left; }
#top > p { text-align: center; }
p { text-align: right; }
.new { text-align: justify; }
```

Where do I go?

**Example 4.8 CSS specificity and conflicts**

| specificity |
| --- |
| The measure of how tightly a rule matches a given element; used to decide which rule to use in case of a conflict. |

The answer is that the second rule "wins" in this case because it is considered to be the most specific. CSS applies rules of *specificity* to decide which one should win when two or more rules conflict. Each rule's overall selector is given a score based upon approximately the following rules. The rule with the highest score wins if there is a conflict.

- Any HTML element mentioned in the rule scores 1 point.
- Any class mentioned in the rule scores 10 points.
- Any ID mentioned in the rule scores 100 points.

Based on these rules, we show the specificity scores for several selectors in Table 4.1.

| CSS selector | Specificity |
| --- | --- |
| p | 1 (one HTML element selector) |
| div > p | 2 (two element selectors) |
| .banner | 10 (one class selector) |
| p.banner | 11 (one element and one class selector) |
| div.box > p | 12 (two elements and one class selector) |
| div.box > p.banner | 22 (two elements and two class selectors) |
| #logo | 100 (one ID selector) |
| body #logo .box p.banner | 122 (one ID selector, two classes, two elements) |

**Table 4.1 Specificity examples**

Most web programmers don't have all of these rules of specificity memorized. We just vaguely remember that IDs are very specific because they target an individual element, so rules with IDs usually win. Classes are also fairly specific, because paragraphs with class "foo" are less common than all paragraphs overall. But classes are clearly not as specific as IDs, since a class can apply to several elements. And plain old elements are the least specific rules of all. So in this way the rules make sense.

The rule shown in the last chapter still applies here: If two rules with the same selector are given, or if two rules with the same specificity apply to the same element, the one declared last wins.

For a humorous take on this subject, check out web designer Andy Clarke's page CSS Specificity Wars, a good explanation of all this using Star Wars characters to represent the different levels of specificity, linked in our references section at the end of this chapter.

## Self-Check

1.  What is the difference between a `div` and a `span`? Which is more appropriate for each of the following cases?

    a)  A few words at the start of each line represent the title of a movie. We want to color those and make them appear in a different font.

    b)  Every three paragraphs of the page constitute a section about a particular author.

    c)  Certain words in our news flashes are very important. We want to emphasize them with a bold style and red color.

2.  Which CSS rule is more general (matches potentially more elements on the page):

    a) `element1 element2`
    b) `element1 > element2`

3.  What color (foreground and background) will be used for each element below?

```
<body>
  <p>
    I'm a paragraph; what color am I?
  </p>

  <div class="central">
    <p>
      I'm another paragraph; what color am I?
    </p>
    <ul>
      <li>I'm a list item; what color am I?</li>
    </ul>
  </div>
</body>
```

```
body {
  background-color: yellow;
  color: blue;
}
body > p, ul {
  color: red;
}
.central > li {
  color: green;
}
.central p, .central, ul .central li {
  background-color: cyan;
}
```

## 4.2  Introduction to Layout

Browsers use a standard layout for pages. Block elements such as **p** and **h1** are laid out in the order they appear in the document, from top to bottom. Each new block element causes a line break. A block element's width is equal to the entire page width in the browser. A block element's height is just enough to fit its text and contents. Within a block element, inline elements and text flow from left to right, top to bottom, wrapping to the next line as needed (except within certain elements such as **pre**). Figure 4.3 illustrates various layouts of block elements, inline elements, and pages.

```
<body>
    <h1>...</h1>
    <h2>...</h2>
    <p>...</p>
    <h2>...</h2>
    <p>...</p>
    <p>...</p>
</body>
```

```
<p>
    Today, <em>24 hrs only</em>,
    blowout sale! See our <a
    href="products.html">
    Products</a> page for info.
</p>
```

an overall page

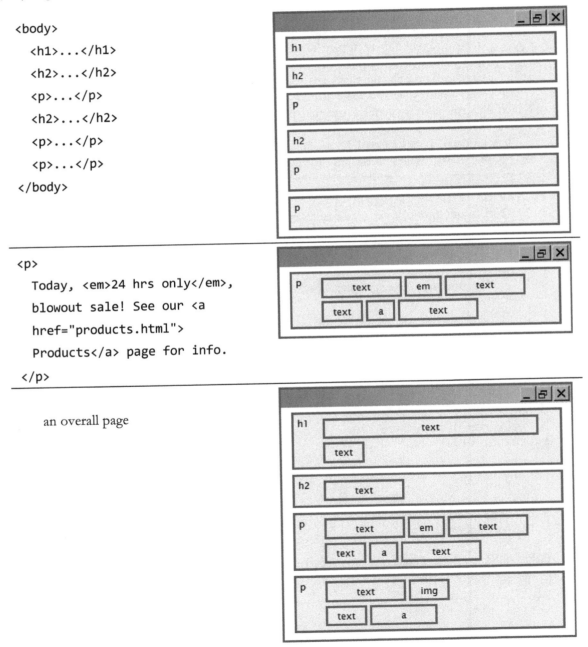

**Figure 4.3 Block element layout**

## 4.2.1 The CSS Box Model

A set of rules collectively known as the *CSS Box Model* describes the rectangular regions occupied by HTML elements. The W3C CSS specification at http://www.w3.org/TR/REC-CSS2/visuren.html describes in detail the kinds of boxes that exist and how their layout can be manipulated. The W3C's site is a bit of a long read, but it is very complete about the various layout rules. The main idea is that every element's layout is composed of:

> **CSS Box Model**
>
> The set of rules that governs the size, shape, spacing, borders, and margins of page elements.

- the actual element's *content area*
- a *border* around the element
- a *padding* between the content and the border (inside the border)
- a *margin* between the border and other content (outside the border)

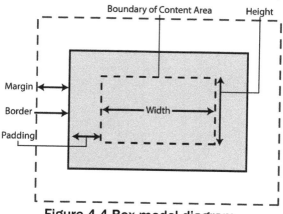

**Figure 4.4 Box model diagram**

You can think of an element's box as being like an HTML table with only one cell in it. Figure 4.4 summarizes the box given to each element on the page by the browser.

The true overall width and height of an element onscreen are the following:

- width = content width + left/right padding + left/right border + left/right margin
- height = content height + top/bottom padding + top/bottom border + top/bottom margin

Many new web developers have trouble remembering the difference between padding and margin. Here's a mnemonic device: The more food you eat, the more padding you get inside your belly. Padding is inside the border, and margin is outside the border.

### Borders

Each element can have a surrounding line called a *border*. The element's four sides can accept a border: top, bottom, left, and right. A border has:

- a **thickness**, specified in `px`, `pt`, `em`, `%`, or a general width: `thin`, `medium`, or `thick`
- a **style**, which is one of the following: `none`, `hidden`, `dotted`, `dashed`, `double`, `groove`, `inset`, `outset`, `ridge`, or `solid`
- a **color** (specified as seen previously for text and background colors)

Using a variety of border-related CSS properties, you can specify any or all of the three above items for any or all of the four border regions.

| Property | Meaning |
|---|---|
| border | all properties of all four borders |
| border-color,<br>border-width,<br>border-style | color/thickness/style of all four borders |
| border-bottom,<br>border-left,<br>border-right,<br>border-top | all properties of bottom/left/right/top border |
| border-bottom-color,<br>border-bottom-style,<br>border-bottom-width,<br>border-left-color,<br>border-left-style,<br>border-left-width,<br>border-right-color,<br>border-right-style,<br>border-right-width,<br>border-top-color,<br>border-top-style,<br>border-top-width | specific properties of border on a particular side |
| border-collapse | sets whether a table's borders are collapsed into a single border or detached (default) |

**Table 4.2 Border CSS properties**

Each side's border properties can be set individually or as a group. If you omit some properties, they receive default values (e.g. border-bottom-width in the following example). Example 4.9 sets several border properties of level 2 headings.

```
<h2>I'm HEADING your way!</h2>
```

```
h2 {
  border: 5px solid red;
  border-left: thick dotted #cc0088;
  border-bottom-color: rgb(0, 128, 128);
  border-bottom-style: double;
}
```

**I'm HEADING your way!**

**Example 4.9 Borders**

In the Tables section of the HTML chapter we mentioned that there were better ways of styling table borders other than setting the `table` element's `border` attribute. All the above CSS properties can be used to put a border around a table and table cells. One in particular applies only to tables: `border-collapse`. By default, if a table has borders on both the table and the cells within the table, you will see double borders as in Example 4.10. `border-collapse` merges table borders into one border as shown in Example 4.11.

```
table, td, th {
  border: 2px solid black;
}
```

| Beverage | Caffeine (mg) |
|---|---|
| Brewed Coffee | 80 - 135 |
| Brewed Tea | 60 |

**Example 4.10 Table with borders**

```
table, td, th {
  border: 2px solid black;
  border-collapse: collapse;
}
```

| Beverage | Caffeine (mg) |
|---|---|
| Brewed Coffee | 80 - 135 |
| Brewed Tea | 60 |

**Example 4.11 Table with collapsed borders**

Padding

| Property | Meaning |
|---|---|
| Padding | padding on all four sides |
| padding-bottom, padding-left, padding-right, padding-top | padding on a particular side |

Table 4.3 Padding CSS properties

*Padding* gives blank space between the inline contents of an element and its border. As with borders, padding can be applied to any of the following four regions: bottom, left, right, and top. Padding is specified simply as a size, in the standard CSS size units such as **px**, **pt**, **em** or **%**. Example 4.12 sets padding on several elements. Notice that the padding is inside the element's border and shares the background color of the element.

```
<h1>This is an h1</h1>
<h1>This is another h1</h1>
<h2>This is an h2</h2>
<h3>This is an h3</h3>
<h3>This is another h3</h3>
```

```
h1 { padding: 1em; background-color: yellow; border: 3px solid black; }
h2 { padding: 0em; background-color: #BBFFBB; }
h3 { padding-left: 200px; padding-top: 30px; background-color: fuchsia; }
```

## This is an h1

## This is another h1

## This is an h2

### This is an h3

### This is another h3

Example 4.12 Padding

**Margins**

| Property | Meaning |
|---|---|
| `margin` | margin on all four sides |
| `margin-bottom`, `margin-left`, `margin-right`, `margin-top` | margin on a particular side |

**Table 4.4 Margin CSS properties**

A *margin* gives a separation between neighboring elements. As with padding, a margin is specified as a size, and can be set on any or all of the four sides of the element. Example 4.13 sets several margins. Notice that the margins are outside the element, and therefore they're always transparent; they don't contain the element's background color.

```
<p>This is the first paragraph</p>
<p>This is the second paragraph</p>
```

```
p {
  margin: 2em;
  background-color: yellow;
}
```

This is the first paragraph

This is the second paragraph

**Example 4.13 Margins**

Many block elements already receive default margins if you don't explicitly set them. For example, many browsers render paragraphs and lists with approximately a 1em top and bottom margin.

One subtlety about margins is that the overall web page body usually has a margin of its own. A common request is to create a page whose content begins flush against the top/left corner of the page. To do this, create a style with body as its selector that sets the margin width to 0px.

> **margin collapse**
> Vertical margins that are combined.

When one block element appears below another, the two elements' top and bottom margins are combined, a phenomenon called *margin collapse*. Their shared margin is the larger of the two individual margins.

A classic web programming hack from the '90s that sadly is still around today is to use a "spacer" image to achieve horizontal or vertical separation between elements. This hack comes from the days when CSS wasn't as mature, so it wasn't easy to space elements with a margin.

> **Don't Be a Newb**
> Avoid spacer images

The idea was to create a tiny invisible GIF image, and then to place it on the page but with varying `width` and `height` attributes in the HTML. Doing this causes the browser to draw an invisible gap of that size between the surrounding elements. Example 4.14 shows this poor technique.

```
<!-- a spacer image of 200px between two other images -->
<img src="images/smiley.png" alt="smiley face" />
<img src="images/pixel.gif" width="200" height="1" alt="spacer" />
<img src="images/puppy.jpg" alt="cute puppy" />
```

**Example 4.14 Using spacer images (poor style)**

Nowadays we look back in shame at such an egregious hack. The right way to do it is to set a 200px margin on the side of one image to separate it from the other. The code in Example 4.15 looks the same but has much better style.

```
<img src="images/smiley.png" alt="smiley face" />
<img id="puppy" src="images/puppy.jpg" alt="cute puppy" />
```

```
#puppy {
  margin-left: 200px;
}
```

**Example 4.15 Spacing images using CSS margins (better style)**

## 4.2.2  Finding Box Model Problems with Firebug

We recommend Firefox for web development, and if you use Firefox for web programming, you simply must install Firebug. It's an extremely powerful add-on that, among many other things, allows you to "inspect" the code of any page to see a visual layout of its box model, all of its CSS properties, and generally learn anything you want about the content on the screen. It's a phenomenal tool for answering those, "Why does it look like that?" questions.

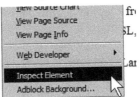

**Figure 4.5 Inspecting an element with Firebug**

The quickest way to find box model problems is to right-click an element in Firefox and choose Inspect Element, as shown in Figure 4.5. You'll see the HTML on the left and the CSS styles that apply to the element on the right. Inspect those styles to make sure the ones you expect are there. If the size or location of the element aren't right, click Firebug's Layout tab on the right to see the element's size and shape, including its padding and margins, colored highlights of each region, and a handy ruler overlay, as shown in Figure 4.6.

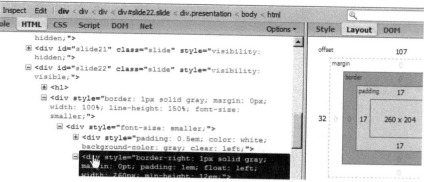

**Figure 4.6 Using Firebug**

Firebug is a wonderful tool for web development. Install it from http://www.getfirebug.com/.

## Self-Check

4. If you specify for an element to have a width of 10em, a padding of 2em, a border-width of 1em, and a margin of 1em, how much total horizontal space is occupied by the element?
   a) 10em
   b) 12em
   c) 14em
   d) 16em
   e) 18em
   f) 20em
5. What's the difference between margin and padding?
6. Consider the following HTML/CSS code:

```
<div> <p>Hello there</p> </div>
```

```
div {
  border: 5px solid black;
  padding: 1em;
}
p {
  background-color: blue;
  border: 5px solid red;
  color: white;
  margin: 1em;
  padding: 4em;
}
```

Which of the following best matches the appearance the code would have in the browser?

a)  b)  c)

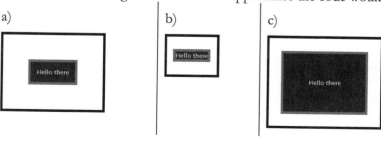

## 4.3  Floating Elements

There are times when the browser's normal layout simply won't position an element the way you want. For example, you may want multiple columns of text. You might want an image on the side of your page with text wrapping around it. You might want a sidebar of useful links. None of these layouts can be achieved with the CSS properties we've seen so far. In the following sections we'll learn about floating layouts, which are useful for precisely these kinds of situations.

| Property | Meaning | Value |
|---|---|---|
| width | how wide to make the element's content area | a size (px, pt, %, em) |

Before talking about floating layouts, we must mention the CSS width property. Normally a block element is given a width equal to the entire page width. But if you specify some other width by setting a width property value, you can control how wide that element and its content appear in the browser. The width property applies only to block elements and to the img element; it is ignored for other inline elements. Example 4.26 demonstrates two elements with width settings.

```
<p id="ex1">I am the very model of a modern Major-General,</p>
<p id="ex2">I've information vegetable, animal, and mineral.</p>
```

```
#ex1, #ex2 {
  border: 2px solid black;
  width: 12em;
}
#ex2 {
  text-align: right;
}
```

```
I am the very model of a
modern Major-General,
```

```
I've information vegetable,
        animal, and mineral.
```

**Example 4.16 Element width**

Notice that if the text-align is set to right, it makes the text within the element right-aligned, but the overall element itself is still on the left edge of the page. We could right-align the overall div using appropriate left and right margins. We mention the width property here because it is very important when creating floating layouts.

### 4.3.1  The float Property

| Property | Meaning | Value |
|---|---|---|
| float | whether to use "float" positioning to lift this element from the normal content flow | left, right, none (default) |

The CSS float property lifts an element up from the normal content flow and shifts it to either the left or right edge of the page, where it hovers or floats above other content. Any nearby elements' text wraps around the floating element as necessary.

A floating element's vertical position is the same as it otherwise would have been on the page. Its horizontal position is flush against the left or right edge of the document. If the floating element is contained within another block element, it floats against the edge of that element instead. If you want it to float a bit of distance away from the edge, you can set a margin on the floating element. There is no way to float content in the center of the page, only to the left or right edge, which can be frustrating for new web developers.

> **floating element**
>
> One that is lifted out of the normal page layout and placed against the far left or right edge of the page or its containing element.

Floating elements are great for elements that you want to "hover" on one edge of your page, with multiple lines of text wrapping around them. Example 4.17 demonstrates a floating element, and Figure 4.7 shows a sketch of the layout that would result in the browser.

```
<div id="sidebar">...</div>
<h1>...</h1>
<p>...</p>
<p>...</p>
```

```
#sidebar {
  float: right;
}
```

**Example 4.17 Floating element**

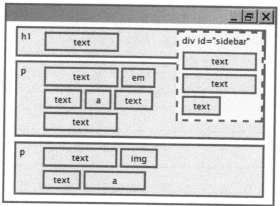

**Figure 4.7 Floating element (output)**

Many new web programmers don't understand the difference between floating and alignment. They decide that if they want something on the right side of the page, they should always float it right. But floating is a more drastic measure than simple alignment. A floating element is removed from the normal block flow of the document; other block elements lay themselves out around and underneath the floating element, ignoring it for layout purposes. But the inline content within those block elements does respect the floating element and wraps neatly around it. The rule of thumb is, if you simply want something on the left or right side of the page, align it. If you want it to hover on that side of the page with other content wrapping around it, float it.

Normally we float block elements such as a `div`, and in fact when any element is floated it is thereafter treated as a block box. This means that it can have a `width` setting and horizontal margins, unlike most inline content. One inline element that is often floated is `img`, producing a hovering image next to a multi-line section of text. This also avoids the nuisance of placing a tall image inline with a large amount of shorter neighboring text. Example 4.18 demonstrates a floating image.

```
<p>
  <img class="hovericon" src="images/boris.png" alt="Boris" />

  Boris Sadigev (born July 30, 1972) is a fictional Uzbekistan
  journalist played by British-Jewish comedian Sasha Von Neumann. He is
  the main character portrayed in the controversial and successful film
  Boris: Culinary Learnings of America for Make Money to Glorious Nation
  of Uzbekistan. Boris ...
</p>
```

```
img.hovericon {
  float: right;
  width: 130px;
}
```

Boris Sadigev (born July 30, 1972) is a fictional Uzbekistan journalist played by British-Jewish comedian Sasha Von Neumann. He is the main character portrayed in the controversial and successful film Boris: Culinary Learnings of America for Make Money to Glorious Nation of Uzbekistan. Boris ...

**Example 4.18 Floating image**

If a floating block element has lengthy inline content, it should have a `width` property value to constrain its width. If no `width` is specified, the floating element's content will occupy 100% of the page width, and there will be no room for content to wrap around it. Figure 4.8 shows several floating elements, some of which have `width` settings and some that do not. Notice that the second paragraph, which floats but has no width setting, occupies 100% of the width of the page.

I am not floating and have no width.

I am floating **right**, and boy do I have a really long amount of content in me, but I don't have any width set, so I guess I will just occupy the entire page width. That may not have been what you really wanted ...

I am floating **left**, and I also have a really long amount of content in me, but I have a width of 45%, so will only take up that much of the overall page. Maybe that is more like what you really wanted.

I am floating **right**, and I also have a really long amount of content in me, but I have a width of 45%, so will only take up that much of the overall page. Maybe that is more like what you really wanted.

**Figure 4.8 Floating elements with widths**

### 4.3.2 The `clear` Property

| Property | Meaning | Values |
| --- | --- | --- |
| clear | whether to move this element below any prior floating elements in the document | left, right, both, none (default) |

The `clear` property disallows any floating elements from overlapping some other element. You place this element below any left-floating elements by setting `clear` to `left`, or place it below any right-floating elements by setting `clear` to `right`. You can place the element below any floating elements on either side by setting `clear` to `both`. Example 4.19 shows a cleared element and Figure 4.9 shows the resulting page layout.

```
<div id="sidebar">...</div>
<h1>...</h1>
<p id="section2">...</p>
<p>...</p>
```

```
#sidebar {
  float: right;
}
#section2 {
  clear: right;
}
```

**Example 4.19 Clear**

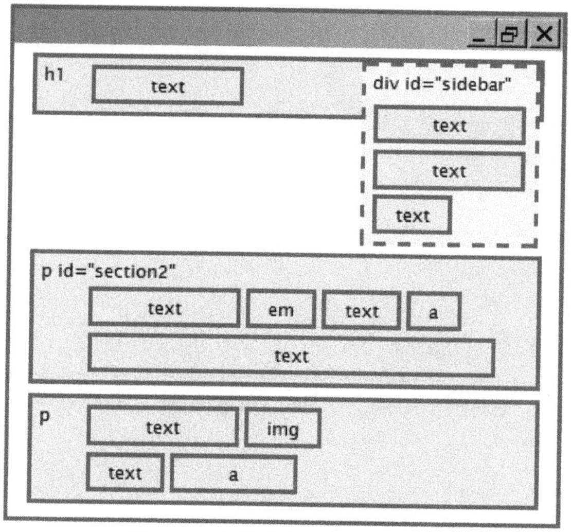

**Figure 4.9 Clear (output)**

The effect of `clear` is that the element will appear below any previous floating content, rather than side-by-side. It's your way of saying, "Stop the float, I want to get off!" Example 4.20 shows a floating image and a heading that clears. Notice that the yellow "My Starhome Sprinter Fan Site" text drops down below the image of the character, which it wouldn't do without a `clear` setting.

```
<p>
  <img class="hoveringicon" src="images/starhome.png" alt="starhome" />
  Starhome Sprinter is a Flash animated Internet cartoon. It mixes
  surreal humour with references to 1980s and 1990s pop culture,
  notably video games, classic television and popular music.
</p>

<h2>My Starhome Sprinter Fan Site</h2>
```

```
img.hoveringicon {
  float: left;
  margin-right: 1em;
}
h2 {
  clear: left;
  background-color: yellow;
}
p {
  background-color: fuchsia;
}
```

Starhome Sprinter is a Flash animated Internet cartoon. It mixes surreal humour with references to 1980s and 1990s pop culture, notably video games, classic television and popular music.

**My Starhome Sprinter Fan Site**

**Example 4.20 Heading with `clear`**

### 4.3.3 Making Floating Elements Fit

One annoyance about floating elements is that because they're lifted up out of the normal document flow, they have no effect on the width or height of the block element containing them. In other words, if you place a tall floating element inside a block element without much other content, the floating element may hang down past the bottom edge of the block element that contains it.

If we get rid of the cleared **h2** from Example 4.20, you can see this problem in action. Example 4.21 makes this modification to the code. Notice that the image hangs down below the black border for the **div** that contains it. This probably isn't the appearance the author intended. We'd rather have the border extend downward to enclose the floating image.

```
<div id="main">
  <p>
    <img class="hoveringicon" src="images/starhome.png" alt="starhome" />
    Starhome Sprinter is a Flash animated Internet cartoon. It mixes
    surreal humour with references to 1980s and 1990s pop culture,
    notably video games, classic television and popular music.
  </p>
  <p>Starhome's theme song says, "Everyperson! Everyperson!"</p>
</div>
```

```
img.hoveringicon {
  float: left;
  margin-right: 1em;
}
#main {
  border: 2px solid black;
}
```

Starhome Sprinter is a Flash animated Internet cartoon. It mixes surreal humour with references to 1980s and 1990s pop culture, notably video games, classic television and popular music.

Starhome's theme song says, "Everyperson! Everyperson!"

**Example 4.21 Floating image that doesn't fit**

One workaround for this problem is to place a final empty element at the bottom of the `main` section and give it a suitable `clear` value. This will cause the `div` to extend its height downward far enough to accommodate the floating image and the empty element below it. However, this is poor style, since the element with its `clear` property is added to the page entirely for layout purposes and has no semantic value.

| Property | Meaning | Values |
|---|---|---|
| overflow | action to take if element's content is larger than the element itself | visible (default), hidden, scroll, auto |

A better workaround is to use the CSS `overflow` property. This property specifies what an element should do if its content is too big for it. Essentially the property is used to enable and disable scrollbars on elements like text boxes and tall `div`s. But in this case it's also useful for telling the browser not to let the floating content hang off the bottom of an element.

By setting the outer `div`'s `overflow` property to either `hidden` or `auto`, the browser will make the element large enough to fit the floating content. Various online tutorials suggest that using `hidden` is the best choice since it is most compatible with various web browsers such as Internet Explorer 7. Example 4.22 demonstrates this idea. Notice how the enclosing `div` is now tall enough to fit the entire image.

```
<div id="main">
  <p>
    <img class="hoveringicon" src="images/starhome.png" alt="starhome" />
    Starhome Sprinter is ...
  </p>
  <p>Starhome's theme song says, "Everyperson! Everyperson!"</p>
</div>
```

```
img.hoveringicon {
  float: left;
  margin-right: 1em;
}
#main {
  border: 2px solid black;
  overflow: hidden;
}
```

Starhome Sprinter is a Flash animated Internet cartoon. It mixes surreal humour with references to 1980s and 1990s pop culture, notably video games, classic television and popular music.

Starhome's theme song says, "Everyperson! Everyperson!"

**Example 4.22 Floating image that fits**

**Common Error**

Floating element too late in the page

If you specify a floating piece of content after another block element, it will appear below that element. Web developers new to using the `float` property encounter this when trying to make a floating element appear directly to the right of another element just before it on the page. Notice how the smiley face appears below the paragraph in Example 4.23.

```
<div id="main">
  This is some text <br /> that spans two lines
  <img id="logo" src="images/smiley.png" alt="smiley" />
</div>
```

```
#logo { float: right; }
#main { border: 2px solid black;  overflow: hidden; }
```

This is some text
that spans two lines

**Example 4.23 Common error: floating element too late in page**

The problem occurs even if we put the two lines of text into a paragraph and set a small `width` value on the paragraph. The proper fix is to define the logo image before the text in the HTML, so its floating position is established before the text is drawn by the browser, as shown in Example 4.24.

```
<div class="main">
  <img id="logo" src="images/smiley.png" alt="smiley" />
  This is some text <br /> that spans two lines
</div>
```

| This is some text |
| that spans two lines |

**Example 4.24 Corrected error with floating image**

## 4.3.4 Multi-Column Floating Layouts

When more than one element floats in the same direction, they stack horizontally. The first one is the furthest toward the float direction (for example, if all the elements float right, the first one will be the furthest right).

This stacking can be useful for creating pages with multi-column layouts. To do this, create multiple `divs`, each with a `float` and `width` attribute. Example 4.25 demonstrates such a multi-column layout. Since the columns float, the paragraph following the columns is given a `clear` value to make sure it is placed below the columns.

```
<div class="column">
  Lorem ipsum dolor sit amet, consectetuer adipiscing elit.
  Integer pretium dui sit amet felis.
</div>
<div class="column">
  Integer sit amet diam. Phasellus ultrices viverra velit.
</div>
<div class="column">
  Beware the Jabberwock, my son!
  The jaws that bite, the claws that catch!
</div>
<p id="aftercolumns">
  I am the text that follows the columns.
  This is some really important text.
  You had better read it if you know what's good for you.
</p>
```

```
div, p {
  border: 2px solid black;
}
.column {
  float: right;
  width: 25%;
}
#aftercolumns {
  background-color: yellow;
  clear: both;
}
```

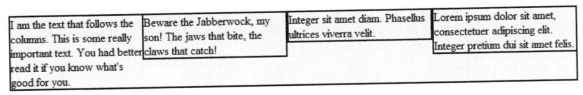

Example 4.25 Multi-column layout

It's important to note that any content to follow these columns should clear the previously set **float**. If this is not done, the following content tries to flow around the floating columns, which usually produces the wrong appearance. If Example 4.25's code had no **clear** attribute set on the last paragraph, it would have the appearance shown in Figure 4.10. The final paragraph actually appears to the left of the column **div**s, which is likely not the appearance intended. Interestingly the paragraph's yellow background also bleeds through into the **div**s. To avoid this we could explicitly give the column **div**s a **background-color** of **white**.

| I am the text that follows the columns. This is some really important text. You had better read it if you know what's good for you. | Beware the Jabberwock, my son! The jaws that bite, the claws that catch! | Integer sit amet diam. Phasellus ultrices viverra velit. | Lorem ipsum dolor sit amet, consectetuer adipiscing elit. Integer pretium dui sit amet felis. |

Figure 4.10 Multi-column layout without **clear**

## Self-Check

7. What is the difference between setting **float: right;** and **text-align: right;** ?
8. If you float two consecutive elements to the same side of the page, what happens? Where will the two elements appear with respect to each other?
9. Why is it important to set a **width** on a floated element? What can happen if it is not set?
10. What is the meaning of the **overflow** property? How is it related to floating elements?
11. Given the following code (abbreviated):

```
<div id="main">
  <h1>My fan site</h1>

  <img src="images/starhome.png" alt="starhome" />

  <p>Starhome Sprinter is a Flash animated Internet cartoon...</p>
  <p>Most of the site's traffic comes from the United States...</p>
  <p>The cartoons are nominally centered on title character ...</p>
  <p>Starhome's theme song says, "Everyperson! Everyperson!"</p>
</div>
```

What CSS code would be necessary to make the page have the following appearance?

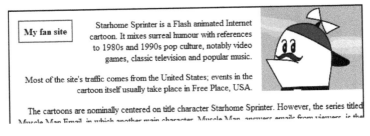

## 4.4 Sizing and Positioning

We've already seen that each element has a default position and size. The default position of block elements is stacked vertically down the page. The default position of inline elements is in a left-to-right flow from top to bottom within their enclosing block elements. A block element's default width is 100% of the page width, and its default height is the height of its inline content. An inline element's default size is just large enough to fit its contents. It's possible to change these defaults using the CSS properties shown in this section.

### 4.4.1 Width and Height

| Property | Meaning |
|---|---|
| `width`, `height` | how wide or tall to make the element's content area |
| `max-width`, `max-height`, `min-width`, `min-height` | the minimum or maximum size of this element |

The size given to an element's content can be changed by setting its CSS `width` and `height` properties. We have already mentioned the `width` property when discussing floating elements. It's also legal to specify minimum and maximum sizes for the element. When a minimum or maximum is set, the browser will try to use the element's default size, but if that would exceed the minimum or maximum, the size is restricted to that bound. All of the properties listed above apply only to block elements and to the `img` element; they are ignored for other inline elements (unless they are floating).

Example 4.26 demonstrates sizing of several elements. Notice that since `h2` is given a height of 3em, its box is now too tall for its contents, so the text inside the heading appears at the top of the element with some empty shaded space underneath. Later in this chapter we'll see how to change that with the `vertical-align` property if we want to do so.

```
<p>This is a paragraph with a fair amount of text</p>
<h2>This is an h2</h2>
```

```
p {
  width: 10em;
  background-color: yellow;
  border: 2px solid black;
}
h2 {
  height: 3em;
  background-color: aqua;
  border: 2px solid black;
}
```

This is a paragraph with a
fair amount of text

**This is an h2**

**Example 4.26 Width and height**

## Centering Block Elements

It's also possible to center a block element on the page using margins. To do so, give a `width` to the element and then set its `margin-left` and `margin-right` to the special value `auto`. A value of `auto` means to let the browser decide the margins. In this case, setting them both to `auto` has the effect of making them both the same size, which places the element horizontally in the center of the page. Example 4.27 illustrates this technique.

```
<p>
  Lorem ipsum dolor sit amet, consectetur adipisicing elit,
  sed do eiusmod tempor incididunt ut la-bore et dolore magna aliqua.
</p>
```

```
p {
  border: 2px solid black;
  margin-left: auto;
  margin-right: auto;
  width: 33%;
}
```

Lorem ipsum dolor sit amet, consectetur adipisicing elit, sed do eiusmod tempor incididunt ut la-bore et dolore magna aliqua.

**Example 4.27 Centering with auto margins**

Centering with `auto` margins only works if the element has a `width` setting; if not, the element occupies 100% of the page width and is too wide to be centered.

It's important to understand the difference between centering a block element and centering the inline content inside it. Notice that the text in the preceding example isn't center-aligned; each line is left-aligned, just not with respect to the left edge of the page. To center inline text within a block element, give the block element a `text-align: center;` instead.

## Inline Elements

You can also adjust the size and position of inline elements, though there are some distinctions between them and block elements:

- The various size properties (`width`, `height`, `min-width`, `max-height`, etc.) are ignored for inline boxes, except when used with the `img` element.
- The `margin-top` and `margin-bottom` properties are ignored. (`margin-left` and `margin-right` do work.)
- The `padding-top` and `padding-bottom` properties cause a padding to appear between an inline element and its border as expected, but they do not cause neighboring lines to be spaced any further apart. This can cause the inline element's border or padding to run over into the lines above and below. The `img` element is the one exception to this rule; `img` elements with vertical padding do cause spacing between themselves and neighboring lines. (The `padding-left` and `padding-right` properties behave as expected on an inline element; they do cause neighboring text content to be spaced farther to the left and right.)
- The containing block element's `text-align` property controls horizontal position of inline boxes within it.

- Each inline box's `vertical-align` property aligns it vertically within its block box.

The `vertical-align` property is a new one we haven't discussed yet, and it has some subtleties, so it deserves its own section.

### Vertical Alignment

| Property | Meaning | Values |
|----------|---------|--------|
| `vertical-align` | vertical alignment of an inline element | `baseline` (default), `top`, `middle`, `bottom`, `sub`, `super`, `text-top`, `text-bottom`, or a size value or % |

The `vertical-align` property specifies where an inline element should be aligned vertically, with respect to other content on the same line within its block element's box. The default value of `baseline` aligns the content vertically with the bottom or baseline of the non-hanging letters of inline text. (Hanging letters are ones such as g or j that have parts that protrude below the normal bottom line of the text.)

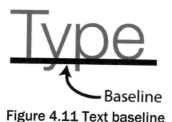

Figure 4.11 Text baseline

Example 4.28 shows several images with different vertical alignments and the way they look with respect to the neighboring text. The paragraph's inline content is wrapped into an overall **span** with a **class** of **inlinestyles**, so that we can apply a border to it to help you see the relative vertical alignment of the images.

```
<p>
  <span class="inlinestyles">
    Don't be sad!  Turn that frown
    <img src="images/sad.png" alt="sad" /> upside down!

    <img class="happy" src="images/smiley.png" alt="smile" />
    Smiling burns calories, you know.

    <img class="puppy" src="images/puppy.jpg" alt="puppy" />
    Anyway, look at this cute puppy; isn't he adorable!  So cheer up,
    and have a nice day.  The End.
  </span>
</p>
```

```
p {
  border: 3px dashed black;
}
.inlinestyles {
  border: 3px solid red;
  vertical-align: bottom;
}
.happy {
  vertical-align: top;
}
.puppy {
  vertical-align: middle;
}
```

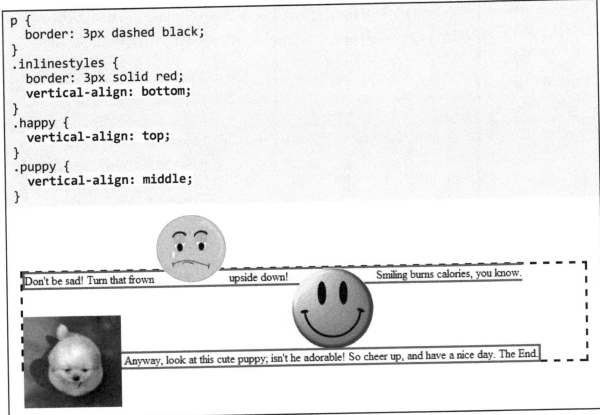

Example 4.28 Vertical alignment

**Common Error**
Space under image

There are cases where you'll want an image inside a block element that is exactly as tall as that image. (We see this a lot when we're placing images into tables. We'll discuss tables in a later chapter.) You'd think it would work to make the block element exactly the right size to fit the image, by setting its padding to 0em. But when you do so, there is a bit of space under the image, as shown in Example 4.29.

```
<p class="alert">
  <img src="images/smiley.png" alt="smile" />
</p>

.alert {
  background-color: red;
  margin: 0px;
  padding: 0px;
}
```

Example 4.29 Common error: space under image

There is red space under the image, despite padding and margin of 0. This is because the image is vertically aligned to the baseline of the paragraph, which isn't the same as the bottom. Setting `vertical-align` to `bottom` as shown in Example 4.30 fixes the problem because it causes the image to also occupy the previously empty baseline area.

```
<p class="alert">
  <img class="bottom" src="images/smiley.png" alt="smile" />
</p>

.alert {
  background-color: red;
  margin: 0px;
  padding: 0px;
}
.bottom {
  vertical-align: bottom;
}
```

**Example 4.30 Corrected error with space under image**

Notice that now the image is flush against both the top and bottom of the area containing it, with no red space showing underneath. Another fix for this problem is to set the `line-height` property to `0px`, which places the baseline into the same position as the bottom, but this is more hackish.

## 4.4.2 Positioning

| Property | Meaning | Values |
|---|---|---|
| position | location of element on page | **static**: default position<br><br>**relative**: offset from its normal static position<br><br>**absolute**: at a particular offset within its containing element<br><br>**fixed**: at a fixed location within the browser window |
| top, bottom, left, right | offsets of element's edges | a size in **px**, **pt**, **em**, or **%** |

There are times when the standard flow of content on the page isn't ideal for presenting your page's information. For example, your page may have a sidebar of links that you want always to be visible even after the user scrolls down the page. Or you may have a pair of block elements that you want to appear next to each other horizontally. To achieve these kinds of effects, we can use the powerful CSS `position` property, which chooses from several models to position an element.

**relative positioning**

Setting the location of an element to an offset from its normal static position.

The default position is `static`, meaning to place the element within the normal document flow. But we can lift the element out of the normal flow in many different ways. Example 4.31 demonstrates *relative positioning*, which lets you shift an element's position slightly relative to its normal static position.

```
<p>
  This example has <span id="lifted">some text</span>
  with a relative position.
</p>

#lifted {
  position: relative;
  left: 0.5em;
  top: 1em;
  border; 2px solid black;
}
```

This example has ⌐some text⌐ with a relative position.

**Example 4.31 Relative positioning**

After setting the `position` to `relative` on the element, you can set its `top`, `bottom`, `left`, or `right` properties to specify the relative adjustments to those respective edges of the element's box.

## Absolute Positioning

**absolute positioning**

Setting the location of an element to an offset from the block element containing it.

Elements with a `position` of `absolute` are given an *absolute position* on the page and are removed from the normal flow. They are positioned at an offset relative to the block element containing them, assuming that block also uses `absolute` or `relative` positioning. (If it doesn't, the position is relative to the edges of the overall web page.)

Other elements on the page completely ignore the absolutely positioned element when laying themselves out. It's as though the element isn't even there, as far as their layout and positioning is concerned. Example 4.32 demonstrates absolute positioning, and Figure 4.12 shows the appearance.

```
<div id="area1">...</div>
<div id="area2">

  ...
  <div id="menubar">...</div>
</div>
<p>...</p>
```

```
#menubar {
  position: absolute;
  top: 20px;
  right: 40px;
  width: 100px;
}
```

**Example 4.32 Absolute positioning**

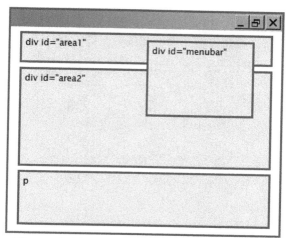

**Figure 4.12 Absolute positioning (output)**

As with relative positioning, the element's placement is determined by the values of its **top**, **bottom**, **left**, and **right** properties. You should generally specify a **width** property as well.

Generally the coordinates of an absolutely positioned element are relative to the entire page. If you want to make them relative to a particular element on the page instead, enclose your absolutely positioned element inside another element that uses absolute or relative positioning. A common idiom is to use an enclosing **div** with relative position, but no **left**, **top**, **right**, or **bottom** values. This will make the outer **div** stay at its normal static position, but also serve as a point of reference for any absolutely positioned elements inside it. Example 4.33 demonstrates this technique.

```
<div id="area1">...</div>
<div id="area2">
  <div id="menubar">...</div>
</div>
<p>...</p>
```

```
#area2 {    /* menubar will be relative to this div's position */
  position: relative;
}
#menubar {
  position: absolute;
  top: 20px;
  right: 40px;
  width: 100px;
}
```

**Example 4.33 Absolute positioning with relative containing element**

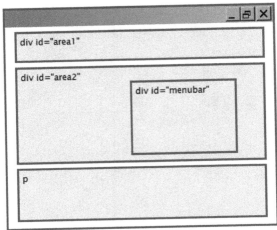

**Figure 4.13 Absolute positioning with relative containing element (output)**

If you use a percentage for your absolute position, you may not see the correct layout in some browsers unless you style the **body** to have a **width/height** of **100%**, as shown in Example 4.34.

```
body {
  width: 100%;
  height: 100%;
}
#menubar {
  position: absolute;
  top: 20px;
  right: 40px;
  width: 20%;
  height: 50%;
}
```

**Example 4.34 Body width and height styles**

An absolute position may sound a lot like floating an element. But a crucial difference is that, unlike absolutely positioned elements, floating ones still affect the flow of nearby inline content. A floating element is removed from the normal block flow of the document, and block elements lay themselves out underneath the floating element, ignoring it for layout purposes. But the inline content within those block elements does respect the floating element and wraps neatly around it. Absolutely positioned elements are ignored by other elements on the page during layout.

### Fixed Positioning

**fixed positioning**

Setting the location of an element to an absolute location on the browser screen.

Elements with a **position** value of **fixed** are given a *fixed position* on the screen and are removed from normal flow. This is much like absolute positioning, except that fixed elements are positioned relative to the overall browser window, not the page or their containing element. In other words, a **fixed** element will stay in exactly the same place on the screen, even if the user scrolls up and down the page. A fixed position is useful for content that you always want to be visible on the page, such as a sidebar of links or (shudder) an advertisement.

The CSS code in Example 4.35 is the same as in Example 4.32 seen previously, except with a fixed instead of absolute position. The screen diagram in Figure 4.14 shows the page after the user has scrolled down. The `menubar` section of the page remains in its original place and does not scroll with the other page contents underneath it.

```
<div id="area1">...</div>
<div id="area2">
  <div id="menubar">...</div>
</div>
<p>...</p>
```

```
#menubar {
  position: fixed;
  top: 20px;
  right: 40px;
  width: 100px;
}
```

**Example 4.35 Fixed positioning**

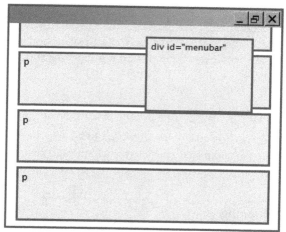

**Figure 4.14 Fixed positioning (output, after scrolling down the page)**

The left, right, top, or bottom value can be negative to cause an element to sit outside the visible browser window. This can create a nice "hanging" effect of an element that's partially off the page. Example 4.36 shows the necessary CSS and Figure 4.15 shows a diagram of the resulting appearance.

```
#menubar {
  position: fixed;
  top: 20px;
  left: -50px;
  width: 100px;
}
```

**Example 4.36 Fixed position with negative offset**

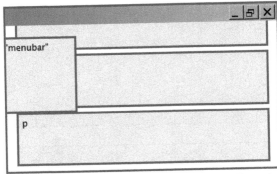

**Figure 4.15 Fixed position with negative offset (output)**

### 4.4.3 Z-indexing

| Property | Meaning | Values |
|---|---|---|
| z-index | element's 3-dimensional ordering | auto (default), or an integer |

The z-index property sets which **absolute** or **fixed** positioned element will appear on top of another that occupies the same space. An element with a greater z-index appears on top of any others on the same part of the screen.

### 4.4.4 Element Visibility

CSS has two properties named display and visibility that let you hide elements on a page. There are a few differences between the two properties, which we'll discuss in the following sections.

**The display Property**

| Property | Meaning | Values | |
|---|---|---|---|
| display | whether an element is displayed as a block or inline element, or not at all | block | (display as a block element), |
| | | inline | (display as an inline element), |
| | | none | (don't display this element), |
| | | ... | |
| visibility | whether an element's content can be seen on the page | visible | (default), or hidden |

The display property sets the type of CSS box the browser should use to display a particular element. This is a powerful property that lets you "play God" a bit with your HTML. For example, you can set an li to display as an inline element even though the browser would normally display it as a block element. Example 4.37 demonstrates headings that display as inline elements.

```
<h2>This is a heading</h2>
<h2>This is another heading</h2>
```

```
h2 {
  background-color: yellow;
  border: 1px solid black;
  display: inline;
}
```

This is a heading This is another heading

**Example 4.37 Displaying a block element as inline**

Setting the `display` property has no effect on what is/isn't valid XHTML. For example, even if you set a `span`'s `display` to `block`, the W3C XHTML validator will complain if the `span` is not placed inside a block element. Use `display` sparingly, because it can radically alter the page layout.

One common use of `display` is to make the contents of a list display horizontally rather than vertically. Most new web developers think of a `ul` as showing on the page as a bulleted list, with each item on its own line. But by setting the list items to display inline, the list flows horizontally with no bullet next to each item. Example 4.38 illustrates this technique.

```
<ul id="menubar">
  <li>News</li>
  <li>Links</li>
  <li>Members Only</li>
  <li>Join</li>
</ul>
```

```
li {
  display: inline;
  padding: 0.5em;
  border: 2px solid gray;
}
```

News Links Members Only Join

**Example 4.38 Displaying a list as inline**

You might ask why we're using an unordered list in Example 4.38, rather than, say, a paragraph with four `span` elements inside it for the list items. But remember that we should choose our HTML tags based on the meaning of the content. The above section headings are a list, not a paragraph. Tagging them as list items is more semantically descriptive than simply labeling them as spans of text.

There are other values `display` can have (such as `compact` and `table-column-group`), but most of them are obscure values dealing with tables, which we'll cover later in this textbook.

An element whose `display` is set to `none` is not shown on the page at all. For example, the code in Example 4.39 produces no visible output in the browser. Right now it might not make sense to set `display` to `none`, rather than just deleting the element from the page's source code altogether or commenting it out. But in later chapters we'll see a common usage of `display` where we'll show and hide an element dynamically in response to user events using JavaScript.

```
<div>
  <p class="secret">No one will be able to see this! :-(</p>
  <p>But you can see this</p>
</div>
```

```
p.secret {
  display: none;
}
```

But you can see this

**Example 4.39 Non-displayed element**

## The visibility Property

The `visibility` property sets whether an element should be shown onscreen. The default visibility for an element is `visible`, but when an element's visibility is set to `hidden`, the element will not be shown on the page. The main difference between the `display` and `visibility` properties is the following:

- `display: none;` means the element does not occupy space on the page ("It's not there")
- `visibility: hidden;` means the element still occupies space on the page, but its contents are not drawn and it is invisible to the user ("It's there, but I can't see it")

Example 4.40 shows a hidden element. It's not very exciting, because you can't see the element. But notice that the area containing the hidden paragraph is large enough to fit the paragraph, unlike the previous example with `display` set to `none`, in which the outer area was smaller.

```
<div>
  <p class="secret">No one will be able to see this! :-(</p>
  <p>But you can see this</p>
</div>
```

```
p.secret {
  visibility: hidden;
}
```

But you can see this

**Example 4.40 Hidden element**

Later we'll use this property to show and hide dynamic HTML content on the page in response to user events in JavaScript. Sometimes a `visibility` of `hidden` is better than a `display` of `none` in such cases because the page layout already has allocated space for the hidden element, so the layout won't change when we instruct the element to appear.

## Self-Check

12. What CSS code would center a paragraph horizontally on the page, making it occupy half the page's width, and with the text right-aligned within the paragraph?

13. What CSS code would place a paragraph against the right edge of the page, making it occupy half the page's width, but with the text left-aligned?

14. Which of the following CSS properties have an effect, when set on an inline element? Choose all that apply.
    a) `margin`
    b) `margin-top`
    c) `margin-left`
    d) `width`
    e) `height`
    f) `padding`
    g) `padding-bottom`
    h) `padding-right`

15. What `vertical-align` value does each of the following images have?

I am fine

16. What is the difference between absolute and fixed positioning? Which is more appropriate for each of the following items you might want to put on your page?
    a) a bar of links that should be visible on the page at all times
    b) a left column of the page's layout showing various news and updates; the updates might be longer than the browser window is tall
    c) an image that you want to appear to the right of some text in a paragraph
    d) a pop-up ad that shows on top of the normal page content and can't be dodged by scrolling down the browser window

17. What is the difference between setting `display: none;` and `visibility: hidden;` on an element? How can you tell them apart by looking at the page?

# 4.5 Internet Explorer Layout Quirks (optional)

One of the sad realities of web programming is that Microsoft's Internet Explorer browser simply does not follow the rules. There are a large number of major bugs and incompatibilities in IE that can make us web coders want to tear our hair out. Microsoft has chosen simply not to follow web standards. In particular, IE does not implement the CSS box model the way it is supposed to be implemented. A page that looks one way in IE may look a completely different way in Firefox or Safari. A page that shows up in one browser may be blank or badly misformatted in another. This leaves web programmers with a tough decision: Which users do I want to be able to see my page correctly?

The worst part is, despite the fact that Microsoft's IE team continues to release new versions of their browser (version 8 is being readied as this book goes to press), they choose not to correct these problems. It's not clear whether this is because they want to retain compatibility with existing pages that use the old incorrect behaviors, or as a way of intentionally balkanizing the web and making it harder for the web as a platform to reduce the importance of Microsoft's Windows operating system. Either way, it can be a royal pain to deal with IE, as you'll see if you try to do so as a web dev.

Fortunately, if you are aware of some of IE's most major deficiencies and workarounds for them, you can often create a page that works in both IE and standards-compliant browsers. In this section, we list some of the more common quirks of IE and suggest ways to deal with them. The section is intentionally kept short, because we generally object to Microsoft's decisions here and want to focus on and follow web standards as much as possible.

### The Broken Box Model

Various versions of Internet Explorer misinterpret the `width` and `height` properties. It considers them to include the padding and border around the element, which it shouldn't. This is disastrous for web developers who want a consistent appearance to their pages, because the width you set for a standards-compliant browser simply won't match that seen in IE, unless your elements have no padding. The element will appear too thin in IE, since the same number of pixels now have to accommodate the padding and border. Thanks a lot, IE development team.

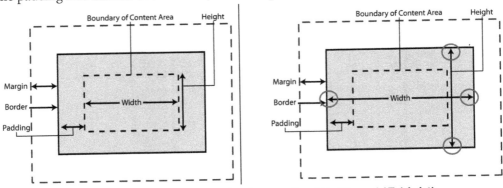

Figure 4.16 Box model, standard-compliant (left) and IE (right)

To make matters worse, Internet Explorer 6 also doesn't support the `min-width`, `min-height`, `max-width`, or `max-height` properties. What a pain! Many web developers have come up with hacks to try to emulate the effect of properties like `min-width` in IE, such as the following sites:

- http://www.cssplay.co.uk/boxes/minwidth.html
- http://www.webreference.com/programming/min-width/

## The Broken Float Model

If you float an element inside another block element and want to space it from the edge a bit, you can set a margin on the appropriate side. For example, the code in Example 4.41 is supposed to space a `div` 100px from the page's left edge. It works properly in standards-compliant browsers.

```css
div#floating {
   float: left;
   margin-left: 100px;
}
```

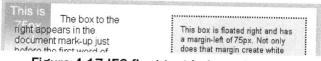

**Example 4.41 Float with left margin**

In Internet Explorer 6 when an element is floated left, its left margin is mistakenly doubled by the browser. In this case our floating element actually appears 200px from the left edge.

This is not the only bug related to floating elements; there is a lengthy list of such bugs. For example, when you float elements, often IE6 will mistakenly indent the first line of nearby text with the same amount of indentation as the floating element's `margin-left` setting.

This is
75... The box to the
right appears in the
document mark-up just
before the first word of

This box is floated right and has
a margin-left of 75px. Not only
does that margin create white

**Figure 4.17 IE6 float text indentation bug**

A suggested workaround for IE is to set the floated element's `display` to `inline`, which does mysteriously fix the bug. But this is simply a hack and shouldn't make such a drastic change to the page's layout.

```css
div#floating {
   display: inline;
   float: left;
   margin-left: 100px;
}
```

**Example 4.42 Display inline hack for float bug**

Here's another float bug. If you float an element to the left and then position other block content underneath it, the block element is supposed to lay itself out normally. But in IE, if the underlying block element has a `width` declaration, it will also be mysteriously turned into a floating element and placed to the side of the floating one. This bug still exists in IE7 (it is fixed in IE8), so the majority of users of the web potentially face this issue. IE also often adds 3px or so of margin between floating elements and other elements, even when they are supposed to touch flush against each other. On and on. The following site has a floating elements test that IE7 and below fail miserably:

* http://css-class.com/articles/explorer/floats/floatandcleartest1.htm

As you can see, getting floating layouts to render correctly in IE can be a grueling experience.

## 4.5.1 Workarounds for IE Flaws

A lot of times you can make a page look right in Internet Explorer if you can apply different CSS rules to it in IE than you do to other browsers. The idea is to supply one set of CSS rules to IE that account for its misbehavior, and another set to everybody else who follows the rules.

### The "Underscore Hack"

Over the years a bunch of CSS "hacks" have been found that can be used to target IE exclusively. For example, recall how IE's box model deals with widths and heights improperly. Some crafty CSS developer discovered that IE will pay attention to CSS rules even if they have certain bad characters in them, such as underscores. For example, if you try to set a property named `_width`, standards-compliant browsers will completely ignore it, but IE will happily set the element's width. People use this to set IE to use a larger width to give space for the element's horizontal padding and borders, as in the code shown in Example 4.43.

```
div {
  width: 100px;
  padding: 10px;
  border: 10px solid black;
  _width: 140px;
}
```

**Example 4.43 IE "underscore hack" (not recommended!)**

There are other equally objectionable hacks, such as calling it `w\idth` or using a bogus context selector that only IE will recognize, such as `* html div { ... }`. We strongly discourage against using hacks like these. Many of them will break your CSS file so that it does not pass the W3C validator. IE support isn't worth that.

Fortunately there's a better way to get this same effect of providing a special set of style rules to IE. This can be achieved by a special IE-only proprietary HTML feature called conditional comments. A *conditional comment* is a comment that can contain an `if` statement in it, causing a piece of HTML to be included only if some condition is met. The syntax for conditional comments is:

```
<!--[if condition]>
  HTML code
<![endif]-->
```

The most common thing to write under condition is simply the letters `IE`, meaning, "if this browser is any version of IE." All other browsers will ignore this text and treat it as a large HTML comment. Another variation of a condition checks for a specific IE version, such as `lte IE 6`, since different versions of IE have had different bugs and require different fixes.

Example 4.44 demonstrates Internet Explorer's conditional comments. The code uses them to link to a file ie_hacks.css on all versions of IE, and to an additional file ie6_more_hacks.css if the browser is specifically IE6. The ie_hacks.css file contains the 140px width to correct for IE's broken box model, so that the actual content width of the element will be the desired 100px to match the standard-compliant browsers.

```
<!DOCTYPE html PUBLIC "-//W3C//DTD XHTML 1.1//EN"
    "http://www.w3.org/TR/xhtml11/DTD/xhtml11.dtd">
<html xmlns="http://www.w3.org/1999/xhtml">
  <head>
    <!--[if IE]>
      <link href="ie_hacks.css" type="text/css" rel="stylesheet" />
    <![endif]-->

    <!--[if lte IE 6]>
      <link href="ie6_more_hacks.css" type="text/css" rel="stylesheet" />
    <![endif]-->
    ...
```

```
/* ie_hacks.css file contents */
div {
  width: 140px;
}
```

Example 4.44 Internet Explorer conditional comments

## 4.6  Case Study: Ultimate Frisbee

At the start of this chapter, we posed the problem of laying out an ultimate Frisbee site. Recall the appearance we wanted it to have, as shown in Figure 4.1. Now, with our new knowledge of CSS ids and classes, `div` and `span`, the box model, and layout, we can achieve the desired layout.

Figure 4.18 Ultimate frisbee page, desired appearance

Let's assume that we're starting out with the HTML code shown in Example 4.45 (abbreviated), and that we want to change the HTML code as little as possible in our process of styling the page.

```
<!DOCTYPE html PUBLIC "-//W3C//DTD XHTML 1.1//EN"
    "http://www.w3.org/TR/xhtml11/DTD/xhtml11.dtd">
<html xmlns="http://www.w3.org/1999/xhtml">
  <head><title>Ultimate Frisbee</title></head>
  <body>
    <h1>News</h1>
    <ul>
      <li>Ultimate frisbee declared an Olympic sport</li>
      ...
    </ul>

    <h1>Marty's Ultimate Page</h1>
    <p>Welcome to my ultimate page! ...</p>

    <h2>2008 College and HS Westerns</h2>
    <p><img src="ultimate.jpg" alt="ultimate" />
      College Championships will be in Boulder, CO ...</p>
    ...
    <h1>Events</h1>
    <ul>
      <li><a href="">January</a></li>
      <li><a href="">February</a></li> ...
    </ul>
  </body>
</html>
```

Example 4.45 Initial HTML code for Ultimate Frisbee page

Let's come up with a strategy to approach this problem step-by step. The following order of operations should help us create the desired page appearance:

1. Look at the desired appearance picture and decide what are the major sections of the page. Change the HTML code to semantically represent these sections as `div` elements.
2. Link the page to a CSS file that we'll create incrementally.
3. Add general styles not related to tricky layout, such as fonts, colors, and alignment.
4. Tackle the layout for each section, starting with the Events calendar, then the News section and central announcements.

## 4.6.1 Page Sections and General Styles

First let's denote the major sections of the page and wrap them in `div`s as appropriate. The news at left and the calendar at right seem to be major page sections, so they each deserve a `div`. Let's also place a `div` on the central section containing the announcements. We'll give each one an `id` for styling, as shown in Example 4.46.

```html
<div id="news">
  <h1>News</h1>
  <ul><li>Ultimate frisbee declared an Olympic sport</li> ...
  </ul>
</div>

<div id="announcements">
  <h1>Marty's Ultimate Page</h1> ...
</div>

<div id="calendar">
  <h1>Events</h1>
  <ul><li><a href="">January</a></li> ...
  </ul>
</div>
```

**Example 4.46 Ultimate frisbee page sections**

Now let's take a stab at a few initial styles, without worrying about the complex layout of the page just yet. We'll edit the HTML page's header to include a link to our CSS file:

```html
<head>
  <link href="ultimate.css" type="text/css" rel="stylesheet" />
```

### General Styles

The overall page body should use a 12pt Tahoma sans-serif font. The central announcements section has a green background and a black border. The level-1 headings on the page should be centered and have reduced margins. Also note how the level-2 headings have a blue background color and white text, and their first word is in a large font. Earlier in this chapter we discussed how to achieve such styles by wrapping text in `span`s. All these initial styles are shown in Example 4.47.

```
body {
  font: 12pt "Tahoma", "Arial", sans-serif;
}
.announcement {  /* text inside h2 headings */
  background-color: #0000cc;
  color: white;
}
#announcements {
  background-color: #ddffdd;
  border: 2px solid black;
}
.firstword {
  font-size: 32pt;
}
h1 {
  margin: 0em 0em 0.5em 0em;
  text-align: center;
}
```

**Example 4.47 Initial page styles**

### Image, Heading, and List Styles using Context Selectors

Some of the announcements have images associated with them, which should hover on the right side of the **main** pane. Rather than styling each of those images with a CSS class, we can use a context selector to float all **img** elements within the **announcements** area. (We'll set a **clear** property on the **h2** elements for each announcement, so that one announcement's image never hangs down into the next announcement.) Example 4.48 shows the related CSS styles.

```
#announcements img {
  float: right;
  margin-left: 2em;
}

#announcements h2 {
  border-bottom: 2px solid black;
  clear: right;
}
```

**Example 4.48 Styles for headings and floating images**

The calendar and news sections have several non-layout styles that we can apply now. The news area should have a small font. Also, you'll notice that in our page the list of news items is a bulleted list, while in the expected page appearance there are no bullets and boxes around each news item. This might make you think that **ul** is the wrong tag for this list of items, but that would be faulty logic. We don't choose our HTML tags based on how content looks; we choose them based on the meaning and semantics of the content. This is still a list of items, so **ul** is the right tag. We'll just remove the bullets by setting a **list-style-type** property on the list in the News area. We don't need to give an **id** to the list to achieve this; we can do it with a CSS context selector that matches any **ul** inside the **#news** area. The list items themselves (**li**) inside this list can be given borders and background colors to make them match the desired appearance. Example 4.50 shows these styles.

```
#calendar {
  background-color: #00eeee;
  border: 2px solid black;
  line-height: 1.5em;
}
#news { font-size: smaller; }
#news > ul {
  list-style-type: none;
  padding-left: 0em;
}
#news li {
  background-color: #ffffcc;
  border: 3px solid #ffff88;
  margin-bottom: 1em;
  padding: 1em;
}
```

**Example 4.49 News and calendar area styles**

After all the preceding styles have been applied, the page has the appearance shown in Figure 4.19 as a split screenshot to show part of the top and bottom of the page.

# News

Ultimate frisbee declared an Olympic sport

George W. Bush hit by frisbee, injured

# Marty's Ultimate Page

Welcome to my ultimate page! Here we have news, links, and other information related to the most underrated sport in America.

## 2008 College and HS Westerns

College Championships will be in Boulder, CO on May 16-18, 2008. The event will be one week earlier than usual, and will be held in conjunction with College Sports Television's (CSTV) Collegiate Nationals event. The UPA is partnering with CSTV and Grass Roots Ultimate to host the event.

High School Westerns will be moving east, at least relatively speaking, to Independence, MO. The Matthew Bourland (matthew@hq.upa.org) if you are interested in receiving an application.

# Events

- January
- February
- March
- April

**Figure 4.19 Ultimate Frisbee page appearance, take 1**

## 4.6.2 Page Layout

Now let's do a bit of layout work. The calendar at right should remain in the same position on the page even after the user scrolls down. To do this, we'll give the calendar area a `fixed` position near the top-right edge of the page. We'll set its width to be 8em, just right for the width of its text.

```
#calendar {
  background-color: #00eeee;
  border: 2px solid black;
  line-height: 1.5em;
  position: fixed;
  right: 1em;
  top: 1em;
  width: 8em;
}
```

**Example 4.50 Calendar area styles**

After these new styles have been applied to the page, it has the appearance shown in Figure 4.20. It still has several glaring flaws. For one, the announcements area is too wide and reaches underneath the fixed Events calendar. Second, the News section is still at the top of the page, rather than on the left where it should be. We'll need to create additional styles to fix these problems.

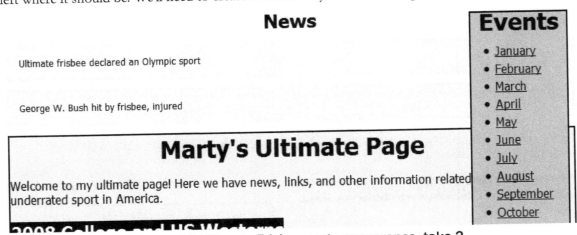

**Figure 4.20 Ultimate Frisbee page appearance, take 2**

First let's fix the announcements area so it doesn't reach underneath the Events calendar. Since the calendar area is 8em wide and 1em from the right edge of the page, we can set a right margin on our announcements area of 10em, which will keep it from colliding.

```
#announcements {
  background-color: #ddffdd;
  border: 2px solid black;
  margin-right: 10em;
}
```

The news bar at left is a little trickier. It should move as the page scrolls, and it should also be contained inside the central announcements area, with the announcement text wrapping around it. This is an ideal case to use a floating layout.

```
#news {
  float: left;
}
```

However, if the `float` style is the only one we set, the appearance still isn't quite right. We get the appearance shown in Figure 4.21, with the News items awkwardly injected into the main announcements area. This is why it's so important to always set a width on any floating content, to keep it from widening and interfering with other contents on the page.

Figure 4.21 Ultimate Frisbee page appearance, take 3

### News and Announcement Section Layout

Let's apply some additional styles to the news section to clean it up. It should have a width of 8em, like the event calendar. Let's also place a 1em margin around it on all sides to distance it from neighboring content.

```
#news {
  float: left;
  font-size: smaller;
  margin-left: 1em;
  width: 8em;
}
```

After these changes, we have the following layout, shown in Figure 4.22 in two sections so you can see the top and bottom of the news area. The appearance is pretty close to what we want, but the text after the News area moves over too far to the left. We want it to stay over to the right of the news section all the way down the page. Also there isn't any spacing between the News section and the announcement text, and the black borders behind the level-2 headings extend left under News.

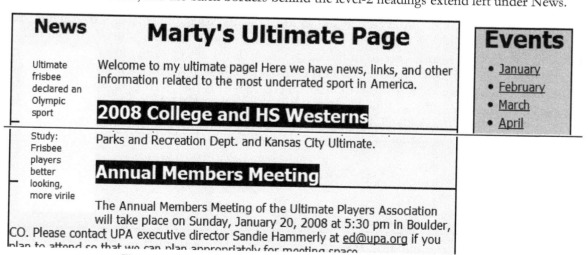

Figure 4.22 Ultimate Frisbee page appearance, take 4

Remembering the right margin we used to separate the announcements section from the events section, we could try setting a similar left margin on the announcements section to distance it from the floating news area. This helps, but it causes the green background and border to move away from the News section, making it differ from the desired appearance, as shown in Figure 4.23.

Figure 4.23 Ultimate Frisbee page appearance, take 5

We want to put a left margin on the announcements area, but not the overall green box and border. How can we do this? The solution is to add an additional outer `div` layer to represent the green background and black border, and place both the News and Announcements sections inside it. Then we can place a margin on the announcements section without moving the border or background.

```
<body>
  <div id="main">
    <div id="news">
      <h1>News</h1> ...
    </div>

    <div id="announcements">
      <h1>Marty's Ultimate Page</h1> ...
    </div>
  </div>

  <div id="calendar">...</div>
</body>
```

Example 4.51 Adding `main` section to page for styling

The styles applied to the main section and announcements section must be chosen carefully. We want the overall background and border on the new `main` section. We want the left margin on the `announcements` section inside `main`, so the margin doesn't move the border. But the right margin, the one to distance the central content from the calendar at right, *must* be on the main section and not the announcements section. If it's placed on the announcements, the green background and border will extend to the right underneath the calendar. Example 4.52 shows the new CSS styles. After adding these final styles, we have the desired appearance from our original screenshot.

```
#main {
  background-color: #ddffdd;
  border: 2px solid black;
  margin-right: 10em;
}
#announcements { margin-left: 8em; }
```

Example 4.52 New CSS styles for main page section

## 4.6.3 Final File Contents

After all of the changes and code in the previous sections, we end up with final files ultimate.html and ultimate.css, shown in Example 4.53 and Example 4.54 respectively.

```html
<!DOCTYPE html PUBLIC "-//W3C//DTD XHTML 1.0 Strict//EN"
    "http://www.w3.org/TR/xhtml1/DTD/xhtml1-strict.dtd">
<html xmlns="http://www.w3.org/1999/xhtml">
  <!-- Chapter 4 case study: XHTML code for Ultimate frisbee page -->
  <head>
    <title>Ultimate Frisbee</title>
    <link href="ultimate.css" type="text/css" rel="stylesheet" />
  </head>

  <body>
    <div id="main">
      <div id="news">
        <h1>News</h1>
        <ul>
          <li>Ultimate frisbee declared an Olympic sport</li> ...
        </ul>
      </div>

      <div id="announcements">
        <h1>Marty's Ultimate Page</h1>
        <p>Welcome to my ultimate page!  Here we have news, ...</p>

        <h2><span class="announcement">2008 College and
            HS Westerns</span></h2>

        <p><img src="ultimate.jpg" alt="ultimate" />
          <span class="firstword">College</span> Championships
          will be in Boulder, CO...</p>

        <h2><span class="announcement">Annual Members Meeting</span></h2>

        <p><span class="firstword">The</span> Annual Members ...</p>
      </div>
    </div>

    <div id="calendar">
      <h1>Events</h1>
      <ul>
        <li><a href="">January</a></li>
        <li><a href="">February</a></li>
        ...
        <li><a href="">December</a></li>
      </ul>
    </div>
  </body>
</html>
```

Example 4.53 Ultimate Frisbee page code `ultimate.html`

```
/* Chapter 4 case study: CSS styles for Ultimate frisbee page */
body { font: 12pt "Tahoma", "Arial", sans-serif; }
.announcement {
  background-color: #0000cc;    color: white;
}
#announcements {
  margin-left: 8em;
  padding: 0em 1em;
}
#announcements h2 {                      /* text inside h2 headings */
  border-bottom: 2px solid black;
  clear: right;
}
#announcements img {
  float: right;     margin-left: 2em;
}
#calendar {
  background-color: #00eeee;
  border: 2px solid black;
  line-height: 1.5em;
  position: fixed;
  right: 1em;
  top: 1em;
  width: 8em;
}
#calendar ul { padding-left: 2em; }
.firstword   { font-size: 32pt; }   /* first word of h2 headings */
h1 {
  margin: 0em 0em 0.5em 0em;
  text-align: center;
}
#main {
  background-color: #ddffdd;
  border: 2px solid black;
  margin-right: 10em;
}
#news {
  float: left;
  font-size: smaller;
  margin-left: 1em;
  width: 8em;
}
#news > ul {
  list-style-type: none;
  padding-left: 0em;
}
#news li {
  background-color: #ffffcc;
  border: 3px solid #ffff88;
  margin-bottom: 1em;
  padding: 1em;
}
```

Example 4.54 Ultimate Frisbee page styles `ultimate.css`

## Chapter Summary

- Block elements in an HTML document are laid out in a standard flow from top to bottom. Inline elements are laid out within block elements from left to right, top to bottom.
- The CSS Box Model describes the regions HTML elements occupy. An element's box has an optional border, with padding inside the border and margins outside it.
- Padding and margins are specified as a size; borders have a thickness, color, and style.
- Elements can be given a width and height. Content's horizontal and vertical position can be affected by setting `auto` margins or changing the `vertical-align` property, respectively.
- Elements can be given custom positions by setting their `position` property. An `absolute` position specifies a particular offset within the surrounding region. A `fixed` position specifies an offset within the browser window.
- The `display` and `visibility` properties set whether an element is displayed as a block element, inline element, or not at all.
- Floating elements are lifted out from the normal document flow and pushed over to the left or right corner of the page.

## References

CSS Specifications and References:

- W3C CSS2 Specification: http://www.w3.org/TR/REC-CSS2/
- W3C Schools CSS2 Reference http://www.w3schools.com/css/css_reference.asp
- W3Schools CSS Tutorial: http://www.w3schools.com/Css/default.asp
- EchoEcho.Com Tutorial: http://www.echoecho.com/css.htm
- CSS by Quirksmode: http://www.quirksmode.org/css/contents.html
- CSS Specificity Wars:
  - http://www.stuffandnonsense.co.uk/archives/css_specificity_wars.html
- CSS Float Theory: Things You Should Know by Smashing Magazine:
  - http://www.smashingmagazine.com/2007/05/01/css-float-theory-things-you-should-know/
- CSS Positioning by Relatively Absolute
  - http://www.autisticcuckoo.net/archive.php?id=2004/12/07/relatively-absolute
- CSS Positioning in 10 Steps
  - http://www.barelyfitz.com/screencast/html-training/css/positioning/
- Web Design from Scratch: Block and Inline elements
  - http://www.webdesignfromscratch.com/css-block-and-inline.cfm
- CSS Zen Garden: http://www.csszengarden.com/
- Most Useful 50 CSS Tips And Tools For Webmasters by Emma Alvarez
  - http://www.emmaalvarez.com/2008/04/most-useful-50-css-tips-and-tools-for.html
- Internet Explorer Layout Hacks and Fixes:
  - http://www.tdrake.net/ie7-hacks/
  - http://www.positioniseverything.net/ie-primer.html
  - http://www.satzansatz.de/cssd/onhavinglayout.html
- Should I Use Tables for Layout?: http://shouldiusetablesforlayout.com/

# Chapter 5  PHP for Server-Side Programming

# Introduction

As you've written web pages so far, you may have found yourself wishing that HTML were more like a programming language. Many pages have large amounts of redundant content that must be copied and pasted many times throughout the page. For example, perhaps your page has 10 `div`s that contain almost identical formatting and text. It's a shame you couldn't have used a `for` loop or a function to capture and eliminate the redundancy. There is also redundancy between pages, where several pages on a site have the same header or footer areas or otherwise share content. HTML itself has no way of expressing this similarity in a compact way.

Another drawback of the pages we've created so far is that their contents are static and never change. It's useful to be able to create dynamic web pages, whose content changes with each visit or upon specified events. For example, you might want a page that counts how many "hits" or visits it receives. Or you might want a page that displays a random quotation at the bottom, or a different header image on each page reload.

In this chapter we'll learn the basics of a language called PHP that enables us to address all of the above issues and more. Using PHP you can create pages that take advantage of data and resources on a web server and present it to the user in dynamic ways.

## 5.1 Server-Side Basics

In this section we'll briefly discuss some background information about how code is run on a web server and what it means to write a dynamic server-side web page. We'll also discuss the PHP language's history and general design philosophies behind it.

### 5.1.1 Lifecycle of a Web Request

When a client's browser requests a simple `.html` file from the server, the web server software (such as Apache or IIS) reads that file from the disk and sends its contents back over the network connection to the client. Such content is called *static content* or *fixed content*. But you have also seen pages that were not static. For example, if two people visit http://www.facebook.com/home.php, they see two very different pages. How does the same URL display two completely different things?

A server can contain web pages that are actually programs written in various languages such as PHP, Java Server Pages (JSP), or Ruby. When the client requests a web program from the server, such as a `.php` file, the server handles this in a different way from static content. The server reads the program file and executes it. The program produces content (usually HTML text) as its output. This output is then sent back to the client over the network. Such web content is called *dynamic content*, and the process of creating programs that generate such content is called *server-side scripting*. The lifecycle of a dynamic server-side web request and response can be summarized by Figure 5.1.

> **dynamic content**
> Web pages generated on-the-fly by a web server at the moment a user requests them.
>
> **server-side scripting**
> Writing programs such as PHP files to generate dynamic content.

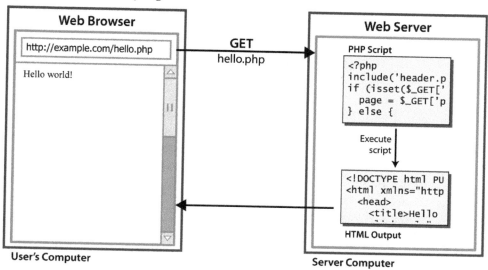

**Figure 5.1 PHP script running on a web server**

If you looked at the source code of Facebook's home.php file on their web server, you'd see a bunch of PHP variables, functions, and statements. If you view the source of **home.php** in your browser, you'll see nothing but HTML code. The former is the server-side program, and the latter is the HTML output it produces. It's important to understand the difference.

Many PHP files are actually written as mixtures of HTML code and PHP program code. When the web server processes such a file, the PHP code is run, and its output is inserted into the HTML around it. Such a mixture of code inside HTML is called *embedded code*. This allows some or all of a page's contents to be created dynamically at the moment the web request is made by the client.

The fact that web programs run on a server means we'll have to make some changes in how we view and test our code. If you direct your browser to open a web program such as a `.php` file on your hard disk, you won't see the program's output. Instead, you may see a blank page or an incomplete file. This is because when you view the file locally, it is being read directly from your hard drive to the browser, and not being processed and run by the web server software. To view it properly, you'll need to upload the web program to a proper web server and point your browser to that URL.

It's also possible to set up a web server on your own computer by installing products such as Apache and PHP, and test that way.

## 5.1.2 Introduction to PHP

PHP is a simple, highly available server-side web programming language. PHP was created by Danish programmer Rasmus Lerdorf in 1995 as a simple way to add small amounts of dynamic content to his personal web pages. The acronym originally stood for "Personal Home Page." PHP was then picked up by other developers and expanded into the language it is today. During this process the acronym PHP was changed to stand for "PHP Hypertext Processor." (That's right; the first P in PHP is short for PHP. It's a recursive acronym.) PHP's current web home is http://www.php.net/, a very useful web site that contains a downloadable installer for PHP, detailed documentation about the language syntax, and API specifications for all PHP classes and functions.

**Figure 5.2 Rasmus Lerdorf, creator of PHP**

PHP is a procedural language that bears many similarities to C and Perl (another scripting language). PHP is dynamically and weakly typed. It is available for many popular operating systems such as Windows, Mac OS X, and Linux. PHP is extremely popular and widespread on the web; it is currently the #1 most widely installed add-on module to the Apache web server. PHP's simplicity and wide availability are two of its strongest benefits, and two reasons we choose it as our server-side language for this textbook. Other benefits of PHP are that it is completely free of charge, is open-source, and is widely compatible with various servers and architectures. PHP is also easy to install on your own computer if you want to do your own PHP coding and testing at home. (Though, there are some who say that the success of a programming language is based solely on whether its creator has a beard! See the References section for a link to some supporting data.)

A lot of the fundamental programming concepts and syntax of PHP will feel familiar to you if you've already learned some Java, C, C++, or a similar language. Since we assume in this textbook that you've learned such a language before, we will move somewhat quickly through PHP's syntax in this chapter except where it differs noticeably from what you've probably seen before.

| interpreted |
|---|
| Translated to machine instructions and executed on the fly, rather than compiled ahead of time. |

However, there are many fundamental differences between PHP and the other languages you've used. Rather than being compiled, PHP source code is translated and executed dynamically, or *interpreted*, by the web server. PHP also has more relaxed syntax than Java and C. It has fewer and looser data types, variables don't need to be declared, and errors are often silent. The key construct in PHP is the function rather than the class, so it is more of a procedural programming language than an object-oriented one. Lastly, rather than running as a stand-alone program, most PHP code is contained within a web page and integrates with that page's HTML content.

PHP popularized the idea of having code embedded inside HTML content. Therefore many PHP programs look like HTML documents, except with **for** loops and function calls injected inside them at various places in the page.

## Self-Check

1.  What is the difference between static and dynamic web content? Which is PHP code?
2.  What computer runs PHP code? When does PHP code run, before or after a web page is sent to a user's computer?
3.  What is the difference between a compiled and interpreted language? Which is PHP?

## 5.2 PHP Basic Syntax

Example 5.1 is our first example of a PHP program. Its code would be saved into a file named with the .php extension, such as **hello.php**. The output shown is what would appear on the resulting web page viewed in the user's browser.

```php
<?php
print "Hello, world!";
?>
```

Hello, world!

**Example 5.1 First PHP program**

Recall from earlier in this chapter that server-side programs must be viewed through web server software such as Apache or Microsoft IIS to see their output. The two screenshots in Figure 5.3 illustrate this. The left image shows what the page looks like if you view it in your browser from your local hard drive. The right image shows the same program when viewed through a web server.

**Figure 5.3 PHP output viewed locally (bad) and on server (good)**

Technically, the output of this PHP program is an HTML page whose entire contents are the message "Hello, world!" A PHP program's general syntax is shown in Example 5.2.

```php
<?php
statements;
?>
```

**Example 5.2 Syntax template for PHP program**

The preceding PHP page shows up in our browser, but it isn't a valid XHTML page. Its entire contents are "Hello, world!", without a !DOCTYPE or <html> and <body> tag and so on. We could insert additional print statements to output these tags, but there's a better way. One of the most powerful features of PHP is that PHP code can be embedded inside regular HTML content. A more accurate description of a PHP page's general syntax is shown in Example 5.3.

```php
HTML content

<?php
statements;
?>

HTML content
```

**Example 5.3 Syntax template for embedded PHP content**

The special tags `<?php` and `?>` can be thought of as mode-switchers. A page can contain any number of these PHP blocks. Any code outside a PHP block is considered to be normal HTML text, but any code inside the block is considered to be PHP code. When the web server is processing the PHP page before sending it back to your browser, it looks for any `<?php ... ?>` blocks within the page, and executes the PHP code inside them. The output from those PHP blocks is inserted into the HTML at that point in the page. Once all PHP blocks are executed and their output inserted into the page, the complete page text is sent back to your browser.

A valid XHTML version of the previous Hello World program, taking advantage of mixing PHP and HTML, is shown in Example 5.4. It looks the same as the previous example, but its output would pass the W3C XHTML validator. We'll explore mixing PHP with HTML in more detail in the later section on embedded PHP.

```
<!DOCTYPE html PUBLIC "-//W3C//DTD XHTML 1.1//EN"
    "http://www.w3.org/TR/xhtml11/DTD/xhtml11.dtd">
<html xmlns="http://www.w3.org/1999/xhtml">
  <head>
    <title>My First PHP Page</title>
  </head>

  <body>
    <p>
      <?php
      print "Hello, world!";
      ?>
    </p>
  </body>
</html>
```

Hello, world!

**Example 5.4 PHP program with valid XHTML**

From a style perspective, it can be a bit confusing to know how to properly indent PHP code that is mixed with HTML code. Our convention is to increase our indent every time we open a new HTML tag (though not when we open a `<?php` tag), and every time we open a new PHP opening { brace, and to decrease the indent when a tag ends or a } brace is reached.

## 5.2.1 Syntax Errors

It's inevitable that you'll type a PHP program that contains a syntax error. Errors are displayed as part of the HTML output. If we had forgotten a quotation mark in Example 5.4, the page would have instead displayed an error message about an unexpected comma. Example 5.5 and Example 5.6 show the erroneous code and the resulting output. Example 5.6's error message is one you'll probably see a lot, about an `"unexpected $end"`. It means that PHP reached the end of the file but didn't see the end of a block, string, or other construct.

```
print Hello, world!";
```

Parse error: syntax error, unexpected ',' in C:\Users\author\examples\error.php on line 11

**Example 5.5 Syntax error: Missing opening quote**

```
print "Hello, world!;
```

Parse error: syntax error, unexpected $end in C:\Users\author\error2.php on line 16

**Example 5.6 Syntax error: Missing closing quote**

## 5.2.2  The `print` Statement

One of the most fundamental tasks in any programming language is producing output. This is done in PHP with the **print** statement. (There is also an **echo** statement that behaves identically, but we find **print** more familiar, so our examples won't use **echo**.) Its syntax is shown in Example 5.7. Example 5.8 demonstrates several **print** statements.

```
print "text";
```

**Example 5.7 Syntax template for `print` statement**

As with all PHP syntax we'll show in this chapter, a **print** statement is only executed if it is placed inside a PHP block. If it's placed outside, the code itself will be shown; the word "print" will appear in the page along with the text to be printed. That's probably not what you want.

```
<!DOCTYPE html PUBLIC "-//W3C//DTD XHTML 1.1//EN"
    "http://www.w3.org/TR/xhtml11/DTD/xhtml11.dtd">
<html xmlns="http://www.w3.org/1999/xhtml">
  <head>
    <title>My First PHP Page</title>
  </head>

  <body>
    <p>
      <?php
      print "Hello, World!\n";
      print "Escape \"characters\" are the same as in Java!\n";

      print "You can have
line breaks in a string\n";

      print 'A string can use "single-quotes". It\'s cool!';
      ?>
    </p>
  </body>
</html>
```

Hello, World! Escape "characters" are the same as in Java! You can have line breaks in a string A string can use "single-quotes". It's cool!

**Example 5.8 The `print` statement**

Looking at Example 5.8's output, you may wonder why all the text appears on the same line, even though there are several print statements each with explicit \n line-break characters at the end. Remember that the output of PHP code is directly inserted into the HTML text and is then treated as part of the HTML. And as you recall, the browser largely ignores whitespace when laying out HTML in a page. If we View Source of the page in our browser, we'd see the text shown in Example 5.9.

```
<!DOCTYPE html PUBLIC "-//W3C//DTD XHTML 1.1//EN"
    "http://www.w3.org/TR/xhtml11/DTD/xhtml11.dtd">
<html xmlns="http://www.w3.org/1999/xhtml">
  <head>
    <title>My First PHP Page</title>
  </head>

  <body>
    <p>
Hello, World!
Escape "characters" are the same as in Java!
You can have
line breaks in a string
A string can use "single-quotes". It's cool!
    </p>
  </body>
</html>
```

**Example 5.9 View Source of PHP output**

If we'd wanted each string to appear on its own line, we'd have to surround them with some sort of HTML tags to achieve that effect, such as placing each into its own paragraph with **<p>**, inserting manual line breaks with **<br />**, or placing a **<pre>** block around the entire PHP block. This is shown in Example 5.10.

```
<!DOCTYPE html PUBLIC "-//W3C//DTD XHTML 1.1//EN"
    "http://www.w3.org/TR/xhtml11/DTD/xhtml11.dtd">
<html xmlns="http://www.w3.org/1999/xhtml">
  <head><title>My First PHP Page</title></head>
  <body>
    <?php
    print "<p>Hello, World!</p>\n";
    print "<p>Escape \"characters\" are the same as in Java!</p>\n";

    print "<p>You can have
line breaks in a string</p>\n";

    print '<p>A string can use "single-quotes". It\'s cool!</p>';
    ?>
  </body>
</html>
```

Hello, World!

Escape "characters" are the same as in Java!

You can have line breaks in a string

A string can use "single-quotes". It's cool!

**Example 5.10 print statements with paragraph tags**

Of course, one might ask why we're using PHP at all, because we could have just placed these paragraphs of text directly into the page as HTML. We technically didn't need PHP to produce this page; its contents aren't dynamic and don't depend on any server-side data. The `print` statement is more useful when we mix it with variables and other statements seen in the following sections.

## 5.2.3 Types

PHP is a loosely typed language, but every value in PHP still does have a type. PHP's basic types are shown in Table 5.1. A value of one of these types, or a set of operations that computes such a value, is called an *expression*. In the following sections we'll see several example expressions and the results they compute when executed.

| Type | Description | Examples |
|------|-------------|----------|
| `int` | integer | `42, -17` |
| `float` a.k.a. `double` | real number | `3.14, 2.4e-6` |
| `boolean` a.k.a. `bool` | logical value | `TRUE, FALSE` |
| `string` | text string | `"Hello there", 'how are you'` |
| `array` | 0-based indexed list of elements | |
| `object` | encapsulation of state and behavior | |
| `NULL` | the absence of an object | |

**Table 5.1 Basic types**

You can manually convert between types by *type casting*, though this is often not necessary. A type cast is a forced type conversion, achieved in PHP by writing the desired type in front of the value to convert. When float values are cast to int, they are rounded down. When string values are cast to numeric types, they are converted to the equivalent number if possible, or to 0 if the string isn't numeric. Type casting has high precedence and only applies to the term directly next to it, unless additional parentheses are used. Table 5.2 shows several examples of type casting.

| Expression | Result |
|------------|--------|
| `(int) 2.71` | 2 |
| `(int) "2.71"` | 2 |
| `(float) "2.71"` | 2.71 |
| `(int) "billybob"` | 0 |
| `(int) 3 / 2` | 1.5 |
| `(int) (3 / 2)` | 1 |

**Table 5.2 Type casting examples**

Not to get ahead of ourselves, but also PHP has some functions related to examining types. A *function* is much like methods or procedures in other languages; they are named groups of statements that you can execute. Some functions can accept values called *parameters* that affect their behavior. Functions are executed (or *called*) in PHP by writing the function's name, and any needed parameter values between parentheses separated by commas, following the syntax shown in Example 5.11. As in other languages, functions can return result values.

```
name(value, ..., value);
```
**Example 5.11 Syntax template for calling a function**

The `gettype` function returns the type of a given value as a string. There is also a set of **is_type** functions that return **boolean** values based on whether a value is of a given type, such as **is_float** which returns TRUE if the value passed to it is of type **float** and FALSE otherwise. Table 5.3 demonstrates both functions.

| Expression | Result |
|---|---|
| gettype(2.71) | "float" |
| gettype(42) | "int" |
| gettype("42") | "string" |
| is_string("hello") | TRUE |
| is_int(3.14) | FALSE |

**Table 5.3 gettype and is_type examples**

We'll explore many other useful built-in functions in the rest of this chapter, as well as how to define your own functions.

## 5.2.4 Arithmetic

PHP supports the usual set of arithmetic operators you would expect from other C-like languages for creating mathematical expressions. Table 5.4 lists these operators.

| Operator | Description |
|---|---|
| + | Addition |
| - | Subtraction, Unary Negation |
| * | Multiplication |
| / | Division |
| % | Modulus |

**Table 5.4 Arithmetic operators**

PHP's operators follow expected rules of precedence, such as computing multiplicative results before additive. When an **int** and **float** are combined, the result is a **float**. Unlike in Java or C, when two integers are divided, the result may be a real number. The expressions in Table 5.5 demonstrate these rules.

| Expression | Result |
|---|---|
| 1 + 2.5 | 3.5 |
| 3 / 2 | 1.5 |

**Table 5.5 Arithmetic expressions**

PHP has several mathematical functions. They can be used directly in your code without any sort of import statement. Table 5.6 lists a subset of these functions. There are also several math constants to represent useful values such as $\pi$ and Euler's constant, listed in Table 5.7. Table 5.8 demonstrates several expressions that use the math functions.

Whenever we need to look up the documentation for a built-in PHP function, we just look them up on php.net by Googling for the word "php" plus the name of the function. For example, the Google query "php sqrt" takes you straight to php.net's reference page about the sqrt function.

| Function | Description |
|----------|-------------|
| abs | absolute value |
| ceil, floor | ceiling (round up) and floor (round down) |
| cos, sin, tan | cosine, sine, tangent (in radians) |
| log, log10 | natural logarithm (or logarithm in any base), and log base-10 |
| min, max | smallest or largest of a set of values |
| pow | exponentiation |
| rand | random integer in a given range, inclusive |
| round | round a number to the nearest integer |
| sqrt | square root |

**Table 5.6 Math functions**

| Constant | Description |
|----------|-------------|
| M_PI | $\pi$, 3.14159265..., ratio of a circle's circumference to its diameter |
| M_E | $e$, 2.7182818..., base of natural logarithms |
| M_LN2 | $\log_e 2$, or 0.693147... |

**Table 5.7 Math constants**

| Expression | Result |
|------------|--------|
| round(3.5) | 4 |
| min(17, 9) | 9 |
| abs(ceil(-3.2)) | 3 |
| max(7.8, 2, 5, round(7.6)) | 8 |
| sqrt(pow(3, 2) + pow(4, 2)) | 5 |

**Table 5.8 Math function expressions**

## 5.2.5 Variables

Like most programming languages, PHP supports storing the result of an evaluated expression into a *variable*. A variable name in PHP is always preceded by a $ sign. Variables are declared by assigning them a value. The syntax for variable declarations is shown in Example 5.12. The code in Example 5.13 declares several variables of various types.

```
$name = expression;
```
**Example 5.12 Syntax template for variable declaration/assignment**

```
$user_name = "billg";
$age = 16;
$drinking_age = $age + 5;
$php_rocks = TRUE;
$drinking_age = "maybe younger overseas";
```
**Example 5.13 Variable declarations**

If you try to use a variable that has not been assigned a value, a default value of 0, 0.0, empty string, or an empty array will be used. The program will continue running, but referring to undeclared variables is considered invalid and will raise a *notice* (a warning message) if you do it.

Variables' types are not declared explicitly. A variable can store a value of any type. In fact, a variable can change types as the program is running, such as the `$drinking_age` variable in the preceding code, which initially stores an integer but later stores a string.

PHP supports the standard set of operators for assigning values to variables and modifying the values stored by variables. These operators are listed in Table 5.9.

| Operator | Description |
| --- | --- |
| = | assign |
| += | add and assign |
| -= | subtract and assign |
| *= | multiply and assign |
| /= | divide and assign |
| %= | modulus and assign |
| .= | concatenate string and assign |
| ++ | increment |
| -- | decrement |

**Table 5.9 Modification/assignment operators**

Normally when one variable is assigned to another, it stores a copy of the variable's value. The variables are not linked in any way. But a variable can also store a reference to other variables, by preceding the assignment with an **&** sign. A *reference variable* is simply an alias or pointer to the original variable. Modifying the reference also modifies the original variable.

```
$age = 16;
$alias = &$age;        # $alias refers to $age
$alias++;              # $age now stores 17
```

Parameters and return values may also be references. We'll explore passing parameters by reference later in this chapter.

## 5.2.6  Strings

Strings in PHP are enclosed in either " quotation marks or ' apostrophe characters. (There is one difference between the two, discussed later.) Strings can contain the usual escape sequences such as \n for a line break and \\ for a backslash. A string can also span multiple lines. Example 5.14 declares two string variables.

```
$str1 = "Joe Biden";
$str2 = "Sarah               # a string that spans two lines
         Palin";
```

**Example 5.14 Declaring string variables**

As in other languages, the characters of a string are associated with integers called *indexes* that begin at 0 with the first character. The string $str1 in Example 5.14 has 9 characters including the space. The indexes associated with those characters are shown in Table 5.10.

| index | 0 | 1 | 2 | 3 | 4 | 5 | 6 | 7 | 8 |
|-------|---|---|---|---|---|---|---|---|---|
| character | J | o | e |   | B | i | d | e | n |

**Table 5.10 Indexes of characters of string $str1, value "Joe Biden"**

You can access the individual characters of a string by writing the string's name followed by the index in square brackets. (This is the same syntax PHP uses for accessing elements of an array, seen later.) You can find out the number of characters in a string by passing it to the strlen function, one of many useful string manipulation functions in PHP. The last character of a string always has an index that is 1 less than the length of the string. Table 5.11 shows several expressions that access characters from $str1.

| Expression | Result |
|------------|--------|
| $str1[0] | "J" |
| $str1[3] | " " |
| $str1[8] | "n" |
| strlen($str1) | 9 |
| $str1[strlen($str1) - 1] | "n" |

**Table 5.11 Index expressions**

You can mix strings and numbers, and PHP will convert the strings to numbers as needed. For example, 1 + "2" produces the int value 3. PHP can also convert strings that begin with numbers, ignoring any characters that follow. For example, "2 live crew" + 5 produces 7. If a string has no equivalent numeric value, 0 is used. For example, 1 + "hello" produces 1.

| Operator | Description |
|----------|-------------|
| . | string concatenation |

**Table 5.12 String concatenation operator**

The + operator is always used for numeric addition in PHP, never to concatenate strings. PHP instead performs string concatenation using the dot . operator. The dot concatenation operator has the same precedence as + and -, so when a mixture of these operators is encountered, it is evaluated left to right. Table 5.13 shows several examples of string addition and concatenation.

| Expression | Result |
|---|---|
| 1 + "2" | 3 |
| 1 + "3 french hens" | 4 |
| 1 . "2" | "12" |
| 1 + "not a number" | 1 |
| 1 + 3 + "5" + 7 + 9 | 25 |
| 1 . 3 . "5" . 7 . 9 | "13579" |
| 1 + 3 . "5" . 7 + 9 | 466 |
| (1 + 3) . "5" . (7 + 9) | "4516" |

**Table 5.13 String concatenation and addition**

PHP has a large number of functions for manipulating strings, which is no surprise since it is used so heavily for text processing. Table 5.15 shows a partial list, and there are many more functions not shown in the table. PHP has a bit of a "kitchen sink" approach, where lots of functions are added to the language if developers find them useful. Table 5.14 demonstrates several string functions.

As we mentioned in the previous section on math functions, the easiest way to find out the details about the parameters and other information for these string functions is to look them up on php.net by Googling for "php" plus the name of the function, or typing "php.net/*functionname*" in your browser's address bar . You can visit http://php.net/strings to find a complete function list.

| Expression | Result |
|---|---|
| strlen("Hello there!") | 12 |
| strtoupper("How are you?") | "HOW ARE YOU?" |
| str_replace("be", "B", "to be or not to be") | "to B or not to B" |
| trim("  hulk smash! !  ") | "hulk smash! !" |
| strrev(strtolower("BOOYAH!")) | "!hayoob" |
| htmlspecialchars("<p>Wow!</p>") | "&lt;p&gt;Wow!&lt;/p&gt;" |
| ord("A") | 65 |
| chr(66) | "B" |
| sprintf("%5s %08d", "hi", 90210) | "   hi 00090210" |

**Table 5.14 String function expressions**

| Function | Description |
|---|---|
| `strlen` | returns a string's length |
| `strtoupper, strtolower` | capitalizes or lowercases a string |
| `trim, ltrim, rtrim` | remove whitespace from edge(s) of a string |
| `strstr, strchr, strrchr` | searches a string to see if it contains another string |
| `str_replace` | replaces all occurrences of one substring with another |
| `explode, implode, str_split` | break apart a string into an array |
| `strcmp, strcasecmp` | compares two strings |
| `str_shuffle` | randomly rearranges the letters in a string |
| `strrev` | reverses a string |
| `htmlspecialchars` | convert characters into HTML entity references for security |
| `ord, chr` | convert between ASCII values and characters |
| `str_pad` | pads a string up to a certain length |
| `str_repeat` | produces a string from repetitions of another string |
| `printf` | prints a formatted string with C-style `printf` syntax |
| `sprintf, sscanf` | returns formatted strings or reads data from a string |

**Table 5.15 String functions**

## Interpreted Strings

PHP makes it easy to format strings containing variables' values with its interpreted strings. An *interpreted string* is one where variables' names can be written inside it, and those variables' values will be inserted into the string when the program runs. PHP strings enclosed in `"` quotation marks are automatically interpreted. (Strings enclosed in `'` apostrophes are not interpreted.) For example, `"hello, $user_name!"` prints as `hello, billg!` The variable may optionally be enclosed in `{}`, which is useful if you want to place the variable right next to other alphabetic characters in the string. Table 5.16 shows several examples of interpreted strings using the variables from Example 5.13 and the resulting printed output.

> **interpreted string**
>
> One with variables' values written directly inside it, and those values will be inserted as the program runs.

| Interpreted String | Appearance When Printed |
|---|---|
| `"$user_name is $age years old."` | `billg is 16 years old.` |
| `'$user_name is $age years old.'` | `$user_name is $age years old.` |
| `"Happy $ageth birthday!"` | Error: undefined variable $ageth |
| `"Happy {$age}th birthday!"` | `Happy 16th birthday!` |

**Table 5.16 Interpreted strings**

Interpreted strings make it easy to build complex strings out of variables' values. This follows PHP's design philosophy of making text processing simple and convenient.

It's important to understand that PHP pages are stateless. That is, if you declare a variable in PHP code in your page, the variable is alive as the web server is building and displaying that page for a particular web request, and then it is discarded. The next time you view the page, or when some other user visits the same page later, the variable's value from past visits will not be remembered. If you want a long-lived state that persists on the server across multiple page loads or visits, we'll need to save the data into someplace such as a file. We'll discuss how to do this later in the chapter.

## 5.2.7 Comments

PHP supports three different syntaxes for comments. It has the expected C-like // single-line comment and /* ... */ multi-line comment, and also a second single-line comment style that begins with #. This comment style is used in several other languages such as many assembly languages and Perl. We prefer the brevity of the # comment style and will use it in our examples.

```
# single-line comment

// single-line comment

/*
multi-line comment
*/
```

**Example 5.15 Syntax template for comments**

## 5.2.8 Boolean Logic

PHP's logical type is called **boolean** but may also be called **bool**. There are two **boolean** literal values: TRUE and FALSE. Their preferred capitalization is entirely uppercase, but they can be written in any case such as True or false. When printed or combined with other values, TRUE evaluates to 1, and FALSE evaluates to "" or 0. PHP's logical operators are shown in Table 5.18.

The == and != operators compare values while ignoring types. So an **int** can be equal to a **float** or string when comparing with ==. But the === and !== operators do consider types; === will only evaluate to TRUE if its operands are equivalent values of exactly the same type. All four of these operators work properly with strings and other built-in types, including arrays, but they do not perform deep comparisons on objects. Table 5.17 demonstrates this difference.

| Expression | Result |
|---|---|
| 42 == "42" | TRUE |
| 42 == 42.0 | TRUE |
| 42 === "42" | FALSE |

**Table 5.17 Equality test expressions**

| Operator | Description |
|---|---|
| == | equality test (ignoring types) |
| != | inequality test (ignoring types) |
| === | equality test (considering types) |
| !== | inequality test (considering types) |
| > | greater than |
| < | less than |
| >= | greater than or equal to |
| <= | less than or equal to |
| && | logical AND |
| \|\| | logical OR |
| ! | logical NOT |

**Table 5.18 Logical operators**

One major difference between PHP and other languages is that PHP can treat *any* value as a **boolean**. There are only two **boolean** literal values in PHP, **TRUE** and **FALSE**, but any other primitive value (i.e. a value of type **int**, **float**, **string**, **array**, etc.) can be used anyplace you'd expect to put a **boolean** value, such as in the test of an **if** statement or **for** loop. Values that are 0-like or empty are considered to be **FALSE**; these are known as *falsey* values. All other values evaluate to **TRUE** and are known as *truthy* values.

The following values are considered falsey. All other primitive values are considered truthy.

- **0** and **0.0**
- **""**, **"0"**, and **NULL**
- arrays with no elements
- variables whose values have not yet been set (undefined variables)

Table 5.19 gives several examples of truthy and falsey values. (Some arrays are shown, which we'll discuss shortly.) You can explicitly cast a value into its **boolean** equivalent by writing (**boolean**).

| Truthy Values | Falsey Values |
|---|---|
| 314, 811, -52, 2.14 | 0, 0.0 |
| "Hello!", 'Hasta Luego.', "0.0", "NULL" | "", '', "0", NULL |
| array(1, 2, 3) | array() |

**Table 5.19 Truthy and falsey values**

## 5.2.9  Control Statements

PHP supports six basic control statements: **if/else**, **for**, **while**, **do/while**, **foreach**, and **switch**. In this section we'll look at the first four; the **foreach** loop isn't useful until we discuss arrays later in this chapter, and **switch** is less commonly used and not covered in this textbook. PHP's control statements behave in very familiar ways; therefore our coverage will be brisk except where subtleties and differences arise.

The `if/else` statement is identical in behavior to what you have seen in other languages, allowing your program to select between several possible paths of code to execute based on the result of boolean tests. As mentioned previously, in PHP any value is inherently considered either "truthy" or "falsey" and can be used as a boolean test. The syntax for an `if/else` statement is shown in Example 5.16. Example 5.17 demonstrates an actual `if/else` statement with three branches.

```
if (test) {
  statements;
} elseif (test) {
  statements;
} else {
  statements;
}
```

**Example 5.16** Syntax template for `if/else` statement

```
if ($a == 5) {
  print "a equals 5";
  print "...";
} elseif ($a == 6) {
  print "a equals 6";
  print "!!!";
} else {
  print "a is neither 5 nor 6";
}
```

**Example 5.17** `if/else` statement

Note that the single keyword `elseif` is commonly used rather than the separate `else if` from most other languages. (The separate `else if` is also legal but less commonly used.)

PHP's `for` loop is used for definite repetition, where the number of iterations is known in advance. Its syntax is the familiar three-part heading with a variable initialization, a **boolean** test (where the loop will stop once the test becomes **FALSE**), and an update to perform after each iteration completes. Example 5.18 shows the general syntax of a `for` loop. The loop in Example 5.19 prints the squares of each integer from 1 to 5 inclusive.

```
for (initialization; test; update) {
  statements;
}
```

**Example 5.18** Syntax template for `for` loop

```
for ($i = 1; $i <= 5; $i++) {
  print "$i squared is " . $i * $i . "...\n";
}
```

1 squared is 1... 2 squared is 4... 3 squared is 9... 4 squared is 16... 5 squared is 25...

**Example 5.19** `for` loop

PHP's `while` and `do/while` loops are used for indefinite repetition, where the number of loop iterations varies or is not known ahead of time. A `while` loop performs its loop test at the start of each iteration, therefore it might execute the body zero times (if the loop's test is initially `FALSE`). A `do/while` loop performs its test at the end of each iteration, so the body will execute at least once even if the test is initially `FALSE`. Their respective syntaxes are shown in Example 5.20.

```
while (test) {
  statements;
}
```

```
do {
  statements;
} while (test);
```

**Example 5.20 Syntax templates for `while`, `do/while` loops**

Anecdotally we'd say that `while` loops are not used as often in PHP as in some other languages. It just turns out that the kind of code you write when producing a web page is more conducive to `for` and `foreach` loops instead.

PHP offers an alternative syntax for its control statements, where you can change the opening brace to a colon (:) and the closing brace to an "end" token matching the control structure, namely `endif;`, `endwhile;`, `endfor;`, or `endforeach;`. The syntax is shown in Example 5.21, where **control** represents a control statement such as `if`, `for`, or `while`. Example 5.22 rewrites some of the preceding control examples equivalently with the alternative syntax.

```
control(...) :
  statements;
endcontrol;
```

**Example 5.21 Alternative syntax template for control statements**

```
if ($a == 5):
  print "a equals 5";
  print "...";
elseif ($a == 6):
  print "a equals 6";
  print "!!!";
else:
  print "a is neither 5 nor 6";
endif;

for ($i = 1; $i <= 10; $i++):
  print "$i squared is " . $i * $i . ".\n";
endfor;
```

**Example 5.22 Control statements using alternative syntax**

This alternative syntax can be useful when writing embedded PHP, which we'll discuss in the next section. One final subtle difference about PHP control statements is that regardless of which syntax you use to create them, they do not introduce a new scope for variables. All variables declared in a function exist until the end of that function unless explicitly unset by the programmer. We'll discuss scope in more detail later in the chapter.

## Self-Check

4. What is the result of each of the following expressions?

   - `4 * 3/8 + 2.5 * 2`
   - `26 % 10 % 4 * 3`
   - `(5 * 7.0/2 - 2.5)/5 * 2`
   - `12/7 * 4.4 * 2/4`
   - `"2 + 2 " . 3 . 4`

   - `3 + 4 . " 2 . 2"`
   - `41 % 7 * 3/5 + 5/2 * 2.5`
   - `27/2/2.0 * (4.3 + 1.7) - 8/3`
   - `89 % (5 + 5) % 5`
   - `4.0/2 * 9/2`

5. Write PHP code to compute the length of a hypotenuse $c$ of a right triangle, assuming that the lengths of the other sides are stored as $a and $b. Recall the Pythagorean theorem:

$$a^2 + b^2 = c^2$$

6. Assuming that you have a string variable stored in a variable $s, what expressions produce:

   - The first letter of the string?
   - The length of the string?
   - The last letter of the string?
   - The middle letter of the string?
   - The first five letters of the string (assuming that $s is at least 5 characters long)?

7. Given the following variable declarations:

```php
$x = 27;
$y = 1;
$z = 32;
$b = FALSE;
```

   What is the result of each of the following boolean expressions?

   - `($x > $y) && ($y > $z)`
   - `($x == $y) || ($x <= $z)`
   - `!$b`
   - `!($x % 2 == 0)`
   - `($x % 2 != 0) && $b`

   - `($x < $y) == $b`
   - `!($x / 2 == 13) || $b || ($z*3 == 96)`
   - `$x === "27"`
   - `$x % 2 === $y`
   - `!($x > 0 && $y < 0)`

8. What is the value of variable $balance after the following code runs:

```php
$balance = 3.00;
if ($balance > 0) {
   $balance -= 5;
}
if ($balance < 0) {
   $balance += 5;
}
```

9. What is the value of variable $sum after the following code runs:

```php
$sum = 0;
for ($i = 1; $i <= 10; $i++) {
   if ($i % 2 == 1) {
      $sum -= $i;
   } else {
      $sum += $i;
   }
}
```

# 5.3 Embedded PHP

We've already seen that output can be produced in PHP using the **print** statement. But **print** can be overused and abused. In this section we'll discuss embedded PHP, which is the act of inserting PHP code into HTML seamlessly so that the PHP code's output mixes with the HTML text in the page to produce a dynamic result.

Consider the poorly written code in Example 5.23, which uses **print** to output large amounts of static HTML text. The program has awful style. An important overall design goal of PHP programs is to maximize the amount of the code that is spent in plain HTML "mode" and to minimize the amount spent in PHP "mode." Any non-dynamic XHTML content of the page should just be written as plain HTML text and not printed using PHP **print** statements. Printing HTML code with **print** statements is ugly and error-prone: You must quote the HTML and escape special characters, e.g. \", insert \n line breaks after each line, and so on.

```php
<?php
print "<!DOCTYPE html PUBLIC \"-//W3C//DTD XHTML 1.1//EN\"\n";
print "    \"http://www.w3.org/TR/xhtml11/DTD/xhtml11.dtd\">\n";
print "<html xmlns=\"http://www.w3.org/1999/xhtml\">\n";
print "  <head>\n";
print "    <title>My web page</title>\n";
print "  </head>\n\n";
print "  <body>\n";

for ($i = 1; $i <= 100; $i++) {
  print "    <p>All work and no play makes Jack a dull boy.</p>\n";
}

print "  </body>\n";
print "</html>\n";
?>
```

**Example 5.23 Poorly written PHP page**

While the above example may seem obviously flawed and easy to improve, many PHP programmers end up writing essentially this kind of code. It's unnecessarily verbose and unpleasant to look at. Fortunately there is a better way.

## 5.3.1 Embedding PHP in HTML

In the case of the preceding program, almost all of the text could be moved out of the **<?php ... ?>** tags. Only the **for** loop really benefits from being produced in PHP mode, since 100 redundant paragraphs in the HTML would be necessary otherwise.

But we can go one step further. Even the print statement in the for loop isn't necessary and can be replaced by plain HTML text output. The way to achieve this is to enter PHP mode with **<?php**, write the **for** loop's header and opening brace, then exit PHP mode with **?>** without closing the **for** loop. Now we're in HTML mode but inside the loop; any HTML we write here will be output for each iteration of the loop. When we're ready to end the loop (when the HTML to repeat has ended), we can return to PHP mode with **<?php** and end the for loop by providing its closing } brace. Example 5.24 utilizes these ideas and is therefore much cleaner than the previous example.

```
<!DOCTYPE html PUBLIC "-//W3C//DTD XHTML 1.1//EN"
    "http://www.w3.org/TR/xhtml11/DTD/xhtml11.dtd">
<html xmlns="http://www.w3.org/1999/xhtml">
  <head>
    <title>My web page</title>
  </head>

  <body>
    <?php
    for ($i = 1; $i <= 100; $i++) {
    ?>
      <p>
        All work and no play makes Jack a dull boy.
      </p>
    <?php
    }
    ?>
  </body>
</html>
```

**Example 5.24 Properly embedded PHP code**

It's important to note that the paragraph above saying, "All work and no play makes Jack a dull boy," is inserted into the resulting HTML 100 times and not just once, because it is inside the bounds of the **for** loop.

Another style is to use the alternative syntax for control structures introduced previously, beginning the loop with a colon and ending it with an **endfor;** token. Example 5.25 demonstrates the relevant changed code.

```
<?php for ($i = 1; $i <= 100; $i++): ?>
  <p>
    All work and no play makes Jack a dull boy.
  </p>
<?php endfor; ?>
```

**Example 5.25 Embedded code using alternative syntax**

The alternative style can be a bit shorter, but we prefer the clarity of the original style with its line breaks and standard syntax. The {} braces to mark the beginnings and ends of control statements are also more familiar to most programmers.

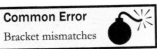

**Common Error**
Bracket mismatches

With all of the various tags and brackets opening and closing in a PHP document, it can be easy to forget to close a set of curly braces. For example, imagine that we had forgotten the **<?php** block containing the **}** for our **for** loop in the previous example, as shown in Example 5.26. In its code, the **</body>** and **</html>** tags are still inside the **for** loop, which is never closed. When you try to view the page on the web server, you'll see an error such as the following:

```
Parse error: syntax error, unexpected $end in example.php on line 16
```

It can be difficult to track down such errors, because the line number given is the last line in the file, which is not usually where the missing brace needs to be inserted. It's helpful to have a text editor that will highlight matching brackets, so you can hover the cursor over various brackets in your code and double-check which bracket elsewhere matches them.

```
<!DOCTYPE html PUBLIC "-//W3C//DTD XHTML 1.1//EN"
    "http://www.w3.org/TR/xhtml11/DTD/xhtml11.dtd">
<html xmlns="http://www.w3.org/1999/xhtml">
  <head>
    <title>My web page</title>
  </head>

  <body>
    <?php
    for ($i = 1; $i <= 100; $i++) {
    ?>
      <p>
        All work and no play makes Jack a dull boy.
      </p>
  </body>
</html>
```

**Example 5.26 Common error: PHP bracket mismatches**

## 5.3.2 Expression Blocks

The preceding examples have shown how to embed HTML text into PHP code. But the syntax shown previously doesn't work well when you want to insert PHP values into the middle of a block of HTML. In this section we will examine a structure called an *expression block* that is used in HTML mode to represent a very short switch into PHP mode to inject the value of a single PHP expression into the page. An expression block has the following syntax:

```
<?= expression ?>
```

**Example 5.27 Syntax template for expression block**

The above syntax is exactly equivalent to writing: `<?php print expression; ?>` But the shorter syntax is much more pleasant to read and to write. Often the expression is just a variable, but it can be any complex expression. For example, the following code shows two expression blocks.

```
<?php
$stuff = "Everything";
?>

<p>
  The answer to the ultimate question of Life, the
  Universe and <?= $stuff ?> is '<?= 6 * 7 ?>'!
</p>
```

The answer to the ultimate question of Life, the Universe and Everything is '42'!

**Example 5.28 Expression blocks**

Notice that the apostrophes and exclamation point around the number 42 are placed flush against the outside of the `<?=` and `?>` tags to make sure that they appear next to the value 42 in the resulting HTML output.

If our example from the previous section were changed to print 100 squared numbers instead of 100 quotes about being a dull boy, its code could be written with the blocks shown in Example 5.29.

```
<body>
  <?php
  for ($i = 1; $i <= 100; $i++) {
    ?>
    <p> <?= $i ?> squared is <?= $i * $i ?> </p>
    <?php
  }
  ?>
</body>
```

**Example 5.29 Expression blocks in loop**

Some would argue that the code would look cleaner in this case without expression blocks, but we disagree. The code below is shorter than the previous code, but we feel that it's important to minimize the number of **print** statements present in a PHP page, if not eliminate them entirely. This way all output is done in HTML mode with proper tags and indentation, and never in a string where text must be quoted, special characters must be escaped, and proper HTML output indentation is hard to maintain. Therefore we do not recommend the style shown in Example 5.30.

```
<body>
  <?php
  for ($i = 1; $i <= 100; $i++) {
    print "    <p> $i  squared is $i * $i </p>\n";
  }
  ?>
</body>
```

**Example 5.30 Printing HTML tags in PHP (not recommended)**

It is legal to place expression blocks anywhere in HTML mode, even inside tags. Example 5.31 displays a stack of headers from **h1** to **h4**.

```
<?php
for ($i = 1; $i <= 4; $i++) {
  ?>
  <h<?= $i ?>>This is a level <?= $i ?> heading.</h<?= $i ?>>
  <?php
}
?>
```

# This is a level 1 heading.

## This is a level 2 heading.

### This is a level 3 heading.

#### This is a level 4 heading.

**Example 5.31 Advanced expression blocks**

New programmers sometimes forget the = sign when opening an expression block, and write `<? expression ?>` by mistake. Without the = sign, PHP treats the block as a normal block of PHP code. `<? expression ?>` is equivalent to `<?php expression ?>`, while `<?= expression ?>` (with an equals sign) is equivalent to `<?php print expression ?>`, the difference being the `print` token. In other words, if you forget your = on an expression block as in Example 5.32, the expression's value is computed but not printed, so you won't see it in the output.

**Common Error**

Missing = in expression block

```php
<?php
for ($i = 1; $i <= 100; $i++) {
  ?>
  <p>
    <? $i ?> squared is <? $i * $i ?>
  </p>
  <?php
}
?>
```

**Example 5.32 Common error: missing = in expression block**

The output from this faulty code is 100 paragraphs saying, " squared is " without any numbers. PHP computes each `$i * $i` expression but does not output its value. It's equivalent to saying:

```php
<?php
$i * $i;
?>
```

If you see unexpectedly missing output from expression blocks, double-check to make sure you've properly opened your expression blocks with `<?=`.

## Self-Check

10. Write code to produce an unordered list of the following format, using embedded PHP:
    - 99 bottles of beer on the wall.
    - 98 bottles of beer on the wall.
    - ...
    - 1 bottles of beer on the wall.
    - 0 bottles of beer on the wall.
11. What is a PHP expression block? Why is it good to use them rather than `print` statements?
12. Assuming your program stores the user's name in a variable named `$name`, write the PHP code that would display a level 1 heading of "Hello, $name" using an expression block.
13. Find the two errors in the following code:

```php
<body>
  <?php
  if ($x > 0) {
    ?>
    <p> Your answer is <? $x ?> </p>
  }
</body>
```

## 5.4  Advanced PHP Syntax

In these sections we'll see more advanced PHP syntax for elements such as functions, arrays, and files. These will allow us to create larger, well-structured programs that interact with interesting data.

### 5.4.1  Functions

Like functions and methods in C, C++, and Java, a PHP *function* is a named group of statements that can be executed many times. PHP functions can accept parameters, which are declared by writing their names with dollar signs in front; no types are declared. Example 5.33 shows the syntax.

PHP functions can also return values. To return a value from a function, place a `return` statement in the function's body, using the syntax shown in Example 5.34. For example, the function shown in Example 5.35 computes the slope of a line based on two points $(x_1, y_1)$, $(x_2, y_2)$.

```
function name($parameterName, ..., $parameterName) {
   statements;
}
```
**Example 5.33 Syntax template for function declaration**

```
   return value;
```
**Example 5.34 Syntax template for `return` statement**

```
function slope($x1, $y1, $x2, $y2) {
   return ($y2 - $y1) / ($x2 - $x1);
}
```
**Example 5.35 Function declaration**

As we've already seen earlier in this chapter, functions are called by writing the function's name and parameter values in parentheses separated by commas. For example, to call the preceding `slope` function, you could write the code shown in Example 5.36.

```
$x = 4;
$y = 6;
$my_slope = slope(0, 0, $x, $y);     # $my_slope stores 1.5
```
**Example 5.36 Function call**

You can specify default parameter values to make a function's parameter optional. The syntax for doing so is to declare the parameter with an equals sign followed by the default value to use if none is passed. Any parameters with default values must appear at the end of the list of parameters. The general syntax is shown in Example 5.37, and a function utilizing the syntax is shown in Example 5.38. The `print_separated` function uses a comma and space as the default separator string when printing its output if the caller passes only one parameter.

```
function name(..., $parameterName = value, $parameterName = value) {
   statements;
}
```
**Example 5.37 Syntax template for default parameter values**

```
function print_separated($str, $separator = ", ") {
  if (strlen($str) > 0) {
    print $str[0];
    for ($i = 1; $i < strlen($str); $i++) {
      print $separator . $str[$i];
    }
  }
}
```

**Example 5.38 Function with default parameter value**

You can call the `print_separated` function two ways: passing one parameter for a string, in which case its letters will be printed separated by commas and spaces; or passing a second parameter for the text to place between the string's characters. Example 5.39 demonstrates both kinds of calls.

```
print_separated("hello");        # h, e, l, l, o
print_separated("hello", "-");   # h-e-l-l-o
```

**Example 5.39 Function calls using default parameter values**

### Value vs. Reference Parameters

Normally parameters are passed by value in PHP, meaning that the actual parameter values passed are copied into the function's formal parameters during each call. The impact of this is that a function cannot change the values of any variables that are passed in to it. Notice that the code in the function in Example 5.40 is not able to modify the value of $x from the main program; $num's value is just a copy of $x's value. They are not linked to each other, so $x is still 5 after the call.

```
function make_bigger($num) {
  $num = $num * 2;
}

$x = 5;
make_bigger($x);
print $x;            # 5
```

**Example 5.40 Value parameter**

Parameters can also be *passed by reference*, which causes the function's parameter to be an alias or link to the original parameter passed from the main program. This means that if the function changes its parameter value, the caller will also see the change in its own parameter. A reference parameter is specified by placing a & before the $ in front of its name. In Example 5.41, parameter $num is a reference, meaning that when it is doubled, $x passed from the main program also doubles.

```
function make_bigger(&$num) {
  $num = $num * 2;
}

$x = 5;
make_bigger($x);
print $x;            # 10
```

**Example 5.41 Reference parameter**

Reference parameters can be very useful in some situations. However, overusing them can lead to abuse of them and can make code more confusing, so we encourage you to limit them to where they are truly useful. For example, in the preceding examples, returning the doubled value would have worked just as well and would have been easier to understand than using a reference parameter.

## Scope

Every variable has a *scope*, or a range of the program where it is accessible. Variables declared outside of any function have *global scope* and can be seen throughout the program. Variables defined inside a function have *local scope* and exist only in that function. Unlike in other languages such as Java, PHP has no narrower scope than function-level. For example, if you declare a variable inside an **if** statement or loop, the variable is destroyed not when that loop ends but when the function returns. This can sometimes lead to bugs where variables are still alive that you assume would have disappeared. Example 5.42 shows a brief example of two variables whose values live on to be printed at the end of a function.

```
function scope_example() {
  for ($i = 0; $i < 10; $i++) {
    print "Hello\n";
    $x = 42;
  }

  # $i and $x are still alive here
  print "i = $i, x = $x\n";    # i = 10, x = 42
}
```

**Example 5.42 Function-level scope of variables**

To avoid name collisions between local and global variables, PHP requires functions to explicitly declare when they want to access global variables. Otherwise any time a function's code refers to a variable, even one that has not yet been declared, PHP treats the variable as local. To access a global variable within a function, use a global declaration statement at the top of the function's body, using the syntax shown in Example 5.43.

```
global $variableName;
```

**Example 5.43 Syntax template for global variable access**

In Example 5.44, the code accesses and modifies the value of a global variable named **$show**. Without the **global** declaration, **$show** would not be visible inside the **downgrade** function.

```
$show = "Star Trek";            # global

function downgrade() {
  global $show;
  $suffix = " Voyager";         # local
  $show = "$show $suffix";
  print "$show\n";
}
```

**Example 5.44 Global variable**

Referring to globals should not be used as a substitute for proper parameter passing. Normally globals contain important values meant to be considered constants to be used throughout your code.

Also note that variable scope is completely unrelated to the start and end of PHP `<?php ... ?>` blocks, so a variable declared in an earlier PHP block is also visible in later PHP blocks in the same page, as shown in Example 5.45. In that example, the variable `$firstname` is declared in the first PHP block, and then it is used successfully in a later block.

```php
<?php
$firstname = "Victoria";
?>

<p>Hello, world!</p>

<?php
# $firstname is still in scope here
$fullname = "$firstname Kirst";
?>

<p>Your full name is <?= $fullname ?></p>

Hello, world!

Your full name is Victoria Kirst
```

**Example 5.45 Scope across PHP blocks**

## 5.4.2  Including Files

PHP has a function named **include** that you can use to inject a file's contents into your page. If the injected file's contents are HTML code, the HTML is displayed on your page. If its contents are PHP code, the code will be executed, and any variables or functions it declares will now be available to any of your subsequent code. The following is the syntax for the **include** function:

```php
include("filename");
```

**Example 5.46 Syntax template for `include` statement**

You can use **include** as a powerful way to eliminate redundancy at the file level. For example, you may have several pages that have a common header or share a common large block of content. Or you may have written useful utility functions and code that you'd like to call in several pages. In either case, you can place the common content into a separate file and have each page include it.

Suppose you have two pieces of important HTML and PHP code whose content you want to include in several pages on your overall web site. The first reused piece of code is a quote from a poem, and a function called **pigLatin** that you want to call in several pages. You can put this partial web content into a file such as **partial1.php** shown in Example 5.47.

```php
<blockquote><p>
  I think that I shall never see <br /> A poem lovely as a tree
</p></blockquote>

<?php
function pigLatin($word) {
  return substr($word, 1) . "-" . $word[0] . "ay";
}
?>
```

**Example 5.47 Partial web page, `partial1.php`**

Suppose the second piece of reused content is a set of sayings from your father, who always repeats the same sayings over and over, so you want to reflect this repetition in your pages. The sayings might be represented as a list, such as the content of `partial2.php` shown in Example 5.48.

```
<ul>
  <li>It's better to be lucky than smart.</li>
  <li>No good deed goes unpunished.</li>
</ul>
```

**Example 5.48 Partial web page, `partial2.php`**

Now let's consider a page that wants to include the partial content from the prior examples. We can use `include` to essentially paste those files' contents into the overall page at whatever place we desire. Example 5.49 shows the overall page's code. Notice that the HTML text from each partial page injects into the overall point at the exact place where the `include` tag appears, so the poem comes before the "My dad always says" paragraph, while the bulleted list comes after, and so on. Also notice that once we've included `partial2.php` in the overall page, we can call the `pigLatin` function that was defined in `partial2.php` in the overall page's code. We use the function to create the text `"arty-may"` in the page.

```
<!DOCTYPE html PUBLIC "-//W3C//DTD XHTML 1.1//EN"
    "http://www.w3.org/TR/xhtml11/DTD/xhtml11.dtd">
<html xmlns="http://www.w3.org/1999/xhtml">
  <head>
    <title>Include Example</title>
  </head>

  <body>
    <?php
    include("partial1.php");
    ?>

    <p>My dad always says:</p>

    <?php
    include("partial2.php");
    ?>

    <p>My name is <?= pigLatin("marty") ?></p>
  </body>
</html>
```

> I think that I shall never see
> A poem lovely as a tree
>
> My dad always says:
>
> - It's better to be lucky than smart.
> - No good deed goes unpunished.
>
> My name is arty-may

**Example 5.49 Overall page that includes other files**

There are some other variations on `include` that can be useful in different situations. There is an `include_once` function that behaves identically to `include`, but it will only include the file once into any given page. This can be useful when several files include a common resource library of code, but you don't want to include multiple copies of it. There is also a `require` function (and related function `require_once`) that behaves identically to `include`, but if the file to be included is not found, require will stop the page from displaying and show a fatal error message instead. Therefore it can be safer to use `require` so that you'll catch errors earlier when you have missing files on your server. Table 5.20 summarizes these functions.

| Function | Description |
|---|---|
| `include` | pastes the contents of one file into another |
| `require` | same as include, but shows an error if the file to include is not found |
| `include_once,`<br>`require_once` | same as `include` and `require`, but prevents the same file's contents from being included in a page multiple times (recommended) |

**Table 5.20 Page inclusion functions**

## 5.4.3 Arrays

PHP's *array* type represents a list of values, each stored with an associated index. Primarily these indexes are a 0-based sequence of integers, though later we'll discuss arrays that use other kinds of indexes. The values stored in an array are called its *elements*.

Arrays in PHP are very similar to arrays in other languages, though they are more flexible than the arrays in C, C++, and Java. PHP arrays can store data of mixed types and can grow or shrink dynamically as new elements are added or removed.

> **array**
>
> An object containing an indexed sequence of element values.
>
> **element**
>
> A single value stored in an array.

A new array is created by writing the **array** keyword followed by parentheses. An empty set of parentheses denotes an empty, 0-element array (to which elements can be added later). You can also write a set of comma-separated values between the parentheses to create an array with an initial set of elements. No element type is specified; the array can store elements of any type, and you can mix types within the same array. Example 5.50 shows the general syntax for array declarations.

```
$name = array();
$name = array(value0, value1, ..., valueN);
```

**Example 5.50 Syntax template for array declaration**

The individual elements of an array are accessed and modified using square `[ ]` brackets. As in most other languages, the index of the element is written between the brackets. To append an element onto the end of an array (increasing its length by 1), use brackets without specifying an index. Example 5.51 demonstrates the syntax for accessing and modifying array elements, and the code in Example 5.52 creates two arrays and manipulates their elements.

```
$name[index]            # get element value
$name[index] = value;   # set element value
$name[] = value;        # append
```

**Example 5.51 Syntax template for array element access**

```
$a = array();          # empty array ($a's length is 0)
$a[0] = 23;            # stores 23 at index 0 ($a's length is now 1)

$a2 = array("some", "strings", "in", "an", "array");
$a2[] = "Ooh!";        # add string to end (at index 5; $a2's length now 6)
```

**Example 5.52 Array creation and element access**

An interesting aspect of PHP arrays is that the indexes of the elements need not be consecutive. If you assign a value at an index that is past the end of the array, the array creates a new index and element at that index. Consider the code shown in Example 5.53. The array contains 4 elements. It contains elements at indexes 0-2 ("Optimus", "Bumblebee", and "Grimlock" respectively), then the indexes 3-99 inclusive are unset. At index 100 the element value "Hotrod" is stored. The array's count is still considered to be 4, but its elements are not stored contiguously at indexes 0-3. Any elements appended to the end of the list at index [ ] will begin at index 101.

```
$autobots = array("Optimus", "Bumblebee", "Grimlock");
$autobots[100] = "Hotrod";
```

**Example 5.53 Non-consecutive array**

Array elements can be printed and can be embedded into interpreted strings. When embedding array elements into an interpreted string, {} braces must be used around the entire expression. For example, to print the second element of the $autobots array defined in the previous example, you could write the code shown in Example 5.54. The same notation can also be used to embed a single letter of a string variable, since string indexing uses the same square brackets as array indexing.

```
print "My favorite robot is {$autobots[1]}.\n";          # Bumblebee
```

**Example 5.54 Array element in embedded string**

### Array Functions

If you try to print the entire contents of an array, the word "Array" will be printed. More likely you want to print the values of the elements of the array. To produce such output, use the **print_r** function, which accepts an array as a parameter and prints its elements as output. The following example demonstrates **print_r**, enclosing its output in a **pre** element to retain its formatting:

```
<pre>
<?php
print_r($autobots);
?>
</pre>

Array
(
    [0] => Optimus
    [1] => Bumblebee
    [2] => Grimlock
    [100] => Hotrod
)
```

The **print_r** function is one of many built-in array functions for examining and manipulating the contents of arrays. Some of the most useful are shown in Table 5.21, and Example 5.55 demonstrates the usage of several of the functions. One of the most commonly used array functions is count, which accepts an array as a parameter and returns the number of elements in the array.

```
$tas = array("MD", "BH", "KK", "HM", "JP");
for ($i = 0; $i < count($tas); $i++) {
  $tas[$i] = strtolower($tas[$i]);
}
$first = array_shift($tas);       # ("md", "bh", "kk", "hm", "jp")
array_pop($tas);                  # ("bh", "kk", "hm", "jp")
array_push($tas, "ms");           # ("bh", "kk", "hm")
array_reverse($tas);              # ("bh", "kk", "hm", "ms")
sort($tas);                       # ("ms", "hm", "kk", "bh")
$best = array_slice($tas, 1, 2);  # ("bh", "hm", "kk", "ms")
                                  # ("hm", "kk")
```

**Example 5.55 Using array functions**

| Function | Description |
|---|---|
| count | returns number of elements in array |
| array_push, array_pop, array_shift, array_unshift | add/remove elements from each end of an array (for using an array as a list, stack, or queue) |
| in_array, array_search | searching for an element in array |
| array_reverse, sort, rsort, shuffle | rearranging order of elements in array |
| array_rand | returns a randomly chosen element from an array |
| array_fill, range | creating arrays with particular contents |
| array_sum, array_product | traversal algorithms |
| array_merge, array_intersect, array_diff, array_slice, array_unique, array_filter, array_reduce | creating, filtering, and combining arrays |
| explode, implode | converting strings to arrays and back |
| list | unpacking the contents of an array into variables |

**Table 5.21 Array functions**

As you can see in Example 5.55, it's relatively easy to add and remove elements from the start and end of an array using the array_push, array_pop, array_shift, and array_unshift functions. It's a bit less intuitive to remove the element at a particular index. You can use the array_splice function, which accepts your array, a starting index, a length, and a list of items to place there. If you don't provide any list of replacement items, the range is replaced with nothing. Example 5.56 demonstrates this idiom.

The example also shows the usage of the unset method, which forcibly removes a single index from an array. However, unlike array_splice, this does not shift other elements over to cover the index of the removed element. Instead it actually leaves a hole in the array, with no element at the vacated index. Notice in the output that the second print_r output text has an element at index [0] and [2] but none at [1]; bizarre. This generally isn't what you want, so we recommend array_splice instead.

```
<pre>
<?php
$grades = array(50, 60, 70, 80, 90, 100);

# removal 1: splice (replaces a range with nothing) (recommended)
array_splice($grades, 2, 3);
print "grades array contains " . count($grades) . " elements.\n";
print_r($grades);

# removal 2: unsetting an element (makes a hole in the array)
unset($grades[1]);
print "grades array contains " . count($grades) . " elements.\n";
print_r($grades);
?>
</pre>
```

```
grades array contains 3 elements.
Array
(
    [0] => 50
    [1] => 60
    [2] => 100
)
grades array contains 2 elements.
Array
(
    [0] => 50
    [2] => 100
)
```

**Example 5.56 Removing elements from an array**

Strings can be split or tokenized into arrays, such as converting "hello how are you" into the array ("hello", "how", "are", "you") and back again. The built-in explode and implode functions break apart a string into an array and merge an array into a unified string respectively. Example 5.57 shows the syntax and Example 5.58 demonstrates the usage of both functions.

```
$array = explode(delimiter, string);
$string = implode(delimiter, array);
```

**Example 5.57 Syntax template for exploding/imploding strings**

```
$s  = "UW CSE 190 M";
$a  = explode(" ", $s);      # ("UW", "CSE", "190", "M")
$s2 = implode("...", $a);    # "UW...CSE...190...M"
```

**Example 5.58 Exploding/imploding strings**

PHP is built for complex text processing. For more complex string splitting and searching, later we'll use a feature called regular expressions.

There's one more useful array function we want to mention briefly, called list. The list function accepts a list of variable names as parameters and is usually used on the left side of an assignment (=) statement, with an array on the right side. A call to list is used to unpack the contents of the right-side array into the variables on the left side. The code in Example 5.59 demonstrates the `list` function. This is useful when you're dealing with an array but want to give names to each of its elements to refer to them later in your program. We'll use this function in this chapter's case study.

```
$stooges = array("larry", "moe", "curly");
list($l, $m, $c) = $stooges;    # $l = "larry", $m = "moe", $c = "curly"
```

**Example 5.59 Unpacking an array with the `list` function**

## 5.4.4  The `foreach` Loop

The contents of an array can be accessed using a `for` loop and an index variable to refer to each element. For example, the **array_max** function in Example 5.60 accepts an array as a parameter and returns the largest integer value in the array.

```
function array_max($a) {
  $largest = $a[0];
  for ($i = 0; $i < count($a); $i++) {
    $largest = max($largest, $a[$i]);
  }
  return $largest;
}
```

**Example 5.60 Traversing array with `for` loop**

Since array traversal loops like the above are so common, PHP has a special loop designed for iteration over arrays. The **foreach** loop is a convenient way to loop over each element of an array, storing each element into a temporary variable instead of accessing it by index. Example 5.61 shows the general syntax. Example 5.62 contains a rewritten **array_max** function using a **foreach** loop.

```
foreach ($array as $element) {
  statements;
}
```

**Example 5.61 Syntax template for `foreach` loop**

```
function array_max($a) {
  $largest = $a[0];
  foreach ($a as $num) {
    $largest = max($largest, $num);
  }
  return $largest;
}
```

**Example 5.62 Traversing array with `foreach` loop**

The **foreach** loop is useful and more pleasant to the eye than the classic **for** loop, but it does have limitations. For example, you cannot use a **foreach** loop to modify the elements, since the variable used during iteration is only a copy of the actual array element it represents. In the above code, if we'd tried to adjust the value of **$num**, it would have changed **$num**'s value but not the value of the corresponding actual element in the array.

A **foreach** loop is also more pleasant to use than a **for** loop in cases where an array has non-contiguous indexes, such as the **$autobots** array from Example 5.53.

## 5.4.5 File I/O

As stated at the beginning of this chapter, one of the most useful reasons for server-side web programming is that it allows you to access resources on the server. One of the most useful resources that can reside on a server is its files. In this section we'll discuss how to open, read and write files. PHP has many functions for accessing the server's file system, listed in Table 5.22.

| Function | Description |
|---|---|
| file_get_contents | returns the text of a given file as a string |
| file_put_contents | writes text into a file, replacing any prior contents |
| file | returns the lines of a given file as an array of strings |
| scandir, glob | returns names of files in a directory as an array of strings |
| file_exists, filesize, filemtime, fileperms, is_dir, is_readable, is_writable, disk_free_space | asking for information about a file, directory, or disk |
| copy, rename, unlink, chmod, chgrp, chown, mkdir, rmdir | manipulating files and directories |

Table 5.22 File I/O functions

You can get a lot of mileage out of **file_get_contents**, which accepts a file path string as a parameter and returns the file's contents as a string. (If the file doesn't exist, an empty string is returned and a warning is issued.) To read and output the contents of **example.txt**, you could write:

```
print file_get_contents("example.txt");
```

(If you're printing the file's contents in a web page, the browser will mangle the whitespace and line breaks in the file unless you enclose it in a **pre** block or otherwise preserve the whitespace.)

You can write new contents into a file using the **file_put_contents** function, which accepts a file name and a string as parameters and writes the string's text to the file, overwriting any previous contents of the file. (If the file did not previously exist, it is created.) The function in Example 5.63 reverses the order of the lines in a file.

```
# Reverses the order of the lines in the file with the given name.
function reverse_lines($filename) {
  $text = file_get_contents($filename);
  $lines = explode("\n", $text);
  $lines = array_reverse($lines);
  $text = implode("\n", $lines);
  file_put_contents($filename, $text);
}
```

Example 5.63 Reading and writing a file

The `reverse_lines` function in Example 5.63 illustrates a useful pattern, reading a file and splitting it into an array of lines with the `explode` function, then manipulating those lines in some way. If you prefer, there is another function named simply `file` that accepts a file name as a parameter and returns an array of strings representing the lines of that file. A more concise version of the `reverse_lines` function is shown in Example 5.64.

```php
function reverse_lines($filename) {
  $lines = file($filename);
  $lines = array_reverse($lines);
  file_put_contents($filename, implode("", $lines));
}
```

**Example 5.64 Reading and writing a file (condensed)**

One minor nuisance to remember about the `file` function is that it returns the lines with their ending \n line breaks still attached. You may need to strip these off depending on what kind of program you're writing.

A concrete example can help to illustrate the difference between the `file_get_contents` and `file` functions. Suppose the file `example.txt` has been placed in the same directory as our PHP program. Table 5.23 summarizes the values returned by calling each function on the file. The `file_get_contents` call returns the entire file's contents as a large string, while `file` returns an array containing 5 elements, one for each line of the file.

| file contents | file_get_contents | file |
|---|---|---|
| Hello<br>how are<br>you?<br><br>I'm fine | "Hello\n<br>how are\n<br>you?\n<br>\n<br>I'm fine\n" | array(<br>  "Hello\n",<br>  "how are\n",<br>  "you?\n",<br>  "\n",<br>  "I'm fine\n"<br>) |

**Table 5.23 Comparison of file functions**

The code in Example 5.65 counts the number of blank lines in a file. Notice that we can directly use the result of the `file` function inside the `foreach` loop header because `file` returns an array.

```php
# Returns how many lines in this file are empty or just spaces.
function count_blank_lines($filename) {
  $count = 0;
  foreach (file($filename) as $line) {
    if (strlen(trim($line)) == 0) {
      $count++;
    }
  }
  return $count;
}
```

**Example 5.65 Counting blank lines**

## Examining Directories

The examples shown previously processed particular files with known names, but sometimes you want to process all files in a directory, or search for a file with an approximate file name. In such cases you'll want to use PHP's directory-reading functions. The most generally useful of these is `scandir`, which accepts a directory name as a parameter and returns an array of the names of all files in that directory. Example 5.66 demonstrates how to use `scandir`.

```
$folder = "images";
$files = scandir($folder);
foreach ($files as $file) {
  print "I found an image: $folder/$file\n";
}
```

**Example 5.66 The `scandir` function**

For example, if the folder `images` contains three images named `huey.jpg`, `dewey.jpg`, and `louie.jpg`, the above function would produce the following output:

```
I found an image: images/.
I found an image: images/..
I found an image: images/dewey.jpg
I found an image: images/huey.jpg
I found an image: images/louie.jpg
```

Annoyingly, the current directory (represented as `"."`) and its parent directory (represented as `".."`) are always included in the array of results returned by `scandir`. You almost never actually want to process these results, so you'll need to skip them in your code. Example 5.67 shows a new version of the prior example's code that contains this fix.

```
$folder = "images";
$files = scandir($folder);
foreach ($files as $file) {
  if ($file != "." && $file != "..") {
    print "I found an image: $folder/$file\n";
  }
}
```

**Example 5.67 The `scandir` function (filtered)**

---

**glob**

A pattern describing a file or set of files.

If you want to process a particular subset of the files in a directory, instead of `scandir` you can use another function named `glob`. A file *glob* is a string specifying a set of files. A glob can contain * wildcards to match a set of files. For example, `"*.mp3"` matches all files with the `.mp3` extension, and `"journal*.d*"` matches all files whose names start with the word "journal" and whose extensions begin with "d", such as `journal2009.doc` and `journalism.dat`.

Earlier in this chapter we wrote a function `reverse_lines` that reversed the order of lines in a file. The code in Example 5.68 would reverse the order of lines of all .txt files in the current directory.

```
foreach (glob("*.txt") as $filename) {
  reverse_lines($filename);
}
```

**Example 5.68 The `glob` function**

A common use of scandir is to obtain a list of files in a particular directory. For example, the call scandir("data") returns an array of all files in the data/ subdirectory of the current directory. However, the code in Example 5.69 does not correctly count the lines of the files in this directory. Can you spot the mistake?

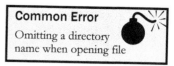

**Common Error**
Omitting a directory name when opening file

```
# count total lines in all files in the data/ directory
foreach (scandir("data") as $filename) {
  $count = 0;
  if ($filename != "." && $filename != "..") {
    $count += count(file($filename));
  }
  print "$count total lines in all files.\n";
}
```

**Example 5.69 Common error: Omitted directory name**

The preceding code produces a bunch of warnings and outputs that there were 0 total lines in all files. The bug is subtle; an incorrect parameter is being passed to the file function.

Suppose that the data directory contains files named example1.txt and example2.txt. The call to scandir("data") returns an array containing four elements: (".", "..", "example1.txt", "example2.txt"). But when we try to open each element with file and count its lines, we have specified only the file name, not the directory. There's no file named example1.txt in the current directory; calling file("example1.txt") would fail.

We should instead be calling file("data/example1.txt") to open this file. In other words, we must attach the directory name we're scanning as a prefix when opening any files in that directory. Example 5.70 shows the corrected code. Notice how we include data/ before the filename.

```
# count total lines in all files in the data/ directory
foreach (scandir("data") as $filename) {
  $count = 0;
  if ($filename != "." && $filename != "..") {
    $count += count(file("data/$filename"));
  }
  print "$count total lines in all files.\n";
}
```

**Example 5.70 Corrected error with directory name**

The glob function doesn't have this problem. If you instead call glob("data/*"), you get complete relative path strings such as "data/example1.txt" in the returned array.

## Self-Check

14. What is the output from the following code?

```php
function mystery($c, $a, $b) {
  print $b . " + " . $c . " = " . $a;
}

$a = 4;
$b = 7;
$c = -2;
mystery($a, $b, $c);
mystery($c, 3, $a);
mystery($a + $b, $b + $c, $c + $a);
```

15. Write a function named quadratic that takes three integer coefficients $a$, $b$, and $c$ as parameters and treats them as the coefficients of a quadratic equation of the form $ax^2 + bx + c = 0$. Solve the equation using the quadratic formula and return one of its roots. The quadratic formula states that the two roots of a quadratic equation can be computed as follows:

$$-b \pm \sqrt{\frac{b^2 - 4ac}{2a}}$$

16. What are the contents of the array $a$ at the end of the code below?

```php
$a = array(1, 2, 3);
```

17. What are the contents of each of the following arrays after function **mystery** runs?

```php
function mystery($list) {
  for ($i = 0; $i < count($list) - 1; $i++) {
    if ($list[$i] > $list[$i + 1]) {
      $list[$i + 1]++;
    }
  }
}
```

- o   `$a = array(14, 7);`
  `mystery($a);`
- o   `$b = array(7, 1, 3, 2, 0, 4);`
  `mystery($b);`
- o   `$c = array(10, 8, 9, 5, 5);`
  `mystery($c);`
- o   `$d = array(12, 11, 10, 10, 8, 7);`
  `mystery($d);`

18. Write a piece of PHP code to read all image files with `.png` extension from the current directory and display each one in an **img** tag.

## 5.5 Case Study: Word of the Day

In this section we'll program a larger example that ties together many of the PHP concepts, syntax rules, statements, and functions we've learned in the chapter so far. Suppose we've been asked to create a web page that will display a "word of the day" to help a person build his/her vocabulary by showing a word, its part of speech (such as noun or verb), and its definition. The input set of words and definitions will come from a text file on our web server. You can find files full of words and definitions in many places on the web by Googling for `words.txt`; the References section of this chapter has a direct link to one such file.

The site will be split into two pages: a main index page that explains the site, and a second page that shows the user's random word of the day. (The site content could probably all be put onto one page, but we want to practice writing multi-page sites.) The bottom of the index page should contain a "hit counter" that tells us how many times the page has been visited. Each time a user fetches the index page, the hit counter should increment. This counter should be stored in a text file on the web server. The desired appearances of the pages are shown in Figure 5.4 and Figure 5.5 respectively.

# GRE Vocab Word of the Day

Welcome to Jessica's GRE vocab word of the day page! Each time you visit, a random word and its definition will be shown.

See my word of the day!

___

This page has been accessed 163 times.

**Figure 5.4 Word of the day, index page**

# GRE Vocab Word of the Day

Your word of the day is:

*pyrrhic* - **adjective**.
*costly to the point of negating or outweighing expected benefits*

**Figure 5.5 Word of the day, word definition page**

The following is a rough outline of how to approach this problem step-by-step:

1. Write the index page without its hit counter. This page has no PHP code in it, so it will be simpler to write.
2. Apply basic styles to the index page with CSS.
3. Add the hit counter to the index page.
4. Write a basic HTML skeleton of the word-of-the-day page.
5. Add any interactive PHP content to that page, such as looking up the random word and displaying it.

## 5.5.1 Index Page

First let's tackle the index page. This will be stored as `index.php`; this file name is useful because it has special meaning to the web server. A file with a name of `index.html` or `index.php` is used as a default file name on a web server if you don't specify a file name. So, for example, if I later upload my `index.php` page to the web server at http://www.example.com/, you can view the page by typing either http://www.example.com/index.php or the shorter http://www.example.com/ (without a filename).

### Initial HTML Content

Let's write an initial stub version of this page, ignoring the hit counter for the moment. Its code is shown in Example 5.71. Referring back to Figure 5.4, the page consists of a level-1 heading, an explanatory paragraph, a link to the word-of-the-day page, and a paragraph showing the hit counter value. We'll also link to a stylesheet named `word.css` that contains the CSS styles for both pages. For now, we'll just place a `???` where the hit counter should go.

```
<!DOCTYPE html PUBLIC "-//W3C//DTD XHTML 1.1//EN"
    "http://www.w3.org/TR/xhtml11/DTD/xhtml11.dtd">
<html xmlns="http://www.w3.org/1999/xhtml">
  <head>
    <title>Word of the Day</title>
    <link href="word.css" type="text/css" rel="stylesheet" />
  </head>

  <body>
    <h1>GRE Vocab Word of the Day</h1>

    <p>
      Welcome to Jessica's GRE vocab word of the day page!  Each time
      you visit, a random word and its definition will be shown.
    </p>
    <p><a href="word.php">See my word of the day!</a></p>
    <hr />
    <p>This page has been accessed ??? times.</p>
  </body>
</html>
```

**Example 5.71 Initial version of `index.php`**

### Basic Styles for Index Page

The CSS rules are fairly simple; just some font/color settings to give the page a clean appearance. Example 5.72 shows the complete CSS file.

```
blockquote {
  font-style: italic;
}
body {
  background-color: white;
  padding: 1em 2em;
  font-family: Garamond, serif;
  font-size: 14pt;
}
```

**Example 5.72 Initial version of word.css**

### Hit Counter

Now let's look at the hit counter. This is active web content, not just part of the static page; it changes each time the page loads. So we'll need to write some PHP code here. The basic idea is that we'll create a text file named hits.txt whose contents are an integer representing the number of hits to the page so far. Each time the page loads, we'll read the integer from the file, increment it, show it on the page, and write this incremented value back to the file. The code would look like the following:

```
$hits = file_get_contents("hits.txt");
$hits++;
file_put_contents("hits.txt", $hits);
```

But the preceding code doesn't use very good style. We should put it into a function for structure, and we should make the file's name a constant so we can change it more easily in one place if necessary. Our function will read the number of hits, increment it, write the incremented value back to the file, and return the hit count. Also the previous code does not take into account that the file might not exist, such as the first time the page is loaded. We can check for this case with the `file_exists` function. The code in Example 5.73 implements the function for our hit counter. The code would go at the top of index.php.

```
<?php
$HIT_COUNTER_FILENAME = "hits.txt";

# Reads hit count from disk, increments/writes it, and returns it.
function hit_counter() {
  global $HIT_COUNTER_FILENAME;
  if (file_exists($HIT_COUNTER_FILENAME)) {
    $hits = file_get_contents($HIT_COUNTER_FILENAME);
  } else {
    $hits = 0;
  }
  $hits++;
  file_put_contents($HIT_COUNTER_FILENAME, $hits);
  return $hits;
}
?>
```

**Example 5.73 Hit counter function**

Now that we have a `hit_counter` function, we need to call it in the page body to display the hit counter on the page. We'll use a PHP expression block for this. The final paragraph with the `???` in Example 5.71 should be replaced with:

```
<p>This page has been accessed <?= hit_counter() ?> times.</p>
```

## 5.5.2 Word Definition Page

Now let's turn our attention to the page that reads and displays the word of the day. Words are stored in the file `words.txt` with one word, its part of speech, and its definition on each line, separated by tabs. Example 5.74 shows a portion of the file's possible contents.

```
prothalamion    noun        a song in celebration of a marriage
atrabilious     adjective   given to or marked by melancholy; GLOOMY
pyrrhic         adjective   costly to the point of negating benefits
```

**Example 5.74 Excerpt from input file `words.txt`**

### Initial HTML Content for Definition Page

Example 5.75 shows an initial stab at the HTML only of `word.php`. Referring back to Figure 5.5, the page should contain a level-1 heading describing it, two rows of six images each (the images will come from a file named `vocab.jpg` in the same directory as our web page), and a couple of paragraphs about the word of the day. For now we'll ignore the trickiest part, reading and displaying the word of the day, and we'll put `???` in its place.

```
<!DOCTYPE html PUBLIC "-//W3C//DTD XHTML 1.1//EN"
    "http://www.w3.org/TR/xhtml11/DTD/xhtml11.dtd">
<html xmlns="http://www.w3.org/1999/xhtml">
  <head>
    <title>Word of the Day</title>
    <link href="word.css" type="text/css" rel="stylesheet" />
  </head>
  <body>
    <h1>GRE Vocab Word of the Day</h1>
    <div>
      <img src="vocab.jpg" alt="vocab guy" />
      <img src="vocab.jpg" alt="vocab guy" />
      <img src="vocab.jpg" alt="vocab guy" />
      <img src="vocab.jpg" alt="vocab guy" />
      <img src="vocab.jpg" alt="vocab guy" />
      <img src="vocab.jpg" alt="vocab guy" /> <br />
      <img src="vocab.jpg" alt="vocab guy" />
      <img src="vocab.jpg" alt="vocab guy" />
      <img src="vocab.jpg" alt="vocab guy" />
      <img src="vocab.jpg" alt="vocab guy" />
      <img src="vocab.jpg" alt="vocab guy" />
      <img src="vocab.jpg" alt="vocab guy" /> <br />
    </div>
    <p>Your word of the day is:</p>
    ???
  </body>
</html>
```

**Example 5.75 Initial version of `word.php`**

## Improving Page Contents with PHP

The code is suboptimal in several ways. For one, it has twelve redundant **img** tags in a row; we could better represent this repetition with a **for** loop:

```php
<?php
for ($row = 1; $row <= 2; $row++) {
  for ($col = 1; $col <= 6; $col++) {
    ?>
    <img src="vocab.jpg" alt="vocab guy" />
    <?php
  }
  ?>
  <br />
  <?php
}
?>
```

Also, the first ten lines of the page (the head section, start of the body, and level-1 heading) are exactly the same as in **index.php**. When we have pages with a large chunk of identical HTML text like this, an elegant way to eliminate the redundancy is to put the repeated code into its own file and include that file into both pages with the **include** function, as explained earlier in this chapter. The contents of this shared file, which we'll call **top.html**, are shown in Example 5.76.

```html
<!DOCTYPE html PUBLIC "-//W3C//DTD XHTML 1.1//EN"
    "http://www.w3.org/TR/xhtml11/DTD/xhtml11.dtd">
<html xmlns="http://www.w3.org/1999/xhtml">
  <head>
    <title>Word of the Day</title>
    <link href="word.css" type="text/css" rel="stylesheet" />
  </head>

  <body>
    <h1>GRE Vocab Word of the Day</h1>
```

**Example 5.76 Shared file top.html**

The repeated content can be removed from both **index.php** and **word.php** and replaced with:

```php
include("top.html");
```

## Displaying the Word of the Day

Now let's turn to the tricky part: reading and displaying the word of the day. Let's create another new function for this called **read_random_word**. The function must grab a random word from the file and display its definition on the page. It will perform the following steps:

- Read the lines of the file using the **file** function. Each line holds a word and its definition.
- Randomly choose one of these lines using the **rand** function.
- Unpack the line's tab-separated tokens (word, part of speech, definition) using **explode**.
- Store these tokens into variables using the **list** function.
- Drop back into HTML mode and display the tokens as output in a **blockquote** tag.

Example 5.77 shows the code for the function that implements each of these steps.

```php
<?php
include("top.html");
$WORDS_FILENAME = "words.txt";

# reads a random word line from disk and displays its text
function read_random_word() {
  global $WORDS_FILENAME;
  $lines = file($WORDS_FILENAME);
  $random_index = rand(0, count($lines) - 1);
  $random_line = $lines[$random_index];
  $tokens = explode("\t", $random_line);
  list($word, $part, $definition) = $tokens;
?>

  <blockquote>
    <p>
      <?= $word ?> -
      <span class="partofspeech"><?= $part ?></span>. <br />
      <?= $definition ?>
    </p>
  </blockquote>

  <?php
}
?>
```

**Example 5.77 Function to read random vocab word**

The portion of word.php with the ??? can now be replaced with a call to our new function.

```php
<p>Your word of the day is:</p>
<?php
read_random_word();
?>
```

We're essentially done now; let's add one more style to our CSS file to make the word's part of speech show up as a span in a monospace font.

```css
.partofspeech {
  font-family: monospace;
  font-weight: bold;
}
```

### 5.5.3 Final File Contents

After all the changes discussed in the preceding sections, we end up with the final four page files shown in Example 5.78 through Example 5.81. These files, plus the vocab.jpg image and the words.txt input file, comprise the entire finished two-page web site.

```php
<?php
include("top.html");
$HIT_COUNTER_FILENAME = "hits.txt";

# Reads hit count from disk, increments/writes it, and returns it.
function hit_counter() {
  global $HIT_COUNTER_FILENAME;
  if (file_exists($HIT_COUNTER_FILENAME)) {
    $hits = file_get_contents($HIT_COUNTER_FILENAME);
  } else {
    $hits = 0;
  }
  $hits++;
  file_put_contents($HIT_COUNTER_FILENAME, $hits);
  return $hits;
}
?>
    <p>Welcome to Jessica's GRE vocab word of the day page!  Each time
      you visit, a random word and its definition will be shown.</p>
    <p><a href="word.php">See my word of the day!</a></p>
    <hr />
    <p>This page has been accessed <?= hit_counter() ?> times.</p>
  </body>
</html>
```

Example 5.78 Final contents of `index.php`

```html
<!DOCTYPE html PUBLIC "-//W3C//DTD XHTML 1.1//EN"
    "http://www.w3.org/TR/xhtml11/DTD/xhtml11.dtd">
<html xmlns="http://www.w3.org/1999/xhtml">
  <head>
    <title>Word of the Day</title>
    <link href="word.css" type="text/css" rel="stylesheet" />
  </head>
  <body>
    <h1>GRE Vocab Word of the Day</h1>
```

Example 5.79 Final contents of `top.html`

```css
blockquote {
  font-style: italic;
}
body {
  padding: 1em 1em;
  font-family: Garamond, serif;
  font-size: 14pt;
}
.partofspeech {
  font-family: monospace;
  font-weight: bold;
}
```

Example 5.80 Final contents of `word.css`

```php
<?php
include("top.html");
$WORDS_FILENAME = "words.txt";

# reads a random word line from disk and displays its text
function read_random_word() {
  global $WORDS_FILENAME;
  $lines = file($WORDS_FILENAME);
  $random_index = rand(0, count($lines) - 1);
  $random_line = $lines[$random_index];
  $tokens = explode("\t", $random_line);
  list($word, $part, $definition) = $tokens;
?>
  <blockquote>
    <p>
      <?= $word ?> -
      <span class="partofspeech"><?= $part ?></span>. <br />
      <?= $definition ?>
    </p>
  </blockquote>
  <?php
}
?>

    <div>
      <?php
      for ($row = 1; $row <= 2; $row++) {
        for ($col = 1; $col <= 6; $col++) {
          ?>
          <img src="vocab.jpg" alt="vocab guy" />
          <?php
        }
        ?>
        <br />
        <?php
      }
      ?>
    </div>

    <p>Your word of the day is:</p>
    <?php
    read_random_word();
    ?>
  </body>
</html>
```

Example 5.81 Final contents of word.php

## Chapter Summary

- PHP is a free, dynamic, loosely-typed procedural programming language for writing programs that execute on a web server.
- When the client requests a web program such as a PHP file from a server, the server reads the program file and executes it. The program's output is then sent back to the client over the network.
- PHP contains types `int`, `float`, `boolean`, `string`, `array`, `object`, and `NULL`. PHP converts between types as needed and usually does "the right thing" without you needing to worry about types.
- The values of variables can be directly injected into strings; this is called an interpreted string.
- PHP can use any value as a `boolean` test; values equal to 0, an empty string, `NULL`, or an empty array are considered "falsey" and all other values are considered "truthy".
- PHP supports the standard control statements such as `if/else`, `for`, and `while`, as well as a special `foreach` loop that iterates over the contents of an array.
- PHP code can be embedded inside an HTML page. This provides more seamless and readable source code and helps you avoid messy print statements that output HTML text.
- Expression blocks are useful for embedding a single expression's result in a page.
- PHP lets you reduce redundancy by putting code into functions and by including entire files inside each other with the include function.
- PHP has a powerful array type that stores a resizable indexed collection of elements. The language has many functions that search, sort, split and join, and otherwise manipulate arrays.
- PHP has simple functions for reading and writing files and directories, such as `file_get_contents`, `file`, and `scandir`.

## References

- PHP home page:      http://www.php.net/
- Types:      http://www.php.net/manual/en/language.types.php
- Operators:      http://www.php.net/manual/en/language.operators.php
- Expressions:      http://www.php.net/manual/en/language.expressions.php
- Math functions:      http://www.php.net/manual/en/ref.math.php
- String functions:      http://www.php.net/strings
- Control statements:      http://www.php.net/if
- Array functions:      http://www.php.net/manual/en/ref.array.php
- File system functions:      http://www.php.net/manual/en/ref.filesystem.php
- W3Schools PHP tutorial:      http://www.w3schools.com/PHP/
- Practical PHP Programming:      http://hudzilla.org/phpwiki/ (free online PHP book)
- PHP Cookbook:      http://commons.oreilly.com/wiki/index.php/PHP_Cookbook
- PHP security guide:      http://phpsec.org/php-security-guide.pdf
- Programming languages and beards:
  - a) http://blogs.microsoft.co.il/blogs/tamir/archive/2008/04/28/computer-languages-and-facial-hair-take-two.aspx
- `words.txt` input file:      http://webster.cs.washington.edu/words.txt

# Chapter 6  HTML Forms and Server-Side Data

## Introduction

The pages we've seen so far have had a one-directional flow of information. The browser asks a web server for a page, and the server sends back that page. Even in dynamic pages generated by languages such as PHP, the user and his/her browser don't have much communication with the web server other than, "Please give me this page."

In this chapter we'll learn about a way for your browser to submit data to a web server. The data might be used for the server to search its databases for information to be sent back to your browser. It might be used to process an order from an online business. Or it might be a message you're sending through a web email system.

The key to sending this kind of information is an HTML element called a form. In this chapter we'll learn how to create forms for storing and retrieving information from web servers, as well as how to write server-side code that processes information sent by a form.

## 6.1  Form Basics

| form |
| --- |
| A group of UI controls on a web page that allows a user to submit information to a web server. |

An HTML *form* is a group of controls that allows a user to submit information to a web server. Controls are elements such as buttons, checkboxes, and text fields. The user types or clicks the relevant information into the form, then presses a button to submit the form data to the server.

Forms are one of several ways to submit information to a server-side web application or service. Another popular way to achieve this is using Ajax, which will be discussed in a later chapter.

### 6.1.1 Parameterized Pages and Query Strings

When you visit Google, the initial front page is just a basic web page. Users love the simplicity of Google's layout; it contains almost nothing but a text box to type your query and a Search button. It turns out that the text box and Search buttons on Google's front page are an example of a form.

When you click Search, the data in the form (the text of your query) is submitted to Google's servers. When you press the Search button, the browser navigates you to a URL that looks something like this (for a query of "Obama"):

```
http://www.google.com/search?q=Obama
```

As we've now seen while learning PHP and other server-side programming languages, some web pages are really programs that run on the server and send back web content as their output. The preceding Google search URL is an example of such a program. The program's URL is http://www.google.com/search. The search program examines your query and outputs the HTML representing the Google results for that query. The page of results you see in your browser is actually the output of this program that runs on Google's servers.

Server-side programs can accept parameters to affect the way they run. This makes sense when thinking about the Google results page: It needs to know your search query in order to produce the proper relevant HTML output. Looking at the URL, you can see the parameter at the end of the URL. These are called *query parameters*.

> **query string**
>
> A set of parameters passed from a browser to a web server, often by placing them at the end of a URL.

A URL may contain multiple query parameters. The set of all parameters in a given URL is called its *query string*. The syntax of a query string begins with a **?** character written at the end of a URL. After this the query string contains a set of **name=value** pairs, separated by **&** characters. The general syntax matches the format shown in Example 6.1.

```
URL?name1=value1&name2=value2&name3=value3...
```

**Example 6.1 Syntax template for URL query string**

For example, in the following URL, the parameter named **q** is given the value **miserable+failure** and the parameter **start** has the value **10**. This URL searches Google for the phrase "miserable failure" and shows the search results starting at the 10th match.

```
http://www.google.com/search?q=miserable+failure&start=10
                            ~~~~~~~~~~~~~~~~~~~~~~~~~~~~~~~~~
                                     query string
```

## 6.1.2 A Simple Form

| Element | form |
|---------|------|
| **Description** | Form of data for the user to fill out and submit to a web server (block) |
| **Syntax** | `<form action="server URL">`<br>    **form controls**<br>`</form>` |

Let's create a simple form for submitting queries to Google. This form will be a replacement for the http://www.google.com/ front page.

A form is essentially a user interface for you to build a query string to pass parameters to a server-side program. A form is represented by the HTML **form** element, which can be placed inside a web page's body. A **form** tag requires an attribute named **action** that specifies the server's target URL to which the form data should be submitted.

As stated previously, the server-side program to which we want to submit information is located at http://www.google.com/search. This program requires a parameter named **q** (short for "query") representing the text to search for. (Google calls their parameter **q** instead of **query** because it's 4 characters shorter, and when you have millions of hits to your site per day, every byte counts.)

The code in Example 6.2 implements a form that can submit a query to Google's server. (The comments are optional and are there merely for clarification purposes.)

```
<form action="http://www.google.com/search">
  <div>
    Type your Google query:
    <input name="q" />            <!-- text box -->
    <input type="submit" />       <!-- submit button -->
  </div>
</form>
```

Type your Google query: [            ]  Submit Query

**Example 6.2 Basic form**

Every form has some set of controls; this one consists of a single text box. A text box is created using the **input** element. An **input** tag contains no content and is self-closing, like **br**, **hr**, **img**, and **link**.

| Element | input |
|---|---|
| Description | User input control (inline) |
| Syntax | `<input type="`**type of control**`" attributes />` |

A form must also have a submit button to allow the user to submit the form data to the web server. A submit button is also created using the **input** element. The two controls are differentiated by the **type** attribute, which specifies what kind of control to display. If no type is given, a single-line text box is displayed. If a type of **"submit"** is specified, the browser displays a Submit Query button. (As we'll see later in this chapter, the **input** element is also used to produce other UI controls including radio buttons and checkboxes.)

When the Submit Query button is clicked, the browser will build a query string URL for us, and request the contents of that URL from the web server. The **name** attribute on each input control tells the browser what query parameter name to give each piece of data. Our text box has a name of "q", so if we type "pretzels" into the text box and click Submit Query, the browser will navigate us to the following URL:

```
http://www.google.com/search?q=pretzels
```

It's important to have a **name** attribute on every control whose value you want to submit. Without it, the browser won't know how to send that control's data to the server and therefore will not send any value for it. Each name should be unique, much like the **id** attribute seen previously.

Another useful attribute on input tags is **value**. The meaning of the **value** attribute differs depending on what kind of input control you're using. When the control is a text box, **value** specifies initial text to place in the text box when the page first loads. This is useful when you have a default initial value you want in the text box. When the control is a submit button, **value** specifies the text to place on the button. The modified version of our form in Example 6.3 demonstrates the **value** attribute. Table 6.1 summarizes the key attributes of the **input** element.

```
<form action="http://www.google.com/search">
  <div>
    Type your Google query:
    <input name="q" value="Captain Planet" />
    <input type="submit" value="Search Google" />
  </div>
</form>
```

Type your Google query: | Captain Planet |    | Search Google |

**Example 6.3 Basic form with `value` attributes**

| Attribute | Value(s) | Definition and Usage |
|-----------|----------|----------------------|
| type | button, checkbox, file, hidden, password, radio, reset, submit, text, ... | type of control |
| name | text | control's parameter name (should be unique) |
| value | text | control's "value" (control-dependent); e.g., when used on a text box, specifies initial text |

**Table 6.1 Common `input` attributes**

The message text, input text box, and Submit Query button in our forms all appear on the same line, even though they are separated by line breaks in the HTML source code. UI controls are inline elements, so they must be nested in a proper block element for the page to be valid XHTML. The form isn't a valid block element for directly storing inline content, so you need to put the controls into some other element. We chose to place the controls into a `div` inside the form.

## Self-Check

1.  What URL and query string would be used to fetch Google's search results for the term "McCain"? What URL would fetch results for "Palin" starting with result #5?
2.  What is the difference between the **name** and **id** attributes on a form control? Can an **id** substitute for a **name**?
3.  What does the **value** attribute do when used on a text box control? On a submit button?

## 6.2 Form Controls

There are a number of HTML elements that represent user interface controls or widgets in a form. These controls allow the user to enter information that will be sent to a web server. The controls we cover in this section are buttons, radio buttons, check boxes, drop-down menus, list boxes, text boxes, and text areas. These controls are depicted in Figure 6.1.

| Control | Example |
|---|---|
| Text Box | Enter your name here. |
| Text Area | Type your comments here. |
| Button | Push my buttons! |
| Check Boxes | ☐ Morning ☐ Afternoon ☐ Evening |
| Radio Buttons | ○ Pick Up ○ Delivery |
| Drop-down Menu | The Godfather ▼ |
| List Box | Brooklyn ▲<br>Manhattan<br>Queens ▼ |

**Figure 6.1 HTML user interface controls**

In all of the examples in this section, we'll have our forms use an **action** URL of http://webster.cs.washington.edu/params.php. This is a page set up by the authors that simply echoes all query parameters that were sent to it.

## 6.2.1 Text Boxes (Single-Line)

| Element | input |
|---|---|
| Description | Box for entering a single line of text (inline) |
| Syntax | `<input type="text" name="name" attributes />` |

The simplest kind of form input is a text box that lets the user enter text input like a street address, name, or ZIP code. HTML has two types of text entry boxes: A single-line text box and a multi-line text area.

As we've already seen, a text box is created using the **input** element. Though it is not required, the tag's **type** attribute should be set to **text** to indicate a text box. We'll also give the tag a **name** attribute with a unique value.

A text box can specify additional attributes in its **input** tag. The **value** attribute specifies any initial text you want in the box. The **size** attribute designates how many characters long the text box should appear on the screen. The user can still type in more than **size** characters, but some will scroll out of view if the user types too many. The **maxlength** attribute constrains the maximum number of characters the user can enter into the text box. Table 6.2 lists these attributes. Example 6.4 demonstrates two text boxes, one with several additional attributes set.

| Attribute | Value(s) | Definition and Usage |
|-----------|----------|----------------------|
| `value` | text | initial text to appear in text box |
| `size` | integer | visible length of text box, in characters |
| `maxlength` | integer | maximum number of characters that may be typed into text box |

**Table 6.2 Attributes for text boxes**

```
<form action="http://webster.cs.washington.edu/params.php">
  <div>
    ID number:
    <input type="text" name="idnumber" /> <br />
    First name:
    <input type="text" name="fname" size="30"
        maxlength="20" value="Jethro" />
    <input type="submit" />
  </div>
</form>
```

ID number: [            ]
First name: [Jethro                    ] [Submit Query]

**Example 6.4 Text boxes**

Recall that text boxes, like all other UI controls, are inline elements. If we want them to appear on separate lines, we must separate them with **br** tags or enclose them in separate block elements such as **div**s.

## 6.2.2  Text Areas (Multi-Line)

| Element | textarea |
|---------|----------|
| **Description** | Box for entering multiple lines of text (inline) |
| **Syntax** | `<textarea name="`**name**`" rows="`**height**`" cols="`**width**`">`<br>**initial text**<br>`</textarea>` |

If you would like to allow the user to enter more than one line of text, use the **textarea** element. Unlike an **input** tag, **textarea** is not self-closing. Despite its multiple lines and potentially large size, a **textarea** is considered an inline element and must be enclosed in a proper block element; for example, a **textarea** cannot be placed directly inside the page's **body**.

Any text placed between the opening `<textarea>` and closing `</textarea>` tags will appear as the initial text in the area when the page loads. If no text is written, the text area will be initially blank.

The **rows** and **cols** attributes designate how many rows and columns the text area should have. These are not hard limits on the amount of text that can occupy the text area; if more text is typed, a scrollbar appears.

Example 6.5 demonstrates a text area. Notice that the closing `</textarea>` tag is not indented. This is because if you do indent it, that whitespace becomes part of the initial text inside the text area. If you don't want this, you must not indent the closing tag.

```
<form action="http://webster.cs.washington.edu/params.php">
  <div>
    Comments: <br />
    <textarea name="comments" rows="4" cols="20">
Type your comments here.
</textarea> <br />
    <input type="submit" />
  </div>
</form>
```

Comments:

```
Type your comments
here.
```

Submit Query

**Example 6.5 Multi-line text area**

By default the words in a `textarea` wrap to the next line if it becomes too long. There is not actually any standards-compliant way to turn this off; currently you must use the non-standard `wrap="off"` attribute in the `textarea` tag.

## 6.2.3 Checkboxes

| Element | input |
| --- | --- |
| Description | Checkbox (inline) |
| Syntax | `<input type="checkbox" name="name" /> text` |

Checkboxes and radio buttons allow the user to choose from a fixed set of options. Checkboxes are used when the options are independent and the user might want to choose none, one, or many of them. For example, photo hosting sites use checkboxes so the user can select to view color photos, black and white, or both. A check box is represented as an `input` tag with a `type` of `checkbox`. Example 6.6 demonstrates the use of check boxes.

```
<form action="http://webster.cs.washington.edu/params.php">
  <div>
    Font options:
    <input type="checkbox" name="bold" /> Bold
    <input type="checkbox" name="italic" checked="checked" /> Italic
    <input type="submit" />
  </div>
</form>
```

Font options: ☐ Bold ☑ Italic  Submit Query

**Example 6.6 Check boxes**

It may seem strange that so many different controls use the same `input` element in HTML. Why isn't there a `checkbox` element? It seems like the designers of forms (which were introduced in HTML 3 in 1996) didn't anticipate how widely they'd be used in the modern web, which is filled with interactive sites. Now we're stuck with these strange design decisions whenever we want to put controls on our page.

When a form with checkboxes is submitted, the browser finds all checkboxes that are checked, and submits them with a value of **on**. Checkboxes that are not checked are not included in the URL. For example, if the user has the Bold box checked and the Italic box unchecked and submits the form, the following URL and query string will be fetched:

```
http://webster.cs.washington.edu/params.php?bold=on
```

If both boxes are checked when the form is submitted, the query string would be the following:

```
http://webster.cs.washington.edu/params.php?bold=on&italic=on
```

The optional **checked** attribute specifies that a checkbox should be checked initially when the page appears. If you do not set the checked attribute, the box will be initially unchecked. Oddly, the only valid value for the **checked** attribute is **"checked"**. In fact, there's no corresponding **"unchecked"** value or any way to specify an unchecked box. To be specific, if you set **checked** to have any value at all, it will check the box, but only **checked="checked"** is valid XHTML. The only way to indicate an unchecked box is by the lack of the **checked** attribute.

The reason the attribute works this way is because in past versions of HTML, you just wrote **checked**, with no equals sign or quoted value. But in XHTML every attribute needs to have a name, an equals sign, and a value in quotes. So the designers of XHTML decided that these kinds of "flag" attributes should be set to values equal to their own names if you want to enable them. We'll see other such attributes later in the chapter, such as **disabled** and **readonly**.

## 6.2.4 Radio Buttons

| Element | input |
| --- | --- |
| Description | Radio button (inline) |
| Syntax | `<input type="radio" name="`**group**`" value="`**param**`" />` **text** |

Radio buttons allow the user to choose one of a set of options. For example, a travel web site may use radio buttons to allow the user to select what kind of flight to search for, such as round-trip, one-way, or multi-city. A radio button is represented as an **input** tag with a **type** of **radio**.

The **name** attribute designates a group of buttons. Normally every control should have a unique name, but if you give several radio buttons the same **name**, the browser will ensure that only one radio button can be checked at a given time. Example 6.7 demonstrates the use of radio buttons.

```
<form action="http://webster.cs.washington.edu/params.php">
  <div>
    Text color:
    <input type="radio" name="color" value="red" /> Red
    <input type="radio" name="color" value="green" /> Green
    <input type="radio" name="color" value="purple"
      checked="checked" /> Purple
    <input type="radio" name="color" value="blue" /> Blue
    <input type="submit" />
  </div>
</form>
```

Text color: ○ Red ○ Green ⦿ Purple ○ Blue  Submit Query

**Example 6.7 Radio buttons**

As with checkboxes, the optional `checked` attribute specifies that a radio button should be checked initially when the page appears. Since groups of radio buttons usually require exactly one choice to be selected at all times, it is usually a good idea to set a choice to be initially checked.

| Common Error |
|---|
| Forgetting **value** on radio buttons |

The `value` attribute is optional on radio buttons, but without it, the buttons are not very useful. If you don't give values for each radio button in a group, then no matter which is checked when the form is submitted, the browser will submit that parameter with a value of **on**.

Consider the code of Example 6.8. If you test the form by submitting it to the server, you'll notice that no matter which credit card you choose, the value submitted to the server for the `ccard` query parameter is simply **on**. The server won't be able to tell which credit card the user selected.

```
<form action="http://webster.cs.washington.edu/params.php">
  <div>
    <input type="radio" name="ccard" /> Visa
    <input type="radio" name="ccard" /> MasterCard
    <input type="radio" name="ccard" /> Discover <br />
    <input type="submit" />
  </div>
</form>
```

**Example 6.8 Common error: Radio buttons without `value` attribute**

This problem is solved using the `value` attribute. A control's `value` attribute represents the value that will be sent to the server for the corresponding query parameter when the form is submitted. The new version of the form shown in Example 6.9 submits the credit card data successfully.

```
<form action="http://webster.cs.washington.edu/params.php">
  <div>
    <input type="radio" name="ccard" value="visa" /> Visa
    <input type="radio" name="ccard" value="mastercard" /> MasterCard
    <input type="radio" name="ccard" value="discover" /> Discover
    <br /> <input type="submit" />
  </div>
</form>
```

**Example 6.9 Corrected error with `value` attributes**

Notice that the value doesn't need to exactly match the text next to the radio button. It can be anything you like; whatever value you need to pass to the server.

## 6.2.5 Labels

| Element | `label` |
|---|---|
| Description | Clickable text label for a control (inline) |
| Syntax 1 | `<label>`**control and label text**`</label>` |
| Syntax 2 | `<label for="`**id of control**`">`**label text**`</label>` |

Radio buttons and check boxes usually come with a bit of text that describes the choice, as in the examples above. However, if you try clicking on that text, you'll notice that it doesn't cause the neighboring box or button to become checked. That's because the browser doesn't have any way of knowing that the text is connected to the button. If you want the browser to associate a piece of text with a nearby radio button or checkbox (and make it clickable), you must wrap that text with another element called `label`.

There are two ways to use the `label` element. The first is to nest the control element and the neighboring text within a `label` element, as shown in Example 6.10. Notice that you'll now be able to click the text and have it check the neighboring checkbox. Also notice that a label has no particular appearance on the page; it just displays the text inside it. The key aspect of the label is that the user can click it to activate the nearby control.

```
<form action="http://webster.cs.washington.edu/params.php">
  <div>
    Font options:
    <label><input type="checkbox" name="bold" /> Bold</label>
    <label><input type="checkbox" name="italic" /> Italic</label>
    <input type="submit" />
  </div>
</form>
```

Font options: ☐ Bold ☐ Italic  Submit Query

**Example 6.10 Labels**

The other way to use a `label` is to give each control an `id` attribute, like the ones we used previously with CSS. Then a label anywhere on the page can target that control by placing a `for` attribute inside it and giving that attribute the same value as the `id` of the control. The `id` doesn't need to be the same as the control's name, though it is in our example.

```
<form action="http://webster.cs.washington.edu/params.php">
  <div>
    Font options:
    <input id="bold" type="checkbox" name="bold" />
    <label for="bold">Bold</label>

    <input id="italic" type="checkbox" name="italic" />
    <label for="italic">Italic</label> <br />
    <br />

    <label for="bold">Click me to check the bold box too!</label> <br />
    <input type="submit" />
  </div>
</form>
```

Font options: ☐ Bold ☐ Italic

Click me to check the bold box too!
Submit Query

**Example 6.11 Labels (second style)**

(Jessica likes the second method because it doesn't really make semantic sense that a control be a child of a label, and because the label can then be anywhere on the page. Marty likes the first way because it is more concise and you don't have to use the `id` attribute on the controls. Both are correct usages and both are valid XHTML, so choose the one you prefer.)

Even though the `label` element isn't required and controls still appear properly without it, we recommend always using the `label` element on your controls for the following reasons:

- **Functionality**: When the user clicks the `label` element text, the cursor will move to that choice and the associated control will be selected without having to click the control itself.
- **Styling**: Many times you want the styling of labels to be different than other text on the page. By using a `label` element you can style labels throughout your web page and site.
- **Accessibility**: Designating the labeling text with the `label` element allows screen readers to know to read the text when a choice has been selected, confirming the choice to the user.

## 6.2.6 Drop-down Menus and Lists

| Elements | select, option |
|----------|----------------|
| Description | A drop-down menu of selectable choices (inline) |
| Syntax | `<select name="`**name**`">`<br>  `<option>`**menu item text**`</option>`<br>  `<option>`**menu item text**`</option>`<br>  `...`<br>  `<option>`**menu item text**`</option>`<br>`</select>` |

Like radio buttons and checkboxes, menus allow the user to select one or more from a list of options. A drop-down menu consists of a `select` element surrounding one or more `option` elements. The `select` element is the overall menu and an `option` element designates each item. Example 6.12 demonstrates a drop-down menu.

```
<form action="http://webster.cs.washington.edu/params.php">
  <div>
    <select name="vehicletype">
      <option>Truck</option>
      <option>SUV</option>
      <option>Car</option>
      <option>Hybrid</option>
      <option>Motorcycle</option>
    </select>
    <input type="submit" />
  </div>
</form>
```

Truck   Submit Query

Example 6.12 Drop-down menu

| Attribute | Value(s) | Definition and Usage |
|-----------|----------|----------------------|
| size | integer | number of options visible at a time (default 1) |
| multiple | "multiple" | whether the user should be allowed to select multiple values at a time (default no) |

Table 6.3 Attributes of `select` element

The `size` attribute can be used to create a list box where a user can see more than one menu item on the screen at a time. The `size` attribute designates how many items can be viewed at a time. The value of the `size` attribute should be an integer, but you must still enclose it in quotes.

To allow the user to select more than one option at a time, you must make two changes to your HTML code:

- set the `multiple` attribute on the select tag
- place a pair of square brackets, [ ], at the end of the `select` element's `name` attribute value

As with the `checked` attribute of radio buttons and checkboxes, the `multiple` attribute is set to `"multiple"`. It generally only makes sense to set `multiple` if you've also set `size` to a value greater than 1. These attributes of the `select` tag are listed in Table 6.3.

When the page first loads, by default the first menu item is selected. If you want a different initially selected item in a drop-down menu or list, use the optional `selected` attribute with the value `"selected"` inside the appropriate `option` tag. Example 6.13 demonstrates a drop-down menu with several additional attributes set.

| Attribute | Value(s) | Definition and Usage |
|---|---|---|
| selected | "selected" | whether the item should be initially selected (default no) |

**Table 6.4 Attributes of `option` element**

```
<form action="http://webster.cs.washington.edu/params.php">
  <div>
    <select name="vehicletype[]" size="4" multiple="multiple">
    <option>Truck</option>
    <option>SUV</option>
    <option>Car</option>
    <option selected="selected">Hybrid</option>
    <option>Motorcycle</option>
    </select>
    <input type="submit" />
  </div>
</form>
```

**Example 6.13 Drop-down menu with additional attributes**

Another handy element to know about when creating menus is `optgroup`, which represents a group of options. Option groups appear as unselectable menu items that group menu choices together. The `optgroup` tag is nested with the `select` and surrounds the group of option items it is meant to label. The required `label` attribute defines the text label for the group. Example 6.14 demonstrates `optgroup`s.

```
<form action="http://webster.cs.washington.edu/params.php">
  <div>
    <select name="vehicletype" size="7">
      <optgroup label="Lots of Gas">
        <option>Truck</option>
        <option>SUV</option>
      </optgroup>
      <optgroup label="Not So Much Gas">
        <option>Car</option>
        <option>Hybrid</option>
        <option>Motorcycle</option>
      </optgroup>
    </select>
    <input type="submit" />
  </div>
</form>
```

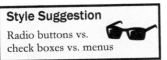

**Example 6.14 Option groups**

---

**Style Suggestion**

Radio buttons vs. check boxes vs. menus

If both checkboxes/radio buttons and menus can be used to allow a user to make choices and can both be set up to allow one or many selections, when should you use radio buttons and checkboxes and when should you use menus? Menus take up less space, especially if there are many choices. The downside to menus is that users cannot see all of their options at once. The number of options viewed in a menu can be adjusted using the size attribute, but for a long list of choices there will likely be some that are still hidden. However, this might not be important if the options are obvious and are ordered well. For example, if you want the user to choose the state they live in, it is likely not important that they see all the options if the options are listed in alphabetical order so it easy to find a state in the list.

Radio buttons/checkboxes have complementary benefits and drawbacks; the user can see all of their choices, but more screen space is taken to display the choices. In the end, you should weigh these factors and use good judgment to choose between radio buttons/checkboxes vs. menus, but a good rule of thumb is that when you have a lot of options to list or limited screen space, use menus. Otherwise, use radio buttons or checkboxes.

## 6.2.7 Reset Buttons

| Element | input |
| --- | --- |
| Description | Reset button (inline) |
| Syntax | `<input type="reset" value="`**button text**`" />` |

HTML supplies another kind of button that resets a form's data to its initial state. A reset button is an **input** element with a type of **reset**. The text on the button is specified by its **value** attribute. (If you don't specify a value, the text is "Reset".) Reset buttons are optional; they were once common, but now many forms do not include them. Example 6.15 shows a form with a reset button. If you were to change some of the values in the controls and then click the Clear button, they would return to their original state.

```html
<form action="http://webster.cs.washington.edu/params.php">
  <div>
    <label>Name: <input type="text" name="name" /></label> <br />
    <label>Meal: <input type="text" name="meal" /></label> <br />
    <label>Meat?
      <input type="checkbox" name="meat" checked="checked" />
    </label> <br />

    <input type="submit" value="Submit Meal Preferences" />
    <input type="reset" value="Clear" />
  </div>
</form>
```

Name: [        ]
Meal: [        ]
Meat? ☑
[Submit Meal Preferences] [Clear]

**Example 6.15 Reset button**

## 6.2.8  Grouping Controls (Field Sets)

| Elements | fieldset, legend |
|---|---|
| Description | A set of related input controls with optional caption (block) |
| Syntax | `<form action="`**server URL**`">`<br>  `<fieldset>`<br>    `<legend>`**caption text**`</legend>`<br>    **elements**<br>  `</fieldset>`<br>`</form>` |

When many controls are on a page, you might want to find ways to group related controls together in order to make input easier for the user. One way to do this is to use the **fieldset** and **legend** elements to group related controls with an optional caption. A **fieldset** is a block element whose default appearance is to place a thin solid border around its contents. Example 6.16 shows a form that uses a **fieldset** and **legend**.

```
<form action="http://webster.cs.washington.edu/params.php">
  <fieldset>
    <legend>Login Information</legend>
    <input type="text" name="username" /> User Name <br />
    <input type="text" name="password" /> Password
  </fieldset>
</form>
```

```
┌─Login Information──────────────────────────────────────────────┐
│ ┌──────────────┐ User Name                                      │
│ └──────────────┘                                                │
│ ┌──────────────┐ Password                                       │
│ └──────────────┘                                                │
└────────────────────────────────────────────────────────────────┘
```

**Example 6.16 Grouping controls with `fieldset`**

The `fieldset` element draws the box around the controls it groups and the `legend` element adds a caption to the box. The `legend` element and all of the related controls should be nested within the `fieldset` element. The `legend` should appear first inside the `fieldset`, before any other elements.

As a side note, one problem with a user name/password form like this one is that the user's password is shown on the page as plain text. If you'd like a more discreet password entry box, HTML includes a simple way to do so by using an `input` element with a `type` of `"password"` instead of `"text"`.

## 6.2.9 Styling Forms

You can use many of the same CSS properties to style HTML forms and controls as you would to style any other element we have learned about. To help you do this, you may want to apply `id` or `class` attributes to the controls of interest. Example 6.17 demonstrates a few controls with styles and their appearance in the Firefox browser.

A particularly useful piece of CSS syntax for styling form controls is a *CSS attribute selector*. Such a selector only applies to an element with a particular attribute set to a particular value. This is very useful with forms because many controls share the same tag, `input`, so an attribute selector can help you to style only the submit button, or only radio buttons, etc. It uses the following syntax:

```
tag[attribute="value"] {
  property: value;
  ...
  property: value;
}
```

Unfortunately, support for styling controls is inconsistent across browsers. For example, Apple's Safari and Microsoft Internet Explorer don't always allow changing borders or fonts on input text boxes, buttons, and other controls. We are not going to go into detail about styling controls here, but the References section of this chapter links to a great blog that details many of the pros/cons and browser consistency issues. Nonetheless, since lots of pages have forms, choosing a good set of styles for your form's controls can set it apart and add a lot to the character of your web page. Be sure to test your styled form in a variety of browsers to make sure it looks the way you want.

```
<form action="http://webster.cs.washington.edu/params.php">
  <div>
    <label for="dreamjobtext">Dream Job:</label>
    <input type="text" name="dreamjob" id="dreamjobtext"
       value="Enter your dream job" />
    <input type="submit" value="Submit!" />
  </div>
</form>
```

```
input[type="text"] {
  background-color: #663AAB;
  border: 2px dashed red;
  color: white;
}

input[type="submit"] {
  background-color: white;
  border: 1px solid black;
  font-family: monospace;
  font-size: 1.5em;
  font-weight: bold;
}
```

Dream Job: Enter your dream job    **Submit!**

**Example 6.17 Styling form controls**

A common layout for forms is to have labels for each control in a column on the left side, right-aligned, with the form controls themselves in a right-hand column, left-aligned. Many web developers use an HTML element called a table for this. But this is poor style; a table is meant to be used to store an actual table of data, not as a hack to get a layout of rows and columns. We can achieve a layout like this by making our labels float to the left with a specific width and a right text alignment.

Suppose we have a form for signing up users to a forum, and we want to arrange it into a two-column layout as just described. We'll target labels for styling by giving them a `class` of `heading`. Example 6.18 shows the form code to be styled, and Figure 6.2 shows its unpleasant appearance.

```
<form action="http://webster.cs.washington.edu/params.php">
  <fieldset>
    <legend>New User Signup</legend>
    <label class="heading" for="name">Name:</label>
    <input type="text" name="name" id="name" /> <br />

    <label class="heading" for="address">Address:</label>
    <input type="text" name="address" id="address" /> <br />

    <label class="heading">Credit Card:</label>
    <label><input type="radio" name="cc" value="visa" /> Visa</label>
    <label><input type="radio" name="cc" value="mc" /> MasterCard</label>
    <br />
    <input type="submit" value="Sign Up" />
  </fieldset>
</form>
```

**Example 6.18 Form to be styled**

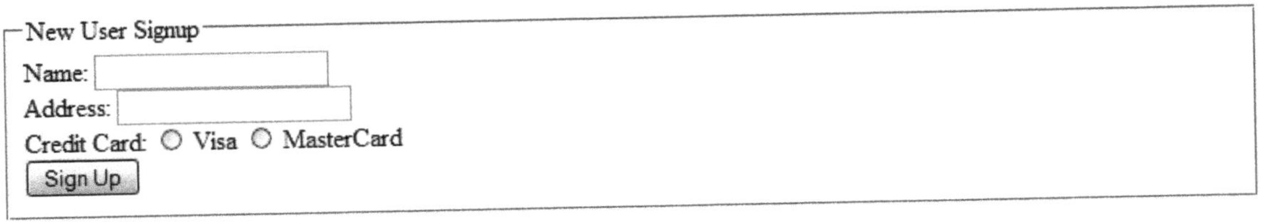

**Figure 6.2 Ugly initial form appearance**

Example 6.19 shows the necessary CSS code for creating the two-column layout. The key aspect is that all **label** elements with **class** of **heading** are set to float left with a width of 7em and a **text-align** of right. We've also cleaned up the overall form by putting some borders, margins, and background colors on its elements, as well as a width and centered margin on the overall **fieldset**. Figure 6.3 shows the much-improved appearance of the form.

```css
fieldset {
  background-color: #ffffcc;
  margin-left: auto;  margin-right: auto;
  width: 21em;
}
form {
  font-family: "Helvetica", sans-serif;
}
input {
  margin-bottom: 0.5em;
}
input[type="submit"] {
  font-weight: bold;
  margin-left: 10em;
}
label.heading {
  float: left;
  margin-right: 1em;
  text-align: right;
  width: 7em;
}
legend {
  background-color: white;
  border: 1px solid black;
  padding: 0.25em;
}
```

**Example 6.19 CSS code for form layout**

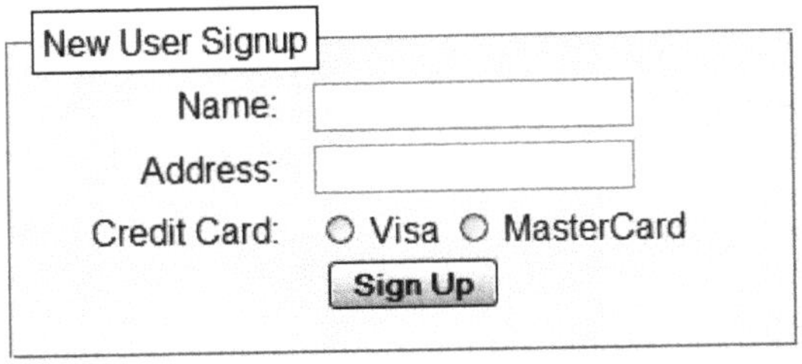

**Figure 6.3 Improved form appearance**

**Self-Check**

4. What is the difference between the `size` and `maxlength` attributes on a text box? These attributes don't work on a `textarea`; what attributes do we use instead to set its size?
5. If the user types a name of "Jessica Miller" and checks both boxes in the form below, what URL will the form fetch, including its full query string? What's bad about the form's code?

```
<form action="http://webster.cs.washington.edu/params.php">
  <div>
    Name: <input type="text" name="name" />
    Gender:
    <input type="checkbox" name="male" /> Male
    <input type="checkbox" name="female" /> Female
    <input type="submit" />
  </div>
</form>
```

6. How do you arrange radio buttons into a group, so that only one can be selected at a time?
7. What's wrong with the following form code?

```
<form action="http://webster.cs.washington.edu/params.php">
  <div>
    Your favorite stooge?
    <input type="radio" name="stooge" /> Larry
    <input type="radio" name="stooge" /> Moe
    <input type="radio" name="stooge" /> Curly
    <input type="submit" />
  </div>
</form>
```

8. What two tags are used to create a drop-down list box? How can you arrange the items in a list box into groups? What differentiates a drop-down list box from a multi-line list box?
9. What's wrong with the following form code?

```
<form action="http://webster.cs.washington.edu/params.php">
  <div>
    <select>
      <option name="stooge">Larry</option>
      <option name="stooge">Moe</option>
      <option name="stooge">Curly</option>
    </select>
    <input type="submit" />
  </div>
</form>
```

## 6.3 Submitting Data

In this section we'll explore some advanced issues relating to how forms and query parameters are submitted. We'll also discuss how form data can be processed on a web server using PHP.

### 6.3.1 URL-encoding

The parameters sent when a form is submitted become part of an HTTP request's URL or request packet, which places some restrictions on what characters can appear in a parameter's value. For example, if you wanted to send a request with a parameter named `icecream` whose value was `Ben&Jerrys`, you might try a URL such as the following:

```
http://webster.cs.washington.edu/params.php?icecream=Ben&Jerrys
```

But this URL would confuse the web server, because `&` is also the character used to separate multiple query parameters. The server would actually think you were sending two parameters: One named `icecream` with a value of `Ben`, and a second named `Jerrys` with an empty value. This isn't what we intended.

---

**URL-encoding**

Replacing characters in query parameters so they can be safely passed to a web server.

---

We have already discussed the concept of HTML-encoding, such as replacing `<` with an `&lt;` entity when writing a web page. There is another type of encoding that is done to query parameters by your browser before they are sent to a web server. Instead of entities starting with `&`, *URL-encoding* uses entities that consist of a `%` character followed by a character code number. For example, the encoding for an `&` sign is `%26`, so the correct way to pass the `Ben&Jerrys` parameter previously shown would be the following:

```
http://webster.cs.washington.edu/params.php?icecream=Ben%26Jerrys
```

There are tables available online of all characters and their URL-encoded equivalents; this chapter's References section points to a good one at w3schools.com. But luckily, you don't often need to know much about URL-encoding to get by. Browsers automatically encode query parameters in forms as they're about to be sent to the server, so you don't need to manually encode them yourself. Also, web servers usually manually decode the parameters for you as well. We mainly introduce URL encoding here so that you are aware of it in case you spot funny characters in query parameters in URLs you submit.

### 6.3.2 Hidden Input Parameters

There are times when you'd like to submit an additional query parameter to a server without it being visible on the form's UI. For example, perhaps you're creating a site for an online store and you have order forms for several products, but all the forms submit to the same URL on the server. You need a query parameter on each order form page to specify which product is being ordered, but you don't really want the user to see it on the page.

This effect can be achieved using a *hidden input parameter*. A hidden parameter is represented by an `input` element with a `type` of `"hidden"`. A hidden parameter must also have `name` and `value` attributes specifying the name/value pair that should be passed to the server.

```
<form action="http://webster.cs.washington.edu/params.php">
  <fieldset>
    <label>Name: <input type="text" name="name" /></label> <br />
    <label>Meal: <input type="text" name="meal" /></label> <br />
    <label>Meat?
      <input type="checkbox" name="meat" checked="checked" />
    </label> <br />

    <!-- two hidden input parameters -->
    <input type="hidden" name="organization" value="ScumCo" />
    <input type="hidden" name="year" value="2008" />
    <input type="submit" value="Submit Meal Preferences" />
  </fieldset>
</form>
```

Name: [                    ]
Meal: [                    ]
Meat? ☑
[ Submit Meal Preferences ]

**Example 6.20 Hidden input parameters**

A hidden parameter has no onscreen appearance, but it will be sent to the server along with all the other parameters on the page. For example, if you type in a name of Jane, a meal of pizza, check the Meat box, and click Submit, the browser will make a request to the web server's page at http://webster.cs.washington.edu/params.php using the following query string:

```
name=Jane&meal=pizza&meat=on&organization=ScumCo&year=2008
```

The submitted value of a hidden input parameter cannot be changed by the user directly, but later we'll learn how to change it using JavaScript code if necessary.

## 6.3.3 HTTP Requests: GET vs. POST

In the first chapter of this textbook when discussing the basics of the HTTP protocol, we briefly mentioned that information can be submitted from your browser using two different HTTP request methods: GET and POST. A *GET request* is supposed to be used when the browser is requesting information from a web server, and a POST request when the browser is submitting new information to the server. A GET request transmits its information as query parameters in the URL it requests from the server. A *POST request* embeds its query parameters into the header of the HTTP request packet, and they are not seen in the URL.

> **GET request**
> Asks for information from a web server, passing query parameters in a URL.

GET requests have some relative advantages over POST requests. Many developers and users find GET requests easier to understand, since parameters are visible in the URL. Also, the result of a GET request can be bookmarked or sent as a link to a friend, because all of the information about the request is in the URL itself.

> **POST request**
> Submits information to a server, passing query parameters inside HTTP packets.

POST requests also have some advantages over GET requests. The amount of information that can be put into a GET request is very limited, since it must be placed in the URL. The maximum length of a query parameter is around 100-200 characters, not long enough for submitting any large amount of data. Also, the fact that POST requests don't show the query parameters in the URL and in the browser's address bar can be desirable, such as if the information is private or sensitive.

Most browsers treat GET and POST requests in slightly different ways. Browsers assume that a GET request is simply asking the server for some information, and that the request could be repeated if necessary without any negative side effects. A POST request, however, might be a more sensitive operation, such as submitting an order to be purchased from an online store. If the user accidentally made the POST request twice (such as by pressing the Submit button twice, or by refreshing the page in the browser after it was submitted), the order might be made twice. To avoid such situations, most browsers prompt the user before re-sending POST requests. For example, Figure 6.4 shows the dialog box that pops up when you try to repeat a POST request in Firefox 3.

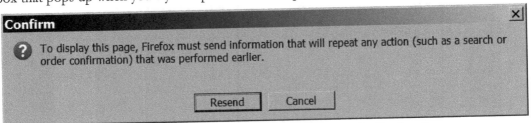

**Figure 6.4 Resubmitting a POST request in Firefox 3**

Because GET requests are slightly simpler to understand, we've been using them in the forms in this chapter so far. But really, many of the forms shown previously in this chapter actually should have used POST requests, since they involve submitting data such as meal preferences to the server, which presumably would save the data into a master list. We chose to use GET requests instead so you could see the parameters being passed more easily, but if this were being used on a real web site, POST would have been better.

It's simple to modify a form to use a POST request. To do so, add a **method** attribute to the form tag with a value of **"post"**. (The attribute values must be lowercase to be considered valid XHTML.) You can also use a **method** value of **"get"** for GET requests, but it isn't necessary to do so since GET is the default.

```
<form action="http://webster.cs.washington.edu/params.php" method="post">
  <fieldset>
    <label>Name: <input type="text" name="name" /></label> <br />
    <label>Meal: <input type="text" name="meal" /></label> <br />
    <label>Meat?
      <input type="checkbox" name="meat" checked="checked" />
    </label> <br />

    <input type="hidden" name="organization" value="ScumCo" />

    <input type="submit" value="Submit Meal Preferences" />
  </fieldset>
</form>
```

**Example 6.21 Form that uses a POST request**

Example 6.21 shows a form that uses a POST request. (Its output is not shown because using a POST request looks no different on the page than using a GET request.) If you were to submit its form, the URL you'd see in the browser's address bar would not contain any query parameter information, but nonetheless the parameters will be transferred to the server. For example, if you type in a name of Jane, a meal of pizza, check the Meat box, and click the Submit button, the browser would make a request to the following URL:

```
http://webster.cs.washington.edu/params.php
```

However, if you were to read the output on the resulting page, you'd see that the page did in fact receive all the parameter names/values that were typed. Later in this chapter we'll learn how server-side programs interact with the query parameters that are sent to them.

When you're creating forms of your own, you should generally choose between GET and POST based on the original meanings of these request types. That is, if you're simply asking the server for some information that requires parameters (such as requesting an article or viewing a particular page of photos from a gallery), a GET request is better. But if you're submitting new data to be saved by the server, POST is the appropriate choice. For example, in our very first form in this chapter that searched Google, GET was the right choice, since we were retrieving information (search results) from Google. But in the forms that submit meal preferences or credit card information, presumably that information is meant to be saved by the server, so it should be sent as a POST.

## 6.3.4 Uploading Files

| Element | input |
|---|---|
| Description | File upload (inline) |
| Syntax | `<input type="file" name="parameter" attributes />` |

A form can also contain a control that allows a user to select a file to be uploaded to the web server. To do this, use an **input** element with a type of **"file"**. The element should have a name attribute as with other query parameters. The single **input** tag will cause both a text field and a Browse button to appear on the page. You can also supply a **size** attribute to control the width in characters of the text field.

To upload files properly, you must also set two attribute values on the **form** tag itself. The first is that the form's **method** must be **"post"**; a GET request wouldn't make sense, since it would be impossible to squish a file into a request's URL. The second attribute that must be set on the **form** tag is a new one named **enctype**. Its value should be set to **"multipart/form-data"**. This parameter tells the browser in what way to encode the pieces of data of the form; we're specifying that the form contains multiple types of data (normal query parameters, and a file to be uploaded). Example 6.22 demonstrates a form with a file upload control.

```html
<form action="http://webster.cs.washington.edu/params.php"
  enctype="multipart/form-data" method="post">
  <fieldset>
    <label>Name: <input type="text" name="name" /></label> <br />
    <label>Meal: <input type="text" name="meal" /></label> <br />
    Your picture:
    <input type="file" name="pic" size="60" /> <br />
    <input type="submit" value="Submit Preferences" />
  </fieldset>
</form>
```

| Name: | |
| Meal: | |
| Your picture: | Browse.. |
| Submit Preferences | |

**Example 6.22 File upload**

If you were to browse to a file and submit the form, you'd notice that the destination web application `params.php` had received the file and displayed its contents as output. Later in this chapter we'll learn how to write server-side code that interacts with uploaded files.

A security-related quirk about file uploads is that unlike most uses of the **input** tag, you aren't allowed to specify a **value** attribute on an **input** with a **type** of **file**. This is for security purposes; if an initial value for the filename were allowed, a malicious web page could use it to specify the name of a sensitive personal file on your disk, then automatically submit the form. The attacker would have your sensitive data without your permission!

## Self-Check

10. What is the properly encoded URL to fetch the page `params.php` with a query parameter **title** with value **Math & Science Basics** and a parameter **equation** with value **1 + 1 = 2** ? (You may need to consult the URL-encoding reference at the end of this chapter to figure out the answer.)

11. How is a hidden input parameter different from a normal text box? Why not just use a text box instead of a hidden input parameter, so that the user can see and change the parameter's value if so desired?

12. What are the major differences between a GET and POST request? How do you know when to use each one?

13. Is a GET or a POST more appropriate for each of the following form requests?
    - a search query to Google
    - a product purchase from Amazon.com
    - submitting your vegan meal preference to an airline
    - asking the latest value of your house on Zillow.com
    - writing a comment on a Youtube video

## 6.4  Processing Form Data in PHP

All of the forms so far have submitted their data either to a pre-existing source (such as Google), or to our own `params.php` that just echoes the query parameter values. Forms are much more interesting when you write code to run on the server to process the form data. In the following sections we'll instruct forms to submit to our own server-side program and learn how to make that program process the data.

### 6.4.1  Superglobal Associative Arrays

A PHP program that processes form data is largely the same as any other PHP program. PHP has several special global variables called *superglobals* that are visible in all code. These variables' names are all uppercase and all begin with an underscore. For example, `$_SERVER` contains information about the current web server, and `$_REQUEST` contains information about the current web request. Table 6.5 lists the most commonly used superglobal arrays.

Each of these superglobals is a special kind of array called an associative array (also sometimes called a dictionary or hash). An *associative array* is an array whose indexes are not integers. Array indexes in PHP can be any type, such as strings or real numbers. For example, the code in Example 6.23 is, perhaps surprisingly, legal. It creates an associative

| **associative array** |
| One whose indexes are not necessarily integers, such as PHP's superglobal arrays. |

array containing two elements. The value **23** is stored at index `"hi"`, and the value **42** is stored at index **3.14**.

```
$a = array();
$a["hi"] = 23;
$a[3.14] = 42;
```

**Example 6.23 Creating an associative array**

If you haven't seen an associative array before, the preceding code may look very strange. The idea of `"hi"` or `3.14` being an index contradicts the notion of 0-based integers as indexes that you're probably comfortable with. A regular array is a way of connecting numbers (indexes) to values (elements); an associative array is just a more generalized version of this same idea. It connects an index to some element value, regardless of what type that index might be or what value it might have. The indexes of an associative array are more commonly referred to as *keys*.

| **key** |
| An index in an associative array that stores an associated element value. |

| Superglobal Array | Description |
|---|---|
| `$_REQUEST` | request query parameters |
| `$_GET`, `$_POST` | request query parameters, for GET or POST requests only, respectively |
| `$_SERVER` | information about the web server |
| `$_FILES` | any files that the user has uploaded in this request |
| `$_SESSION`, `$_COOKIE` | information related to stateful web sessions and user cookies |
| `$_ENV` | environment variables that are set on the web server |

**Table 6.5 PHP superglobal associative arrays**

PHP stores any query parameters submitted to your program in a global associative array named **$_REQUEST**. To retrieve the value of a query parameter, you write that parameter's name in quotes as the key when accessing **$_REQUEST**. The general syntax is shown in Example 6.24.

```
$_REQUEST["parameter name"]
```

**Example 6.24 Syntax template for accessing query parameters**

Earlier in this chapter we wrote a form for submitting a credit card number. Let's now write a modified version of that form that instead submits to a program we'll write named **process.php**. The form code is shown in Example 6.25.

```
<form action="process.php">
  <div>
    <input type="radio" name="ccard" value="visa" /> Visa
    <input type="radio" name="ccard" value="mastercard" /> MasterCard
    <input type="radio" name="ccard" value="discover" /> Discover <br />

    Credit card number:
    <input type="text" name="ccnumber" size="20" /> <br />

    <input type="submit" />
  </div>
</form>
```

○ Visa ○ MasterCard ○ Discover
Credit card number: [        ]
[ Submit Query ]

**Example 6.25 Form that submits to a custom PHP script**

Suppose we'd like to display a message informing the user that the credit card has been charged a large sum of money. When we submit the form to **process.php**, the type of card used will be in the **$_REQUEST** array at index **"ccard"**, and the credit card number at index **"ccnumber"**. Our PHP code can extract the parameter values from the array and use them in the page it outputs.

Example 6.26 demonstrates processing form parameters. The code would go into a file named **process.php** in the same folder as the HTML file, to match the form's **action** attribute. The indexes to use with **$_REQUEST** must match up exactly with the **name** attribute of the corresponding HTML form parameter. The example also shows the HTML output that would appear in the browser if the user chose a card type of MasterCard, a number of 4000100020003000, and submitted the form.

```php
<?php
  $creditcard = $_REQUEST["ccard"];
  $ccnum = $_REQUEST["ccnumber"];
?>
<!DOCTYPE html PUBLIC "-//W3C//DTD XHTML 1.1//EN"
    "http://www.w3.org/TR/xhtml11/DTD/xhtml11.dtd">
<html xmlns="http://www.w3.org/1999/xhtml">
  <head>
    <title>Credit Card Billing</title>
  </head>
  <body>
    <h1>Thank You</h1>
    <p>
      Your <?= $creditcard ?> card, number <?= $ccnum ?>, has
      been successfully charged $1,000,000.  Thank you!
    </p>
  </body>
</html>
```

## Thank You

Your mastercard credit card, number 4000100020003000, has been successfully charged $1,000,000. Thank you!

**Example 6.26 PHP form-processing code**

## 6.4.2 Working with **$_REQUEST**

$_REQUEST and other associative arrays can be examined and manipulated in many of the same ways as regular arrays. The **count** function reports the number of elements in an associative array. The **print_r** function prints a display of the contents of an associative array. (This is what our params.php service does.) It is a useful debugging tool to print the **$_REQUEST** array's contents to see what query parameters were passed to your PHP program. This is shown in Example 6.27.

```php
<pre>
<?php
  print_r($_REQUEST);
?>
</pre>
```

**Example 6.27 Printing request parameters for debugging**

Notice how the **print_r** call is wrapped in a **pre** block so you'll see it in a monospace font with whitespace preserved. If the above code were placed into the body of **process.php**, and the previous form was submitted with the same example input, the following output would be produced:

```
Array
(
    [creditcard] => mastercard
    [ccnumber] => 4000100020003000
)
```

The `foreach` loop still works on associative arrays, but it produces only the elements' values, not their associated indexes. If you want both, you must use a modified version of the `foreach` syntax, following the template shown in Example 6.28.

```
foreach ($array as $index => $element) {
    statements;
}
```

**Example 6.28 Syntax template for `foreach` loop over associative array**

The code in Example 6.29 demonstrates this syntax. The output shown is what would appear if the user chose MasterCard and a credit card number of 4000100020003000 and submitted the form.

```
<ul>
  <?php
    foreach ($_REQUEST as $param => $value) {
      ?>
      <li>The parameter named <?= $param ?> has value <?= $value ?></li>
      <?php
    }
  ?>
</ul>
```

- The parameter named ccard has value mastercard
- The parameter named ccnumber has value 4000100020003000

**Example 6.29 Traversing an associative array with `foreach` loop**

PHP has several functions that can be used with associative arrays. For example, you don't want to use the `sort` function on an associative array, because it destroys its keys and replaces them with sequential integer indexes. But `ksort` and `asort` will correctly sort an associative array by its keys' ordering or its element values' ordering respectively. Table 6.6 lists several other useful associative array functions.

| Function | Description |
|---|---|
| ksort, krsort | sorts by key (index), in normal or reverse order |
| asort, arsort | sorts by element value, in normal or reverse order |
| array_keys, array_values | an array holding all keys or values in the given associative array |

**Table 6.6 Associative array functions**

We saw previously that when a form has a checkbox, if the box is checked it will be submitted as a query parameter with the value **on**, and if unchecked it will not be submitted. Suppose we add a checkbox to our credit card form for choosing express shipping on the transaction. Example 6.30 shows the form and the output that would be produced by `process.php` if the user again chose a card type of MasterCard, a number of 4000100020003000, checked the express shipping checkbox, and submitted the form.

```
<form action="process.php">
  <div>
    <input type="radio" name="ccard" value="visa" checked="checked" />
    Visa
    <input type="radio" name="ccard" value="mastercard" /> MasterCard
    <input type="radio" name="ccard" value="discover" /> Discover <br />

    Credit card number:
    <input type="text" name="ccnumber" size="20" /> <br />

    <label>
      <input type="checkbox" name="express" />
      Express shipping? ($10 extra)
    </label> <br />
    <input type="submit" />
  </div>
</form>
```

- The parameter named ccard has value mastercard
- The parameter named ccnumber has value 4000100020003000
- The parameter named express has value on

**Example 6.30 Processing form with checkbox**

If the box is unchecked when the form is submitted, the parameter express will not be submitted and therefore there will be no value at index "express" in the $_REQUEST array. In that case we would instead see the output shown in Example 6.31.

- The parameter named ccard has value mastercard
- The parameter named ccnumber has value 4000100020003000

**Example 6.31 Form output when checkbox is unchecked**

Your form-processing code probably should produce different output for express vs. non-regular customers. You might be tempted to write a statement such as:

```
if ($_REQUEST["express"] == "on") {
  ...
}
```

However, this code will cause warning messages to appear if the user does not check the box. Because express may not be submitted, there might not be a value stored in $_REQUEST at index ["express"]. And if a variable is unset like that, you can't check to see if it is equal to a value like "on". PHP has a function named isset that you can use to test whether a given variable has been set and has any value. The proper test is the following:

```
if (isset($_REQUEST["express"])) {
  ...
}
```

Example 6.32 shows a new version of process.php demonstrating a test that uses isset to display a different message to express customers. The output shown is what would appear if the user chooses a card type of MasterCard, types a number of 4000100020003000, checks the express shipping box, and submits the form.

```php
<?php
  $creditcard = $_REQUEST["ccard"];
  $ccnum = $_REQUEST["ccnumber"];
?>

<!DOCTYPE html PUBLIC "-//W3C//DTD XHTML 1.1//EN"
    "http://www.w3.org/TR/xhtml11/DTD/xhtml11.dtd">
<html xmlns="http://www.w3.org/1999/xhtml">
  <head>
    <title>Credit Card Billing</title>
  </head>

  <body>
    <h1>Thank You</h1>

    <p>
      Your <?= $creditcard ?> card, number <?= $ccnum ?>, has
      been successfully charged $1,000,000.  Thank you!
    </p>

    <?php
      if (isset($_REQUEST["express"])) {
        ?>
        <p>
          Thanks for using express shipping.
          Your card was charged an additional $10.
        </p>
        <?php
      }
    ?>
  </body>
</html>
```

# Thank You

Your mastercard card, number 4000100020003000, has been successfully charged $1,000,000. Thank you!

Thanks for using express shipping. Your card was charged an additional $10.

**Example 6.32 Form that processes checkbox**

**Security Note**

HTML-encode
query parameters

Believe it or not, the simple form processing examples we've shown contain a major security problem! Our `process.php` code reads the query parameters and immediately echoes them back in the resulting page. But if the user types HTML tags as the credit card number, those tags will be injected into the `process.php` result page. This can be dangerous because it allows the form submitter to inject text, HTML tags, and/or images into your page. Before placing any PHP programs that process forms onto public web pages, you may want to look up more information about the `htmlspecialchars` function that encodes these values into HTML-safe equivalents.

```php
<?php
$name = htmlspecialchars($_REQUEST["name"]);  # prevent HTML injection
?>
<h1>Welcome, <?= $name ?></h1>
```

One special case for query parameters is when the form has a **select** box with the **multiple** attribute enabled, as in the code of Example 6.33. In this case, more than one value from the list may have been selected by the user.

```html
<select name="vehicletype[]" size="4" multiple="multiple">
  <option>Truck</option>
  <option>SUV</option>
  <option>Car</option>
  <option>Hybrid</option>
  <option>Motorcycle</option>
</select>
```

**Example 6.33 Form with select box with multiple attribute**

PHP represents this by having the corresponding **$_REQUEST** element store an array instead of a single value. Your PHP code can access this array by first pulling it out of the request associative array and then looping over its elements to process them as you see fit, as shown in Example 6.34.

```php
$vehicles = $_REQUEST["vehicletype"];
for ($i = 0; $i < count($vehicles); $i++) {
  print "You selected the following vehicle: {$vehicles[$i]}\n";
}
```

**Example 6.34 Accessing multiple selected elements**

## 6.4.3 Processing Uploaded Files

Though almost all query parameters are stored into PHP's **$_REQUEST** array, uploaded files are handled differently. A two-dimensional superglobal associative array named **$_FILES** stores information about any uploaded files. The keys of the **$_FILES** array are the names of any file input parameters. For example, if your form has an **input** tag with a **type** of **"file"** and a **name** of **"bizreport"**, there will be a value stored in **$_FILES["bizreport"]**.

Here's where it gets confusing: The values associated with each key in **$_FILES** are themselves associative arrays, whose keys are various attributes about the file such as **"name"** and **"size"**. So if you uploaded a 1066-byte file named **"sales.txt"** for that **bizreport** file parameter, the following statements would be true:

- **$_FILES["bizreport"]["name"] == "sales.txt"**
- **$_FILES["bizreport"]["type"] == "text/plain"**
- **$_FILES["bizreport"]["size"] == 1066**

It's easier to understand with a complete example. Recall Example 6.22's form seen in the Uploading Files section earlier in this chapter, displayed again here as Example 6.35. We've set the form's action to a new page we'll create called **upload.php**.

```
<form action="upload.php" enctype="multipart/form-data" method="post">
  <fieldset>
    <label>Name: <input type="text" name="name" /></label> <br />
    <label>Meal: <input type="text" name="meal" /></label> <br />

    Your picture:
    <input type="file" name="pic" size="60" /> <br />

    <input type="submit" value="Submit Preferences" />
  </fieldset>
</form>
```

**Example 6.35 File upload form**

The initial contents of upload.php are shown in Example 6.36, which also shows the output that would result if the user typed a name of Suzie, a meal of pizza, and uploaded a 3023-byte file named smiley.jpg for her image.

```
<pre>
<?php
  print "contents of REQUEST array:\n";
  print_r($_REQUEST);

  print "\ncontents of FILES array:\n";
  print_r($_FILES);
?>
</pre>

contents of REQUEST array:
Array
(
    [name] => Suzie
    [meal] => pizza
)

contents of FILES array:
Array
(
    [pic] => Array
        (
            [name] => smiley.jpg
            [type] => image/jpeg
            [tmp_name] => C:\WINDOWS\TEMP\php39B.tmp
            [error] => 0
            [size] => 3023
        )
```

**Example 6.36 Contents of upload.php**

It's one thing to print information about the file that was uploaded, but how do you actually access and process that file on the server? That's where it gets a little tricky. When the user uploads a file, PHP doesn't save it in your program's current directory with its uploaded file name; this would pose a security risk, because users could upload PHP scripts and other files and then cause the server to execute them. Instead, PHP stores the uploaded file in a temporary directory with a nonsense filename like php39B.tmp. You can find out any uploaded file's temporary file name by accessing the "tmp_name" within the associative array for that query parameter inside $_FILES. In other words:

```
$_FILES["parameter"]["tmp_name"]
```

If your program wants to store the file in a more permanent location, you need to use the `move_uploaded_file` function, which accepts two parameters: a source and destination filename. You should also use the `is_uploaded_file` function to make sure the file was uploaded successfully to the server before trying to move it. Table 6.7 summarizes these functions.

| Function | Description |
|---|---|
| is_uploaded_file | returns TRUE if the given file name exists and represents an uploaded temporary file |
| move_uploaded_file | moves an uploaded file from its temporary location to a location you specify |

Table 6.7 PHP uploaded file functions

Our overall suggested template for grabbing and saving an uploaded file is the following:

```php
if (is_uploaded_file($_FILES["parameter"]["tmp_name"])) {
   move_uploaded_file($_FILES["parameter"]["tmp_name"],
                 "destination filename");
}
```

For example, suppose we want to save each image the user uploads into our **images/** subdirectory on the server. We'll give the image a file name related to that of the user who uploads it. Once we save the image, we'll display all user-uploaded images on the page, each in its own **img** tag.

```php
<?php
$name = $_REQUEST["name"];
if (is_uploaded_file($_FILES["pic"]["tmp_name"])) {
   move_uploaded_file($_FILES["pic"]["tmp_name"], "images/$name.jpg");
}
foreach (glob("images/*.jpg") as $image) {
   ?>
   <img src="<?= $image ?>" alt="user image" /> <?= $image ?> <br />
   <?php
}
?>
```

Example 6.37 File upload processing code

## Self-Check

14. What is a superglobal? What is the difference between an associative array and normal array?
15. What PHP expression will retrieve the value of the query parameter named **address**? How can you check to see whether the user has checked a checkbox for a parameter named **vegetarian**?
16. Assume that the user has submitted a name with a query parameter of **name**, and an age with a parameter of **age**. Write PHP code to process this and display a message such as: "Hello Jim, you are 47. That is old!" or, "Hello Suzy, you are 19. What a whipper-snapper!"
17. What superglobal array contains information about uploaded files? What code would grab an uploaded file from a query parameter **turnin** and save it to a filename of **hw/HW1.java**?
18. What code would ensure that the previous problem's uploaded file would only be accepted if it had a file name that ends with **.java** and a file size of at least 256 bytes?

## 6.5  Case Study: Vocab Quiz

In this section we'll build a larger program for quizzing the user about GRE vocabulary words. This program bears some similarity to the Word of the Day case study from the previous chapter. We'll use the same `words.txt` file of words and definitions, only this time rather than simply showing the user a random word and its definition, we'll choose a random word and present the user with 5 random definitions and ask them to guess which one is right. Once the user submits his/her answer, we'll tell whether it was right or wrong and ask another question. The page will keep track of how many questions the user has answered and how many were correct. Figure 6.5 shows the desired appearance of the page.

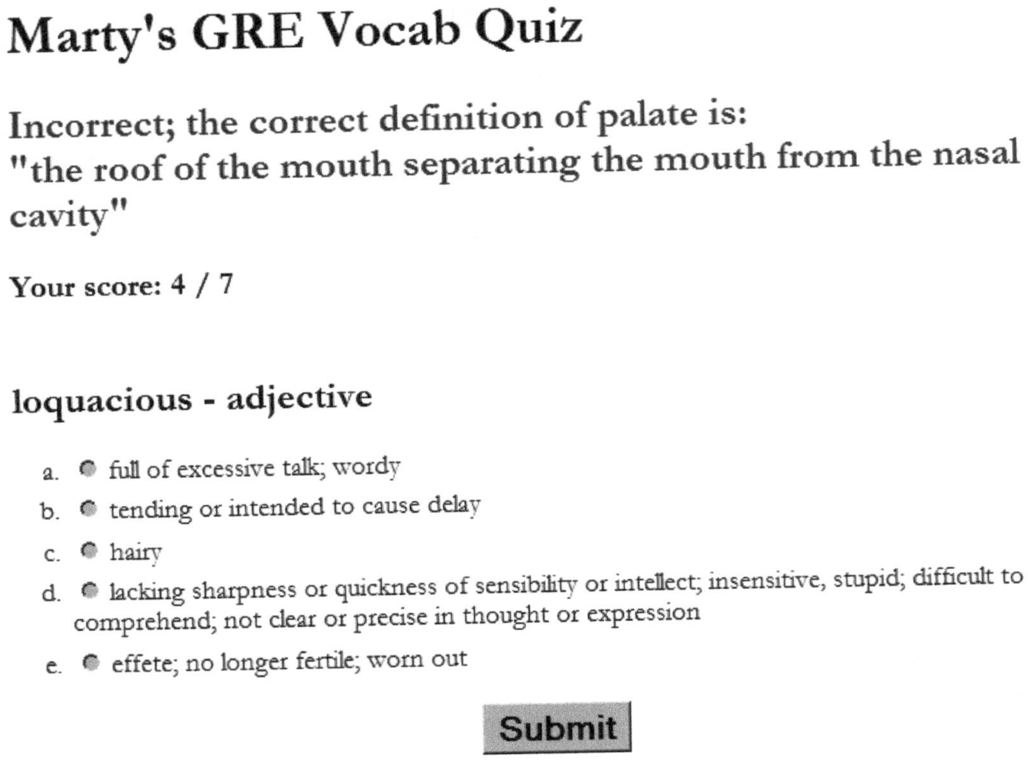

# Marty's GRE Vocab Quiz

**Incorrect; the correct definition of palate is: "the roof of the mouth separating the mouth from the nasal cavity"**

**Your score: 4 / 7**

## loquacious - adjective

    a.   ● full of excessive talk; wordy

    b.   ● tending or intended to cause delay

    c.   ● hairy

    d.   ● lacking sharpness or quickness of sensibility or intellect; insensitive, stupid; difficult to comprehend; not clear or precise in thought or expression

    e.   ● effete; no longer fertile; worn out

**Submit**

**Figure 6.5 Desired vocab quiz page appearance**

A complex page like this is best completed in stages. Here is a suggested ordering for us to approach this problem step-by-step:

1. Write the PHP code for randomly choosing a part of speech (noun, verb, or adjective) and then randomly grabbing 5 words from the file that use that part of speech.
2. Display the 5 words on the HTML page for the user to choose from.
3. Add HTML code so that the user can submit a guess for the correct definition.
4. Write PHP code to process submitted guesses so that the server can recognize whether the guess is correct.
5. Enhance our code to keep score of how many answers are correct and incorrect.

## 6.5.1 Selecting Random Words

In order to quiz the user, we'll need to be able to select 5 random words from the file to display on the page. We should probably pick 5 words that use the same part of speech (all adjectives, all nouns, etc.), so that it isn't easy for the user to eliminate a definition that way. So our algorithm should choose a random part of speech, open the input file, and repeatedly grab lines until it has chosen 5 that share that same part of speech.

### Choosing a Random Part of Speech

Let's assume that each word in our vocabulary quiz input file is either a noun, verb, or adjective. So we simply need to choose one of those three strings at random. An easy way to randomly choose an element from an array is to shuffle the order of the array's elements and then grab the last element. We can randomize an array using PHP's shuffle function and grab the last element using the array_pop function, like so:

```
$parts_of_speech = array("noun", "verb", "adjective");
shuffle($parts_of_speech);
$answer_part = array_pop($parts_of_speech);
```

### Reading 5 Random Words from the Input File

Now it's time to open the file, read its lines, and choose 5 random lines that use this part of speech. We already saw some similar code in the previous PHP chapter's case study; you may want to go back and review it. Recall that the file contains lines consisting of a word, its part of speech, and its definition, separated by tabs. Example 6.38 shows an excerpt from the input file, words.txt.

```
prothalamion    noun        a song in celebration of a marriage
atrabilious     adjective   given to or marked by melancholy; GLOOMY
souse           verb        pickle
pyrrhic         adjective   costly to the point of negating benefits
```

**Example 6.38 Excerpt from input file words.txt**

We'll open the file and split it into its lines using the **file** function. We can use the same **shuffle** technique shown above to randomly reorder the lines. As we look at each line, we'll split it into its three tokens (word, part of speech, definition) using the **explode** function. If the current line has the right part of speech, we'll add it to the end of an array until we have found 5 legal choices.

All of this I/O code can be wrapped into a function that accepts the input file name as a parameter. Example 6.39 shows the complete function.

```php
function read_words($filename) {
  $parts_of_speech = array("noun", "verb", "adjective");
  shuffle($parts_of_speech);
  $answer_part = array_pop($parts_of_speech);

  $lines = file($filename);
  shuffle($lines);

  $choices = array();
  while (count($choices) < 5) {
    $line = array_pop($lines);
    list($word, $part, $defn) = explode("\t", $line);

    if ($part == $answer_part) {
      $choices[] = $line;
    }
  }
  return $choices;
}
```

**Example 6.39 Function to choose 5 random words from input file**

### Displaying 5 Random Definitions on the Page

Now let's write the HTML to display the page; this code will call the **read_words** function we just wrote. The method will return to us an array of the 5 lines containing 5 suitable words to show on the page. We'll create an unordered list (**ul**) and use a **foreach** loop to display each of the 5 definitions in its own **li** as a radio button. Since these radio buttons will eventually be part of a form the user submits, we'll label them with a query parameter name of **guess**. We will use PHP expression blocks between **<?=** and **?>** to inject each word's definition onto the page.

Recall from earlier in this chapter that the **value** attribute is especially relevant when placing radio buttons into forms. If we don't set a unique **value** for each of the 5 choices, the server won't be able to tell which choice the user made. The simplest solution is to take the text of each definition and make that the **value**. We can get away with this because the definitions don't have special characters like quotation marks or **<** signs in them. (If they did contain such characters, we'd have to remove them with PHP's **htmlspecialchars** function.) Here is the code in question:

```php
<ul>
  <?php
  $choices = read_words("words.txt");
  foreach ($choices as $line) {
    list($word, $part, $defn) = explode("\t", $line);
  ?>
    <li><label>
      <input type="radio" name="guess" value="<?= $defn ?>" />
      <?= $defn ?>
    </label></li>
    <?php
  }
  ?>
</ul>
```

We also need a way to decide which of the 5 randomly chosen words to present to the user. Any of the five returned from **read_words** will do, so let's randomly pick one using the **rand** function:

```
$answer_index = rand(0, count($choices) - 1);
list($answer, $part, $defn) = explode("\t", $choices[$answer_index]);
```

Let's inject this code into the context of a larger HTML page. The page will show its title as an h1, the word to guess and its part of speech in an h2, the list of 5 choices inside a **form**, along with a Submit button. The form will submit back to the same page itself. Example 6.40 shows the code.

```html
<!DOCTYPE html PUBLIC "-//W3C//DTD XHTML 1.1//EN"
    "http://www.w3.org/TR/xhtml11/DTD/xhtml11.dtd">
<html xmlns="http://www.w3.org/1999/xhtml">
  <head>
    <title>GRE Vocab Quiz</title>
    <link href="quiz.css" type="text/css" rel="stylesheet" />
  </head>
  <body>
    <h1>Marty's GRE Vocab Quiz</h1>

    <?php
    $choices = read_words("words.txt");
    $answer_index = rand(0, count($choices) - 1);
    list($answer, $part, $defn) = explode("\t", $choices[$answer_index]);
    ?>

    <h2><?= $answer ?> - <?= $part ?></h2>
    <form action="quiz.php" method="post">
      <ul id="choices">
        <?php
        foreach ($choices as $line) {
          list($word, $part, $defn) = explode("\t", $line);
          ?>
          <li><label>
              <input type="radio" name="guess" value="<?= $defn ?>" />
              <?= $defn ?> </label></li>
          <?php
        }
        ?>
      </ul>
      <div><input type="submit" value="Submit" /></div>
    </form>
  </body>
</html>
```

**Example 6.40 HTML to display 5 random words in a form**

The form is submitting new data to the server, which is why a request method of **post** is appropriate for this form. The HTML code in Example 6.40 produces a page that looks pretty close to what we want. Figure 6.6 shows the output so far. We've also applied a bit of CSS to the page that is largely straightforward, including an attribute selector for **input[type="submit"]** to make the Submit button's text bigger and bolder so it's easier to click.

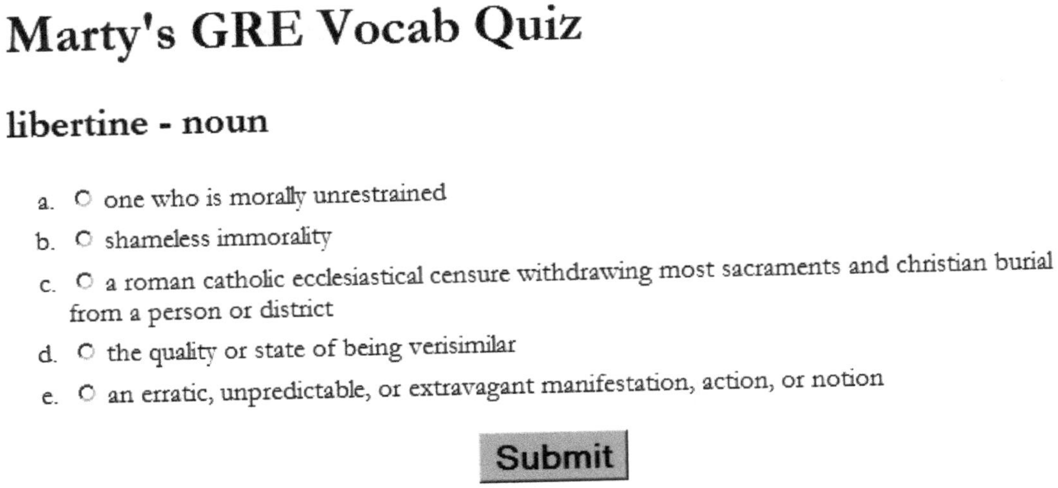

# Marty's GRE Vocab Quiz

## libertine - noun

a.  ○ one who is morally unrestrained

b.  ○ shameless immorality

c.  ○ a roman catholic ecclesiastical censure withdrawing most sacraments and christian burial from a person or district

d.  ○ the quality or state of being verisimilar

e.  ○ an erratic, unpredictable, or extravagant manifestation, action, or notion

**Submit**

**Figure 6.6 Initial vocab quiz appearance**

## 6.5.2 Submitting Guesses

As we saw in this chapter, form query parameters are accessible in PHP through the superglobal $_REQUEST associative array. So if the user saw the screen in Figure 6.6 and chose option "b", the element $_REQUEST["guess"] would have a value of "shameless immorality".

Now we need to think about things from the server's perspective. The page will need to be usable in two ways: The initial visit, matching what we've already written, where a random word should be chosen and 5 random definitions presented for it; and the response to form posts, which includes the previous contents plus a display of whether the user guessed the last word correctly.

Right now our code is submitting only the guess, such as "shameless immorality" in the previous example. But if all it has to go on is the guess, the server isn't going to be able to tell whether we got the word right or not. Remember that web requests are stateless, so the server won't remember what word it was we were trying to guess unless we remind it. The server is also going to need to know how many words we've guessed total so far, and how many we have guessed correctly.

### Query Parameters for Word, Correct, and Total

To provide this information to the server, we'll need additional form query parameters. We'll add a parameter named **word** for the word the user is guessing, as well as parameters named **total** and **correct** for the total words guessed and correct guesses respectively. But we don't want these parameters to appear on the page visible to the user, and we especially don't want the user to change their values. Therefore the best choice to represent them is to use hidden input tags. Assuming we'll end up with variables named $total and $correct for the totals, the tags will look like this:

```
<input type="hidden" name="word" value="<?= $answer ?>" />
<input type="hidden" name="total" value="<?= $total ?>" />
<input type="hidden" name="correct" value="<?= $correct ?>" />
```

Now when the user submits a guess, the contents of $_REQUEST will look more like this:

```
Array
(
    [guess] => full of excessive talk; wordy
    [word] => loquacious
    [total] => 0
    [correct] => 0
)
```

So as we said, the page now operates in two modes: The mode where the user has submitted a guess and we need to see if it's right, and the mode where the user has just arrived on the page. To tell which mode we're in, we'll examine the contents of **$_REQUEST**. If it has elements in it for the query parameters we expect, this must be a post of a guess. If one of the parameters exists, we'll unpack the contents of **$_REQUEST** into variables for further processing.

```
$correct = 0;
$total = 0;
if (isset($_REQUEST["guess"])) {
  # a form post
  $answer = $_REQUEST["word"];
  $guess = $_REQUEST["guess"];
  $correct = $_REQUEST["correct"];
  $total = $_REQUEST["total"];
  $total++;   # because the user has now answered one more question
  ...
}
```

## Checking Whether the User's Guess is Correct

Now that we have the information from the post, we must see whether the user's guess was correct. To do this, we'll need to open the input file and find the line for the word the user is guessing, and compare the word's actual definition to the user's guess. If they match, we'll give the user a point and display a "Correct" message. If not, we'll display an "Incorrect" message and tell the user the correct definition as found in the line of the file. One quirk here is that the **file** function leaves the \n characters at the ends of each line, which can mess up our comparisons of guesses to line definitions, so we'll remove any potential stray whitespace by calling **trim** on each line before we **explode** it.

To help us do this, let's write a function **get_definition** that searches the file for the line containing a particular word and returns the definition of that word:

```
function get_definition($answer, $filename) {
  foreach (file($filename) as $line) {
    list($word, $part, $defn) = explode("\t", trim($line));
    if ($answer == $word) {
      return $defn;
    }
  }
  return NULL;  # word not found; should not ever get here
}
```

Now we can write code in the page that uses **get_definition** to check whether the user guessed correctly or incorrectly.

```php
$defn = get_definition($answer, $FILENAME);
if ($defn == $guess) {    # user guessed definition correctly
  $correct++;
?>
  <h2>Correct!</h2>
<?php
} else {
?>
  <h2>Incorrect; the correct definition was:<br /> "<?= $defn ?>"</h2>
<?php
}
```

After all of the preceding processing, we know everything we need to know about the user's guess, total guesses, and number of correct guesses. We can display these in a heading on the page:

```html
<h3>Your score: <?= $correct ?> / <?= $total ?></h3>
```

### 6.5.3 Final File Contents

After all of the changes in the preceding sections, the complete code for `quiz.php` and `quiz.css` are shown in Example 6.41 and Example 6.42 respectively.

```html
<!DOCTYPE html PUBLIC "-//W3C//DTD XHTML 1.1//EN"
    "http://www.w3.org/TR/xhtml11/DTD/xhtml11.dtd">
<html xmlns="http://www.w3.org/1999/xhtml">
  <head>
    <title>GRE Vocab Quiz</title>
    <link href="quiz.css" type="text/css" rel="stylesheet" />
  </head>

  <body>
    <h1>Marty's GRE Vocab Quiz</h1>

    <?php
    $FILENAME = "words.txt";
    $correct = 0;
    $total = 0;

    if (isset($_REQUEST["guess"])) {
      $answer = $_REQUEST["word"];
      $guess = $_REQUEST["guess"];
      $correct = $_REQUEST["correct"];
      $total = $_REQUEST["total"];
      $total++;

      $defn = get_definition($answer, $FILENAME);
      if ($defn == $guess) {   # user guessed definition correctly
        $correct++;
      ?>

        <h2 class="correct">Correct!</h2>
```

```php
      <?php
    } else {
      ?>

      <h2 class="incorrect">
        Incorrect; the correct definition was: <br />
        "<?= $defn ?>"
      </h2>

      <?php
    }
    ?>

    <h3>Your score: <?= $correct ?> / <?= $total ?></h3>

    <?php
  }

  $choices = read_words($FILENAME);
  $answer_index = rand(0, count($choices) - 1);
  list($answer, $part, $defn) = explode("\t", $choices[$answer_index]);
  ?>

  <h4><?= $answer ?> - <?= $part ?></h4>

  <form action="quiz.php" method="post">
    <ul id="choices">
      <?php
      foreach ($choices as $line) {
        list($word, $part, $defn) = explode("\t", trim($line));
        ?>

        <li>
          <label>
            <input type="radio" name="guess" value="<?= $defn ?>" />
            <?= $defn ?>
          </label>
        </li>

        <?php
      }
      ?>
    </ul>

    <div>
      <input type="hidden" name="word" value="<?= $answer ?>" />
      <input type="hidden" name="total" value="<?= $total ?>" />
      <input type="hidden" name="correct" value="<?= $correct ?>" />
      <input type="submit" value="Submit" />
    </div>
  </form>
</body>
</html>
```

```php
<?php
# Reads the given file name looking for a line about the given word.
# Returns the definition of that word.
function get_definition($answer, $filename) {
  $lines = file($filename);
  foreach ($lines as $line) {
    list($word, $part, $defn) = explode("\t", trim($line));
    if ($answer == $word) {
      return $defn;
    }
  }
  return NULL;  # word not found; should not ever get here
}

# Reads the given file name and returns an array of 5 randomly
# chosen lines representing 5 words of the same part of speech.
function read_words($filename) {
  $parts_of_speech = array("noun", "verb", "adjective");
  shuffle($parts_of_speech);
  $answer_part = array_pop($parts_of_speech);

  $lines = file($filename);
  shuffle($lines);

  $choices = array();
  while (count($choices) < 5) {
    $line = array_pop($lines);
    list($word, $part, $defn) = explode("\t", $line);

    if ($part == $answer_part) {
      $choices[] = $line;
    }
  }

  return $choices;
}
?>
```

Example 6.41 Final contents of `quiz.php`

```
body {
  background-color: white;
  font-family: Garamond, serif;
  font-size: 14pt;
}


.correct   { color: #00aa00; }
.incorrect { color: #aa0000; }

div { text-align: center; }
h1  { margin-top: 0em; }

h4 {
  font-size: 20pt;
  margin-bottom: 0em;
  margin-top: 2em;
}

input[type="submit"] {
  font-size: 18pt;
  font-weight: bold;
}

ul#choices {
  list-style-type: lower-alpha;
}

ul#choices li {
  font-size: 14pt;
  padding-bottom: 0.2em;
  padding-top: 0.2em;
}
```

**Example 6.42 Final contents of `quiz.css`**

## Chapter Summary

- An HTML form is a group of UI controls on a web page that allows a user to submit information to a web server.
- Information is sent to a server through text at the end of a URL, called a query string.
- HTML has elements for creating user interface controls, such as **select** and **textarea**.
- The **input** tag is used to make many controls such as check boxes, radio buttons, and text boxes, depending on the **type** attribute given inside the tag.
- Controls can be grouped inside a **fieldset** with an optional **legend** label.
- Controls can be styled like other elements using CSS, often by placing **id** or **class** attributes on the controls. CSS attribute selectors can help you to select specific form controls.
- Query parameters must be URL-encoded to make sure that special characters in a URL are not misinterpreted.
- Form data can be sent in two ways in HTTP: a GET request, which encodes the form parameters into the request URL; and a POST request, which places the form parameters into the request's data packet.

- PHP has associative arrays, whose indexes can be non-integer values. There is a special set of useful associative arrays called superglobals that can be accessed anywhere in your code.
- Form data can be processed in PHP by examining the contents of the superglobal $_REQUEST array. Information about uploaded files is stored in the $_FILES array.

## References

- W3C XHTML Controls:           http://www.w3.org/TR/html4/interact/forms.html
- W3Schools HTML forms tutorial    http://www.w3schools.com/html/html_forms.asp
- EchoEcho.com UI controls tutorial:   http://www.echoecho.com/htmlforms04.htm
- Browser Compatibility and Styling Form Controls:
    a) http://www.456bereastreet.com/archive/200409/styling_form_controls/
- List of character URL-encodings:
    b) http://www.w3schools.com/TAGS/ref_urlencode.asp
- PHP superglobals:           http://www.php.net/manual/en/reserved.variables.php
- Styling and laying out forms:    http://www.quirksmode.org/css/forms.html
- CSS fun with forms:        http://www.picment.com/articles/css/funwithforms/
- Fancy form design using CSS:   http://www.sitepoint.com/article/fancy-form-design-css/
- PHP handling file uploads:     http://www.php.net/features.file-upload

# Chapter 7  JavaScript for Interactive Web Pages

# Introduction

So far we have seen how to make web pages programmable on the server-side. Though server-side programming is very powerful, its power ends when the page is sent from the server to the browser. Once the browser renders the page, it is static and rigid.

This chapter begins our discussion of how to program web pages on the client side, creating elements and controls that react when users interact with them. The programming language we'll use to implement dynamic client-side interfaces is called JavaScript. Most of the complex web user interfaces you've interacted with are full of Java-Script code that makes the page respond interactively to your behavior and actions.

JavaScript is a much-maligned but very powerful language that, when used properly, can be both elegant and pleasant to work with. We will discuss basic JavaScript syntax as compared to that of other languages you may have learned such as Java or C.

A key aspect of JavaScript code is its ability to interact with the content of a web page and change that content in response to user actions. To this end we'll learn a bit about the Document Object Model (DOM) that gives us programmatic access to the elements of a web page so that we can manipulate those elements' content. We will also introduce you to some useful tools for debugging JavaScript code.

This book gives an introduction to the language. If you want to learn JavaScript at a more expert level, we recommend Douglas Crockford's excellent book, *JavaScript: The Good Parts*.

## 7.1 Key JavaScript Concepts

*JavaScript* is a lightweight, dynamic scripting language that is most often used to make web pages interactive. Some of the things JavaScript allows you to do are:

- insert dynamic text into HTML (e.g., a user's name),
- react to events (e.g., when the user clicks a button),
- get information about a user's computer (e.g., browser type), and
- perform calculations on user's computer (e.g., make sure a date the user entered is valid).

JavaScript is actually an implementation of a web standard called *ECMAScript*. Technically speaking, JavaScript is Netscape's dialect of ECMAScript. Netscape was the first to develop JavaScript as a scripting language for their browsers. The second-most popular dialect is that used in Microsoft Internet Explorer, called JScript. Unfortunately, as with most of the web languages we are learning, JavaScript is not supported identically by all browsers. We'll have to take special care to make our scripts cross-browser compatible (and, in some cases, ignore browsers that misbehave such as IE6).

**Figure 7.1 JavaScript's design philosophy**

Since we assume in this textbook that you've learned a similar language before, we will move quickly through JavaScript's syntax in this chapter except where it differs noticeably from what you've probably seen before. Our overall impression of JavaScript is that it's essentially a "hippy" version of Java where much of the syntax and rules are relaxed. (JavaScript's name makes it sound like it must be related to Java, but the two are unrelated other than some syntactic similarities.) Like PHP, JavaScript has much more relaxed syntax than Java and C. It has loose data types, variables don't need to be declared, and errors are often silent. The key construct in JavaScript is the function, but JavaScript is a powerful object-oriented language at its heart.

In the following sections we'll discuss some important background concepts about when and how JavaScript programs run and how JavaScript code interacts with web pages.

### 7.1.1 Client-Side Scripting

The key difference between JavaScript code and server-side code is where and when the code runs. Server-side code (such as PHP or JSP code) runs on the web server before the page is sent to the user's browser. Server-side code might be used to help create the page and put text into it. JavaScript code runs inside the user's web browser when the page arrives and is displayed. JavaScript code allows you to make the page behave interactively without having to send any information back to the web server. For example, using JavaScript you can pop up a message box when the user clicks a button, or turn text red when it is misspelled, or make a section of text blink or animate in response to mouse clicks.

Like with PHP code, JavaScript source code is translated and executed dynamically, or *interpreted*, on the fly as each statement runs. But while PHP runs on a web server before a page is sent to the user, JavaScript code runs on the user's computer in the web browser after the page arrives. Figure 7.2 shows the overall flow of requests, responses, and code executing. Notice that any JavaScript code executes last, after the page is requested, retrieved by the web server (possibly using a server-side language such as PHP to construct the page), and sent back to the browser.

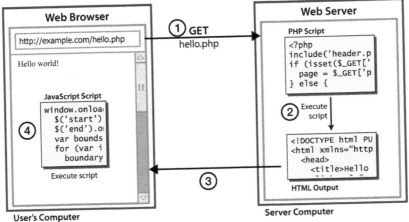

**Figure 7.2 JavaScript code running in web browser**

| client-side scripting |
| --- |
| Writing programs (such as JavaScript files) that run in a user's web browser. |

Rather than running as a stand-alone program, JavaScript code is contained within a web page and integrates with that page's HTML and CSS content. Since it runs in a user's (the client's) web browser, we sometimes refer to JavaScript programming as *client-side scripting*. As we'll discuss in a moment, most of this code consists of specifying code to run when the user interacts with the page in various ways. For example, you could write JavaScript code to turn a paragraph blue when the user clicks a button on the page.

Client-side scripting is important because there are things that can be done in a client-side script that cannot be done on the server side. Only on the client are we able to examine the user's interactions with the web page and directly respond to them. For example, when the user clicks various elements or types text into the page, client-side code can be used to respond to these actions, such as by popping up message boxes or changing the page's text and styles. It would be impossible to write programs of that nature in a language like PHP because PHP code doesn't interact with the browser. The server's PHP code is finished running once it builds and sends the page to the client's browser.

## 7.1.2 Event-Driven Programming

So JavaScript code runs in a browser. But what does the code look like? When and how does it execute? What kind of statements do we execute in a JavaScript program? Before we jump into the details of JavaScript syntax, we need to understand the programming model that JavaScript uses to make web pages interactive: event-driven programming.

| event |
| --- |
| A user action such as clicking on a button, checking a checkbox, or typing text into a text field. |

Many people begin learning how to program in a language that uses a sequential or procedural programming model, where a particular entry point of code (often called **main**) is called to begin the program's execution. Sequential programs run one statement after another from main until completion. The flow of execution is driven by main and by the statements and calls made there.

In JavaScript programs, the flow of execution is instead determined by the user. In an *event-driven program*, the program waits for a user interaction like a key press or button click. These interactions are called *events*. We can write code to respond to various events as the user generates them. To respond to events, we write a JavaScript function and attach it to a control so that the function will be called when an event occurs. Such a function is called an *event handler*. Figure 7.3 summarizes the flow of execution in an event-driven program, from the user interacting with a control on a page to an event occurring and the response to the event being executed.

> **event-driven programming**
>
> Writing programs whose execution is driven by events and user interaction, rather than by an overall "main" function that runs all the others.

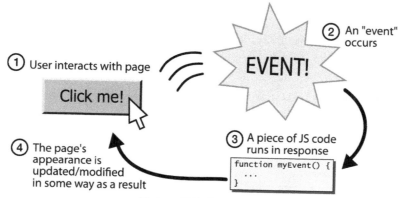

**Figure 7.3 An event**

To respond to an event in JavaScript, we use the following steps:

1. decide which element or control we want to respond to
2. write a JavaScript function with the code we want to run
3. attach that function to the control's event

> **event handler**
>
> A piece of code (in JavaScript, a function) that runs when an event occurs.

In the Forms chapter we discussed the HTML UI controls such as buttons and checkboxes. JavaScript code is often attached to such controls to respond when the user clicks or types on them.

One more key question remains: What should the function do when it is called? Generally event handler functions cause some sort of change to be made to the web page, such as changing text on the page, dynamically adjusting styles of elements on the page (turning a paragraph red, for example), or adding/removing content from the page. We'll tackle this a bit later in the chapter when we discuss the "DOM" of a page. For now, let's explore a simpler example that uses JavaScript to handle an event by displaying a message box.

## 7.1.3 A JavaScript Program

Suppose we want to make a page with a button that will cause some code to run when it is clicked. Following the steps listed above, in this section we'll create our page with a button, write a JavaScript function to run when the button is clicked, and attach the function to the button so that it will be executed.

### Step 1: Creating the HTML Control

In the Forms chapter, we talked about using the **input** tag to create submit and reset buttons for forms. There is also a **button** HTML tag for times when you just want a button on your page that is unrelated to any form.

| Element | button |
|---|---|
| Description | A clickable button (inline) |
| Syntax | `<button>`**text/images**`</button>` |

A `button` element can be styled and customized in many ways. For example, it can have an `img` inside to place an icon on it, or it can use a large bold font or a padding to make it bigger, more visible, and easier to click. For our page, let's just make a simple button with some text on it, like the one shown in Example 7.1.

```
<!DOCTYPE html PUBLIC "-//W3C//DTD XHTML 1.1//EN"
    "http://www.w3.org/TR/xhtml11/DTD/xhtml11.dtd">
<html xmlns="http://www.w3.org/1999/xhtml">
  <head><title>JavaScript example</title></head>
  <body>
    <div>
      <button>Say the Magic Word</button>
    </div>
  </body>
</html>
```

`Say the Magic Word`

**Example 7.1 Page with button**

## Step 2: Write JavaScript Event-Handling Function

Right now, nothing would happen if we were to click our button, because we haven't specified any action to take. Let's make it so that when the user clicks the button, a message box pops up saying, "PLEASE!"

To do this, we will need to create a JavaScript (`.js`) file and link it to our page. The `.js` file will contain a function to execute when the button is clicked. A function consists of the keyword `function`, a name, parentheses containing any parameters, and a body between braces. Example 7.2 lists the complete contents of our file, which we'll save as `please.js`. We will place this file in the same folder on our disk as the .html page file.

```
function sayMagicWord() {
  alert("PLEASE!");
}
```

**Example 7.2 JavaScript file `please.js`**

In our `sayMagicWord` function we use a built-in JavaScript command named `alert`. Calling alert causes the browser to show a pop-up message dialog box.

| Function | `alert("`**message**`")` |
|---|---|
| Description | Shows **"message"** to user in a pop-up dialog box |

At this point, if the user views our web page and clicks the button, it still does nothing. We have not attached the .js file to the .html page, nor have we told the browser to execute our `sayMagicWord` function. We have only declared it.

### Step 3: Attach Event Handler to Control

Now that we've written our JavaScript code, we need to connect it to our page. There are two changes that must be made. First, we must place a `script` tag in the HTML header to tell the page to load our script code. This is analogous to using a `link` tag to include a CSS file.

| Element | script |
|---|---|
| Description | Defines or links to a script |
| Syntax | `<script src="URL" type="text/javascript"></script>` |

In this case, the script is saved into a file named `please.js`, so we would place the following text in our page's header:

```
<script src="please.js" type="text/javascript"></script>
```

Unlike the `link` tag, the `script` tag unfortunately isn't self-closing. You must include a separate `</script>` tag to end your script.

There's one more thing we need to do. We must attach our `sayMagicWord` function so it will be called when the user clicks the button. There are several ways to do this. The most stylistically pure way to attach an event handler is a bit complicated, so we'll discuss it in the next chapter. For now, we'll use a simpler way that is easier to understand.

Every HTML element has special *event attributes* that represent actions you can perform on it, such as clicking, moving the mouse, pressing keyboard keys, and so on. The attributes' names all begin with `on`, such as `onclick`, `onkeydown`, `onchange`, and `onsubmit`. To listen to an event on an element, you set a value for one of the element's event attributes. Example 7.3 shows the general syntax for attaching an event handler in this way.

```
<element onevent="functionName();"> ... </element>
```
**Example 7.3 Syntax template for attaching an HTML event handler**

For example, to listen to clicks on a button, set its `onclick` attribute to the JavaScript function you want to run when it is clicked. Example 7.4 shows the complete page that links to the JavaScript file and attaches an `onclick` event handler to its button. When the user clicks the "Say the Magic Word" button, the browser calls our `sayMagicWord` JavaScript function. The box that pops up is shown in Figure 7.4.

```
<!DOCTYPE html PUBLIC "-//W3C//DTD XHTML 1.1//EN"
    "http://www.w3.org/TR/xhtml11/DTD/xhtml11.dtd">
<html xmlns="http://www.w3.org/1999/xhtml">
  <head>
    <title>JavaScript example</title>
    <script src="please.js" type="text/javascript"></script>
  </head>
  <body>
    <div>
      <button onclick="sayMagicWord();">Say the Magic Word</button>
    </div>
  </body>
</html>
```

Say the Magic Word

**Example 7.4 Page with event handler**

**Figure 7.4 Alert box that appears when user clicks button**

Again, it's important to understand when our JavaScript code executes. The `sayMagicWord` function doesn't run when the page first loads up. The page sits and waits for the user to interact with the page, and only in response to user interaction (events) does JavaScript code become invoked. Getting used to this kind of event-driven programming model is a major step toward becoming a skilled JavaScript programmer.

## 7.1.4 The Document Object Model (DOM)

The `alert` in our previous example is probably the simplest statement that produces a visible output. But in most situations users prefer when the response to their action appears within the web page itself, such as new text on the page, altered styles of the page's elements, or added content on the page. In order to produce effects like these, we must learn the basics of how a JavaScript program interacts with a web page's content.

| Document Object Model (DOM) |
|---|
| A set of JavaScript objects representing the content of the current HTML page. |

JavaScript has a set of objects and functions that allow us to access and modify the content of the current web page. Each tag on the page (such as a paragraph, heading, or list item) is represented as an object. This set of objects is collectively referred to as the *Document Object Model*, or *DOM*. Interacting with DOM objects in your JavaScript code allows you to dynamically manipulate the web page's appearance on the screen.

Figure 7.5 shows a piece of HTML code and a diagram of its corresponding DOM element object.

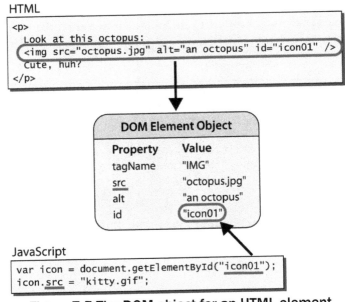

**Figure 7.5 The DOM object for an HTML element**

The Document Object Model acts as the glue between web page content and JavaScript. We will use it to create dynamic and interactive web pages.

### Accessing DOM Objects by ID

DOM objects can be accessed in several ways. The simplest way to get a DOM object is to ask for it by specifying the element's **id** attribute. Once our code has access to such an object, we can send commands to it, such as:

- Capitalize the text inside this element.
- Set the element's **background-color** style to **yellow**.
- For each tag inside of this element, clear out that tag's text content.
- Add a new **li** item inside of this list element.

The DOM exposes some global JavaScript objects that allow you to access the elements of the current web page. One of these is the **document** object. The **document** object represents the entire HTML document and is used to access all of the other DOM objects representing each page element.

The **document** object has a **getElementById** method that accepts an **id** string as a parameter and returns the DOM object for the HTML element with that **id**. If no element with the specified **id** is found, **null** is returned. The syntax of the method is shown in Example 7.5. (Recall that a *method* is a function that exists inside of an object.)

```
var name = document.getElementById("id of desired element");
```

**Example 7.5 Syntax template for getting a DOM object by ID**

Suppose we want to change the code from Example 7.4 so that the magic word of "PLEASE!" will display in the page rather than popping up as an **alert**. In the code, the **button's onclick** attribute has specified to call the **sayMagicWord** function when clicked. Let's make two changes to this program. First, let's add a paragraph to the HTML with an **id** of **result** with some initial text in it. When the user clicks the button, we want the paragraph's text to change to "PLEASE!" Example 7.6 shows the modification to the HTML.

```
<button onclick="sayMagicWord();">Say the Magic Word</button>
<p id="result">What do you say?</p>
```

Say the Magic Word

What do you say?

**Example 7.6 Modified page code with paragraph**

Now we'll have to make some changes to our JavaScript code to achieve the desired behavior. (There's a bit of new syntax in this example that we'll explain later in this chapter.) The first line of the new **sayMagicWord** function body calls the **document.getElementById** method to access the DOM object representing our newly added **result** paragraph. This DOM object is stored as a variable named **paragraph**. The second line accesses the **paragraph** object's **innerHTML** property (which represents the text or HTML content inside an element) and sets it to be **"PLEASE!"** The result is that when the "Say the Magic Word" button is clicked, the text of the paragraph on the page changes from "What do you say?" to "PLEASE!" Example 7.7 shows the code and resulting page appearance after the button is clicked.

```
function sayMagicWord() {
  var paragraph = document.getElementById("result");
  paragraph.innerHTML = "PLEASE!";
}
```

Say the Magic Word

PLEASE!

**Example 7.7** Modified `sayMagicWord` function and resulting click behavior

It's important to understand that the above code does not permanently modify the web page. If some other user visits the page later, or if you refresh the page, the paragraph will go back to its original message of "What do you say?" The changes made to the page using the DOM affect only what the current user sees in the browser on that viewing of the page. If we want to make more permanent changes to page content, we'll have to learn more about JavaScript and Ajax in subsequent chapters.

There are ways to access and manipulate DOM elements other than by **id**. We will explore this in much more detail in the next chapter. For now, `document.getElementById` is our choice.

## Self-Check

1. When and where does a JavaScript program execute, as opposed to a PHP program?
2. What is an event? What's the difference between event-driven and normal programming?
3. Write a line of HTML code that attaches a JavaScript file **example.js** to a web page.
4. What does the **alert** JavaScript function do?
5. What is the Document Object Model (DOM)? How can you use the DOM to modify the contents of a web page?

## 7.2 JavaScript Syntax

Now that we have seen the general idea of how to attach JavaScript code to a web page, in this section we'll explore the syntax of the JavaScript language in much more detail.

### 7.2.1 Types

JavaScript contains eight fundamental types, shown in Table 7.1. We'll discuss most of these in the upcoming sections, saving arrays and objects for a bit later in the chapter.

| Type | Description | Examples |
|------|-------------|----------|
| Number | integer or real number | 42, -17, 3.14, 2.4e-6 |
| Boolean | logical value | true, false |
| String | text string | "Hello there", 'how are you' |
| Array | indexed list of elements | [12, 17, -5, 42] |
| Object | entity containing data and behavior | {name: "Marty", age: 12} |
| function | group of statements to execute | function message() {<br>    alert("Hello, world!");<br>} |
| null | an empty value | null |
| undefined | the lack of a value; an undefined value | undefined |

**Table 7.1 JavaScript's types**

Like PHP and many other web languages, JavaScript is loosely and dynamically typed. This means that you almost never need to specify types in expressions. JavaScript also converts transparently between types as needed in many cases.

### 7.2.2 Numbers and Arithmetic

JavaScript has a single **Number** type to represent both integers and real numbers. One effect of this is that JavaScript (like PHP) always performs real-number division even when dividing two integers. For example, while **7 / 2** is 3 in Java, it is **3.5** in JavaScript. If you're curious, all numbers in JavaScript are internally represented as 64-bit floating-point numbers. Table 7.2 gives several examples of number literals.

| | | |
|---|---|---|
| 3 | 110 | 52 |
| 3.14 | 1042.3567 | 82.4564 |
| .3333333 | 3.1E12 | 2E-12 |

**Table 7.2 Some Number literal values**

There are also several constants in the Number class representing extreme values, such as infinity, and the largest or smallest possible number values, and the special **NaN** value that means "not a number," the result of invalid computations such as **1 / "huh?"**. These constants are listed in Table 7.3. You can test whether a number is **NaN** by passing it to JavaScript's **isNaN** function.

| Constant | Description |
|---|---|
| `Number.MAX_VALUE` | Largest possible finite number value |
| `Number.MIN_VALUE` | Smallest possible finite number value |
| `Number.NaN` (or just `NaN`) | Not a number |
| `Number.NEGATIVE_INFINITY` | Value of out of range of negative numbers |
| `Number.POSITIVE_INFINITY` (or just `Infinity`) | Value of out of range of positive numbers |

Table 7.3 Number constant values

**expression**

A value or set of operations that computes a value.

A JavaScript *expression* is a value or a set of operations that computes a value. The value can be a number, string, or other type. Expressions and operators in JavaScript generally work as they do in other high-level programming languages.

JavaScript supports the expected set of arithmetic operators from other C-like languages. If the two operands supplied are not of **Number** type, JavaScript automatically attempts to convert them into the **Number** type. This most frequently happens when one of the operands is a string. If JavaScript is unable to convert one of the operands into a numerical value, the value **NaN** is the result. JavaScript's arithmetic operators are listed in Table 7.4. Example expressions are shown in Table 7.5.

| Operator | Description |
|---|---|
| + | Addition |
| - | Subtraction, Unary Negation |
| * | Multiplication |
| / | Division |
| % | Modulus |

Table 7.4 Arithmetic operators

| Expression | Result |
|---|---|
| `5 * 8` | `40` |
| `1 + 2.5` | `3.5` |
| `5 / 8` | `0.625` |
| `1 / 0` | `Infinity` |
| `10 / "oops"` | `NaN` |

Table 7.5 Arithmetic expressions

## 7.2.3 Variables

A *variable* in JavaScript is much the same thing as in other high level programming languages: a named piece of memory for storing a value. JavaScript variable names are case-sensitive and can consist of letters, numbers, and underscores, but must start either with a letter or an underscore.

To declare and initialize a variable you begin the declaration with the keyword `var` followed by the variable name, an equals sign, and the value to store in the variable, as shown in Example 7.8. We briefly saw this syntax in our earlier "say please" DOM example.

```
var name = value;
```

**Example 7.8 Syntax template for variable declaration/initialization statement**

Notice that the type of the variable is not specified. Unlike in many other programming languages, in JavaScript variables are *loosely typed*. It's not that the variable has no type; it's that the programmer doesn't have to explicitly say what type it is. JavaScript determines the type dynamically based on the kind of value you assign to the variable.

> **loose typing**
>
> JavaScript's syntax where values do have types, but they do not need to be declared or stated in most code.

The variable declaration and assignment is an example of a JavaScript statement. A *statement* is a single command to be executed, the fundamental unit of execution of most programming languages.

JavaScript statements don't have to end with semicolons; unlike in many other languages, the semicolon is optional. But most JavaScript programmers do include them by convention, and we strongly recommend using them. This is for reasons of familiarity and to avoid subtle bugs that can occur when omitting them. We'll use semicolons after all statements in our examples.

To assign a different value to a variable later, use an assignment statement with the = operator. You don't need to write the word `var` when reassigning the variable a new value, but the code will still work the same if you do write `var`. Example 7.9 shows the syntax for assignment.

```
name = value;
```

**Example 7.9 Syntax template for assignment statement**

In Example 7.10, the variable `theAnswer` is of a different type on each line. On the first line, we assign the variable a value of `Number` type. Then on the second line it is assigned a value of `String` type. This is legal since the type of the variable is bound at assignment, not at declaration.

```
var theAnswer = 42;
theAnswer = "Jessica";
```

**Example 7.10 Variable changing types**

It's also legal to declare a variable without the `var` keyword; this is called an *implicit variable declaration* as opposed to an explicit declaration. We don't recommend implicit declaration because it can make it harder to tell the programmer's intent; did you mean to declare the variable or merely to change its value? Also implicit declarations have different scoping rules in some cases, which we'll discuss later. Example 7.11 demonstrates such a declaration.

> **implicit declaration**
>
> Behavior where a variable can be assigned without having previously declared.

```
var userName1 = "Jessica";
userName2 = "Marty";
```

**Example 7.11 Implicit variable declaration (discouraged)**

In summary, the changes between JavaScript's variables and other languages' are the following:

- JavaScript's variables are loosely typed (and can change types).
- JavaScript variables don't need to be explicitly declared before they are used.

JavaScript has several arithmetic assignment operators that perform an arithmetic operation on a variable and then assign the result back into the variable. These same operators exist in C, C++, and Java. Table 7.6 lists these operators and gives an example of each.

| Operator | Example | Same As |
|----------|---------|---------|
| ++ | x++; | x = x + 1; |
| -- | x--; | x = x - 1; |
| += | x += y; | x = x + y; |
| -= | x -= y; | x = x - y; |
| *= | x *= y; | x = x * y; |
| /= | x /= y; | x = x / y; |
| %= | x %= y; | x = x % y; |

**Table 7.6 Modify-and-assign operators**

## 7.2.4 Comments

JavaScript syntax for comments is identical to C, C++, and Java. Single-line comments begin with //, and multi-line comments are between /* and */. Example 7.12 shows the syntax.

```
// single-line comment

/*
multi-line comment
*/
```

**Example 7.12 Comments**

## 7.2.5 Using DOM Objects

An element's DOM object has properties that the programmer can use to dynamically access and alter page content. Table 7.7 lists some of the most commonly used properties shared by all DOM element objects. Particularly useful will be the **innerHTML** property, which represents the text and/or tags inside the element. We'll use this property in several examples to modify text on the page.

| Property | Type | Description |
|----------|------|-------------|
| className | string | The **class** attribute of the element ("" if no **class** is set) |
| id | string | The **id** attribute of the element (**undefined** if no **id** is set) |
| innerHTML | string | The HTML markup and content inside the element, i.e., between its opening and closing tags ("" if there is no content) |
| style | object | An object representing the element's style attributes |
| tagName | string | The element's HTML tag, in uppercase (such as "DIV") |

**Table 7.7 DOM element properties**

In addition, if the HTML element being represented by the DOM object has any other attributes, those attributes and their values are also represented as properties in the element's DOM object. For example, if an `img` tag has a `src` attribute set to `"dog.gif"`, that element's DOM object will have a `.src` property whose value is `"dog.gif"`. In your JavaScript code you can examine these properties' values or change them to alter the appearance of the page. Most DOM object property names are identical to names of the corresponding attributes in the HTML, with a few notable exceptions such as the `class` HTML attribute that maps to the `className` DOM property. Table 7.8 lists some other properties you may expect to find in various DOM objects.

| Property | Type | Description |
|----------|------|-------------|
| checked | boolean | Whether a checkbox or radio button is checked |
| disabled | boolean | Whether a form control is disabled |
| href | string | Target URL for a link (a) |
| src | string | Source URL for an image (img) |
| value | string | Text inside a form control such as an input or textarea |

Table 7.8 Additional properties of some DOM objects

For example, suppose there is an image on the page that you want to change from displaying a picture of a cat stored in `cat.jpg`, represented by the following HTML code:

```html
<img id="mypet" src="cat.jpg" alt="my favorite pet" />
```

Suppose you want to the image's source URL to instead show an image of a dog stored in `dog.jpg`. Recall that you can access an HTML element's corresponding DOM object by calling `document.getElementById`. Therefore the following JavaScript code would do the trick:

```javascript
var myImage = document.getElementById("mypet");
myImage.src = "dog.jpg";
```

There are a lot more properties inside each DOM object that we will explore in the next chapter, such as properties related to the styling and appearance of the element.

### Example Program: Multiplier

Let's write a page that acts as a simple multiplication calculator. The page will contain two input text boxes. When the user types an integer into each box and presses a Compute button, the numbers will be multiplied and the answer will be shown. Example 7.13 shows the initial HTML code.

```html
<h1>The Amazing Multiplier</h1>
<div>
  <input type="text" size="3" /> * <input type="text" size="3" /> =<br />
  <button>Compute!</button>
</div>
```

# The Amazing Multiplier

[ ] * [ ] =
[Compute!]

Example 7.13 Multiplier initial HTML code

To bring this page to life with JavaScript, we'll first need to link the page to a JavaScript file. This is done by adding a **script** reference to the page's header:

```
<script src="multiply.js" type="text/javascript"></script>
```

In the previous section about the DOM, we saw that JavaScript code can interact with elements on the page. Conceptually what we'd like to do is fetch the integers inside both text boxes, multiply them together, and display the result on the page. To do this, we'll need to access the DOM objects for both text boxes.

Earlier in this chapter we saw that you can access an HTML element's DOM object using the **document.getElementById** method. This means that in order to grab the integers to multiply, we'll need the two **input** elements to have **id** attributes. We will also need a place to display the answer on the page. Let's create an empty **span** with an **id** of **answer** and put the result into that span. Lastly, we want our JavaScript code to run when the Compute button is clicked, so let's add an **onclick** attribute that calls a JavaScript function named **compute** that we'll write in multiply.js.

```
<h1>The Amazing Multiplier</h1>
<div>
  <input id="num1" type="text" size="3" /> *
  <input id="num2" type="text" size="3" /> =
  <span id="answer"></span> <br />
  <button onclick="compute();">Compute!</button>
</div>
```

**Example 7.14 Multiplier improved HTML code**

Now that our HTML page is more JavaScript-friendly, let's write the **compute** function to be called when our button is clicked. We start by retrieving three elements by their ids: the two **input** boxes and the answer **span**. We can grab the text out of an input control by accessing its **value** property, which directly mirrors the **value** attribute in the HTML. Once we've multiplied the two numbers, we can store the result into the answer **span** by setting its **innerHTML** property. Example 7.15 shows the complete code and a screenshot of the appearance after the button is clicked.

```
// Multiplies two numbers typed into input boxes on the page,
// and displays the result in a span on the page.

function compute() {
  var input1 = document.getElementById("num1");   // fetch the 2 numbers
  var input2 = document.getElementById("num2");
  var answer = document.getElementById("answer");
  var result = input1.value * input2.value;       // compute result
  answer.innerHTML = result;
}
```

# The Amazing Multiplier

6  *  7  = 42

Compute!

**Example 7.15 JavaScript multiplier code**

Many students get the `value` and `innerHTML` properties mixed up. It can be a bit confusing that most elements' DOM objects hold their inner content in `innerHTML`, but that controls like text boxes store their values in `value`. The thing to remember is that `innerHTML` is analogous to text between an element's opening and closing tag. An `input` element has no such inner content because it is a self-closing tag. The difference can be summarized by the following example:

```
<div>this is innerHTML inside a div element</div>
<input type="text" value="this is value inside an input element" />
```

## 7.2.6 Debugging Common Errors (a.k.a., "Why Doesn't My Program Do Anything?")

By far, the most common report we hear from students learning JavaScript is, "When I press the button, nothing happens! What's wrong?" Unfortunately, the web browser isn't a very friendly environment for software development. By default if anything is wrong with your JavaScript program, you will see nothing. The browser won't show any error message, and nothing will appear on the page to indicate an error. Nothing will happen, as though you didn't write any JavaScript code at all. New JavaScript programmers can become very frustrated by programs that won't respond and give no hint of what is causing the problem.

There are several reasons a JavaScript program might do nothing. In this section we explore a few of the most common ones and give general tips about how to diagnose the problem.

If you specified the wrong file name in the script tag at the top of your page, the browser will be unable to load your JavaScript code, and no error message will be initially shown. Let's consider our previous Multiplier example. Imagine that the programmer has misspelled the name of the JavaScript file multilpy.js (sic) in the HTML header, as shown in Example 7.16.

**Common Error**

Failing to link to JavaScript file properly

(Fix: Place an **alert** at the top of your .js file as a sanity check, and/or use Firebug)

```
<script src="multilpy.js" type="text/javascript"></script>
```
**Example 7.16 Common error: misspelled script file name**

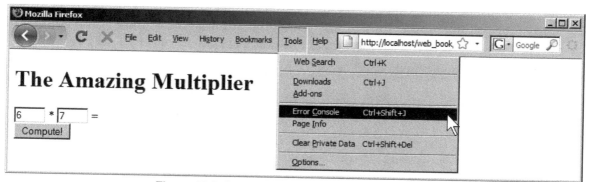

**Figure 7.6 Opening the Firefox Error Console**

The page shows up in the browser without any problems, but when you click the Compute button, nothing happens. No hint of any error is shown. In some browsers, you can view a log of JavaScript errors to help diagnose what is wrong. In Firefox, you can access an Error Console by clicking Tools, Error Console, as shown in Figure 7.6.

After clicking the Compute button error message shows up in our Error Console stating that the `compute` function is not defined, as shown in Figure 7.7. If you install the Firebug add-on for Firefox (which we *highly recommend* when debugging JavaScript programs), the moment you click the Compute button, you will see a red message in the bottom-right of your browser window indicating an error. Clicking this message shows more information about the error, as shown in Figure 7.8.

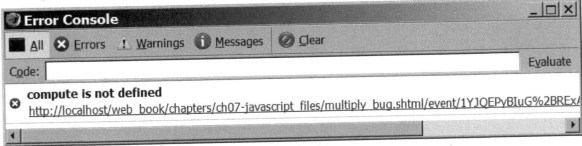

Figure 7.7 Error console displaying an error message

Figure 7.8 Firebug add-on displaying error message

Now that we see this error, we double-check our code and are sure that we defined a function named `compute`. The fact that the browser cannot find this function indicates that it may not be properly finding our JavaScript file. Firebug provides evidence of this if you click its Net tab. This tab shows all of the files the browser has tried to fetch during the loading of the page. As seen in Figure 7.9, the browser got an HTTP 404 error (file not found) when trying to load the script multilpy.js.

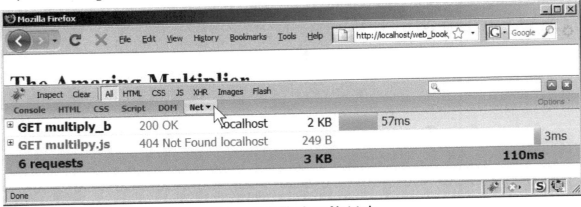

Figure 7.9 Firebug Net tab

Another good sanity check to make sure the browser is loading your file is to insert an `alert` statement at the very top of your file, outside of any function. If the browser loads your .js file, it will immediately show this `alert` message box on the screen. If you don't see the `alert` box, you know that the browser didn't load the script file. Example 7.17 shows an example of this technique and a screenshot of the appearance that would result if the box popped up. The box would not pop up with our buggy code, but once we discover the error, fix it, and reload the page, the `alert` appears.

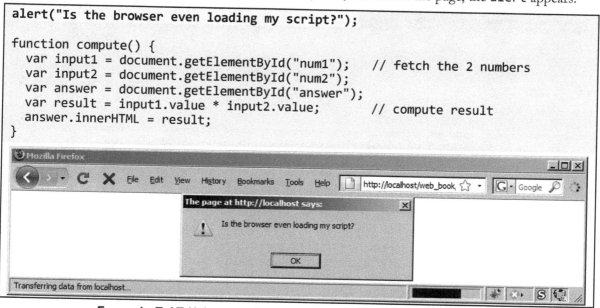

```
alert("Is the browser even loading my script?");

function compute() {
  var input1 = document.getElementById("num1");   // fetch the 2 numbers
  var input2 = document.getElementById("num2");
  var answer = document.getElementById("answer");
  var result = input1.value * input2.value;        // compute result
  answer.innerHTML = result;
}
```

**Example 7.17 Using an `alert` to test whether a script is loaded**

The `alert` trick isn't limited to the top of the file. You can imagine a similar bug where the HTML file misspells the name of the `compute` function we're trying to call, writing it as `copmuet` or similar. In a case like this, we'll again get a message saying that the function is undefined. If you put an `alert` statement at the start of the `compute` function, you'd notice that it was not being called, which should give a strong hint that the page is not correctly naming the function it is trying to call.

Let's examine another error many students make. Recall that our Multiplier page has two input elements with `id`s of `num1` and `num2` into which the user types the two numbers to multiply.

> **Common Error**
>
> Trying to access an undefined object or property
> (Fix: Use Firebug to find the line with an error, and double-check relevant expressions.)

```
<input id="num1" type="text" size="3" /> *
<input id="num2" type="text" size="3" /> =
```

Suppose we have a bug in our JavaScript code where we accidentally try to fetch the DOM objects for these elements using the wrong `id`s (in this case, `number1` and `number2` instead of `num1` and `num2`). Again, when we go to use the web page and click the Compute button, the symptom we get is that nothing happens. Luckily, Firebug again shows the helpful error message to indicate that our page has an error.

Example 7.18 shows the faulty code and the error that shows up in Firebug. The error says that the variable `input1` is `null`. The value `null` is a special empty value returned by some functions to indicate an empty value or an error condition. The `document.getElementById` method returns `null` when there is no element on the page with the `id` specified.

```
function compute() {
  var input1 = document.getElementById("number1");
  var input2 = document.getElementById("number2");
  var answer = document.getElementById("answer");
  var result = input1.value * input2.value;
  answer.innerHTML = result;
}
```

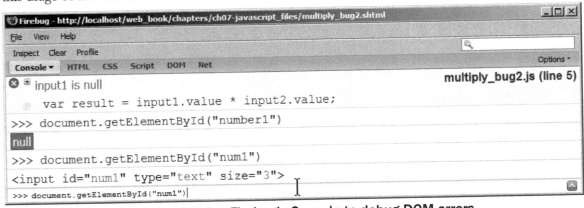

**Example 7.18 Incorrect JavaScript multiplier code (wrong ids)**

A very helpful facility in Firebug is its Console, where you can type in arbitrary JavaScript statements or expressions. The Console will execute the expression or statement and immediately show its result. We encourage our students to try typing in short pieces of their code into this console to see what the results are, in the hope of finding an error. In this case, since the error stated that `input1` was `null`, perhaps we'll decide to double-check the lines of code that fetched `input1`'s value. If you type `document.getElementById("number1")` into the console, it shows `null` as the result. Hopefully at this moment we double-check the HTML and realize our mistake, then try it again in Firebug with `num1` instead of `number1`, and the `input` tag is shown as originally intended. Figure 7.10 shows this usage of the Console.

**Figure 7.10 Using Firebug's Console to debug DOM errors**

Another very useful utility for finding JavaScript errors is JSLint, by Douglas Crockford of Yahoo. JSLint is a web page that attempts to make up for the fact that JavaScript has no compiler by analyzing your JavaScript code and reporting possible errors in it. Its author Douglas Crockford is considered one of the preeminent authorities on JavaScript programming. If your code doesn't work and you're not sure why, you may want to paste it into JSLint at http://www.jslint.com/ and see if any helpful error messages present themselves. Figure 7.11 shows a screenshot of JSLint in action.

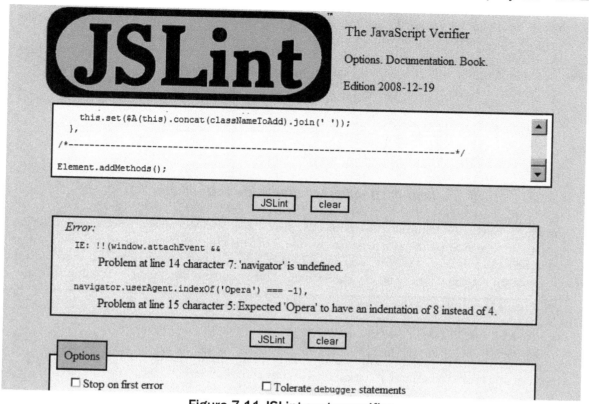

**Figure 7.11 JSLint syntax verifier**

## 7.2.7 Strings

JavaScript strings represent sequences of characters. Unlike C or Java, there is no `char` type to represent individual characters; even a single character is represented as a string.

JavaScript string literals can be specified with either single quotes such as `'Hola'` or double quotes such as `"Salut"`. There is no difference between the two except the fact that if you want an apostrophe inside a single-quoted string, you must escape it as `\'`, while in a double-quoted string if you want a quotation mark you must escape it as `\"`. We generally use double-quoted strings in our examples.

Other special characters within a JavaScript string literal, such as `'` and `"`, can be escaped with a backslash just like in Java and C. Table 7.9 lists the common escape sequences.

| Name | Escape Sequence |
|---|---|
| single quote | `\'` |
| double quote | `\"` |
| backslash | `\\` |
| new line | `\n` |
| horizontal tab | `\t` |

**Table 7.9 Escape sequences**

Strings are *concatenated* (joined together) with the + operator. For example, `"hello" + "there"` produces `"hellothere"`. When you concatenate strings with numbers, JavaScript will convert the numbers to strings as needed. For example, `1 + "2"` produces the string `"12"`. When + operators occur multiple times in the same expression, they are evaluated left to right.

| Expression | Result |
|---|---|
| `1 + "2"` | `"12"` |
| `1 + 3 + "5" + 7 + 9` | `"4579"` |
| `1 + (3 + "5") + (7 + 9)` | `"13516"` |

**Table 7.10 String concatenation and addition**

String concatenation with the + operator can cause some unexpected bugs. For example, let's revisit the multiplier example from a previous section, but let's convert it into an adder. The user will type numbers in two text boxes, and after pressing a button, the two numbers will be added and the result shown on the page. Example 7.19 shows the HTML code, modified from the multiplier code.

```html
<h1>The Amazing Adder</h1>
<div>
  <input id="num1" type="text" size="3" /> +
  <input id="num2" type="text" size="3" /> =
  <span id="answer"></span> <br />
  <button onclick="compute();">Compute!</button>
</div>
```

# The Amazing Adder

[    ] + [    ] =
Compute!

**Example 7.19 Adder HTML code**

One might assume that the only change to be made to the JavaScript code is to replace the * operator with a +, as shown in Example 7.20. But the code doesn't work. As shown in the screenshot, JavaScript appears to have some serious math issues: It reports that 6 plus 7 equals 67!

```javascript
function compute() {
  var input1 = document.getElementById("num1");
  var input2 = document.getElementById("num2");
  var answer = document.getElementById("answer");
  var result = input1.value + input2.value;   // add, not multiply
  answer.innerHTML = result;
}
```

# The Amazing Adder

6 + 7 = 67
Compute!

**Example 7.20 Adder JavaScript code, incorrect version**

The reason the math is incorrect is that JavaScript isn't performing numeric computations at all, but rather string concatenations. The `value` attribute of a DOM object is actually represented as a string. When we write `input1.value + input2.value`, we are actually concatenating the strings `"6" + "7"`, which results in the string `"67"`. You may wonder why we didn't encounter this bug earlier with the similar Amazing Multiplier program. The answer is that JavaScript doesn't have a `*` operator for strings, so when you multiply strings it converts them to numbers, producing the result we wanted. With `+`, JavaScript assumes we want string concatenation, so we're not so lucky.

To get a numeric addition, we'll need to convert these strings into integers. This can be done with JavaScript's `parseInt` function, which accepts a value as a parameter and returns an integer. If the value is a non-numeric string such as `"Jimmy"`, `parseInt` returns NaN.

| Function | parseInt(**value**) | parseFloat(**value**) |
|---|---|---|
| Description | Converts a value into an integer and returns the integer<br><br>(returns **NaN** if the value cannot be converted to an integer) | Converts a value into a real number and returns the number<br><br>(returns **NaN** if the value cannot be converted to a real number) |

The `parseInt` and `parseFloat` functions are able to convert any string into a number so long as its first meaningful characters are numbers. Table 7.11 shows several example calls.

| Expression | Result |
|---|---|
| parseInt("42") | 42 |
| parseInt("12pt font") | 12 |
| parseInt("    4ever young!") | 4 |
| parseInt("") | NaN |
| parseInt("Sacha Baron Cohen") | NaN |
| parseInt("2.56") | 2 |
| parseFloat("2.56") | 2.56 |
| parseFloat("3.14159ppp09348") | 3.14159 |
| parseFloat("0000000000.0000") | 0 |

Table 7.11 Numeric parsing expressions

Armed with this new knowledge, we can correct the error in our adding program. By calling `parseInt` on each of the input box values we retrieve, we will achieve a numeric addition. Example 7.21 shows the code and the resulting behavior in the browser.

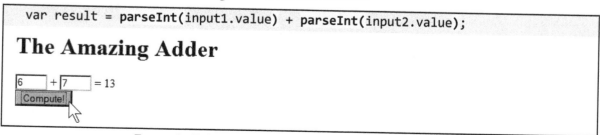

Example 7.21 Adder JavaScript code, correct version

## String Properties and Methods

In JavaScript, every value is also an object, meaning that it may contain properties and methods that you can access in your code. The syntax for accessing properties and methods of objects is the same as Java's and are shown in Example 7.22.

```
object.property
object.method(parameters)
```

**Example 7.22 Syntax template for object properties and methods**

String objects provide a number of useful properties and methods. To find the length of a string, use its `length` property. Empty strings have length 0.

```
var name = "L. Croft";
var len = name.length;      // len = 8
```

**Example 7.23 String `length` property**

In addition to the `length` property, there are a number of methods that the **String** object provides. A subset of these methods is listed in Table 7.12. Several of these methods have optional parameters; in such cases, the Method Name column lists each way of calling the method. The optional parameters may be included if so desired; if omitted, reasonable default values will be chosen.

| Method Name | Description |
|---|---|
| charAt(**index**) | Returns the character at the specified index |
| charCodeAt(**index**) | Returns the ASCII numeric value of a character |
| String.fromCharCode(**value**) | Converts an ASCII numeric value into a string |
| indexOf(**searchStr**)<br>indexOf(**searchStr**, **fromIndex**) | Returns the index within the calling string of the first occurrence of search string, or -1 if not found. Starts at index 0 unless **fromIndex** is specified |
| split(**delimeter**)<br>split(**delimeter**, **howMany**) | Breaks into an array of strings using a delimiter. Returns all matches unless **howMany** is specified |
| substring(**start**)<br>substring(**start**, **stop**) | Returns the characters between two specified indices. Grabs characters until the end of the string unless **stop** is specified |
| toLowerCase() | Returns the calling string converted to lower case |
| toUpperCase() | Returns the calling string converted to uppercase |

**Table 7.12 Useful String methods**

## Example Program: Name Converter

Let's write a small program that uses string methods. This program will allow the user to type his/her name in a (*firstName lastName*) format, then once the user clicks a button, the name will be converted into (*LAST NAME, firstInitial*) format. Example 7.24 shows the relevant HTML code, including an **input** box with an **id** for holding the name, and a button with an **onclick** attribute. The example also shows a screenshot of the page appearance after a name is typed into the box.

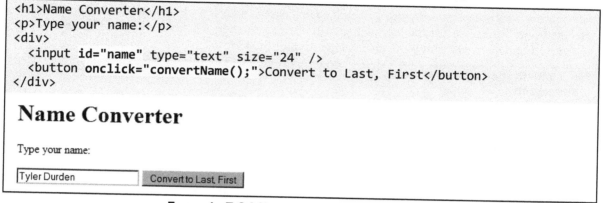

```
<h1>Name Converter</h1>
<p>Type your name:</p>
<div>
  <input id="name" type="text" size="24" />
  <button onclick="convertName();">Convert to Last, First</button>
</div>
```

**Name Converter**

Type your name:

`Tyler Durden`  `Convert to Last, First`

**Example 7.24 Name converter HTML code**

In the JavaScript code we attach to this page, we'll fetch the text from the **name** box and manipulate that text. First we'll split it into a first and last name using the **substring** and **indexOf** methods. Then we'll capitalize the last name using the **toUpperCase** method and grab the first initial of the first name with the **charAt** method. Lastly we'll inject the text back into the page as the value of the **name** box. Example 7.25 shows the complete JavaScript code and the page behavior when a name is typed and the button is clicked.

```
// Converts a name in first-last order to last, first order.
function convertName() {
  var input = document.getElementById("name");
  var name = input.value;
  var spaceIndex = name.indexOf(" ");
  var firstName = name.substring(0, spaceIndex);
  var lastName = name.substring(spaceIndex + 1);
  lastName = lastName.toUpperCase();
  var firstInitial = firstName.charAt(0);
  input.value = lastName + ", " + firstInitial + ".";
}
```

**Name Converter**

Type your name:

`DURDEN, T.`  `Convert to Last, First`

**Example 7.25 Name converter JavaScript code**

In addition to accessing characters through the **charAt** method, you can also treat a string as an array of characters where each index corresponds to an individual character using the [] operator. Although this method of accessing characters of a string is intuitive and popular, it is not part of the ECMAScript specification, so some browsers (chiefly Internet Explorer) do not support it. In such browsers, **charAt** must be used to access characters of a string. It's also important to remember that you cannot use this notation to set a character of a string, only to access or examine the character.

## 7.2.8 for Loops

A **for** loop repeats a group of statements a definite number of times. The syntax for JavaScript **for** loops is very similar to other programming languages, containing an initialization statement to be executed once at the start of the loop, a logical test indicating how long the loop should keep repeating, and an update to perform between each iteration of the loop.

```
for (initialization; test; update) {
    statements;
}
```

**Example 7.26 for loop**

The initialization is usually a variable declaration and initialization, such as `var i = 0;`. The test is usually a logical expression related to the loop variable just declared, such as `i < 10`. (We'll cover logical expressions in detail in a few sections; they are nearly identical to logical tests used in other languages.) The update is a statement that modifies the loop variable's value, such as `i++`.

Example 7.27 uses a **for** loop to calculate the factorial of an integer. Recall that a factorial, designated as *n*! where *n* is a non-negative integer, is the product of all positive integers less than or equal to *n*. For example, $5! = 1 * 2 * 3 * 4 * 5 = 120$. The computed factorial is placed into the page in a **span** with **id** of **result**.

```html
<h1>Factorializer</h1>
<p>Type an integer:</p>
<div>
    <input id="number" type="text" size="4" />
    <button onclick="factorial();">Compute</button>
    <span id="result"></span>
</div>
```

```javascript
function factorial() {
    var input = document.getElementById("number");
    var number = input.value;
    var result = 1;
    for (var i = 1; i <= number; i++) {
        result = result * i;
    }
    var span = document.getElementById("result");
    span.innerHTML = result;
}
```

# Factorializer

Type an integer:

5 [Compute] 120

**Example 7.27 The for loop**

One bug we often make is to accidentally write `int` instead of `var` in a **for** loop's header. Having written so many **for** loops that way in C and Java makes it an easy mistake to make. If you do this, you'll see a syntax error about a missing semicolon in your loop header; basically JavaScript doesn't understand the keyword `int`. Figure 7.12 shows the Firebug output from such an error.

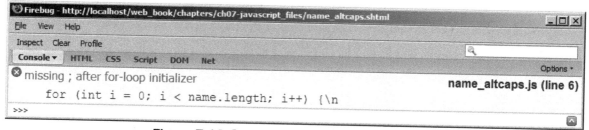

Figure 7.12 **for** loop with **int** instead of **var**

Another subtle difference between **for** loops in JavaScript and Java is that the loop counter variable **i** still exists when the loop finishes. We'll talk more about variable scope in a later section.

## 7.2.9  The Math Object

The **Math** object is a predefined global JavaScript object which contains properties and functions for mathematical constants and functions. You access properties and functions contained within the **Math** object as you would static members and methods in Java. Table 7.13 and Table 7.14 list the most commonly used constants and functions found in the **Math** object. Math has a few other properties and functions not listed, such as **LOG10E** and **atan**.

```
Math.property
Math.method(parameters)
```

Example 7.28 Syntax template for **Math** properties and methods

| Constant | Description |
|---|---|
| Math.E | Euler's Number, the Base of Natural Logarithms |
| Math.LN2 | Natural logarithm of 2, approximately 0.693 |
| Math.PI | Ratio of the circumference of a circle to its diameter, approximately 3.14159 |

Table 7.13 Math constants

Example 7.29 shows an example of using various **Math** methods.

```
var r = 5;
var circleArea = Math.PI * Math.pow(r, 2);
var randNum = Math.random() * 10;
var smaller = Math.min(circleArea, randNum);
```

Example 7.29 Using the **Math** object

If you want to generate a random number, use the **Math.random** function, which returns a random real number between 0 and 1. If you want a random number in a different range, multiply and/or add to the result of **Math.random**. If you want an integer instead of a real number, call **Math.floor** or **parseInt** on the result of **Math.random** after scaling it to your desired range. For example, to produce a random integer between 1 and 10, use the following code:

```
var rand = parseInt(Math.random() * 10) + 1;    // integer from 1-10
```

| Function | Description |
|---|---|
| `Math.abs(`**x**`)` | Returns the absolute value of a number, **x** |
| `Math.ceil(`**x**`)` | Returns the smallest integer ≥ a number, **x** |
| `Math.cos(`**x**`)` | Returns the cosine of an angle in radians **x** |
| `Math.floor(`**x**`)` | Returns the largest integer ≤ a number, **x** |
| `Math.log(`**x**`)` | Returns logarithm of **x**, base *e* |
| `Math.max(`**x, y**`)` | Returns the larger of **x** and **y** |
| `Math.min(`**x, y**`)` | Returns the smaller of **x** and **y** |
| `Math.pow(`**base, exponent**`)` | Returns **base** to the **exponent** power |
| `Math.random()` | Returns a pseudo-random number between 0 (inclusive) and 1 (exclusive) |
| `Math.round(`**x**`)` | Returns the value of a number, **x**, rounded to the nearest integer |
| `Math.sin(`**x**`)` | Returns the sine of an angle in radians **x** |
| `Math.sqrt(`**x**`)` | Returns the square root of a number, **x** |
| `Math.tan(`**x**`)` | Returns the tangent of an angle in radians **x** |

**Table 7.14 Math functions**

## 7.2.10 Null and Undefined Values

JavaScript has two special "empty" values that differ in subtle ways. The value `null` indicates the lack of a value, much like it does in other programming languages. The value `undefined` is actually not a value at all; it represents something that is not specified, declared, or defined. A variable that has not been declared yet has the value `undefined`, not `null`. `undefined` is also what is returned by functions that do not return a value.

Students are often confused about the difference between these two values; they both seem to indicate a lack of a value. Sometimes we describe `null` as the *"no"* value and `undefined` as the *"huh?"* value. A function that gives you back a `null` is trying to say, "No, I don't have any result for you." An `undefined` value is JavaScript's way of saying, "Huh? I don't understand what you mean here." Stated another way, if a variable holds the value `null`, the variable does exist, but it does not have any meaningful or usable value yet; but if a variable has an `undefined` value, it means that the variable hasn't been declared at all and essentially does not exist.

You may encounter each of these two values in various places as you write JavaScript programs. For example, as we saw previously, the function `document.getElementById` returns `null` when you pass it an `id` that is not found on the page. You're more likely to encounter `undefined` if your program has a bug and tries to access a variable or other identifier that has not been declared.

**Common Error**

Program says "undefined"

The `null` and `undefined` values are confusing to new students. The place where you may see them is when your code has a bug. For example, if you try to `alert` the value of a variable you haven't declared yet, the message box will often display the word `undefined` instead.

Consider the previous Name Converter example. What would happen if we accidentally mis-capitalized the variable **lastName** as **lastname** on the last line of code? Since **lastname** is not a variable that has been declared, its value is **undefined**. When the **undefined** value is concatenated with a string such as **", "** in our code, it converts into the string **"undefined"**, leading to the bizarre output shown in Example 7.30.

```
function convertName() {
  var input = document.getElementById("name");
  var name = input.value;
  var spaceIndex = name.indexOf(" ");
  var firstName = name.substring(0, spaceIndex);
  var lastName = name.substring(spaceIndex + 1);
  lastName = lastName.toUpperCase();
  var firstInitial = firstName.charAt(0);
  input.value = lastname + ", " + firstInitial + ".";
}
```

# Name Converter

Type your name:

| undefined, M. | Convert to Last, First |

**Example 7.30 Common error: undefined result**

Luckily Firebug does still show an error message to us indicating that the variable **lastname** is undefined, as shown in Figure 7.13, helping us to track down the error. What a life-saver Firebug is!

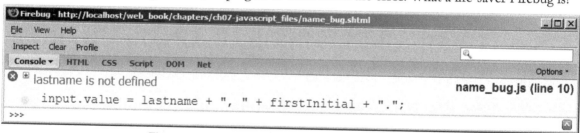

**Figure 7.13 Firebug displaying error message**

## Self-Check

6. What JavaScript type is equivalent to Java's int (integer)? To double (real numbers)? *Number*
7. Write a line of code declaring a numeric variable named gpa with value 2.7. *var gpa = 2.7;*
8. What happens if you assign a value to a variable without having previously declared it? *legal*
9. Name three things you can do when your program does not work and does nothing. *error console, alert, Firebug's console*
10. Compute (without a computer!) the result of each of the following numeric expressions:

   - 12 - 2 - 3 *7*
   - 12 - (2 - 3) *13*
   - 22 + 4 * 2 *30*
   - 3 * 4 + 2 * 3 *18*
   - 4 * 3 / 8 + 2.5 * 2
   - 26 % 10 % 4 * 3
   - "2 + 2 " + 3 + 4

   - 3 + 4 + " 2 + 2"
   - 10.0 / 2 / 4
   - 23 % 8 % 3
   - 17 % 8 / 4
   - (2.5 + 3.5) / 2
   - 9/4 * 2.0 - 5/4
   - "$" + 9.0 / 4.0 + 1

11. Compute the result of each of the following Math expressions:
   - Math.abs(-1.6) *1.6*
   - Math.abs(2 + -4) *2*
   - Math.pow(6, 2) *36*
   - Math.ceil(9.2) *10*
   - Math.max(4, 7) *7*
   - Math.min(-2, -5) *-5*
   - Math.sqrt(64) *8*
   - 100 + Math.floor(41.1 + 1.7) *142*
   - Math.sqrt(16) * Math.max(Math.abs(5), Math.abs(3)) *20*
   - ✗ 7 - 2 + Math.log(Math.pow(Math.E, 5))

12. Given the following variable declarations:

```
var str1 = "Q.E.D.";
var str2 = "Arcturan Megadonkey";
var str3 = "Sirius Cybernetics Corporation";
```

   Compute the result of each of the following string expressions:
   - str1.length *6*
   - str1.toLowerCase() *q.e.d.*
   - ✗ str2.substring(10, 14) *donk*
   - ✗ str1.indexOf(".") *1*
   - str2.indexOf("donkey") *10*
   - ✗ str3.indexOf("X") *Null*
   - str2 + str3.charAt(17)
   - str3.substring(7, 12)
   - str3.substring(9, str3.indexOf("e"))
   - str2.toLowerCase().substring(9, 13)

13. Why does JavaScript have both a null and undefined value? How do they differ?

*The null indicates the lack of a value.*

*The undefined is actually not a value at all.*

*A variable has not been declared yet is undefined, is also what is returned by functions that do not return a value.*

## 7.3 Program Logic

In this section we will discuss Boolean logic and how to use conditional statements with `if/else`. Lastly, we'll talk about `while` loops for indefinite repetition. Conditional statements can also be written using the JavaScript `switch` statement, but we do not cover it in this book.

### 7.3.1 Comparison Operators

*Comparison operators* (also called *relational operators*) examine a pair of operands and produce a `boolean` result. If two operands are not of the same type, JavaScript automatically attempts to convert them into the same type. Table 7.15 summarizes the common comparison operators.

| Operator | Description |
|---|---|
| > | Greater than |
| >= | Greater than or equal |
| < | Less than |
| <= | Less than or equal |
| == | Equal (tests whether values match, ignoring types) |
| === | Strictly equal (tests whether both values and types match) |
| != | Not equal (tests whether values differ, ignoring types) |
| !== | Strictly not equal (tests whether either values or types do not match) |

**Table 7.15 Comparison operators**

All of the operators are familiar if you have read the chapters about PHP. If not, the === and !== operators are perhaps the only unfamiliar ones. Since JavaScript tries to automatically convert two operands of different types into two operands that can be compared, there are situations where you want to be able to actually test both value and type. The === and !== will test both for value and type while the == and != operators will test only for value. Table 7.16 demonstrates several kinds of tests.

| Expression | Result |
|---|---|
| `5 < 10.0` | true |
| `7 == "7"` | true |
| `7 === "7"` | false |
| `7 != "7.0"` | false |
| `7 !== "7.0"` | true |
| `42 < "hello"` | false |
| `42 >= "hello"` | false |
| `10 > "3 french hens"` | false |

**Table 7.16 Logical tests**

While JavaScript tries its best to do the right thing when you mix types, sometimes a test contains values that simply cannot be compared. In such a case the test's result will always be `false`. For example, the string `"hello"` has no numeric value, so the test `"hello" < 42` will be `false`.

The precedence of the relational operators is the same as in many other languages. The relational operators (`<`, `<=`, `>`, `>=`) have lower precedence than addition and subtraction, and the equality operators (`==`, `!=`, `===`, `!==`) are just below that. A full table detailing operator precedence in JavaScript is given at the end of this section. Parentheses can be used to force any desired evaluation order.

## 7.3.2 Conditional Statements: `if/else`

The syntax of JavaScript's `if` and `if/else` statements is virtually identical to other languages.

```
if (test) {
  statements;
}
```

```
if (test) {
  statements;
} else if (test) {
  statements;
} else {
  statements;
}
```

**Example 7.31 Syntax template for `if` and `if/else` statements**

Example 7.32 uses an `if/else` statement to capitalize every other letter of a string. This is done by looping over each character. If its index is even, we capitalize it, otherwise we lowercase it. The string called `newName` grows to contain the complete re-capitalized name at the end of the loop.

```html
<h1>Name Capitalizizizer</h1>
<p>Type your name:</p>
<div>
  <input id="name" type="text" size="24" />
  <button onclick="capitalize();">Capitalizizize it!</button>
</div>
```

```javascript
// Capitalizes every other letter of a given name.
function capitalize() {
  var input = document.getElementById("name");
  var name = input.value;
  var newName = "";
  for (var i = 0; i < name.length; i++) {
    if (i % 2 == 0) {
      newName += name.charAt(i).toUpperCase();
    } else {
      newName += name.charAt(i).toLowerCase();
    }
  }
  input.value = newName;
}
```

**Example 7.32 `if/else` statement**

## 7.3.3 Boolean Values

Another difference between JavaScript and C or Java is the way JavaScript evaluates any primitive value as a `Boolean`. There are only two `Boolean` literals in JavaScript, `true` and `false`, but any other primitive value (i.e. values of type `Number`, `String`, `null`, and `undefined`) can also be evaluated as a `Boolean` value. Values that are treated as `false`, but aren't the `false` literal value are known as *falsey* values. Likewise values that evaluate to `true`, but aren't the `true` literal value are known as *truthy* values.

**truthy**

Interpreted as being true in a logical expression.

**falsey**

Interpreted as being false in a logical expression.

The following values are considered falsey:

- `0`
- `NaN`
- `""`, the empty string
- `null`
- `undefined`

All other values are considered truthy. Table 7.17 shows examples of truthy and falsey values.

In Example 7.33, the first `alert` will show because the string is truthy. (Fittingly, `"Stephen Colbert"` has truthiness in JavaScript.) The second will not show because both `0` and `null` are falsey. Table 7.17 lists some other values and whether they are truthy or falsey.

```
var msg = "Stephen Colbert";
if (msg) {
  alert("And that's The Word.");   // this message will show
}
var x = 0;
var y = null;
if (x || y) {
  alert("This message is not going to show.");
}
```

**Example 7.33 Using truthy and falsey values**

| Truthy Values | Falsey Values |
|---|---|
| `314, 811, -52, 2.14` | `0, 0.0, 0.000,` `NaN` |
| `"Hello!", 'Hasta Luego.'` | `"", ''` |
| `"0", "0.0", "null", "undefined"` | `null, undefined` |

**Table 7.17 Truthy and falsey values**

It's often important to check if a variable has a value before using it. Many new JavaScript programmers forget to do this. Then on top of that, they forget they also must check if a variable is `undefined`. Checking for both `null` and `undefined` values is especially important if you

**Don't Be a Newb**

Testing for **null** or **undefined**

will be writing functions that others will use. You don't want somebody else's bad value to break your code. Example 7.34 tests whether a variable is defined and has a value, but it has poor style.

```
if (myVariable != null && myVariable != undefined) {
    ...
}
```

**Example 7.34 Newb way of testing for a `null`/`undefined` value**

Since both `null` and `undefined` are falsey values, we can more easily check if a variable has a value using the more concise `if` statement shown in Example 7.35.

```
if (myVariable) {
    ...
}
```

**Example 7.35 Jedi way of testing for a `null`/`undefined` value**

## 7.3.4 Logical Operators

Just like in Java, C, and C++, you can form more complex Boolean expressions using the logical operators `&&` (AND), `||` (OR), and `!` (NOT). Table 7.18 lists these operators.

| Operator | Meaning | Description |
|---|---|---|
| **value1 && value2** | AND | true if both values are "truthy" |
| **value1 \|\| value2** | OR | true if either value (or both) is "truthy" |
| **!value** | NOT (Negation) | true if the value is "falsey" |

**Table 7.18 Logical operators**

When these operators have Boolean values as their operands, they work just as in Java and C. JavaScript performs *short-circuit evaluation* of the `&&` and `||` operators as seen in other languages. In other words, if the left operand of an `&&` evaluates to `false` or if the left operand of an `||` evaluates to `true`, the result of the overall test is already known, so the right operand is not evaluated.

Unlike in other programming languages, JavaScript's `&&` and `||` can produce non-boolean results if they have non-boolean operands. When `&&` is used with non-boolean values, it will return the left hand operand if it can be converted to `false` and otherwise returns the right hand operand.

```
var a = 15 && 30;             // a is 30
var b = "Tea" && "Coffee";    // b is "Coffee"
var c = null && "Coffee";     // c is null
var d = "Coffee" && "";       // d is ""
```

**Example 7.36 The && operator**

When `||` is used with non-Boolean values, it will return the left hand operand if it can be converted to `true` and otherwise returns the value of the right hand operand. Because of this behavior, the `||` operator is also called the "default operator". We can use `||` in situations where we want to assign a variable a value if and only if it is valid (not `null`, `undefined`, or some other falsey value) when otherwise we'd want to assign it a default value. Example 7.37 shows some examples of `||`.

```
var s = "Espresso";
var n = null;

var e = s || "Coffee";      // e is "Espresso"
var f = n || "Coffee";      // f is "Coffee"
var g = n || s;             // g is "Espresso"
var h = 0 || n;             // h is null
```

**Example 7.37 The || operator**

A clever way to use this "default operator" concept is to provide a default value in case of failure. For example, the code in Example 7.38 causes the program to use a donation amount of $5.00 if the user has typed an empty or invalid value into the **donationamount** text box.

```
var textField = document.getElementById("donationamount");
var donation = textField.value || 5.00;
```

**Example 7.38 Using the || operator to provide a default value**

The ! operator always produces a Boolean value. It evaluates to **false** if its single operand is truthy; otherwise, it evaluates to **true**.

Logical operators have very low precedence but higher precedence than assignment operators. Furthermore, **&&** has higher precedence than ||. Now that we have discussed many of the basic JavaScript operators, we can list a full table of precedence of all common operators. Table 7.19 lists them in decreasing order.

| Category | Operator(s) |
|---|---|
| Member | . [] |
| Call/create instance | () new |
| Negation and increment | ! - ++ -- |
| Multiply/divide | * / % |
| Addition/subtraction | + - |
| Relational | < <= > >= |
| Equality | == != === !== |
| Logical AND | && |
| Logical OR | \|\| |
| Assignment | = += -= *= /= %= |

**Table 7.19 Operator precedence (decreasing order)**

## 7.3.5 While Loops

A `while` loop is another statement like the `for` loop that is used to achieve repetition. Unlike `for` loops, `while` loops are most often used for what is called *indefinite repetition*, where the number of repetitions is not known in advance. The syntax and behavior of the `while` loop in JavaScript is the same as what you would expect from Java, C, or C++, and is shown in Example 7.39.

```
while (test) {
   statements;
}
```

**Example 7.39 Syntax template for `while` loop**

For example, Example 7.40 uses a `while` loop to find the next 10 leap years after a given year typed by the user. Recall that a leap year is one that is divisible by 4, except for multiples of 100 that are not divisible by 400 (such as 1900 and 2100). A `while` loop is appropriate to solve this problem because we must check each year after the one typed by the user, and we don't know exactly how many years we'll need to test before we'll find the 10th leap year.

```html
<h1>Leap Years</h1>
<p>Type a year:</p>
<div>
   <input id="year" type="text" size="24" />
   <button onclick="leapYears();">Compute Leap Years</button> <br />
   <span id="output"></span>
</div>
```

```javascript
// Displays the next 10 leap years after a given year.
function leapYears() {
   var input = document.getElementById("year");
   var year = parseInt(input.value);
   var output = document.getElementById("output");
   output.innerHTML = "Next 10 leap years after " + year + ": ";

   var count = 0;
   while (count < 10) {
      if (year % 400 == 0 || (year % 100 != 0 && year % 4 == 0)) {
         count++;
         output.innerHTML += " " + year;
      }
      year++;
   }
}
```

# Leap Years

Type a year:

```
2076                    Compute Leap Years
```
Next 10 leap years after 2076: 2076 2080 2084 2088 2092 2096 2104 2108 2112 2116

**Example 7.40 `while` loop**

JavaScript also has **do/while** loops, using the same syntax and behavior as C and Java. A do/while loop performs its test at the end of each pass of the loop rather than at the start, so it is guaranteed to execute its body at least once. The syntax is shown in Example 7.41, but we will not cover **do/while** in detail.

```
do {
    statements;
while (test);
```

**Example 7.41 Syntax template for do/while loop**

## Self-Check

*[handwritten: loose typed language  == value  === type and value]*

14. Why does JavaScript have both an == and === operator? What is the difference?
15. Are each of the following expressions "truthy" or "falsey"?
    ○  `0.000`  *[handwritten: f]*
    ○  `"no"`  *[handwritten: t]*
    ○  `null`  *[handwritten: f]*
    ○  `""`  *[handwritten: f]*
    ○  `"false"`  *[handwritten: t]*
    ○  `parseInt(0.97)`  *[handwritten: f]*
    ○  `42 / "ten"`  *[handwritten: NaN  f]*
16. What value is stored in each variable in each of the following expressions?
    ○  `var a = 2 || 3;`
    ○  `var b = 0 || 42;`
    ○  `var c = 0 && 42;`
    ○  `var d = "you" && "me";`
    ○  `var e = "ok" && null;`
    ○  `var f = "" && "0" || "1";`
    ○  `var g = null || 1 || null || 2;`
17. Write a better version of the following code with a more concise **if** test:

```
if (amount == null || amount == undefined) {
    var warning = document.getElementById("warningarea");
    warning.innerHTML = "You did not type an amount! Try again.");
}
```

## 7.4 Advanced JavaScript Syntax

In this section we cover some of the more advanced syntax of JavaScript, such as subtleties of variable scope, arrays for storing lists of data, functions that use parameters and return values, and dialog boxes for user input.

### 7.4.1 Scope and Global Variables

| |
|---|
| **local variable** |
| One that exists only within a particular function. |
| **global variable** |
| One that can be seen and modified by any JavaScript code on the page. |

In JavaScript, there are two types of variable scope: local and global. A *local variable* is one that is declared with the `var` keyword inside of a function. A local variable is only available inside the function in which it was declared. A *global variable* is declared outside a function or implicitly declared. Even variables that are implicitly declared within a function are considered global variables. Global variables are usually declared at the top of a JavaScript file so they are easy to find and notice.

Because implicitly declared variables are always global, we highly recommend you always use `var` to declare your variables. Declaring variables with `var`, especially those within functions, can prevent confusing bugs where the programmer intends to have two local variables in two separate functions with the same name, but gets one global variable with the common name because the programmer used implicit declaration. Example 7.42 shows a mixture of global and local variables and the behavior of each.

```
var a = 2;         // global variable

// out here,  a = 2, b = undefined, c = undefined

function scopeTest() {
  a = 2 * 2;       // implicitly declared (global) by assignment
  b = 3;           // local variable
  var c = 8;       // local variable

  // in here,  a = 4, b = 3, c = 8
}

scopeTest();
// out here, a = 4, b = 3, c = undefined
```

**Example 7.42 Global and local variables**

It should be noted that in most languages global variables are considered poor style, and in JavaScript we try to minimize their use as much as possible. Sometimes a global variable is the best way to store a long-lived piece of data that we want to exist outside of any particular function, but programs with lots of global variables usually show a lack of understanding of proper ways to share data between functions, such as parameters and returns, which we'll discuss later in this section.

### 7.4.2 Arrays

JavaScript provides an `Array` type; an array stores an indexed list of values. The syntax for creating an array is shown in Example 7.43.

```
var name = [];                           // empty array
var name = [value, value, ..., value];   // array with initial values
```

**Example 7.43 Syntax template for constructing an array**

JavaScript array indexes are 0-based, and you can access elements in the array using the [ ] operator. An array has a `length` property storing its number of elements, or more precisely, one more than the highest index stored in the array. Example 7.44 shows how to assign to elements in an array, access the elements, and iterate through its elements using the `length` property and a `for` loop.

```
var xgames = [];                 // an empty array
xgames[0] = "Freestyle BMX";
xgames[1] = "MotoX";
xgames[2] = "Skateboarding";
xgames[3] = "Surfing";
xgames[4] = "Rallying";          // xgames.length is 5 now
for (var i = 0; i < xgames.length; i++) {
  alert(xgames[i]);              // alert all games stored in the array
}
```

**Example 7.44 Using an array**

In addition to the `length` property, there are a number of methods that the `Array` object provides, summarized in Table 7.20. Several methods have optional parameters, so multiple ways of calling them are shown as appropriate.

| Method | Description |
|---|---|
| concat(**array1**, ..., **arrayN**) | Joins two or more arrays and returns a new array |
| join()<br>join(**separator**) | Returns a string of joined array elements separated by an optional separator (default is a comma) |
| pop() | Removes last element from array and returns it |
| push(**value**)<br>push(**value1**, ..., **valueN**) | Adds one or more elements to end of array |
| reverse() | Reverses order of the elements of array, in place |
| shift() | Removes and returns the first element from an array |
| slice(**startIndex**)<br>slice(**startIndex**, **endIndex**) | Returns a sub-array of an existing array, from **startIndex** (inclusive) to **endIndex** (*exclusive*). If **endIndex** is omitted, goes to end of array |
| splice(**index**, **count**,<br>     **value1**, ..., **valueN**) | Removes **count** elements from array starting at the given index, and inserts the given new elements there |
| sort() | Sorts the elements of an array in place |
| toString() | Converts an array into a string such as "1,2,3" |
| unshift(**value**)<br>unshift(**value1**, ..., **valueN**) | Adds one or more elements to the front of an array |

**Table 7.20 Array methods**

The `slice` and `splice` methods are particularly useful. The `slice` method returns a smaller array based on a sub-range of the elements of an existing array. For example:

```
//       index    0       1       2       3        4          5
var a1 = ["Leo", "Mike", "Don", "Raph", "Splinter", "April"];
var a2 = a1.slice(2, 5);    // ["Don", "Raph", "Splinter"]
var a3 = a1.slice(0, 1);    // ["Leo"]
```

The `splice` method is a Swiss army knife of adding and removing array contents. It should not be confused with `slice`. By passing it a start index and a count, it can be used to remove that many elements starting from that index from an array, shifting elements to the left to fill the holes:

```
//       index    0       1       2       3        4          5
var a1 = ["Leo", "Mike", "Don", "Raph", "Splinter", "April"];
a1.splice(2, 3);            // a1 is now ["Leo", "Mike", "April"]
```

Rather than returning a new array, `splice` modifies the existing array. The `splice` method can be used to insert new elements into an array by providing values after the start index and count. To insert new elements without deleting existing ones, use a count of 0. To replace, use a count above 0.

```
//       index    0       1       2       3        4          5
var a1 = ["Leo", "Mike", "Don", "Raph", "Splinter", "April"];

// replace 4 elements at index 1 with "Bebop", "Krang"
a1.splice(1, 4, "Bebop", "Krang"); // ["Leo", "Bebop", "Krang", "April"]

// insert new element "Don" at index 2
a1.splice(2, 0, "Don");     // ["Leo", "Bebop", "Don", "Krang", "April"]
```

### Example Program: Favorite Bands

Suppose we want to write a program that displays a list of the user's favorite rock bands. Our web page will have a method to add to the end of the list, a method for reversing the order of the list, and a method for clearing the list. On any change to the list, a `span` with `id` of `list` will be updated to show the current list of favorite bands. Example 7.45 shows the relevant HTML code.

```html
<h1>Rock Bands</h1>
<p>Type a band's name:</p>
<div>
  <input id="band" type="text" size="24" /> <br />
  <button onclick="addToList();">Add</button>
  <button onclick="reverseList();">Reverse</button>
  <button onclick="clearList();">Clear</button> <br />
  <span id="list"></span>
</div>
```

# Rock Bands

Type a band's name:

| Add | Reverse | Clear |

**Example 7.45 Rock band HTML code**

Now let's look at the relevant JavaScript code. An array is an ideal structure for storing the list of favorite bands. But we should not declare it inside any one particular method, because then it will only exist until the end of that method. To make it survive throughout the lifetime of the page, we can declare the band list as a global variable at the top of our code. All of the functions can refer to this global variable.

```
var bandList = [];     // global list of favorite bands
```

Each operation (add, reverse, clear) will modify the contents of the array in some way. We'll have to take the contents of the list, format them into a string, and place this string into the page in the **span** with **id** of **list**. Since we don't want to repeat this code in every method, let's make a helping method called **updateList** that performs this operation. The event-handling methods can call the **updateList** method, which turns the array into a string by using its **join** method.

```javascript
function updateList() {
  var output = document.getElementById("list");
  output.innerHTML = "[" + bandList.join(", ") + "]";
}
```

The code for adding a value to the list will fetch the value from the **input** box with **id** of **band** and add this to the end of our array with its **push** method. The code for reversing the list will call the array's **reverse** method; the code for clearing the list will set the list to an empty array, **[ ]**. After each of these operations we'll call **updateList** to make sure the screen updates to show the array's current contents. Without this call nothing would happen to the list on the screen. Example 7.46 shows the complete code and a screenshot of the list after several items have been added.

```javascript
var bandList = [];     // global list of favorite bands

function addToList() {
  var input = document.getElementById("band");
  bandList.push(input.value);
  input.value = "";   // clear the text box
  updateList();
}

function clearList() {
  bandList = [];
  updateList();
}

function reverseList() {
  bandList.reverse();
  updateList();
}

function updateList() {
  var output = document.getElementById("list");
  output.innerHTML = "[" + bandList.join(", ") + "]";
}
```

Weird Al Yankovic

Add   Reverse   Clear

[Prince, Rick Astley, Madonna]

**Example 7.46 Rock band JavaScript code and output**

### 7.4.3 Function Parameters and Returns

| parameter |
| --- |
| A value passed to a function by its caller that affects the function's execution. |

Like functions and methods in C, C++, and Java, a JavaScript *function* is a group of statements that is given a name and can be called (executed) elsewhere in your program. We have already used functions in all of our JavaScript examples to handle events. As we saw in the last Bands example, a function can call other functions.

JavaScript functions can accept input values called *parameters* to guide their behavior. Parameters allow the caller of a method to pass information in to that method. Parameters are useful for writing general methods that can handle a family of similar tasks. Up until now, none of the functions we've written have accepted any parameters, but Example 7.47 shows the template for declaring a function that does have parameters. Example 7.48 shows a function that accepts two parameters and uses them to display a name on an element on the page.

```
function name(parameter1, parameter2, ..., parameterN) {
    statements;
}
```

Example 7.47 Syntax template for function with parameters

```
// Accepts a first and last name as parameters and displays them on
// the page in "LAST NAME, First Initial." format.
function convertName(firstName, lastName) {
    lastName = lastName.toUpperCase();
    var firstInitial = firstName.charAt(0);

    var input = document.getElementById("name");
    input.value = lastName + ", " + firstInitial + ".";
}
```

Example 7.48 Function with parameters

To declare a parameter, all that is needed is its name; types are not written, nor is the keyword var used. Though no types are specified, often the programmer makes assumptions about what type of value is being passed. The code in the **convertName** function would only work properly if string values were passed to it; any other type of value would likely produce an error about a missing **toUpperCase** method or similar.

If the wrong number of parameters are passed to a function, there is no compiler error or warning given by the interpreter like you might expect from C, C++, or Java. If too many parameters are passed, the extra parameters are ignored. If too few parameters are passed, the remaining parameters' values are **undefined**. This can be used to implement a function with optional parameters.

A function can also *return* a value, sending that value back to its caller. A function can accept arbitrarily many parameters but can return at most one value. A value is returned using a *return statement*, as shown in Example 7.49. Notice that return types are not explicitly written when declaring a function. If you want to return something, you just return it and JavaScript figures things out.

```
function name(parameter1, parameter2, ..., parameterN) {
    statements;
    return value;
}
```

Example 7.49 Syntax template for function with return

Example 7.50 shows a function that accepts two parameters and returns a value. Example 7.51 shows a call to this function.

```
function rightTriangleArea(base, height) {
  return 0.5 * base * height;
}
```

**Example 7.50 Function with return**

```
var tArea = rightTriangleArea(5, 3);
```

**Example 7.51 Function call with return**

The **return** statement stops the execution of the function. If it is followed by a value, the value is returned to the caller. If no value is specified after the **return** statement or if a function has no **return** statement, the function exits and the value returned is **undefined**.

## 7.4.4  Input Dialog Boxes

We can achieve a sophisticated user interface using the form controls we've already seen. But sometimes you want to pop up a dialog box to ask the user for information or to inform about an important event. In these cases you may want to use JavaScript's built-in functions for dialog boxes. We have already seen the **alert** function, which pops up a message dialog box.

In order to get user input in the above example, we have to use a second kind of popup box: the **prompt** box. The **prompt** function takes two parameters: a string message and a default initial value. The second parameter is optional; in fact, we often omit it so that the box's initial text is empty. In contrast with the **alert** box, the prompt box has two buttons: OK and Cancel. If the user presses OK or presses Enter, the **prompt** function returns the string in the dialog's text box. (An empty string is returned if no text is entered.) If Cancel is pressed or the user presses the Escape key, **null** is returned from the **prompt** function, regardless of the text in the text box.

| Function | prompt("**message**") |
| --- | --- |
| | prompt("**message**",  "**default value**") |
| Description | Prompts the user for a value in a pop-up box |
| Returns | the string the user enters, or **null** if user cancels |

```
var year = prompt("Please enter your birth year.");
```

**The page at http://localhost says:**    ✕

? Please enter your birth year.

[                    ]

OK      Cancel

**Example 7.52 prompt box**

One thing web programmers commonly want to do is confirm a user action, such as confirming that a user really intends to submit information that they have just entered. This can be accomplished using the third kind of input dialog: the **confirm** box. The **confirm** function is used to verify some-

thing with the user. The box has two buttons: OK and Cancel. If the user presses OK, `confirm` returns `true`. If the user presses Cancel, the function returns `false`.

| Function | `confirm("`**message**`")` |
|---|---|
| Description | Confirms a user's decision |
| Returns | `true` if user clicks OK, and `false` if user clicks Cancel |

In Example 7.53, if the user clicks the OK button, the hypothetical function `closeAccount` executes. Otherwise, the body of the `if` statement is not entered and the function is not called.

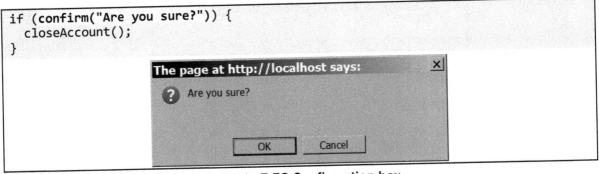

```
if (confirm("Are you sure?")) {
    closeAccount();
}
```

The page at http://localhost says:

? Are you sure?

OK    Cancel

**Example 7.53 Confirmation box**

## Self-Check

18. What are the values of variables **a**, **b**, **c**, **d**, and **e** at the marked point in the following code?

```
var a = 1;
b = 2;
var c = 3;
function f() {
    a = 4;
    var c = 5;
    var d = 6;
    e = 6;  global
}
f();    // call the f function
// marked point, here
```
a=4  b=2
c=5. d undefined  e=6

19. Write code to construct a new array containing 3 elements: Your first, middle, and last name.
20. What do the **slice** and **splice** methods do on arrays? How do they differ?
21. What elements are in the array after the following code?    var name = [ ] ; ... [ ].
var name : [ first, last ].

```
var a = ["Stef", "Amit"];
a.push("Brian");   ["s","A","B"]
a.unshift("Morgan");   ["M","s","A"]
a.pop();   ["s"]
a.shift();
a.sort();   ["A","s"],
a.splice(1, 0, "Victoria");   ["s","v","A"],
```
insert

22. Write a function that accepts a string as a parameter and alerts a message if that string is a pa-
lindrome (the same forwards as backwards).
23. Write a function that accepts a Fahrenheit temperature and converts it to (returns in) Celsius.

## 7.5 Case Study: Hangman

In this section we'll build a JavaScript-powered web page for playing the game of Hangman. In this game, the computer randomly chooses a word, and the player attempts to figure out the word by guessing letters. Initially the player sees a series of blanks representing the letters of the word. Each time the player guesses a letter that does appear in the word, every occurrence of the letter is revealed. If the player guesses a letter that does not appear in the word, a body part of a hanging man is drawn on the screen. First the head, then the body, then the left arm, right arm, left leg, and right leg are drawn. If the player guesses six incorrect letters, the complete hanging man is drawn and the player loses the game. If the player is able to guess all letters of the word without getting 6 wrong, the player wins the game. Figure 7.14 shows the desired appearance of our page in the middle of a game.

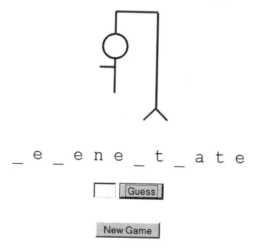

Figure 7.14 Hangman page expected appearance

The page itself will be written in HTML/CSS, but all of the various behavior and user interaction must be done in JavaScript. This page is complex and won't be easy to code, so we should follow a step-by-step process to implement it. The following are our suggested steps for solving this problem:

1. Set up the initial HTML and CSS code.
2. Implement the New Game behavior in JavaScript, so that we can press the New Game button and see a word full of blank _ characters appear on the page.
3. Implement behavior so that the user can guess letters and display guesses on the page.
4. Determine whether a given letter is found in the word or not; write code to handle each case.
5. Add polish to the game, such as the ability to play multiple games, preventing the user from making the same guess twice, and so on.

### 7.5.1 Initial HTML/CSS Code

The overall page has several major elements in its body. There is an image of the hanging man, which will change to show different images as the game is played. We've got 7 GIF images representing the hanging man in his various states. Figure 7.15 shows several of these images. The initial empty hangman is `hangman6.gif`, meaning that the player has 6 guesses remaining. The fully formed "dead" hangman is `hangman0.gif`, meaning that the player has 0 guesses remaining.

hangman6.gif       hangman3.gif       hangman0.gif

**Figure 7.15 Hangman images**

On the page there is an area that shows the current state of the hidden word and which of its letters are visible; we'll call this the "clue" area. Since we'll need JavaScript to show proper word clues, for now we'll just put initial text of "Press New Game to play!" here. We'll need a text box and a button for typing and submitting guesses. The text box will have a `size` and `maxlength` of 1 since the user is supposed to type only single letters. Example 7.54 shows the complete initial HTML code and its appearance in the browser.

```
<!DOCTYPE html PUBLIC "-//W3C//DTD XHTML 1.1//EN"
    "http://www.w3.org/TR/xhtml11/DTD/xhtml11.dtd">
<html xmlns="http://www.w3.org/1999/xhtml">
  <head>
    <title>Hangman</title>
  </head>

  <body>
    <div><img src="hangman6.gif" alt="hangman" /></div>
    <div id="clue">Press New Game to play!</div>

    <div>
      <input type="text" size="1" maxlength="1" />
      <button>Guess</button>
    </div>

    <div id="newgamearea"><button>New Game</button></div>
  </body>
</html>
```

Press New Game to play!

[ ] Guess

New Game

**Example 7.54 Hangman initial HTML code**

Let's also add some CSS to give the page a slightly less plain look. We'll center the content on the page and give the word clue a large Courier font with a bit of padding. Example 7.55 shows the complete CSS code and the updated page appearance.

```
<link href="hangman.css" type="text/css" rel="stylesheet" />
```

```
body {
  text-align: center;
}
#clue {
  font-family: monospace;
  font-size: 2em;
  padding: 1em;
}
#newgamearea {
  margin-top: 2em;
}
```

Press New Game to play!

&#91;   &#93; Guess

New Game

**Example 7.55 Hangman initial CSS code**

So far the page is lifeless and the player cannot play a game. We'll do that next.

## 7.5.2 Choosing a Word with JavaScript

Now let's write some initial code to randomly select a word and display that word on the page. We'll do this using JavaScript. First we'll add a line to our HTML page's header linking the page to a JavaScript file:

```
<script src="hangman.js" type="text/javascript"></script>
```

The random word should be chosen when the user clicks the New Game button; let's decide that this code will be in a function named newGame. We specify an onclick handler on our New Game button to call this (as yet unwritten) function.

```
    <button onclick="newGame();">New Game</button>
```

What should the newGame function do? For starters, we'll need a list of words to choose from. You can make up any word list you want, but we'll just put a few words into an array and declare this array as a global variable. You could always add to this list later for a more challenging game.

```
// list of random words to choose from
var POSSIBLE_WORDS = ["obdurate", "verisimilitude", "defenestrate",
    "obsequious", "dissonant", "toady", "idempotent"];
```

Our newGame function must choose a random element from this array. Recall that you can choose a random real number from 0-1 with Math.random. We can use it to choose a random array index by multiplying it by the array's length and then truncating it to an integer using parseInt.

```
// choose a random word
var randomIndex = parseInt(Math.random() * POSSIBLE_WORDS.length);
var word = POSSIBLE_WORDS[randomIndex];
```

Now that we've chosen our word, we must display the clue to the user on the page. Since the user hasn't initially guessed any of the letters, all of the letters of the word should appear as underscores, with spaces between them. For example, if the word is "toady", the clue string should be " _ _ _ _ _ ". We can generate such a clue string using a for loop, then inject it into the page using document.getElementById to fetch the DOM object representing the div with id of clue. Example 7.56 shows the complete code for the newGame function so far and the web page's appearance after the New Game button has been clicked.

```
// Chooses a new random word and displays its clue on the page.
function newGame() {
  // choose a random word
  var randomIndex = parseInt(Math.random() * POSSIBLE_WORDS.length);
  var word = POSSIBLE_WORDS[randomIndex];

  // show initial word clue - all underscores
  var clueString = "";
  for (var i = 0; i < word.length; i++) {
    clueString += "_ ";
  }
  var clue = document.getElementById("clue");
  clue.innerHTML = clueString;
}
```

Example 7.56 New Game JavaScript code

## 7.5.3 Making Guesses

Now let's write code so that the player can guess letters in the hidden word. The user will type a guess letter into the text box and click the Guess button, so we need to listen to clicks on that button. Our event handler function will need to grab the letter from the text box, then search through the letters of our **word** variable string and see whether any of them match it. If so, it should reveal them on the screen, replacing the underscores that used to be there. To do this we'll set an **onclick** attribute for the Guess button and an **id** attribute on the text box so our code can grab its value. We'll also need a place on the page to show the user's guesses, so let's add a **div** to the HTML:

```
<div>
  <input id="guess" type="text" size="1" maxlength="1" />
  <button onclick="guessLetter();">Guess</button>
</div>
...
<div id="guesses"></div>
```

At this point in our JavaScript code we will want to access the **word** variable in multiple functions. Both the **newGame** function that chooses the random word and the **guessLetter** function will want to access it. Therefore we'll change `word` into a global variable. We're going to need another global variable to keep track of all the letters the user has guessed. Let's store them as a string named `guesses` that is initially empty but grows as letters are added:

```
// global variables
var word = "";      // the random word the user is trying to guess
var guesses = "";   // letters the player has guessed

// Chooses a new random word and displays its clue on the page.
function newGame() {
  // choose a random word
  var randomIndex = parseInt(Math.random() * POSSIBLE_WORDS.length);
  word = POSSIBLE_WORDS[randomIndex];
  ...
```

Our `guessLetter` method will fetch the letter to guess from the text box and add it to the global `guesses` string. Then we'll need to update the display of the word so that any relevant underscores are changed into visible letters. The `newGame` function currently has a loop that creates a string of underscores to update the text of the `clue` area on the page. Since we'll want to update the page appearance in different places, let's create a helper function for it called `updatePage` that examines the guesses we've made, uses them to build a string, and displays it. In this string the letters from the clue that have been guessed are visible, and those that aren't are shown as underscores. We'll also make the `updatePage` function display all guesses currently made by the player:

```
// Updates the word clue to the current game state.
function updatePage() {
  var clueString = "";
  for (var i = 0; i < word.length; i++) {
    var letter = word.charAt(i);
    if (guesses.indexOf(letter) >= 0) {    // letter has been guessed
      clueString += letter + " ";
    } else {                               // not guessed
      clueString += "_ ";
    }
  }
  var clue = document.getElementById("clue");
  clue.innerHTML = clueString;

  // show guesses made by player
  var guessArea = document.getElementById("guesses");
  guessArea.innerHTML = "Guesses: " + guesses;
}
```

After adding this function, the `newGame` function is shortened to the following code:

```
// Chooses a new random word and displays its clue on the page.
function newGame() {
  // choose a random word
  var randomIndex = parseInt(Math.random() * POSSIBLE_WORDS.length);
  word = POSSIBLE_WORDS[randomIndex];
  updatePage();   // show initial word clue - all underscores
}
```

Our `guessLetter` function will fetch the letter typed by the user and add it to the list of guesses. It will then call `updatePage` to display all guesses in the `guesses` area.

```
// Guesses a letter.  Called when the user presses the Guess button.
function guessLetter() {
  var input = document.getElementById("guess");
  var letter = input.value;
  guesses += letter;
  updatePage();    // rebuild word clue
}
```

Figure 7.16 shows the appearance of the page after some guesses have been made.

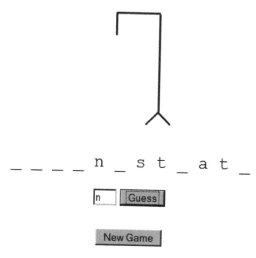

Guesses: itsuoan

**Figure 7.16 Hangman page appearance, phase 3 (after several guesses)**

## 7.5.4 Right and Wrong Guesses

We still haven't addressed the most memorable part of the game of Hangman: The image of the hanging man with progressively more body parts as the user makes incorrect guesses. We need to write code to distinguish which guesses are correct and which are incorrect, and use this to update the hanging man image and to detect when the game is over.

In our game we'll give the player 6 guesses before the game is over. Let's represent this as a global constant, and also declare a global variable representing how many guesses the player has left:

```
var MAX_GUESSES = 6;              // number of total guesses per game

var guessCount = MAX_GUESSES;   // number of guesses player has left
```

When a new game is started, we should reset the guess count to the max and clear our guesses:

```
function newGame() {
  var randomIndex = parseInt(Math.random() * POSSIBLE_WORDS.length);
  word = POSSIBLE_WORDS[randomIndex];
  guessCount = MAX_GUESSES;
  guesses = "";
  ...
```

Now we need to modify our `guessLetter` function to check whether the guess was correct or incorrect. We can check whether the guess appears in the random word using its `indexOf` method:

```
// Guesses a letter.  Called when the user presses the Guess button.
function guessLetter() {
  var input = document.getElementById("guess");
  var letter = input.value;
  if (word.indexOf(letter) < 0) {
    guessCount--;        // an incorrect guess
  }
  guesses += letter;
  updatePage();
}
```

Now that we're counting how many guesses the user has left, when updating the page appearance we can update the hangman image to reflect this. To manipulate the image in our JavaScript via the DOM, we must give it an `id` attribute in the HTML code:

```
<div><img id="hangmanpic" src="hangman6.gif" alt="hangman" /></div>
```

Recall that we have images hangman6.gif through hangman0.gif, each representing the picture to show when the user has a given number of guesses left. So we'll need to set the `src` attribute of the image to the proper picture based on our guess count:

```
// Updates the hangman image, word clue, etc. to the current game state.
function updatePage() {

  ...
  // update hangman image
  var image = document.getElementById("hangmanpic");
  image.src = "hangman" + guessCount + ".gif";
```

We should also make it so that the game tells the player when he/she has won or lost the game. We can figure this out by examining our global variables. If the user has no guesses left, the game is lost. Otherwise, if there are still some underscores left in the clue string on the page, the game is still in progress. Otherwise, the user has won the game. Therefore we can add the following code to the end of the `updatePage` function:

```
  // show the guesses the player has made
  var guessArea = document.getElementById("guesses");
  if (guessCount == 0) {
    guessArea.innerHTML = "You lose.";      // game over (loss)
  } else if (clueString.indexOf("_") < 0) {
    guessArea.innerHTML = "You win!!!";     // game over (win)
  } else {
    guessArea.innerHTML = "Guesses: " + guesses;
  }
```

Figure 7.17 shows the appearance of the page in two different states: one where the user has lost the game and one where the game is won.

**Figure 7.17 Hangman page appearance, phase 4**

Our game at this point has a serious bug: It allows the user to make guesses after the game is over. If the game is lost (0 guesses remaining) or won (no underscores remain in the page's clue string), we shouldn't let the user make more guesses. While we're at it, we should prevent the user from guessing the same letter twice. The following modifications to guessLetter achieve this:

```
function guessLetter() {
  var input = document.getElementById("guess");
  var clue = document.getElementById("clue");
  var letter = input.value;
  if (guessCount == 0 || clue.innerHTML.indexOf("_") < 0 ||
     guesses.indexOf(letter) >= 0) {
   return;   // game over, or already guessed this letter
  }
  ...
}
```

At this point our game is finished! Certainly the game could be improved and expanded, such as by keeping score records or having 26 buttons, one for each letter, so that the user could play without the keyboard. But we'll leave such enhancements as an exercise to the reader.

## 7.5.5 Final File Contents

After all of the changes in the preceding sections, the complete code for hangman.html, hangman.css, and hangman.js are shown in Example 7.57, Example 7.58, and Example 7.59 respectively.

```
<!DOCTYPE html PUBLIC "-//W3C//DTD XHTML 1.1//EN"
    "http://www.w3.org/TR/xhtml11/DTD/xhtml11.dtd">
<html xmlns="http://www.w3.org/1999/xhtml">
  <!-- Hangman game HTML code -->

  <head>
    <title>Hangman</title>
    <link href="hangman.css" type="text/css" rel="stylesheet" />
    <script src="hangman.js" type="text/javascript"></script>
  </head>

  <body>
    <div><img id="hangmanpic" src="hangman6.gif" alt="hangman" /></div>
    <div id="clue">Press New Game to play!</div>
    <div>
      <input id="guess" type="text" size="1" maxlength="1" />
      <button onclick="guessLetter();">Guess</button>
    </div>
    <div id="newgamearea">
      <button onclick="newGame();">New Game</button>
    </div>
    <div id="guesses"></div>
  </body>
</html>
```

Example 7.57 Final contents of `hangman.html`

```
/* Hangman game CSS code */
body {
  text-align: center;
}

/* bottom area containing the New Game button */
#newgamearea {
  margin-top: 2em;
}

/* large courier font for word clues and guesses */
#clue, #guesses {
  font-family: monospace;
  font-size: 2em;
  padding: 1em;
}
```

Example 7.58 Final contents of `hangman.css`

```
// Hangman game JavaScript code
// This file defines the event behavior for the Hangman game.

// constants
var MAX_GUESSES = 6;              // number of total guesses per game
var POSSIBLE_WORDS = ["obdurate", "verisimilitude", "defenestrate",
    "obsequious", "dissonant", "toady", "idempotent"];

// global variables
var word = "";                   // random word user is trying to guess
var guesses = "";                // letters the player has guessed
var guessCount = MAX_GUESSES;    // number of guesses player has left

// Chooses a new random word and displays its clue on the page.
function newGame() {
  // choose a random word
  var randomIndex = parseInt(Math.random() * POSSIBLE_WORDS.length);
  word = POSSIBLE_WORDS[randomIndex];
  guessCount = MAX_GUESSES;
  guesses = "";
  updatePage();    // show initial word clue - all underscores
}


// Guesses a letter.  Called when the user presses the Guess button.
function guessLetter() {
  var input = document.getElementById("guess");
  var clue = document.getElementById("clue");
  var letter = input.value;
  if (guessCount == 0 || clue.innerHTML.indexOf("_") < 0 ||
      guesses.indexOf(letter) >= 0) {
    return;    // game is over, or already guessed this letter
  }

  guesses += letter;
  if (word.indexOf(letter) < 0) {
    guessCount--;          // an incorrect guess
  }

  updatePage();    // update word clue, image, etc.
}

// Updates the hangman image, word clue, etc. to the current game state.
function updatePage() {
  // update clue string such as "h _ l l _ "
  var clueString = "";
  for (var i = 0; i < word.length; i++) {
    var letter = word.charAt(i);
    if (guesses.indexOf(letter) >= 0) {   // letter has been guessed
      clueString += letter + " ";
    } else {                              // not guessed
      clueString += "_ ";
    }
  }
  var clue = document.getElementById("clue");
  clue.innerHTML = clueString;
```

```
var guessArea = document.getElementById("guesses");    // show guesses
if (guessCount == 0) {
  guessArea.innerHTML = "You lose.";      // game over (loss)
} else if (clueString.indexOf("_") < 0) {
  guessArea.innerHTML = "You win!!!";     // game over (win)
} else {
  guessArea.innerHTML = "Guesses: " + guesses;
}
var image = document.getElementById("hangmanpic");    // update hangman image
image.src = "hangman" + guessCount + ".gif";
}
```

**Example 7.59 Final contents of `hangman.js`**

## Chapter Summary

- JavaScript is a lightweight scripting programming language that is most often used to make web pages interactive. A lot of the syntax and rules are more relaxed than Java or C.
- In user interfaces, the flow of execution is determined by the user interacting with controls. These actions are called events, and such a program is called an event-driven program.
- The Document Object Model (DOM) is a set of JavaScript objects that your code can interact with to manipulate the contents of the current web page.
- Each HTML element's DOM object can be used to ask for information about the element, such as to get its text or find out whether it is checked, or to dynamically change styles of the element. You can access a DOM object using the `document.getElementById` function.
- JavaScript has five primitive types: `Number`, `String`, `Boolean`, `null`, and `undefined`. The common arithmetic and logical operators on numbers, strings, and boolean values from Java are also present in JavaScript. The syntax for commenting is also the same.
- In JavaScript, any value can be treated as a `boolean` test. The values `0`, the empty string `""`, `null`, and `undefined` are considered `false`, and all other values are considered `true`.
- Arrays are similar in JavaScript to Java, except that they grow in size as needed.

## References

- ECMAScript Specification:
    a) http://www.ecma-international.org/publications/standards/Ecma-262.htm
- Mozilla Developer Center – Core JavaScript 1.5 Guide:
    b) http://developer.mozilla.org/en/docs/Core_JavaScript_1.5_Guide
- Mozilla Developer Center – Core JavaScript 1.5 Reference:
    c) http://developer.mozilla.org/en/docs/Core_JavaScript_1.5_Reference
- Microsoft Developer Network – JScript Language Reference:
    d) http://msdn2.microsoft.com/en-us/library/yek4tbz0(VS.85).aspx
- W3 Schools `style` DOM object properties:
    e) http://www.w3schools.com/HTMLDOM/dom_obj_style.asp
- W3 Schools JavaScript Tutorial:            http://www.w3schools.com/js/default.asp
- JavaScript: The Definitive Guide:          http://books.google.ie/books?id=VOS6IlCsuU4C
- ppk on JavaScript by Quirksmode:           http://www.quirksmode.org/js/contents.html
- JSLint syntax checker:                     http://www.jslint.com/

# Chapter 8  The Document Object Model (DOM)

# Introduction

In the previous chapter we saw an introduction to JavaScript for producing interactive client-side user interfaces in web pages. A key feature provided to JavaScript by the web browser is its Document Object Model (DOM) that represents the contents of the page as JavaScript objects that the user can examine and manipulate to produce changes on the page.

In this chapter we'll learn much more about how the DOM works. We'll become able to manipulate elements on the page, add and remove elements from the page, change onscreen text, styles, images, and more. We'll also see the structure of the DOM as a tree of connected objects and learn how to crawl and change the contents of the tree to dynamically add and remove content from a page.

## 8.1  Global DOM Objects

Web browsers provide six important global objects that you can access in your JavaScript code. These objects allow your code to learn about the current document, browser window, URL, and so on. The six objects are shown in Table 8.1.

| Object Name | Represents |
|---|---|
| document | The current web page |
| history | The list of pages the user has visited previously |
| location | The URL of the current web page |
| navigator | The web browser you're using |
| screen | The screen area occupied by the browser and page |
| window | The browser window |

Table 8.1 Global DOM objects

For now, we're most interested in the `window` object. This object represents the entire browser window, and is the top-level object in DOM hierarchy. The `window` object has several useful methods, shown in Table 8.2. Also, the global functions we've seen so far such as `alert` are actually methods of the `window` object. Even the other global objects such as `document` and `navigator` are actually properties inside the `window` object, and you can optionally refer to them by their full names such as `window.location` or `window.history`. All of the code and variables you write in your JavaScript program become part of the `window` object.

| Method Name(s) | Description |
|---|---|
| `alert`, `confirm`, `prompt` | popup boxes (see JavaScript chapter) |
| `setInterval`, `setTimeout`, `clearInterval`, `clearTimeout` | timers (see Events chapter) |
| `open(`**`URL, name, options`**`)` `close()` | popping up new browser windows |
| `print()` | sending a web page to the printer |
| `blur()`, `focus()` | bringing a window to the foreground or background |
| `moveBy(`**`dx, dy`**`)` `moveTo(`**`x, y`**`)` | move browser window to an (x, y) position on the screen |
| `resizeBy(`**`dw, dh`**`)` `resizeTo(`**`width, height`**`)` | resizing the browser window |
| `scrollBy(`**`dx, dy`**`)` `scrollTo(`**`x, y`**`)` | scrolling up and down the page to a particular point |

**Table 8.2 Methods of the `window` object**

The `document` object represents the current web page and is the top-level object for all HTML elements on the current web page. We have already interacted with the `document` object by calling its `getElementById` method to access objects on our web page. Table 8.3 lists some useful properties of this object. The `document` object also contains some array-like properties such as `forms[]` and `images[]` and some methods such as `open`, `close`, and `writeln`, but we consider it poor style to use these features, so they are not listed here.

| Property Name | Type | Description |
|---|---|---|
| `body` | DOM element | the DOM object for the page's body |
| `cookie` | string | a string representation of all "cookies" (client-side data) supplied to this page |
| `referrer` | string | the URL of the document the user was viewing before this one |
| `title` | string | title of the web page as shown in title bar |
| URL | string | complete URL of this web page |

**Table 8.3 Properties of the `document` object**

The properties in the `document` object can be quite useful. For example, the `document.body` property provides direct access to the DOM object for the page's `<body>` tag and can be used to set a style on the entire page body or add/remove content directly from the body of the page. Later in this chapter we will learn more about **document** methods and properties for accessing DOM elements on the page.

The **navigator** object represents the user's browser. Table 8.4 lists its most useful properties.

| Property Name | Type | Description |
|---|---|---|
| appName | string | browser's name |
| appVersion | string | browser's version number |
| cookieEnabled | boolean | **true** if the browser supports cookies |
| language | string | user's language such as **"en-US"** |
| platform | string | user's operating system, such as **"Win32"** |
| userAgent | string | a lengthy "user agent" string representing the user's browser, OS, and version |

Table 8.4 Properties of the **navigator** object

Perhaps the most common use of the **navigator** object is to learn which browser the user is using by examining the property **navigator.appName**, which will have a value such as **"Microsoft Internet Explorer"** in IE or **"Netscape"** in Firefox. But this is a poor usage of the object, both because browsers' features are always changing and because the user can set the browser to "spoof" its app name to any string they want. Instead of checking for a particular browser, you should test for specific JavaScript objects and features.

The **history** object represents the list of previous pages that the user has visited in the browser. By calling its methods, you can force the browser to go back or forward to a different page. (This is often used to implement a "Back" button on a web page.) Table 8.5 lists the methods and properties.

| Method/Property Name | Description |
|---|---|
| back(), forward() | redirect the browser to its previous or next page |
| go(**index**) | redirect the browser to a specific page in the history |
| length | number of URLs in history (property) |

Table 8.5 Methods and properties of the **history** object

The **screen** object represents the browser window and the user's screen as a whole. Its properties can tell you the dimensions of the screen as well as the number of colors the user has available on the system. Table 8.6 summarizes the useful properties.

| Property Name(s) | Type | Description |
|---|---|---|
| availHeight, availWidth | integer | width/height of display screen, excluding taskbar |
| colorDepth | integer | bits of color depth available on user's monitor |
| height, width | integer | width/height of display screen |

Table 8.6 Properties of the **screen** object

The **location** object represents the URL of the current web page. Table 8.7 lists the useful properties of this object, as well as what their values would be if the current page's URL were:

```
http://www.example.com:8080/foo/bar/index.html?a=b&c=d#link05
```

| Name | Type | Description | Example |
|------|------|-------------|---------|
| hash | string | anchor (part of URL after #) | `"#link05"` |
| host | string | host name and port number | `"www.example.com:8080"` |
| hostname | string | host/domain name | `"www.example.com"` |
| href | string | entire URL | (the entire above URL) |
| pathname | string | directory/filename | `"/foo/bar/index.html"` |
| port | string | port number ("" if unspecified) | `"8080"` |
| protocol | string | protocol, followed by a colon | `"http:"` |
| search | string | query string (part of URL after ?) | `"?a=b&c=d"` |

**Table 8.7 Properties of the `location` object**

Example 8.1 shows the use of a couple of the global DOM objects. In the screenshot we have pressed the "Browser Info" button which shows we are working on a Windows machine in a Netscape (Firefox) browser. In our case, if we had just been browsing kayak.com (a travel search site) before this page and then clicked the Go Back button, we would return to that site.

```html
<div>
  <button onclick="getInfo();">Browser Info</button>
  <button onclick="goBack();">Go Back</button><br /><br />
  <span id="output"></span>
</div>
```

```javascript
function getInfo() {
  var span = document.getElementById("output");
  span.innerHTML = "Browser: " + navigator.appName +
                   "; System: " + navigator.platform;
}

function goBack() {
  history.back();
}
```

    [Browser Info] [Go Back]

Browser: Netscape; System: Win32

**Example 8.1 Using Global DOM Objects**

## 8.1.1  `window.onload` and Unobtrusive JavaScript

The JavaScript event code seen previously in this textbook was technically poor style. It's what we call obtrusive JavaScript, because the event handlers were attached in the HTML. This clutters our HTML code with lots of JavaScript and blurs the distinction between content and behavior.

| **unobtrusive JavaScript** A set of best practices for producing well-styled JavaScript code that is kept separate from webpage content. |
|---|

In this section, we'll see how to write unobtrusive JavaScript code. *Unobtrusive JavaScript* describes a way of attaching event handlers without putting any JavaScript into the body of your HTML page. This will give us much cleaner HTML code and a clear separation of content, presentation, and behavior.

The global `window` object provides features that can help us write unobtrusive JavaScript code. Recall that in the previous chapter we wrote a JavaScript-powered web page called the Amazing Multiplier. In that example and the others done so far, we've attached our event handlers by placing an event attribute in the HTML code, like in the code shown in Example 8.2. It turns out that attaching event handlers in HTML code like this is poor style and a habit we'll need to unlearn in this chapter.

```
<!DOCTYPE html PUBLIC "-//W3C//DTD XHTML 1.1//EN"
  "http://www.w3.org/TR/xhtml11/DTD/xhtml11.dtd">
<html xmlns="http://www.w3.org/1999/xhtml">
  <head>
    <script src="multiply.js" type="text/javascript"></script>
  </head>

  <body>
    <h1>The Amazing Multiplier</h1>
    <div>
      <input id="num1" type="text" size="3" /> *
      <input id="num2" type="text" size="3" /> =
      <span id="answer"></span> <br />
      <button onclick="compute();">Compute!</button>
    </div>
  </body>
</html>
```

**Example 8.2 Event handler attached in HTML code (bad style)**

```
// Multiplies two numbers typed into input boxes on the page,
// and displays the result in a span on the page.
function compute() {
  var input1 = document.getElementById("num1");   // fetch the 2 numbers
  var input2 = document.getElementById("num2");
  var answer = document.getElementById("answer");
  var result = input1.value * input2.value;        // compute result
  answer.innerHTML = result;
}
```

**Example 8.3 Multiplier original JavaScript code**

The reason it is bad style to attach the `onclick="compute();"` event handler in the HTML code is that it provides a poor separation of content from code. Recall from early in this textbook that an ideal web site separates the page into three parts: *content* (in the HTML files), *presentation* / style information (CSS files), and *code* / scripts (JS files). Our page unnecessarily blends the HTML content and the JavaScript event behavior. This is poor programming style, much like it would be poor style to put the visual styles directly into the HTML rather than separating them into their own CSS file.

We can separate the HTML from the script code by attaching and removing event handlers in our JavaScript code. If we take advantage of this ability, we'll be able to remove all the `onclick=`...

attributes from our HTML code. The key to attaching event handlers in JavaScript code is to take advantage of event properties of DOM objects.

DOM objects have properties matching the HTML event attributes, such as `onclick` and `onchange`. The syntax for attaching to such an event is shown in Example 8.4.

```
element.event = functionName;
```

**Example 8.4 Syntax template for attaching an event handler through the DOM**

For example, if your page has a button with an `id` of `"ok"` and you'd like to set an event handler on this button that calls a `booyah` function, previously you would have said:

```
<button id="ok" onclick="booyah();">Okay</button>
```

But in our new unobtrusive style, you would instead attach the handler in your JavaScript code, as shown in Example 8.5:

```
<button id="ok">Okay</button>
```

```
// attach onclick handler to Okay button
var okayButton = document.getElementById("ok");
okayButton.onclick = booyah;
```

**Example 8.5 Event handler attached unobtrusively**

Notice that you don't put parentheses after the function name, since the line of code is simply assigning the function, not calling it. That's it! If we do this for all of our event handlers, we can now remove all JavaScript code from our HTML, except for the initial `script` tag in the page header to load the JS file in the first place.

The next natural question to ask is, where should you put this code to attach the event handler? If you put the handler-attaching code in the global code of your `.js` file, it won't work properly. You'll get errors such as, "okayButton has no properties." This is because the browser runs your global code at the moment that it loads the `script` tag, which is when it is reading the page header. At this point in time, the page's body hasn't been read yet by the browser, nor have the DOM objects representing its elements been created. So you can't attach event handlers to the elements yet.

What we'd like is a way to run some code right when the browser has finished reading and creating the page's body. The `window` object can help us with this effort. It exposes several events of its own that relate to the page overall. Table 8.8 lists some of the most useful ones.

| Event Name | Description |
|---|---|
| `onerror` | an error occurs when loading a document or an image |
| `onload` | the browser loads the page |
| `onresize` | the browser window is resized |
| `onunload` | the browser exits the page |

**Table 8.8 Events of the `window` object**

The `window.onload` event occurs when the browser has finished loading the page. That's exactly when we want to attach our handlers. A template for this code is shown in Example 8.6.

```
window.onload = functionName;
...

function functionName() {
  code to attach event handlers;
}
```

**Example 8.6 Syntax template for `window.onload` handler**

Example 8.7 demonstrates the unobtrusive JavaScript technique. Notice that we've succeeded in removing the `onclick` code from the HTML code, leaving it cleaner and more readable.

```
...
  <button id="compute">Compute!</button>
...
```

```
window.onload = pageLoad;

// called when page loads; sets up event handlers
function pageLoad() {
  var computeButton = document.getElementById("compute");
  computeButton.onclick = compute;
}

// Multiplies two numbers typed into input boxes on the page,
// and displays the result in a span on the page.
function compute() {
  var input1 = document.getElementById("num1");   // fetch the 2 numbers
  var input2 = document.getElementById("num2");
  var answer = document.getElementById("answer");
  var result = input1.value * input2.value;        // compute result
  answer.innerHTML = result;
}
```

**Example 8.7 Unobtrusive multiplier code**

The resulting HTML code is cleaner, but the JavaScript is a bit less so. It's important to understand exactly when each piece of code executes. When the browser loads the HTML file for the page and reaches the **script** tag in the **head** section, it declares (but does not run) the **pageLoad** and **compute** functions, and also attaches **pageLoad** to be an event handler for when the page finishes loading. The browser goes on loading the rest of the page. When it finishes loading the very end of the HTML file (the `</html>` tag), it then fires the **window.onload** event, which causes the **pageLoad** function to execute. This attaches the **compute** function as an **onclick** event handler to the Compute! button, so that if the user clicks the button later, that function will execute. Phew!

**Common Error**

Parentheses and capitalization in event handlers

Many students mistakenly write **()** when attaching their event handlers in **window.onload**. Presumably this is because we're used to calling functions with parentheses. But attaching a function as an event handler is not the same as calling it. We're actually specifying that we want the browser to call it later, when the event occurs. This mistake can be made both when attaching the **window.onload** handler and when attaching other handlers inside its function. Example 8.8 shows an incorrect example and a corrected version.

```
window.onload = pageLoad();        // incorrect
window.onload = pageLoad;          // correct
...
okayButton.onclick = okayClick();  // incorrect
okayButton.onclick = okayClick;    // correct
```

**Example 8.8 Common error: Parentheses when attaching event handler**

If you run your code through the JSLint checker linked from our web site, it should catch this mistake and report an error to help you find it. While we're at it, another common bug is to incorrectly capitalize the event property names. Event names are all lowercase, not capitalized like most variables. Example 8.9 shows an incorrect capitalization for an event followed by a correct version.

```
window.onLoad = pageLoad;   // incorrect
window.onload = pageLoad;   // correct
```

**Example 8.9 Common error: Incorrectly capitalized event name**

## 8.1.2 Anonymous Functions

Sometimes you want to quickly create a function without bothering to give it a name. For example, the function you attach as the handler for the `window.onload` event is a function that you'll never call again. It wastes a few lines to declare it and name it, when you'll never refer to it by its name again in the rest of your code. For cases like these, JavaScript allows you to declare anonymous functions. An *anonymous function* is one that is not given a name and therefore can only be called if it is stored as a variable, attached to an event handler, etc. at the moment it's being declared. The syntax for creating an anonymous function is shown in Example 8.10.

> **anonymous function**
>
> One that is not given a name; useful for quickly creating and attaching an event handler.

```
function(parameters) {
    statements;
}
```

**Example 8.10 Syntax template for anonymous function declaration**

Generally you create an anonymous function and immediately assign it as an event handler or pass it as a parameter. The most common place we'll use anonymous functions in this textbook is as `window.onload` handlers. The syntax for attaching an anonymous function as a `window.onload` handler is shown in Example 8.11. Notice that you should still place a semicolon after the anonymous function's closing brace.

```
window.onload = function() {
    statements;
};
```

**Example 8.11 Syntax template for anonymous `window.onload` handler**

Example 8.12 revises our previous Multiplier code to use an anonymous `window.onload` handler. The code is a few lines shorter and saves us the drudgery of coming up with a name for our `onload` handler function.

```
...
  <button id="compute">Compute!</button>
...
```

```
// called when page loads; sets up event handlers
window.onload = function() {
  var computeButton = document.getElementById("compute");
  computeButton.onclick = compute;
};

// Multiplies two numbers typed into input boxes on the page,
// and displays the result in a span on the page.
function compute() {
  var input1 = document.getElementById("num1");     // fetch the 2 numbers
  var input2 = document.getElementById("num2");
  var answer = document.getElementById("answer");
  var result = input1.value * input2.value;          // compute result
  answer.innerHTML = result;
}
```

Example 8.12 Anonymous `window.onload` handler

### 8.1.3 The Keyword `this`

> **this**
>
> A keyword that refers to the current object. In event handlers, refers to the element to which the handler was attached.

Attaching event handlers unobtrusively has another benefit we haven't discussed yet. When they're attached, the event handlers are *bound* to the element objects. This means that the handler function's code knows what element it is listening to and can refer to that object in its code. The keyword for referring to the element object is `this`.

Suppose we want to write a page with a simple tip calculator. The user will type in a subtotal amount, then click one of three buttons to indicate a tip of 10%, 15%, or 18%. Upon clicking the button, the proper tip amount will be computed and shown on the page. Example 8.13 shows the relevant HTML code.

```
<h1>Tip Calculator</h1>

<div>
  $<input id="subtotal" type="text" size="5" /> subtotal <br />

  <button id="tenpercent">10%</button>
  <button id="fifteenpercent">15%</button>
  <button id="eighteenpercent">18%</button>

  <span id="total"></span>
</div>
```

# Tip Calculator

$[      ] subtotal
[ 10% ] [ 15% ] [ 18% ]

Example 8.13 Tip calculator HTML code

Let's write the code to handle just the 10% tip button. We'll set up a `window.onload` handler to run when the `tenpercent` button is clicked. (We use a slightly abbreviated syntax to do this, calling `document.getElementById` and directly setting the `.onclick` property of the DOM object returned.) Example 8.14 shows the code. In the `computeTip10` event handler function, we grab the subtotal amount from the page and parse it into a real number. Then we compute 10% of this amount and insert the result into the page in the `span` with `id` of `total`.

```
window.onload = function() {
  document.getElementById("tenpercent").onclick = computeTip10;
};


// Computes proper tip amount based on the subtotal and 10% tip.
function computeTip10() {
  var subtotal = parseFloat(document.getElementById("subtotal").value);
  var tipAmount = subtotal * 10 / 100.0;
  document.getElementById("total").innerHTML = "Tip: $" + tipAmount;
}
```

**Example 8.14 Tip calculator initial JavaScript code**

As you can imagine, the code for a 15% and 18% tip looks almost identical to the 10% tip code. We don't want to redundantly copy and paste the same code three times.

Often new students misguidedly try to attach event handlers with parameters. For example, in this tip calculator program, students try to write a `computeTip` function that accepts a tip percentage as a parameter and call that function when attaching the event handlers. The code of Example 8.15 does not attach its event handlers properly.

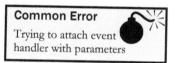

**Common Error**

Trying to attach event handler with parameters

```
// This does not work!
window.onload = function() {
  document.getElementById("tenpercent").onclick    = computeTip(10);
  document.getElementById("fifteenpercent").onclick = computeTip(15);
  document.getElementById("eighteenpercent").onclick = computeTip(18);
};
```

**Example 8.15 Common error: Passing parameters when attaching event handler**

The reason the code doesn't work is because event handlers cannot have parameters. When you write `computeTip(10);`, you aren't attaching the `computeTip` function as an event handler to be executed later. You're *calling* the `computeTip` function, and whatever value it returns is attached as the `onclick` handler. The function returns nothing, so the `onclick` handler is set to `undefined`.

This isn't what we want; you'll probably get an error such as "subtotal is not defined" or "Tip: $NaN". This is because the `computeTip` function is being called immediately in the `window.onload` handler, not later when the button is clicked. So the DOM objects aren't properly set up yet.

The proper way to attach the same tip calculating behavior to each button is to take advantage of the `this` keyword. We can use the same event handler on all three buttons. First, we'll attach the same `computeTip` function to all three buttons in our `window.onload` handler:

```
window.onload = function() {
  document.getElementById("tenpercent").onclick = computeTip;
  document.getElementById("fifteenpercent").onclick = computeTip;
  document.getElementById("eighteenpercent").onclick = computeTip;
};
```

When we attach `computeTip` to each button, it makes it so that inside the code of `computeTip`, we can refer to the DOM object of the button that was clicked each time by the keyword `this`. We can find out the tip amount from this button by looking at the `innerHTML` in the button. The `innerHTML` text will be a string such as `"10%"` or `"18%"`. If we call JavaScript's `parseInt` function on this string, it will strip the % sign and return the corresponding integer such as `10` or `18`. Example 8.16 shows the code.

```
// Computes proper tip amount based on the subtotal and tip percentage.
function computeTip() {
  var subtotal = parseFloat(document.getElementById("subtotal").value);
  var tipPercent = parseInt(this.innerHTML);
  var tipAmount = subtotal * tipPercent / 100.0;
  document.getElementById("total").innerHTML = "Tip: $" + tipAmount;
}
```

**Example 8.16 Improved tip calculator event handler**

Now we're able to reuse the same event handler to listen to three different elements, and it does the right thing for each one that is clicked. This only works when you attach your event handlers unobtrusively in your JavaScript code; if they are attached as attributes in your HTML, the code won't bind properly and the `this` keyword doesn't work as expected. (In such code, `this` actually refers to the global `window` object, which probably isn't what you want.)

## Self-Check

1. What is unobtrusive JavaScript? Why is it poor style to use obtrusive JavaScript, and what are the key changes one makes to cause JavaScript code to become unobtrusive?
2. What are the six global JavaScript DOM objects, and what does each one represent?
3. What is a "user agent" string? Why is it poor form to examine browser names and user agent strings in JavaScript code and use their values to govern a program's behavior or features?
4. Describe the specific changes that must be made to the Hangman JavaScript code from the previous chapter's case study in order to make it use unobtrusive JavaScript.
5. What is an anonymous function, and how can it be useful in JavaScript code?
6. Suppose a page has the following HTML code containing four buttons representing football scoring options. When each button is clicked, the appropriate number of points is added to the player's total score. Describe a way to write the JavaScript code for this page, avoiding redundancy by using the `this` keyword.

```
<button id="touchdown">6 points (touchdown)</button>
<button id="fieldgoal">3 points (field goal)</button>
<button id="safety">2 points (safety/2-point conversion)</button>
<button id="extrapoint">1 point (extra point)</button>

<input id="total" type="text" value="0" />
```

## 8.2  DOM Element Objects

In our previous examples we have seen DOM objects for elements on a page. But our interaction with these objects has been very limited: we've set the `innerHTML` for `span` elements and we've interacted with the `value` of text boxes. These DOM objects are actually rich with other properties and methods we can use in our JavaScript code. In this section we'll explore some of the basic features of DOM objects and interacting with them. We'll explore DOM interactions in much more detail in the next chapter.

### 8.2.1  Interacting with Text

Much of the manipulation we want to perform on DOM objects involves getting, manipulating, and setting text. The text inside an element is accessible as a string, and we can manipulate these strings using the string methods shown in the previous chapter. But the means of accessing the element text differs for various elements, so it merits some discussion here. There are also some browser incompatibilities related to text content.

The ECMAScript-standard way of changing the text inside an element is to set its `textContent` property. This property is supported by all standards-compliant browsers, but unfortunately not by Internet Explorer, which uses a non-standard property named `innerText` instead. Because of this ugly incompatibility, so far in this textbook we've used the `innerHTML` property instead to set text. Even though `innerHTML` is not currently part of the ECMA JavaScript standard, it will be in the next version of the ECMAScript standard and is already supported by every major browser. These properties are summarized in Table 8.9.

| Property Name | Description | Supported By |
|---|---|---|
| `innerHTML` | text and/or HTML tags inside a node | all browsers (non-standard) |
| `innerText` | text (without HTML tags) inside a node | IE only |
| `textContent` | text (without HTML tags) inside a node | all browsers except IE |
| `value` | text value inside a form control | all browsers |

Table 8.9 Various DOM properties for getting text/HTML content

For example, to set the paragraph with an `id` of `error` to show a particular error message, you could write the following code, which would work on standards-compliant browsers:

```
var errorArea = document.getElementById("error");
errorArea.textContent = "Error: Missing last name";
```

If you want the code to work on all browsers including Internet Explorer, you could write:

```
// more cross-browser compatible
var errorArea = document.getElementById("error");
errorArea.innerText = errorArea.textContent = "Error: Missing last name";
```

We find the dual assignment tedious and therefore use the `innerHTML` property instead to set the text. Technically setting `textContent` would be more stylistically correct, but the browser compatibility problems make it too cumbersome for our taste.

```
// also cross-browser compatible
var errorArea = document.getElementById("error");
errorArea.innerHTML = "Error: Missing last name";
```

An interesting feature of the `innerHTML` property is that it can be used not only to get/set text content, but also to add new HTML elements and tags to a page. This ability is very powerful, but it can be abused and often leads to ugly code. Example 8.17 demonstrates the use of `innerHTML` to add tags to a page. We strongly discourage this style; we'll show a better style later in this chapter for adding new elements to a page using a method called `document.createElement`.

```
// bad code (don't insert HTML tags using innerHTML!)
var div = document.getElementById("mainarea");
div.innerHTML = "<a href=\"foo/bar.html\">Check it out!</a>";
```

**Example 8.17 Abusing `innerHTML`**

### Example Program: Shuffler

We've already seen that to get and set the text of most normal elements, you use the previous properties such as `innerHTML`. If the element in question is a form control, such as an `input` text box or `textarea`, we access the text using the `value` property instead. You can also set new text to appear in the element by assigning `value` a new string.

Suppose we want to write a page that lets the user type in lines of input into a `textarea`, with a Shuffle button below that randomly rearranges the order of the lines when clicked. Example 8.18 shows the relevant HTML code and its appearance in the browser.

```
<h1>Ye Old Shuffle Tool</h1>
<div>
  Items (one per line): <br />
  <textarea id="items" rows="10" cols="80"></textarea>
  <button id="shuffle">Shuffle It!</button>
</div>
```

# Ye Old Shuffle Tool

Items (one per line):

Shuffle It!

**Example 8.18 Shuffler HTML code**

Probably the trickiest part of this program is the actual algorithm for shuffling the array. Since it is difficult and also might be of general use in other programs, let's write a function called `shuffle` that accepts an array as a parameter and shuffles that array's elements. Keeping the shuffling algorithm from the DOM and event code will help us keep the code cleaner and avoid bugs.

A simple algorithm for shuffling is to loop over the elements of the array, choosing a new random index for each element and swapping it to that index. To make sure that the algorithm is fairly balanced (that each arrangement of the elements is equally likely), we must make sure to choose a random index greater than or equal to the element's current position. (The proof that our algorithm is balanced is outside the scope of this textbook.) Example 8.19 shows the code.

```javascript
// Randomly rearranges the elements of the given array.
function shuffle(a) {
  for (var i = 0; i < a.length; i++) {
    // pick a random index j such that i <= j <= a.length - 1
    var j = i + parseInt(Math.random() * (a.length - i));

    // swap the element to that index
    var temp = a[i];
    a[i] = a[j];
    a[j] = temp;
  }
}
```

**Example 8.19 Array shuffle code**

It can be tough to get a tricky function like this working straight away. We suggest typing in the shuffle function into your .js file, then opening the page in Firefox and popping up the Firebug console. Then declare one or two short arrays and call the shuffle function on them. Inspect the results to make sure that they look suitably random. Once we're convinced that our function works, we go on to the rest of the code. Figure 8.1 demonstrates this technique.

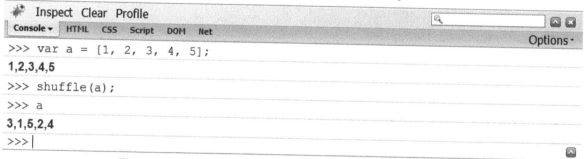

**Figure 8.1 Testing shuffle function in Firebug console**

Now that our shuffling algorithm is implemented, the rest of the code to attach the event handlers can be written. When the Shuffle button is clicked, we'll grab the text from the **items** text area, split it into an array of lines using its **split** method, and then call the **shuffle** function on that array of lines. Example 8.20 shows the code.

```javascript
window.onload = function() {
  document.getElementById("shuffle").onclick = shuffleClick;
};

function shuffleClick() {
  var items = document.getElementById("items");
  var lines = items.value.split("\n");   // split into lines
  shuffle(lines);
  items.value = lines.join("\n");        // put back into text area
}
```

**Example 8.20 Shuffler JavaScript code**

## 8.2.2 Adjusting Styles

The DOM can be used to modify the styles and onscreen appearance of page elements. This is done through the DOM object's **style** property. This property represents the HTML element's **style** attribute and directly connects to the CSS for that element. The **style** property is not a string but instead an object that contains dozens of properties, one for each possible CSS property of that element. The syntax for accessing these properties is shown in Example 8.21.

```
element.style.property           // get value
element.style.property = value;  // set value
```

**Example 8.21 DOM style property**

For most of the CSS properties, there is a corresponding DOM **style** object property with the same name. For example, suppose you have the following HTML code in your page:

```
<p id="slogan">Eat at Joe's.  You can't beat our prices!</p>
```

To set the preceding paragraph's text color to red, you would use the following JavaScript code:

```
var paragraph = document.getElementById("slogan");
paragraph.style.color = "red";
```

The names of the DOM style properties are as similar as possible to their CSS counterparts, but there are a few small differences. DOM style properties can't have dashes in them because - is the subtraction operator in JavaScript. Wherever there would have been a dash, the DOM property's name capitalizes the next letter. For example, the CSS **background-color** property is called **backgroundColor** in the DOM.

Table 8.10 lists several examples of the mapping between CSS property names and DOM property names. This is obviously an incomplete list, since there are too many style properties to list here. But this chapter's References section points to a page on the W3Schools web site that has a complete list of all style properties. All values for DOM style properties are stored as strings, with an empty string " " as the value if the property is not set.

| CSS Property Name | DOM Property Name | Example |
|---|---|---|
| background-color | backgroundColor | "#ff00dd" |
| border | border | "1em solid red" |
| border-top-width | borderTopWidth | "3px" |
| color | color | "red" |
| float | cssFloat | "left" |
| font-weight | fontWeight | "bold" |
| font-size | fontSize | "12pt" |
| z-index | zIndex | "456" |

**Table 8.10 DOM style property names**

A DOM object's **style** property is useful for setting new styles but has some issues when trying to examine pre-existing element styles defined in CSS, which we'll explore in a later section. In the next chapter we will learn a workaround for this limitation.

### Example Program: Never Gonna Give You Up

You may be familiar with the popular internet meme of "Rick rolling" where one person dupes another into viewing a video of Rick Astley's 1987 hit song, "Never Gonna Give You Up." Let's write a short page that shows the lyrics of that song along with some controls beneath the lyrics. The controls will enable the user to change the font family and style of the lyrics. Figure 8.2 shows the desired page appearance.

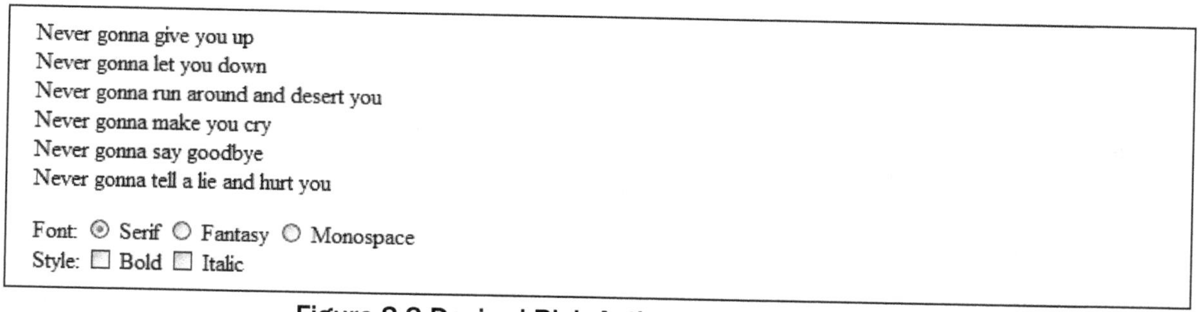

```
Never gonna give you up
Never gonna let you down
Never gonna run around and desert you
Never gonna make you cry
Never gonna say goodbye
Never gonna tell a lie and hurt you

Font: ⦿ Serif  ◯ Fantasy  ◯ Monospace
Style: ☐ Bold  ☐ Italic
```

**Figure 8.2 Desired Rick Astley page appearance**

Let's begin with the HTML code for this page. The lyrics themselves are just a paragraph with line breaks. We'll give it an **id** of **lyrics** since we will want to access this paragraph using the DOM later. Below the lyrics are two **div**s with controls. The first has three radio buttons for the font family to use. Recall that in order to ensure that only one radio button can be checked at a time, we must group them by giving each of the three buttons a **name** attribute with the same value. Below the font radio buttons are two checkboxes for bold and italic styles. These make more sense as checkboxes than radio buttons because a font could be both bold and italic, or one or the other, or neither. We'll also wrap each radio button and checkbox and its text in a **label** so that its text is clickable. Example 8.22 shows the HTML code.

```html
<p id="lyrics">
  Never gonna give you up <br /> Never gonna let you down <br />
  Never gonna run around and desert you <br />
  Never gonna make you cry <br /> Never gonna say goodbye <br />
  Never gonna tell a lie and hurt you
</p>

<div>
  Font:
  <label><input id="serif" type="radio" name="font" checked="checked" />
    Serif</label>
  <label><input id="fantasy" type="radio" name="font" />
    Fantasy</label>
  <label><input id="monospace" type="radio" name="font" />
    Monospace</label>
</div>

<div>
  Style:
  <label><input id="bold" type="checkbox" /> Bold</label>
  <label><input id="italic" type="checkbox" /> Italic</label>
</div>
```

**Example 8.22 Rick Astley HTML code**

Now let's write the JavaScript code to give behavior to the controls. Let's begin with the bold and italic checkboxes. We need `onclick` handlers on each of them, so we'll set up a `window.onload` handler to attach these handlers. The `boldClick` and `italicClick` functions aren't written yet:

```
window.onload = function() {
  document.getElementById("bold").onclick = boldClick;
  document.getElementById("italic").onclick = italicClick;
};
```

An initial stab at the `boldClick` function is shown in Example 8.23. Recall that `font-weight` is the CSS property for boldness. So to make the font bold, we access the DOM object for the `lyrics` paragraph and set its `style` property's `fontWeight` to the string `"bold"`.

```
function boldClick() {
  var lyrics = document.getElementById("lyrics");
  lyrics.style.fontWeight = "bold";
}
```

**Example 8.23 Flawed `boldClick` function**

The problem with our initial `boldClick` function is that it always makes the text bold, even if the user unchecks the box. The code should actually check whether the box is checked, and if so, set the font weight to bold, but otherwise set it to normal. Recall that the checkbox that was clicked can refer to itself as `this`. A similar pattern should be followed for the italic checkbox, but the CSS property to use for italic is `font-style`, corresponding to the `fontStyle` property in the DOM. Example 8.24 shows the corrected code, which now works properly when attached to the page.

```
// Called when the Bold checkbox is clicked.
function boldClick() {
  var lyrics = document.getElementById("lyrics");
  if (this.checked) {
    lyrics.style.fontWeight = "bold";
  } else {
    lyrics.style.fontWeight = "normal";
  }
}

// Called when the Italic checkbox is clicked.
function italicClick() {
  var lyrics = document.getElementById("lyrics");
  if (this.checked) {
    lyrics.style.fontStyle = "italic";
  } else {
    lyrics.style.fontStyle = "normal";
  }
}
```

**Example 8.24 JavaScript code to set font weight and style**

Now it's time to write the code to change the font used for the song lyrics. The radio buttons each need `onclick` handlers, so we'll attach them in our `window.onload` function. Recall that to set a font like Serif or Monospace, we must change the CSS `font-family` property of the paragraph, which corresponds to the `fontFamily` property of its DOM object. So for example, if the `monospace` radio button is clicked, we must set the paragraph's `fontFamily` to `"monospace"`.

You may think we need 3 functions here, one for each radio button. But in this case we can use a clever trick to avoid redundancy. The value we want for the fontFamily is the same as the id of whichever radio button is clicked. (We sneakily chose those id values on purpose to make the Java-Script code easier to write later; a good trick.) The radio button can refer to itself inside the event handler as this. So we can ask for this.id and set the font family to that value. Example 8.25 shows the modified JavaScript code and the resulting appearance in the browser after clicking some of the buttons.

```
window.onload = function() {
  document.getElementById("serif").onclick = fontClick;
  document.getElementById("fantasy").onclick = fontClick;
  document.getElementById("monospace").onclick = fontClick;
  document.getElementById("bold").onclick = boldClick;
  document.getElementById("italic").onclick = italicClick;
};

// Called when one of the font radio button is clicked.
function fontClick() {
  var lyrics = document.getElementById("lyrics");
  lyrics.style.fontFamily = this.id;
}
```

Never gonna give you up
Never gonna let you down
Never gonna run around and desert you
Never gonna make you cry
Never gonna say goodbye
Never gonna tell a lie and hurt you

Font: ○ Serif ◉ Fantasy ○ Monospace
Style: ☑ Bold ☑ Italic

**Example 8.25 JavaScript code to set font family**

Let's add one last feature to our page to illustrate a few gotchas of styling with the DOM. Let's make it so that every time you change the font family, the font size changes to a larger size. At first, let's just try to set the size to 20pt when the font is changed. Recall that the font size of the lyrics is represented by the CSS font-size property, which corresponds to the fontSize property in the DOM. Example 8.26 shows an incorrect initial attempt at increasing the font size.

```
// Called when one of the font radio button is clicked.
function fontClick() {
  var lyrics = document.getElementById("lyrics");
  lyrics.style.fontFamily = this.id;
  lyrics.style.fontSize = 20;   // does not work!
}
```

**Example 8.26 Failed attempt to enlarge font size**

The bug in our code is that the fontSize property is not an integer such as 20. Instead it must be a string with a unit attached such as px, pt, em, etc. The correct line of code is the following:

```
lyrics.style.fontSize = "20pt";
```

Let's modify this feature slightly to demonstrate another common gotcha of DOM styling. Suppose that instead of setting the font size to 20pt every time, we want to enlarge the font size by 2pt each time the font family is changed. The following code is a failed attempt to do this:

```
lyrics.style.fontSize += 2;
```

Again we remember that we cannot just add 2 to a string such as `"12pt"` to get a new string such as `"14pt"`. The following also does not work properly:

```
lyrics.style.fontSize += "2pt";
```

The correct start toward increasing the font size is to get its old size value *as an integer* by calling `parseInt` on the old `fontSize` value. Then we increase this integer by 2, and set this new larger value to be the font size of the paragraph, making sure to append the suffix `"pt"`. The following code is an improvement:

```
var oldSize = parseInt(lyrics.style.fontSize);   // e.g. 12
lyrics.style.fontSize = (oldSize + 2) + "pt";    // e.g. "14pt"
```

But believe it or not, this code *still* does not work. The problem is that the `fontSize` property will only have a value if the page's HTML, JavaScript, or CSS code has explicitly set a font size on that element. The first time the page loads there is no explicitly set font size on our `lyrics` paragraph element – it relies on the browser's default font size initially for the paragraph. So the first time a font radio button is clicked, `lyrics.style.fontSize` has the value `""` (empty string), and when we call `parseInt` on the empty string, we get `NaN` as our result. For now our workaround for this problem is to use the `||` operator to default to a font size of 12 if none is specified. Once the `fontSize` is explicitly using the DOM in our JavaScript, the font will increase by 2pt as expected each time a font is chosen. In the next chapter we'll see a better way to find out style information for page content even if none is explicitly set in the HTML or CSS.

```
// Called when one of the font radio button is clicked.
function fontClick() {
  var lyrics = document.getElementById("lyrics");
  lyrics.style.fontFamily = this.id;

  // enlarge font size by 2pt
  var oldSize = parseInt(lyrics.style.fontSize) || 12;   // default 12
  lyrics.style.fontSize = (oldSize + 2) + "pt";
}

Never gonna give you up
Never gonna let you down
Never gonna run around and desert you
Never gonna make you cry
Never gonna say goodbye
Never gonna tell a lie and hurt you

Font: ◯ Serif  ◯ Fantasy  ◉ Monospace
Style: ☑ Bold  ☐ Italic
```

**Example 8.27 Corrected font-enlargement code**

## 8.2.3 Unobtrusive Styling

We've discussed unobtrusive JavaScript as a way to improve the separation between content and code. But there's a more subtle separation that we should also discuss: the one between JavaScript code and styling/presentation.

So far, our JavaScript code has had a lot of statements that directly modify CSS style properties of elements. This is actually poor style (no pun intended), because we're hard-coding styles, fonts, colors, and so on into our JavaScript code. Suppose our code makes it so that every time you click a button, that button's text turns red, as shown in Example 8.28.

```
// called when a button is clicked on the page
function buttonClick() {
  this.style.color = "red";    // set the button's text to a red color
}
```

**Example 8.28 JavaScript code that restyles a button (poor style)**

What if we decide to redesign our site later, changing the site's look and wanting the buttons green instead of red? We'll have to edit not only our CSS files but also our JavaScript code. Ideally we should have to change only our CSS files to change the site's presentation, not anything in our JavaScript.

A well-styled JavaScript code should contain as little CSS style code as possible. Whenever you can, you should instead use JavaScript to modify classes and/or IDs on elements, and then define the appearance of those classes and IDs in your CSS files. DOM element objects contain properties named `className` and `id` to help us. Example 8.29 demonstrates this idea.

```
/* CSS style for buttons that have been clicked. */
.clickedbutton {
  color: red;
}
```

```
// called when a button is clicked on the page
function buttonClick() {
  this.className = "clickedbutton";
}
```

**Example 8.29 Setting a CSS class using the DOM**

The `className` property is a bit clunky because it's just a string. If the button already had a pre-existing class, our code that sets `className` would obliterate this and replace it with the `clickedbutton` class; it's hard to add and remove multiple classes this way. In the next chapter we'll see a way to gracefully handle multiple classes on the same element using the DOM.

## Self-Check

7. What are the differences between the `textContent, innerText, innerHTML`, and `value` properties? When should each be used?

8. How would you change an element's background color using the DOM? What object(s) do you interact with, and what is the style property name? What property would you access to make an element float to the left?

9. Write a line of code that changes the width of an element stored in a variable named `myBox` to 500 pixels.

10. How can you change what CSS class(es) apply to a given element using the DOM?

11. What is unobtrusive styling, and why is it beneficial?

12. A previous problem asked you to change an element's width to 500 pixels. Modify this code to use unobtrusive styling; assume that the reason we are setting the width to 500 pixels is because our pages has information boxes on it and we want all information boxes to be 500 pixels wide. Create appropriate CSS style content to achieve this.

## 8.3 The DOM Tree

In this section we'll discuss ways to traverse and access DOM objects in our JavaScript code. We'll learn about the connections between related DOM objects, how to examine groups of elements with loops in our code, and how to dynamically add and remove elements from a page.

As we discussed in the previous chapter, JavaScript represents each element on the page as an object. These objects are connected to each other in a tree-like structure with parent, child, and sibling links between them, sometimes called the *DOM tree* for the page. The structure of a page's DOM tree mirrors the structure of the HTML content of the page. For example, if a `div` section contains a `ul` list with three `li` items inside it, the JavaScript object representing the `ul` will have a reference to the `div` as its parent and the `li` items as its children. The `li` items have references to the other `li`s as siblings and to the `ul` as their parent.

DOM objects are sometimes also called DOM *nodes* because they are like nodes of a linked list or a tree data structure. Each node has references to its parent (the element that contains it), its siblings (other elements with the same parent), and its children (elements contained inside this one). Figure 8.3 displays a short web page and a diagram of its resulting DOM tree (elements only).

```
<!DOCTYPE html PUBLIC "-//W3C//DTD XHTML 1.1//EN"
  "http://www.w3.org/tr/xhtml11/dtd/xhtml11.dtd">
<html xmlns="http://www.w3.org/1999/XHTML">
  <head>
    <title>Page Title</title>
    <meta name="description" content="A really great web site" />
  </head>

  <body>
    <h1>This is a heading</h1>
    <p>A paragraph with a <a href="http://www.google.com/">link</a>.</p>
    <ul>
      <li>a list item</li>
      <li>another list item</li>
      <li>a third list item</li>
    </ul>
  </body>
</html>
```

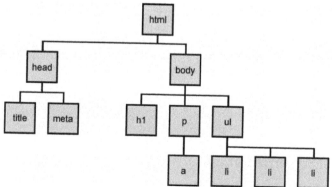

**Figure 8.3 A basic web page and its resulting DOM tree**

## 8.3.1 DOM Nodes

There are three types of nodes representing different kinds of content that can appear on a page:

- An *element node* represents an HTML tag. It can have children and/or attributes.

- A *text node* represents inline text inside a block element. It always occurs as a child within an element node. It cannot have children or attributes.

- An *attribute node* represents an attribute name/value pair inside an element's opening tag. It is related to an element but is not considered a child of that node. An attribute node cannot have any children or attributes.

Consider the short HTML code fragment shown below in Figure 8.4. Its HTML would be represented as the DOM tree shown below the code.

```
<p>This is a paragraph of text with a
    <a href="/path/to/another/page.html">link</a>.</p>
```

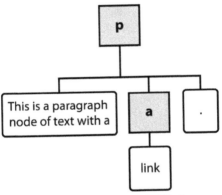

**Figure 8.4 DOM tree for HTML fragment**

There are a few things to notice about the tree:

- The plain text such as "This is a paragraph..." gets represented as text nodes. We don't think of text as an element, but it is still part of the tree.
- The text after the link, consisting of only a period, does get its own text node as well.
- The link consists of an element node, with a child text node inside it representing the word "link", the link's inner text content.

Most of the nodes we'll want to deal with in this textbook are element nodes, but it's important to understand that the other nodes are there. Sometimes the other nodes (particularly text nodes) crop up and we must navigate around them or otherwise interact with them.

## 8.3.2 Traversal Properties and Methods

Every DOM node object has several properties that connect it to other nearby nodes. Many of these are listed in Table 8.11. Each of these properties is a reference to another DOM object. If no such object exists (such as if the node has no children or no next sibling), the property is `null`.

| Property Name | Description |
|---|---|
| parentNode | the element that contains this node |
| previousSibling, nextSibling | neighboring nodes that have the same parent |
| firstChild, lastChild | start/end of this node's list of children |
| childNodes | an array of all this node's children |

**Table 8.11 DOM node properties**

These properties link the DOM nodes into a tree structure that can be traversed in your Java-Script code. Some of the links that would be created to represent Figure 8.4's HTML code are shown in Figure 8.5. The `firstChild` of the paragraph is a text node representing the text "This is a paragraph of text with a". That text node's `nextSibling` is an element node representing the **a** link tag. The **a** node's `firstChild` is a text node representing the word "link" inside the node.

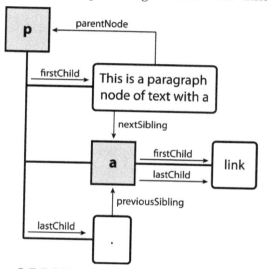

**Figure 8.5 DOM tree structure for HTML fragment**

For example, if you have a reference to the paragraph element stored in a variable named `myParagraph` and want to change the link's text from "link" to "foosball", you could write the following JavaScript code (the comments indicate the node to which each reference refers):

```
//    <p>      "This..."       <a>        "link"
myParagraph.firstChild.nextSibling.firstChild.textContent = "foosball";
```

### 8.3.3 Traversing Elements

The tree link properties such as `firstChild` and `nextSibling` are useful, but they have some serious drawbacks. For one, they can be tedious to use when you're trying to worm your way into a deeply nested set of tags. Second, there are subtle bugs that are easy to encounter when using them.

For example, consider the following HTML code. Looking at the **div** with **id** of **foo**, how many child nodes does it have (in other words, how many elements are in its `childNodes` array)?

```
<div id="foo">
  <p>
    This is a paragraph of text with a
    <a href="page.html">link</a>
  </p>
</div>
```

Most people say 1, representing the paragraph. Others see the `<a>` tag inside that paragraph and mistakenly count it as a child of the `div`, so they guess 2. But the correct answer is 3 children:

- a text node representing `"\n\t"` (before the paragraph)
- an element node representing the `<p>`
- a text node representing `"\n"` (after the paragraph)

Technically the `div` also has an attribute node representing its `id` attribute. But that attribute node doesn't show up in the `childNodes` of the `div`'s DOM object.

What a pain. We usually don't want to interact with attribute or text nodes directly; the elements are much more interesting. Therefore, if we really want to walk the DOM tree and manipulate its elements in interesting ways, a more powerful set of tools is needed.

### 8.3.4 Selecting Groups of Elements

We've seen many examples of accessing a particular element by its `id`. But often we're instead concerned with groups of elements. For example, how would we do each of the following in our JavaScript code?

- When the "Go" button is clicked, move all `div`s of class `puzzle` to random x/y locations.
- When the user hovers over the maze boundary, turn all maze walls red.
- Change every other item in the `ul` list with `id` of `students` to have a gray background.

Each task involves modifying a group of elements to have a common new feature or style. In this section we'll see how to select such a group of elements and process each one. The global `document` object (as well as every DOM element object) contains methods that return a node or array of nodes that match certain criteria. The methods provided are shown in Table 8.12.

| Method Name | Description |
| --- | --- |
| getElementById | returns a DOM element with the given HTML `id` attribute |
| getElementsByTagName | returns an array of DOM elements with the given HTML element, such as `"div"` |
| getElementsByName | returns an array of DOM elements with given `name` attribute (e.g. all radio buttons in a group) |

Table 8.12 DOM node selection methods

For example, to set every paragraph on the page to have a yellow background color, you could write the code shown in Example 8.30.

```
// set all paragraphs to have a yellow background color
var allParagraphs = document.getElementsByTagName("p");
for (var i = 0; i < allParagraphs.length; i++) {
  allParagraphs[i].style.backgroundColor = "yellow";
}
```

**Example 8.30 Getting elements by name**

The DOM node selection methods actually exist for every DOM element object (not just the parent **document** object). You can call these methods on any element inside the DOM to select only those sub-elements contained within the element. For example, the following HTML code contains 3 paragraphs, the latter 2 of which will be returned by the JavaScript code in Example 8.31.

```
<p>This paragraph won't be affected!</p>
<div id="footer">
  <p>1234 Street</p>
  <p>Atlanta, GA</p>
</div>
```

```
var footer = document.getElementById("footer");
var footerParagraphs = footer.getElementsByTagName("p");
for (var i = 0; i < footerParagraphs.length; i++) {
  footerParagraphs[i].style.backgroundColor = "yellow";
}
```

**Example 8.31 Selecting elements within another element**

## Example Program: Searchable Text

Many sites want a Search feature that allows the user to search for a given string or keyword in a page. Suppose we have set up a fan site about our favorite sports team and want the site to have such a feature. The site's main text content is placed into paragraphs inside a **div** with an **id** of main. Example 8.32 shows the initial HTML code and its appearance in the browser.

We'd like to make it so that the Search highlights in yellow any paragraph containing the phrase that is searched for. Before starting with JavaScript, let's set up a CSS class for highlighted paragraphs with the desired appearance. That way, in our JS code we can unobtrusively set matching paragraphs to use the CSS class rather than setting all of the style properties using the DOM. Example 8.33 shows the CSS code. (We'd also have to insert a **link** tag in the HTML page's header to attach this CSS file to the page.)

```
<div id="main">
  <p>The Phoenix Suns are a professional basketball team based in
    Phoenix, Arizona. They are members of the ...</p>
  <p>The Suns have been generally successful since they began play as an
    expansion team in 1968. In forty years of play they have posted ...</p>
  <p>On January 22, 1968, the NBA awarded expansion franchises to an
    ownership group from Phoenix and one from Milwaukee. ...</p>
  <ul>
    <li>Richard L. Bloch, investment broker/real estate developer...</li>
    <li>Karl Eller, outdoor advertising company owner and former...</li>
    <li>Donald Pitt, Tucson-based attorney;</li>
    <li>Don Diamond, Tucson-based real estate investor.</li>
  </ul>
</div>

<p>Page by Marty Stepp. <br />
  Some (all) information taken from Wikipedia.</p>
<hr />
<div>
  Search for text:
  <input id="searchtext" type="text" />
  <button id="searchbutton">Search</button>
</div>
```

The Phoenix Suns are a professional basketball team based in Phoenix, Arizona. They are members of the Pacific Division of the Western Conference in the National Basketball Association (NBA). ...

The Suns have been generally successful since they began play as an expansion team in 1968. In forty years of play they have posted seventeen fifty-win seasons ...

On January 22, 1968, the NBA awarded expansion franchises to an ownership group from Phoenix and one from Milwaukee. ...

- Richard L. Bloch, investment broker/real estate developer and former Tucson resident;
- Karl Eller, outdoor advertising company owner and former Arizona football player;
- Donald Pitt, Tucson-based attorney;
- Don Diamond, Tucson-based real estate investor.

Page by Marty Stepp.
Some (all) information taken from Wikipedia.

Search for text: [          ] [ Search ]

**Example 8.32 Searchable fan site HTML code**

```
/* A style for paragraphs that have been highlighted from a search. */
.highlighted {
  background-color: yellow;
  border: 1px dashed #666600;
  font-weight: bold;
}
```

**Example 8.33 CSS code for searchable fan site highlighting**

Now let's write the JavaScript code. When the page loads, we'll attach a function to the Search button as an `onclick` event handler:

```
window.onload = function() {
  document.getElementById("searchbutton").onclick = searchClick;
};
```

In the `searchClick` function, we need to examine every paragraph in the main section of the page to see whether it matches the search phrase typed by the user. To do this, first we'll fetch the DOM object for the main section, then we'll ask it for all of its elements by tag name `"p"`:

```
function searchClick() {
  var main = document.getElementById("main");
  var mainParas = main.getElementsByTagName("p");
  for (var i = 0; i < mainParas.length; i++) {
    ...
  }
}
```

To see whether a paragraph's text matches the search phrase, first we must grab the search phrase itself as the `value` of the `searchtext` element. Then we can test it for a match against each paragraph by calling the `indexOf` method on the `innerHTML` in the paragraph. Recall that `innerHTML` is a string and that the `indexOf` method returns one string's index location inside another (-1 if not found). So an index ≥ 0 indicates that the search phrase is contained in the paragraph. If the paragraph contains the search phrase, we'll set it to have a class attribute of `"highlighted"` using the paragraph's `className` property. Example 8.34 shows the complete JavaScript code for the page. Figure 8.6 shows the resulting appearance in the browser after searching for a given string.

```
window.onload = function() {
  document.getElementById("searchbutton").onclick = searchClick;
};

// Called when the Search button is clicked.
// Looks for paragraphs matching a search string and highlights them.
function searchClick() {
  var searchPhrase = document.getElementById("searchtext").value;

  var main = document.getElementById("main");
  var mainParas = main.getElementsByTagName("p");

  for (var i = 0; i < mainParas.length; i++) {
    if (mainParas[i].innerHTML.indexOf(searchPhrase) >= 0) {
      mainParas[i].className = "highlighted";   // highlight
    } else {
      mainParas[i].className = null;            // un-highlight
    }
  }
}
```

Example 8.34 Searchable fan site complete JavaScript code

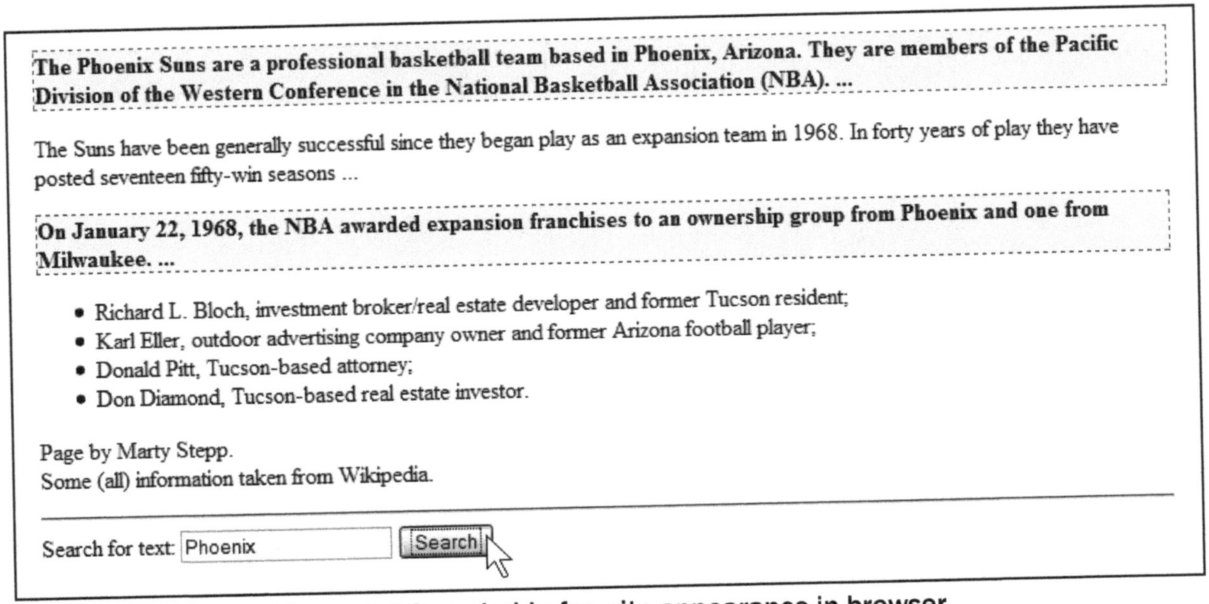

The Phoenix Suns are a professional basketball team based in Phoenix, Arizona. They are members of the Pacific Division of the Western Conference in the National Basketball Association (NBA). ...

The Suns have been generally successful since they began play as an expansion team in 1968. In forty years of play they have posted seventeen fifty-win seasons ...

On January 22, 1968, the NBA awarded expansion franchises to an ownership group from Phoenix and one from Milwaukee. ...

- Richard L. Bloch, investment broker/real estate developer and former Tucson resident;
- Karl Eller, outdoor advertising company owner and former Arizona football player;
- Donald Pitt, Tucson-based attorney;
- Don Diamond, Tucson-based real estate investor.

Page by Marty Stepp.
Some (all) information taken from Wikipedia.

Search for text: Phoenix    [Search]

**Figure 8.6 Searchable fan site appearance in browser**

In a later chapter we'll learn about the Prototype JavaScript library, which can make it even easier to select complex groups of nodes from the page and manipulate them.

## 8.3.5 Creating and Removing Nodes

At times it is useful to add and remove entire elements from the page in JavaScript code. The `document` object has a method `createElement` that creates and returns a new empty DOM node representing an element of a given type. This new node object's properties can be set just like any other DOM object. Code to create a new `h2` element is shown in Example 8.35.

```
// create a new <h2> node
var newHeading = document.createElement("h2");
newHeading.style.color = "green";
newHeading.innerHTML = "This is a heading";
```

**Example 8.35 Creating a new DOM node object**

Just creating a node won't make it appear on the page, though. You must explicitly add the newly created node to the page by adding it to the child list of some existing element on the page. DOM element objects have the following methods for changing their children lists, listed in Table 8.13.

| Method Name | Description |
|---|---|
| `appendChild(node)` | places given node at the end of this node's child list |
| `insertBefore(new, old)` | places given new node in this node's child list just before *old* |
| `removeChild(node)` | removes given node from this node's child list |
| `replaceChild(new, old)` | replaces given child with new node |

**Table 8.13 DOM node methods for adding nodes**

The code in Example 8.36 adds a paragraph to an existing `div` each time a button is clicked.

```
<div id="paragrapharea">
  <button id="add">Add a paragraph</button>
</div>
```

```
window.onload = function() {
  var button = document.getElementById("add");
  button.onclick = addParagraphClick;
};

function addParagraphClick() {
  var paragraph = document.createElement("p");
  paragraph.innerHTML = "All work and no play makes Jack a dull boy";
  var area = document.getElementById("paragrapharea");
  area.appendChild(paragraph);
}
```

**Example 8.36 Adding a node to the page**

## Self-Check

13. How are the various DOM objects connected to each other?
14. What are the three types of DOM nodes? Which types appear in lists of children and siblings of other nodes?
15. Consider the following code fragment. How many children does the **footer** node have, and what are they? How many siblings does it have, and what are they?

```
<p>This paragraph won't be affected!</p>
<div id="footer">
  <p>1234 Street</p>
  <p>Atlanta, GA</p>
</div>
```

16. How can you avoid text nodes and focus only on element nodes when traversing a page using the DOM? What methods are provided to help with this goal?
17. Suppose a page has a **div** with an **id** of **main**. Write the JavaScript code that would change every list item (**li**) within this **div** to use an italic font.
18. Suppose a page has a **div** with an **id** of **main**. Write the JavaScript code to insert a new **h1** heading at the top of this **div** with the text of, "Welcome to my page!"
19. Suppose a page has a **div** with an **id** of **main**. Write the JavaScript code to delete every other paragraph from this **div**. For example, if the **div** contains six paragraphs, the second, fourth, and sixth should be deleted.

## 8.4 Case Study: Colored Squares

Suppose we want to write a page that displays a bunch of randomly colored and positioned squares. Because they'll be randomly positioned, some of the squares will appear partially on top of other squares. When the user clicks on a square, the square moves to the top, so that no others obscure it from view. If the user double-clicks a square (or clicks on a square that is already on top), the square will be deleted from the page. The page will also have buttons allowing the user to add a single square or to choose new random colors for all squares. Figure 8.7 shows its desired appearance.

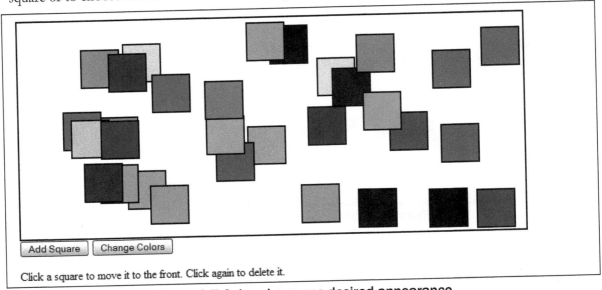

**Figure 8.7 Colored squares desired appearance**

We'll break our exploration of this problem into the following steps:

1. Create the initial HTML and CSS code for the page.
2. Use JavaScript code to create squares with random positions and colors.
3. Implement the buttons to add a square or change the colors of existing squares.
4. Handle clicking on squares to bring them to the front or delete them.

### 8.4.1 Initial HTML/CSS Code

Let's begin with the HTML body code shown in Example 8.37. There's not much to the file, because we will do most of the heavy lifting in JavaScript. In fact, the page doesn't even have any squares on it at first. We'll create them using the DOM and add them to the page.

```
<div id="squarearea"></div>
<div>
  <button id="add">Add Square</button>
  <button id="colors">Change Colors</button>
</div>
<p>Click a square to move it to the front.</p>
```

**Example 8.37 Squares HTML code**

Suppose that each is an absolutely-positioned 50x50px square `div` with a 2px black border. Since we'll be creating squares in our JavaScript code later, we could set all of those styles in the DOM. But since these are common styles shared by all squares, it is cleaner to set these using CSS. Example 8.38 shows the common CSS code. The code also defines the styles for the overall square area. It is a 700x300px box with a black border of its own. Recall from the Layout chapter we must set its position to `relative` so that absolutely-positioned elements inside it are placed relative to the square area, not the top/left of the page.

```css
/* Style sheet for colored squares example */
.square {
  width: 50px;
  height: 50px;
  border: 2px solid black;
  position: absolute;
}

#squarearea {
  width: 700px;
  height: 300px;
  border: 2px solid black;
  position: relative;
}
```

```
+---------------------------------------------------+
|                                                   |
|                                                   |
|                                                   |
|                                                   |
|                                                   |
|                                                   |
|                                                   |
|                                                   |
|                                                   |
|                                                   |
+---------------------------------------------------+
 [ Add Square ]  [ Change Colors ]
Click a square to move it to the front. Click again to delete it.
```

**Example 8.38 Squares CSS code**

## 8.4.2 Creating Squares

When the page loads we want to create a random number of squares; suppose the desired range is between 30 and 50 squares inclusive. To generate a random number in that range, we can call the `Math.random` function and multiply it by the size of the random range (50 - 30 + 1 = 21), then add the range's minimum value (30).

```javascript
var squareCount = parseInt(Math.random() * 21) + 30;
```

We want a loop that creates `squareCount` number of randomly positioned and colored shapes. We want to create many `div`s and give them random positions. Each of these `div`s will use the CSS class of `square` that we just defined. We'll use `document.createElement` here to create each div. The following code gets us started:

```
var square = document.createElement("div");
square.className = "square";
```

The squares must be randomly positioned and colored. Let's ignore colors for now and leave them all white, focusing on position first. To position a square, we must set its `left` and `top` style properties to random values in the bounds of the 700x300px `squarearea`. Since a square is 50px in size, this means we're choosing a random left x value between 0 and 650, and a random y value between 0 and 250. Recall that properties like `left` and `top` are strings and must have units after their values. We don't set `left` to 346, we set it to a string such as `"346px"`. For example:

```
square.style.left = parseInt(Math.random() * 650) + "px";
```

Once we've set up the various properties of our new square, we add it to the `squarearea` by calling its DOM object's `appendChild` method. Example 8.39 shows the complete code. Upon loading the page we now see several randomly positioned clear rectangles as expected.

```
window.onload = function() {
    var squareArea = document.getElementById("squarearea");
    var squareCount = parseInt(Math.random() * 21) + 30;
    for (var i = 0; i < squareCount; i++) {
        var square = document.createElement("div");   // create a square
        square.className = "square";
        square.style.left = parseInt(Math.random() * 650) + "px";
        square.style.top = parseInt(Math.random() * 250) + "px";
        squareArea.appendChild(square);
    }
};
```

Add Square    Change Colors

Click a square to move it to the front. Click again to delete it.

**Example 8.39 Randomly positioned squares**

Next let's give a random color to each square. Generating random colors is a useful general ability to have, so let's create a `getRandomColor` function that returns a random color string such as `"#f08a7c"`. We just need to choose 6 characters in the range 0-9 or a-f. A clever trick for doing this is to put all the legal character choices into a string or array and then choose a random character from that string/array 6 times. Example 8.40 shows the function's complete code.

```
// Generates and returns a random color string such as "#f08a7c".
function getRandomColor() {
  var letters = "0123456789abcdef";
  var result = "#";
  for (var i = 0; i < 6; i++) {
    result += letters.charAt(parseInt(Math.random() * letters.length));
  }
  return result;
}
```

**Example 8.40 Code to generate a random color**

Now that we have this function, we can call it in our `window.onload` handler to set each square's random color as its `backgroundColor` style property. Example 8.41 shows the new code. The squares still do nothing when clicked, and the two buttons still do nothing.

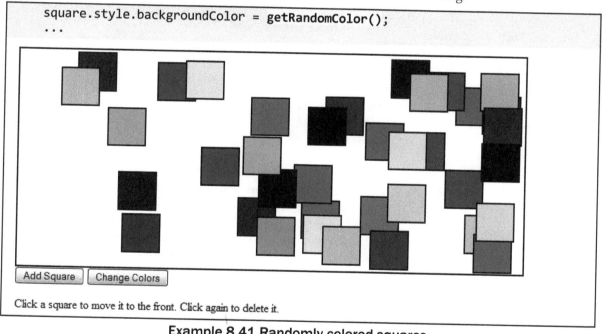

```
square.style.backgroundColor = getRandomColor();
...
```

Add Square   Change Colors

Click a square to move it to the front. Click again to delete it.

**Example 8.41 Randomly colored squares**

## 8.4.3 Add Squares, Change Colors

Now let's address the two buttons. Clicking the Add Square button should add a single square to the page. We have already written the code to add a square to the page, but it's currently written directly in the `window.onload` handler and is therefore not very reusable. Let's put this code into its own function so that we can call it both when the page loads and also when the Add Square button is clicked. Example 8.42 shows the code for this function, cut from `window.onload`.

```
// Creates and adds a new square div to the page.
function addSquare() {
  var square = document.createElement("div");
  square.className = "square";
  square.style.left = parseInt(Math.random() * 650) + "px";
  square.style.top = parseInt(Math.random() * 250) + "px";
  square.style.backgroundColor = getRandomColor();

  var squareArea = document.getElementById("squarearea");
  squareArea.appendChild(square);
}
```

**Example 8.42 Function to add a square**

The `window.onload` handler should of course call this function rather than repeating the same code. We'll also need to attach a click handler for the two buttons in our `window.onload` code. Example 8.43 shows the modifications to the code; the `changeColors` function is not yet written.

```
window.onload = function() {
  var add = document.getElementById("add");
  add.onclick = addSquare;
  var colors = document.getElementById("colors");
  colors.onclick = changeColors;

  // create several randomly positioned squares
  var squareCount = parseInt(Math.random() * 21) + 30;
  for (var i = 0; i < squareCount; i++) {
    addSquare();
  }
};
```

**Example 8.43 Refactored `window.onload` handler**

Now that the Add Square button code is written, it's time to address the Change Colors button. When clicked, this button should give a new random color to each square on the page. We already wrote logic to assign random colors to squares using the `getRandomColor` function, so we'll need to fetch the DOM object for every square on the page and reapply that logic to each of them.

We can grab all DOM objects with the same HTML tag by calling `getElementsByTagName` on the `document` object or on an existing element. The squares all use the `div` tag. We don't want to fetch every single `div` on the page, just the ones within the `squarearea` section of the page. So we'll get the `squarearea` `div` object by ID and then ask it for all the `div`s it contains. Then we loop over each of those `div`s and apply a new background color to it. Example 8.44 shows this function's code.

```
// Gives a new randomly chosen color to every square on the page.
function changeColors() {
  var squareArea = document.getElementById("squarearea");
  var squares = squareArea.getElementsByTagName("div");
  for (var i = 0; i < squares.length; i++) {
    squares[i].style.backgroundColor = getRandomColor();
  }
}
```

**Example 8.44 Function to recolor every square**

Figure 8.8 shows the initial appearance of the page, the appearance after clicking the Add Square button several times, and the appearance after clicking the Change Colors button.

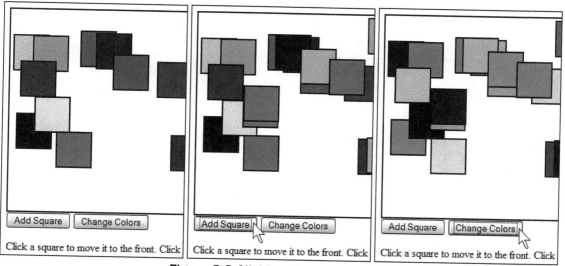

**Figure 8.8 Clicking the two buttons**

## 8.4.4 Clickable Squares

Lastly let's make the squares clickable to move them to the front. To make them clickable we must attach an **onclick** handler to each square as it's being created in the **addSquare** function, as shown in Example 8.45. The actual handler function **squareClick** is not written yet.

```
function addSquare() {
  var square = document.createElement("div");
  ...
  square.onclick = squareClick;

  var squareArea = document.getElementById("squarearea");
  squareArea.appendChild(square);
}
```

**Example 8.45 Attaching click handler to squares**

To move a square to the front, the click handler should set a large value for the **z-index** property of the square that was clicked. Let's initialize a global variable to store the current maximum z-index, choosing a safely large number such as 1000 that will be higher than any of the squares' default z-indexes. Every time a square is clicked, we'll set it to use our large z-index value and increase the value by 1 so that the next click will lead to an even larger value. Example 8.46 shows the new code.

```
var maxZ = 1000;    // z-index of rectangle that gets clicked
...

// Called when a square is clicked; moves it to the top.
function squareClick() {
  maxZ++;
  this.style.zIndex = maxZ;
}
```

**Example 8.46 Clickable squares code**

We must also make it so that if the user clicks on the square that is already on top, the square will be deleted from the page. We can detect if a square is already on the top of all the others by checking its `zIndex` property to see if it is equal to the max z value set so far. To remove a square from the page, we must contact its parent node and tell it to remove that square as a child. Since the square refers to itself as `this` in the `onclick` handler, the code to remove it is the following:

```
this.parentNode.removeChild(this);    // remove this square
```

Example 8.47 shows the complete modified `squareClick` handler code, along with the page's appearance as a square is clicked once and then a second time.

```
// Called when a square is clicked; moves it to the top or removes it.
function squareClick() {
  var oldZ = parseInt(this.style.zIndex);
  if (oldZ == maxZ) {
    this.parentNode.removeChild(this);    // square is on top; remove it
  } else {
    maxZ++;
    this.style.zIndex = maxZ;
  }
}
```

**Example 8.47 Clickable squares code**

## 8.4.5 Final File Contents

After all of the changes in the preceding sections, the complete code for coloredsquares.js is shown in Example 8.48. The HTML/CSS did not change from its initial version, so it is not shown.

```javascript
var maxZ = 1000;    // z-index of rectangle that gets clicked
window.onload = function() {
  var add = document.getElementById("add");
  add.onclick = addSquare;
  var colors = document.getElementById("colors");
  colors.onclick = changeColors;
  var squareCount = parseInt(Math.random() * 21) + 30;
  for (var i = 0; i < squareCount; i++) {  // create random squares
    addSquare();
  }
};
// Gives a new randomly chosen color to every square on the page.
function changeColors() {
  var squareArea = document.getElementById("squarearea");
  var squares = squareArea.getElementsByTagName("div");
  for (var i = 0; i < squares.length; i++) {
    squares[i].style.backgroundColor = getRandomColor();
  }
}
// Creates and adds a new square div to the page.
function addSquare() {
  var square = document.createElement("div");
  square.className = "square";
  square.style.left = parseInt(Math.random() * 650) + "px";
  square.style.top = parseInt(Math.random() * 250) + "px";
  square.style.backgroundColor = getRandomColor();
  square.onclick = squareClick;
  var squareArea = document.getElementById("squarearea");
  squareArea.appendChild(square);
}
// Generates and returns a random color string such as "#f08a7c".
function getRandomColor() {
  var letters = "0123456789abcdef";
  var result = "#";
  for (var i = 0; i < 6; i++) {
    result += letters.charAt(parseInt(Math.random() * letters.length));
  }
  return result;
}
// Called when a square is clicked; moves it to the top or removes it.
function squareClick() {
  var oldZ = parseInt(this.style.zIndex);
  if (oldZ == maxZ) {
    this.parentNode.removeChild(this);   // square is on top; remove it
  } else {
    maxZ++;
    this.style.zIndex = maxZ;
} }
```

Example 8.48 Final contents of `coloredsquares.js`

## Chapter Summary

- Unobtrusive JavaScript is a way of attaching event handlers without putting any JavaScript into the body of your HTML page, giving you much cleaner HTML code and a clear separation of content, presentation, and behavior.
- Web browsers provide six important global objects that you can access in your JavaScript code: `document`, `window`, `location`, `navigator`, `screen`, and `history`.
- Unobtrusive JavaScript is achieved by attaching event handlers in your JavaScript code inside a handler for the `window.onload` event.
- The Document Object Model (DOM) contains node objects representing elements, attributes, and text on the page. DOM objects have properties that mimic the corresponding attributes in the HTML, such as `src` and `id`.
- You can set styles of a DOM object by setting properties of its `style` object.
- DOM nodes are connected to each other in a treelike structure. You can traverse the structure of the DOM tree using node properties like `firstChild` and `nextSibling`.
- You can select and manipulate groups of DOM element nodes using methods such as `document.getElementsByTagName`.
- Nodes can be dynamically created and added or removed from the page. Nodes are created with the `document.createElement` method.

## References

- Seven Rules of Unobtrusive JavaScript:
  - http://icant.co.uk/articles/seven-rules-of-unobtrusive-javascript/
- Mozilla DOM reference, `window`:     https://developer.mozilla.org/En/DOM:window
- W3Schools DOM tutorial:     http://www.w3schools.com/htmldom/
- W3Schools, DOM node reference:     http://www.w3schools.com/dom/dom_node.asp
- Quirksmode DOM tutorial:     http://www.quirksmode.org/dom/intro.html
- Ryan's DOM tutorial:
  - http://www.pageresource.com/dhtml/ryan/part4-1.html
- GUIStuff, DOM Modifications:
  - http://www.guistuff.com/javascript/js_dom_a2.html

# Chapter 9  Events and the Prototype Library

# Introduction

In this chapter we'll explore more kinds of events that occur in JavaScript programs and interesting ways of handling those events. Examples of these events include mouse gestures, key presses, general page events such as loading and unloading, form submit events, and animation with timers.

We will also explore the Prototype JavaScript library, which includes many useful additions to JavaScript to make the language more pleasant to use. Prototype adds lots of features to the JavaScript language as well as improving the DOM and event-driven programming. It will assist us in writing powerful applications that are compatible with a number of web browsers.

## 9.1 The Prototype JavaScript Library

JavaScript is a powerful language, but it has many flaws. The DOM can be clunky to use. There are a number of objects and methods that would be very useful, but do not exist in the ECMA Standard. In addition, the same code doesn't always work the same way in every browser. Code that works great in Firefox, Safari, and others will fail in IE and vice versa. Many web developers work around these problems with hacks, testing explicitly for what browser is being used and using different code in each case.

Many groups have tried to work around these problems by creating standard libraries of functionality to add to your JavaScript programs. Some of the most popular libraries include jQuery, Dojo, MooTools, Scriptaculous, and Prototype. All of these libraries extend JavaScript to more easily walk the DOM, respond to events, and handle browser compatibility. We prefer Prototype as its syntax is closest to traditional JavaScript, it holds solid alliances within the web development community, and it is the foundation for Scriptaculous, another free JavaScript library that allows the web programmer to spice up their web page with neat visual effects. We talk first about Prototype in this chapter which will allow us to get more into the "guts" of JavaScript and the DOM in powerful ways and will introduce Scriptaculous later in the book.

### 9.1.1 Introduction to Prototype

Prototype adds many useful features to JavaScript. Prototype's primary features are the following:

- Additional methods for common objects such as `String`, `Array`, `Number`, and `Object`.
- Extensions to the DOM.
- Improvements for event handling and event-driven programming.

- Cross-browser compatibility fixes.
- Easier object-oriented programming and class creation.
- Ajax programming utilities (which we'll see in the next chapter).

The Prototype library is implemented in a large .js file. Just like any other JavaScript file, you must link to Prototype in your web page. But first you must download the Prototype library to your own computer or web server by going to the Prototype home page, http://prototypejs.org/. Assuming that you download the Prototype library to a file named **prototype.js** and save the file in the same folder as your web page, the code to include Prototype in your page would look like that shown in Example 9.1.

```
<script src="prototype.js" type="text/javascript"></script>
```
**Example 9.1 Link to Prototype library**

That's it! Once the script loads into your page, you can use Prototype's features in your code. We are going to demonstrate a lot of the neat features that come with Prototype, but there is even more documentation and examples on the Prototype API Documentation web site found at: http://www.prototypejs.org/api Be sure to check it out!

## 9.1.2 Language Improvements

The following tables show some of the useful methods Prototype adds to various existing JavaScript objects.

Prototype adds several methods to array objects as shown in Table 9.1. Example 9.2 demonstrates the usage of several of these methods.

```
var a = [1, 2, 3, 3, 3, 4, 5, 5, 5, 5, 5];
a = a.without(5);          // [1, 2, 3, 3, 3, 4]
a.reverse();               // [4, 3, 3, 3, 2, 1]
var index = a.indexOf(3);  // 1
a = a.uniq();              // [4, 3, 2, 1]
```
**Example 9.2 Using Prototype's array methods**

Numbers (integers and real numbers) are technically objects in JavaScript, and those objects have methods. Prototype adds several methods to numbers, many of which are similar to methods found in the **Math** class. Though these methods are equivalent to those found in the **Math** class, some users prefer the abbreviated syntax Prototype provides. The additional methods for converting an integer to a hexadecimal color part and to a padded string are also convenient. Table 9.2 lists the useful methods and Example 9.3 demonstrates their use.

```
var n = -42.1;
var k = 167.25;
n = n.round();             // -42
n = n.abs();               // 42
k = k.ceil();              // 168
var c = k.toColorPart();   // "a8"
var s = n.toPaddedString(5); // "00042"
```
**Example 9.3 Using Prototype's Number methods**

| Method Name | Description |
|---|---|
| clear() | removes all elements from an array |
| clone() | returns a copy of an array |
| compact() | returns a new version of the array but with no null / undefined values |
| first() | returns the array's first element (or undefined if the array is empty) |
| flatten() | converts a multi-dimensional array into a 1-D array and returns it |
| indexOf(value) | returns index of first occurrence of value within array, or -1 if not found |
| inspect() | returns a string representing the array, such as "[10, 20, 30]" |
| last() | returns the array's last element (or undefined if the array is empty) |
| reverse()<br>reverse(inline) | places the elements of the array into the opposite order; if false is passed for optional parameter inline, returns a reversed copy of this array |
| uniq() | returns a new array the same as this one but with all duplicates removed |
| without(value) | returns a new array the same as this one but with all occurrences of the given value removed |

Table 9.1 Prototype's Array methods

| Method Name | Description |
|---|---|
| abs() | returns absolute value |
| ceil() | returns number rounded up to nearest integer |
| floor() | returns number rounded down to nearest integer |
| round() | returns number rounded up or down to nearest integer |
| toColorPart() | returns number as a 2-digit hex string, such as "7f" |
| toPaddedString(length)<br>toPaddedString(length, base) | returns number converted to a string with leading 0s; uses base-10 (decimal) unless base is specified |

Table 9.2 Prototype's Number methods

Prototype also adds methods to strings, many of which are listed in Table 9.3. Example 9.4 uses several of the methods. Notice that like the Number methods, these methods return a new string object value rather than modifying the string upon which it was called. If you want to modify the value of an existing string variable, you must reassign it.

```
var s = " Jessica ";
s = s.times(3);              // " Jessica  Jessica  Jessica "
s = s.strip();              // "Jessica  Jessica  Jessica"
if (s.endsWith("ica") && s.include("Jess")) {
  s = s.truncate(7);        // "Jess..."
}
var a = s.toArray();        // ["J", "e", "s", "s", ".", ".", "."]
```

Example 9.4 Using Prototype's String methods

| Method Name | Description |
|---|---|
| blank() | returns **true** if the string is empty or contains only whitespace |
| camelize() | converts dashed-strings to camelCased strings |
| capitalize() | capitalizes the first letter of a string and lowercases all others |
| dasherize() | converts all underscores ('_') in the string into dashes ('-') |
| empty() | returns **true** if this is the empty string |
| endsWith(**string**) | returns **true** if this string ends with the given string parameter |
| escapeHTML() | converts HTML special characters to their entity equivalents |
| include(**string**) | returns **true** if this string contains the given string parameter |
| startsWith(**string**) | returns **true** if this string begins with the given string parameter |
| strip() | removes all initial and ending whitespace from the string |
| stripTags() | removes any HTML tags from the string |
| times(**count**) | concatenates the string together **count** times |
| toArray() | returns the characters of this string as an array |
| toQueryParams()<br>toQueryParams(**sep**) | parses a URL-like query string and returns an object composed of parameter/value pairs, separated by **&** or by the value of **sep** |
| truncate(**length**)<br>truncate(**length, suffix**) | returns this string limited to the given length; if more characters exist than the given length, appends "..." or the value of **suffix** |
| underscore() | converts a camel-cased string into a series of words separated by underscores ('_') |
| unescapeHTML() | strips tags and converts entities of HTML characters to their normal forms |

**Table 9.3 Prototype's String methods**

Prototype also has a set of methods to be used with any object in general. These methods are not actually added to every JavaScript object, but they can be called externally by writing the word `Object` followed by a dot and the method name and passing the object of interest as a parameter. Particularly useful are the **isType** methods, which provide a simple way to test the type of an object. This can be done without Prototype using the **typeof** function, but **typeof** is quirky and not always reliable. For example, it reports that the type of an array is `"object"` rather than something more specific like `"array"` and that the type of `null` is also `"object"`, which is dangerous and misleading. You can also ask for a list of an object's property names and values using the `keys` and `values` methods respectively. Table 9.4 lists the useful methods and Example 9.5 uses them.

| Method Name | Description |
|---|---|
| `Object.clone(`**`obj`**`)` | returns a shallow copy of the object |
| `Object.extend(`**`obj`**`)` | adds Prototype's functionality to an object |
| `Object.inspect(`**`obj`**`)` | returns a debug string representing the object |
| `Object.isArray(`**`obj`**`)` | returns **true** if the object is an array |
| `Object.isElement(`**`obj`**`)` | returns **true** if the object is a DOM element |
| `Object.isFunction(`**`obj`**`)` | returns **true** if the object is a function |
| `Object.isHash(`**`obj`**`)` | returns **true** if the object is an associative array |
| `Object.isNumber(`**`obj`**`)` | returns **true** if the object is a number |
| `Object.isString(`**`obj`**`)` | returns **true** if the object is a string |
| `Object.keys(`**`obj`**`)` | returns an array of all property/method names of this object |
| `Object.toQueryString(`**`obj`**`)` | converts the object's properties into a returned string of name/value pairs such as `"action=ship&orderid=123"` |
| `Object.values(`**`obj`**`)` | returns an array of all property values in this object |

**Table 9.4 Prototype's Object methods**

```
var a = [10, 20, 30];
if (Object.isArray(a)) {         // true
  var a2 = Object.clone(a);      // [10, 20, 30]
}
if (Object.isNumber(a2[0])) {    // true
  var keys = Object.keys(a2[0]); // ["abs", "ceil", "floor", ...]
}
```

**Example 9.5 Using Prototype's Object methods**

### 9.1.3 Prototype and the DOM

Many of Prototype's more interesting features are designed to make JavaScript's HTML Document Object Model easier to use. In this section we explore several of those features.

#### The $ Function

Prototype provides the convenient **$** function, a shorthand for `document.getElementById`. You may have noticed that we're using `getElementById` a lot to grab DOM objects for various HTML elements on the page. Since the name is so long to type, Prototype provides a shorter version of the same functionality whose name is just a single letter: the dollar sign, **$**. It may seem strange, but the function's name is **$**, it accepts a string **id** as a parameter, and it returns the same result as `document.getElementById`. The syntax of the **$** function is shown in Example 9.6.

```
$("id")
```

**Example 9.6 Prototype's $ function (gets a DOM element by ID)**

The $ may seem like a useless function since we can already do the same thing with `document.getElementById`. But trust us: Less typing is good. Once you go $, you don't go back. For example, if your page has a paragraph with an `id` of `welcome` and you want to change its text to say "Thanks for visiting!", you previously would have written:

```
var paragraph = document.getElementById("welcome");   // old and busted
paragraph.innerHTML = "Thanks for visiting!";
```

With Prototype, you can instead write the following:

```
$("welcome").innerHTML = "Thanks for visiting!";      // new hotness
```

Example 9.7 shows a refactored version of an example from the previous DOM chapter that increased the size of an element's font. Using $ makes the code shorter and cleaner.

```
// Called when one of the font radio buttons is clicked.
function fontClick() {
  $("lyrics").style.fontFamily = this.id;
  var oldSize = parseInt($("lyrics").style.fontSize) || 12;
  $("lyrics").style.fontSize = (oldSize + 2) + "pt";
}
```

**Example 9.7 Improved DOM font manipulation code**

## Extended DOM Elements

Prototype also adds dozens of new methods to each DOM element object such that the objects you retrieve using the $ function are more powerful and easier to use. These methods are automatically available if you use the $ function to access DOM elements. To use these methods on an element retrieved by the traditional `getElementByID` method, you would have to either use the Prototype `extend` method or pass the element in as the first parameter to the method.

Table 9.5 lists many of these methods. The methods are grouped by the type of functionality they provide. There are quite a few new methods to choose from; you may be overwhelmed when looking at the list at first. But you don't need to use all of them. We'll point out a few we find most useful.

The `scrollTo` method is useful when you have a tall page and want the browser to scroll up or down until a particular element is in view:

```
if ($("mycheckbox").checked) {
  $("orderform").scrollTo();       // scroll until order form is in view
}
```

Some of the methods are meant to make it easier to manipulate the DOM node structure and walk the DOM tree. The `remove` method makes it easier to remove an element from the page. For example, the following code (if attached as an `onclick` handler to a button) causes a button to remove itself:

```
function buttonClick() {
  this.remove();   // remove the button that was clicked from the page
}
```

The `hide` and `show` methods are useful for making an element disappear or reappear on the page in response to an event. The `identify` method is nice for assigning `id` values to elements that may not have them initially, such as ones you create using `document.createElement`.

Some of the methods might seem unnecessary, such as `setOpacity`, which sets the opacity style of the element. Why not just do it yourself by referring to `element.style.opacity`? The reason for some of these methods is to work around various browser incompatibilities.

Most of Prototype's DOM methods that don't otherwise return a value actually return the element object upon which they were called. This allows you to chain calls together, such as:

```
$("mytextdiv").cleanWhitespace().show().scrollTo();
```

The References section of this chapter links to a page from Prototype's official web site called "How Prototype Extends the DOM," describing how to use many of these additions in your DOM code.

| Method Name | Description |
|---|---|
| **Position/Size** ||
| `absolutize()`, `relativize()` | changes object to be absolutely or relatively positioned |
| `cumulativeOffset()`, `cumulativeScrollOffset()`, `positionedOffset()`, `viewportOffset()` | returns a 2-element array containing this element's x/y offset relative to the very top/left corner of the page, its containing scrolling container, its closest positioned ancestor, or the visible portion of the page respectively |
| `getHeight()`, `getWidth()` | returns the element's computed height or width |
| `scrollTo()` | scrolls page until this element appears at top of window |
| **Visibility** ||
| `hide()`, `show()` | makes element invisible (sets `display` to `none`) or visible |
| `toggle()` | toggles the element between being visible and invisible |
| `visible()` | returns **true** if the element is currently visible |
| `setOpacity(`**value**`)` | sets the opacity of the element to **value** (between 0.0-1.0) |
| **Information About the Element** ||
| `empty()` | returns **true** if the element contains only whitespace |
| `identify()` | returns element's **id**, or gives it a unique one if no **id** found |
| `inspect()` | returns a string of the element's state (useful for debugging) |
| `match(`**selector**`)` | returns **true** if the given CSS selector matches this element |
| **Modifying the Element** ||
| `cleanWhitespace()` | removes this element's children that contain only whitespace |
| `remove()` | removes the element from the page |
| `replace(`**html**`)` | replaces the element with the given text or HTML code |
| `update(`**content**`)` | sets element's inner HTML content to the given value (essentially the same as setting the element's `innerHTML`) |

Table 9.5 Prototype's DOM object methods

## 9.1.4 Accessing Styles

| Method Name | Description |
|---|---|
| getStyle(**name**) | returns the element's style for the given CSS property name |
| setStyle(**styles**) | uses the given object of name/value pairs to set the element's styles for various CSS property names |

**Table 9.6 Prototype's DOM styling methods**

In the last chapter we saw that you could use the **style** property of DOM element objects to set styles on them. However, we also saw (in our Rick Astley font-changing example) the **style** property does not work for reading existing styles on elements. It can only read existing styles if they were declared inline in the HTML (which we discourage) or were previously set via JavaScript DOM code.

So how does one find out information about existing styles on an element? There are ways of doing this, but they are specific to particular browsers. Firefox, Opera, and Safari have a method named **document.getComputedStyle** that helps with this. Internet Explorer instead gives DOM elements a **currentStyle** property that behaves similarly. It's a pain to write a script that plays nicely with both of these and their various incompatibilities.

Enter Prototype. Prototype extends every DOM element object by giving it a **getStyle** method, as shown in Table 9.6. This method accepts a string parameter representing the name of the style property of interest, and it returns that property's current value. The property name can be hyphenated like **"font-size"** or camel-cased like **"fontSize"**. (There is also a **setStyle** method, but it's less useful for our purposes. We can just use the element's **style** object to set styles.)

Using this new method, the code to set the font for our old Rick Astley text can be written more correctly and easily. We no longer have to use a default font size of 12; we can now just ask for the existing size and add 2 to it. Example 9.8 shows the improved code.

```
// Called when one of the font radio button is clicked.
function fontClick() {
  $("lyrics").style.fontFamily = this.id;
  var oldSize = parseFloat($("lyrics").getStyle("font-size"));
  $("lyrics").style.fontSize = (oldSize + 2) + "px";
}
```

**Example 9.8 Improved code to enlarge font size by 2px**

Although **getStyle** and **setStyle** make it easier to manually adjust style properties using CSS property names, more generally we'd like to practice unobtrusive styling by adding and removing CSS class names from elements. We saw in the previous chapter that DOM element objects have a **className** property that we can use to implement unobtrusive styling. But it has its drawbacks. Notably, its value is just a string. This makes it ugly to figure out whether a given class is contained in the string value of **className** and even uglier to remove a single class from a **className** value that has 4 or 5 others in it that we want to retain.

Luckily Prototype also includes functionality to help us manage the class names attached to DOM elements. Table 9.7 lists several of the methods Prototype adds to each DOM element object for setting CSS classes.

| Method Name | Description |
|---|---|
| addClassName(**name**) | adds the given CSS class to this element's set of classes |
| classNames() | returns a list of the CSS classes applied to this element |
| hasClassName(**name**) | returns true if the given CSS class is applied to this element |
| removeClassName(**name**) | removes the given class attribute from this element's set of classes |
| toggleClassName(**name**) | adds the given class if not present, otherwise removes it |

**Table 9.7 Prototype's DOM element CSS class methods**

In the previous chapter we wrote a program with searchable text that would highlight every paragraph that contained a given search phrase. The code for that program can be improved with Prototype by calling addClassName and removeClassName to manage the classes applied to the paragraphs. This way if any of the paragraphs had other existing classes attached to them, those would not be lost by our DOM code. The new code is shown in Example 9.9.

```
// Called when the Search button is clicked.
// Looks for paragraphs matching a search string and highlights them.
function searchClick() {
  var main = document.getElementById("main");
  var mainParas = main.getElementsByTagName("p");

  for (var i = 0; i < mainParas.length; i++) {
    if (mainParas[i].innerHTML.indexOf($("searchtext").value) >= 0) {
      mainParas[i].addClassName("highlighted");
    } else {
      mainParas[i].removeClassName("highlighted");
    }
  }
}
```

**Example 9.9 Using Prototype to set CSS classes**

## 9.1.5 Traversing the DOM

Prototype provides several additional methods to DOM element nodes that let us walk the DOM tree and access an element's ancestors, siblings, and children more easily. One of the most important benefits Prototype provides is that its methods deal with element nodes only, without any text or attribute nodes getting in the way. Another nice benefit is that Prototype lets us reach further up or down the tree than the standard DOM. Rather than only being able to look at the parent of a node, we can ask for all of its *ancestors*, nodes that are above this one in the tree: parents, grandparents, and so on. Similarly, rather than only being able to look at a node's direct children, we can ask for all of its *descendants*, nodes that are below this one in the tree: children, grandchildren, etc. We can even do filtering, asking for only the ancestors/siblings/descendants that match some criteria. Table 9.8 lists the relevant methods. Figure 9.1 shows the methods in relation to the current DOM element.

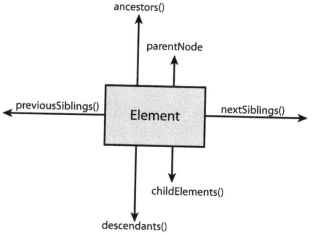

**Figure 9.1 An element and its neighboring nodes**

| Method Name | Description |
|---|---|
| ancestors() | returns an array of the object's ancestors in the DOM tree: parent, grandparents, ... |
| siblings() | returns an array of all siblings of this element (elements only) |
| previousSiblings(), nextSiblings() | returns an array of all sibling elements before or after this element |
| previous() previous(**selector**) next() next(**selector**) | returns the sibling prior to or after this element (elements only), optionally matching the given CSS selector; if no previous or next sibling is found **undefined** is returned |
| adjacent(**selector**) | returns an array of all siblings of this element that match the given CSS selector(s) |
| childElements() | returns an array of this element's children (elements only) |
| descendantOf(**element**) | returns **true** if this element is a child, grandchild, etc. of **element** in the page's DOM tree |
| descendants() | returns an array of the object's children, grandchildren, etc. |
| down(**selector**) down(**selector**, **index**) | returns the element's first (or **index**th) descendant that matches the given optional CSS selector; if no selector is given, all descendants are considered |
| up(**selector**) up(**selector**, **index**) | returns the element's first (or **index**th) ancestor that matches the given optional CSS selector; if no selector is given, all ancestors are considered |

**Table 9.8 Prototype's DOM node traversal methods**

For example, if you have an element on your page with an **id** of **main** and you want to change the text of its neighbors to end with an exclamation point, you could write the code in Example 9.10.

```
var siblings = $("main").siblings();
for (var i = 0; i < siblings.length; i++) {
  siblings[i].innerHTML += "!";
}
```

**Example 9.10 Processing siblings using Prototype's DOM node methods**

Notice that `siblings`, like the rest of Prototype's DOM additions, is a method and must be called with parentheses, unlike the built-in DOM properties `firstChild`, `nextSibling`, etc.

### Selecting Groups of Nodes

In the previous chapter we saw that you can call `document.getElementsByTagName` to get an array of DOM elements using a given HTML tag. This was useful for looping over many elements and processing them. We used this technique in our searchable fan site example in the DOM chapter.

But the ability to process all nodes with a given tag is not very versatile. Often we want to process a group of nodes that are related in some other way, such as all elements that have the `urgent` CSS class, or all `li` items that are inside an `ol` inside a particular `div` on the page. The existing DOM doesn't make it easy to do these kinds of manipulations. But Prototype comes to our rescue.

Prototype adds some methods to the `document` object (and to all other DOM objects) for accessing groups of nodes. The most useful of these methods is listed in Table 9.9. The `$$` function is especially useful for processing all elements that match a given CSS selector. You can set up your page so that the elements of interest use a particular class, and then target that class.

| Method Name | Description |
| --- | --- |
| select(**selector**)<br>(a.k.a. $$ when called on **document**) | returns array of all DOM elements that match the given CSS selector string, such as "div#sidebar > li" |

**Table 9.9 Prototype's DOM selection methods**

But even more useful is Prototype's ability to select a group of elements based on CSS selector strings. Recall that a selector is the part of a CSS rule that comes before the { brace, that determines which parts of the page the rule will affect. Selectors can be simple, such as `"p"` to select all paragraphs, or complex, such as `"div#topmenu > img.banner"` to select all `img` elements with a `class` of `banner` that reside directly inside the `div` element with an `id` of `topmenu`.

Prototype's mighty `select` method, which has been added to the `document` object as well as to every other DOM object, accepts a string parameter representing a CSS selector, and returns an array of all DOM objects for elements that match that selector. The selector you pass is a string that follows the same syntax as a CSS selector does. For example, if you want to hide all paragraphs with the class of `announcement` that are contained within the `div` with `id` of `news`, you could write:

```
var paragraphs = document.select("div#news p.announcement");
for (var i = 0; i < paragraphs.length; i++) {
  paragraphs[i].hide();
}
```

Since you often want to call `select` on the overall `document` object, and to reduce typing, Prototype introduces a `$$` function that is a shorthand for `document.select`. You can select a group of elements using `$$` even if your CSS file has no style rule for that group. For example, it is fine to use `$$` to select all paragraphs even if your CSS file does have a rule for the `p` tag. (We jokingly refer to

$$ as the "mo' money" function with our students.) For example, Example 9.11 accomplishes the same thing as the previous code, hiding the same group of paragraphs.

```
var paragraphs = $$("div#news p.announcement");
for (var i = 0; i < paragraphs.length; i++) {
  paragraphs[i].hide();
}
```

**Example 9.11 Selecting elements with $$**

$$ can also be used in a `window.onload` handler to attach event handlers to a group of elements. For example, the code in Example 9.12 listens to clicks on all buttons with a class of `control` directly inside of the section with `id` of `game`.

```
window.onload = function() {
  var gameButtons = $$("#game > button.control");
  for (var i = 0; i < gameButtons.length; i++) {
    gameButtons[i].onclick = gameButtonClick;
  }
};

function gameButtonClick() {
  ...
}
```

**Example 9.12 Attaching event handlers with $$**

$$ effectively replaces all of the other multi-element selection techniques and is simpler and more pleasant to use. Therefore it's our recommended way of accessing groups of nodes, and it's what we'll use in our examples in the rest of the textbook.

Many students make simple mistakes when first using Prototype's $$ function. For example, it's easy to forget to write . or # in front of a desired `class` or `id` that you want to select. Example 9.13 shows two attempts to use $$ to fetch all elements with the `class` of `control`. But the first call will return an empty array, because there is no element with a tag of `control`. The second line shows a correct call.

**Common Error**
Misusing **$$**

```
var gameButtons = $$("control");   // incorrect
var gameButtons = $$(".control");  // correct
```

**Example 9.13 Common error: Forgetting . or # when using $$**

Another important thing to remember is that $$ does not return the same type of value as $. While $ returns a single DOM element object, $$ returns an array of the elements it matched. If you want to do something to those DOM objects, you must loop over the results and process each one. The first line in Example 9.14 incorrectly attempts to set buttons with a `class` of `control` to have red text. The code afterward correctly loops over each element and applies the style to it.

```
$$(".control").style.color = "red";      // incorrect

var gameButtons = $$(".control");
for (var i = 0; i < gameButtons.length; i++) {
  gameButtons[i].style.color = "red";     // correct
}
```

**Example 9.14 Common error: Treating $$ return value as a single element**

Even if the selector you pass to **$$** matches only a single element, the result is still returned as an array (an array containing just one element). You must either loop over the elements returned (if there will be many of them) or access elements at particular indexes. If you're sure the array will contain just one element, you can just directly refer to its element [**0**], as shown in Example 9.15.

```
$$(".control")[0].style.color = "red";    // correct
```

**Example 9.15 Modifying a single element using $$**


## 9.1.6 Prototype and Forms

Prototype includes several useful features for dealing with HTML forms. Since a common JavaScript usage pattern is to get a DOM object for a form control and then examine or set its value, Prototype also includes a variant of **$** called **$F**. The **$F** function accepts a form control's **id** string as its parameter and returns the **value** of that control. For example, for an input text control, **$F** returns the text typed into that text box. Example 9.16 shows the syntax for the **$F** function.

```
var name = $F("id");
```

**Example 9.16 Syntax template for accessing form control values**

**$F** does not provide any functionality that cannot be achieved through other means such as the **$** function and the **value** property, but it is a concise way to get a form control's value.

Prototype also adds a set of additional methods to every form control that are useful for manipulating the control and its value. Several of the useful methods are shown in Table 9.10. For example, if a form has a text box with an **id** of **tip** and you want to clear the box's text if it represents an integer less than 10, you could write code such as the following:

```
if ($F("tip") < 10) {
  $("tip").clear();     // erase text if number typed is too small
}
```

| Method Name | Description |
|---|---|
| activate() | gives the control focus and selects its text, if any |
| clear() | removes any text from the control |
| disable(), enable() | disables or enables the form control's value from being changed |
| focus() | gives the control focus |
| getValue() | returns the current value of the control (usually a string, but an array of strings for multiple-select list boxes); a longhand for $F |
| present() | returns **true** if there is any text typed into the control |
| select() | selects/highlights the text in the control |

Table 9.10 Prototype form control element methods

## Self-Check

1.  What are the contents of the following array after the following code runs?

```
var nums = [2.7, 5.1, 18.6, 5.1, 2.7, 16, 27];
nums = nums.uniq().without(16);
for (var i = 0; i < nums.length; i++) {
  a[i] = a[i].round();
  if (a[i] % 2 == 0) {
    a[i] = a[i].toColorPart().times(3);
  }
}
```

2.  Suppose we have an element with **id** of **box**. How would we use Prototype to make this element invisible on the page? How would we delete the element from the page?
3.  Suppose we have an element with **id** of **box**. How would we use Prototype to check whether the element's font is bold, and if so, to also make the font become italic?
4.  In Prototype's terminology, what is the difference between a parent node and an ancestor node? Between a child and a descendant?
5.  How would you use Prototype to retrieve the DOM objects for all paragraph (**p**) elements on the page that have the CSS class of **story** that are inside the div with **id** of **container**?

## 9.2 Event-Handling

In the past couple of chapters we've seen how to handle basic mouse clicks using the `click` event (by attaching `onclick` handlers to elements), but this is just one of many events that can be handled in JavaScript. In this section we'll explore other kinds of events and write programs that handle them. Recall the way to attach an event handler to an element as shown in Example 9.17.

```
element.onevent = function;
```

**Example 9.17 Syntax template for attaching an event handler**

For example, later in this chapter we'll learn about the `mousemove` event that occurs when the user moves the mouse over a given element. To attach an event handler named `myHandler` to this event for an element with an `id` of target, we would write:

```
$("target").onmousemove = myHandler;
```

The event's name is similar to but not quite the same as the DOM element's property for that event. For example, the `click` event corresponds to the `onclick` event property in the DOM. When you see event names in the tables in this chapter such as `load` or `mouseup`, the corresponding event property is `onload` or `onmouseup`.

Unfortunately, there is currently no W3C standard for how events should work. Therefore each organization that has built a browser has essentially invented its own event system. The systems are largely similar, but if you're doing anything complex you'll quickly bump into frustrating incompatibilities and bugs.

Prototype does a great job of repairing and standardizing events in JavaScript. In order to fully take advantage of its features, however, we must attach our event handlers in the Prototype way. If we attach our event handlers using Prototype's syntax, Prototype will do some extra work under the hood to make sure that any events that occur will be modified to work the same way on any browser.

Prototype attaches event handlers by calling an `observe` method on the element and passing two parameters: The event name as a string, without the "on" prefix, and the function to use as the event handler. The syntax is shown in Example 9.18.

```
element.observe("eventName", function);
```

**Example 9.18 Syntax template for attaching an event handler (Prototype)**

For example, the `mousemove` event handler above would be attached in Prototype as follows:

```
$("target").observe("mousemove", myHandler);
```

Another nice thing about attaching event handlers the Prototype way is that you can attach more than one handler for the same event if so desired.

To maintain our sanity, we have chosen to use Prototype to help us handle events in all the examples in this section. Going through all of the various incompatibilities and how to solve them using traditional JavaScript is confusing and wastes page space, especially given that Prototype fixes most of the problems for us. If you don't want to use Prototype and want to learn how to wade through the muck yourself, see the Quirksmode pages in this chapter's References section for more information.

### 9.2.1 The Event Object

Whenever any event handler is called, it is passed a parameter representing the event that occurred. The event-handling functions we've written so far did not declare any such parameter, because we didn't need to interact with it. But if you like, you can declare this parameter in your handler and examine its state to learn more about the event that occurred. The syntax template for declaring such a handler is shown in Example 9.19.

```
function name(event) {
   statements;
}
```

**Example 9.19 Syntax template for event handler with event parameter**

It may seem odd that just by declaring an `event` parameter you get access to information about the event. You don't even need to change anything about the code that attaches the event handler. But that's how it works in JavaScript; the parameter is optional, and if you declare it, you'll receive it and can examine it. Event objects have several properties, depending on the type of event that occurred. Every event has a `type` property, as shown in Table 9.11. We don't use that property very much, because usually we know what kind of event occurred simply by what function is called.

| Property Name | Type | Description |
|---|---|---|
| type | string | kind of event, such as `"click"` or `"mousedown"` |

**Table 9.11 Properties common to all event objects**

(FYI, if we weren't using Prototype, Internet Explorer would not work with this model of declaring the `event` parameter. We'd have to access another event object called `window.event` instead. Thanks to Prototype we don't need to fret about such things!)

Prototype also adds several methods to enhance every event object. These methods are listed in Table 9.12. Particularly useful is the `stop` method, which aborts the normal behavior of an event. For example, when a mouse button is pressed or a key is typed, if we handle that event and call `stop()` on it, the normal click/key behavior goes away. So it is possible to make unclickable buttons or text boxes that accept only certain characters (e.g. only letters or numbers) as user input. We'll explore this in a later section of this chapter.

| Method Name | Description |
|---|---|
| element() | element on which event occurred (replaces `which`, `srcElement`) |
| stop() | cancels the event's normal behavior |
| stopObserving() | removes an event handler |

**Table 9.12 Prototype's event methods**

## 9.2.2 Mouse Events

JavaScript contains events related to mouse actions such as movement, pressing and releasing a button, entering and exiting an element, and double-clicks. These events are listed in Table 9.13. Some relate to the pressing of buttons, such as `mousedown`, `mouseup`, and `click`. Others relate to the movement of the cursor, such as `mousemove`, `mouseover`, and `mouseout`.

When the user clicks the mouse button, a series of events occurs. First a `mousedown` event occurs as the user presses down the mouse button. Then, when the user lifts up the button, first a `mouseup` event occurs, then a `click` event occurs. You may wonder why there is both a `mouseup` event and a `click` event. It's possible to press the mouse down and up without it being a click. If the mouse cursor moves more than a few pixels between the button being pushed down and lifted up, the browser assumes that the user is dragging rather than clicking, so no **click** event occurs. The **mousedown** and **mouseup** events do still occur, though (with several **mousemove** events between).

| Event Name | Occurs When... |
|---|---|
| click | an object is clicked (mouse is pressed then released) |
| dblclick | an object is double-clicked (two rapid clicks in a row) |
| mousedown | a mouse button is pressed |
| mousemove | the mouse cursor moves within this element |
| mouseout | the mouse cursor exits this element |
| mouseover | the mouse cursor enters this element |
| mouseup | a mouse button is released |

Table 9.13 Mouse events

The **mouseover** and **mouseout** events occur when the mouse cursor enters or exits the part of the screen occupied by a given element respectively. This can be useful to cause hover effects, like elements that enable/disable or highlight when the mouse cursor is on top of them. Example 9.20 shows a page with a paragraph that, when the mouse enters it, decrements the count of how many bottles of beer are left.

```
<p id="beercounter">99 bottles of beer</p>
```

```
var beerCount = 99;

window.onload = function() {
    $("beercounter").observe("mouseover", countBeers);
};

function countBeers() {
    $("beercounter").innerHTML = (--beerCount) + " bottles of beer";
}
```

| | |
|---|---|
| 99 bottles of beer | 98 bottles of beer |

Example 9.20 The mouseover event

## Mouse Event Properties

Mouse events in particular have lots of other properties related to the x/y position where the event occurred and which button (if any) was pressed. But there are lots of incompatibilities between various browsers in terms of which properties are provided. Some of the common properties are listed in Table 9.14, but we actually don't recommend that you use any of them, because your code is unlikely to work in multiple browsers.

Often we want to know the x/y coordinates at which a mouse event occurred. You can ask a mouse event for its x/y position relative to the top/left corner of the following four places:

- the user's computer screen (screenX and screenY)
- the overall web page (pageX and pageY)
- the visible portion of the page on the screen (clientX and clientY)
- the element in which the event occurred (offsetX and offsetY) (missing in Firefox)

Figure 9.2 diagrams the difference between several of these properties. The clientX and clientY change as you scroll the browser window, but the pageX and pageY do not.

Though things have improved recently, mouse position has historically been an area rife with browser incompatibilities. Even now, for example, Firefox does not support the offsetX and offsetY properties that other browsers support. And older versions of the browsers provide incorrect values for clientX and clientY, among other incompatibilities.

| Property Name | Description |
|---|---|
| clientX, clientY | coordinates relative to the top/left corner of the browser window/tab |
| screenX, screenY | coordinates relative to the top/left corner of the entire screen |
| offsetX, offsetY | coordinates from top/left of element in which event occurred (does not work in Firefox) |
| pageX, pageY | coordinates relative to the top/left corner of the overall document |

Table 9.14 Mouse event coordinate properties

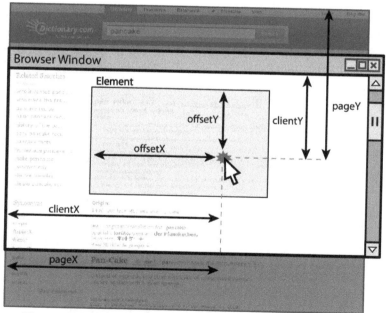

Figure 9.2 Relative x/y coordinates of mouse events

Example 9.21 sets up a single event handler to listen to three different kinds of mouse events. When an event occurs, text is put onto the page showing the event's type (such as mousedown or mousemove), along with the x/y coordinates at which the event occurred relative to the top/left corner of the page.

Many mousemove events can occur in a short time. As the mouse moves around on the element, each time its position changes, which can happen many times per second, another mousemove event occurs. The change in x/y position between each event is generally just a few pixels unless the user is moving the mouse very quickly.

```
<div id="status">Move the mouse on me!</div>
```

```
window.onload = function() {
  $("status").observe("mousemove", showCoordinates);
  $("status").observe("mousedown", showCoordinates);
  $("status").observe("mouseup", showCoordinates);
};

// Called when any of several mouse events occurs on the status area.
function showCoordinates(event) {
  $("status").innerHTML = "A " + event.type + " event occurred at (" +
    event.pageX + ", " + event.pageY + ")";
}
```

| | |
|---|---|
| Move the mouse on me! | A mousemove event occurred at (133, 20) |

**Example 9.21 Using the mouse event object**

There are some other things you can ask the mouse event object, but not in a very standard way. For example, the event stores a reference to the element on which it occurred, but this is nonstandard between browsers. Firefox calls it `target`, while other browsers call it `srcElement`. You can also ask the mouse event which button was pressed, if it was a button-related event such as `click` or `mousedown`. The property to examine is called button, but its value is not standard between browsers. Firefox gives the left button a value of 0; IE gives it a value of 1. Table 9.15 lists these poorly standardized mouse event properties. We suggest that you not use them (Prototype offers a better way to get this information, as we'll see in a moment).

Browser incompatibilities like these are frustrating. Depending on what you're trying to do, it can be very difficult to make things work in all browsers without testing in your JS code for what browser the user is using by examining `navigator.appName`. But we want to avoid doing so if possible, because it creates brittle scripts that may not work in the future or on browsers we didn't check.

| Property Name | Description |
|---|---|
| button | which mouse button was pressed/released, if any; IE returns 1/2/4 for left/right/middle buttons (nonstandard); Firefox/others return 0/1/2 for left/right/middle buttons |
| layerX, layerY | equivalent to pageX/Y; nonstandard, do not use |
| srcElement | element that fired the event; does not work in Firefox |
| target | element that fired the event; Firefox only |

**Table 9.15 JavaScript mouse event properties (non-standard and discouraged)**

Prototype tries to help us by adding a new set of methods to all event objects, as shown in Table 9.16. We recommend using these methods as it helps you avoid the non-standard properties from Table 9.15. The `isLeftClick` method helps you conclusively test whether the left or right button was pressed. The `element` method conclusively returns the element on which the event occurred (though we don't often use the method, because usually `this` stores the same information).

| Method Name | Description |
|---|---|
| isLeftClick() | true if this event was a left click (replaces button, which) |
| pointerX(), pointerY() | coordinates relative to overall document (same as pageX, pageY) |

**Table 9.16 Prototype's mouse event methods**

Example 9.22 demonstrates the use of some of these methods. Notice that like all of Prototype's features, these are methods and not properties, so you must write () when calling them.

```
function handleClick(event) {
  if (event.isLeftClick() && event.pointerX() < 100) {
    alert("You clicked on this element: " + event.element());
  }
}
```

**Example 9.22 Using Prototype's event methods**

## Example Program: Colored Squares Revisited

In the previous chapter we wrote a program to randomly create 50x50px squares and allow the user to click each one to move it to the top of the field of view. Let's revisit that page and add the ability to drag squares around with the mouse. The relevant HTML code is shown in Example 9.23, mostly unmodified except for a few new words about being able to drag squares around.

```
<div id="squarearea"></div>
<div>
  <button id="add">Add Square</button>
  <button id="colors">Change Colors</button>
</div>
<p>Click a square to move it to the front, or drag it around.</p>
```

**Example 9.23 Colored squares HTML code**

If we want squares to be draggable, we'll need to detect several events: pressing down the mouse button on a square (**mousedown**), moving the mouse (**mousemove**) with the button held down, and releasing the button (**mouseup**). We previously wrote an **addSquare** function to create random squares and attach an **onclick** handler to each square. Let's modify this code to also attach these three event handlers. While we're at it we will modify the existing code to attach the click handler using Prototype's **observe** method. We'll write the code for the new event-handling functions next.

```
// Creates and adds a new square div to the page.
function addSquare() {
  var square = document.createElement("div");
  $("squarearea").appendChild(square);
  ...
  square.observe("click", squareClick);
  square.observe("mousedown", squareMouseDown);
  square.observe("mousemove", squareMouseMove);
  square.observe("mouseup", squareMouseUp);
}
```

**Example 9.24 Attaching mouse event handlers to squares**

If we want to be cross-browser compatible, we should add one more line of code. In Internet Explorer, when we create new elements with `document.createElement`, they are not properly enhanced with Prototype's features. This means they don't have the `observe` method, so our code to attach the event listeners will fail. But we can fix this by calling the `$` function and passing it the new element we are creating. `$` automatically enhances the DOM object so it will work properly:

```
var square = $(document.createElement("div"));
...
```

Now let's try to implement dragging of squares. It's easy to get this code wrong and have the wrong squares move, squares start flying around the page, squares disappearing altogether, and so on. The crucial aspect to solving this is keeping track of the change in x and y between each `mousemove` event. For example, if the user moves the mouse over a square and starts dragging it, if the user's cursor moves left by 5px, we must move the square's x-coordinate left by 5px.

To know the distance traveled by the mouse cursor between each event, we will declare global variables named `oldX` and `oldY` to remember where the mouse cursor was on the previous event. Each time an event occurs, we'll compare the mouse's new position to the old one, and update the old position to be the current position. Example 9.25 shows the code.

```
var oldX = null;       // x/y position of last mousemove event
var oldY = null;

// Called when the user moves the mouse.  Drags a square.
function squareMouseMove(event) {
  if (oldX !== null && oldY !== null) {
    var dx = event.pointerX() - oldX;
    var dy = event.pointerY() - oldY;
    this.style.left = parseInt(this.style.left) + dx + "px";
    this.style.top  = parseInt(this.style.top)  + dy + "px";

  }
  oldX = event.pointerX();     // update old x/y to current position
  oldY = event.pointerY();
}
```

**Example 9.25 Colored squares mouse movement code**

This code does cause squares to move on the page when we test it. But it doesn't pay attention to the mouse button; it moves any square that the mouse moves onto. That isn't quite what we wanted.

To implement the behavior properly, there are actually three events to consider: pressing the button, moving the cursor, and releasing the button. When the user presses down the button on a square, that is the one and only square that we should now allow to be dragged. So we'll store the element on which the event occurred in a variable named `moving`, so that when future `mousemove` events occur, we'll know which square to move. When the user lifts the mouse button, we'll erase our memory of the moving square so that it no longer drags. We'll also modify our mouse-move code so that we only move a square if it is the square that is being clicked and moving. Example 9.26 shows the new code, which now behaves as desired, and the appearance in the browser before and after dragging.

```
var moving = null;    // square that is moving, if any

// Called when the user presses down the mouse button.
// Moves the clicked square to the top and starts moving it.
function squareMouseDown(event) {
  this.style.zIndex = (++maxZ);    // move clicked square to top
  moving = this;
  oldX = event.pointerX();         // remember this square for
  oldY = event.pointerY();         //    future mousemove events
}

// Called when the user lifts the mouse button.  Stops dragging.
function squareMouseUp(event) {
  moving = null;
}

// Called when the user moves the mouse.  Drags a square if
// the mouse button is being held down.
function squareMouseMove(event) {
  if (this === moving && oldX !== null && oldY !== null) {
    ...
  }
}
```

Click a square to move it to the front, or drag it around.        Click a square to move it to the front, or drag it around.

**Example 9.26 Colored squares mouse down/up code**

## 9.2.3 Keyboard and Text Events

JavaScript has several events related to text on the page and to typing keys on the keyboard, shown in Table 9.17. There are three main keyboard events you can handle in your code: **keydown** (when the user presses a key), **keyup** (when the user releases a key), and **keypress** (when a key character has been typed). If the user holds down a key and the keyboard starts auto-repeating the key, multiple **keydown** and **keypress** events occur. These three key events are analogous to the **mousedown**, **mouseup**, and **click** events when dealing with the mouse.

| Event Name | Occurs When... |
|---|---|
| blur | this element loses keyboard focus |
| focus | this element gains keyboard focus |
| keydown | a user presses a key while this element has keyboard focus |
| keypress | a user presses and releases a key while this element has keyboard focus (not well standardized across browsers) |
| keyup | a user releases a key while this element has keyboard focus |
| select | the user selects text in an element |

**Table 9.17 Keyboard and text events**

The difference between `keydown` and `keypress` is like the difference between `mousedown` and `click`. A `keypress` event will only occur if a character is typed that appears on the page, such as a letter or number; it won't occur if the user presses an arrow key or Enter, for example. There are some inconsistencies to how `keydown` and `keypress` work on various browsers and operating systems. We have found the `keydown` event more reliable in our own testing and recommend using it and ignoring `keypress`.

**focus**

An element has keyboard focus if the key cursor is on that element and the user can type text into the element.

Another important concept when dealing with key events is the notion of keyboard focus. An element has keyboard *focus* if the key cursor is on that element and the user is currently able to type text into it. For example, there might be several text boxes on the page, but only one at a time (the one the user clicks) will receive the key cursor and focus. There are two events related to keyboard focus: `focus` (when the event gains focus) and `blur` (when the event loses focus).

There is also a `select` event that fires when the user selects text in an element. This can be useful if you're implementing esoteric features such as a text highlighter.

Every keyboard event object has some additional properties, shown in Table 9.18. The most important is the `keyCode` property, which gives you the ASCII value of the key the user pressed. For example, if the user presses the "a" key, the `keyCode` of the event will be 65. You don't need to have any ASCII values memorized; the `String.fromCharCode` method accepts an integer ASCII code as its parameter and returns the corresponding character as a string.

| Property Name | Type | Description |
|---|---|---|
| keyCode | integer | the ASCII value of the character that was pressed (convert to a character using `String.fromCharCode`) |
| charCode | string | the character that was typed (non-standard; do not use) |
| altKey, ctrlKey, shiftKey | boolean | `true` if Alt, Ctrl, or Shift is being held down respectively |

**Table 9.18 Key event properties**

For example, suppose your page has a text box with `id` of `words`, and you want the page to pop up an alert box whenever the user types the character "c". Example 9.27 demonstrates how to test for this character. Case sensitivity can be an issue; the `keyCode` you receive for an event will always be the `keyCode` for the uppercase version of a character, regardless of whether the Shift key is being held down. Note that we check for an uppercase "C" in our code.

```
window.onload = function() {
  $("words").observe("keydown", wordsKeyDown);
};

function wordsKeyDown(event) {
  var letter = String.fromCharCode(event.keyCode));
  if (letter == "C") {
    alert("C is for cookie.  That's good enough for me!"):
  }
}
```

**Example 9.27 Detecting a specific character**

Sometimes you specifically want to look for a non-alphanumeric character such as an arrow key or the Escape key. Normally you have to do this by looking up the ASCII value for said key and testing whether the event's `keyCode` equals that number. But Prototype provides several useful constants in its global **Event** (capital E) object that correspond to the ASCII values of various special characters. These constants are shown in Table 9.19.

| KEY_BACKSPACE | KEY_DELETE | KEY_DOWN | KEY_END | KEY_ESC |
| KEY_HOME | KEY_INSERT | KEY_LEFT | KEY_PAGEDOWN | KEY_PAGEUP |
| KEY_RETURN | KEY_RIGHT | KEY_TAB | KEY_UP | |

**Table 9.19 Prototype's key code constants (part of Event object)**

Example 9.28 demonstrates using one of these key constants. When the Escape key is pressed, the contents of the text box are cleared.

```
function textBoxKeyDown(event) {
  if (event.keyCode == Event.KEY_ESC) {
    this.clear();   // clear text when Esc is pressed
  }
}
```

**Example 9.28 Using Prototype's key code constants**

## Example Program: Valid ZIP Code

Suppose our page has a form that lets the user type in a ZIP code, and that we'd like to make sure the user types only numbers into the ZIP code box. Example 9.29 shows the initial HTML.

```
<form action="http://webster.cs.washington.edu/params.php" method="get">
  ZIP code:
  <input id="zip" type="text" size="5" maxlength="5" />
</form>
```

**Example 9.29 ZIP code HTML code**

We'll need to detect key press events so that we can filter out any unwanted (non-numeric) characters typed into the text box. Example 9.30 shows the initial setup of the JavaScript code.

```
window.onload = function() {
  $("zip").observe("keydown", zipKeyDown);
};

// Called when a key is pressed on the zip code field.
// Disallows non-numeric characters from being typed.
function zipKeyDown(event) {
  ...
}
```

**Example 9.30 ZIP code initial JavaScript skeleton**

Every time a key is pressed, we should look at the keyCode of the event and see whether or not it was a number that was typed. But how do we detect numbers? There are ten key codes we'd like to allow: Those of "0", "1", "2", ..., and "9". Keep in mind that the ASCII key code for "0" is not 0; it's actually 48. We could look up the ASCII key codes for the numbers 0-9, but instead we can just ask JavaScript what they are by calling the charCodeAt method on the strings "0" and "9" to find the range of values we want to allow. If the event's keyCode is outside this range, we don't want that key. The way to disallow a key from being typed into the text box is to call Prototype's stop method on the event object. Example 9.31 shows the code to achieve this.

```
function zipKeyDown(event) {
  var zero = "0".charCodeAt(0);
  var nine = "9".charCodeAt(0);
  if (event.keyCode < zero || event.keyCode > nine) {
    event.stop();
  }
}
```

ZIP code: 85704

**Example 9.31 ZIP code excluding keys outside 0-9 range**

One problem with our code is that it disallows ALL key presses other than the numbers 0-9. For example the user can't even erase a mistyped number by typing Backspace because we disallow all non-numeric keys. One workaround for this problem is to create a list of other allowed keys in an array and test whether the user's keyCode is found in that array. Example 9.32 shows this code.

```
var ALLOWED = [Event.KEY_BACKSPACE, Event.KEY_LEFT, Event.KEY_RIGHT];
...
function zipKeyDown(event) {
  var zero = "0".charCodeAt(0);
  var nine = "9".charCodeAt(0);
  if ((event.keyCode < zero || event.keyCode > nine) &&
      ALLOWED.indexOf(event.keyCode) < 0) {
    event.stop();
  }
}
```

**Example 9.32 Allowing additional characters**

(Side note: Even the above code has a slight problem. If you enter numbers using your numeric keypad, it won't work on some browsers because they return different key codes. Addressing that issue is beyond the scope of this section; Google about this issue if you are curious about fixing it.)

## 9.2.4 Form Events

There are several JavaScript events related to forms and form controls, shown in Table 9.20. The main purpose of handling form events is to detect when the user is about to submit a form and perform some important action before the form data is sent to the server. For example, you might want to reformat the information the user typed before sending it, to remove unwanted characters or correct spelling and capitalization. Another use is to abort the submitting of a form if the data typed into the page is invalid.

| Event Name | Occurs When... |
|---|---|
| change | the value of a control (e.g., `select` box) changes |
| reset | the form is being reset |
| submit | the form is being submitted |

Table 9.20 Form events

You attach the **submit** or **reset** event handlers to the form itself, not to any particular control inside the form.

You may wonder why these events exist when we already have the **click** event. Why not just listen for clicks on the specific form controls of interest? The answer is that a form can have more than one way to submit itself, such as multiple submit buttons or by pressing Enter on a text box. Using a **submit** event handler makes sure that no matter how the user attempts to submit the data, our code will catch the event and respond accordingly.

### Example Program: Valid ZIP Code Revisited

Let's revisit our previous example with the ZIP code box. We already wrote code to ensure that only digits are typed into the box. And the user is prevented from typing too many digits because the **maxlength** attribute of the text box element is set to 5. But what if the user types too few characters? Let's block the form from being submitted by handling its **submit** event. If not enough digits are typed, we'll stop the form submit, light up the input box in red, and show a text error message.

Example 9.33 shows the revised HTML code for the form. We have given the **form** element an **id** so that we can access it in our JavaScript code, and we have inserted a submit button and an initially empty **span** called **ziperror** where we'll insert any error messages that we want to show to the user.

```
<form id="zipform" action="http://webster.cs.washington.edu/params.php"
  method="get">
  ZIP code:
  <input id="zip" type="text" size="5" maxlength="5" />
  <span id="ziperror"></span> <br />
  <input type="submit" />
</form>
```

ZIP code: 234

Submit Query

Example 9.33 ZIP code revised HTML code

When the ZIP code is invalid and the user tries to submit, we want it to light up in red with yellow text. In Example 9.34 we define a CSS class for bad form data that contains these style properties. Later in our JavaScript code we'll attach that class to the **zip** text box if necessary.

```
/* CSS code for ZIP code example */
.badformdata {
  background-color: #FF6666;
  color: yellow;
}
```

**Example 9.34 ZIP code CSS code**

Now we are ready to revise the JavaScript code for the page. This program already has a `window.onload` handler to attach a handler for `keydown` events on the `zip` text box. We can add a second handler that listens for `submit` events on the `zipform`, as shown in Example 9.35.

```
window.onload = function() {
  $("zip").observe("keydown", zipKeyDown);
  $("zipform").observe("submit", zipFormSubmit);
};
```

**Example 9.35 Handler for form submit events**

The `zipFormSubmit` function will check to see whether the `zip` box's text length is exactly 5. If not, we'll do three things: Show an error message in the `ziperror` span, set the `zip` box to use the class `badformdata` to make the text yellow and the background red, and stop the event to prevent the form from submitting. Example 9.36 shows the complete code for the function and the appearance in the browser when a bad ZIP code has been entered.

```
// Called when the user tries to submit the form.
function zipFormSubmit(event) {
  if ($("zip").value.length != 5) {
    // bad ZIP code; stop form from submitting and show error msg
    $("ziperror").innerHTML = "ZIP code must be 5 characters.";
    $("zip").addClassName("badformdata");
    event.stop();
  }
}
```

ZIP code: 984    ZIP code must be 5 characters.

Submit Query

**Example 9.36 Form submit event handler**

The **change** event is used to detect when a form control's state changes. This has several uses. The most common place we use this event is to detect when a **select** box's selected element changes. You attach a **change** handler to the **select** box itself (not to each **option** inside it). This works much better than trying to use an **onclick** handler on each **option** to detect changes. Example 9.37 demonstrates this event. If the **select** box changes to select **"Toyota"**, the Hybrid option enables.

The **change** event also occurs when the text changes in a **textarea** or in an **input** element with a type of **text**. The text is defined to have "changed" when the user presses Enter or when the keyboard focus leaves the element. The idea is that not every keystroke will result in a **change** event, but when the user is "finished" typing the new value, the event will occur. This will be useful for us in this chapter's case study example.

```
<select id="car">
  <option value="Chevy">Chevy</option>
  <option value="Ford">Ford</option>
  <option value="Toyota">Toyota</option>
</select>

<label>
  <input id="hybrid" type="checkbox" disabled="disabled" /> Hybrid?
</label>
```

```
window.onload = function() {
  $("car").observe("change", carChange);
};

// Enables hybrid option when Toyota is chosen as car maker
function carChange(event) {
  $("hybrid").disabled = (this.value != "Toyota");
}
```

**Example 9.37 Handling the onchange event**

## 9.2.5  Page Events

There are some events that relate to the overall web page, shown in Table 9.21. You can handle these events by attaching handlers to the global **window** object. We have already seen the **load** event since we've been attaching **window.onload** handlers for the last few chapters. There is also an **unload** event that fires as the user is about to leave the page. Prototype currently doesn't let you **observe** the **unload** event, but you can attach an **onunload** handler to it directly. You can stop this event to prevent the user from leaving the page. (There's nothing like a captive audience!) Example 9.38 shows an example that prompts the user before leaving the page if any text exists in the **message** element.

| Event Name | Occurs When... |
|---|---|
| abort | the user cancels the loading of the page |
| contextmenu | the user right-clicks to pop up a context menu |
| load | the page has finished loading |
| unload | the user chooses to leave the page |

**Table 9.21 Page events**

```
window.onunload = pageUnload;

function pageUnload(event) {
  if ($("message").length > 0 &&
      !confirm("You have unsaved data!  Are you sure?")) {
    event.stop();
  }
}
```
**Example 9.38 Observing the unload event**

The contextmenu event occurs when the user clicks the right mouse button to bring up a menu. Some web sites stop this event to try to prevent the user from saving images on the site (by default, right clicking an image gives a context menu with an option to save the image clicked on). A more relevant reason to handle this event would be to pop up your own context menu with custom menu options when the user right-clicks.

Prototype offers an additional page event called dom:loaded, shown in Table 9.22. This event fires when the page has finished loading all of its HTML DOM content. This is very similar to window.onload, except that it occurs sooner. The window.onload event doesn't occur until the entire page and all of its resources (image files, etc.) have been fully downloaded and displayed on the screen. The dom:loaded event fires as soon as the browser is done downloading the page's HTML file and has created the corresponding DOM tree of objects for all of the page's elements. This event occurs on the global document object, so if you want to handle it, you attach your handler there.

In many cases, you can notice a significant speed boost in the time it takes your page to be ready by listening to the dom:loaded event instead of window.onload. You will especially notice the difference if your window.onload function does any DOM manipulations like showing/hiding elements or dynamically adding elements to the page.

| Event Name | Occurs When... |
|---|---|
| dom:loaded | the page's HTML DOM content has finished loading |

**Table 9.22 Prototype's dom:loaded event**

Just as with window.onload, we often attach our event handler for dom:loaded as an anonymous function. Example 9.39 shows a syntax template for attaching a handler in such a way. The anonymous function is passed as the second parameter to the document.observe method. Be careful to get the closing operators right: The last line of the template has a } brace to end the anonymous handler function, followed by a ) right-parenthesis and semicolon to end the call to document.observe.

```
document.observe("dom:loaded", function() {
  statements;
});
```
**Example 9.39 Syntax template for dom:loaded handler**

Example 9.40 updates our ZIP code example to use a dom:loaded handler.

```
document.observe("dom:loaded", function() {
  $("zip").observe("keydown", zipKeyDown);
  $("zipform").observe("submit", zipFormSubmit);
});
```

**Example 9.40 Using Prototype's dom:loaded event**

## 9.2.6 Timer Events

JavaScript contains the powerful notion of *timers*, which allow you to run a piece of code after a specified delay. Timers are useful for many purposes, such as:

- requests or questions to the user that "time out" after a given interval
- retrying an action repeatedly
- contacting a server at given intervals to request data
- drawing animations on a page

There are two integral functions for using timers, named **setTimeout** and **setInterval**. Each of these functions accepts two parameters: a function to call, and an integer delay in milliseconds. The difference between them is that **setTimeout** calls the function a single time, while **setInterval** calls it repeatedly. There are also functions called **clearTimeout** and **clearInterval** that stop a timer. Each of these functions accepts a timer ID as a parameter. Timer IDs are returned by **setTimeout** and **setInterval**, so you can store your timer's ID in a variable if you may want to cancel it later. Table 9.23 summarizes these functions.

| Method Name(s) | Description |
|---|---|
| setTimeout(**function, delayMS**) | starts a timer to call the given function *once* after **delayMS** milliseconds; <br><br> returns a timer ID that can be passed to clearTimeout later if so desired |
| setInterval(**function, delayMS**) | starts a timer to call the given function *repeatedly* every **delayMS** milliseconds; <br><br> returns a timer ID that can be passed to clearInterval later if so desired |
| clearTimeout(**timerID**) | aborts the timer associated with the given ID |
| clearInterval(**timerID**) | stops the timer associated with the given ID |

**Table 9.23 Timer functions**

For example, to call the function **blingBling** after 3 seconds, you would write:

```
setTimeout(blingBling, 3000);   // call blingBling function after 3 sec
```

(There is another older way to call **setTimeout** and **setInterval** where the first parameter is not a function name but instead a string of code to run when the time elapses. This older style was required by some browsers such as older versions of Internet Explorer, but is no longer required on modern browser versions. To use the older style, you would write code such as the following:)

```
setTimeout("blingbling();", 3000);    // older style; do not use!
```

Some students have trouble understanding the flow of execution of the code when using timers, because the execution occurs asynchronously. In other words, the event does not occur at the same time you call the `setTimeout` function. When you call `setTimeout`, the call returns immediately. The call doesn't cause your page to halt or wait at that line of code for 3 seconds. But the call does set up the internal plumbing of the browser so that 3 seconds from now, `blingBling` will be called.

If we had wanted to potentially be able to cancel this event later, we could have stored the return value from `setTimeout` into a global variable. Example 9.41 shows a piece of code where a click of one "stopwatch" button begins a timer and a click of another "abort" button stops the timer.

```
var timerID = null;

function stopwatchClick() {
  timerID = setTimeout(blingBling, 3000);    // start/save timer
}

function abortButtonClick() {
  clearTimeout(timerID);                      // cancel timer
}
```

**Example 9.41 Canceling a timer with `clearTimeout`**

Prototype contains a `PeriodicalExecuter` object that represents an action to repeat at regular intervals; it serves as a wrapper for `setInterval`. It can be created by passing a function to call and an interval in **seconds** (not milliseconds) between calls, as shown in Example 9.42. The timer repeatedly executes the function until the page unloads or until you call its `stop` method on it.

```
var name = new PeriodicalExecuter(function, delaySeconds);
```

**Example 9.42 Syntax template for Prototype's PeriodicalExecuter**

We do not consider Prototype's way of doing things to be significantly better than the existing functionality in JavaScript, therefore in our future examples we'll continue to use `setInterval`.

## Self-Check

6. Using Prototype's event attachment function, how would you attach the function `kaboom` as a handler for the `mouseover` event for an element with `id` of `bomb`?
7. How do you abort an event? Why is it sometimes useful to do so?
8. What is the difference between a `click` event and a `mousedown` event?
9. How do you tell whether the left or right mouse button was clicked?
10. When dealing with mouse events, you can ask for the x/y position at which the event occurred relative to various other points. What are three of these other points? What is one case where several of these values would be the same, and when would they differ?
11. When a key event occurs, how do you figure out which character was typed? How do you tell whether a special modifier such as Shift or Ctrl is being held down?
12. What is keyboard focus? How does a user tell what part of the page has the focus?
13. What is the difference between the `setTimeout` and `setInterval` functions?
14. How do you abort a timer?

## 9.3 Case Study: Multiplication Quiz

Suppose we want to write a page that asks the user multiplication problems between two numbers. When the user types an answer and presses Enter, the program will see whether the guess was correct, and give the user a point if so. The quiz is timed; the page will show a timer that starts at 5 seconds and counts downward. If the user cannot make a guess before the 5 seconds are up, the next problem will be shown and the user will receive no points. The desired appearance of the page is shown in Figure 9.3.

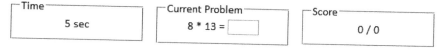

# Multiplication Quiz

You have 5 seconds for each problem. How many can you solve?

**Figure 9.3 Multiplication quiz, desired appearance**

Since this is a large and tricky problem to solve, we'll need to break it down into steps. A good set of steps for solving this problem are the following:

1. Create the initial HTML and CSS code.
2. Write the JavaScript code to create a random multiplication problem.
3. Write the JavaScript code to let the user make a guess and determine whether that guess is correct or incorrect, giving points accordingly.
4. Add the timer code so that the user is limited to 5 seconds and is marked incorrect if the problem is not solved within that time.

### 9.3.1 Initial HTML/CSS Code

The page will need to have some CSS and JavaScript code, so let's begin our file by creating a head section that links to `multquiz.css` and `multquiz.js` files, both as yet unwritten. We will also want to link to the Prototype library. Example 9.43 shows the relevant portion of the HTML.

```
<!DOCTYPE html PUBLIC "-//W3C//DTD XHTML 1.1//EN"
 "http://www.w3.org/TR/xhtml11/DTD/xhtml11.dtd">
<html>
  <head>
    <title>Marvelous Multiplication Quiz</title>
    <link href="multquiz.css" type="text/css" rel="stylesheet" />
    <script src="prototype.js" type="text/javascript"></script>
    <script src="multquiz.js" type="text/javascript"></script>
  </head>

  <body>
    <!-- body contents ... -->
  </body>
</html>
```

**Example 9.43 Page head section**

The **body** section of the page should start with a heading and then contain a main section with three field sets in it, one for each of the boxes shown in the expected output. Example 9.44 shows the outline of this HTML code.

```
<body>
  <h1>Multiplication Quiz</h1>

  <div id="main">
    <!-- 3 fieldsets ... -->
  </div>

  <p>You have 5 seconds for each problem.  How many can you solve?</p>
</body>
```

**Example 9.44 Skeleton of page body**

The first field set, shown in Example 9.45, has a label of "Time" and will display how many seconds are left to guess the current problem. This number of seconds will change as time passes, so we'll wrap a **span** around the number of seconds with an **id** of **time** so we can manipulate it using the DOM later.

```
<fieldset>
  <legend>Time</legend>
  <div><span id="time">5</span> sec</div>
</fieldset>
```

**Example 9.45 Time field set**

The second field set displays information about the current multiplication problem. There will be two numbers to multiply, which we'll represent as **span**s with **id**s of **num1** and **num2**. Next to these **span**s there will be an input text box for the user to type his/her guess. Let's restrict ourselves to numbers between 1 and 20 to keep the game from being too difficult. The product of any two numbers in that range will be three digits or fewer, so we'll use 3 as our **size** and **maxlength** for the text box. Example 9.46 shows the code.

```
<fieldset>
  <legend>Current Problem</legend>
  <div>
    <span id="num1"></span> * <span id="num2"></span> =
    <input id="guess" type="text" size="3" maxlength="3" />
  </div>
</fieldset>
```

**Example 9.46 Current problem field set**

The third and final field set shows information about the player's current score; its code is shown in Example 9.47. As with the other field sets, we use **span**s to represent text that will change in our JavaScript code, namely the number of correct guesses and the total problems shown so far.

```
<fieldset>
  <legend>Score</legend>
  <div>
    <span id="correct">0</span> / <span id="total">0</span>
  </div>
</fieldset>
```

**Example 9.47 Score field set**

The appearance of the page after writing all of the preceding code is shown in Figure 9.4.

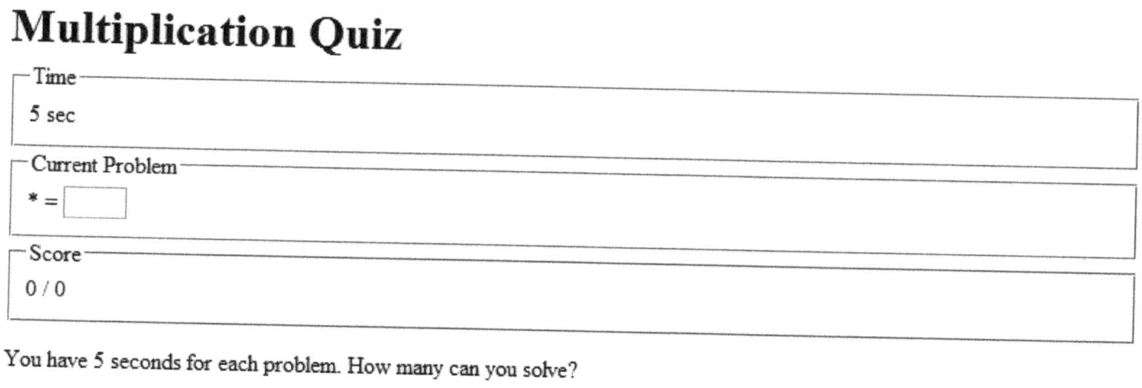

# Multiplication Quiz

┌─ Time ──────────────────────────────────────────────┐
│ 5 sec                                                │
└──────────────────────────────────────────────────────┘

┌─ Current Problem ───────────────────────────────────┐
│ * = [    ]                                           │
└──────────────────────────────────────────────────────┘

┌─ Score ─────────────────────────────────────────────┐
│ 0 / 0                                                │
└──────────────────────────────────────────────────────┘

You have 5 seconds for each problem. How many can you solve?

**Figure 9.4 Multiplication quiz HTML-only appearance**

The CSS code for the page and its resulting appearance are shown in Example 9.48. Most of the code is straightforward stuff like fonts and margins. The trickiest part is lining up the field sets into a single horizontal row. We'll achieve this by making them float to the left and setting each to have a width of 12em. We'll make the overall `main` area 40em wide and centered horizontally using `auto` margins. An important detail is to set the `overflow` of `main` to `hidden` so it will extend downward to contain its floating content, so the paragraph below is not covered up. (See the Layout chapter if you need to review the material about making floating elements fit.)

```
/* CSS code for multiplication quiz example */
body, input {
  font-family: "Calibri", "Verdana", "Arial", sans-serif;
}
fieldset {
  float: left;
  margin-left: 1em;
  width: 12em;
}
fieldset, h1, p {
  text-align: center;
}
#main {
  margin-left: auto;
  margin-right: auto;
  overflow: hidden;
  width: 40em;
}
```

# Multiplication Quiz

| ┌Time──────────── | ┌Current Problem─── | ┌Score─────────── |
|---|---|---|
| 5 sec | * = [    ] | 0 / 0 |

You have 5 seconds for each problem. How many can you solve?

**Example 9.48 Multiplication quiz CSS code**

## 9.3.2 Problems and Guesses

Now let's tackle some JavaScript code for our page. There are a lot of aspects to the page's behavior, and it would be difficult to tackle all of them at once. For now let's ignore the timer and just give the user infinite time to think of an answer. Let's focus first on the task of creating random multiplication problems for the user to solve and on determining whether the user has solved a given problem correctly. There are several subtasks here:

- When the page first loads up, we need to create a random multiplication problem. To do this, we must choose two random numbers and put them onto the page.
- When the user presses Enter on the input text box, we should check if the guess is correct.
- If so, we should give the user a point. We should also increment the total problems by 1.
- After any guess (correct or not), we need to create and display the next random problem.

It sounds like in a couple of places we'll need to be able to create a new random problem. Since we don't want to redundantly repeat this code, let's create a nextProblem function that picks the two random values from 1-20. The user will also want us to clear the text in the input box when each new problem starts, in case anything had been typed there previously. Example 9.49 shows the code.

```
var MAX_VALUE = 20;      // largest number that could be used in a problem

// Chooses two new random numbers for the next quiz problem.
function nextProblem() {
  $("num1").innerHTML = parseInt(Math.random() * MAX_VALUE) + 1;
  $("num2").innerHTML = parseInt(Math.random() * MAX_VALUE) + 1;
  $("guess").clear();
}
```

**Example 9.49 Creating a random problem**

When the window loads, we should call this `nextProblem` function to set up the first multiplication problem. Rather than `window.onload`, we'll use Prototype's `dom:loaded` event for better responsiveness. Example 9.50 shows this code and the page's new appearance, now with a different random problem displayed each time you reload it.

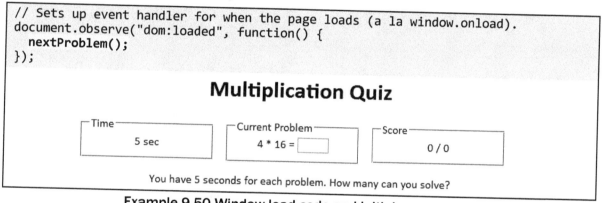

**Example 9.50 Window load code and initial appearance**

Now let's tackle the behavior for when the user makes a guess. We could attach an event handler to the **keydown** event of the text box, but the only key that interests us is when the user presses the Enter key after typing an answer. If that's all you want to handle, the better way is to attach a **change** handler to the input box, as shown in Example 9.51.

```
document.observe("dom:loaded", function() {
  nextProblem();
  $("guess").observe("change", guessChange);
});

// Called when player's guess changes.  Checks whether guess is correct.
function guessChange(event) {
  ...
}
```

**Example 9.51 Listening to change event**

To detect whether the player's guess is correct, we must grab the user's guess (the **value** of the **guess** text box) with the **$F** function and also grab the two numbers that we've previously chosen. We can check whether the guess is equal to the product of the two randomly chosen numbers. If so, we should give the player a point. Regardless of whether it is correct, we should increment the total number of problems shown so far, then move on to the next problem. The implementation is shown in Example 9.52, along with the page appearance after a few correct and incorrect guesses.

```
// Called when player's guess changes.  Checks guess is correct.
function guessChange(event) {
  var guess = $F("guess");
  var answer = $("num1").innerHTML * $("num2").innerHTML;

  if (guess == answer) {
    // user got the right answer; give a point
    $("correct").innerHTML = parseInt($("correct").innerHTML) + 1;
  }

  // move on to next problem
  $("total").innerHTML = parseInt($("total").innerHTML) + 1;
  nextProblem();
}
```

## Multiplication Quiz

| Time | Current Problem | Score |
|------|----------------|-------|
| 5 sec | 6 * 12 = 72 | 3 / 4 |

You have 5 seconds for each problem. How many can you solve?

**Example 9.52 Checking for correct guesses**

Notice that in two places we read the `innerHTML` of an element, parsing it into an integer value, then adding 1 to that value and putting it back into the element. (We have to call `parseInt`; otherwise JavaScript does a string concatenation.) Since this is a bit hard to read and will be repeated throughout our program, let's write a helper function called `increment` that accepts an element's `id` and increments the integer value stored in that element's text by 1. Example 9.53 shows the code.

```
// Increases value of text of element with given id by 1.
function increment(id) {
  $(id).innerHTML = parseInt($(id).innerHTML) + 1;
}
```

**Example 9.53 Helper to increment an element's integer value**

Example 9.54 shows the improved version of our `guessChange` function that uses the new `increment` helper we just wrote.

```
// Called when player's guess changes.  Checks guess is correct.
function guessChange(event) {
  var guess = $F("guess");
  var answer = $("num1").innerHTML * $("num2").innerHTML;
  if (guess == answer) {
    increment("correct");   // user got the right answer; give a point
  }
  increment("total");       // move on to next problem
  nextProblem();
}
```

**Example 9.54 Improved guessChange function**

## 9.3.3 Time Limits

So far the game affords the player infinite time to answer each problem. Our next challenge is limiting the user to a 5-second time limit. We'll need to use one of JavaScript's timer functions such as `setTimeout` or `setInterval`. But where/when do we start the timer? When does it stop? How long should we make its delay in milliseconds?

The player has 5 seconds to answer each problem, so 5000ms might seem like the right delay amount for our timer. But this provides an unpleasant user experience, because suddenly without warning the page will mark the user incorrect. The player will want to know how much time is left at any given moment. Instead of a 5-second timer delay, let's make a timer that ticks once per second, decreasing the visible time display by 1 second each time, until we hit 0.

Timer code can be hard to test and debug, and most students approach it in the wrong order. You may be tempted to rush in and start writing code to call `setTimeout` or `setInterval`. But let's take a different approach: Let's focus on the code that should run each the timer ticks, once per second, and manually test that code in Firebug before proceeding. Once we're pretty sure that code is done properly, we'll turn to the actual timer code.

On each tick, we should get the text from the `span` with `id` of `time`, which contains the number of seconds remaining (initially 5), and decrease this number by 1. If it reaches 0 without the user making a guess, we'll mark it as an incorrect answer and go to the next problem.

The task of grabbing the time text and decreasing it by 1 is a lot like the increment helper code we just wrote, except that it goes down by 1 instead of up by 1. Let's modify our increment method so that it accepts an optional second parameter: the amount to adjust the element's value by, with a default of 1. Let's also make `increment` return the new numeric value so that the caller can examine it if so desired. Example 9.55 shows this code, which uses the `||` operator to allow for the default increment of 1 if no amount (`undefined`) is passed.

```
// Adjusts the integer value of the text for the element with the
// given id by the given amount (by 1 if no amount is passed).
function increment(id, amount) {
  var number = parseInt($(id).innerHTML) + (amount || 1);
  $(id).innerHTML = number;
  return number;
}
```

**Example 9.55 Improved `increment` function**

Now that we have a more flexible `increment` function, we can implement the timer-tick function with just a few lines of code. Every time a second passes, we should decrease the amount of time left by 1 using our `increment` function. If it hits 0, we should increment the total number of problems (to indicate that the user ran out of time and therefore got this problem incorrect), then advance to the next problem. Example 9.56 shows this code.

```
// Called by timer once per second
function tick() {
  var seconds = increment("time", -1);
  if (seconds <= 0) {    // time up!
    increment("total");
    nextProblem();
  }
}
```

**Example 9.56 Timer tick code**

So far `tick` is not being called anywhere in the code. Eventually our timer will call it once per second, but we can test it before ever implementing a timer. By loading your page in the browser and then opening Firebug's console, you can manually call `tick();` and observe the results. This allows us to test our code thoroughly to make sure that it behaves properly. Figure 9.5 shows this technique in action. The importance of coding and testing incrementally like this cannot be overstated.

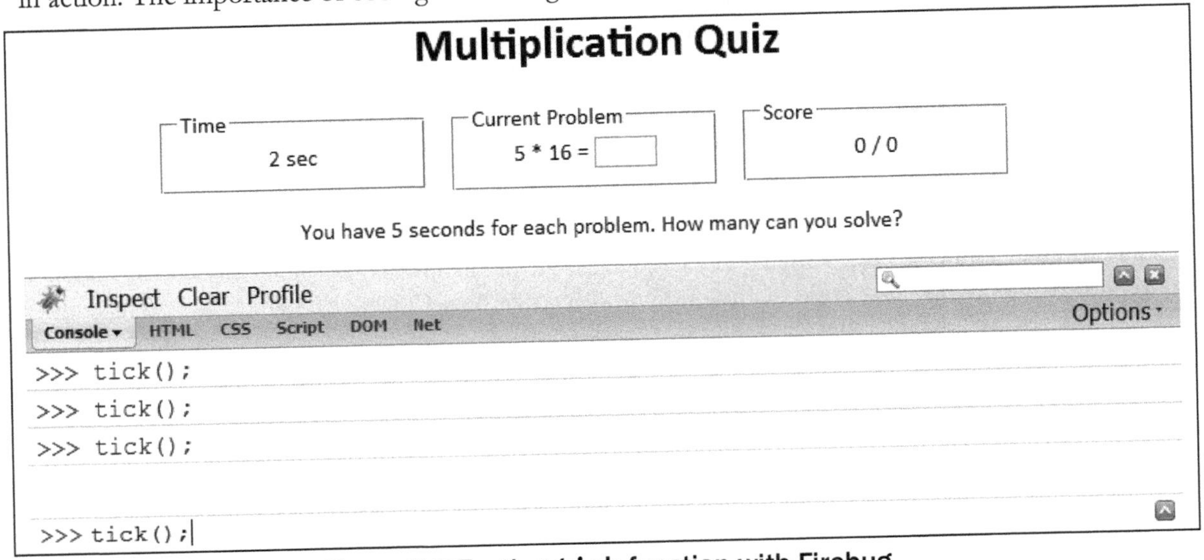

## Multiplication Quiz

Time
2 sec

Current Problem
5 * 16 = [    ]

Score
0 / 0

You have 5 seconds for each problem. How many can you solve?

Inspect  Clear  Profile

Console ▾    HTML   CSS   Script   DOM   Net

```
>>> tick();
>>> tick();
>>> tick();

>>> tick();|
```

**Figure 9.5 Testing `tick` function with Firebug**

As we test the code, we notice that it works fine in general, decreasing the remaining time and giving the user credit for an incorrect answer. But it is unfinished because once it hits 0, it fails to reset the remaining time to the full amount of 5 seconds. First of all, when the page loads we should grab the value of the max time remaining and hold onto that while the game is in progress. This way we don't lose track of the fact that 5 seconds is the maximum for each problem. Example 9.57 shows the modifications to the code. We could just hard-code the value of 5 into the program, but this way if the author modifies the max value in the HTML, the JavaScript code will update properly.

```
var MAX_TIME = null;    // number of seconds for each question

// Sets up event handler for when the page loads (a la window.onload).
document.observe("dom:loaded", function() {
  MAX_TIME = parseInt($("time").innerHTML);
  nextProblem();
  $("guess").observe("change", guessChange);
});
```

**Example 9.57 Grabbing the maximum time limit**

Now whenever we move on to the next problem, we will make sure to reset the time remaining to this maximum value. Example 9.58 shows the modification to the `nextProblem` function. After this modification the `tick` behavior now appears to work properly in all cases. When we call `tick` in Firebug, the time remaining decreases. If the time hits 0, the user is given an incorrect answer and the time resets to 5 seconds.

```
function nextProblem() {
  $("num1").innerHTML = parseInt(Math.random() * MAX_VALUE) + 1;
  $("num2").innerHTML = parseInt(Math.random() * MAX_VALUE) + 1;
  $("guess").clear();
  $("time").innerHTML = MAX_TIME;
}
```

**Example 9.58 Resetting the time after each game**

Now that our `tick` function is working, it should be fairly straightforward to implement the actual timer. The main question is where to start the timer: When the page loads? When the user makes a guess?

It might seem adequate to start the timer when the page loads and let it run for the entire time the page is on the screen, as shown in the following code:

```
document.observe("dom:loaded", function() {
  MAX_TIME = parseInt($("time").innerHTML);
  nextProblem();
  $("guess").observe("change", guessChange);
  setInterval(tick, 1000);    // timer tick 1x/sec (not quite right)
});
```

But there's a subtle issue here that may not be obvious if you haven't programmed much with timers. Recall that the timer will tick once per second. Suppose that the player has 0.1 seconds left; at this point the time shown on the screen will say 1 second. Now suppose that with 0.1 seconds left the player finishes typing an answer and presses Enter. The code will give the player a point and advance to the next problem and will update the time remaining to 5. But the timer will tick its event 0.1 seconds later and will decrease the time remaining to 4. So really the user only has 4.1 seconds to work on the next problem.

To avoid this problem and make sure that the player gets a full 5 seconds to think, we must reset the timer every time we advance to the next problem. Recall that you can reset a timer by storing the returned result from `setTimeout` or `setInterval` into a global variable and later passing that variable to the `clearTimeout` or `clearInterval` function. Every time a new problem begins (every time `nextProblem` is called) we'll stop the timer and start a new one. Example 9.59 shows the new `nextProblem` code, which now ticks properly and completes the page behavior.

```
var timer = null;        // holds ID of timer

function nextProblem() {
  $("num1").innerHTML = parseInt(Math.random() * 20) + 1;
  $("num2").innerHTML = parseInt(Math.random() * 20) + 1;
  $("guess").clear();
  clearInterval(timer);
  timer = setInterval(tick, 1000);
}
```

**Example 9.59 Stopping/starting a timer on each problem**

We can now remove the call to `setInterval` from the `document.observe` code because it already calls `nextProblem`, which sets up a new timer each time.

## 9.3.4 Final File Contents

After all of the changes in the preceding sections, the complete code for multquiz.html and mult-quiz.js is shown in Example 9.60 and Example 9.61 respectively. (The code for the CSS file did not change from our original version shown in Example 9.48.)

```
<!DOCTYPE html PUBLIC "-//W3C//DTD XHTML 1.1//EN"
  "http://www.w3.org/TR/xhtml11/DTD/xhtml11.dtd">
<html>
  <head>
    <title>Marvelous Multiplication Quiz</title>
    <link href="multquiz3.css" type="text/css" rel="stylesheet" />
    <script src="prototype.js" type="text/javascript"></script>
    <script src="multquiz3.js" type="text/javascript"></script>
  </head>

  <body>
    <h1>Multiplication Quiz</h1>

    <div id="main">
      <fieldset>
        <legend>Time</legend>
        <div><span id="time">5</span> sec</div>
      </fieldset>

      <fieldset>
        <legend>Current Problem</legend>
        <div>
          <span id="num1"></span> * <span id="num2"></span> =
          <input id="guess" type="text" size="3" maxlength="3" />
        </div>
      </fieldset>

      <fieldset>
        <legend>Score</legend>
        <div>
          <span id="correct">0</span> / <span id="total">0</span>
        </div>
      </fieldset>
    </div>

    <p>You have 5 seconds for each problem.  How many can you solve?</p>
  </body>
</html>
```

Example 9.60 Final contents of `multquiz.html`

```javascript
var MAX_VALUE = 20;       // largest number that could be used in a problem
var MAX_TIME = null;      // number of seconds for each question
var timer = null;         // holds ID of timer

// Sets up event handler for when the page loads (a la window.onload).
document.observe("dom:loaded", function() {
  MAX_TIME = parseInt($("time").innerHTML);
  nextProblem();
  $("guess").observe("change", guessChange);
});

// Chooses two new random numbers for the next quiz problem.
function nextProblem() {
  $("num1").innerHTML = parseInt(Math.random() * MAX_VALUE) + 1;
  $("num2").innerHTML = parseInt(Math.random() * MAX_VALUE) + 1;
  $("guess").clear();
  $("time").innerHTML = MAX_TIME;
  clearInterval(timer);
  timer = setInterval(tick, 1000);    // timer tick 1x/sec
}

// Called when player's guess changes.  Checks whether guess is correct.
function guessChange(event) {
  var guess = $F("guess");
  var answer = $("num1").innerHTML * $("num2").innerHTML;
  if (guess == answer) {
    increment("correct");   // user got the right answer; give a point
  }
  increment("total");       // move on to next problem
  nextProblem();
}

// Adjusts the integer value of the text for the element with the
// given id by the given amount (by 1 if no amount is passed).
function increment(id, amount) {
  var number = parseInt($(id).innerHTML) + (amount || 1);
  $(id).innerHTML = number;
  return number;
}

// Called by timer when time has elapsed (user ran out of time)
function tick() {
  var seconds = increment("time", -1);
  if (seconds <= 0) {    // time up!
    increment("total");
    nextProblem();
  }
}
```

Example 9.61 Final contents of `multquiz.js`

## Chapter Summary

- The Prototype library adds many useful features to JavaScript, such as extensions to the DOM, event-driven programming improvements, and cross-browser compatibility fixes.
- Prototype adds a lot of methods to the standard JavaScript types such as arrays, numbers, strings, and other objects.
- Prototype allows you to access elements by **id** with its **$** function.
- Prototype can access elements' styles with its **getStyle** method.
- Prototype provides easier ways to traverse the DOM tree, especially its **$$** function that accepts a CSS selector string parameter and returns all DOM elements that match the selector.
- JavaScript can handle many kinds of events including mouse movement and key presses.
- Every event function can accept a parameter that contains information about the event.
- There are several browser incompatibilities in event handling, but Prototype provides ways to avoid many of them, such as the **observe** method and **Event** object improvements.
- Mouse events are available for cursor movement, clicks, button press/releases, and more. You can examine the x/y position of a mouse event relative to various points on the page.
- Key events are available for key presses/releases, focus, and more. You can examine the key that was pressed and what modifier keys (such as Shift or Ctrl) were held down.
- Form events are available for submitting or resetting a form or changing a form control's value. You can cancel a form submit event to abort the sending of form data to the server.
- Timers can be created with the **setTimeout** and **setInterval** functions to execute a particular action after a given interval of time has passed. This is useful for delayed actions, repeated actions, animation, and more.

## References

- Prototype home page:        http://www.prototypejs.org/
- How Prototype Extends the DOM:    http://www.prototypejs.org/learn/extensions
- Prototype reference chart:
    - http://www.developer.com/img/2007/01/prototype1280.png
- Quirksmode, intro to events:     http://www.quirksmode.org/js/introevents.html
- Quirksmode, event compatibility:   http://www.quirksmode.org/dom/events/
- Quirksmode, mouse events:      http://www.quirksmode.org/js/events_mouse.html
- Quirksmode, detecting keystrokes:   http://www.quirksmode.org/js/keys.html
- Wikipedia, ASCII tables:       http://en.wikipedia.org/wiki/Ascii
- Switch on the Code, Using **setInterval** and **setTimeout**:
    - http://blog.paranoidferret.com/index.php/2007/09/06/javascript-tutorial-using-setinterval-and-settimeout/
- JavaScript Madness, Keyboard Events:   http://unixpapa.com/js/key.html

# Chapter 10    Ajax and XML for Accessing Data

## Introduction

Most of the interesting web sites today revolve around data. Google, IMDB, Digg, Facebook, MySpace, YouTube, and Rotten Tomatoes are all examples of sites whose main reason for existence is to serve you interesting data. You may not think of MySpace as a data-driven web site, but all of the content created by users, such as their profiles, journals, and photos, is data. The data on a web site can take many formats, such as text, HTML, XML, or multimedia.

The web has more data than a person can possibly consume in his or her lifetime, so a key to a useful web site is that it connects to data seamlessly and presents it to the user in a pleasant and useful way. In this chapter we'll discuss Ajax, which is a way to inject new data into an existing web page. The core of Ajax is a JavaScript object called `XMLHttpRequest`, so in this chapter we'll learn how to use it and also learn a bit about the XML data formatting language.

## 10.1   Ajax Concepts

*Ajax*, short for Asynchronous JavaScript and XML, is a way to dynamically update a page using data fetched from a web server. The basic idea of Ajax is the following:

- The user's web browser creates a JavaScript object called an `XMLHttpRequest`.
- The `XMLHttpRequest` requests some data from a web server.
- The data is sent back from the web server in a format called XML.
- Once the XML data arrives at your browser, JavaScript code injects that data into the web page and displays it to the user.

**Ajax**

A set of concepts and technologies for dynamically requesting web content from a server and using it to update a page in the browser.

There is some confusion about what Ajax actually is. Ajax is not a programming language, nor is it a product that you need to install. It's just a catchy name for a group of existing ideas and technologies built into your web browser, along with some clever ways of using those technologies.

Ajax is a departure from the normal flow of traffic between a browser and a web server. The normal flow is that when you click a link in your browser, an entire web page is loaded. That page stays on the screen until you click a link to move to a new page. This is called *synchronous communication*, because you must wait for the page to load before you can do anything else on the page. This is indicated by the breaks in user activity in Figure 10.1. Notice that the user must sit idle while waiting for the server to respond, which can be an unpleasant user experience.

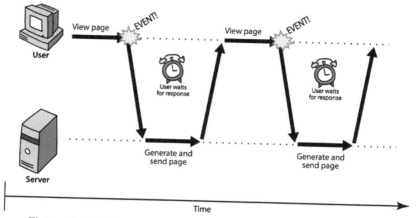

**Figure 10.1 Classic web application model (synchronous)**

When you use Ajax, your interactions trigger a request to receive a small amount of data. When the data arrives, rather than taking you to a new page with a different URL, you remain on the same page and the JavaScript code updates the page you're already viewing. All of this happens in the background, hidden to you.

> **synchronous communication**
>
> Interaction that only allows one action at a time and forces the user to wait for that action to complete.

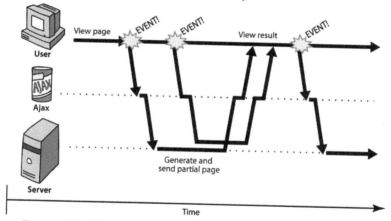

**Figure 10.2 Ajax web application model (asynchronous)**

This is called *asynchronous communication*, because multiple things can happen at the same time without needing to wait for each other. This asynchronous flow and ability to update an existing page are what powers modern web applications like Gmail and Flickr. The web site feels more like a coherent desktop application, because when you interact with it, small changes and updates occur to the page, rather than waiting for a lengthy reloading of a brand new page. In this way Ajax can greatly enhance the user experience of a web site. This is shown in Figure 10.2.

> **asynchronous communication**
>
> Interaction where many actions can occur at a time, in any order, without waiting for each other; the style of communication used by Ajax.

Ajax has many uses on the web today. Among these are the following:

- **Real-time form data validation**: Form data such as user IDs, serial numbers, postal codes, or even special coupon codes that require server-side validation can be validated in a form before the user submits a form.

- **Auto-completion**: A specific portion of form data such as a search term, email address, name, or city name may be auto-completed as the user types.
- **Load on demand**: Based on a client event, a web page can fetch more data in the background, allowing the browser to load pages more quickly.
- **Sophisticated user interface controls and effects**: Controls such as trees, menus, data tables, rich text editors, calendars, and progress bars allow for better user interaction with web pages, generally without requiring the user to reload the page.
- **Refreshing data and server push**: Web pages can repeatedly request or poll a server for up-to-date data to retrieve sports scores, stock quotes, weather, application-specific data, etc. Ajax techniques can be used to get a set of data without reloading a full page. Polling is not the most efficient means of ensuring that data on a page is the most current, but it is normally the best option for web pages at the moment due to the nature of HTTP.
- **Partial submit**: A web page can submit form data without requiring a full page refresh.
- **Mashups**: A web page can obtain data using a server-side proxy or by including an external script to mix external data with your application's or your service's data. You can mix content or data from a third-party application such as Google Maps with your own page.
- **Web applications**: Ajax techniques can be made to create single-page marshaled applications that look and feel much like a desktop application.

## 10.1.1 History and Compatibility

The term "Ajax" was coined by Jesse James Garrett in February 2005, but the technologies that make it possible have been around for many years. Microsoft invented the object that would become today's `XMLHttpRequest`. The object, which was then called `Microsoft.XMLHTTP`, served as a way to fetch data from a web server dynamically. It was created as part of an effort to build a more interactive web version of Microsoft Outlook. Once web developers discovered the existence of this object, they began experimenting with using it for their own dynamic web sites.

Over time, a standardized version of this object was proposed to the W3C, called `XMLHttpRequest`. This has become a web standard that is part of every modern browser, including Firefox, Safari, Opera, and others. Ironically, one browser not to support `XMLHttpRequest` is Microsoft Internet Explorer 6 and prior, which still use their old `Microsoft.XMLHTTP` object. In Internet Explorer 7, Microsoft added `XMLHttpRequest` support to match the other browsers.

The fact that IE did not support `XMLHttpRequest` object until IE7 has made it more cumbersome to write Ajax applications. Developers who want compatibility with older versions of IE and with compliant browsers must insert checks in their code to see which object to use. Thankfully, there is not much code needed to work around this, because once the object is created, it behaves the same way whether it's a `Microsoft.XMLHTTP` object or the standard `XMLHttpRequest` object.

## Self-Check

1. What does the term "Ajax" stand for? Is Ajax a programming language? What language(s) and technologies are involved in Ajax?
2. Name three situations in which it would be useful to use Ajax on a web site.
3. What is the difference between synchronous and asynchronous communication between a web browser and web server? Which style does Ajax use, and why is this helpful?
4. Who created the technologies necessary to do Ajax? Which browsers support Ajax today?

## 10.2 Using XMLHttpRequest to Fetch Data

Since fetching data with Ajax can be complicated, we'll explain the Ajax process step-by-step. We'll begin with text data rather than complex XML data. We'll also begin with a simpler synchronous program rather than asynchronous. Each step will provide a working program that downloads and displays data using Ajax, with each version improving on previous ones. The steps will be:

- Synchronized JavaScript and text-only data (perhaps we'd call this "Sjat"?)
- Asynchronous JavaScript and text-only data (Ajat?)
- Asynchronous JavaScript and text-only data, using Prototype (Ajap?)
- Asynchronous JavaScript and XML data (true Ajax)

### 10.2.1 Synchronous Requests

Enough talk; let's write some Ajax code. Imagine that we have a web site with a text file of data. We also have a page with a button and a text area. We'd like to make it so that when the user clicks the button, the contents of the data file will be downloaded and shown inside the text area.

The basic code you need to synchronously fetch text data using XMLHttpRequest follows:

```
// this code is in some onscreen control's event handler
var ajax = new XMLHttpRequest();
ajax.open("GET", "url", false);
ajax.send(null);

// at this point in the code, the web request has completed
do something with ajax.responseText;
```

**Example 10.1 Syntax template for synchronous Ajax request**

Generally you have some kind of button or control that, when clicked, causes JavaScript code like the above to execute. You create an XMLHttpRequest object and ask it to retrieve data from the URL of interest. The contents of the response (i.e., the data) are stored into a property of the request object called responseText. You can do anything you like with this text, such as put it directly onto the page or process it in other ways. For example, the short page in Example 10.2 has a Load button that, when clicked, will retrieve data from the file notes.txt and place that data inside a textarea with the ID of output.

```
<textarea id="output" rows="4" cols="40"></textarea><br />
<button id="load">Load</button>
```

```
window.onload = function() {
  $("load").onclick = loadClick;
};          = document.getElementById

function loadClick() {
  var ajax = new XMLHttpRequest();
  ajax.open("GET", "notes.txt", false);
  ajax.send(null);
  $("output").value = ajax.responseText;    // request has completed
}
```

**Example 10.2 Synchronous Ajax request**

The action of fetching text from a URL is common enough that we could make a helper function for it, which would be reusable in many different situations. Example 10.3 gives such a helper function. The `loadClick` function could be modified to use our new helper function.

```
// Fetches the text at the given URL using XMLHttpRequest and returns it.
function downloadText(url) {
  var ajax = new XMLHttpRequest();
  ajax.open("GET", url, false);
  ajax.send(null);
  return ajax.responseText;
}

function loadClick() {
  $("output").value = downloadText("notes.txt");
}
```

**Example 10.3 `downloadText` synchronous helper function**

Now that we have a helper to fetch text from a URL, let's write a more complex example. Suppose you have a text file named transcript.txt that represents a transcript of a chat between two users, like the following:

```
1:57 | Jessica Miller | yeah i have been thinking about that
1:57 | Marty Stepp | in what order should the book cover various topics?
1:57 | Jessica Miller | i have been thinking about that too
...
```

**Example 10.4 Contents of `transcript.txt`**

Imagine you want to write a page that fetches the text of this file dynamically and converts its contents into a bulleted list on the page. The code in Example 10.5 uses our new `downloadText` function to do exactly that.

```
<div id="transcriptarea"></div>
<button id="displaytranscript">Display Transcript</button>
```

```
// called when the Display Transcript button is clicked
function displayTranscriptClick() {
  var text = downloadText("transcript.txt");   // fetch the text
  var lines = text.split("\n");

  var ul = document.createElement("ul");   // convert lines into DOM list items
  for (var i = 0; i < lines.length; i++) {
    var li = document.createElement("li");
    li.innerHTML = lines[i];
    ul.appendChild(li);
  }

  // place the list onto the page in the transcriptarea div
  $("transcriptarea").appendChild(ul);
}
```

**Example 10.5 Using `downloadText` helper**

What we've done so far is much like Ajax, but it's not quite the same. For one, the request we have made is synchronous. The call of `ajax.send(null);` waits for the request to finish before returning, which means that when the next line of code is reached we know that the request has completed. This makes our programming easier, but the user experience can be unpleasant, because the user's browser locks up until we receive a response and our code finishes processing.

Another difference is that Ajax usually transmits its data in XML format, not as plain text. Plain text is easier for a beginner to understand than XML, but from the previous example you can already see a major drawback of plain text: it can be a bit of work to extract meaningful information from plain text and display it to the user in a useful way.

What we've just done isn't asynchronous, nor is it XML. So really we've only discussed the J in Ajax so far. Making our code asynchronous and being able to process XML data are useful qualities, so we'll address both of these issues in subsequent sections.

## 10.2.2 Checking for Ajax Errors

A lot of things can go wrong when you make a web request. The user's network connection could be down. The URL could be incorrect. The web server could be down or experiencing too much traffic. And so on. In cases like these, your `XMLHttpRequest` object may not succeed in downloading the data you've requested. It indicates this to you by placing an HTTP error code value into the request object's `status` property. Another property named `statusText` indicates any message related to the error status. Examining these properties can help you identify and respond to anything that went wrong with the request.

The version of our `downloadText` helper function in Example 10.6 shows an error message if something goes wrong with the request. Recall that HTTP error code 200 represents success. For example, if the file is not found the output from the function would look something like the screenshot shown in Figure 10.3.

```
// Downloads text at the given URL using XMLHttpRequest and returns it.
function downloadText(url) {
  var ajax = new XMLHttpRequest();
  ajax.open("GET", url, false);
  ajax.send(null);

  if (ajax.status != 200) {    // warn user if there was an Ajax error
    alert("Error fetching text of " + url + ":\n"
        + ajax.status + " " + ajax.statusText);
  }

  return ajax.responseText;
}
```

Example 10.6 Checking for Ajax errors

Figure 10.3 Ajax error message

## 10.2.3 Asynchronous Requests

The synchronous Ajax code we wrote is somewhat simple to program, but it can lead to an unpleasant user experience. You may not notice on a fast web server, but once you click the Load button the entire web browser halts and waits until the request is done before anything else can happen. This would prevent the user from scrolling on the page or interacting with any other page controls. The reason the browser halts is because your JavaScript code waits for the **XMLHttpRequest** object's **send** method to receive the file from the web server before your code continues execution. If the server is slow or the file is large, this can take a long time. For the duration of that time, the browser completely locks up; your page won't respond to any other user input or mouse clicks.

By contrast, an asynchronous operation is one that does not block others from occurring while it is completing its own processing. Most **XMLHttpRequest**s are made asynchronously, so that the user can still use and interact with the page while the request is being completed. The drawback is that it's a little trickier to program an asynchronous request properly, but we'll tackle that now.

> **callback**
>
> A general term for a function that is to be called later, often in response to an event.

The idea with an asynchronous request is that your code initiates the **XMLHttpRequest**, and rather than your code waiting for the request to finish, you instead get the request started, send it to the server, and specify a function that you'd like to be called when a response is received. You specify this function by attaching it to an event on the **XMLHttpRequest** object, just like we attached event handlers on UI controls in Chapter 3. In this case the event we are listening to is the **onreadystatechange** event, which occurs whenever the request's state changes. A function that is called later is also sometimes referred to as a *callback*.

To initiate an asynchronous request, you must make the following changes to our previous code:

- Pass **true** instead of **false** as the third parameter when calling **open** on the request object. (By doing this, the send method returns immediately rather than it waiting for the request to be completed before returning.)

- Attach a function as an event handler to the request's **onreadystatechange** event, containing the code you want to use to handle the request. The **onreadystatechange** event occurs when the status of the request changes, such as when the request is complete.

> **nested function**
>
> One declared inside another function.

One problem we encounter when writing our function to handle **onreadystatechange** is that we'd like to have access to the **XMLHttpRequest** object, which we called **ajax**, in that function's code. But if we define the function separately in our JavaScript file, the **ajax** variable will be out of scope. One solution to this problem would be to declare **ajax** as a global variable, but this is poor style. A better approach is to declare our event handler as an anonymous function inside the function that creates **ajax**. A function declared inside another is called a *nested function*. A nice benefit of nested functions is that they can see and access all the variables of the outer function in which they're declared. This idea is also called a *closure*.

> **closure**
>
> The useful ability for nested functions to see variables of the outer function in which they were declared.

Another important detail about our new asynchronous code is that the **onreadystatechange** event doesn't just occur when the request is completed. Technically, the event occurs whenever the value of the **XMLHttpRequest**'s **readyState** property changes. This property is an integer representing the state of the request, which goes through several state changes as the request is being made, from 0 (not initialized) to 3 (in progress) to 4 (completed). To make sure that we only run our code when the request is fully completed, we'll include a test that the **readyState** is 4 in our function. It's a bit ugly to have to check for a "magic number" like 4 in our code, but this is what we're forced to do.

The template in Example 10.7 represents an asynchronous Ajax request. Our previous Display Transcript example, implemented asynchronously, would use the code shown in Example 10.8.

```
// an asynchronous Ajax request
// (this code is in some onscreen control's event handler)
var ajax = new XMLHttpRequest();
ajax.onreadystatechange = function() {
  if (ajax.readyState == 4) {
    do something with ajax.responseText;
  }
};
ajax.open("GET", "url", true);
ajax.send(null);
```

**Example 10.7 Syntax template for asynchronous Ajax request**

```
// called when the Display Transcript Async button is clicked
function displayTranscriptClickAsync() {
  var ajax = new XMLHttpRequest();

  // attach event handler to be executed when request is done
  ajax.onreadystatechange = function() {
    if (ajax.readyState == 4) {
      var lines = ajax.responseText.split("\n");

      // convert the lines of text into DOM items in an unordered list
      var ul = document.createElement("ul");
      for (var i = 0; i < lines.length; i++) {
        var li = document.createElement("li");
        li.innerHTML = lines[i];
        ul.appendChild(li);
      }

      // place the list onto the page in the transcriptarea div
      $("transcriptareaasync").appendChild(ul);
    }
  };

  ajax.open("GET", "transcript.txt", true);
  ajax.send(null);
}
```

**Example 10.8 Asynchronous Ajax request**

We've used several properties and methods of the request without yet showing a proper reference. Table 10.1 and Table 10.2 list the properties and methods of the XMLHttpRequest object.

| Property Name | Meaning or Value |
|---|---|
| onreadystatechange | an event that fires when the web request's state changes |
| readyState | the current state of the web request, which is either:<br>• 0: not initialized<br>• 1: set up, but not sent<br>• 2: sent<br>• 3: in progress<br>• 4: completed |
| responseText | a string representing the data that has been fetched |
| responseXML | the XML data that has been fetched, as a DOM **Document** object |
| status | the HTTP status code sent back by the web server, such as 200 for OK or 404 for Not Found (0 means that the request is not finished yet) |
| statusText | the text sent back by the web server about its status, such as "File Not Found" for a 404 status or "OK" for a 200 status |

Table 10.1 **XMLHttpRequest** properties

| Method Name | Behavior |
|---|---|
| abort() | halts a web request in progress |
| open(**method, url, async**) | begins a web request with the following parameters:<br>• a string representing the method of retrieval of the data (either "GET" or "POST")<br>• a string representing the URL to fetch<br>• a boolean representing whether to fetch the data synchronously (**false**) or asynchronously (**true**) |
| send(**data**) | called after **open** to complete a web request, sending the given string of POST data to the web server (data should be **null** for GET requests) |

Table 10.2 **XMLHttpRequest** methods

One thing we've lost in our transition from the synchronous to asynchronous request is the nice error message that would pop up if the request failed. We also lost the convenient downloadText wrapper function. We can create a similar function downloadTextAsync, but it will require a few changes. The synchronous helper function returned the fetched text, but we can't do that in an asynchronous request. Instead, we'll have our downloadTextAsync function accept your onreadystatechange handler function as a parameter. When the request is done, downloadTextAsync will call your handler and pass the XMLHttpRequest object, ajax, to you.

Example 10.9 shows the complete code for the downloadTextAsync helper function. An example usage of this function is shown in Example 10.10.

```
// Downloads the text at the given URL using XMLHttpRequest,
// then calls the given function, passing the XMLHttpRequest to it.
function downloadTextAsync(url, fn) {
  var ajax = new XMLHttpRequest();

  // Call the function fn if the request completes successfully,
  // or show an error message if the request failed
  ajax.onreadystatechange = function() {
    if (ajax.readyState == 4) {
      if (ajax.status == 200) {
        fn(ajax);    // call function fn; pass ajax as parameter to it
      } else {
        alert("Error fetching text of " + url + ":\n"
            + ajax.status + " " + ajax.statusText);
      }
    }
  };

  // begin the request
  ajax.open("GET", url, true);
  ajax.send(null);
}
```

Example 10.9 downloadTextAsync asynchronous helper function

```
// called when the Display Transcript Async button is clicked
function displayTranscriptClickAsync2() {
  downloadTextAsync("transcript.txt", ajaxCompleted);
}

// event handler to be executed when request is done
function ajaxCompleted(ajax) {
  var lines = ajax.responseText.split("\n");

  // convert the lines of text into DOM items in an unordered list
  var ul = document.createElement("ul");
  for (var i = 0; i < lines.length; i++) {
    var li = document.createElement("li");
    li.innerHTML = lines[i];
    ul.appendChild(li);
  }

  // place the list onto the page in the transcriptarea div
  $("transcriptareaasync").appendChild(ul);
}
```

Example 10.10 Using downloadTextAsync helper

## 10.2.4    Prototype's Ajax Features

The Ajax we've seen so far has some drawbacks. It's clunky and not the most readable code. It refers to "magic numbers" such as a ready state of 4. And, worst of all, it doesn't work in Internet

Explorer 6 and below. As discussed previously IE6 implements a different object for doing Ajax requests, called `Microsoft.XMLHTTP`.

Enter Prototype. The Prototype library offers a friendlier set of Ajax wrapper objects that help us to implement cross-browser Ajax functionality more easily. The most fundamental of these is the `Ajax.Request` object. (Yes, the name has a period in it; technically it's a nested object named `Request` inside one named `Ajax`.) Simply constructing an `Ajax.Request` object with the proper parameters will initiate an asynchronous Ajax request to any URL you like and call any function you like when it is complete.

```
new Ajax.Request(
  "url",
  {
    option : value,
    option : value,
    ...
    option : value
  }
);
```

**Example 10.11 Syntax template for Prototype's `Ajax.Request` object**

The syntax for using `Ajax.Request` is shown in Example 10.11. The syntax is a bit odd and deserves some discussion. First, the overall statement is just constructing an object of type `Ajax.Request`. The object is not being stored into any variable; its constructor does all the work we need. The constructor accepts two parameters: the URL to be fetched as a string, and a group of options within braces. The options are written as an option name followed by a colon and the option's value, and are separated by commas. Technically this syntax of option/value pairs between braces is a declaration of an *anonymous object*, which is being passed as a parameter to the `Ajax.Request`. This is a common idiom used by JavaScript libraries to allow the passing of a large number of optional parameters.

**anonymous object**

One that is declared but not given a name or stored into a variable.

There are quite a few options that can be passed to the `Ajax.Request`. Table 10.3 provides a partial list of the most useful ones. The most common option we'll set will be **method**, but later in this chapter we'll also use the **parameters** option to make a request that uses query parameters.

| Option Name | Description |
|---|---|
| method | how to fetch the request from the server; either "get" or "post" (default "post") |
| parameters | query string parameters to pass to the server, if any, as a string or object |
| asynchronous | whether the request should be sent asynchronously (default true) |

**Table 10.3 Ajax.Request options**

For this example the first option we'll pass is **method**, which we'll set to `"get"` instead of the default `"post"`. As discussed previously in the chapter on HTML forms, an HTTP GET request is generally one that just fetches a file or retrieves information, while a POST request is one that often submits information back to a web server to be saved or processed. At the moment all we are doing is downloading plain text files so a GET request is the appropriate for now.

The `Ajax.Request` object also exposes a number of event options, also called callbacks, which can be assigned event handlers to be called when various stages of the request cycle are reached. You can attach event handler functions to these event options by passing them to the request's constructor. The most common event option to set is `onSuccess`, which occurs when the request completes successfully. Notice the capital S in `onSuccess`; unfortunately the designers of Prototype decided to break from the standard all-lowercase naming convention of events (such as `onclick`) and chose to camel-case their event names. Example 10.12 illustrates a complete usage of `Ajax.Request`:

```
// called when the Display Transcript Async button is clicked
function displayTranscriptClickAsync3() {
  new Ajax.Request(
    "transcript.txt",
    {
      method: "get",
      onSuccess: ajaxCompleted
    }
  );
}


// event handler to be executed when request is done
function ajaxCompleted(ajax) {
  var lines = ajax.responseText.split("\n");

  // convert the lines of text into DOM items in an unordered list
  var ul = document.createElement("ul");
  for (var i = 0; i < lines.length; i++) {
    var li = document.createElement("li");
    li.innerHTML = lines[i];
    ul.appendChild(li);
  }

  // place the list onto the page in the transcriptarea div
  $("transcriptareaasync").appendChild(ul);
}
```

**Example 10.12 Using `Ajax.Request`**

Notice that when Prototype calls the event handler, it passes the underlying `XMLHttpRequest` object, which we called `ajax`, as its first parameter. This allows the event handler to still be able to access the `responseText` and other properties from this object as before.

Table 10.4 lists common event options exposed by the `Ajax.Request` object:

| Event Option | Occurs When... |
|---|---|
| onSuccess | the request completes successfully |
| onFailure | the request was unsuccessful |
| onComplete | the request completes, whether successful or unsuccessful |
| onException | an exception occurs during the request |
| on### | the request fails with an error code of ### (e.g. on404, on500, ...) |

**Table 10.4 Event options exposed by `Ajax.Request`**

## Handling Errors

Two other commonly handled events are the onFailure and onException events. If something goes wrong with the request, it's important to know about it so that we can correct the problem. Example 10.13 shows a modified version of the previous program with an error handler, along with a screenshot of the window that would appear if a request failed.

The function to handle the error accepts an optional second parameter representing any exception that occurred. We use the exception object's message property to display information about the error that occurred. An onException event will also occur if there's some sort of syntax error in our Ajax code, so it's important to set an event handler to tell us if something is wrong; otherwise debugging a badly written Ajax request can be next to impossible. JavaScript exceptions are not discussed in detail in this textbook, but see this chapter's References section if the topic interests you.

```javascript
// called when the Display Transcript Async button is clicked
function displayTranscriptClickAsync3() {
  new Ajax.Request(
    "ajax_files/transcript.txt",
    {
      method: "get",
      onSuccess: ajaxCompleted,
      onFailure: ajaxFailed,
      onException: ajaxFailed
    }
  );
}

function ajaxCompleted(ajax) {
  // ...
}

function ajaxFailed(ajax, exception) {
  var msg = "Error making Ajax request:\n\n";
  if (exception) {
    msg += "Exception: " + exception.message;
  } else {
    msg += "Server status:\n" + ajax.status + " " + ajax.statusText +
                    "\n\nServer response text:\n" + ajax.responseText;
  }
  alert(msg);
}
```

Example 10.13 Prototype Ajax request with error handling

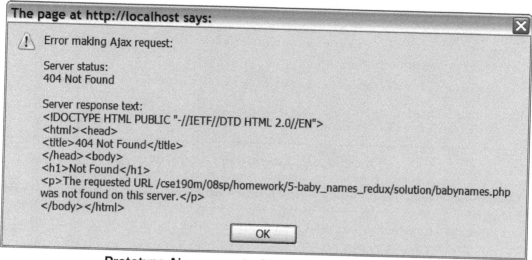

**Prototype Ajax request with error handling (output)**

In most pages you probably wouldn't `alert` the error message but would instead inject it into an element on the page using the DOM. We encourage you to use the `ajaxFailed` function as a template to provide more user-friendly error handling.

### Ajax.Updater

A common pattern in Ajax programming is to fetch text or HTML data from a server, then put that data directly into an element on the page. To facilitate this, Prototype provides an object named `Ajax.Updater`. This object's constructor accepts three parameters: a string representing the `id` of a page element, a string representing the URL to fetch, and a collection of additional options in braces (the latter two parameters are the same as the first two parameters of the `Ajax.Request` object). Its general syntax is shown in Example 10.14.

```
new Ajax.Updater(
  "id",
  "url",
  {
    option: value,
    option: value,
    ...
    option: value
  }
);
```

**Example 10.14 Syntax template for `Ajax.Updater`**

For example, our first synchronous Ajax code example in this chapter fetched text from a file named `notes.txt` and put it directly into an element with `id` of `output`. To do the same thing using `Ajax.Updater`, you'd write the code shown in Example 10.15.

```
function loadClick() {
  new Ajax.Updater(
    "output",
    "ajax_files/notes.txt",
    {
      method: "get"
    }
  );
}
```

**Example 10.15 Using Ajax.Updater**

There are some other useful Prototype Ajax features that we won't discuss in detail. For example, DOM objects of forms have a powerful method named **request** that auto-submits the form using Ajax in a single call. There is also a method **serialize** that packs up all query parameters and values from the form and returns them as a string.

Prototype offers some other useful Ajax objects. One of these is **Ajax.PeriodicalUpdater**, which is like **Ajax.Updater** but repeatedly updates an element's content by fetching the URL's data at given intervals. This is useful in situations when you want to poll a server for the most up-to-date data. Another is **Ajax.Responders**, which lets you create common handlers that process events on any Ajax request on an entire page. These objects are not discussed in detail in this textbook, but Prototype's web site provides documentation and examples.

## 10.2.5 Ajax Security and Debugging

**Security Note**

Ajax code can only connect to the current page's web server.

There are limits to the power of Ajax. Ajax code can fetch files only from the same web server where your page is hosted. This can be frustrating, because it means you can't reliably test your Ajax code from your hard drive. You need to upload it to the web to get it to work.

This restriction is in place for good reason. If Ajax code could connect to arbitrary sites, it would be easy for malicious sites to steal personal information and cause mischief in your browser. The restrictions help keep the web safe from attacks.

If you try to connect to a URL that isn't allowed, an exception will be raised by your code. If you're using Prototype, its **Ajax.Request** object will fire an **onException** event, which you can choose to handle if you like. The exception output in Firebug is shown in Figure 10.4.

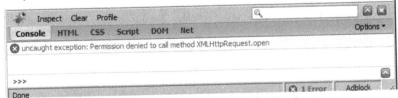

**Figure 10.4 Ajax exception in Firebug**

Ajax also raises some unique issues for debugging. A small bug in your code can cause nothing to change on your page, or for an undefined value to appear on the page. It can be difficult to tell whether you've even requested any data from the web server, and if so, what data was sent back.

Firebug has a Net tab that shows all HTTP requests initiated by the browser for your page. Checking this tab can tell you whether your Ajax HTTP request was sent out. If not, you should check the line that constructs the request object carefully for errors. If the request was in fact sent out, you can click the [+] next to it to inspect its URL, any parameters sent with it, and the exact response that was sent back. Figure 10.5 shows the appearance of Firebug's Net tab.

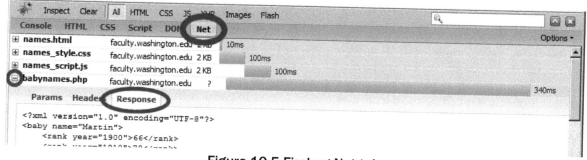

**Figure 10.5 Firebug Net tab**

If your requests aren't working, inspect the request URL to make sure it is what you expect. You can also test this URL by copying/pasting it into the browser's address bar in a new window or tab to see if you can fetch the data normally in the browser. If the URL checks out, look at the Response sub-tab and see what data the server sent back. Is it the data you expect? If so, the problem lies in your code to process that data and you can fall back on traditional JavaScript debugging techniques to figure out what is wrong.

## Self-Check

5. The XMLHttpRequest object has several important properties. How are each of the following properties used: onreadystatechange, readyState, and status?
6. How does your JavaScript code know when the result of an Ajax request arrives? (How does the answer differ depending on whether you're performing a synchronous or asynchronous request?) How do you access the text data that has been retrieved from the web server?
7. In what ways does Prototype make Ajax programming easier?
8. When creating an Ajax request with Prototype, how do you specify whether the request is an HTTP GET or POST?
9. What is the difference between Prototype's Ajax.Request and Ajax.Updater? When is it appropriate to use each of them?
10. What security restrictions are placed on Ajax code, and why was Ajax designed with these security restrictions? How can you detect when your program has violated such a restriction?

## 10.3 XML

So far we have completed the first three steps of the Ajax process by using the `XMLHttpRequest` object (and the Prototype AJAX wrappers) to asynchronously connect our web sites to dynamic data. But the request is only as useful as the data it fetches. The data we fetched in our previous examples was plain text, but much of the useful data on the web is in other formats. In this section, we'll discuss a very widely used data format called XML and how to parse XML data in Ajax code and thus complete the Ajax process.

### 10.3.1 What is XML?

Historically a lot of data has been stored as plain text, using whitespace, line breaks, and various other characters to delimit pieces of data. For example, the data in Example 10.16 might represent a log of chat messages, where the time is followed by a |, followed by the user name, followed by another |, followed by the message.

```
1:57 | Jessica Miller | So do we have a title yet?
1:58 | Marty Stepp | i was hoping we'd use one that glorifies my name
2:03 | Jessica Miller | sheesh
...
```

**Example 10.16 Chat transcript as formatted text**

To process or restructure the text chat data, first you need to split the string by \n line breaks, then split each line by |, and so on; what a pain. Plus, there's no standardization here; we just made up the above format, and no other software is likely to use that same format. So you're unlikely to find any off-the-shelf tools to help you break apart the data and process it.

XML is a more formalized way of storing structured text data, an attempt to standardize the way data is stored and get rid of hackish formats like the above. In many cases XML data is easier to deal with than plain text. XML is a specification for creating markup to store hierarchical data. XML describes a tag-based syntax for marking up text, but does not describe what tags should or should not be used. One can create an XML-based format by creating a set of tags, attributes, and deciding which tags should be nested inside of other tags, and so on.

Think of XML as HTML but with no pre-defined rules about what the legal tags are. XML syntax looks a lot like HTML syntax, with tags in < and >, but XML is designed for storing data, not just representing web pages. Instead of having a fixed set of tags to use, you can make up tags that will help you to best organize your data. The previous chat message data, when converted into XML, could have the appearance shown in Example 10.17.

```xml
<?xml version="1.0" encoding="UTF-8"?>
<messages>
  <message time="1:57" sender="Jessica Miller">
    So do we have a title for the book yet?
  </message>
  <message time="1:58" sender="Marty Stepp">
    i was hoping we'd use one that glorifies my name
  </message>
  <message time="2:03" sender="Jessica Miller">sheesh</message>
</messages>
```

**Example 10.17 Chat transcript as XML**

The reason we say that it *could* have that appearance as XML is that the person writing this software system can make up any set of tags and attributes they want. We chose to make a tag named `message` with an attribute named `sender`. Someone else writing this application might come up with a different set of tags, but the overall tag syntax and format of the language would be the same.

When looking at the preceding XML chat message data, your reaction might be, "I don't like the XML version; it's a bigger data file, and it's actually harder for me to read than before." But the important thing is that XML is easy for a *computer* to read and process. One of the biggest benefits to using XML is that since it's prolific and heavily standardized there are lots of great tools and libraries that exist for parsing (reading and interpreting) XML data. If you format your data as XML, you won't have to write a bunch of string-splitting and error checking code to process it. Example 10.18 shows another example made-up XML file for representing the data of an email message.

```
<?xml version="1.0" encoding="UTF-8"?>
<email>
  <to>Tove</to>
  <from>Jani</from>
  <subject>Reminder</subject>
  <body>
    Hey honey,
    Don't forget to pick me up this weekend!
    Love, Jani
  </body>
</email>
```

**Example 10.18 Email message as XML**

As we said, XML looks a lot like HTML. That's no coincidence: XHTML is actually a language created using XML's ideas and specifications, an adaptation of older HTML to fit XML's syntax requirements.

XML is used in lots of places on the web and elsewhere. Many web servers and databases display their data in XML format for processing. Apps called "web services" use XML to exchange messages and send commands over the web. RSS news feeds are stored in an XML format. Even several common document formats such as OpenOffice.org's documents are stored as XML internally.

## 10.3.2   XML Document Structure, Schemas, and DTDs

A legal XML document must follow a standard structure. It begins with an *XML prologue*, which declares that this is an XML document as well as the version and language in which it is written. After the prologue comes the *document tag*, the single outermost tag that encloses all other content in the document. In XHTML, this is the `html` tag. In our preceding XML examples, it was the `messages` and `email` tags respectively.

In general, any combination of tags, attributes, and text can appear inside an XML document's document tag. However, if validity of XML documents is of great importance, you can define rules for what tags and attributes are allowed where. A *schema* is an optional document that describes which tags and data are legal in your XML language. Tools can validate XML files to make sure they match a given schema. XHTML has a schema; this allows the W3C validator to check HTML files to make sure they comply with the XHTML standards.

> **schema**
>
> A document that describes which tags and data are legal in a given XML language.

XML schemas can be specified in many different languages, including *Document Type Definition* (*DTD*) and W3C XML Schema. While schemas are very useful and many times necessary in formal settings, we won't explore them in more detail in this textbook.

## 10.3.3 Processing XML Data

Suppose we have a data source available on a web server that can accept queries and return results as XML. Data sources are very commonly accessed as such on the web. For this section let's consider a data source `books.php` that allows searching an online bookstore's catalog of books for sale. You can query the `books.php` in two ways. If you request the page with no query parameters, such as by requesting the following URL in your browser:

```
http://webster.cs.washington.edu/books.php
```

You'd receive an XML response of all categories of books for sale, as shown in Example 10.19.

```
<categories>
  <category>children</category>
  <category>computers</category>
  <category>cooking</category>
  <category>finance</category>
</categories>
```

**Example 10.19 Books XML output, no query parameters**

You can also request the page with a `category` parameter:

```
http://webster.cs.washington.edu/books.php?category=cooking
```

In such a case you would see details about all books for sale in that category, as in Example 10.20.

```
<books>
  <book category="cooking" year="2009" price="22.00">
    <title>Breakfast for Dinner</title>
    <author>Amanda Camp</author>
  </book>
  <book category="cooking" year="2010" price="75.00">
    <title>21 Burgers for the 21st Century</title>
    <author>Stuart Reges</author>
  </book>
  <book category="cooking" year="2005" price="30.00">
    <title>The Four Food Groups of Chocolate</title>
    <author>Victoria Kirst</author>
  </book>
</books>
```

**Example 10.20 Books XML output, with `category` parameter**

We'd like to write a web page that allows the user to search the bookstore's inventory using Ajax. The page would dynamically read and processes this XML data and display it on the page. We'll start with the HTML code shown in Example 10.21. The page contains a list with **id** of **categories** into which we want to inject all categories of books when the page loads. When these categories appear and the user clicks on one of them, the books for sale in that category should appear inside the list with **id** of **books**.

```
<div>
  <p>Categories:</p>
  <ul id="categories">
    <li>Fetching...</li>
  </ul>
</div>

<div>
  <p>Books for sale:</p>
  <ul id="books">
    <li>Choose a category...</li>
  </ul>
</div>
```

Categories:

- Fetching...

Books for sale:

- Choose a category...

**Example 10.21 Relevant HTML for fetching book XML data**

Assume that the HTML page containing the code from Example 10.21 links to a JavaScript file. The rest of our discussion will center on the contents of that JavaScript file and how to fetch and display the XML category/book data using Ajax.

### The responseXML Property

XML data is fetched in JavaScript using Ajax, much like text data. The XMLHttpRequest object contains a responseXML property that is the key to processing XML data in JavaScript. The responseXML property is similar to responseText, but instead of representing the data as a long string, it represents it as a tree of linked objects. Specifically, the value of the responseXML property is an XML Document Object Model object that is the root of this tree. The way the XML DOM tree represents each tag and attribute in the XML data is similar to the way the HTML DOM tree represents all elements in a web page as seen in the DOM chapter.

The revised template for fetching and processing XML data is shown in Example 10.22. The steps are the same as when dealing with text data in Ajax, except that we refer to ajax.responseXML.

```
new Ajax.Request("URL",
  {
    method: "get",
    onSuccess: name
  }
);
}

function name(ajax) {
  do something with ajax.responseXML;
}
```

**Example 10.22 Syntax template for processing XML data with Ajax**

## JavaScript's XML DOM

The `responseXML` property of the `XMLHttpRequest` object represents the overall XML document that was sent back from the server. This document has child references to all the XML elements and content of the document. For example, if we fetch the list of bookstore categories from Example 10.19, the first child of the `responseXML` document represents the `<categories>` tag. This first child in turn has child references to the content inside it, such as each `<category>` tag.

As with the HTML DOM, you generally don't navigate the XML DOM tree by directly walking the child references. Instead you call methods on a node to ask it for a list of its children that match a certain tag or class name. The most common method for accessing such child nodes is named `getElementsByTagName`. Example 10.23 demonstrates the use of this method, and Table 10.5 lists the relevant methods of XML DOM nodes.

```
var name = ajax.responseXML.getElementsByTagName("tag");
for (var i = 0; i < name.length; i++) {
    do something with the node at name[i];
}
```

**Example 10.23 Syntax template for processing child nodes of an XML document**

| Method Name | Description |
|---|---|
| getElementsByTagName | returns an array of elements inside the current element that match the given tag name |
| getAttribute | returns the value of the node's attribute with the given name (null if the attribute is not found) |

**Table 10.5 XML DOM element node methods**

Once you've asked the `responseXML` for the set of relevant nodes to process, you can interact with those nodes by examining their properties. Many relevant properties are listed in Table 10.6.

| Property Name | Description |
|---|---|
| tagName, nodeName | the node's tag, such as `"book"` or `"categories"` |
| nodeValue | the text content directly inside the node |
| nodeType | an integer representing the kind of node: 1 for an element, 2 for an attribute, 3 for text, ..., 9 for a document node |
| attributes | an array of nodes representing the attributes of this element |
| childNodes | an array of the child nodes contained inside this node |
| firstChild, lastChild | references to the first/last elements of this node's list of children |
| nextSibling, previousSibling | references to the previous/next nodes with the same parent |
| parentNode | a reference to the node above this one in the tree |

**Table 10.6 XML DOM element node properties**

In order to understand how to properly walk the XML DOM tree, it's important to understand the nodes that the tree contains and how they are connected. It is very similar to the HTML DOM, except that Prototype doesn't extend the XML DOM, so it is a bit harder to use. Specifically, there are two gotchas in the XML DOM that you should look out for:

1. The DOM tree contains nodes for not only the elements in the XML data but also for any whitespace or text between those elements. These text nodes must usually be avoided when walking the DOM tree but must be examined when retrieving the text inside an element.
2. You cannot access an element's attributes directly by name, as we could in the HTML DOM. You have to use the **getAttribute** method on the element's node to access its attributes.

Let's examine these two confusing aspects one at a time. Consider the XML from Example 10.19:

```
<categories>
  <category>children</category>
  <category>computers</category>
  ...
</categories>
```

As expected, the **firstChild** of **ajax.responseXML** refers to the DOM node representing the **categories** tag. But the **firstChild** of the categories tag is *not* the node representing the children category. Instead, it is a plain-text node representing the blank spaces that precede the **<category>** tag on the second line of the XML. That's right; the designers of the XML DOM felt that we might want to examine the whitespace between nodes. It gets worse: If you're trying to read the text of each **category** node to display each category's name on the page, you can't just access it directly from the category DOM node. You have to ask for the **firstChild** of the category node, which is a text node containing the text inside the **category** tag, and then ask *that* text node for its **nodeValue** property, which finally gives you the text back as a string.

The authors are baffled by this design decision, and more so by the fact that there is no way to toggle it. Nevertheless this is the way the DOM works, so we'll have to ignore these text nodes when they crop up. Figure 10.6 shows a diagram of the DOM tree for part of the preceding XML.

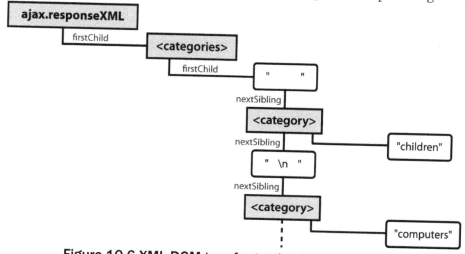

**Figure 10.6 XML DOM tree for textbook category data**

The best way to get around the annoying whitespace text nodes is to always fetch groups of nodes by calling `getElementsByTagName` on some parent node (or on the overall `responseXML` document) and avoiding the relative links like `firstChild` and `nextSibling` whenever possible.

Armed with this new knowledge we can write the code to process the bookstore categories. First let's use a `window.onload` handler to start an Ajax request to `books.php`, as shown in Example 10.24. When the Ajax data arrives, the as-yet-unwritten `showCategories` function will be called.

```
window.onload = function() {
  new Ajax.Request("books.php",
    {
      method: "GET",
      onSuccess: showCategories,
      onFailure: ajaxFailed,      // function shown in previous sections
      onException: ajaxFailed
    }
  );
};
```

**Example 10.24 JavaScript code to fetch bookstore categories using Ajax**

The `showCategories` code in Example 10.25 asks the `responseXML` for all nodes representing `<category>` tags. The `getElementsByTagName` method returns an array, so we will loop over each of its elements from 0 to the array's length. (Technically it is not an array but a `NodeList` object that acts much like an array, allowing you to access the nodes by indexes and having a `length` property.)

We want to add an `li` tag to the page for each category. We retrieve the category's name by examining the `firstChild` of the XML category node, which is a text node containing the category text. The `nodeValue` of this text node is the text we're looking for. We create a new `li` DOM element and place the category name into its `innerHTML`, then place it onto the page.

```
function showCategories(ajax) {
  // add all categories from the XML to the page's bulleted list
  var categories = ajax.responseXML.getElementsByTagName("category");
  for (var i = 0; i < categories.length; i++) {
    var categoryName = categories[i].firstChild.nodeValue;

    // create a new <li> tag and add it to the page
    var li = document.createElement("li");
    li.innerHTML = categoryName;
    $("categories").appendChild(li);
  }
}
```

Categories:

- children
- computers
- cooking
- finance

Books for sale:

- Choose a category...

**Example 10.25 JavaScript code to process bookstore categories XML**

Now let's examine the second XML DOM gotcha, related to examining attributes. When we used the HTML DOM we were able to access the attributes of a node by their names. For example, if a variable `textbox` refers to the DOM element for an `input` tag, we could write expressions like `textbox.value` or `textbox.disabled` to examine the `value` or `disabled` attributes of that `input` tag respectively.

With the XML DOM you cannot access attributes directly in that way. Instead, you must call a method `getAttribute` on the DOM node object, which accepts the attribute's name as a parameter and returns the attribute's value. If the node has no such attribute, `null` is returned. This change isn't too difficult to make, but it can be hard to remember, and forgetting it can cause tricky bugs.

To illustrate this issue let's continue our book example. When the user clicks a category name, we'd like a list of all books from that category to appear on the page in the `books` list. To do this we'll need to attach an `onclick` handler to each category's `li` item, as shown in Example 10.26.

```
var li = document.createElement("li");      // add a new <li> to the page
li.innerHTML = categoryName;
li.onclick = categoryClick;
$("categories").appendChild(li);
```

**Example 10.26 Attaching `onclick` handler to category list items**

The `categoryClick` handler function should open a second Ajax request to `books.php`, this time with a query parameter named `category` whose value is the category name. By requesting `books.php` with this parameter, rather than sending us back a list of all categories as its result, it will send us an XML list of all books in that category. Example 10.27 shows the code for this function.

```
function categoryClick() {
  new Ajax.Request("books.php?category=" + this.innerHTML,
    {
      method: "GET",
      onSuccess: showBooks,
      onFailure: ajaxFailed,
      onException: ajaxFailed
    }
  );
}
```

**Example 10.27 Click handler for categories**

Once we're making Ajax requests that require query parameters, the URL parameter to the `Ajax.Request` object can get messy. It's a pain to specify several query parameters by manually concatenating together a long string of `?` and `&` signs. Also, that approach wouldn't work if this were a POST request. To get around this, Prototype provides a `parameters` option you can pass to `Ajax.Request` to specify your parameters in a **name: value** format, as shown in Example 10.28.

```
new Ajax.Request("URL",
  {
    parameters: {name: value, name: value, ..., name: value},
    onSuccess: functionName,
    ...
  }
);
```

**Example 10.28 Syntax template for `Ajax.Request` with parameters option**

The code in Example 10.29 utilizes this improved style to keep the request URL and parameters separate and cleaner.

```
function categoryClick() {
  new Ajax.Request("books.php",
    {
      method: "GET",
      parameters: {category: this.innerHTML},
      onSuccess: showBooks,
      onFailure: ajaxFailed,
      onException: ajaxFailed
    }
  );
}
```

**Example 10.29 Improved click handler with `parameters`**

When the XML data arrives the `showBooks` function will be called. Let's write that function now. Recall that the XML output from `books.php` when a `category` parameter is specified has the following format, also shown in Example 10.20.

```
<books>
  <book category="cooking" year="2009" price="22.00">
    <title>Breakfast for Dinner</title>
    <author>Amanda Camp</author>
  </book>
  <book category="cooking" year="2010" price="75.00">
    <title>21 Burgers for the 21st Century</title>
    <author>Stuart Reges</author>
  </book>
</books>
```

Suppose we want to show each book in the XML as a bullet on the page, in a format such as:

- Breakfast for Dinner, by Amanda Camp (2009)

To do this we'll need to examine each **book** node in a way that is more complex than we examined the **category** nodes previously. We'll start with code such as the following:

```
function showBooks(ajax) {
  var books = ajax.responseXML.getElementsByTagName("book");
  for (var i = 0; i < books.length; i++) {
    do something with books[i];
  }
}
```

We need each book's title, author, and year. The **title** and **author** are children of the **book** node, but which child are they? The `firstChild.nextSibling.nextSibling`? It's not worth trying to hunt down the nodes that way. Instead, you can again call `getElementsByTagName` but this time on the **book** node object itself, passing it **title** and **author** as the tag names. Even though there will be exactly one of each of these tags inside each **book** node, `getElementsByTagName` returns an array, so we must access element `[0]` from this array:

```
var authorNode = books[i].getElementsByTagName("author")[0];
```

We can then access `authorNode.firstChild.nodeValue` to get the author's name.

The year the book was published is not a child element inside the **book** node; it's an attribute named **year**. (Why? Because whoever designed the XML for this application decided it should be that way.) To retrieve the **year** attribute's value, we can call **getAttribute** on the **book** node object, passing **"year"** as the parameter.

Example 10.30 shows the complete code for the **showBooks** function. The code loops over each of the **book** node objects, retrieving the various sub-element text and attributes from each. It then creates a new **li** HTML DOM object displaying this information and inserts it into the page. The code example also shows the page output after the user clicks the "cooking" category.

```javascript
function showBooks(ajax) {
  // add all books from the XML to the page's bulleted list
  var books = ajax.responseXML.getElementsByTagName("book");
  for (var i = 0; i < books.length; i++) {
    var titleNode  = books[i].getElementsByTagName("title")[0];
    var authorNode = books[i].getElementsByTagName("author")[0];
    var title  = titleNode.firstChild.nodeValue;
    var author = authorNode.firstChild.nodeValue;
    var year = books[i].getAttribute("year");

    var li = document.createElement("li");
    li.innerHTML = title + ", by " + author + " (" + year + ")";
    $("books").appendChild(li);
  }
}
```

Categories:

- children
- computers
- cooking
- finance

Books for sale:

- Breakfast for Dinner, by Amanda Camp (2009)
- 21 Burgers for the 21st Century, by Stuart Reges (2010)
- The Four Food Groups of Chocolate, by Victoria Kirst (2005)

**Example 10.30 JavaScript code to process books XML**

The user will probably want to be able to view several different categories. When a category is clicked on the page, it should probably clear any books from the last category. To do this, the start of **showBooks** needs a loop that removes the first child from the **books** list until no children remain.

```javascript
while ($("books").firstChild) {    // clear out the list of categories
  $("books").removeChild($("books").firstChild);
}
```

## Self-Check

11. What is XML? What is the primary motivation for using XML to represent data?
12. XML code looks a lot like HTML. What is the relationship between the two languages? How are the syntaxes of XML and HTML similar and how are they different? What tags are legal to use in XML?
13. How are schemas and DTDs useful when dealing with XML data?
14. How do you fetch XML data using JavaScript? What set of objects represents XML data from a web server?
15. Name two useful methods that every XML DOM node object contains, and three useful properties.
16. What statement would retrieve all `vehicle` tags from an XML data set sent back from a server using Ajax? What statement would access the `model` attribute of the first vehicle?

## 10.4 Case Study: Animal Game

The game of "20 Questions" is a classic problem in computer science. In this game, the user thinks of an object, and a program asks the user a series of yes/no questions, trying to figure out what the object is. Eventually the computer makes a guess ("Is your object a screwdriver?"), and the user inputs whether the guess was correct. In some versions of the game, if the guess is wrong, the user enters a new question/answer pair to the program, making it smarter for the next game.

This case study implements a version of this game where all of the objects are animals. The user thinks of a kind of animal, and the computer asks a series of yes/no questions trying to guess that animal. You can play a real version of this game at http://www.animalgame.com/. (The maintainer of animalgame.com, Guy Carpenter, was kind enough to lend us his data for use in this project.) Figure 10.7 shows the desired appearance of the game.

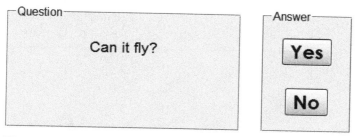

**Figure 10.7 Animal game web page, desired appearance**

The data representing the computer's set of questions to ask and guesses to make is already provided for us on our web server; we just have to fetch it, one question/guess at a time, and display it on a web page as the user plays the game. Conceptually you can think of the questions and answers as a tree, as depicted in Figure 10.8.

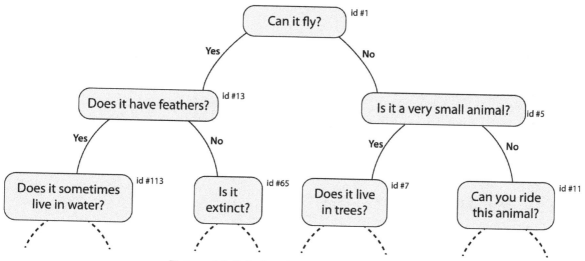

**Figure 10.8 Animal game question tree**

Each question for the computer to ask has an ID number, a string of the question's text, and references to the ID numbers of two other children. Each child represents the next question to ask if the user says "yes" and if the user says "no." Eventually you reach the bottom of the tree, finding nodes that represent answer guesses, such as "Is it a horse?" These nodes in the question tree don't have any children.

The animal game data is accessible to us via a web service called `animalgame.php` available at the following URL:

```
http://webster.cs.washington.edu/animalgame.php
```

To fetch data from this service, you must supply a query parameter named `nodeid` storing the integer of the question/answer you want to retrieve from the data set. The root question of the tree, "Can it fly?", has the special ID of 1. To retrieve this question, you would fetch the following URL:

```
http://webster.cs.washington.edu/animalgame.php?nodeid=1
```

The service sends back its data as XML in the format shown in Example 10.31. The overall document has the tag `node`, and inside this tag are three relevant elements: a `question` element whose inner text content is the question to ask; a `yes` element whose `nodeid` attribute is the ID of the next question to fetch if the user says "yes" to the current question; and a `no` element whose `nodeid` attribute is the ID of the next question to fetch if the user says "no" to the current question.

```
<node id="1">
  <question>Can it fly?</question>
  <yes nodeid="13" />
  <no nodeid="5" />
</node>
```

**Example 10.31 Animal game question XML**

Once the user reaches the eventual dead-end node at the bottom of the tree, the XML will have a slightly different format as shown in Example 10.32. The overall `node` element will contain only an `answer` element whose inner text content is the item to guess.

```
<node id="23428">
  <answer>God</answer>
</node>
```

**Example 10.32 Animal game answer XML**

The following set of tasks will help us to solve this problem step-by-step:

1. Create the initial HTML/CSS for the page.
2. Write the JavaScript code to display the game's initial yes/no question.
3. Write the code to fetch additional questions and answers using Ajax.
4. Add polish and finish up the overall game flow.

## 10.4.1 Initial HTML/CSS Content

Re-examining the desired appearance screenshot in Figure 10.7, we can see that the major elements of the page include a field set displaying a question, and another field set with two "Yes" and "No" buttons for the user to give a response to that question. We can represent each area with a `fieldset` element with a `legend` for its titled border.

Since we'll be inserting the text of various questions into the page, we have created an initially empty paragraph with an **id** of **question** inside the question area. We've also given the Yes / No buttons **id** values of **yes** and **no** respectively, since we'll eventually need to handle clicks on those buttons. Example 10.33 shows the complete code and its initial appearance in the browser.

```html
<!DOCTYPE html PUBLIC "-//W3C//DTD XHTML 1.1//EN"
  "http://www.w3.org/TR/xhtml11/DTD/xhtml11.dtd">
<html xmlns="http://www.w3.org/1999/xhtml">
  <head>
    <title>The Animal Game</title>
    <link href="animalgame.css" type="text/css" rel="stylesheet" />
    <script src="prototype.js" type="text/javascript"></script>
    <script src="animalgame.js" type="text/javascript"></script>
  </head>

  <body>
    <h1>The Animal Game</h1>

    <p>Think of an animal, then let me guess it!</p>

    <div id="container">
      <fieldset>
        <legend>Question</legend>
        <p id="question"></p>
      </fieldset>

      <fieldset id="answer">
        <legend>Answer</legend>
        <button id="yes">Yes</button>
        <button id="no">No</button>
      </fieldset>
    </div>
  </body>
</html>
```

# The Animal Game

Think of an animal, then let me guess it!

┌─ Question ─────────────────────────────────────────────────────┐
│                                                                 │
│                                                                 │
└─────────────────────────────────────────────────────────────────┘
┌─ Answer ───────────────────────────────────────────────────────┐
│  Yes   No                                                       │
└─────────────────────────────────────────────────────────────────┘

**Example 10.33 Animal game HTML code**

A bit of CSS will give the page a much more pleasing appearance. We'll create a style sheet file **animalgame.css** that floats both of the **fieldset**s into a two-column layout, sets a few fonts and alignment of various text, and so on. Since CSS is not the focus of this chapter and since the CSS content here contains nothing we haven't seen before, we'll just show the style sheet code and move on. Example 10.34 shows the CSS content and the page's improved appearance after linking this style sheet to the page.

```
#answerarea {
  width: 100px;
}
body {
  font: 12pt "Century Gothic", "Helvetica", "Arial", sans-serif;
}
button {
  font-size: 20pt;
  font-weight: bold;
  margin: 15px auto;
}
#container {
  margin: auto;
  width: 520px;
}
fieldset {
  background-color: #F0F0F0;
  float: left;
  height: 150px;
  margin-right: 15px;
  text-align: center;
}
h1, p {
  text-align: center;
}
#question {
  font-size: 16pt;
  text-align: center;
  width: 300px;
}
```

# The Animal Game

Think of an animal, then let me guess it!

┌─Question─────────────┐  ┌─Answer─┐
│                      │  │  Yes   │
│                      │  │        │
│                      │  │  No    │
└──────────────────────┘  └────────┘

Example 10.34 Animal game CSS style sheet

## 10.4.2   Fetching Question Data Using Ajax

So far our game doesn't actually display any of the yes/no questions or answers from the XML data. To do this, we'll need to start working on `animalgame.js`, the JavaScript code attached to the page. First let's make our game fetch and display the game's initial question, "Can it fly?"

When the page loads, we must fetch the initial question XML using Ajax. In a `window.onload` handler we'll create a Prototype Ajax.Request that fetches `animalgame.php` with a parameter of `nodeid` whose value is `1`, since ID #1 represents the root of the question tree. We'll follow our usual Ajax template, specifying the request's `onSuccess`, `onFailure`, and `onException` properties. We'll specify a function named `displayQuestion` (as yet unwritten) to run if the Ajax data comes back successfully. If anything goes wrong, it will run our standard `ajaxFailed` function from earlier in this chapter (not repeated here). Example 10.35 shows the code.

```javascript
window.onload = function() {
  // initialize the game at the first node of data
  new Ajax.Request("/animalgame.php",
    {
      method: "get",
      parameters: { nodeid: 1 },
      onSuccess: displayQuestion,
      onFailure: ajaxFailed,
      onException: ajaxFailed
    }
  );
};
```

**Example 10.35 Page loading code to fetch root question XML**

Now let's write the `displayQuestion` function. Recall that the data sent back from `animalgame.php` has the following format, as shown in Example 10.31:

```xml
<node id="1">
  <question>Can it fly?</question>
  <yes nodeid="13" />
  <no nodeid="5" />
</node>
```

For now, all we care about is the content of the XML `question` element. So in our `displayQuestion` function, we'll ask the Ajax object's `responseXML` property to give us the first element with a tag of `question`. We do this by calling `getElementsByTagName` with a parameter of `"question"`, which returns an array of matching elements, and then accessing element `[0]` of this array. We want the text inside that `question` element, so we ask for its `.firstChild.nodeValue`. We place this node value into the page as the `innerHTML` of the paragraph with the `id` of `question`. Example 10.36 shows the complete code.

```javascript
// Parses the XML for the question and yes/no answers.
function displayQuestion(ajax) {
  var question = ajax.responseXML.getElementsByTagName("question")[0];
  var questionText = question.firstChild.nodeValue;
  $("question").innerHTML = questionText;
}
```

**Example 10.36 Code to display question XML**

Figure 10.9 shows the new initial appearance of the page, which now displays the initial question.

# The Animal Game

Think of an animal, then let me guess it!

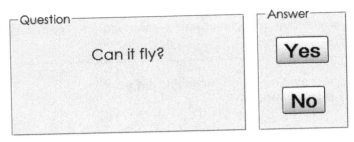

Figure 10.9 Animal game revised initial appearance

Now that the page displays the initial question, we also want it to move on to subsequent questions when the user clicks Yes or No. We'll attach `onclick` handlers to each of these buttons when the page loads. When the user clicks one of these buttons, we're going to need to fetch another question from the server and display its information. This means that we'll be performing more Ajax requests just like the one we already wrote, but each will have a different `nodeid` query parameter value. A good way of doing this without redundancy is to turn our Ajax request code into a helper function that accepts the node id as a parameter, as shown in Example 10.37.

```
window.onload = function() {
  $("yes").onclick = yesClick;   // not written yet
  $("no").onclick = noClick;     // not written yet
  getNode(1);    // initialize the game at the first node of data
};

// Fetches the next node of the game using Ajax.
function getNode(id) {
  new Ajax.Request(
    "/animalgame.php",
    {
      method: "get",
      parameters: { nodeid: id },
      onSuccess: displayQuestion,
      onFailure: ajaxFailed,
      onException: ajaxFailed
    }
  );
}
...
```

Example 10.37 Code to fetch any node from the XML

We could test the code by changing the number 1 in `window.onload` to some other id, such as 13, and noticing that the page now loads with a new initial question showing.

Now let's write the event handlers for clicks on the Yes and No buttons. When one of these buttons is clicked, we must fetch a new question from the XML data. But what question? When we fetched the game's initial question, "Can it fly?", that XML also contained information about which IDs represent the next question to ask if the user says yes or no. Our current code ignored that information, so we don't know what question to ask next. To fix this, we must add some new code to our `displayQuestion` method that extracts the yes/no IDs from the XML.

Recall that the yes/no IDs are stored in the XML as **yes**/**no** elements with **nodeid** attributes:

```
<node id="1">
  <question>Can it fly?</question>
  <yes nodeid="13" />
  <no nodeid="5" />
</node>
```

To retrieve the yes/no ID values, we'll fetch the first element node from `responseXML` that has a **yes** tag and the first that has a **no** tag. We'll then ask each of these nodes for its **nodeid** attribute by calling `getAttribute` on it. To keep the IDs around for later when the user clicks the Yes or No button, we'll put the yes/no IDs into global variables named `yesID` and `noID` respectively. Example 10.38 shows the code.

```
var yesID;    // globals to remember next ID to fetch on Yes/No clicks
var noID;

// Parses the XML for the question and yes/no answers.
function displayQuestion(ajax) {
  var question = ajax.responseXML.getElementsByTagName("question")[0];
  var yesNode  = ajax.responseXML.getElementsByTagName("yes")[0];
  var noNode   = ajax.responseXML.getElementsByTagName("no")[0];

  var questionText = question.firstChild.nodeValue;
  $("question").innerHTML = questionText;

  yesID = yesNode.getAttribute("nodeid");
  noID = noNode.getAttribute("nodeid");
}
```

**Example 10.38 Code to display a question from XML and remember yes/no IDs**

Lastly, when the user clicks Yes or No, we want to display the next question on the page. We can do this in our event handler functions `yesClick` and `noClick` by calling the new `getNode` helper function we wrote and passing it one of the globals `yesID` or `noID` as its parameter. This will fetch the appropriate node's XML from the server and display the question on the page.

```
// Called when 'Yes' is clicked; requests next node and updates page.
function yesClick() {
  getNode(yesID);
}

// Called when 'No' is clicked; requests next node and updates page.
function noClick() {
  getNode(noID);
}
```

Figure 10.10 shows the page's new appearance after the user has answered a few questions. We have now completed the main flow of the animal game, and our page is mostly playable.

# The Animal Game

Think of an animal, then let me guess it!

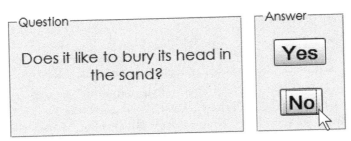

Figure 10.10 Page appearance with ability to answer questions

## 10.4.3 End-of-Game and Adding Polish

The game as written so far mostly works, but it crashes and burns when we reach the bottom of the data tree. After several questions have been asked and Yes or No has been clicked several times, eventually the page displays an error as shown in Figure 10.11.

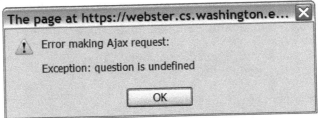

Figure 10.11 Ajax error on animal game page

The problem is that eventually the server has asked enough yes/no questions that it's ready to make a guess about what animal the user is thinking of. In such cases, the XML response from the server has a different format than before: It contains an `answer` element rather than `question`, `yes`, and `no` elements. The format is the following, first shown in Example 10.32:

```
<node id="23428">
  <answer>God</answer>
</node>
```

When an "answer" XML response like this is sent back to the browser, our JavaScript code is trying to access an element with tag name `question`, but no such element exists. Our code needs to be modified to handle this end-of-game case. When we receive an answer XML response, we should ask the user if this answer is his/her animal. Based on the user's response, we should display whether the computer won or lost the game.

We'll need to modify our `displayQuestion` function to treat question XML responses differently than answer XML responses. The easy way for us to do this is to use the XML DOM to check whether the response contains a `question` element or an `answer` element. Currently our function requests an array of elements with tag name `"question"` and saves element `[0]` of this array into a variable named `question`. If the XML is actually an answer, there will be no elements with tag name `"question"`, so the variable `question`'s value will be `undefined`. We can test whether it is defined by using the variable `question` itself as the test in an `if` statement. Recall that if `question` is a "truthy" value (an actual defined object), the `if` test will pass. But if `question` is undefined, the test will fail and the code will execute its `else` branch. Example 10.39 shows partial code.

```
// Parses the XML for the question and yes/no answers.
function displayQuestion(ajax) {
  var question = ajax.responseXML.getElementsByTagName("question")[0];
  if (question) {
    // this XML represents a question and its yes/no response
    var yesNode  = ajax.responseXML.getElementsByTagName("yes")[0];
    var noNode   = ajax.responseXML.getElementsByTagName("no")[0];

    var questionText = question.firstChild.nodeValue;
    $("question").innerHTML = questionText;

    yesID = yesNode.getAttribute("nodeid");
    noID = noNode.getAttribute("nodeid");
  } else {
    // this XML represents an answer to guess
    ...
  }
}
```

**Example 10.39 Code to display a question or answer from XML**

Now let's consider what code should be run in the `else` branch to handle answer XML responses. Instead of getting the first element with tag name `question`, we should get the first element with tag name `answer`. The text inside this node should be displayed on the page, but not by itself as questions are. Since the text will be an animal name like "horse" or "elephant", we should surround it with a few words so that the page will ask the user if this is the correct animal, such as, "Is your animal: horse?" Example 10.40 shows the code that should go in the `else` branch in place of `...` above.

```
  } else {
    // this XML represents an answer to guess
    var answerNode = ajax.responseXML.getElementsByTagName("answer")[0];
    var answerText = answerNode.firstChild.nodeValue;
    $("question").innerHTML = "Is your animal: " + answerText + "?";
  }
```

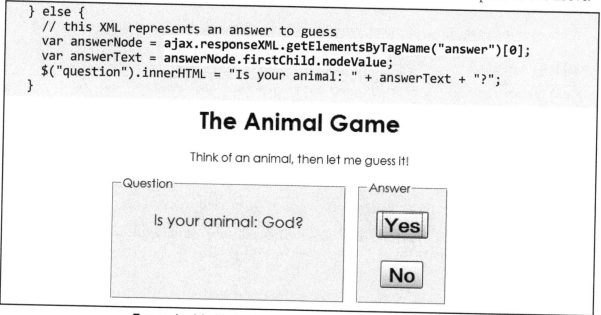

**Example 10.40 Code to display an answer from XML**

Now the game correctly displays answer guesses. But from there it doesn't quite behave properly. At this point in the game the computer is making its final guess about what the item is. If the user says Yes, the computer should display a message such as "I won!" and if the user clicks no, "I lost." Right now it doesn't do this; instead it contacts the server and requests another set of XML data.

To make our page handle the end of the game, we need to modify the event handlers on our Yes and No buttons. If the game is guessing an answer, clicking Yes/No should result in a win/lose message being shown. Right now our game doesn't remember whether it is showing a question or answer. We could try to deduce this by looking for the text "Is your animal: " in the question paragraph on the page, but this is a kludge; it's possible that a question could contain that text. A better way to remember which state we're in is to keep a global boolean value representing whether the answer has been given. If not (initially), the boolean value is `false`. But once we display the answer node in our `displayQuestion` function, the boolean switches to `true`. Example 10.41 shows the code.

```
var answerGiven = false;    // true if the game has guessed an answer yet

// Parses the XML for the question and yes/no answers.
function displayQuestion(ajax) {
  var question = ajax.responseXML.getElementsByTagName("question")[0];
  if (question) {
    ...
  } else {
    // this XML represents an answer to guess
    var answerNode = ajax.responseXML.getElementsByTagName("answer")[0];
    var answerText = answerNode.firstChild.nodeValue;
    $("question").innerHTML = "Is your animal: " + answerText + "?";
    answerGiven = true;
  }
}
```

**Example 10.41 Global boolean variable to remember question/answer state**

The purpose of the new global boolean value is so that later, when the user clicks Yes or No, we can show an appropriate win/lose message on the page. We'll have to modify our `yesClick` and `noClick` event handlers to accommodate this case, as shown in Example 10.42.

```
// Called when 'Yes' is clicked; requests next node and updates page.
function yesClick() {
  if (answerGiven) {    // computer guessed an answer; it was correct
    $("question").innerHTML = "Yay, I won!";
  } else {
    getNode(yesID);
  }
}
// Called when 'No' is clicked; requests next node and updates page.
function noClick() {
  if (answerGiven) {    // computer guessed an answer; it was incorrect
    $("question").innerHTML = "Aww, I lost.  :-(";
  } else {
    getNode(noID);
  }
}
```

**Example 10.42 Improved Yes/No button event handler code**

# The Animal Game

Think of an animal, then let me guess it!

**Figure 10.12 Animal game appearance after answer shown and Yes clicked**

Figure 10.12 shows the appearance after an answer is shown and the user clicks Yes. At this point the game is done except for a bit of polish. Right now when the game is over the user can click Yes/No again. This is undesirable because if the game says "Yay, I won!" and the user clicks No, it changes to "Aww, I lost." The fix is to disallow the user from clicking Yes/No once the game is over by inserting the following lines when the "Yay" or "Aww" message is being displayed:

```
$("yes").disabled = true;
$("no").disabled = true;
```

If we wanted the page to allow multiple games to be played, we could add a Start Over button to the HTML. Example 10.43 shows the necessary additional HTML and CSS code and its appearance.

```
<div id="startoverarea">
   <button id="startover">Start Over</button></div>
```

```
#startoverarea {
  clear: both;
  text-align: center;
}
```

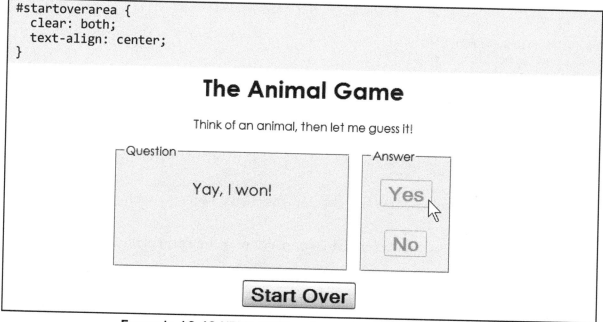

**Example 10.43 HTML/CSS code to add Start Over button**

To make the Start Over button functional we'll factor out some of our previous `window.onload` code for starting the game and place it into a function named `startGame`, which we can call both when the window loads and when the Start Over button is clicked. The `startGame` function can enable the Yes/No buttons (in case they had been previously disabled by ending the game) and fetch the XML node with ID #1 to start the game. Example 10.44 shows the code.

```
window.onload = function() {
  $("yes").onclick = yesClick;
  $("no").onclick = noClick;
  $("startover").onclick = startGame;
  startGame();
};

// Called when a new game begins
function startGame() {
  $("yes").disabled = false;
  $("no").disabled  = false;
  getNode(1);   // initialize the game at the first node of data
}
```

**Example 10.44 Code to enable starting multiple guessing games**

### 10.4.4   Final File Contents

After all of the changes in the preceding sections, the complete code for <u>animalgame.js</u> is shown in Example 10.45.

```
// globals
var yesID;               // ID of next 'yes' answer on server
var noID;                // ID of next 'no' answer on server
var answerGiven = false; // true if the game has guessed an answer yet

window.onload = function() {
  $("yes").onclick = yesClick;
  $("no").onclick = noClick;
  $("startover").onclick = startGame;
  startGame();
};

// Called when a new game begins.
function startGame() {
  $("yes").disabled = false;
  $("no").disabled  = false;
  getNode(1);   // initialize the game at the first node of data
}

// Called when game is over to disable buttons from further clicking.
function endGame() {
  $("yes").disabled = true;
  $("no").disabled  = true;
}
```

```
// Fetches the next node of the game using Ajax.
function getNode(id) {
  new Ajax.Request("/animalgame.php",
    {
      method: "get",
      parameters: { nodeid: id },
      onSuccess: displayQuestion,
      onFailure: ajaxFailed,
      onException: ajaxFailed
    }
  );
}

// Called when 'Yes' is clicked; requests next node and updates page.
function yesClick() {
  if (answerGiven) {
    $("question").innerHTML = "Yay, I won!";
    endGame();    // computer guessed an answer, and "Yes" it was correct
  } else {
    getNode(yesID);
  }
}

// Called when 'No' is clicked; requests next node and updates page.
function noClick() {
  if (answerGiven) {
    $("question").innerHTML = "Aww, I lost.  :-(";
    endGame();    // computer guessed an answer, and "No" it was not correct
  } else {
    getNode(noID);
  }
}

// Parses the XML for the question and yes/no answers.
function displayQuestion(ajax) {
  var question = ajax.responseXML.getElementsByTagName("question")[0];
  if (question) {  // XML represents a question and its yes/no response
    var yesNode  = ajax.responseXML.getElementsByTagName("yes")[0];
    var noNode   = ajax.responseXML.getElementsByTagName("no")[0];

    var questionText = question.firstChild.nodeValue;
    $("question").innerHTML = questionText;

    yesID = yesNode.getAttribute("nodeid");
    noID = noNode.getAttribute("nodeid");
  } else {          // XML represents an answer to guess
    var answerNode = ajax.responseXML.getElementsByTagName("answer")[0];
    var answerText = answerNode.firstChild.nodeValue;
    $("question").innerHTML = "Is your animal: " + answerText + "?";
    answerGiven = true;
  }
}
```

Example 10.45 Final contents of `animalgame.js`

## Chapter Summary

- Ajax (Asynchronous JavaScript and XML) is a set of technologies that allows a web page to fetch data from a web server in the background and display it on the page dynamically.
- The key facility in JavaScript to enable Ajax is the `XMLHttpRequest` object, which lets you request data from a server and be notified when the data arrives.
- Ajax requests can be made either synchronously (making the user wait until the request is complete), or asynchronously (in the background, without making the user wait). Asynchronous requests provide a more pleasant user experience and are therefore recommended.
- Ajax code is subject to various security restrictions. Most notably, an Ajax request can fetch data only from the server hosting that web page.
- Prototype provides an `Ajax.Request` object that wraps up the functionality of `XMLHttpRequest` and Ajax in a more usable way, along with other Ajax improvements.
- XML is a syntax for creating languages to store hierarchical data and information about that data. XML syntax uses tags, elements, and attributes much like HTML, but the set of tags allowed is unrestricted and therefore up to the developer.
- JavaScript can examine and process XML data using its XML Document Object Model (DOM) that represents an XML document and each of its elements and attributes as objects. XML data from a server can be fetched using Ajax and processed using the XML DOM.


## References

- Ajax, A New Approach to Web Applications, by Jesse James Garrett (coined "Ajax" term):
  - http://www.adaptivepath.com/ideas/essays/archives/000385.php
- Google Code University Ajax Tutorial:
  - http://code.google.com/edu/ajax/tutorials/ajax-tutorial.html
- W3Schools Ajax tutorial: http://www.w3schools.com/Ajax/
- Tizag Ajax tutorial: http://www.tizag.com/ajaxTutorial/
- Prototype, Introduction to Ajax:
  - http://www.prototypejs.org/learn/introduction-to-ajax
- Modelworks Ajax tutorial: http://www.modelworks.com/ajax.html
- Wikipedia, `XMLHttpRequest`: http://en.wikipedia.org/wiki/XMLHttpRequest
- Wikipedia, XML: http://en.wikipedia.org/wiki/XML
- W3Schools XML DOM tutorial: http://www.w3schools.com/dom/default.asp
- Microsoft beginner's guide to the XML DOM:
  - http://msdn.microsoft.com/en-us/library/aa468547.aspx
- DevGuru XML DOM reference:
  - http://www.devguru.com/Technologies/xmldom/QuickRef/xmldom_intro.html
- Mozilla Developer Center, JavaScript exception-handling statements:
  - https://developer.mozilla.org/en/Core_JavaScript_1.5_Guide/Exception_Handling_Statements

# Chapter 11    Relational Databases and SQL

## Introduction

Up until now the data that we have been accessing with our web applications have been stored on the server as flat files such as text or XML files. Storing data as flat files is okay for small, single-user web applications, but to support web applications that access huge amounts of data accessed by millions of users, a more advanced data storage system is needed. Enter the relational database.

Databases have been around since the 1970s and are the backbone of the majority of the web applications out there. To properly design, create, and maintain a busy database takes years of experience and is usually done by high-paid, database administrator geek types. In this chapter, we will leave the complicated stuff to them and will focus on the tasks of accessing data in a database from a web application.

## 11.1   Database Basics

**relational database**

A set of data organized into tables, with rows representing records, columns representing data fields within each record, and relationships connecting tables to each other.

**relational database management system (RDBMS)**

A software package for managing databases and allowing you to query them.

A *database* is a structured collection of related data. The most common type is the *relational database*, invented by E. F. Codd in 1970 at IBM. The data are stored in two-dimensional *tables* of rows and columns, and relations are connections between pieces of data. Each row (also called a *tuple* or *record*) is a data item or object, and each column (or *field*) is an attribute of that object. A table is like a C++ or Java class, where each row is an object and the columns store the fields of the object.

In order to use a database on your web server, you must install software called a Relational Database Management System (*RDBMS*). There are a number of commercial database management systems such as Oracle Corp.'s Oracle, IBM's DB2, and Microsoft's SQL Server. There are also very good open-source RDBMSs including PostgreSQL and MySQL from Sun Microsystems. Which RDBMS you choose depends on your needs and your budget. We prefer MySQL because it is a simple, solid, free, open-source product used by many industry leaders.

Throughout this chapter we will be using data from an Internet Movie Database (IMDb) which stores information about movies, actors, and directors. For example, it has an **actors** table where each row represents information about one individual actor that has appeared in one or more movies. The `actors` table has columns for the first name, the last name, and the gender of each actor.

Since databases may contain thousands or millions of rows of data, it isn't practical to write a program that loops over each row to search for a specific piece(s) of data. Instead, you ask the RDBMS to search the database for you by sending it a request called a *query*. A query can be thought of as a declarative statement such as, "Show me all rows of actors where the actor's first name is Jessica," or, "Show me the titles of all movies that were released in the year 2005."

> **query**
>
> A request for data submitted to a database.

Some students get confused about the difference between a database and a table. A database is a collection of one or more tables. IMDb contains tables `actors`, `movies`, `directors`, and more.

Students also get confused about the difference between a database and a spreadsheet such as from Microsoft Excel. Both store data in 2D tables, but each is optimized for different usage. Spreadsheets are often for smaller amounts of data to be viewed in charts or reports. Databases are for large amounts of data to be searched or used for fast calculations. There are also structural differences: database rows are unordered (but can be retrieved in a variety of orders); database columns hold data of a specific type; and databases don't allow swapping rows for columns, ensuring that rows are objects and columns are attributes.

## 11.1.1   Motivation

Up until now we have been using simple files to store the data for our web applications. You may wonder why databases are necessary. Databases provide the following advantages over regular files:

- **Power**. With a database you can quickly and easily learn the answer to complex questions as, "How many of our customers bought both diapers and beer?" or, "Which users' accounts have shown no activity in the last 2 months other than checking deposits?"

- **Speed**. Databases are specifically designed to allow data to be searched and filtered very quickly, even with large amounts of data. For example, consider a web app for a medical company with hundreds of thousands of patients. If you use a file to store the data, the system would have to search it sequentially for a particular patient a doctor is treating.

- **Reliability**. Imagine that a large bank's web app is in the middle of transferring $1000 from one customer's account to another and the server power goes out. The money could be lost or doubly credited, which is not acceptable in a professional system. Databases provide "transactions" that guarantee that any actions performed will leave data in a reliable state.

- **Concurrency**. Databases can be accessed by up to thousands or millions of users at once, unlike ordinary file systems that often lock an entire file when one user is making changes to it. If a customer is making a purchase from your online store, you wouldn't want to lock the entire "shopping carts" file and leave other customers unable to add items to their carts.

- **Abstraction**. Databases provide a standard layer between data and applications and use a common language (SQL) understood by programmers and by applications and libraries. Even if you were able to create your own home-grown file system that had similar power to a database, it would be unfamiliar to all but the few people who created it.

## 11.1.2 Example Database: `imdb`

Figure 11.1 shows the `imdb` database tables we'll use in this chapter and a few rows from each table. Tables can contain data and/or information about relationships. For example, the `roles` table contains information about the relationship of which actors appeared in which movies.

| id | first_name | last_name | gender |
|---|---|---|---|
| 172424 | Mel | Gibson | M |
| 666662 | Scarlett | Johansson | F |

**actors**

| id | first_name | last_name |
|---|---|---|
| 15901 | Francis Ford | Coppola |
| 78273 | Quentin | Tarantino |

**directors**

| director_id | genre | prob |
|---|---|---|
| 15901 | Mystery | 0.0689655 |
| 78273 | Romance | 0.125 |

**directors_genres**

| id | name | year | rank |
|---|---|---|---|
| 46169 | Braveheart | 1995 | 8.3 |
| 194874 | Lost in Translation | 2003 | 8 |

**movies**

| director_id | movie_id |
|---|---|
| 15906 | 194874 |
| 28395 | 46169 |

**movies_directors**

| actor_id | movie_id | role |
|---|---|---|
| 172424 | 46169 | William Wallace |
| 666662 | 194874 | Charlotte |

**roles**

| movie_id | genre |
|---|---|
| 46169 | Action |
| 194874 | Drama |

**movies_genres**

**Figure 11.1 imdb database tables**

If you choose to set up MySQL on your own computer, you may download the `imdb` database (along with other databases we use in this chapter) from the book's accompanying web site. In the next section, we will focus on writing queries to search for information in this database and talk a bit about adding, updating, and deleting data to give you a flavor for data manipulation.

## Self-Check

1. What is a relational database? How are data organized in a relational database?
2. In RDBMSs, what is another name for a table? A column? A row?
3. Name a few of the RDBMSs out there. Which are commercial? Which are open source?
4. Which table(s) from the `imdb` database might we look at if we wanted to find out which actors have appeared in one or more comedy movies?
5. What are the standard capabilities of SQL regardless of which software you use?

## 11.2   SQL

Database queries are written in a standard declarative language called *Structured Query Language* (*SQL*), maintained as an international standard by ISO (International Organization for Standardization). SQL provides a standard way to interact with RDBMS software to define, manage, and search for data. Unfortunately each RDBMS vendor has slightly different implementations of and unique extensions to the language, but the majority of the common syntax is equivalent across all systems. The SQL code we show in this book will work properly on MySQL and other major software.

SQL provides the following capabilities:

- Queries: Retrieving desired information from the database
- Data Manipulation: Adding, updating, and deleting data in tables
- Transactions: Ensuring that data is always in a consistent state
- Data Definition: Creating and altering the structure of tables
- Data Control: Specifying permissions for access to databases

SQL differs from most other programming languages because it is a *declarative programming language* rather than an *imperative programming language*. In an imperative programming language such as Java, C, or JavaScript, you tell the computer exactly how to perform the desired computation step by step. In a declarative language like SQL, we describe to the computer what we want but not how to do it. In our SQL statements we will tell the RDBMS, "I want the data that meet the following criteria," and the RDBMS figures out how best to get that data for us.

Since SQL is a declarative programming language, writing SQL comes down to writing commands called *statements* as opposed to programs, scripts, or functions. A statement is made up of a number of *clauses*. Every clause begins with a SQL keyword. Figure 11.2 shows the components of a basic SQL statement. Don't worry about the specifics for now – we'll break those down step by step in the following sections.

| **statement** |
| --- |
| An SQL command. Statements perform queries and changes to database tables. |
| **clause** |
| A component of a SQL statement. Some are optional. |

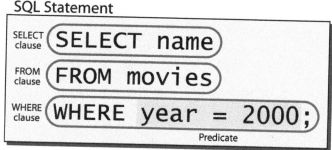

**Figure 11.2 Components of a SQL Statement**

## 11.2.1 Connecting to MySQL

Eventually we will write code in a server-side language such as PHP to connect to a database and query it. But that code will contain SQL statements in it, and before we begin to write such code we should practice bare SQL syntax in the simplest environment possible. The easiest way to practice SQL queries is to log in to a web server using an SSH terminal program, type the commands directly in to the MySQL command-line interpreter, and examine the results.

First you will need to connect to a MySQL database server that has a database to query. There may already be a database server set up for you to which you have credentials (a user name and password). If not, you can install MySQL on your own computer from the MySQL web site listed in the References section of this chapter.

First, log onto the server that is hosting the MySQL database. Once logged into the server, you should be able to connect to MySQL.

- Run your computer's SSH or terminal program and connect to your database server.
- Run the **mysql** program to start the MySQL client. Type your password when prompted.
- At the **mysql>** prompt, type an SQL query and press Enter to view its results.

Example 11.1 shows the syntax for the **mysql** command-line interpreter program. The **-u** option specifies the MySQL user name to use. The **-p** option specifies that your user requires a password. After logging in successfully, you should see some introductory information followed by a **mysql>** prompt where you can now type queries. Figure 11.3 shows the appearance on one Windows system.

```
mysql -u username -p
```

Example 11.1 Syntax template for MySQL command line

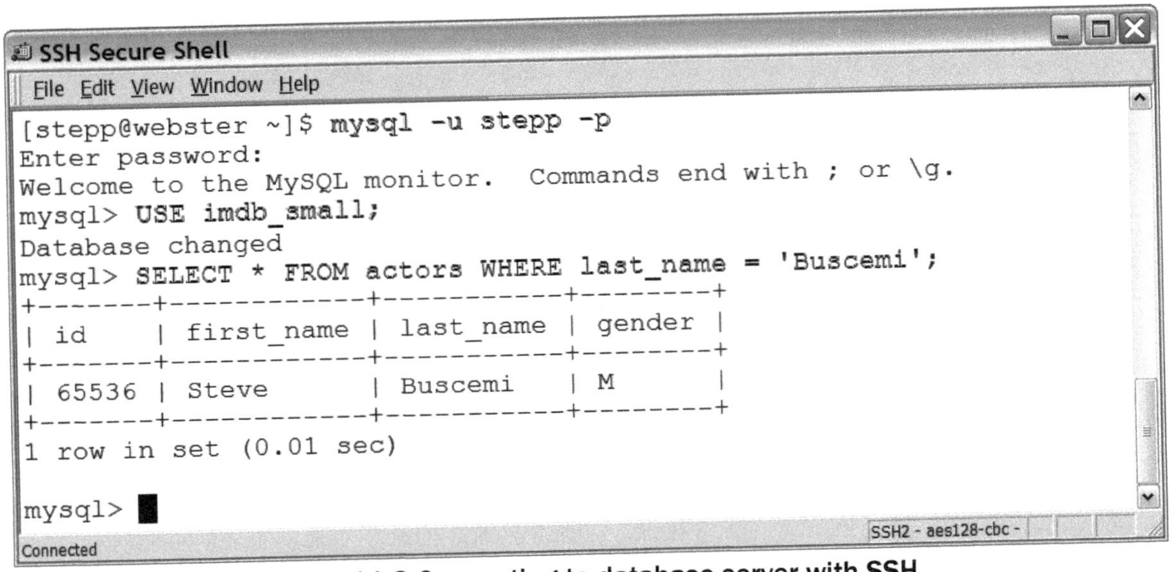

```
SSH Secure Shell
File Edit View Window Help

[stepp@webster ~]$ mysql -u stepp -p
Enter password:
Welcome to the MySQL monitor.  Commands end with ; or \g.
mysql> USE imdb_small;
Database changed
mysql> SELECT * FROM actors WHERE last_name = 'Buscemi';
+-------+------------+-----------+--------+
| id    | first_name | last_name | gender |
+-------+------------+-----------+--------+
| 65536 | Steve      | Buscemi   | M      |
+-------+------------+-----------+--------+
1 row in set (0.01 sec)

mysql>
Connected                                          SSH2 - aes128-cbc -
```

Figure 11.3 Connecting to database server with SSH

You can quit the MySQL client at any time by typing QUIT or \q at the MySQL prompt.

## 11.2.2    Database/Table Information

| SQL Statement | Meaning |
|---|---|
| SHOW DATABASES; | Lists all available databases on this server |
| USE **database**; | Chooses a database to use as the target of queries |
| SHOW TABLES; | Lists all tables in the current database (must USE a database first) |
| DESCRIBE **table**; | Lists information about the columns of a table (must USE first) |

Table 11.1 SQL statements for database/table information

Once successfully logged into MySQL, you must choose a database to query. You can find out the names of all available databases on a server by typing the SHOW DATABASES statement. An example call to this command on our IMDb server is shown in Example 11.2.

```
mysql> SHOW DATABASES;
+--------------------+
| Database           |
+--------------------+
| information_schema |
| animalgame         |
| imdb               |
| imdb_small         |
| mysql              |
| simpsons           |
| world              |
+--------------------+
7 rows in set (0.01 sec)
```

Example 11.2 SHOW DATABASES command

SHOW DATABASES is our first SQL statement. All statements consist of a sequence of SQL keywords and operators, ending with a semicolon and a line break (pressing Enter). The keywords do not need to be capitalized, but many programmers do so for consistency and for good style.

To choose a database to query, you use the USE statement. For the rest of this chapter we'll use the imdb_small database, so you can type the text in Example 11.3 into the MySQL client. If the database you want to query was successfully selected, you will see a **Database changed** message.

```
mysql> USE imdb_small;
Database changed
```

Example 11.3 USE command

MySQL also has commands that allow you to get information about tables in a database. The first is the SHOW TABLES command, which lists all of the tables in the selected database. The output of the SHOW TABLES command on the imdb_small database is shown in Example 11.4.

```
mysql> USE imdb_small;
Database changed
mysql> SHOW TABLES;
+----------------------+
| Tables_in_imdb_small |
+----------------------+
| actors               |
| directors            |
| directors_genres     |
| movies               |
| movies_directors     |
| movies_genres        |
| roles                |
+----------------------+
7 rows in set (0.00 sec)
```

Example 11.4 SHOW TABLES command

If you want to get information about a particular table's columns, you can use the DESCRIBE command. The output of this command for the `directors` table is shown in Example 11.5.

```
mysql> DESCRIBE directors;
+------------+--------------+------+-----+---------+-------+
| Field      | Type         | Null | Key | Default | Extra |
+------------+--------------+------+-----+---------+-------+
| id         | int(11)      | NO   | PRI | 0       |       |
| first_name | varchar(100) | YES  |     | NULL    |       |
| last_name  | varchar(100) | YES  |     | NULL    |       |
+------------+--------------+------+-----+---------+-------+
3 rows in set (0.03 sec)
```

Example 11.5 DESCRIBE command

The DESCRIBE output has six columns, but for now we'll only focus on the first two. The Field column lists the names of the columns. The second column, Type, tells the type of the data found in each column. In the example, `id` is an integer of up to 11 bytes, and `first_name` is a string of up to 100 characters. We'll discuss SQL data types in more detail later in the chapter.

## 11.2.3 The SELECT Statement

The query is the most commonly performed SQL operation. To perform a query, you use the SELECT statement, which retrieves information from a specified table and returns the result of the query in another table. The basic syntax of the SELECT statement is shown in Example 11.6.

```
SELECT column1, column2, ..., columnN
FROM   table
```

Example 11.6 Syntax template for SELECT statement

In the SELECT clause you designate which table columns you want to see in the query results. In the FROM clause you designate the table to query. Example 11.7 shows a query that retrieves the first and last names of all of directors in the `directors` table of the `imdb_small` database.

```
mysql> SELECT first_name, last_name
    -> FROM directors;
+--------------+------------+
| first_name   | last_name  |
+--------------+------------+
| Andrew       | Adamson    |
| Darren       | Aronofsky  |
| Zach         | Braff      |
| James (I)    | Cameron    |
| Ron          | Clements   |
| Ethan        | Coen       |
| Joel         | Coen       |
| ...          | ...        |
| Paul (I)     | Verhoeven  |
| Andy         | Wachowski  |
| Larry        | Wachowski  |
+--------------+------------+
33 rows in set (0.00 sec)
```

**Example 11.7 Simple SELECT statement (some rows omitted)**

Though the SQL keywords and column names are not case-sensitive, the database and table names are case-sensitive in MySQL and some other RDBMS programs. Since the table name is **directors** with a lowercase **d**, we're careful to type it that way in our query.

A SQL statement is not considered finished until a semi-colon followed by a newline is entered. In the above example, we pressed Enter after **last_name**. The interpreter moved to the second line and indicated that the query was still incomplete by leading the next line with a **->** arrow marker. Once we entered the semicolon after **directors** and pressed Enter, the query was executed.

Although SQL keywords and column names are not case-sensitive, database and table names sometimes are. This can depend on the underlying operating system of the database server hosting the MySQL RDBMS. In some operating systems (e.g., Windows) database and table names are not case-sensitive, but in others (e.g., most varieties of Unix) database and table names are case-sensitive. Our **imdb_small** database is stored on a server that is running the Fedora Linux operating system, so case sensitivity is an issue. Example 11.8 shows the result when we run the previous query while capitalizing the d of the **directors** table.

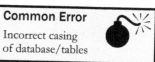

**Common Error**
Incorrect casing
of database/tables

```
mysql> SELECT first_name, last_name
    -> FROM Directors;
ERROR 1146 (42S02): Table 'imdb_small.Directors' doesn't exist
```

**Example 11.8 Common error: Incorrect capitalization of database or table name**

It is easy to incorrectly capitalize a table or database name, but the error message you get doesn't tell you that is the problem. It tells you that the database or table doesn't exist. Before you freak out and think that you lost your data, check the capitalization of your database and table names first.

You can use * as a wildcard to specify all columns of a table. The query in Example 11.9 displays everything about directors in the **imdb_small** database, including the **id**, **first_name**, and **last_name** columns. The same number of rows (33) are returned, but with more columns in each.

```
mysql> SELECT *
    -> FROM directors;
+-------+--------------+------------+
| id    | first_name   | last_name  |
+-------+--------------+------------+
|   429 | Andrew       | Adamson    |
|  2931 | Darren       | Aronofsky  |
|   ... | ...          | ...        |
| 83617 | Larry        | Wachowski  |
+-------+--------------+------------+
33 rows in set (0.00 sec)
```

**Example 11.9 SELECT statement with * wildcard**

### DISTINCT Modifier

To prevent the **SELECT** statement from returning repetitions in the results, you can use the **DISTINCT** modifier. The syntax for using the **DISTINCT** modifier is shown in Example 11.10.

```
SELECT DISTINCT column(s)
FROM table
```

**Example 11.10 Syntax template for DISTINCT modifier**

For example, from Example 11.7 we can see that there are some directors in our database with the same last name, such as Coen. The query in Example 11.11 gives all unique last names of directors.

```
mysql> SELECT DISTINCT last_name
    -> FROM directors;
+------------+
| last_name  |
+------------+
| Adamson    |
| Aronofsky  |
| Braff      |
| Cameron    |
| Clements   |
| Coen       |
| Coppola    |
| ...        |
| Verhoeven  |
| Wachowski  |
+------------+
30 rows in set (0.00 sec)
```

**Example 11.11 DISTINCT modifier**

Notice that there are now only 30 rows returned as opposed to 33. This is because there is now only one copy of the last names Coen, Coppola, and Wachowski. If you specify more than one column after **SELECT DISTINCT**, the query will strip out any records in which all columns are duplicates of another record already being returned.

## 11.2.4 Filtering Results with the WHERE Clause

So far our queries have returned all rows in the database table. More often you want only the rows that meet certain conditions. This is achieved using a WHERE clause, which is made up of some number of *predicates* that specify conditions to limit which rows are returned. In SQL, predicates are logical expressions that evaluate to an answer of true, false, or unknown. The syntax of the WHERE clause is shown in Example 11.12.

> **predicate**
>
> A logical expression or condition. Composed of an operator and one or two arguments.

```
SELECT column1, column2, ..., columnN
FROM table
WHERE predicate(s)
```

**Example 11.12** Syntax template for WHERE clause

The query in Example 11.13 searches for movies that were released in 1995.

```
mysql> SELECT *
    -> FROM movies
    -> WHERE year = 1995;
+-------+------------+------+------+
| id    | name       | year | rank |
+-------+------------+------+------+
| 18979 | Apollo 13  | 1995 | 7.5  |
| 46169 | Braveheart | 1995 | 8.3  |
+-------+------------+------+------+
2 rows in set (0.00 sec)
```

**Example 11.13** WHERE clause

The example above uses the equality operator, =, to filter the rows returned from the query. This is much like the == or === operator in most programming languages. Table 11.2 summarizes other common operators. The MySQL Reference for functions and operators in this chapter's References section gives a full listing of available operators.

| Operator | Description |
|---|---|
| = | Equal |
| > | Greater than |
| >= | Greater than or equal |
| < | Less than |
| <= | Less than or equal |
| <> | Not equal |
| AND (or &&) | Logical AND |
| BETWEEN **min** AND **max** | Values within a particular range |
| IN(**value1, ..., valueN**) | Check whether a value is within a set of values |
| LIKE **pattern** | Values that match a pattern |
| NOT (or !) | Negation |
| OR (or ||) | Logical OR |

Table 11.2 SQL logical operators

### The BETWEEN, IN, and LIKE Operators

Most of the operators work as in Example 11.13, but BETWEEN, IN, and LIKE deserve some more explanation. BETWEEN can be used to check whether a value is within a range of values. For example, the query in Example 11.14 searches for movies that were released between 1995 and 1999. Notice that it is inclusive and returns movies that were released in 1995 and 1999.

```
mysql> SELECT *
    -> FROM movies
    -> WHERE year BETWEEN 1995 AND 1999;
+--------+----------------+------+------+
| id     | name           | year | rank |
+--------+----------------+------+------+
|  18979 | Apollo 13      | 1995 |  7.5 |
|  46169 | Braveheart     | 1995 |  8.3 |
| 109093 | Fargo          | 1996 |  8.2 |
| 112290 | Fight Club     | 1999 |  8.5 |
| 207992 | Matrix, The    | 1999 |  8.5 |
| 238695 | Office Space   | 1999 |  7.6 |
| 254943 | Pi             | 1998 |  7.5 |
| 314965 | Stir of Echoes | 1999 |    7 |
| 333856 | Titanic        | 1997 |  6.9 |
+--------+----------------+------+------+
9 rows in set (0.00 sec)
```

Example 11.14 BETWEEN operator

The IN operator checks that a value is one of a given set of values. For example, the query in Example 11.15 searches for movies released in either 1995 or 1999 (but not between).

```
mysql> SELECT *
    -> FROM movies
    -> WHERE year IN (1995, 1999);
+--------+---------------+------+------+
| id     | name          | year | rank |
+--------+---------------+------+------+
|  18979 | Apollo 13     | 1995 |  7.5 |
|  46169 | Braveheart    | 1995 |  8.3 |
| 112290 | Fight Club    | 1999 |  8.5 |
| 207992 | Matrix, The   | 1999 |  8.5 |
| 238695 | Office Space  | 1999 |  7.6 |
| 314965 | Stir of Echoes| 1999 |    7 |
+--------+---------------+------+------+
6 rows in set (0.00 sec)
```

Example 11.15 IN operator

The LIKE operator is useful to filter on strings. LIKE can be used with the % wildcard placeholder, which signifies any character or sequence of characters. % can specify patterns in strings in three different ways as shown in Table 11.3.

| Usage | Description |
|---|---|
| LIKE 'text%' | text that starts with a given prefix |
| LIKE '%text' | text that ends with a given suffix |
| LIKE '%text%' | text that contains a given substring |

Table 11.3 The LIKE operator with % wildcard

Example 11.16 finds all actors whose first names begin with 'cla'. Patterns with LIKE are not case-sensitive; although the pattern 'cla%' is lowercase, the results contain rows where the first name begins with a capital C.

```
mysql> SELECT *
    -> FROM actors
    -> WHERE first_name LIKE 'cla%';
+--------+------------+-----------+--------+
| id     | first_name | last_name | gender |
+--------+------------+-----------+--------+
|  59824 | Clancy     | Brown     | M      |
| 319795 | Clark      | Middleton | M      |
| 794261 | Claire     | Slemmer   | F      |
| 795587 | Claire     | Smithies  | F      |
+--------+------------+-----------+--------+
4 rows in set (0.00 sec)
```

Example 11.16 LIKE operator

% matches one or many characters, but the _ placeholder matches exactly one character. Example 11.17 finds all actors whose first names contain exactly two letters.

```
mysql> SELECT *
    -> FROM actors
    -> WHERE first_name LIKE '__';
+--------+------------+-----------+--------+
| id     | first_name | last_name | gender |
+--------+------------+-----------+--------+
| 163893 | Ed         | Gale      | M      |
| ...    | ...        | ...       | ...    |
| 275761 | Al         | Lettieri  | M      |
| ...    | ...        | ...       | ...    |
| 434562 | Sy         | Sher      | M      |
| 445292 | Ed         | Snodderly | M      |
| 461413 | Bo         | Svenson   | M      |
| 477860 | Cy         | Town      | M      |
| ...    | ...        | ...       | ...    |
+--------+------------+-----------+--------+
13 rows in set (0.02 sec)
```

Example 11.17 LIKE operator with _ wildcard

### Multiple Predicates with AND and OR

So far we have only been filtering our queries using a single predicate. Many times you want to get a set of results based on a number of different conditions. You can do this by sequencing a number of different predicates together using the AND and OR operators. For example, the query in Example 11.18 retrieves all movies made between 1990 and 2000 with a ranking above 8.5.

```
mysql> SELECT *
    -> FROM movies
    -> WHERE year BETWEEN 1990 AND 2000
    ->       AND rank > 8.5;
+--------+------------------------+------+------+
| id     | name                   | year | rank |
+--------+------------------------+------+------+
| 210511 | Memento                | 2000 | 8.7  |
| 267038 | Pulp Fiction           | 1994 | 8.7  |
| 297838 | Shawshank Redemption, The | 1994 | 9 |
+--------+------------------------+------+------+
3 rows in set (0.00 sec)
```

Example 11.18 WHERE clause with multiple conditions

AND has higher precedence than OR, but parentheses can be used to enforce a specified precedence. The MySQL Reference gives a full listing of operator precedence.

### 11.2.5 Ordering Results: ORDER BY

If you want the results of your query to be returned in a particular order, you can request this using an ORDER BY clause. Its syntax is shown in Example 11.19.

```
SELECT column(s)
FROM table
WHERE predicate(s)
ORDER BY column(s) [ASC | DESC]
```

**Example 11.19 Syntax template for ORDER BY clause**

You list the column(s) you want your results sorted by, and the results will be sorted in order of those columns. If you list multiple columns, the data will first be sorted by the first column and will use subsequent columns to break ties. By default the results are shown in ascending (increasing) order, but you can change this by specifying ASC (ascending) or DESC (descending) after each column in the ORDER BY clause. Example 11.20 lists the last names of all directors in alphabetical order.

```
mysql> SELECT last_name
    -> FROM directors
    -> ORDER BY last_name;
+------------+
| last_name  |
+------------+
| Adamson    |
| Aronofsky  |
| Braff      |
| ...        |
| Verhoeven  |
| Wachowski  |
+------------+
33 rows in set (0.00 sec)
```

**Example 11.20 ORDER BY clause**

Example 11.21 demonstrates sorting by multiple columns by retrieving all directors' first and last names, first sorted by last name ascending (A-Z) and then by first name descending (Z-A).

```
mysql> SELECT *
    -> FROM directors
    -> ORDER BY last_name, first_name DESC;
+-------+--------------+------------+
| id    | first_name   | last_name  |
+-------+--------------+------------+
|   429 | Andrew       | Adamson    |
|  2931 | Darren       | Aronofsky  |
|  9247 | Zach         | Braff      |
| 11652 | James (I)    | Cameron    |
| 14927 | Ron          | Clements   |
| 15093 | Joel         | Coen       |
| 15092 | Ethan        | Coen       |
| 15906 | Sofia        | Coppola    |
| 15901 | Francis Ford | Coppola    |
| ...   | ...          | ...        |
| 83617 | Larry        | Wachowski  |
| 83616 | Andy         | Wachowski  |
+-------+--------------+------------+
33 rows in set (0.05 sec)
```

**Example 11.21 ORDER BY clause sorting on multiple columns**

## 11.2.6 Modifying Data: INSERT, UPDATE, and DELETE

In addition to using SQL to write queries, you can also use SQL for data manipulation like adding, updating, and deleting data via the INSERT, UPDATE, and DELETE statements. Your database administrator may have turned off these capabilities for your MySQL user account as your changes affect others if many people are sharing the same database. However, we'll talk briefly about data manipulation in SQL to give you a flavor of what it is like.

The INSERT statement is used to add new rows to a database table. The syntax to add a single row to a database table is shown in Example 11.22. The column names listed in [] are optional; if omitted, the command will assume that the first value listed goes into the first column, and so on.

```
INSERT INTO table [(column1, column2, ..., columnN)]
VALUES (value1, value2, ..., valueN)
```

**Example 11.22 Syntax table for INSERT INTO statement**

The values listed in the VALUES clause must match the order and data type of the columns listed in the INSERT INTO clause. Example 11.23 adds a row in the actors database and then queries for the newly inserted row.

```
mysql> INSERT INTO actors (id, first_name, last_name, gender)
    -> VALUES (723208, 'Jessica', 'Miller', 'F');
Query OK, 1 row affected (0.02 sec)

mysql> SELECT *
    -> FROM actors
    -> WHERE first_name = 'Jessica';
+--------+------------+-----------+--------+
| id     | first_name | last_name | gender |
+--------+------------+-----------+--------+
| 723208 | Jessica    | Miller    | F      |
| 789764 | Jessica    | Shepherd  | F      |
| 791422 | Jessica    | Siemens   | F      |
+--------+------------+-----------+--------+
1 row in set (0.00 sec)
```

**Example 11.23 INSERT statement**

If you like, you can omit the names of the columns when doing an INSERT, in which case the values you write will be implicitly mapped to the table columns in their order of declaration:

```
mysql> INSERT INTO actors
    -> VALUES (723208, 'Jessica', 'Miller', 'F');
```

The UPDATE statement shown in Example 11.24 is used to modify the data in a database table.

```
UPDATE table
SET column1 = value1, column2 = value2, ..., columnN = valueN
WHERE predicate(s)
```

**Example 11.24 Syntax template for UPDATE statement**

Example 11.25 modifies the row we inserted previously to contain a male actor with the name of 'Marty Stepp' and then queries for the updated row.

```
mysql> UPDATE actors
    -> SET first_name = 'Marty', last_name = 'Stepp', gender = 'M'
    -> WHERE id = 723208;
Query OK, 1 row affected (0.00 sec)
Rows matched: 1  Changed: 1  Warnings: 0

mysql> SELECT *
    -> FROM actors
    -> WHERE id = 723208;
+--------+------------+-----------+--------+
| id     | first_name | last_name | gender |
+--------+------------+-----------+--------+
| 723208 | Marty      | Stepp     | M      |
+--------+------------+-----------+--------+
1 row in set (0.00 sec)
```

**Example 11.25 UPDATE statement**

The DELETE statement shown in Example 11.26 is used to delete rows from a database table.

```
DELETE
FROM table
WHERE condition(s)
```

**Example 11.26 Syntax template for DELETE FROM statement**

Example 11.27 deletes the row that we inserted and modified, because we lowly authors are just wannabe movie stars and shouldn't be in the real data set.

```
mysql> DELETE
    -> FROM actors
    -> WHERE id = 723208;
Query OK, 1 row affected (0.00 sec)
```

**Example 11.27 DELETE FROM statement**

The optional WHERE clause of the UPDATE and DELETE statements is used to filter which rows are updated or deleted just as it is used in the SELECT statement. If you don't include a WHERE clause in the UPDATE and DELETE statements, all rows of the table are modified or deleted. This is probably not what you want, so be sure to include a WHERE clause with the appropriate predicates.

The UPDATE and DELETE statements are scarily permanent; once you update or delete data it is a hassle to undo. Moreover, there is no confirmation message that asks you whether or not you are sure you want to update or delete before the changes are committed. So it bears repeating that before using the UPDATE and DELETE statements make sure you have filtered the rows you want to modify or delete properly in the WHERE clause. You may want to SELECT those rows first with a test query before you manipulate or delete them.

## Self-Check

6. Explain the difference between declarative and an imperative programming language. Give examples of each.
7. Describe the structure of a SQL statement.
8. What SQL statement allows you to view the databases you can query?
9. What SQL statement allows you to view the tables within a database?
10. Describe in English what the following query will return:

```
mysql> SELECT last_name
    -> FROM actors
    -> WHERE first_name = 'Ed';
```

11. Describe in English what the following query will return:

```
mysql> SELECT year
    -> FROM movies
    -> WHERE name LIKE '%star%'
    -> ORDER BY year ASC;
```

12. Write the query that will return all movies that have a two letter name.
13. Write a query that returns the first name of all actresses whose last names begin with W.
14. Write a query that returns all movies made after 2000 that had a rating between 7 and 8.
15. Write the query that would update Brad Pitt to have the same first name as yours.

## 11.3    Interacting with a Database using PHP

Now that we know how to access a database and do some basic SQL queries in a terminal window, let's learn how to do the same in our web pages using PHP.  PHP has several functions for accessing a MySQL database. All of these functions have names that begin with `mysql_`. Table 11.4 summarizes the PHP MySQL functions we will use in this section.

| Function | Description |
| --- | --- |
| mysql_close | Closes a database connection |
| mysql_connect | Opens a connection to a MySQL database server |
| mysql_fetch_array | Returns the next row from an SQL query as an associative array |
| mysql_query | Performs a SQL query on the database |
| mysql_real_escape_string | Encodes a value to make it safe for inclusion in a query |
| mysql_select_db | Opens a particular database on the server |

**Table 11.4 Key PHP MySQL Functions**

Connecting to and querying a MySQL database in a web page involves three steps:

1. Establish a connection to the database server (`mysql_connect`)
2. Choose a database to query (`mysql_select_db`)
3. Query the database (`mysql_query`) and examine the results (`mysql_fetch_array`)

When you perform a query from the MySQL client in a terminal window, you see the results immediately as text output. But when you make a query in PHP, you fetch the resulting rows of the query one at a time with the `mysql_fetch_array` function. Each row is represented as an array.

```php
<h1>Movies Made in 2000</h1>
<ul>
<?php
  $db = mysql_connect("localhost", "jessica", "guinness");
  mysql_select_db("imdb_small");
  $results = mysql_query("SELECT * FROM movies WHERE year = 2000;");
  while ($row = mysql_fetch_array($results)) {
    ?>
    <li><?= $row["name"] ?></li>
    <?php
  }
  mysql_close($db);
?>
</ul>
```

# Movies Made in 2000

- Hollow Man
- Memento
- O Brother, Where Art Thou?
- Snatch

**Example 11.28 movies2000.php**

Example 11.28 shows a brief yet complete example that queries the `imdb_small` database to find all movies that were made in the year 2000. This information is presented on the page as a bulleted list. In the following sections we'll go step by step through each of the functions and how it is used.

## 11.3.1 Connecting to a Database

The `mysql_connect` function opens a connection to a MySQL server. Its syntax is shown in Example 11.29.

```
$db = mysql_connect("server", "user name", "password");
```

**Example 11.29 Syntax template for `mysql_connect` function**

The first parameter is the name or IP address of the MySQL server. If this parameter is omitted, `localhost` is assumed. The second parameter is the MySQL user name and the third parameter is the MySQL user's password. The second and third parameters can also be omitted and by default they are anonymous and the empty string, `""`, respectively. However, this won't work on many systems, because allowing anonymous access to your MySQL server is a security risk.

If the connection is successful, `mysql_connect` returns an object called a *resource* that represents the database connection. You should store this resource into a variable so that you can pass it as an argument to other functions later. If the connection fails, such as if the user name or password are incorrect, the function returns `FALSE`.

Once you connect to a MySQL server you must choose a database to query. The function used to do this is called `mysql_select_db`. Its syntax is shown in Example 11.30. Note that even though the function has the word `select` in its name, it does not perform a `SELECT` SQL query on the database; it only selects which database our future queries will target.

```
mysql_select_db("database name");
```

**Example 11.30 Syntax template for `mysql_select_db` function**

The name of the database you would like to use is the first parameter. An optional second parameter is the resource representing the database connection to use (i.e. the object returned from `mysql_connect`). If this second parameter is not passed, the last connection established through `mysql_connect` is assumed, so many times this second parameter is not necessary. The function returns `TRUE` if it succeeded or `FALSE` if it failed. The function could fail if, for example, there is no database with the given name or if it is accidentally called before you call `mysql_connect`.

## 11.3.2 Performing Queries

Once you have connected to a server and chosen a database, you can query it. This is done via the `mysql_query` function. Its syntax is shown in Example 11.31.

```
$results = mysql_query("SQL query");
```

**Example 11.31 Syntax template for `mysql_query` function**

The parameter is a string containing a SQL query. Example 11.31 demonstrates its usage.

```php
<?php
$db = mysql_connect("localhost", "jessica", "guinness");
mysql_select_db("imdb_small");
$results = mysql_query("SELECT name FROM movies WHERE name LIKE '%oo%'");
?>
```

Example 11.32 Calling `mysql_query` function

## Including Parameters in a Query

Many web pages execute queries based on form parameters. Say we have web page where the user types the title of a movie into a form, then the server shows the year the movie was made. We can implement this page using a form with a text box with a **name** of **movietitle**. When the user submits the form, we access the movie title from the **$_REQUEST** array:

```php
# get query parameter for name of movie
$title = $_REQUEST["movietitle"];
...
```

To search for the year in which the user's movie was made, the variable **$title** can be included in the query string. Since our query is in " double-quote marks, it is an interpreted string, meaning that variables can be inserted into it directly. The code in Example 11.33 creates and issues the query.

```php
<?php
# connect to imdb_small database on local computer
$db = mysql_connect("localhost", "jessica", "guinness");
mysql_select_db("imdb_small");

# execute a SQL query on the database (not secure)
$results = mysql_query("SELECT year FROM movies WHERE name = '$title';");
?>
```

Example 11.33 Form query parameter in SQL query

Notice that since the title is a string, we must surround it with quotes in the query string just as we would if we were typing directly into the command line. Suppose that the user types Fight Club as the movie title. With the quotes shown in Example 11.33, the query would be sent to the server as:

```
SELECT year FROM movies WHERE name = 'Fight Club';
```

Without the quotes, the query would be sent with the following invalid syntax:

```
SELECT year FROM movies WHERE name = Fight Club;
```

The return type of **mysql_query** depends on the kind of SQL statement. If your query was a SELECT and the query was successful, **mysql_query** returns a PHP resource that allows us to access the query results. If there was an error, the function will return **FALSE**. If the SQL statement was an INSERT, UPDATE, or DELETE, the result will be **TRUE** on success or **FALSE** on failure.

When using PHP variables in interpreted strings to construct MySQL queries, it is easy to forget the quotes that should go around arguments of type string. If you forget, the query will fail and the value returned from **mysql_query** will be **FALSE**, as shown in Example 11.34. If the author of that code tries to use **$results**, he/she will get unexpected error messages. In a later section we'll describe how to perform proper error checking to catch when the result of **mysql_query** is FALSE.

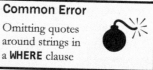

**Common Error**

Omitting quotes around strings in a **WHERE** clause

```php
<?php
$db = mysql_connect("localhost", "jessica", "guinness");
mysql_select_db("imdb_small");
$title = 'Pi';
$results = mysql_query("SELECT year FROM movies WHERE name = $title;");
?>
```

**Example 11.34 Common error: Omitting quotes around a string variable**

**SQL injection**

A common security attack on a web site that uses databases where the attacker is able to execute unauthorized SQL by taking advantage of insecure code.

If you are inserting query parameters typed by the user into your SQL query, you should be aware that there are some security issues here. The user could try to type a malicious parameter value (such as one that begins with a ' quote mark followed by some SQL commands) that would trick your query into returning other people's private data or into deleting data from the database. This kind of security breach is called *SQL injection*. To prevent such things from happening, we can encode the parameter into a safe form by calling the `mysql_real_escape_string` function, which accepts a value as a parameter and returns a string that is safe to use in your query. Example 11.35 demonstrates the use of this function.

```php
<?php
# get query parameter for name of movie
$title = mysql_real_escape_string($_REQUEST["movietitle"]);

# connect to imdb_small database on local computer
$db = mysql_connect("localhost", "jessica", "guinness");
mysql_select_db("imdb_small");

# execute a SQL query on the database (securely)
$results = mysql_query("SELECT year FROM movies WHERE name = '$title';");
?>
```

**Example 11.35 Securely including form parameter in SQL query**

### Reading Query Results: `mysql_fetch_array`

It would be natural to think that `mysql_query` would return the results of the query in some sort of table or 2-dimensional array, like when you perform queries from the command line. But PHP instead returns a special object called a MySQL *resource*. A resource is used to grab each result of the query, one at a time. This approach is used because queries can return thousands or even millions of rows. Returning all the results of a query at once could overload the server's memory.

The `mysql_fetch_array` function accepts a resource as a parameter and uses it to fetch and return the query's next result. The result returned by `mysql_fetch_array` is a single result row from the query or `FALSE` if there are no more rows available. The row is returned as an associative array.

The associative array returned uses column names as its indexes. For example, suppose you perform the following query to find all actors whose last names begin with "Del":

```php
$results = mysql_query("SELECT first_name, last_name FROM actors
                        WHERE last_name LIKE 'Del%';");
```

The code in Example 11.36 shows some calls to `mysql_fetch_array` from this query result resource. The first few rows' contents are shown in comments. Eventually the result is FALSE.

```php
$row = mysql_fetch_array($results);
# $row["first_name"] == "Benicio",  $row["last_name"] == "Del Toro"

$row = mysql_fetch_array($results);
# $row["first_name"] == "Michael",  $row["last_name"] == "Delano"

...
$row = mysql_fetch_array($results);
# $row = FALSE
```

**Example 11.36 Examining result rows with `mysql_fetch_array`**

It's best to use a `while` loop to fetch and display each result on your page. The loop should stop when the row returned is FALSE. So we make the loop's test be the assignment of the row itself. If the value assigned is FALSE, the loop will stop. Example 11.37 demonstrates this technique.

```php
<h1>Actors whose names begin with &quot;Del&quot;</h1>

<ul>
  <?php
    $db = mysql_connect("localhost", "jessica", "guinness");
    mysql_select_db("imdb_small");
    $results = mysql_query("SELECT first_name, last_name FROM actors
                        WHERE last_name LIKE 'Del%';");
    while ($row = mysql_fetch_array($results)) {
    ?>
    <li> First name: <?= $row["first_name"] ?>,
        Last name: <?= $row["last_name"] ?> </li>
    <?php
    }
  ?>
</ul>
```

# Actors whose names begin with "Del"

- First name: Benicio, Last name: Del Toro
- First name: Michael, Last name: Delano
- First name: Brian, Last name: Delate
- First name: Charlie, Last name: Dell
- First name: Michael, Last name: DeLorenzo
- First name: Maria, Last name: Del Rosario Gutiérrez

**Example 11.37 Using `mysql_fetch_array` in a loop**

It is easy to make mistakes in the query sent to `mysql_query`. The first kind of mistake is sending a query with incorrect SQL syntax. This can be caused by any number of things including misspelling keywords, table or column names, forgetting a clause, ordering clauses incorrectly (e.g., putting the WHERE clause before the FROM clause), or forgetting quotes around string parameters. Recall that when you send a malformed query to `mysql_query`, FALSE is returned. If you pass FALSE to `mysql_fetch_array`, you get an error like the following in your browser:

**Common Error**
Malformed queries

**Warning**: mysql_fetch_array(): supplied argument is not a valid MySQL result resource in **myfile.php** on line **27**

Even if the syntax of the query is correct, the query may be logically incorrect. In this case, you will get a valid MySQL resource object, but the results won't contain the data you expect. Suppose we are trying to find all movies released in the year 2000. We could use the following query:

```
SELECT id FROM movies WHERE year = 2000;
```

The query returns **id** numbers. But now suppose we try to display the name of each movie on the web page. When we try to access **$row["name"]**, we are going to get an error like the following:

**Notice**: Undefined index: name in **myfile.php** on line **34**

To avoid these kinds of errors, before inserting your MySQL into a PHP page, **construct your query in the MySQL console and make sure it is correct there first**. Once your query works in the console, then insert it into your page replacing any parameters with variables where necessary.

When you have a long query, you can store your query string into a variable first and then call **mysql_query** with the string as a parameter. Having readable queries will help you and others who have to work with your code to see what is going on and debug errors more quickly. You can also print the query out onto your PHP page to make sure it is correct, as shown in Example 11.38.

```php
<?php
  $query = "SELECT * FROM movies WHERE name LIKE Fight Club;";
  print "<p> DEBUG: My query is: $query </p>";
  $results = mysql_query($query);
?>
```

DEBUG: My query is: SELECT name, year FROM movies WHERE name LIKE Fight Club;

**Warning**: mysql_fetch_array(): supplied argument is not a valid MySQL result resource in **/var/www/html/stepp /php/query_debug.php** on line **21**

```
2:webster.cs.washington.edu - webster* - SSH Secure Shell

mysql> SELECT name, year FROM movies WHERE name LIKE Fight Club;
ERROR 1064 (42000): You have an error in your SQL syntax; check the
 manual that corresponds to your MySQL server version for the right
 syntax to use near 'Club' at line 1
mysql>

Connected to webster.cs.washington.edu    SSH2 - aes128-cbc - hmac-md5   67x5
```

**Example 11.38 Printing a query and testing it in the MySQL console**

You can copy the query from the webpage and paste it into the console to double-check it. In the console you get the full advantage of the MySQL interpreter's more detailed error messages.

## Disconnecting: mysql_close

After you are finished using the results returned to you by **mysql_query** and are finished with the database connection, it is good practice to explicitly close the connection. To do so, use the **mysql_close** function, which accepts as a parameter the resource for the database connection as returned by **mysql_connect**. **mysql_close** returns **TRUE** on success or **FALSE** on failure. Technically **mysql_close** is not required, as connections are automatically closed at the end of the script's execution, but it is good practice to call it when you know you no longer need the connection.

### 11.3.3 Error Checking

When connecting to and querying a database, there are many things that can go wrong including the database being down, passing the wrong username or password, not having appropriate permissions on the database or tables, and passing malformed or incorrect queries (as discussed above). For these reasons, it is important to perform error checking in your code.

As we have gone through each of the functions above, you might have noticed that as a general rule if the function fails it returns **FALSE**. We can write code to explicitly look for a **FALSE** result from any of our MySQL functions and take appropriate action to report the failure. The **mysql_error** function returns a string representing an error message describing the last MySQL-related error that has occurred. We can call this function and print the cause of the failure.

If there is a serious error in our database connection, we may also want to stop the rest of the page from displaying. To do so, when we detect an error we can use PHP's **die** function, which accepts a string parameter. When you call **die**, the string you pass is printed and then the page's code stops executing. Table 11.5 shows these functions and Example 11.39 demonstrates their usage.

| Function | Description |
|---|---|
| mysql_error | Returns a message describing the most recent MySQL-related error |
| die | Prints a message and exits the current PHP script |

**Table 11.5 PHP functions for SQL error checking**

```
$db = mysql_connect("localhost", "jessica", "guinness");
if (!$db) {
  die("SQL error occurred on connect: " . mysql_error());
}
```

**Example 11.39 Using mysql_error and die to catch SQL errors**

You should check for errors after almost every call to a PHP MySQL function. But this clutters your script with lots of **if** blocks. Alternatively, most PHP coders use the PHP **or** operator and the **die** function to perform error checking, as shown in Example 11.40.

```
$db = mysql_connect("localhost", "jessica", "guinness")
  or die("SQL error occurred on connect: " . mysql_error());
mysql_select_db("imdb_small")
  or die("Could not select database" . mysql_error());
$results = mysql_query("SELECT * FROM movies WHERE year = 2000;")
  or die("Query failed: " . mysql_error());
...
```

**Example 11.40 Using or die**

The **or** operator is just like the **||** operator except that it has a lower precedence, ensuring anything to the left of **or** is executed before evaluating the right operand. Both **||** and **or** perform short circuit evaluation such that if the left operand evaluates to **TRUE**, the right operand is not evaluated.

This basic type of error handling is likely sufficient for personal projects and homework assignments, but if you are developing a web site that will go live to the public, you probably want to handle errors more gracefully than just printing PHP MySQL error messages that will probably be confusing to the user. Production sites try to handle errors more gracefully for the user, such as by redirecting the user to a page that says the service is down and to try later, or giving a means to contact the administrators of the web site. A production site also probably records the error into an error log or automatically emails the administrator about the error. If you want to learn more about more gracefully handling errors in PHP, refer to the References section.

## Other Functions

There are many other functions in the PHP MySQL library. Table 11.6 lists a few of them. For a full reference, visit the PHP MySQL functions manual in the References section of this chapter.

| Function | Description |
|---|---|
| mysql_free_result | Deallocates the memory associated with a query or connection |
| mysql_list_dbs | Returns a list of databases on this server |
| mysql_num_fields | Returns number of columns per result in the query |
| mysql_num_rows | Returns number of rows matched by the query |
| mysql_ping | Checks to see whether or not a database connection is working and if it is not attempts a reconnect |

**Table 11.6 Other PHP MySQL Functions**

For example, to free any resources associated with a query, use mysql_free_result. This function takes as its parameter the resource object that you get from mysql_query and frees any memory associated with it. It returns TRUE on success or FALSE on failure. Luckily, if you forget to do this, PHP automatically releases any memory used at the end of the script's execution. However, explicitly freeing the resource object is good practice and can be particularly useful when you want to free up memory between multiple queries that return large result sets.

## Self-Check

16. Name the PHP MySQL functions that allow you to access, select, and query a database from your page. What is the function that allows you to read each result from your queries?
17. Why is it advantageous to use double-quoted strings for your PHP MySQL queries?
18. What is wrong with the following code? (There are at least three problems with it.)

```
$name = $_REQUEST["actor_name"];
$results = mysql_query("SELECT * FROM actor
                        WHERE first_name = $name");
```

19. What does the mysql_query function return? How is it used to read results from a query?
20. What does mysql_fetch_array return? How is it used to read results from a query?
21. If you are not getting the results you were expecting or received an error using MySQL PHP, what steps would you make to debug the issue?

# 11.4 Multi-table Queries

So far our queries have selected from a single table to answer simple questions, but where database queries really get interesting is when you have queries that involve many tables. We will want to use the **imdb** database to answer queries like: "Show all actors that have been in a horror movie" or, "Who played Neil Armstrong in Apollo 13?" or, "Who directed Pi?" All of these can be answered using our **imdb_small** database, but we'll need to connect the data from multiple tables. For example, if we want to know which actors have been in a horror movie, we need to connect actors to their roles, and connect roles to movies and genres, and so on.

## 11.4.1 Cartesian Product

The SQL **JOIN** keyword connects two or more tables into a larger combined result. Example 11.41 shows a query with the **actors** and **movies** tables joined together. This isn't quite what we want, because it includes all possible combinations of rows between all of the tables listed, otherwise known as the *Cartesian product* of the tables. This is usually very large because the number of rows returned will be the product of the number of rows of each table included (1907 actors x 36 movies = over 68,000 rows in our example).

```
mysql> SELECT * FROM actors JOIN movies;
+------+------------+------------+--------+--------+--------------+------+------+
| id   | first_name | last_name  | gender | id     | name         | year | rank |
+------+------------+------------+--------+--------+--------------+------+------+
| 933  | Lewis      | Abernathy  | M      | 10920  | Aliens       | 1986 | 8.2  |
| 933  | Lewis      | Abernathy  | M      | 17173  | Animal House | 1978 | 7.5  |
| 933  | Lewis      | Abernathy  | M      | 18979  | Apollo 13    | 1995 | 7.5  |
| 933  | Lewis      | Abernathy  | M      | 30959  | Batman Begins| 2005 | NULL |
| 933  | Lewis      | Abernathy  | M      | 46169  | Braveheart   | 1995 | 8.3  |
| 933  | Lewis      | Abernathy  | M      | 109093 | Fargo        | 1996 | 8.2  |
| ...  | ...        | ...        | ...    | ...    | ...          | ...  | ...  |
+------+------------+------------+--------+--------+--------------+------+------+
68652 rows in set (0.45 sec)
```

**Example 11.41 Cartesian product**

The result output is trimmed in our example, but the complete output would list every actor paired with every movie, regardless of whether the actor appeared in that movie. In the output shown, the first actor in the **actors** table, Lewis Abernathy, is getting coupled with all the movies in the database (even though the only movie he appeared in is **"Titanic"**).

One way you could deal with the large set of results is to filter it in your code (i.e. your PHP script) using **if** statements. But filtering results in code is an inefficient solution that would waste lots of time and memory. RDBMS software is specifically optimized to handle filtering multi-table joins, which we'll learn about in the next section.

## 11.4.2 Joins

A *join* between tables is a subset of the Cartesian product of the tables, where the records are connected to each other only if they meet certain conditions, specified by the **ON** keyword. The conditions capture relationships and how values in each table relate to those in other tables. The proper syntax of a **JOIN** in a query is shown in Example 11.42.

> **join**
>
> A SQL operation that relates two or more tables, usually by means of values that are common between them.

```
SELECT column(s)
FROM table1
     JOIN table2 ON condition(s)
     ...
     JOIN tableN ON condition(s)
WHERE condition(s);
```

**Example 11.42 Syntax template for JOIN clause**

For example, let's say we want to know under which genres the movie *Memento* is classified. We can use the **id** of the **movies** table and link it with the **movie_id** in the **movies_genres** table to figure out the answer to this question, as shown in Example 11.43.

```
mysql> SELECT *
    -> FROM movies
    ->     JOIN movies_genres ON id = movie_id
    -> WHERE name = 'Memento';
+--------+---------+------+------+----------+----------+
| id     | name    | year | rank | movie_id | genre    |
+--------+---------+------+------+----------+----------+
| 210511 | Memento | 2000 | 8.7  | 210511   | Drama    |
| 210511 | Memento | 2000 | 8.7  | 210511   | Mystery  |
| 210511 | Memento | 2000 | 8.7  | 210511   | Thriller |
+--------+---------+------+------+----------+----------+
3 rows in set (0.00 sec)
```

**Example 11.43 JOIN clause**

We start with the enormous Cartesian product (all movies joined with all genre records, even genres of unrelated movies), but then we use **ON** to filter out all rows except those where the **id** of the movie is the same as the **movie_id** of the genre record. We're left with all movies joined with their own genres. We additionally filter in the **WHERE** clause, asking only for results where the movie's name is **'Memento'**. What's left is the movie Memento joined to all of its associated genres.

## Referring to Tables by Name

Sometimes when you perform a join, you want to link tables by columns that have the same name. In these cases you must disambiguate column names by their tables' names using the syntax **table.column**. For example, if we want to know which actresses have the same first name as a director in the database, we can disambiguate the join as demonstrated in Example 11.44.

```
mysql> SELECT *
    -> FROM actors
    ->     JOIN directors ON actors.first_name = directors.first_name
    -> WHERE actors.gender = 'F';
+--------+------------+-----------+--------+-------+------------+-----------+
| id     | first_name | last_name | gender | id    | first_name | last_name |
+--------+------------+-----------+--------+-------+------------+-----------+
| 586071 | Sofia      | Coppola   | F      | 15906 | Sofia      | Coppola   |
| 602370 | Cameron    | Diaz      | F      | 16816 | Cameron    | Crowe     |
+--------+------------+-----------+--------+-------+------------+-----------+
2 rows in set (0.01 sec)
```

**Example 11.44 Disambiguating columns**

This syntax can become quite verbose. One thing you can do to make the syntax more compact is to give names to tables. You can give names to tables much like giving names to variables in programming languages. All you have to do to give a table a name is list the name you want to give the table right after the table is listed in the FROM or JOIN clause. Example 11.45 is the same query to find the female actresses with the same first name as a director, but this time we give the name a to the actors table and d to the directors table, making the query syntax more compact.

```
mysql> SELECT *
    -> FROM actors a
    ->      JOIN directors d ON a.first_name = d.first_name
    -> WHERE a.gender = 'F';
+--------+------------+-----------+--------+-------+------------+-----------+
| id     | first_name | last_name | gender | id    | first_name | last_name |
+--------+------------+-----------+--------+-------+------------+-----------+
| 586071 | Sofia      | Coppola   | F      | 15906 | Sofia      | Coppola   |
| 602370 | Cameron    | Diaz      | F      | 16816 | Cameron    | Crowe     |
+--------+------------+-----------+--------+-------+------------+-----------+
2 rows in set (0.01 sec)
```

**Example 11.45 Giving names to tables**

## 11.4.3   Keys

Now that we are performing complex queries, let's look at a quirk of the imdb database design. You may notice that every table has one or more id columns. The id doesn't mean anything outside the database; no one refers to Cameron Diaz as actress #602370. So why are these columns there? Some tables consist of almost nothing but ids, such as movies_directors or roles.

The answer is related to duplicates. It is possible for two actors to have the same name; there are 20 actors named "Will Smith," for example (but only one who played the Fresh Prince). It is also possible for two movies to have the same title, such as when Hollywood churns out yet another remake of a classic film. It would be bad if these similar actors or movies had identical records in the database, because we would not be able to distinguish them. The id columns ensure that each row of each table is unique. Even if two actors have exactly the same name, the records for those actors have different id values. A column that must be unique for each row of a table is called a *key*.

> **key**
>
> A column in a database table whose value must be unique for every row in the table.

A database's designer (the person who decides what tables and columns should be in the database) will designate a column or set of columns that uniquely identify each row. A table can have more than one key column; if so, one or more are chosen to be the main or *primary key*. Often the keys are large integer ids. One reason integer ids are used is that integer comparisons are computationally cheap, so the RDBMS is able to quickly perform large queries and join tables together by integer id values.

> **primary key**
>
> The main column or group of columns that uniquely identify every row in a table.

As we said, some tables such as roles consist almost entirely of ids. Each row of roles contains three columns: actor_id, movie_id, and role. A role connects an actor with a given actor_id to the movie_id of the movie in which that actor appeared. These columns in the roles table are examples of another kind of key called a foreign key. A *foreign key* is a column containing values from the primary key of another table. In this case, the foreign key actor_id refers to the primary key id from actors, and foreign key movie_id refers to movie's primary key id. Values for a foreign key don't have to be unique; for example, the same actor could appear in many films, which would lead to many rows in the roles table with the same actor_id.

You may wonder why some of these tables even exist. Why have a table called `movies_genres` to store each movie's genre, rather than just including a `genre` column in the `movies` table? Why not include the director's id in the movie table rather than having a separate `movies_directors` table? These kinds of decisions are part of the process of designing a database. Some decisions are made to reduce redundancy or keep the database's memory size smaller. Others are made to keep the database cleaner or to keep its design more conceptually pure. If you are interested, please refer to our appendix on database definition and design for more information.

You can see which columns serve as keys for a given database table using the `DESCRIBE` command in the MySQL command-line interpreter, as shown in Example 11.46.

```
mysql> DESCRIBE movies;
+--------+--------------+------+-----+---------+-------+
| Field  | Type         | Null | Key | Default | Extra |
+--------+--------------+------+-----+---------+-------+
| id     | int(11)      | NO   | PRI | 0       |       |
| name   | varchar(100) | YES  |     | NULL    |       |
| year   | int(11)      | YES  |     | NULL    |       |
| rank   | float        | YES  |     | NULL    |       |
+--------+--------------+------+-----+---------+-------+
4 rows in set (0.01 sec)
```

**Example 11.46 Using DESCRIBE to find keys**

When we use `DESCRIBE` with `movies` we see that the fourth column tells us whether or not the column is a key. The word `PRI` indicates that `id` is the primary key for the `movies` table.

Keys are crucial in `JOIN`s because keys are often connected in `ON` conditions. A frequent pattern is to compare the primary key of one table with a foreign key in a second table that refers to it.

Databases commonly have two types of tables: ones with names of objects (e.g., `actors`, `directors`, and `movies`) and ones with names of relationships (e.g., `directors_genres`, `movies_directors`, `movies_genres`, and `roles`). Object tables usually contain a primary key column to uniquely identify the object in each row. Relationship tables usually contain foreign keys referring to the objects that are involved in the relationship. Figure 11.4 shows the tables of the `imdb` database and how they connect to each other.

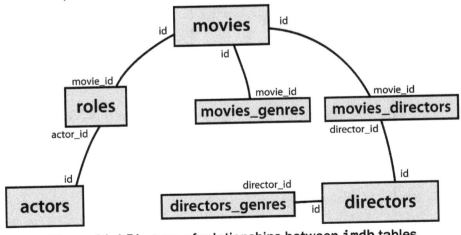

**Figure 11.4 Diagram of relationships between imdb tables**

## 11.4.4    Designing a Query

When working with multi-table queries, it can be hard to see how tables should be joined and the query created to answer your question. You can follow the steps below to help you understand how to think through how to create multi-table queries.

- Use SHOW TABLES to figure out which tables are available and DESCRIBE to see what information each table contains. Once you have figured out which tables contain the data you need, you know they will be present in the FROM clause.
- Use DESCRIBE to figure out which columns connect the tables found in Step 1. Look for primary and foreign keys, if appropriate. Sometimes there is no direct connection between two tables, but rather a third table that connects the two. Again, use SHOW TABLES and DESCRIBE to find such connecting tables. Once you have figured out how tables are connected, you know what conditions should be present in the ON condition of the JOIN.
- Think about any other conditions the query needs that don't have to do with linking tables, such as a name of 'Memento'. This will go in the WHERE portion of your query.
- Lastly, think about what columns you want to display. This goes in the SELECT clause.

### Example Query: Comediennes Since 2002

Using these guidelines, let's try to find out the answer to a complex query: Which actresses have starred in a comedy made after 2002? First, let's think about which tables have information we need.

- Actors' names and genders are found in the actors table.
- To know whether a film is a comedy, we can look in the movies_genres table.

How do we link this information? We need to know which actors appeared in a comedy film. There is no direct link between actors and movies_genres, so we must take a more roundabout route. If we knew what movies each actor has been in, we could check to see whether any of those films is a comedy. So it seems we need a third table in our query:

- Movies' information is in the movies table.

But again, there is no direct link from actors to movies. If we want to know which movies every actor has appeared in, we must use a fourth table in our query. From looking at the relationships between tables shown in Figure 11.4, we can see the connection between actors and movies:

- Actors are connected to the movies they appeared in through the roles table.

The roles table will link actors to movies. So in our query, we will join the following tables:

```
FROM actors a
    JOIN roles r
    JOIN movies m
```

The above FROM clause is too general because it links every actor with every role (even roles that actor did not perform) and with every movie (even movies in which that actor did not appear). We must use ON conditions to make sure that we connect actors to *their* roles, and only connect those roles to the movies that the role was part of:

```
FROM actors a
     JOIN roles r ON r.actor_id = a.id
     JOIN movies m ON m.id = r.movie_id
```

Now we're getting all actors and the movies they appeared in, but we want only the ones that appeared in a comedy film. We can tell whether a film is a comedy by looking at its genre, so we still need to connect **movies_genres** to our query. We can do this be adding one additional JOIN clause. Once again we need a proper **ON** condition. The condition is that we want the genre of the movie the actor appeared in, so this means that the **movie_id** of the genre record must match the **id** of the movie record:

```
FROM actors a
     JOIN roles r ON r.actor_id = a.id
     JOIN movies m ON m.id = r.movie_id
     JOIN movies_genres mg on mg.movie_id = m.id
```

The hardest part of our query is now written. You may be saying, "What about the rest of the conditions, such as making sure it is a female actor?" These are also important conditions, but they are not related to the connecting of tables, so they do not belong as part of our **JOIN** clauses. Instead they will be part of the query's **WHERE** clause. There are three filtering conditions that have nothing to do with joining tables: we are looking for female actresses only, only comedies, and the movie must have been made after 2002. Therefore, our **WHERE** clause should be:

```
WHERE a.gender = 'F'
      AND mg.genre = 'Comedy'
      AND m.year > 2002
```

The last part of our query to build is the **SELECT** clause. We want only the actress' names, so we'll select the first and last name from **actors**. The complete query is shown in Example 11.47.

```
mysql> SELECT a.first_name, a.last_name
    -> FROM actors a
    ->      JOIN roles r ON r.actor_id = a.id
    ->      JOIN movies m ON m.id = r.movie_id
    ->      JOIN movies_genres mg ON mg.movie_id = m.id
    -> WHERE a.gender = 'F'
    ->       AND mg.genre = 'Comedy'
    ->       AND m.year > 2002;
+----------------+--------------+
| first_name     | last_name    |
+----------------+--------------+
| Pamela         | Abdy         |
| Tracey         | Antosiweicz  |
| Debbon         | Ayer         |
| ...            | ...          |
| Akiko          | Takeshita    |
| Lisle          | Wilkerson    |
+----------------+--------------+
27 rows in set (0.00 sec)
```

Example 11.47 Complete query with JOINs

## Self-Check

22. What is a Cartesian product? If you do a Cartesian product between one table that has M rows and another table that has N rows, how many results would be produced?

23. This query below is meant to return all the movies and their genres. Is there anything wrong with it? If so, how would you fix it?

```
SELECT m.name, mg.genre
FROM movies m
     JOIN movies_genres mg
```

24. What is a join?
25. What is a key? What is a primary key? What is a foreign key?
26. Write the query that will list the first/last names of all actresses that have starred in a thriller.
27. Write the query that will list director first/last names by their likelihood to direct a comedy.
28. Write a concise English sentence that describes what the following query returns:

```
SELECT a.first_name, a.last_name
FROM actors a
     JOIN roles r ON a.id = r.actor_id
WHERE role IN ('Herself', 'Himself');
```

## 11.5   Case Study: Adventure Recommender

In this section we build a web application that ties together many of the concepts learned in this chapter including SQL **SELECT** statements, queries to more than one table, and connecting and querying a database using PHP MySQL functions. This program recommends developing countries for a user to visit based upon a continent and official languages spoken in the country. Given these preferences, our program will consult a new database, the **world** database, and return to the user countries that match their criteria for their next adventure.

Part of the task of building a database-driven web site like this one is designing the database that will store the data (i.e., deciding what tables the database should have and what columns the tables should have). Since database design is a more advanced topic we have not included material on it in this chapter. If you want to learn about database design, before continuing with this case study you might want to refer to the Database Design Appendix and learn how we designed the **world** database.

The **world** database contains information about countries, cities and languages. The tables contained in the **world** database can be found in Figure 11.5.

| code | name | continent | sur-face_area | population | life_expectancy | gnp | ... |
|------|------|-----------|---------------|------------|-----------------|-----|-----|
| ITA | Italy | Europe | 301316.00 | 57680000 | 79.0 | 1161755.00 | ... |
| NPL | Nepal | Asia | 147181.00 | 147181.00 | 57.8 | 4768.00 | ... |

**Countries (partial list of columns)**

| id | name | country_code | district | popula-tion |
|----|------|--------------|----------|-------------|
| 1464 | Roma | ITA | Latium | 2643581 |
| 3816 | Seattle | USA | Washington | 563374 |

**Cities**

| country_code | language | official | percentage |
|--------------|----------|----------|------------|
| NPL | Nepali | T | 50.4 |
| USA | Spanish | F | 7.5 |

**CountriesLanguages**

**Figure 11.5 world database tables**

The site will be split into two pages: a main page that explains the site and displays the form the user fills out and a second page that shows the countries that fulfill the user preferences. The desired appearances of the main page is shown in Figure 11.6. Notice that the user can only choose one continent but may select many languages for their adventure.

Choose characteristics a developing nation you'd like to visit.

## Which continent and language(s) do you prefer?

**Figure 11.6 Developing World Adventure Recommender, index page**

The desired appearance for the results page is shown in Figure 11.7.

### Countries that fit your preferences for your next adventure are:

- Laos
- North Korea
- South Korea

**Figure 11.7 Developing World Adventure Recommender, results page**

A complex page like this is best completed in stages. Here is a rough outline of how to approach this problem step-by-step:

1. Write the index page, but leave the continents and language list boxes unpopulated. This page will have no PHP and no MySQL, but will provide the framework for us to use PHP and MySQL to populate the list boxes.
2. Apply basic styles to the index page with CSS.
3. Using the MySQL client, figure out the SQL that returns all the continents and languages stored in our database.
4. Add the PHP MySQL code that queries the database from our index page and fills in the list boxes' values with the countries and languages.
5. Write the HTML skeleton for the results page.
6. Using the MySQL client, figure out the SQL needed to recommend countries to visit.
7. Programmatically build the SQL query above and write PHP functions to retrieve the recommendations and display them to the user.

## 11.5.1   Index Page

We'll first tackle the index page. This will be stored as `index.php` and contain a form that will allow the user to input their preferences for the next developing nation they want to visit.

### Initial HTML Content

First we will write a stub version of this page, ignoring the fact we have to populate the list boxes with data the user can choose. Its code is shown in Example 11.48. Referring back to Figure 11.6, the page consists of a level-1 heading with an image and text for the site logo, an explanatory paragraph, and a form with a level-2 heading asking the user their preferences, one list box with choices for continents, a second list box with languages, and a button for the user to submit their preferences. We'll also link to a style sheet `adventure.css` that contains the CSS styles for both pages. For the `index.php` stub, we'll place `???` where the function calls to fill in the list boxes should go.

Since there are many continents and languages to choose from, we choose list boxes to display the options for continents and languages. Additionally, we want the user to be able to select more than one language as a choice – recall from the Forms Chapter you have to indicate the list box accepts multiple choices by putting `[]` at the end of the list box's name. If you do not do this you only receive the last of the choices selected in the query parameters.

```
<!DOCTYPE html PUBLIC "-//W3C//DTD XHTML 1.1//EN"
  "http://www.w3.org/TR/xhtml11/DTD/xhtml11.dtd">
<html xmlns="http://www.w3.org/1999/xhtml">
  <head>
    <title>Developing World Adventure Recommender</title>
    <link href="adventure.css" type="text/css" rel="stylesheet" />
  </head>

  <body>
    <div class="logo">
      <h1>
        Developing <img src="world.jpg" alt="world" /> Adventure Recommender
      </h1>
    </div>

    <p>Choose characteristics of a developing nation you'd like to visit.</p>

    <form action="adventure_recommendations.php" method="get">
      <div>
        <h2>Which continent and language(s) do you prefer?</h2>

        <select name="continent" size="5">???</select>
        <select name="languages[]" size="5" multiple="multiple">???</select>
      </div>

      <div>
        <input type="submit" value="Submit" />
      </div>
    </form>
  </body>
</html>
```

**Example 11.48 Initial version of `index.php`**

### Basic Styles for Index Page

The styles for our Developing World Adventure Recommender are fairly straightforward. In the `body` selector we choose a font and font size and center the entire page by setting `margin-left` and `margin-right` to `auto`. Similarly, we set up the `logo div` so that it is in the very center of the page by setting its `margin-left` and `margin-right` to `auto`. To vertically align the image in the center of the `logo div`, we set the height of the `logo div` to be a bit larger than the height of the image and set the `vertical-align` property of the image to `middle`. Lastly, to horizontally align all contents of the `h1` of the `div` to the center, we set its `text-align` property to `center`. Now we have a nice, clean style with a centered logo for our page.

```
body {
  font-family: "Helvetica", sans-serif;
  font-size: 14px;
  margin-left: auto;
  margin-right: auto;
  width: 60%;
}

h1 {
  margin: 0em;
  text-align: center;
}

.logo {
  height: 75px;
  margin-left: auto;
  margin-right: auto;
  width: 80%;
}

.logo img {
  height: 63px;
  vertical-align: middle;
  width: 69px;
}
```

**Example 11.49 Initial version of `adventure.css`**

## SQL for Continents and Languages

Before adding any PHP MySQL to our `index.php` stub we practice and perfect our queries in the MySQL client. First we want to figure out the query that will bring back all the continents the user can select from. Using the **DESCRIBE** statement in the client we notice that the **Countries** table has a column named **continent**. Our first stab at the query is found in Example 11.50.

```
mysql> SELECT continent
    -> FROM Countries;
+----------------+
| continent      |
+----------------+
| Asia           |
| Europe         |
| North America  |
| Europe         |
| ...            |
+----------------+
239 rows in set (0.00 sec)
```

**Example 11.50 First try to bring back choices for continent in MySQL Client**

The query in Example 11.50 isn't quite right. Every row in the **Countries** table has an entry for continent and since there are 239 countries in our database, this query brings back 239 choices for continent. Since we don't want the continent names to be repeated in our continents list box we use the **DISTINCT** keyword to only bring back distinct continent names. The resulting query can be found in Example 11.51.

```
SELECT DISTINCT continent
FROM Countries
```

**Example 11.51 SQL query to fetch data for continents list box**

Now we want to bring back all the languages that are in the database that the user can choose from, but we want to be a little picky here as we only want officially recognized languages. Again, using DESCRIBE statement in MySQL client we see that it is the CountriesLanguages table that contains possible languages. The query that pulls back languages will be against this one table and will have a WHERE clause specifying we only want official languages. Again, since we don't want language choices to be repeated in the list box we use SELECT DISTINCT. The resulting query can be found in Example 11.52.

```
SELECT DISTINCT language
FROM CountriesLanguages
WHERE official = 'T'
ORDER BY language
```

**Example 11.52 SQL query to fetch data for languages list box**

### Populating list boxes with data

To populate the continents list box with the continents data, we need a function that will connect to the database, execute the query in Example 11.51, and iterate through the results, printing out an option element for each continent returned. The function in Example 11.53 does just this.

```php
<?php
function populate_continents() {
  $db = mysql_connect(server, user, password);
  mysql_select_db("world");

  $query = "SELECT DISTINCT continent
            FROM Countries";

  $results = mysql_query($query);

  while ($row = mysql_fetch_array($results)) {
    $choice = $row["continent"];
    ?>
    <option value="<?= $choice ?>"><?= $choice ?></option>
    <?php
  }

  mysql_free_result($results);
  mysql_close($db);
}
?>
```

**Example 11.53 Initial function to populate continents list box**

With a little tweaking we can make this function more generic and use it to also populate the languages list box. The two things we need to abstract from this function to make it reusable to generate language options are the query to retrieve the options and the name of the column holding the values we want to appear in the list box. Instead of copy and pasting all the code and tweaking the few needed spots to accommodate filling the languages list box, we make a more generic function that takes a query and a column name to generate list box choices from a database query. Additionally, we add in some database error handling code. Example 11.54 shows the resulting function.

```php
<?php
function get_and_print_options($query, $column) {
  $db = mysql_connect(server, user, password)
    or die("Could not connect to database: " . mysql_error());
  mysql_select_db("world")
    or die("Could not select database" . mysql_error());
  $results = mysql_query($query)
    or die("Query (" . $query . ") failed" . mysql_error());

  while ($row = mysql_fetch_array($results)) {
    $choice = $row[$column];
    ?>
    <option value="<?= $choice ?>"><?= $choice ?></option>
    <?php
  }

  mysql_free_result($results);
  mysql_close($db);
}
?>
```

**Example 11.54 Functions to populate continent and language lists**

Now that we have functions that will fill the list boxes with options, we need to call the functions in the page body so that the list boxes are populated when the page loads. We'll use a PHP expression block for this. The two **select** elements containing the **???** in Example 11.48 should be replaced by the two **select** elements below:

```php
<select name="continent" size="5">
  <?php
  $query = "SELECT DISTINCT continent FROM Countries";
  get_and_print_options($query, "continent");
  ?>
</select>

<select name="languages[]" size="5" multiple="multiple">
  <?php
  $query = "SELECT DISTINCT language
            FROM CountriesLanguages
            WHERE official = 'T'
            ORDER BY language";
  get_and_print_options($query, "language");
  ?>
</select>
```

## 11.5.2 Adventure Recommendations Page

Now let's turn our attention to the page that gets and displays adventure recommendations according to the users' preferences.

## Initial HTML and PHP Content for Adventure Recommendations Page

Again, we begin by writing the recommendations results page as a stub. The stub code is shown in Example 11.55. Referring back to Figure 11.7, the page consists of the same image and text for the site logo as the index page, a level-2 heading indicating the results, and an unordered list of the results themselves. For the stub, we place a **???** where the function call to print out the results of the users' request should go.

Since the index and results pages have the same HTML to declare the page and show the logo, we have decided to make a shared file called **top.html** as shown in Example 11.56.

```php
<?php
include("top.html");
include("adventure_shared.php");
?>

    <h2>Countries that fit your preferences for your next adventure are:</h2>
    ???
  </body>
</html>
```

**Example 11.55 Adventure recommendations results stub**

```
<!DOCTYPE html PUBLIC "-//W3C//DTD XHTML 1.1//EN"
"http://www.w3.org/TR/xhtml11/DTD/xhtml11.dtd">
<html xmlns="http://www.w3.org/1999/xhtml">
  <head>
    <title>Developing World Adventure Recommender</title>
    <link href="adventure.css" type="text/css" rel="stylesheet" />
  </head>

  <body>
    <div class="logo">
      <h1>
        Developing <img src="world.jpg" alt="world" /> Adventure Recommender
      </h1>
    </div>
```

**Example 11.56 Shared file top.html**

## SQL for Getting Adventure Recommendations

Now we turn our attention to taking a user's preferences and turning those into a SQL query that will bring back recommendations. Since we will first develop and perfect our queries in the MySQL client we pick an example continent (Africa) and a couple languages (Portuguese and Swazi) to filter on and test in the client.

Let's break down the query that will bring back recommendations for these preferences by first considering how to build a query that will bring back countries that are only in Africa. For this query, we only need to select country names from the **Countries** table based on whether or not they are in Africa. An example query for filtering based on countries in Africa can be found in Example 11.57.

```sql
SELECT name
FROM Countries
WHERE continent = 'Africa'
```

**Example 11.57 SQL query to fetch countries filtered by continents**

Now let's add to the query what is needed to further filter results by official languages spoken. To perform this query, we join the Countries table with the CountriesLanguages table on the country code. We can use the IN operator to filter based on a list of languages. Example 11.58 gives a query that filters countries on Africa and Portuguese and Swazi.

```sql
SELECT c.name
FROM Countries c
    JOIN CountriesLanguages cl ON c.code = cl.country_code
WHERE c.continent = 'Africa'
    AND cl.language in ('Portuguese', 'Swazi') AND cl.official =  'T'
```

**Example 11.58 SQL query to fetch countries filtered by continents and languages**

The last filter we need to add to this query determines the results are only developing countries. Whether or not the economy is developed or not is a somewhat arbitrary measure, but two generally accepted indicators that a country is developing are a GNP per capita of less than $10,000 and an average life expectancy of less than 70 years. The data stored in the GNP column of the Countries table is stored in millions (we figured this out manually be comparing the data in the table to data on the Internet), so our formula for calculating GNP per capita is (c.gnp * 1000000) / c.population. Taking these two additional filters into account, Example 11.59 shows an example query that returns adventure recommendations for a traveler that wants to go to a developing African country that officially speaks Portuguese or Swazi. We test this query in MySQL Client to be sure we get the expected results in Example 11.59.

```
mysql> SELECT DISTINCT c.name
    -> FROM Countries c
    ->      JOIN CountriesLanguages cl ON c.code = cl.country_code
    -> WHERE continent = 'Africa'
    ->      AND cl.language IN ('Portuguese', 'Swazi') AND cl.official = 'T'
    ->      AND (((c.gnp * 1000000) / c.population) < 10000
    ->      OR c.life_expectancy < 70);
+----------------+
| name           |
+----------------+
| Swaziland      |
| Cape Verde     |
| Guinea-Bissau  |
+----------------+
3 rows in set (0.00 sec)
```

**Example 11.59 SQL query to get adventure recommendations**

## PHP to Retrieve and Display Recommendations

Now that we have an idea of what the recommendations query should look like, we need to build this query dynamically in PHP using user input, execute it, and print out the given results in HTML unordered list. To dynamically build the query we need to get the continent and languages the user has specified. To get the continent we use $_REQUEST["continent"]. To build the list of languages to insert into the query, we can use the PHP implode function to concatenate all the strings in $_REQUEST["languages"] separated by ', '. In order to make the string correct for the IN predicate, we need to concatenate it with a beginning and ending quote as well. Lastly, we add an ORDER BY clause to the query to make the results more easily read by the user.

To perform the query, we use the same MySQL PHP code as in Example 11.54 so we put this common code in its own function called **perform_query** in a file called **adventure_shared.php** (Example 11.63).

Lastly, if there are any results, we will iterate through them dynamically building an unordered list. If there are no results, we will let the user know by displaying a message. The resulting function is shown in Example 11.60.

```php
<?php
function print_countries() {
  $languages = "'" . implode("', '", $_REQUEST["languages"]) . "'";

  $query = "SELECT DISTINCT c.name
            FROM Countries c
            JOIN CountriesLanguages cl ON c.code = cl.country_code
            WHERE c.continent = '" . $_REQUEST["continent"] . "'
              AND cl.language IN ($languages) AND cl.official = 'T'
              AND (((c.gnp * 1000000) / c.population) < 10000
              OR c.life_expectancy < 70)
            ORDER BY c.name";
  $results = perform_query($query);

  if (mysql_num_rows($results) > 0) {
    ?>
    <ul>

    <?php
    while ($row = mysql_fetch_array($results)) {
      ?>
      <li><?= $row["name"] ?></li>
      <?php
    }
    ?>

    </ul>
    <?php
  } else {
    ?>

    <p>Sorry there were no countries matching your preferences.</p>
    <?php
  }
}
?>
```

**Example 11.60 PHP function to print out adventure recommendations**

## 11.5.3    Final File Contents

After all the changes discussed in the preceding sections, we end up with the final four page files shown in Example 11.61 through Example 11.65. These files, plus the **world.jpg** image, comprise the entire finished two-page web site.

```php
<?php
include("top.html");
include("adventure_shared.php");
?>

    <p>Choose characteristics of a developing nation you'd like to visit.</p>

    <form action="adventure_recommendations.php" method="get">
      <div>
        <h2>Which continent and language(s) do you prefer?</h2>

      <select name="continent" size="5">
        <?php
        $query = "SELECT DISTINCT continent FROM Countries ORDER BY continent";
        get_and_print_options($query, "continent");
        ?>
      </select>

      <select name="languages[]" size="5" multiple="multiple">
        <?php
        $query = "SELECT DISTINCT language
                  FROM CountriesLanguages
                  WHERE official = 'T'
                  ORDER BY language";
        get_and_print_options($query, "language");
        ?>
      </select>
    </div>

    <div>
      <input type="submit" value="Submit" />
    </div>
    </form>
  </body>
</html>

<?php
function get_and_print_options($query, $column) {
  $results = perform_query($query);
  while ($row = mysql_fetch_array($results)) {
    $choice = $row[$column];
    ?>
    <option value="<?= $choice ?>"><?= $choice ?></option>
    <?php
  }
}
?>
```

Example 11.61 Final contents of `index.php`

```
<!DOCTYPE html PUBLIC "-//W3C//DTD XHTML 1.1//EN"
"http://www.w3.org/TR/xhtml11/DTD/xhtml11.dtd">
<html xmlns="http://www.w3.org/1999/xhtml">
  <head>
    <title>Developing World Adventure Recommender</title>
    <link href="adventure.css" type="text/css" rel="stylesheet" />
  </head>
  <body>
    <div class="logo">
      <h1>
        Developing <img src="world.jpg" alt="world" /> Adventure Recommender
      </h1>
    </div>
```

Example 11.62 Final content of `top.html`

```php
<?php
function perform_query($query) {
  $db = mysql_connect("webster.cs.washington.edu", "jkmiller", "9v3nTBWiL2eBC")
    or die("Could not connect to database: " . mysql_error());
  mysql_select_db("world")
    or die("Could not select database" . mysql_error());
  $results = mysql_query($query)
    or die("Query (" . $query . ") failed" . mysql_error());
  return $results;
}
?>
```

Example 11.63 Final content of `adventure_shared.php`

```css
body {
  font-family: "Helvetica", sans-serif;
  font-size: 14px;
  margin-left: auto;
  margin-right: auto;
  width: 60%;
}
h1 {
  margin: 0em;
  text-align: center;
}
.logo {
  height: 75px;
  margin-left: auto;
  margin-right: auto;
  width: 80%;
}
.logo img {
  height: 63px;
  vertical-align: middle;
  width: 69px;
}
```

Example 11.64 Final contents of `adventure.css`

```php
<?php
include("top.html");
include("adventure_shared.php");
?>

    <h2>Countries that fit your preferences for your next adventure are:</h2>

    <?php
    print_countries();
    ?>
  </body>
</html>

<?php
function print_countries() {
  $languages = "'" . implode("', '", $_REQUEST["languages"]) . "'";

  $query = "SELECT DISTINCT c.name
            FROM Countries c
            JOIN CountriesLanguages cl ON c.code = cl.country_code
            WHERE c.continent = '" . $_REQUEST["continent"] . "'
                AND cl.language IN ($languages)
                AND cl.official = 'T'
                AND (((c.gnp * 1000000) / c.population) < 10000
                OR c.life_expectancy < 70)
            ORDER BY c.name";
  $results = perform_query($query);

  if (mysql_num_rows($results) > 0) {
    ?>
    <ul>

      <?php
      while ($row = mysql_fetch_array($results)) {
        ?>
        <li><?= $row["name"] ?></li>
        <?php
      }
      ?>

    </ul>
    <?php
  } else {
    ?>

    <p>Sorry there were no countries matching your preferences.</p>
    <?php
  }
}
?>
```

Example 11.65 Final contents of `adventure_recommendations.php`

## Chapter Summary

- Databases are frequently used for applications that heavily rely on data and need concurrency, speed, reliability, and abstraction.
- Relational databases organize data into tables where columns represent attributes of objects and rows represent single objects.
- SQL is a declarative programming language that allows the user to define, manage, and search for data in relational database management systems.
- A SQL statement is made up of clauses. Each clause begins with a SQL keyword.
- The SQL SELECT statement is used to perform queries on a database.
- The SQL WHERE clause is used filter out rows that are affected by SQL statements.
- `mysql_connect`, `mysql_select_db`, `mysql_query`, and **`mysql_fetch_array`** are PHP functions that a web programmer can use to connect to and query a MySQL database from inside a web page.
- Joins are used to make queries that involve multiple tables.
- Database design is the process that decides the schema of a database. During this process, system objects and their attributes are identified, those objects and attributes are mapped into tables, and data types for those attributes are chosen.

## References

- FirstSQL.com SQL tutorial:  http://www.firstsql.com/tutor1.htm
- PHP MySQL manual:  http://www.php.net/mysql
- Wikipedia - SQL:  http://en.wikipedia.org/wiki/SQL
- W3Schools PHP database tutorial:  http://www.w3schools.com/PHP/
- Custom error handling in PHP:  http://php.dzone.com/news/custom-error-handling-php
- PHP error handling:  http://www.w3schools.com/php/php_error.asp
- PHP MySQL functions:  http://www.php.net/manual/en/ref.mysql.php
- SQL for Web Nerds:  http://philip.greenspun.com/sql/
- Tutorials Point, MySQL tutorial:  http://www.tutorialspoint.com/mysql/
- MySQL home page:  http://www.mysql.com/
- MySQL documentation:  http://dev.mysql.com/doc/
- MySQL operators and function reference:
  - http://dev.mysql.com/doc/refman/6.0/en/func-op-summary-ref.html
- MySQL operator precedence:
  - http://dev.mysql.com/doc/refman/6.0/en/operator-precedence.html

# Chapter 12    Web 2.0 and Scriptaculous

## Introduction

The phrase "*Web 2.0*" is a general term that describes a set of technologies and ideas related to creating interactive web sites and applications. Web 2.0 is not any particular technology, product, or language; it is a general concept implying an evolution in thinking about web sites and design. Web 2.0 is made possible by recent advances in browser technology such as JavaScript and Ajax.

This chapter begins with a set of design guidelines for creating sites that adhere to Web 2.0 principles. We also discuss a JavaScript framework called Scriptaculous (available from http://script.aculo.us/) that helps you produce complex visual effects and animations on your pages.

## 12.1 Designing for Web 2.0

**Web 2.0**

A set of ideas and technologies for creating modern interactive web applications.

To a web programmer, the "hard" part of creating a web site likely involves getting the *backend* of a web site working; that is, setting up the database, getting the PHP web services working properly, and writing the code that does much of the heavy-lifting for the web site. The *front-end* element of web programming – such as writing the HTML, CSS, and JavaScript that interfaces with the users – may seem deceptively trivial in comparison. As a result, sometimes web programmers do not take the design aspect of web site creation very seriously.

But the front-end of your web site is crucial: it is the only method through which the user interacts with your site. If your web site is confusing, difficult to use, or even just ugly, visitors will leave your page and all your hard work in the backend will be for naught.

In the era of Web 2.0 web applications, the user experience has never been more important. The proliferation of attractive, easy-to-use web sites has raised the expectations of the modern day web user, and because millions of alternative sites are often just a Google search away, users are not willing to give a site a chance if it doesn't immediately "seem" promising. The study of design in computing is so important that there is an entire field of computer science devoted to the interaction between computers and people, appropriately titled Human-Computer Interaction (HCI).

The importance of design in applications may seem discouraging to developers who do not think themselves very artistic, as some may believe that creating a well-designed web site requires a lot of artistic talent. However, "design" in this case is not so much about aesthetics as it is about user experience. The experience your web site provides to its users is the result of a wide spectrum of factors, from the aesthetics of the page to the organization of content to the usability of controls.

While art is something that is difficult to teach, design is not; there are rules and principles that one can follow to build well-designed applications. In this section we introduce a set of guidelines and tips to help you create attractive, usable web sites.

## Usability and the User

With all this attention placed on user experience, it's important to understand who exactly this "user" is. Although the typical user varies greatly depending on the web site, there are some generalizations that can be made to characterize the majority of web users.

You can think of visitors as being on a feverish search for information, functionality, or products. The visitor quickly scans a page's headers, links, and icons in search for something that remotely looks like it will take them to what they're searching for. They click the first promising link and scan the page. If there is nothing of interest on this new page, the visitor will click the Back button and continue his or her search.

In this rapid and hasty search process, instructions and long passages of text are often ignored. Users want to browse pages efficiently, and reading takes up valuable time. When a user visits your page, its functionality should be immediately clear. The visitor should be able to very quickly determine, "Does this web site have value to me? Can I use it to get what I want?"

Visitors are not going read instructions on a web site; you must design for instant gratification.

- **Summarize:** Users hate to read. Pages should be easy to scan: use headings, lists, bold keywords, and short paragraphs. Write straightforward and informative headings and page titles.
- **Organize:** Your content should be structured to avoid long pages. Break up large articles of text into sub-pages, and provide an overview that explains the content in the separate parts.
- **Write succinctly:** Don't waste words or bloat the page with unnecessary flourishes.
- **Don't be too creative:** A unique look isn't always good. Conventional designs have the advantage of being familiar, thus reducing the time needed to get comfortable with the site.

> **usability**
>
> The measure of how effectively a person can navigate an interface, find information on it, and achieve specific goals.

## Example: Admissions Page

To give an example of usability, let's examine the differences between admission pages for the University of Washington (the authors' alma mater) and Washington State University, UW's rival.

Suppose we are a transfer student from a community college, trying to find what courses will transfer from our community college to these universities. UW's admission page is shown in Figure 12.1. The image is numbered in the order of what catches the eye first.

The first thing we focus on is "Admissions." From there our eye starts moving down the yellow column. We skim the column and infer that it's discussing undergraduate enrollment, and the column ends in a button to "Apply Now." We don't want to apply to UW yet; we just wanted to see what courses would transfer, so we start looking for an option for transfer students. The next column talks about graduate enrollment, which we skip, and then we see a circle for "other options." The list of other options doesn't match what we're looking for, but "Continuing Education" is the closest match, so we click that. This doesn't lead us to what we want, so we have to go back and try again.

Contrast UW's admissions page with WSU's admissions page shown in Figure 12.2. Navigating WSU's admissions page requires very little thinking. The titles are ordered naturally, so the eye flows from the first level heading to the subheading, down the bulleted list. Quickly skimming down this list shows us there's a link called "Transfer information." We click this link, and one of the first links on the page gives us "Transfer Course Equivalencies."

WSU's admission page has a clean, simple design. The colors have a nice contrast, and navigating the page is pleasant. Contrarily, it is a more cognitive process to find information from UW's admissions page. It has a more creative design, but as a result it's more confusing to navigate. It's not clear if the page will give us the information we are seeking, so we have to examine the page elements more carefully. Even when we settle on a link to click, the link takes us to the wrong page.

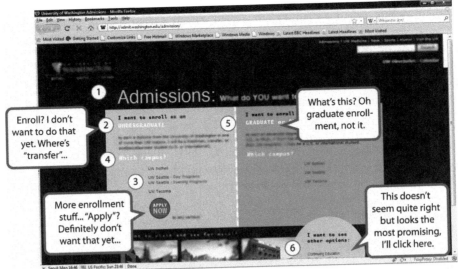

**Figure 12.1 University of Washington Admissions Page**

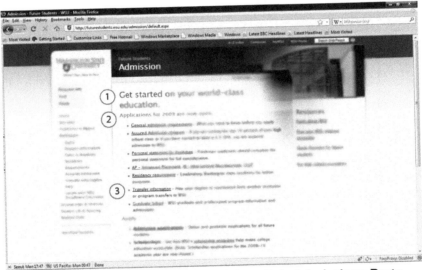

**Figure 12.2 Washington State University's Admissions Page**

From a usability standpoint, WSU is the clear winner over UW in this case. We hope that the usability of the admissions page is not a large factor in a student's college decision!

## 12.1.1    Page Layout

Much of the "feel" of your web site comes from the layout of your pages. A page that is clean, organized, and easy to navigate makes the visitor feel comfortable using your web site. A page that is confusing or chaotic makes the visitor feel impatient and frustrated.

Clutter is a large cause of visual distraction for visitors. Layouts look cluttered when there are too many things trying to draw the user's attention, resulting in a messy, confusing appearance. Haphazardly placed elements, distracting backgrounds, animations, and excessive use of graphics are all signs of clutter. Structure and organization are keys to creating a pleasant user experience.

## Grid-based Layout Design

Designing clean, organized layouts on a completely blank canvas can be difficult. Web pages often consist of several components (e.g. a header, footer, navigation bar, body), and figuring out how to size and place everything while keeping the layout organized is not an easy task.

One strategy is to design your layouts on a grid. Using a grid can help ensure your design stays organized and balanced, as the structure of a grid lends itself to organization. The locations and sizes of different components are also significantly narrowed down from the "blank canvas" approach so layouts can be designed faster. Figure 12.3 shows an example of this technique.

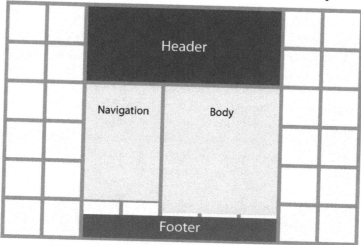

**Figure 12.3 Using a grid for layout design**

The exact size and shape of your grid depends on your preference, though the columns should be evenly spaced and of equal size to each other (without being cut off at the edge). An excellent article discussing the specifics of grid design is listed in the resources.

## Screen Resolution

Screen resolution is another thing to keep in mind when designing a layout. Not every visitor of your site will have the same monitor size, so it is important to think about the layout width and how it looks on other screens. A layout that's too wide could result in ugly horizontal scrollbars. Using fluid layouts (sizes based on percentages and not exact numbers) can help avoid resolution problems.

Some designers don't like fluid layouts because they place difficult limitations on design. The vast majority of users on the web have a screen resolution of 1024x768 or higher, so many feel it is safe to use 1024px as a minimum expected screen width. A popular layout width is around 950px, since browsers need some extra pixels to accommodate the scrollbar.

## Design Inspiration

While web design is not entirely an art, it is still a skill that takes practice to perfect. One of the best ways to learn how to design a usable, visually appealing web site is from the sites that do it right. When you visit a web site with a layout you like, try to figure out what it is about the layout that strikes you as appealing. See how the web site differs from your own design and see how you could incorporate such elements in your own layouts.

Of course, we don't suggest you blatantly rip-off a web site's look and feel, but this technique can help quickly and rapidly improve your skills as a designer. Several web sites exist solely to showcase well-designed web sites, and some of their links can be found in the references.

## 12.1.2    Navigation and Links

Before anyone can use your application, they must be able to find it. Ambiguous or clunky navigation is a common source of frustration for visitors, as witnessed in our example earlier in the chapter. Here we list some commonly dreaded navigation schemes:

- **Frames:** Not only are frames ugly, out of date, and incompliant of W3C standards, they are a classic hallmark of an inexperienced web programmer. The only reason to use frames is when you actually want multiple web pages side by side, where the navigation of one frame is independent of the navigation of another. For example, the online API of several programming languages uses frames to separate function and class names from their documentation.

- **Splash screens:** A splash screen is a page that is shown before the user can access the actual main page of a web site. While there are certain cases where splash screens may be useful or even required by law (such as legal warning before a gambling web page), most of the time they just serve to annoy the visitor.

- **"Creative" navigation systems:** Navigation should be clear and easy to click. Do not try to make a game out of your navigation system. For example, horizontally scrolling layouts (as opposed to the standard vertically scrolling layouts) are inflexible and awkward. It minimizes the ability for users to scan the page and it doesn't take advantage of navigation shortcuts like the Page Down key or the scroll wheel on a mouse.

We have mentioned several times that it is a good idea to follow conventions when designing a web site. But how does a new web developer know what the conventions are?

| web pattern |
| --- |
| A solution to a common software or design problem that is given a name. |

There are groups and individuals who study design trends on the web. In software engineering, a *design pattern* is a solution to a common software problem in a certain context. *Web patterns* are a variant of design patterns that are specific to web sites. Studying web patterns can be a great way to find design solutions that fit the needs of your web site.

### Horizontal Menu

A horizontal menu is a form of main navigation. It is a bar placed at the top of a web page with links to major sections of the site, and it does not change in appearance between different pages.

**Figure 12.4: Horizontal menu on Barnes & Noble website**

It is good to have some indication of what is the currently selected page, and this should not be a clickable link. Links that go nowhere are pointless and misleading to the user.

The biggest drawback of using a horizontal menu is the limited number of items in the menu. Depending on the size of each menu item and the width of the layout, a horizontal menu will likely fit at most 6-8 items. This does not give much flexibility for expansion and requires you to maintain a fairly general information structure.

## Vertical Menu

A vertical menu is a vertical column placed on the side of a web page (usually the left) that serves as the source of main navigation for the page. When a vertical menu is used, the page has been split into at least 2 columns: one for the menu, the other for the rest of the page.

**Figure 12.5: Vertical Menu on Google News**

A vertical menu has some advantages over a horizontal one. It scales well because the navigation grows downward instead of horizontally, so there is not a limitation on the number of menu items. It is also next to the body of the page instead of on top of it, so the body is not pushed down and more body text is visible "above the fold," or in the top of the page that can be viewed without scrolling.

The disadvantages are perhaps obvious. The menu grows downward, so a long list of menu items may not be visible above the fold. If the selected item is below the fold as well, then the menu does not serve as good visual feedback for where the user is currently located.

## Fly-out Menu

A fly-out menu looks like a horizontal or vertical menu, but an additional submenu appears after hovering or clicking on a menu item. The navigation system is good for large web sites with hierarchical structures, and it is especially useful when there is limited space to devote to navigation.

**Figure 12.6: Fly-out menu on Amazon.com**

Fly-out menus also have their drawbacks. Individual items in the submenu may be hard to click if the submenus disappear after mouse out. Having multiple submenus is an especially bad idea because of the difficulty in clicking. Fly-out menus are space-efficient, but they also hide the majority of the navigation. It is important to make it clear that the fly-out menu is indeed a menu.

## Breadcrumbs

Breadcrumbs show a clickable path from the top level of the web site hierarchy to the current page. Breadcrumbs are not usually a form of main navigation, but can add unobtrusive usability to your site. They are a convenient way to let users know exactly where they are.

> **breadcrumbs**
> A series of links to navigate between the current page and higher levels of a site.

Target : Baby : Baby Brands : **Classic Pooh**

**Figure 12.7: Breadcrumbs on Target.com**

The web patterns shown here are just the tip of the iceberg. The web is constantly evolving and new trends appear regularly. For more information, visit the links in the references section.

## Body Links

While main navigation may be the most obvious form of navigation on a web page, links in the body of the page should also be clear and easy to read. A few simple guidelines can improve the usability of body links:

- Users should not have to guess what a link is. Links should be **colored** and should stand out against the body text.
- Don't underline text that's not a link, even if you choose not to underline your links. Don't use text in the same font color as your links unless it's a link.
- Visited links should be in a different, duller color than unvisited links.
- Be wary of using hover effects on a link. A subtle hover effect (such as removing the underline of a link on hover) provides a source of user feedback, but too much styling is distracting. Links should never turn bold on hover, as it shifts the position of the surrounding text.
- Using link titles can be an effective way to give the user more information about where a link takes them before they click.

Avoid using "click here" links and instead use descriptive links that clearly explain where the link takes the user. As mentioned previously, users don't read; they scan. Links stand out and act as keywords in your web page. Link text should be kept short and to the point, not exceeding 4-5 words.

In Figure 12.8, notice what stands out in the three paragraphs. In the first paragraph, you have to search the text surrounding the link to intuit its destination, but in second paragraph you immediately know where the link will take you. The third paragraph isn't as bad as the first, but it looks a bit cluttered and doesn't communicate as well as the second.

| The school year has begun! I am taking a course called Advanced Topics in HCI this quarter. Click **here** to see the website for my course. We have a lot of reading to do before each class, but it's a lot of fun! | The school year has begun! I am taking a course called **Advanced Topics in HCI** this quarter. We have a lot of reading to do before each class, but it's a lot of fun! | The school year has begun! **I am taking a course called Advanced Topics in HCI this quarter**. We have a lot of reading to do before each class, but it's a lot of fun! |
|---|---|---|

**Figure 12.8 Examples of link text**

There's another advantage to using descriptive links. Search engine spiders look at link text when cataloguing pages, and links like "click here" are not helpful for this purpose.

## 12.1.3    Forms and UI Controls

Forms and controls comprise a large part of the way users interact with a web site. Users post comments, sign up for accounts, and send feedback via forms. Controls can be used to increase font sizes, change settings, and manipulate the content of a web page.

## Efficient Forms

Forms are the online version of paperwork. Just as people don't like to fill out paperwork, people don't like to fill out online forms. Users want to be able to post their content or register for accounts quickly and efficiently, and they will get fed up if there's a cumbersome process involved.

- Minimize number of fields required. Don't require anything users don't need to give you.
- Minimize number of non-required fields on forms. If you don't need it, don't ask for it. Long pages of input fields make a form confusing, and it gets hard to determine what is required and what is not. A compromise is to put non-required fields in an "expandable" section: hide them by default, but show them if a user clicks on a button or text to expand the options.
- Group related fields and arrange fields in a logical order. You should also make sure that a user can tab through your form in a logical manner.
- Use default values. Default values give the user an example of what is expected in the form and reduce errors. It also speeds up the process if the user is content with the default values.
- Use the label tag on checkboxes and radio buttons. The checkbox and radio button elements are small and hard to click. Using the label tag greatly increases the clickable area and is a subtle way to improve the usability of a form.
- Use JavaScript to validate prior to submission. It is annoying to have to reenter values after submitting a form. Use the appropriate event handling to let the user know immediately when there are problems with the submission. For example, if a password must be at least 8 characters in length, make use of the onkeyup JavaScript event to tell the user how many characters he or she needs to add until the password is valid.

## Use Proper Input Elements

The built-in HTML input elements are not particularly customizable, so it is important to use them as they're meant to be used.

- **Single Choice:** User is to select exactly one among several choices
  - Checkbox for yes/no, true/false
  - Radio buttons for < 5 options
  - List box for 5-10 options
  - List box or text input for >10 options
    - If there are many options, but not necessarily infinite options, consider making a text input with auto-completion.
- **Multiple Choice:** User is to select multiple options from a list of choices
  - Checkboxes for finite number of options
  - Text box for short lists, textarea for long lists
    - Consider giving your form a flexible number of text boxes by using JavaScript to add additional or remove excess text boxes.

## Exploring Widgets

Sometimes your input needs do not fit the limited selection of the built-in HTML input elements. For example, if you want to ask your user to select a color, it would be nice to provide a color palette from which the user can select. Unfortunately, HTML does not provide color palettes as a built-in input device. One way to solve this problem is to create your own input devices using a combination of HTML and JavaScript, called widgets. You could create the color palette input device we described by creating a grid of small divs with appropriate onclick handlers attached to each.

But it's not always easy to create the widget you need. Dates are another piece of data that you may want to collect but are not well represented in HTML. Users want to be able to choose from a calendar view of available dates. Implementing a date widget is a messy task that is prone to bugs.

Instead of creating your own widgets from scratch, you may consider using a free Widgets toolkit such as Dijit. Using a lightweight widget library can increase the usability of your forms without taking up too much development time. A link to the Dijit web site can be found in the references.

## 12.1.4   Accessibility

Accessibility is an often overlooked issue when designing sites and applications for the web. Users with visual impairments or other disabilities will want to use your web site, too. The W3C has published Web Content Accessibility Guidelines on how to make web pages accessible for all users, and the link to this is included in the references. We will not attempt to recreate the W3C list, but we will mention some of the more important issues here.

### Accessible HTML

Many devices used by those with physical disabilities (e.g. screen readers) ignore the CSS and JavaScript of a web page and rely solely on your HTML to provide the content of page. This doesn't mean that you should avoid using CSS and JavaScript, but you should ensure that your HTML is written well enough so it could stand alone from these visual and interactive enhancements. Here are some tips on writing accessible HTML:

- Organize your HTML so it can be read without a stylesheet and write W3C valid HTML. This is good web programming practice anyway.
- Always use `alt` tags on images. Audio files and video should have `alt` descriptions as well.
- Do not rely on images, CSS, or JavaScript to convey large or crucial portions of information.
- For tables, use `th` elements for headers and `td` for data. Write tables with headers on the leftmost column instead of headers on the top of the column so that tables are readable from markup. If this is not possible, provide an alternative version of the information in the table.

### Legibility

Illegible font styling is frustrating for all users, with or without vision impairments. Even if the page as a whole is visually pleasing, usability should be the greatest priority.

- Have a clear contrast between fonts and backgrounds; contrast is more important than color.
- Words in mixed case are more legible than WORDS IN UPPERCASE.
- On a monitor, Serif fonts are less legible than Sans Serif fonts due to the limitations in font rendering. When using smaller text, you should use Sans Serif fonts.
- Fonts should be set at a large enough size to be read comfortably; body text should usually be at least 10pt font.

## 12.2   Scriptaculous

Adding polish to your web site might seem like a lot of work for relatively little gain. Suppose you're writing a simple web application to maintain a user's grocery list. When the user adds an item to the list, you'd like the item to fade in gradually instead of appearing instantly. You'd also like to allow users to reorganize the list by dragging each item to its new location and to edit a list item by double-clicking on it. These small enhancements would take a lot of code and testing to get working correctly, which takes away from time used to write and maintain the core functionality of your app.

Luckily, there are several free JavaScript libraries that specialize in visual effects and other UI enhancements. In this section we will use a library called Scriptaculous to enhance the appearance and usability of our web apps.

Scriptaculous is built upon the Prototype library and can be used for the following purposes:

- Visual effects (animation, fade in/out, highlighting, etc.)
- Drag-and-drop behavior
- Ajax widgets
  - Auto-complete text fields (predictive drop-down list similar to Google Suggest)
  - In-place editors (clickable text that you can edit and send to a server)
- DOM builder and other enhancements
- Unit testing and other utilities

In this text, we will not cover the DOM builder or the testing utilities of Scriptaculous, but the documentation regarding these topics is listed in the references of this chapter.

### Using Scriptaculous

In order to use the Scriptaculous library, you must download and link in the library from the Scriptaculous web site, as we did with Prototype. Because Scriptaculous is built upon the Prototype library, the Prototype library must be linked to the page before the Scriptaculous library. Last comes your own .js file, which depends on both of these libraries.

Example 12.1 shows how you would link in a JavaScript file called `script.js` that uses the Scriptaculous library.

```
<script src="prototype.js" type="text/JavaScript"></script>
<script src="scriptaculous.js" type="text/JavaScript"></script>
<script src="script.js" type="text/JavaScript"></script>
```

**Example 12.1 Linking to Scriptaculous**

It is also worth mentioning that Scriptaculous is a relatively new library, and is therefore not as robust as the Prototype library. Sometimes you may find parts of Scriptaculous to be buggy or you may run into some strange behavior. What's worse is the API for Scriptaculous is incomplete, so some of the functionality is completely undocumented. Nonetheless, Scriptaculous is an easy-to-use library to provide lots of great functionality to web sites.

### 12.2.1   Visual Effects

Scriptaculous provides a variety of simple-to-use animated effects for block-level elements. To use an effect on an element, call the effect's corresponding method on the element. The syntax to add an effect to an element is as follows:

```
$(element or id).effectName();
```

**Example 12.2 Syntax template for starting a Scriptaculous effect**

Example 12.3 makes the doughboy shake left and right when you click on it. Note that the method call to `shake()` must be on the div and not the img because an img is not a block-level element. The effect works best when there is a CSS style indicating the height and a width of the element; by default, a block element's width is the length of the page, and you may get horizontal scrollbars if the animation goes off-screen when the effect is in place.

```
<h1>Tickle the Doughboy!</h1>
<div id="doughboy">
  <img src="doughboy.jpg" alt="dough boy" />
</div>
```

```
window.onload = function() {
  $("doughboy").onclick = tickle;
};

function tickle() {
  $("doughboy").shake();
}
```

**Example 12.3 A Scriptaculous effect**

Notice that the object was referenced via the Prototype $ function. Prototype's $ function is not simply a shortcut for `document.getElementById`. By calling $, you are also extending the object with additional functionality that does not exist in normal JavaScript objects, and this allows you to call Scriptaculous methods directly on the elements. In certain browsers (such as Firefox), Prototype is able to add methods to the native JavaScript language so you do not have to use $, but certain browsers (namely Internet Explorer) will not let external files extend JavaScript's native objects. Therefore, to ensure your method calls will work for all browsers, you should always obtain the element through $ (or $$).

```
// this code always works
var boy = $("doughboy");
boy.shake();

// this code always works
var items = $$("img");
for(var i = 0; i < items.length; i++) {
  items[i].shake();
}

// this code does NOT always work
var girl = document.getElementById("doughgirl");
girl.shake();
```

**Example 12.4 $ and $$ vs. getElementById for effects**

Scriptaculous visual effects fall into three general categories: showing, hiding, and calling attention. The "showing" methods will make the element visible if it was previously set to `display:`

none. Many of the most common effects are listed in the following tables, though we encourage you to view the animations on the Scriptaculous demo page to see the effects in action.

| Method Name | Behavior |
|---|---|
| `appear()` | fades in the element |
| `blindDown()` | the elements "rolls" down |
| `grow()` | grows from the center |
| `slideDown()` | slides in from the bottom |

Table 12.1 Scriptaculous entrance effects

| Method Name | Behavior |
|---|---|
| `blindUp()` | rolls up from the bottom |
| `dropOut()` | drops off the page |
| `fade()` | fades out element |
| `fold()` | rolls up element, then squishes left |
| `puff()` | expands element off page |
| `shrink()` | shrinks to center |
| `slideUp()` | rolls up top-first |
| `squish()` | shrinks to upper-left corner |
| `switchOff()` | flickers then shrinks to middle |

Table 12.2 Scriptaculous exit effects

| Method Name | Behavior |
|---|---|
| `pulsate()` | flashes in and out |
| `shake()` | shakes back and forth |

Table 12.3 Scriptaculous attention effects

There is an annoying quirk when dealing with the visible effects that make elements appear. In Example 12.5, there is a joke and a punch line. Instead of showing the punch line right away, we'd like the answer to "fade in" when you click the button. We initially hide the punch line by setting the `punchline` element to `display: none` in our CSS because we don't want the joke's punch line to show before the button click, as shown in Example 12.5.

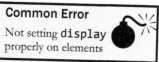

**Common Error**

Not setting `display` properly on elements

```
<p>
  What do you get if you cross an apple with a Christmas tree?
  <button id="answerbutton">Show</button>
</p>
<p id="punchline">
  A pineapple!
</p>
```

```
#punchline {
  display: none;
}
```

```
window.onload = function() {
  $("answerbutton").onclick = showPunchline;
};

function showPunchline() {
  $("punchline").appear();
}
```

Example 12.5 Common error with hidden elements and effects

If you tried running that code, though, the punch line wouldn't appear. The problem is that Scriptaculous requires you to set the **display: none** in an *inline* style attribute of the element for effects like Appear to work; setting the **display** property in a CSS stylesheet will not work. Example 12.6 shows the corrected HTML. You could also leave out the **punchline** element from the HTML entirely and use JavaScript to create and attach the element to the DOM; while this would avoid inline styles, it may become cumbersome if there are a lot of elements in need of hiding.

```
<p>
  What do you get if you cross an apple with a Christmas tree?
  <button id="answer_button">Show</button>
</p>
<p id="punchline" style="display: none;">
  A pineapple!
</p>
```

Example 12.6 Corrected hidden element code

Another way to add a visual effect to an object is by constructing an **Effect** object and passing either a reference to the element or the element's **id**:

```
new Effect.name(element or id);
```

Example 12.7 Syntax template for alternate effect syntax

This syntax for invoking a visual effect does the same thing as the method calls described earlier; in fact, each method call is actually a shortcut for the code above. This syntax to construct **Effect** objects to set off a visual effect is somewhat unintuitive, though, since a visual effect is a behavior, and usually behaviors are represented in computer programming as method calls. Because we feel the method call syntax more clearly shows the programmer's intent, this is the syntax we will use in the text.

The visual effects in the preceding tables are all actually composed of six core effects: `Effect.Highlight`, `Effect.Morph`, `Effect.Move`, `Effect.Opacity`, `Effect.Scale`, and `Effect.Parallel`. These effects have no shortcut methods and can only be invoked by constructing an `Effect` object.

## Effect Options and Events

The default settings for a visual effect may not perfectly fit your needs. Effects can be customized by passing additional options as a parameter to the method call. Example 12.8 shows the syntax:

```
$(element or id).name(
  {
    option: value,
    ...
    option: value
  }
);
```

**Example 12.8 Syntax template for passing options to an effect**

Here we see the method takes as a parameter an anonymous object storing a collection of option/value pairs, an idiom seen first in the Ajax chapter with `Ajax.Request`.

There are several options available to the visual effects, some that are unique to the effect itself. Table 12.4 below lists several of the more commonly used options and their descriptions.

| Option Name | Type | Description |
| --- | --- | --- |
| duration | Number | Duration of the effect, in seconds |
| from | Number | Sets how transparent the image is at the beginning of the effect, from 0.0 and 1.0 |
| to | Number | Sets how transparent the image is at the end of the effect, from 0.0 and 1.0 |
| delay | Number | Seconds to wait before the effect begins |

**Table 12.4 Common effect options**

In addition to options, you can set various event methods or "callbacks" to be triggered at certain points of the effect's animations. The possible callbacks are listed in Table 12.5. Each of these methods takes a reference to the `Effect` object that fired off the event as a parameter. The `Effect` object has several useful properties and methods, some of which are listed in Table 12.6.

| Method Name | Description |
| --- | --- |
| beforeStart | Called before effect begins |
| beforeUpdate | Called on each iteration of the effect's animation, before it draws a frame |
| afterUpdate | Called on each iteration of the effect's animation, after it has drawn a frame |
| afterFinish | Called after the effect finishes |

**Table 12.5 Effect events**

| Property Name | Description |
|---|---|
| `element` | Element the effect is applied to. |
| `options` | Options given to the effect. |
| `startOn,finishOn` | Start and finish times |

| Method Name | Description |
|---|---|
| `cancel()` | Stop the effect |

**Table 12.6 Properties and methods of effect events**

As an example, let's revisit the exercise at the beginning of the chapter involving the doughboy. We'll make a few simple modifications to the example: the duration of the shaking should be sped up to 0.3 seconds (the default is 0.5 seconds) and after the effect has finished, the **h1** heading should read, "Hoo-hoo!" Example 12.9 shows a naïve approach to the code.

```
<h1 id="title">Tickle the Doughboy!</h1>
<div id="doughboy">
  <img src="doughboy.jpg" alt="dough boy" />
</div>
```

```
window.onload = function() {
  $("doughboy").onclick = tickle;
};

function tickle() {
  $("doughboy").shake({
    duration: 0.3
  });
  $("title").innerHTML = "Hoo-hoo!";
}
```

**Example 12.9 Incorrect attempt to show text after an effect**

If you ran this code, you should see that this doesn't quite work: the text content changes immediately after the effect *starts*, not after it stops. Scriptaculous visual effects are run asynchronously, so the flow of control returns back to the caller immediately after the animation starts. This allows you to continue executing code while the animation is running. If we want to run some special code when the animation stops, we have to put that code in a callback method for **afterFinish**. Example 12.10 shows the corrected procedure.

```
window.onload = function() {
  $("doughboy").onclick = tickle;
};

function tickle() {
  $("doughboy").shake({
    duration: 0.3,
    afterFinish: cheer
  });
}

function cheer(effect) {
  $("title").innerHTML = "Hoo-hoo!";
}
```

Example 12.10 Showing text after an effect

### Toggling Effects

You can also toggle an element's visibility by constructing the `Effect.toggle` object. The first parameter of the constructor is its only required parameter, the reference or `id` of an element. The optional second parameter indicates what type of animation to use when toggling (Appear/Fade, Slide, Blind) and the optional third parameter is the anonymous options object.

```
new Effect.toggle(element or id, ['appear'|'slide'|'blind'], [options]);
```
Example 12.11 Syntax template for toggling effects

## 12.2.2   Drag-and-Drop

In addition to animations, Scriptaculous offers simple ways to implement drag-and-drop behaviors. The library's drag-and-drop capabilities are encapsulated in two classes, `Draggable` and its counterpart `Droppable`. `Sortable` is another useful Scriptaculous class built on top of these two classes involving rearrangeable lists.

### Draggable Elements

Scriptaculous considers an element to be "draggable" if you can move it by clicking on it, holding down, and dragging it to a new location. You can make an element draggable by using the now-familiar Scriptaculous idiom: construct a `Draggable` object using the `id` of or reference to the element as a parameter.

```
new Draggable(element or id, [options]);
```
Example 12.12 Syntax template for constructing Draggable element

Like with visual effects, the `Draggable` constructor can take a variety of options and callback methods via an anonymous object with option/value pairs. A portion of these options are listed in Table 12.7. Note that `revert` and `snap` can be assigned either literal values or callback methods, and the behavior slightly differs depending on the type of value passed.

| Option Name | Type | Description |
|---|---|---|
| handle | Element or string | Reference or id of the element you click on to "drag" the Draggable object; defaults to the Draggable element itself. |
| revert | boolean, string, or function | If set to true, the element returns to its original position when drag ends; if false, element always stays where it is dragged. If set to "failure", the element stays where it is dragged only if it's moved into a Droppable area; otherwise it returns to its original position. The Droppable area must have onDrop defined. Can also be a callback function. |
| snap | boolean, integer, or function | If set to false, no snapping occurs. If set to an integer, uses that integer as a minimum delta value for horizontal and vertical snapping. If set to a function, uses its return value for snapping. |
| zindex | integer | Z-index of the draggable item; defaults to 1000. |
| constraint | string | If set to "horizontal" or "vertical", the drag will be constrained to take place only horizontally or vertically. |
| ghosting | boolean | If true, clones the element and drags the clone, leaving the original in place until the clone is dropped. Defaults to false. |
| starteffect, endeffect | Effect | The visual effect used when the element starts or stops being dragged. Defaults to Effect.Opacity. |
| scroll | Element | Specifies an element to scroll when you get to the boundary; off by default. For example, set to window if you want the browser to scroll when you drag to the edge of the window. |

**Table 12.7 Draggable options**

### Droppable Target Elements

The meaning of "droppable" in Scriptaculous doesn't quite match up with its linguistic connotation: Droppable elements are not "things that can be dropped", but they are areas that react to Draggable objects that are dropped on them. You can think of Droppable elements as drop-off areas or landing pads for Draggable items. When a Draggable element is dragged to a Droppable area, the area will either "accept" the object or it will ignore it; various settings for both the Draggable and Droppable elements define what happens to the object upon acceptance or failure.

The syntax for Droppable is also a bit different from what we've seen in the past. To declare an area Droppable, add the element to the global Droppables object.

```
Droppables.add(element or id, [options]);
```

**Example 12.13 Syntax template for creating Droppable element**

This too can accept the standard anonymous object of options as a parameter, and a selection of options and callbacks is listed in Table 12.8.

| Option Name | Type | Description |
|---|---|---|
| accept | string or array | The Droppable element will only accept Draggable elements that have one of these class(es) listed. |
| hoverclass | string | The Droppable element will have this additional CSS class when an accepted Draggable is hovered over it. <br> **Note:** You *must* define the CSS rule as **#id.classname** for this to work. Simply putting **.classname** may not work. |
| greedy | boolean | If **true**, doesn't look for other Droppables that are under the Draggable |

| Callback Name | Description |
|---|---|
| onHover | Called when a Draggable is moved over the Droppable and the Droppable would accept it. Accepts the Draggable and Droppable as parameters. |
| onDrop | Called when a Draggable is released over the Droppable and the Droppable accepts it. Takes the Draggable element, the Droppable element and the event as parameters. onDrop needs to be defined if Droppable is to accept Draggable objects with **revert** of **"failure"**. |

Table 12.8 Droppable options and callbacks

Draggable and Droppable elements should always have defined heights and widths. Therefore most Draggable elements are block-level elements, but **img** elements have implicitly defined heights and widths and can also be used.

### Example Program: Paper Dolls

One fun application of drag-and-drop is a paper doll page. The clothes and accessories of the paper doll are the Draggable elements (images with transparent backgrounds), and the doll itself (another image) is the Droppable area. Our desired page appearance is shown in Figure 12.9.

Figure 12.9 Paper dolls expected appearance

First let's write the HTML code. The page is organized into two sections: the image of the doll and the images of the clothes. We make `div`s for each section, label them with `id`s, and fill the `div`s with their respective images. To give the page more organization, we add CSS styles to float the doll to the left and allow the clothes to wrap around it. We give a gray border and background to the doll as well as 20px of margin for aesthetics. (We would have to worry about z-indexes of the clothes and accessories, but we purposely chose non-overlapping accessories to avoid this.)

```
<div id="dollbody">
  <img src="body.png" alt="doll body"/>
</div>
<div id="dollcloset">
  <img src="blackhair.png" alt="black hair" />
  <img src="blondehair.png" alt="blonde hair" /> <br />
  <img src="bluedress.png" alt="blue dress" />
  <img src="reddress.png" alt="red dress" />
  <img src="casual.png" alt="casual" /> <br />
  <img src="shoes.png" alt="shoes" />
</div>
```

```
#dollbody {
  background-color: #FCFCFC;
  border: solid 2px gray;
  float: left;
  height: 616px;   /* dimensions of image */
  margin: 20px;
  width: 388px;
}
```

**Example 12.14 Paper dolls HTML/CSS code**

Now we write and attach our JavaScript code. Let's start by making the clothes draggable. To do so, use the `$$` function to grab all the `img` elements in the `dollcloset` area, then construct a new `Draggable` object for each of the `img` elements.

```
window.onload = function() {
  var clothes = $$("#dollcloset img");
  for (var i = 0; i < clothes.length; i++) {
    new Draggable(clothes[i]);
  }
};
```

**Example 12.15 Making clothes draggable**

With those few lines of code, much of the functionality of our program is already complete: you can drag and drop the clothes onto the doll. Hooray!

But before we celebrate, let's make a couple of improvements to our program. One subtle bug with the code we've just written becomes apparent if the doll buys too many articles of clothing. Let's say there are 50 different dresses in our doll's closet. If we want our doll to try on the 50th dress, we have to scroll down to the bottom of page, leaving the doll off-screen at the top. But when we try to drag the 50th dress back up to the doll, we get stuck: the window does not scroll when we get to a boundary. To fix this, we must set the `scroll` option to `window`. (Note we are referring to the window DOM object, not a string setting.)

```
window.onload = function() {
  var clothes = $$("#dollcloset img");
  for (var i = 0; i < clothes.length; i++) {
    new Draggable(clothes[i], {
      scroll: window
    });
  }
};
```

**Example 12.16 Revised draggable code**

Another enhancement we'd like to make improves the organization of the clothes. Right now, we can move the clothing wherever we'd like, quickly cluttering the screen and making the clothes selection difficult to see. We can improve this by restricting the movement of the **Draggable** objects: if the **Draggable** element is moved to the **Droppable** area (i.e. the doll's body), the element should be freely moveable; otherwise, it should return back to where it came from.

This movement behavior can be obtained by the setting the **revert** option on the **Draggable** elements. When **revert** is set to **true**, the element returns back to its original position after dragging. We don't want the elements to always revert, though – instead we set revert to **"failure"**, which is a special string that tells Scriptaculous to let the element stay where it's been dragged only if it's been dropped into and accepted by a **Droppable** area.

Therefore we must also register the **dollbody** element as a **Droppable** area. We do this by calling the **add** method from the **Droppables** object and passing the **dollbody** id to the method.

Finally, we must also define the **onDrop** callback method for the **Droppable**. This is a silly Scriptaculous quirk: the **Droppable** won't accept any **Draggable** objects unless the **Droppable**'s **onDrop** callback method is defined. This appears to be a bug and will hopefully be fixed in future versions of Scriptaculous. For now, we simply set **onDrop** to a blank, anonymous function.

```
window.onload = function() {
  var clothes = $$("#dollcloset img");
  for (var i = 0; i < clothes.length; i++) {
    new Draggable(clothes[i], {
      scroll: window,
      revert: "failure"
    });
  }

  Droppables.add("dollbody", {
    onDrop: function() {}        // hack so that Droppables accept Draggables
  });
};
```

**Example 12.17 Final paper dolls code**

## Sortable Lists

The Scriptaculous library also provides the means to make a list "sortable" by dragging and dropping list items into any order. The behavior is implemented in the **Sortable** class, and you can give a list this behavior by calling **Sortable**'s **create** method. This method takes as a parameter the parent element of the sortable items, e.g. a reference to the **ul** or **ol** of the list. (Technically, **Sortable** can be used to make *any* container's child elements sortable by drag-and-drop, but in this book we will discuss lists only. More information on other types of sortable containers can be found in the Scriptaculous documentation in the references.)

```
Sortable.create(element or id, [options]);
```

**Example 12.18 Syntax template for creating a sortable list**

`Sortable.create` can also be given an anonymous object of options, some of which are listed in Table 12.9 below. Internally, Scriptaculous uses the `Draggable` and `Droppables` objects to implement `Sortable` behavior, so some of the options are very similar to ones we have seen previously in those sections.

| Option Name | Type | Description |
|---|---|---|
| only | string or array | The list will only sort `li`s with at least one of these classes. (Similar to `Droppables`' `accept` option) |
| constraint | string | Restricts movement of list items to `"horizontal"` or `"vertical"`. Identical to the option for `Draggable`. |
| containment | boolean | When true, enables dragging and dropping between different `Sortable` lists. |
| ghosting | boolean | If set to `true`, dragged elements of the `Sortable` will be cloned and appear as "ghost", i.e. a representation of their original element, instead of directly dragging the original element. See below for more details. Defaults to `false`. |
| dropOnEmpty | boolean | If set to `true`, the `Sortable` container will be made into a `Droppable` that can receive a `Draggable` (as according to the containment rules) as a child element when there are no more elements inside. Defaults to `false`. |
| scroll | Element | Specifies an element to scroll when you get to the boundary; off by default. Identical option to `Draggable`. |

| Callback Name | Description |
|---|---|
| onChange | Called whenever the sort order changes while dragging. When dragging from one `Sortable` to another, the callback is called once on each `Sortable`. Accepts the affected element as its parameter. |
| onUpdate | Called when the drag ends and the `Sortable`'s order is changed in any way. When dragging from one `Sortable` to another, the callback is called once on each `Sortable`. Accepts the container as its parameter. Note that the `id` attributes of the elements contained in the `Sortable` must be named as described in the chapter. |

**Table 12.9 Sortable options and callbacks**

Sortable lists come in handy for a wide range of applications, especially for forms and user-generated content. For example, the following code allows a user to order their prediction for football team standings at the end of the season. We put an `id` on the list we want to sort, then we call `Sortable.create` on that list.

```
<h1>NFC North Division Standings: Make your prediction</h1>
<ol id="teams">
  <li>Green Bay Packers</li>
  <li>Chicago Bears</li>
  <li>Minnesota Vikings</li>
  <li>Detroit Lions</li>
</ol>
```

```
window.onload = function() {
  Sortable.create("teams");
};
```

**Example 12.19 Creating a sortable list**

However, the sortable lists do not automatically "remember" the rearranged order of the list if the page is revisited. In the example, the football teams revert back to the original order when the page is refreshed. Saving the newly reordered list must be implemented on your own through a post to a server via Ajax or form submission.

Two callback methods that may be helpful in this task are **Sortable**'s **onChange** and **onUpdate**, described in Table 12.9. For example, to save the order of the list to the server every time a user makes a rearrangement, you can make an Ajax set request to post the revised order of the list to the server in the list's **onUpdate** handler. Then when the page is refreshed, you can retrieve the saved values via an Ajax GET request and populate the list through the DOM. Some starter code for this is shown in Example 12.20, but the details of the code are left as an exercise to the reader.

```
var WEB_SERVICE = 'http://www.example.com/service.php';

window.onload = function() {
  // ajax request to get saved order of list
  new Ajax.Request(WEB_SERVICE, {
    method: "get",
    onSuccess: loadList
  });
};

function loadList(ajax) {
  // process ajax.responseText, order elements in list ...

  Sortable.create("teams", {
    onUpdate: saveList
  });
}

function saveList() {
  // make an Ajax request to save the list ...
}
```

**Example 12.20 Sortable list Ajax code**

There is a very important thing to know about using **onUpdate**: the **onUpdate** event *will not work* unless each **li** has an **id** of the form **listID_index**, e.g. "teams_0". The updated HTML code is shown in Example 12.21.

```
<h1>NFC North Division Standings: Make your prediction</h1>
<ol id="teams">
  <li id="teams_0">Green Bay Packers</li>
  <li id="teams_1">Chicago Bears</li>

  <li id="teams_2">Minnesota Vikings</li>
  <li id="teams_3">Detroit Lions</li>
</ol>
```

**Example 12.21 Sortable list updated HTML code**

Often you'd like to make sortable lists that can grow and shrink through the addition and removal of li elements via DOM manipulations. If you try to implement this using what we've learned so far, you may run into some strange errors: some list items may no longer become draggable, or some items won't let you drag other items around them. This is due to yet another Scriptaculous quirk: every time you modify a sortable list or its elements in the DOM, you must call Sortable.create on the list again to maintain the correct sorting behavior.

Occasionally you may want to deactivate sorting on a list entirely. This can be accomplished by calling Sortable.destroy on the list.

```
Sortable.destroy(element or id);
```

**Example 12.22 Syntax template for deactivating sorting**

### 12.2.3 Controls and Sounds

Controls are the last component of the Scriptaculous library we will examine. Scriptaculous supplies a handful of slick UI enhancements for input controls. Scriptaculous is not primarily a widget library, however, and we suggest you investigate a library such as Dijit if you're in need of additional interesting controls to your web site.

#### Auto-Complete

Auto-complete is a feature for text input boxes that suggests possible "completions" for the values being typed in the box. The input box guesses what words the user might be trying to write and provides a dynamically changing drop-down menu of suggestions that the user may use to complete the field. Auto-complete is a great way to enhance UI: it helps reduce errors in typing and helps the user fill in the form or search box efficiently.

Scriptaculous offers a way to make a text box that auto-completes based on prefix strings. There are two ways it can fetch the auto-completion options: through a local array or through an Ajax request to a database, but we will only cover the local array in this text. To enable auto-completion for a text box, create an Autocompleter.Local object using the format shown in Example 12.23.

```
new Autocompleter.Local(
    element or id of text box,
    element or id of div,
    array of choices,
    {
        options
    }
);
```

**Example 12.23 Syntax template for auto-completing text box**

You must create an empty div that will store the auto-completion matches. Scriptaculous will insert a ul of possible matches into this div. To control its formatting, you must use CSS to style the list to make it look more presentable. The user can select items by pressing the up and down arrows, and each selected item is given a class of "selected" which you can style in your CSS to give a highlighting effect. Example 12.24 shows auto-completion for a list of bands from the 70s.

```
<input id="bands70s" size="40" type="text" />
<div id="bandlistarea"></div>
```

```
window.onload = function() {
  new Autocompleter.Local(
    "bands70s",
    "bandlistarea",
    ["ABBA", "AC/DC", "Aerosmith", "America", "Bay City Rollers", ...],
    {}
  );
};
```

Example 12.24 Auto-completing text box

### In-Place Editor

Scriptaculous provides functionality for in-place editing of text items; for example, when the user clicks text in a div, it turns into a text input box for changing that text. To make an element in-place editable, create a new Ajax.InPlaceEditor object using the syntax shown in Example 12.25.

```
new Ajax.InPlaceEditor(
  element,
  url,
  {
    options
  }
);
```

Example 12.25 Syntax template for in-place editable element

Scriptaculous will POST the changed content to the URL listed with a parameter called value when a user edits the item. There are several options described in the Scriptaculous documentation.

### Sound

Playing sounds can be cumbersome because it requires you to understand HTML tags for multimedia, and because it involves browser plugins for playing media types. Scriptaculous has a helpful Sound object to make this easier. It can play WAV, MP3, MIDI, and many other formats, limited only by the user's browser and what types it supports. You have to upload your multimedia files to the web; it can't play files on your local hard drive. Table 12.10 lists the methods.

| Method Name | Description |
|---|---|
| Sound.play("**url**"); | plays a sound or music file |
| Sound.disable(); | stops future sounds from playing (doesn't stop a sound currently playing) |
| Sound.enable(); | re-enables sound to be playable (after a call to Sound.disable()) |

Table 12.10 Sound playing methods

## Chapter Summary

- Web 2.0 is a set of ideas, technologies, and guidelines for creating modern web applications.
- A clean design and layout is important for a web site. Consider using a grid to sketch out a rough template of your layout before coding it, and always consider that some users have higher or lower screen sizes and resolutions than your own.
- Navigation between pages of your site should be clear and simple, with "breadcrumb" links from any page to the others and with descriptive link text.
- Forms should use minimal sets of controls to reduce user confusion/frustration. You should choose the proper controls for each UI choice.
- Accessibility involves creating sites that everyone can use, regardless of their computer, disabilities, etc. Having a well laid-out, legible web site with alternate text in place of any images and multimedia helps make your site more accessible.
- Scriptaculous is a JavaScript library built on top of Prototype that allows you to add animations, drag-and-drop, and other useful effects to your pages.
- The visual effects in Scriptaculous are added as methods to each DOM element object, such as the `shake` and `fade` methods. Calling these on an element produces the effect. Each effect method can accept a set of options as a parameter, represented as an anonymous object.
- Scriptaculous implements its drag-and-drop functionality through a type called `Draggable` for objects that can be dragged and `Droppable` for targets where objects can be dropped.
- Scriptaculous allows you to rearrange the contents of lists by making the list into a `Sortable` object. The rearranged order can also be backed up to a server using Ajax.
- Scriptaculous allows you to create an auto-completing list that examines the text the user types and suggests longer strings that start with this text. The auto-completer can get its list of candidate strings from a server using Ajax.

## References

- Wikipedia - Web 2.0:      http://en.wikipedia.org/wiki/Web_2.0
- Grid Design Basics:
  - http://dev.opera.com/articles/view/grid-design-basics-grids-for-web-page-1/
- Smashing Magazine, Design Reference:   http://www.smashingmagazine.com/
- 10 Principles of Effective Web Design:
  - http://www.smashingmagazine.com/2008/01/31/10-principles-of-effective-web-design/
- Patterns in Interaction Design:    http://www.welie.com/
- W3C content accessibility guidelines:   http://www.w3.org/TR/WAI-WEBCONTENT/
- Designing accessible tables:
  - http://www.netmechanic.com/news/vol4/accessibility_no16.htm
- Scriptaculous home page:    http://script.aculo.us/
- Scriptaculous wiki (API):    http://wiki.github.com/madrobby/scriptaculous
- Scriptaculous tutorial:    http://www.tutorialspoint.com/script.aculo.us/
- Dijit Toolkit:    http://dojotoolkit.org/developer/dijit

# Chapter 13   Going Live: Creating/Launching a Website

By guest author, Alex Loddengaard
Professional software developer and
University of Washington Computer Science graduate

# Introduction

This book has discussed the process one goes through to build a web site from the ground up. At this point you possess most of the skills needed to build a web site, but there is still much to be learned about how to put the web site in production on the Internet for the world to use. In web-speak this process is called "going live".

This chapter will discuss many different areas of knowledge that a site owner needs to be aware of when launching a site. These areas of knowledge include driving traffic to your web site, testing and maintaining your code, tracking your site's growth, and finding ways to make money.

The great thing about the internet is that the gap between personal projects and money-making, professional web sites is small. Many popular web sites, such as YouTube, Yahoo!, and Facebook, started with a young team trying to make something fun and useful. Those sites have grown to be some of the most visited on the entire web, employing hundreds or thousands of employees. This chapter is an attempt to show you the true beauty of the internet: right now you are in a great position to achieve the skills needed to make a useful, popular web site. This chapter also augments the skills you have learned so far with those you'll need to launch, grow, and maintain a web site.

| | |
|---|---|
| **13.1** | **Refine Your Idea** |
| 13.1.1 | Talk to Your Users |
| 13.1.2 | Look at Your Competition |
| 13.1.3 | Decide on Technology |
| 13.1.4 | Encouragement |
| | |
| **13.2** | **Get Your Site on the Internet** |
| 13.2.1 | Running a Web Server |
| 13.2.2 | Web Hosting |
| 13.2.3 | Debugging/Testing a Live Site |
| | |
| **13.3** | **Driving Traffic to Your Web Site** |
| 13.3.1 | Google AdWords |
| 13.3.2 | Viral Marketing Features |
| 13.3.3 | Search Engine Optimization |
| 13.3.4 | PageRank |
| 13.3.5 | Google Analytics |
| | |
| **13.4** | **Making Money** |
| 13.4.1 | Google AdSense |
| 13.4.2 | Referral Programs |
| 13.4.3 | Banner Advertisements |
| 13.4.4 | Other Options |
| 13.4.5 | Fund Your Site |
| | |
| **13.5** | **Legal Issues** |
| 13.5.1 | Intellectual Property |
| 13.5.2 | Legal Liabilities |
| 13.5.3 | Security Issues |
| 13.5.4 | Conclusion |

Hi, I'm Alex Loddengaard, the guest author of this chapter. I created a web site called Cellarspot, a social network for wine lovers, in Spring 2007. I created, launched, and maintained the site with classmates while studying computer science at the University of Washington.

Throughout this chapter you will see boxes such as this one; these boxes tell my Cellarspot story. The intention is to give you a taste of what we did with Cellarspot and about the decision-making process we went through about technology, features, and everything else.

I was once in your shoes, learning about the web and the technologies that power it. I took what I had learned about PHP, MySQL, etc, and used it to build Cellarspot. This chapter is a result of my learning about what's involved with launching, maintaining, and growing a real web site. These boxes tell my Cellarspot story, a story that started where you are now. You are entirely capable of one day being able to tell perhaps an even more successful story, and this chapter will try its best to help you along the way. I hope this chapter motivates and teaches you how to create something real, something that others can use and benefit from. You're much closer to achieving this than you may think.

Thanks for listening.

## 13.1 Refine Your Idea

The purpose of a web site is to solve a problem. Take YouTube, for example. Without You-Tube, none of us would be able to easily find that silly video of the guy dancing and lip-syncing from behind his computer. YouTube solves a problem: It fulfills people's desire to find videos. The purpose of refining your web site idea is to guarantee that your web site will solve a problem, which in turn will increase your chances of people using and benefiting from your web site. Let's face it, making a web site is always cool, but making web sites that people use is much more satisfying.

### 13.1.1 Talk to Your Users

The first step to refine a web site idea is always to talk to potential users, or users who at some point might use your web site. When ideas are first concocted, they are generally not well thought-out and lack the specifics necessary to create a web site that people will actually use. You, the inventor of an idea, are only one person. Unless you speak with others, you will have no way to validate that the idea you have will actually solve a problem.

The key to talking to users is asking good questions. By asking your potential users good questions, you are starting a specific dialog that, once synthesized, will serve as a basis to evaluate the problems your site will solve. Consider the following questions when speaking to potential users:

1. Do you think my web site would be useful?
2. How could I improve my web site to better cater to your needs?
3. Do you use any other web sites similar to my web site, and if so, would you prefer to use my web site or the other web site? Why or why not?
4. What factors would most motivate you to return to my web site? Good information? An aesthetic design? Desire to be part of a community? Lots of functionality?
5. Do you know of anyone that would use the site, and how do their needs differ from yours?

Make sure to speak to more than one potential user. The more conversations you have, the more diverse your understanding will be. It is also a good idea to approach potential users with a site prototype that you can demo. Prototypes can provide concreteness in a dialog, making it more effective.

My father is absolutely nuts over wine. He has been collecting wine for many years now; he even has a large refrigerated wine cellar in his house. I interviewed my father many times when refining my ideas around Cellarspot. I also had him organize a wine dinner with friends, which gave me a great opportunity to hear each of their individual opinions. I asked them questions about what mediums they use to discuss wine. I also asked them how willing they would be to insert information about their entire collections of wine into Cellarspot. From these interviews I learned more about the older wine-loving male demographic, which constitutes a large portion of Cellarspot's user base. Looking back, I should have also interviewed other demographics such as younger users.

Once you have spoken to a few different potential users, you must start to synthesize all of their feedback into one cohesive idea. A good approach to doing this is to define specific *use cases*, which are general actions that a user will perform while using your web site. With use cases defined, you can start proposing web site features to satisfy each use case. Let's look at YouTube, for example. YouTube's web site offers lots of features such as searching, categorizing, and browsing videos, to let users discover new videos and find familiar ones. These example features – searching, categorizing, and browsing – each satisfy a high-level use case. Table 13.1 lists a few YouTube use cases, along with some features that satisfy them.

**use case**

A description of a high-level action that a user might perform when using your site.

| Use Case | Satisfying Feature |
|---|---|
| Find a familiar video | Search, video categorization |
| Discover new videos | Related videos, response videos, top-rated videos, most-viewed videos |
| Get involved with the community | Video uploading, friends, channel subscriptions |

Table 13.1 YouTube use cases and their satisfying features

Use cases and features lay the groundwork for all web sites, whether they are formally defined or not. With well-thought-out, well-defined use cases and features created with the feedback from potential users in mind, the chances of web site success are much greater than they would be otherwise.

> Some example use cases that we considered in Cellarspot are: users will want to share tasting experiences with their friends; users will want to remember what they have tasted; users will want to inventory their wine collections. I believe we were successful in creating a list of good use cases that, if executed correctly, would solve a true problem. However, I do not believe we built the right features to satisfy these use cases.
>
> Defining good use cases is the first step. However, the next important step is creating features that satisfy those use cases. One of the features we created to facilitate taste experience sharing was a blog, or a pseudo-journal. Blogging is very prevalent on the internet these days, and at the time when we created the blog feature, we knew nothing about blogging. We ended up creating a terrible excuse for a blog, which nearly none of our users used. Prior to considering a blog, we should have done more research about blogs in order to better address the use case that it was attempting to solve.

## 13.1.2 Look at Your Competition

Many web developers regard competition as a potential threat, which is not necessarily wrong. After all, your competition is stealing your users and money! However, your competition is already one step ahead of you. They have already seen the ways in which their users use their web site, and they have already begun to think about how to improve their web site.

Competition can be a threat, but it should also be a source for ideas. While refining your idea, look closely at your competition to see what they do well and how they could improve. Try to speak to their users to get a better sense of what is good and what could be improved. The practice of comparing yourself to your competition will help you better understand your idea and how it fits with the users in the particular space, or industry, that you and your competition are involved in.

Cloning a competitor's web site is probably a bad idea (if not illegal), but implementing features that are similar is generally a good idea. Often users in a particular space, such as social networks, video web sites, etc., get comfortable with certain features and expect others' web sites to have them. For example, try to name a social network that does not have a messaging feature. All social networks have this feature because users expect it. If you are entering a space with at least one big competitor, then you should try and determine what the key features are that your site must also have.

You can also examine a competitor's web site to get ideas for design and code. It is easy to view the code of any given web page, simply by right-clicking on the page and clicking "View Source." Viewing the source of a web page can help you learn how certain features or tricks are done. But do not copy/paste source code from one page to yours. This may violate copyright laws, which could put you in legal trouble. We will discuss copyright law in more detail later.

Competitors should not be taken lightly. They should be monitored, analyzed, and thought about when creating the idea for a site. They can help you, but they should not be the sole purpose behind a feature or focus of your site. They should be included in the debate that goes on either in your own head or amongst your teammates when deciding on features.

> The two largest competitors to Cellarspot are Cellartracker and Corkd. Taking a quick glance at each of these two web sites tells you two things: Cellartracker is plain and Corkd is rich and beautiful. A deeper use of each of these web sites reveals other differences, such as the detail given to users to describe wines that they have tasted. We analyzed these web sites to understand why their users enjoyed using them. We were worried about Corkd and its elegant and useful design; we were confident we could outperform Cellartracker. In hindsight, we should have realized that the Cellartracker's large user base was a good indication that they were doing many things right.

## 13.1.3    Decide on Technology

Once you have refined your web site idea and have a better sense of the problem you're going to try to solve and the features you're going to build, the next logical step is to decide on the technology to use. Though this may seem like an obvious decision, deciding on technology can be more complex. Some types of technology allow you to develop a web site very rapidly or simply, while others may help you develop your web site in a very flexible or expandable way. All of these ideas – speed, simplicity, maintainability, and expandability – should be considered when deciding on technology. *Expandable code* is code that can be easily expanded to perform other tasks and features. Similarly, a *maintainable* web site is one that is easy to keep running, debug, and modify in minor ways as needed. Nearly all sites have small bugs here and there, and if yours is maintainable, then those bugs will be easier to discover and fix than they would be otherwise.

> **maintainable code**
>
> Code that makes bug fixing, and feature changing easier at times after you have already launched the first version of your web site.
>
> **expandable code**
>
> Code that makes feature addition easy at times after you have already launched the first version of your web site.

Many new web programmers begin by learning PHP, but PHP may not be the best language to use for every project. Other technologies called *rapid application development (RAD) frameworks* such as Django, Ruby on Rails, and CakePHP can automatically generate code for you, making your job easier and quicker. These frameworks allow you to develop maintainable, expandable code quickly, but they do not give you as much control over your code as you would have designing a site from scratch with PHP. They are worth learning in greater detail, but a review of them requires an entirely separate book. Rapid development frameworks exist to make your job easier, but hand-coded web sites can work just as well. Table 13.2 shows a comparison of several server-side web technologies.

> **rapid development (RAD) framework**
>
> A technology that does a lot of work for you by generating code and providing common features.

> Cellarspot was implemented in JSP, using the Spring framework and Hibernate persistence layer. I personally regret using JSP, because too much of our programming time was spent writing code that a rapid development framework would have generated for us. We chose JSP because we were all proficient in Java. However, after working through two versions of Cellarspot, both written in JSP, I have felt the pain of not using a rapid development framework. My current preference for a rapid development framework is Django, because I love Python, and I find it intuitive and easy to use.

| Web Technology | Pros | Cons |
|---|---|---|
| PHP | Fast and very widely used | Encourages non-maintainable and non-expandable code |
| CakePHP | Rapid development compared to plain PHP | Not as intuitive and clean as Ruby on Rails or Django |
| JSP (Java) | Based on Java | Usually requires lots of code |
| Ruby on Rails | Rapid development; widely used | Reinvents a lot of traditional web practices that do not necessarily need to be reinvented. Not as intuitive as Django |
| .NET | Any Microsoft languages (C++, C#, Visual Basic) can be used | Usually requires lots of code to be written; requires IIS web server |
| Django (Python) | Rapid development; intuitive | Somewhat immature, not as many features as Ruby on Rails |

Table 13.2 Server-side technologies and their tradeoffs

There are other tradeoffs that one should consider when deciding on technology. For example, MySQL, the database that you have learned in this book, is great for most web sites. However, certain web sites, in particular web sites that use maps and geo-coded (latitude and longitude) coordinates, benefit much more by using PostgreSQL, a competitor of MySQL. Microsoft SQL Server, SQLite, and Oracle are also very widely used database implementations. Each database implementation does certain things better, and it is important to understand their pros and cons when deciding what to use. Table 13.3 discusses the pros and cons of various database implementations.

| Database Software | Pros | Cons |
|---|---|---|
| Microsoft SQL Server | Good at optimizing large queries | Expensive; must run on Windows |
| MySQL | Free; widely used; fast for single-table queries | Slow for complex queries/operations |
| Oracle | Reliable, good for data analysis | Expensive and complicated |
| PostgreSQL | Free; good at optimizing complicated queries and other operations | Complicated to get running |
| SQLite | Free; simple; fast for reading data | Slow for writes; dangerous for sites with many insert/update operations |

Table 13.3 Database implementations and their tradeoffs

We used MySQL for Cellarspot, because our database schema was relatively simple. All of us were also already familiar with MySQL. MySQL worked out fine for Cellarspot, because the site is relatively simple, and the amount of traffic we see is relatively small. In most cases, MySQL is a great database choice for its simplicity.

In addition to software tradeoffs, one should also consider the learning curve associated with learning new technologies. In order to give competing databases or rapid development frameworks a full evaluation, someone will have to install and try out each of the choices. This can be a long process, and if your web site has to be developed very quickly, the best way to decide on new technology may be to choose technology that is already familiar.

You will also need to make decisions about what web browsers you want your site to support. Certain web sites (such as sites that target Mac users) do not support Internet Explorer because it does not exist for recent versions of Mac OS X. Similarly, some web sites such as Facebook need to support all browsers, including mobile browsers on devices such as the iPhone. Your browser compatibility should be based on your user base. If you are building a general web site, then you will most likely have to support Internet Explorer. As of this writing, most IE users use version 6, 7 or now 8. (Just be glad that Internet Explorer 5 is no longer widely used!) According to hitslink.com, Internet Explorer still constitutes 71% of all browser usage across the world. Firefox constitutes nearly 20%, Safari constitutes 6.5%, and the remaining percentage is split across a number of less common browsers such as Google Chrome and Opera.

> Cellarspot chose to support both Internet Explorer 6 and 7, because an overwhelming majority of older men (the majority of the Cellarspot user base) use IE. Cellarspot also had to support Firefox and Safari, because these two browsers are most commonly used by younger, more internet-savvy wine lovers. We had to bear the brunt by supporting so many browsers, but our work paid off. About half of our users use IE, and none complained of browser-specific bugs.

In conclusion, there are many tradeoffs between frameworks and pieces of software, and these tradeoffs should be considered when determining the technology to use. Learning curves should be considered, along with expandability, maintainability, speed to develop, simplicity, and compatibility.

## 13.1.4 Encouragement

The truth is that the distance between a single person's personal project and a widely-used money-making web site is not large. This is the true beauty of the web: that anyone of any level of experience can create a web site that other people use and benefit from. You have seen this happen with large web sites such as Facebook and YouTube. They both started off small, perhaps as personal projects, and they have since developed into gigantic, famous, world-wide businesses. This truth is the driving reason behind many programmers' love for the web, and it is a truth that you should accept and exploit. You have the knowledge and ability to make something great, just as others in your position have done before you. Dream big, and execute effectively. Even if you create a failed web site, then you will make up for it with gained experience and knowledge.

> Cellarspot failed to generate lots of traffic and money, but it is not a failed web site or a failed learning experience. I cannot begin to explain the significance that Cellarspot has played in my computer science career thus far. Cellarspot has been brought up in nearly all of my technical interviews, and it manages to impress nearly all of my interviewers, despite its inability to solve the problem that we hoped it would solve. Most importantly, Cellarspot taught me about the process one must go through when creating a web site. I would not be writing this chapter without the experience I gained from Cellarspot. I do not regret the many, many hours I spent working on Cellarspot; the experience I gained and the knowledge I acquired could not have been achieved from a book or lecture. Cellarspot was a real world experience, and it taught me how I can change my practices in the future to increase my probability of creating a successful web site. With each "failure" comes new perspectives and new insights that make all other future attempts more probable for success. As the ancient Chinese proverb goes, "The gem cannot be polished without friction, nor man perfected without trials."

## 13.2 Get Your Site on the Internet

Building your web site is the natural next step after refining your idea. However, given that this entire book thus far has been about building web sites, this chapter will continue with the step following building: launching your site and making it accessible to the world, or at least to the Internet.

### 13.2.1 Running a Web Server

Thus far you have learned how to accept information from the client in the form of query variables, and similarly you have written HTML, JavaScript, and CSS that the client's web browser understands. This simple interface -- accepting variables and writing text -- is made possible by web server software. Web server software is a program that waits for an HTTP request from a client and sends that request to your web application. Finally, the web server then takes your web page's HTML, JavaScript, and CSS output and sends it back to the client. Though this seems rather simple, web servers in practice, such as Apache HTTP and Microsoft IIS, are insanely complicated.

> **data center**
>
> A room or building that is filled with computers, power backups, and cooling supplies, with a very fast connection to the internet.

The most common place a web server is run is on a server in a distant *data center*, a building full of servers and computers and a fast internet connection. However, if while developing and testing your web site, you use a server to serve your web site, you will have to make code changes, upload these changes to the server via a transfer protocol such as FTP or SSH, and refresh the page to see your change. For this reason, developing and testing on a server is rather cumbersome. A much more efficient solution to developing and testing a web site is to run a web server on your own personal computer. Even though web servers are meant to be run on servers in datacenters, they can be run on your person computer, which makes applying code changes much more simple and quick.

> When we were developing Cellarspot, we were all able to run the web site from our desktops and laptops. Once we all agreed that what was running on our local computers was sufficiently stable and ready for the internet, we deployed our software to a real web server in a data center.

Unfortunately, installing a web server is not as easy as just installing Apache. Apache by itself is capable of serving static content such as HTML, CSS, and image files, but in order to run PHP or query MySQL, special software packages need to be installed alongside the web server. Fortunately, hordes of web developers have installed Apache, PHP, and MySQL together, so installers exist that can install and configure everything automatically. Surprisingly enough, Mac OS 10.5 (Leopard) comes installed with Apache and PHP, only requiring MySQL to be installed. Refer to the following links to learn how to install Apache, PHP, and MySQL on either Windows or Mac:

Lean more about installing Apache, PHP, and MySQL from the links below:

- Windows:    http://www.wampserver.com/en/
- Mac OS X:    http://www.mamp.info/en/index.php
- Linux:    http://www.howtoforge.com/ubuntu_debian_lamp_server

### 13.2.2 Web Hosting

Running your own web server on your personal computer is great for developing and testing your web site. However, this setup will most likely not suffice for a web site that is publicly available. If you plan to use your personal computer to serve your public web site, then your computer must remain turned on at all times, which is impractical. Users would not be able to access your site if your computer were turned off.

Fortunately, many different web hosts offer hosting services that provide a web server for you on a server in a datacenter. Many of these web hosts are very cheap; rates can start as low as $3.00 per month for access to a web server, PHP, and MySQL. Web hosts come in many different flavors, but they all accomplish the same goal: to allow web site owners without their own servers and datacenters to run public sites.

> **web host**
>
> A company that provides its clients with a web server on a server in a data center, making it cheaper and easier for a site owner to host their web site.

The first, simplest type of hosting is referred to as simply *web hosting*. A web host will host many different web sites on a single server, allowing the host to charge less per web site, but forcing the server to do more work. You connect to the server using SSH and upload your files into a particular directory on the server, which maps to some URL on the public internet. Using web hosts is relatively cheap, but if your web site traffic increases to a certain threshold, your host will not be able to reliably serve your web site. Given that many different web site owners are hosted from the same server, web hosts typically have to limit the technologies their customers are allowed to use. Typically certain web hosts will only provide one specific server-side web technology, such as PHP, Ruby on Rails, etc. When choosing a web host, make sure they provide the technology that you are interested in using. Certain technologies may cost more to host than others. For example, JSP hosting is typically more expensive than Python and PHP hosting.

Another form of hosting is known as *virtual private server* or *VPS* hosting. A VPS is essentially a virtual server, or a VPS instance, that is run alongside other VPS instances on the same physical server. A single physical server can have many VPS instances installed, where each VPS is essentially its own server. It follows that VPS hosting is more power-

> **virtual private server**
>
> A virtual server that runs alongside other virtual servers on the same physical server.

ful in that web site owners have total control over what technology they can use, because they have total control over their VPS instance. However, because VPS hosts have many VPS instances on a single server, if your web site ever became very popular, your host would not be able to reliably serve your web site. VPS hosting is also on the order of four times as expensive as standard web hosting.

A much newer form of hosting called *cloud hosting* has recently become popular, where web applications are hosted from a "cloud" of computers. The two leaders in this type of hosting are Google's App Engine and Amazon's Elastic Compute Cloud (EC2). The idea behind this type of hosting is that you can host a web site for any number of users. Web sites with both large and small traffic can be hosted without

> **cloud hosting**
>
> A new type of hosting, which serves web sites from a cloud of computers, allowing web sites to be reliable with large amounts of traffic growth.

drops in reliability, and the host will automatically handle large increases in traffic for you. The idea is that a "cloud" of computers is serving your web site. When your web site traffic is small, maybe only one computer is serving your web site, but when your web site traffic is large, maybe hundreds of computers are serving your web site. Though cloud and VPS hosting are very different, each solves the problem of web site reliability when an infrequently visited web site is visited much more frequently. The cost of cloud hosting is typically somewhere between a basic web host and a VPS host.

The last, most common type of hosting among professional businesses is known as collocation. *Collocation* is the service one purchases when they own their own rack-mounted servers. A rack-mounted server is a special server that is very thin and that can be installed on a rack, which houses many of these special servers. A photo of a rack-mounted server can be seen in Figure 13.1.

> **collocation**
>
> A type of hosting which involves installing a rack-mounted server in a data center, where it has backup power, air conditioning, and a fast connection to the internet.

**Figure 13.1 Rack-mounted server that can be collocated**

Collocating a rack-mounted server means installing a server in a data center that is managed by a collocation host. Once installed in the data center, the server is given backup power in case of power outages, along with a fast internet connection. Collocation is by far the most customizable solution, but it is also the most expensive. Collocation costs start at around $100 per month, and can go as high as many tens of thousands of dollars per month depending on the number of servers.

You should choose hosting based on your site's amount of traffic and the technology your site uses. Table 13.4 does a side-by-side comparison of all the hosting options from this section.

| Hosting Type | Pros | Cons |
| --- | --- | --- |
| Standard Web Host (Dreamhost.com, InMotion.com) | Cheap; simple; easy | Cannot handle large traffic; only certain technologies |
| Virtual Private Server (VPS) (Slicehost.com, Rackspace.com) | Cheap; customizable; has any technology you need | Cannot handle large amounts of traffic |
| "Cloud" Hosting (Google App Engine, Amazon EC2) | Cheap; can handle small and large traffic | May support only limited choice of web technologies |
| Collocation Host (adtaq.com, Rackspace.com) | Customizable; can handle small and large traffic | Expensive; requires you to configure the server(s) |

**Table 13.4 Web hosting options**

Cellarspot was hosted on a powerful Dell rack-mount server and collocated in Seattle. We chose this hosting thinking that we would see lots of traffic right away, and at the time cloud hosting was not very popular. We did not recognize that most web sites grow slowly, and that choosing collocation right away is economically risky. We learned a lot about Linux server administration by collocating a rack-mounted server, but we spent much more money than we otherwise would have. The server cost upwards of $2000, and the collocation service cost around $100 per month. Given these figures, Cellarspot cost us around $3200 for the first year. Fortunately for us, we managed to collect around $100 in revenues for the first year, giving us an overall net loss of $3100. (Ouch!) This section will later discuss means for making money. In hindsight, we should have chosen a basic web host to start, and upgraded to a collocated rack-mount as our traffic increased.

Web hosting provides you with space on a server and a connection to the internet, but web hosting does not always include a domain name, which is a web site name that ends with .com, .net, etc. In order to register a domain name to allow your web site to be accessed like all other web sites, you have to also sign up with a registrar and register a domain name. Nearly all web hosting companies, such as Dreamhost, Slicehost, etc, offer both web hosting services and domain registration services. In fact, they usually make it very easy to sign up for each of these services at the same time. When signing up for a web host, be sure to also register a domain name with them if you don't have one already.

> **domain name**
>
> A name that is superseded by ".com," ".net," ".edu," etc. Domain names are registered with domain name registrars, which are often web hosts as well.

## 13.2.3   Debugging and Testing a Live Web Site

In the motion picture *Spider-man*, Peter Parker's uncle Ben said, "With great power comes great responsibility." This advice applies when running a web site. When making a web site for a homework assignment or just for fun, it's generally acceptable to have little problems with the site. But when you are running a real site, problems can be a drastic deterrent, depending on their severity. For this reason, special measures should always be put in place to help you understand when your web site has a problem. These measures should also make debugging and understanding the problem as easy as possible. This section discusses mechanisms for debugging and testing a live web site.

### Logging

The first and simplest approach that you should put in place to make debugging problems easier is *logging*. All widely used programming languages such as Python, Java, C++, PHP, etc., have tools and libraries to make logging easier for developers. A *log file* is a text file to which a web site, or any program for that matter, can append messages. These messages describe what the program is doing at a certain time. For example, log messages can contain information about when a certain database row was inserted, or when a certain operation was performed for a user. Log messages can be anything that you want them to be, so it's important to choose log messages that will be helpful for debugging purposes when a problem is discovered.

> **log file**
>
> A file that contains an execution log for a given program, where each message in the log describes what the program is doing at a certain time.

Java's most common logging tool is the Apache Commons log4j library, and Python's most common logging tool is the built-in logging module. PHP, like Python, has built-in support for logging via a few functions such as **error_log**. On top of logging for your web site, your web server and database will also create their own logs, which may be useful to you for certain problems. Usually, in Linux systems, web server and database logs are found in /var/log. If this directory does not appear to have information about your web server or database, then take a look at their respective configuration files. Usually Linux configuration files can be found in /etc.

```
127.0.0.1 - - [25/Jan/2009:12:57:51 -0800] "GET /show_ads.js HTTP/1.1" 404 216
[Sun Jan 25 12:57:51 2009] [error] [client 127.0.0.1] File does not exist:
/pagead, referer: http://speeddemosarchive.com/KungFu.html
```

**13.1 Apache log example output**

## Error and Exception Handling

**Security Note**

Don't display error messages with code details on your site; attackers can use this information to better target your web server.

While developing your web site, you probably became familiar with errors and exceptions that were created because of bad code. When working on a site in progress, it's useful to have the site display any error messages directly on the page so you can see them and quickly fix them. But in a live web site, you want to hide these errors from users' eyes. Partly this is to maintain professionalism, because exception messages confuse or frustrate users. Another reason is because giving a malicious user a lot of information about a site crash can create a security risk or give an attacker information to use against your site.

So you don't want every user to see detailed error messages when your site fails, but you still want to expose these errors to yourself (the developer) so you can find and fix them. All popular web technologies such as PHP, Python, JSP, etc, allow you to do this. To learn more, do a web search for error and exception handling for the technology that you are using. The most common implementation of error and exception handling is to display a plain error message to users and to send an email with the full error message to the maintainers of your web site.

## Automated Testing

**cron job (service)**

Cron jobs are Linux's way of automatically executing a program every so often, while services are Window's way of doing the exact same thing.

One last measure that can be put in place to help debug and guarantee web site nirvana (that is, zero problems) is to setup recurring testing programs to analyze your database and look for problems and inconsistencies. These recurring programs are called *cron jobs* in Linux and *services* in Windows. You can configure these programs to run as often as you would like. For example, you can run certain programs every minute, others every hour, and some every week, month, or year. Cron jobs and services can be used to run a test program that analyzes your database. Below are some common things you can check in a data validation program:

1. Empty fields that should be required (for example, user emails, etc)
2. Special characters that may not display correctly on your site (<, >, &, ", etc.)
3. Bad relationships (for example, if your user table references a nonexistent second table)

Depending on your web site, you may even be able to have your cron job or service correct issues that it finds. For example, it would be relatively simple to create a script that looked for bad characters (<, >, etc.) and change them to HTML-safe equivalents (&lt;, &gt;, etc.).

We did not have any notifications or automated testing in place in Cellarspot, and for this reason we had a few bugs that persisted for a long time without notice. For example, one user was able to hack our web site by inserting custom JavaScript. This hack is known as an XSS attack. Another user was not able to register for an account because his last name contained a hyphen (-), which our web site considered a bad character. Another user wasn't able to register for an account because his zip code started with a zero (0), which made Cellarspot think their zip code was four characters long, and hence invalid. Had we not known these users personally, we would have never known that these issues existed. We needed to have put automated tests in place to verify our database, along with a notification framework that told us about errors that users came across while using our web site.

## Browser Compatibility

Another key piece of debugging and testing your web site is browser compatibility, and unfortunately, ensuring your web site works in different browsers can be a painstaking process. That said, there are ways to distribute this manual process to make your life a little easier. Most web sites provide an easy way for their users to submit problems, issues, and feature requests. A great trick when accepting this information is to automatically include the user's browser information, which can be fetched by JavaScript and by most server-side languages such as JSP, PHP, etc. Providing this information will allow you to try and reproduce the problem that the user has encountered, which may not necessarily be a problem in other browsers. Browser compatibility is not a very intellectual aspect of web programming, but efforts must be made to ensure your web site works in all necessary browsers. You should not only do your own testing, but also allow your users to tell you about problems. Make sure you have a bug reporting mechanism on your web site and that you test extensively for cross-browser compatibility both with JavaScript and CSS.

> Fortunately for Cellarspot, we did lots of testing in Internet Explorer 6 and 7, and we were never aware of an issue related to browser compatibility. However, we did not have a user-submitted issues tool in place, so there could exist a few small browser incompatibilities that are still around today.

## Site Environments: Staging and Production

Once a web site goes live and new changes are being introduced, the source code that powers that web site should be run in two different locations called *environments*. A *staging environment* is a version of your web site that is only accessible to the site developers; it gives the developers a place to test new changes to the web site. A *production environment* is the place storing the actual live web site. The reason for having two different environments is to ensure that certain changes work in staging before they are applied to the production web site.

> **environment**
>
> A context that a web site runs in. Typically most professional web sites have a staging environment for development purposes and a production environment, which houses their live web site.

It is never a good idea to make live changes to a production web site, because you will run the risk of making a mistake and causing your site to create an error or perform strangely for the user. Your staging and production environments will differ only slightly; one common difference between the two environments is database configuration. Staging environments can be configured to use an entirely different database than production: a testing database that can be tampered with. Your staging environment can be on your local computer, but generally you want your staging environment to be as similar to your production environment as possible. For this reason, most web sites have two different hosting plans with the same host: one for staging, and the other for production; typically the only difference between the staging and production environments are configuration settings. The important aspect of having two different hosting plans is to have two isolated environments that are mirror copies of one another.

Launching a web site is like freeing a caged animal into the wild. Without certain precautions in place, you may launch a web site with errors and problems that wouldn't look good in the eyes of your users. The most common way to avoid having problems with your web site is to create error email alerts, deploy testing programs that guarantee data validity, write comprehensive log messages, and allow for user-submitted feedback. Without monitoring, your web site will have a higher potential to be hacked or to appear to be lower quality, which can deter users. Testing and debugging efforts are an up-front cost that will make maintaining your web site and furthering its excellence much, much easier. Accept the cost up front; you will be glad you did when you are further down the road of web site maintenance.

## 13.3   Driving Traffic to Your Web Site

By this time you have seen how to build and launch a web site. Next is possibly the most difficult challenge in web site success: getting people to use it. This section will talk about strategies to drive traffic to your web site.

### 13.3.1   Google AdWords

**Google AdWords**

A service that allows you to purchase keywords, whereby an advertisement you specify is displayed when your keywords are searched for.

Though you may not have heard of Google AdWords, you have certainly seen them in action. Google AdWords are the sponsored advertisements you see on Google's search results page. AdWords allow web site owners to purchase specific keywords. By purchasing these keywords, Google will guarantee that your ad is displayed a certain percentage of the time when these keywords are searched. Figure 13.2 shows examples of AdWords displaying ads on Google search results.

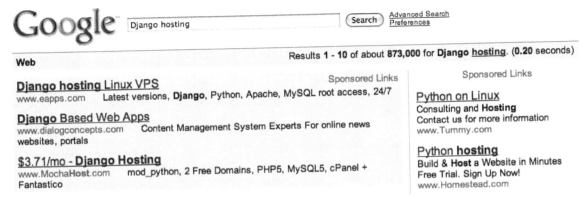

**Figure 13.2 Google AdWords**

**Cost Per Click (CPC)**

A form of advertising where the advertiser pays each time their ad is clicked.

In the figure, the web sites displayed in the "Sponsored Links" sections, both directly under the search box and in the right sidebar, purchased "Django hosting" AdWords. If a Google user clicks on any of these links, the web site whose link was clicked will be charged a small amount. This model of advertising is called *cost per click*, or CPC. Google uses a complex algorithm to determine how much each ad click costs, but most clicks generally cost between $.25 and $1.50. For most keywords, there exist more advertisers than spots for advertisements, which means that your ad is not guaranteed to be displayed each time a certain keyword is searched. Google will cycle advertisements depending on the frequency at which each advertisement has been shown. Google also allows its customers to spread their clicks out as much as they would like. For example, customers can purchase $100 worth of clicks for a keyword and request that the $100 be spent as quickly as possible, or be spread out over a timeframe that the customer can specify.

Google AdWords advertisements can also be displayed on web sites that run AdSense (another Google product that we'll discuss in more detail later). This allows AdWords to display advertisements on non-Google web sites. Google first started selling ads on their search results page, but once they started selling ads on others' web sites by means of the AdSense product, their business took off and revenues skyrocketed. AdWords makes up most of Google's total revenues because it is such a useful product for advertisers.

Google AdWords are an easy way to get your web site name and description in front of people's eyes, but AdWords cost money and may not be as cost effective as other mediums of marketing discussed later in this section. However, AdWords is the most cost effective way to advertise on the internet. They allow an advertiser to display ads to users who are interested in them, and they are paid for on a pay-per-click basis, which means advertisers only pay when a user visits their web site.

> We never purchased any keywords with Google AdWords for Cellarspot, because we didn't have much money to spend on advertising. AdWords may have driven traffic to our web site, but this new traffic may not have necessarily been helpful. I make this claim because we had a problem with converting new visitors to registered users. That is, most new Cellarspot visitors did not sign up for an account. Purchasing AdWords would have increased our traffic, but an increase in traffic probably wouldn't have meant an increase in account registration. For Cellarspot, like most social networks, account registration is more important than new visitor traffic, because registered users are the users who will be spending the most time on social networks. Cellarspot did, however, have Google AdSense, which will be discussed in more detail later.

As of this writing, Marty Stepp, one of the authors of this book, has had AdWords keywords purchased for his name. This means that if you search Google for "marty stepp," you'll notice a sponsored ad with some interesting text. Figure 13.3 shows the ad. You'll notice that the text was not written by Marty; it turns out that one of his friends purchased this ad for him as a joke.

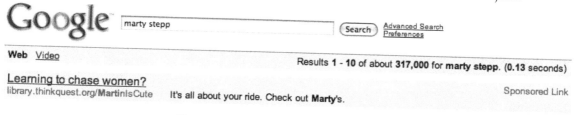

**Figure 13.3 Marty Stepp's AdWords**

To sign up for Google AdWords, visit http://adwords.google.com/. Other search engines such as Live Search and Yahoo! provide similar services as well.

## 13.3.2    Viral Marketing

A free and very effective mechanism for generating traffic is to create certain features that will help your web site spread virally. *Viral marketing* is marketing that spreads by word of mouth. Friends will naturally want to tell their friends about a web site that they have gotten involved with, and you should make that communication as easy and seamless as possible. Though the word "viral" usually has a negative connotation, it is a cost effective way to increase your web site's traffic. Included below are a few examples of viral features that are commonly found in modern web sites.

> **viral marketing**
>
> Allows a user to get friends involved in advertising a web site.

### Invites

Invites usually come in the flavor of a single "Invite" link, which prompts the user for a list of their friends' email addresses. Upon submission, invitations are sent to each email address that was included. The email contains information about the web site, the user who created the invite, and a call to action to create an account. Invites can also help bootstrap a user's activity on the web site. For example, if an invitee signs up for a social network, the chances are good that they will be friends with the inviter. For this reason, registrations from invites can create friend relationships automatically. Invites are a great way to get new users registered on your web site.

Invites can also be incentivized. That is, if your web site provides some sort of credit or score for its users, then users who invite their friends could receive free credits or increased scores. Giving users incentives to invite their friends will increase the number of invitations that your users send, which increases your user base and traffic. Netflix is a good example of an incentivized invite system. Users who invite their friends to use Netflix get discounts on their Netflix services, which encourages users to invite friends.

## Address Book Searching

When a user first signs up with a web site, the chances are good that some of their friends are already on the web site. For this reason, many web sites allow their users to upload an address book or even provide login information to their email accounts, which the web site will use to look for friends that are already signed up. This feature helps to bootstrap a new user's activity on the web site by automatically creating friend relationships. Address book searching is a great way to get your users started using your web site.

## Sharing

All web sites have content or material that can be consumed by a user. This consumable material can come in the form of funny images, videos, political analysis, etc. The chances are good that some consumers will want to inform their friends of the material that they have recently consumed. A sharing feature would allow users to send emails to their friends, where each sent email would contain the consumable material, along with some information about your web site. Sharing is a great way to drive traffic to your web site.

## RSS Feeds

| **RSS feed** |
| :--- |
| A special type of content that usually represents recent activity and is subscribable by feed readers. |
| **RSS feed reader** |
| A program that syndicates a number of subscribed feeds into a single consumable list. |

RSS feeds are a very effective way to make your web site more viral, but they are somewhat complicated. *RSS feeds* are a special type of content that are subscribable and that usually display some notion of recent activity. They allow users who are interested in seeing recent activity to subscribe to this recent activity with a feed reader. An *RSS feed reader* is a special type of program that allows users to add RSS feeds that they are interested in subscribing to. Every time one of their RSS feeds has a new item, that item is displayed in a list alongside other new items, allowing the user to effectively read new items from all of their subscriptions in a single consumable list. Some example feed readers are Google Reader, FeedReader.com, and Netvibes.com. Figure 13.4 shows a screen shot of Google Reader.

RSS feeds are most commonly used in news web sites and blogs. However, they also allow other web sites to very easily fetch data from your web site, which means that other web sites can programmatically display your content, making your content visible to a broader audience. RSS feeds provide a "readers digest" version of a web site. They provide a recent snapshot of a web site, and feed readers combine recent snapshots from many different web sites together into a single digest.

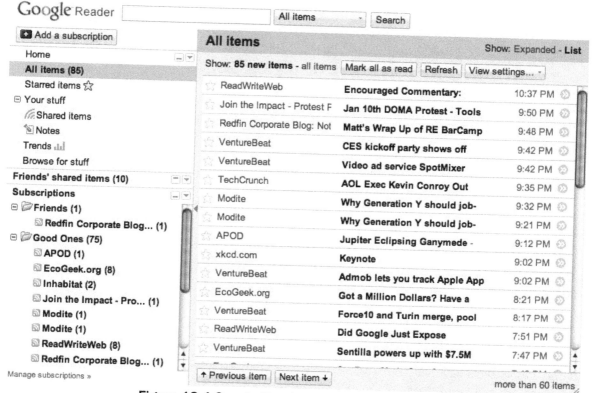

**Figure 13.4 Google Reader (an RSS feed reader)**

RSS feeds allow your users to subscribe to your web site, which effectively keeps them coming back for more. They also allow your data to be more portable, which broadens your audience. Most technologies such as Java, PHP, and Python also provide tools and libraries to create RSS feeds.

### Embedded Features

As was the case with AdWords, you may not have heard of embedded features before, but you have most certainly seen them. *Embedded features* are features of your site that can be included on other web sites. The most known use of this feature is YouTube's ability to let users embed YouTube videos on their web sites. YouTube provides a snippet of HTML code that can merely be copied and pasted into another web site's HTML source code; the copy-pasted HTML is all the user needs to get the video playing on their web site. Embedded features broaden your audience and generate incoming links to your web site, which can drive more traffic and also improve your search engine optimization. Search engine optimization will be covered in detail later in this chapter.

Specific viral features are not always relevant, depending on the goals of your web site. You should decide which of these features is most relevant and include them in your web site. You should also pay close attention to which features are most useful to you and bear this in mind when creating other features. This chapter will also cover ways to determine how users find your web site.

Cellarspot implemented one viral feature: invites. The invite feature noticeably increased the number of registered users we had. Cellarspot didn't launch with the invite feature, because at the time we didn't think it was a priority. However, we convinced ourselves that we needed the invite feature, and its usage proved that viral features can increase traffic to your web site.

## 13.3.3    Search Engine Optimization (SEO)

Nearly all Internet users use search engines as a starting point for finding something on the internet. Studies have also shown that most search engine users consider only the first page of results, which makes having a good search engine ranking very important.

| search engine optimization (SEO) |
| --- |
| The practice of optimizing your web site in such a way that it performs better in search engine rankings. |

*Search engine optimization (SEO)* is the practice of designing your web site in such a way to make it perform better in search engines. A web site that has good SEO will appear high in search engines' search results for keywords relating to that web site. For example, if your web site is about cats, and a search for "cats" on a search engine displays your web site at the very top of the search results, your web site has great SEO. SEO is perhaps the most effective way to drive traffic to your web site.

Search engines succeed when they provide a useful, relevant link to a user who searches for a specific set of keywords. SEO is about understanding how search engines determine relevancy of each web site for a given set of keywords. The catch is that search engines don't always make these techniques publicly available, because they need to stay competitive with other search engines. However, given how important SEO is for a web site, a large amount of research has been done to determine the techniques one should follow to have good SEO.

A few years ago, one of Google's ranking algorithms was discovered and exploited by bloggers on the internet. Thousands of bloggers all linked to <u>whitehouse.gov</u>, which at the time was a biography of President George W. Bush. These bloggers linked with an anchor text of "miserable failure." As a result, searching for "miserable failure" on Google would display <u>whitehouse.gov</u> as the first result. Google changed their search algorithm to not be susceptible to an exploit like this one, which is now known as a *Google bomb*.

Some techniques to improve SEO have to do with the way you design and code your web site, while others focus on how other web sites affect your web site's SEO. Let's first look at the former set of techniques: ways to design and code your web site to improve SEO.

### Descriptive Titles and Headings

An easy way for a search engine to determine the essence of a web site is to analyze the site's `<title>` and `<h1>` tags. These tags are meant to describe the web site in a single sentence, so the keywords used in this sentence are often very similar to the general categorization of the web site itself. For example, if the `<title>` and `<h1>` tags have the words "online," "shopping," and "electronics," then the web site is probably an online technology store. Take a look at the `<title>` of Amazon.com's front page, which at the time of this writing was, "Amazon.com: Online Shopping for Electronics, Apparel, Computers, Books, DVDs & more." Search engines consider the `<title>` and `<h1>` tags to be great descriptors of a site, so make sure these tags describe yours in a concise way.

### Meta Tags

The `<meta>` tag is another easy way for search engines to understand your web site. However, not all meta tags are totally relevant anymore. At the time the HTML specification that introduced meta tags was released, search engines were not capable of analyzing the entire internet and coming up with keyword descriptions of each web site. For this reason, the meta "keywords" tag was necessary to describe a web site according to a few keywords. In today's day and age, all reputable search engines such as Google, Yahoo!, and Live Search can determine the mapping of keywords to web sites by analyzing the actual content of each web site, not just its meta tags. That is, search engines no longer need (nor entirely trust) a site's meta "keywords" tag to determine a site's relevance. However, the meta "description" tag is important for SEO for two reasons. First, it gives a mechanism for a web site owner to describe their web site. And second, it's often used as the text that search engines display on their search results page. You probably want control over this aspect of your site's appearance in the search rankings, so always make sure to use a meta "description" tag on your site's pages.

## Descriptive, Plain, Discoverable Text

More and more web sites these days are written entirely using technologies such as Flash, JavaScript, or images. These web sites, though fancy and fun to use, provide hardly any information to search engines, because search engines are poor at analyzing this kind of content. Search engines are most capable of analyzing plain text found in HTML source code. For this reason, try to avoid making web sites that rely too heavily on images, JavaScript, or Flash to display their core content. Try to have descriptive, plain text on every page. The more consumable content search engines have, the better job they'll do at categorizing your pages.

Search engines also aren't generally able to make Ajax queries. If your entire web site's content is served from an Ajax query, then search engines won't be able to see your content. The solution to using Ajax and providing content to search engines is to use a combination of Ajax and non-Ajax. For example, if your web site has a list that is sortable and searchable with Ajax, make sure that your server-side language populates this list on the first page load. Doing so will give search engines at least part of your list, along with allowing you to provide your users with a fancy Ajax interface. A good rule of thumb when determining what content search engines can and cannot see is to simply view the source of a web site in your browser. You'll notice that you will see the content that was created on the initial page load, and not content that was a result of Ajax queries. The source code that you see when viewing the source of a web site is the same source that a search engine will see.

Search engines aren't able to see content that requires logging in with a user name and/or password. If every page on your web site requires being logged in, search engines won't be able to learn anything about your web site. For this reason, a common practice is to offer two versions of each page: one that is viewable by users that are logged in, and another that is viewable by users that aren't logged in. Typically the version that is viewable by users who aren't logged in is more minimal and exposes only a small amount of the page. Again, offering two versions of every single page is excessive; only offer two versions for pages that you want to affect your SEO.

## Frequent Updates

Most search engines value web sites that are frequently updated more than web sites that are stagnant. For this reason, typically blogs and news sources perform better in search engines. However, update frequency is only a small part of the equation. If you have a really good cat web site, then the chances are good that you'll rank highly in search results even if your web site isn't updated very frequently. Update frequency isn't something you should worry about much when designing your web site; it has been included just for completeness.

The techniques described above have shown ways to improve SEO from a design and code point of view. These techniques are very important, but they aren't the largest factors that affect SEO. The most influencing factor of SEO is the way that other web sites link to your web site. The reason search engines rely on other web sites to gauge your web site is because web site owners can lie about their content. That is, spoofing the `<title>`, `<h1>`, `<meta>` tags, and content of a web site is as easy as changing the HTML. If I run a web site that sells advertisements, I could create a web site that, when described by my tags and content, looks like a web site about the 2008 presidential election. If search engines didn't rely on other web sites to describe my web site, then my advertisement site that really just consists of a lot of meaningless content or ads might be the top search result for searches about the 2008 presidential election. Clearly this is problematic, so by using lots of other web sites to characterize a single web site, search engines are able to create a very accurate categorization for a certain web site, without relying on liar web site owners.

| link analysis |
|---|
| The analysis of incoming and outgoing links for a certain web site. |

Search engines consider two properties when analyzing a web site according to its incoming and outgoing links: PageRank and link anchor text. PageRank and link anchor text are both means of *link analysis*, the task of examining incoming and outgoing links on a page to make conclusions about its content and relevance. Both are discussed in detail in the following sections.

## 13.3.4   PageRank

| PageRank |
|---|
| An algorithm created by Google that assigns relevance to a page based upon the number and relevance of other sites that link to it. |

*PageRank* ranks your web site relative to the rest of the internet, based on the links that point to your web site. PageRank is an algorithm created by Google that revolutionized the search engine industry and is a large reason why Google was significantly better than its competition in its early days. PageRank is one of the largest factors in a web site's search ranking. The algorithm is fairly complex, but the circumstances it creates are easy to understand. In general, web sites with lots of incoming links have better PageRank than web sites that do not have many incoming links. Furthermore, if a web site has incoming links from web sites who themselves have high PageRank, then that web site will have a better PageRank.

To be even more general, your web site will have better ranking if it has lots of incoming links and if those incoming links are coming from web sites with high PageRank. Figure 13.5 shows a graphical representation of PageRank, where each circle represents a web site. The diameter of the circle represents the PageRank for that web site, and the arrows represent links. If an arrow travels from A to B, then this means that web site B has an incoming link from web site A. The diameters are meant to be general comparisons of ranking and are not necessarily drawn "to scale."

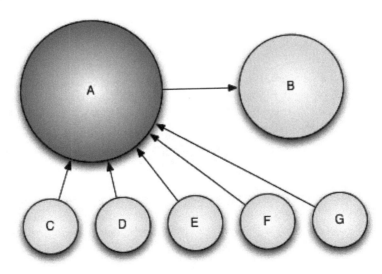

**Figure 13.5 PageRank algorithm**

Notice that web sites C through G have a relatively small PageRank. This is because they do no contain any incoming links. In contrast, web site A has a large PageRank because it contains many incoming links. Similarly, web site B has a large PageRank because its single incoming link comes from web site A, which has a very large PageRank. The reason for web site A having a larger PageRank than web site B is complicated and requires a much deeper understanding of the PageRank algorithm. Consult Wikipedia if you are interested in understanding this difference.

The takeaway from PageRank is that your web site will have significantly better search ranking if it has incoming links and if those incoming links are from reputable web sites. Some companies whose businesses rely on good SEO employ teams of people who literally contact web sites and ask for incoming links from them. Some companies also hire PR firms who try and get news sources and high-profile blogs to write stories about these companies, which generate incoming links. Having a dedicated team or a PR firm getting incoming links for your web site may not be in the cards, but that doesn't mean you won't get incoming links.

If you make a good, useful web site, then you will naturally get links to your web site, either from bloggers who use your site or maybe even from news sites that are interested in your web site for a certain journalism piece. Furthermore, you can try to do the following to improve your PageRank:

- Get friends with blogs to write about your web site, which can help get you started.
- Create embedded features (like YouTube's embedding) and include a link to your web site in the embedded HTML, giving you an incoming link for each site that embeds your feature.
- Try to create incentives for people to link to your web site.

### Incoming Link Anchor Text

PageRank tells search engines the overall rank of a page relative to the rest of the internet, but it doesn't help search engines create keyword mappings for each web site on the internet. For keyword mapping, search engines look at the anchor text of incoming links, because the chances are good that this anchor text will describe the web site being linked to. For example, if I link to CNN with a link that says, "Great News Source," then I've essentially told search engines that my site thinks CNN is a "Great News Source." Search engines value incoming link anchor text very highly when determining the keywords that a certain web site is associated with. That is, the links to your web site from other web sites will largely impact your SEO.

> **anchor text**
>
> The text that is displayed to the user in a hyperlink between the `<a>` and `</a>` tags.

Not only should you strive for incoming links, but you should also push for incoming links with anchor text that matches the keywords that you want your web site to be associated with. For example, if you have a cat web site, then you want incoming links to your web site to have "cat" in the anchor text. Similarly, if you're Amazon.com, then you want incoming links to have an anchor text of "online shopping," etc. Again, search engines value incoming link anchor text highly. Unfortunately you can't usually control incoming link anchor text; instead the web site linking to you controls the link anchor text. However, there are certain situations when you can control the incoming link anchor text. For example, if you create an embedded feature like YouTube videos, then you can include in the embedded HTML a link to your web site with whatever anchor text you want.

External links from other web sites impact SEO greater than incoming links from one of your pages to another. However, the anchor text used in your internal links also helps search engines create a keyword mapping for your web site. For this reason, be thoughtful when choosing the text for links that link to other pages within your web site. For example, try to avoid using anchor texts link like "this," or "here," or "view more." Instead, use links like "More Cat Information," or "See more online shopping results," etc. You'll notice that keyworded anchor text is longer, requiring more space on your web site. Though keyworded anchor text may improve your search rankings, it might also hinder your user experience. You should never let SEO interfere with your web site's ability to be easy to use, because in most cases your users' love for your web site outweighs your SEO.

## "nofollow" Tags

Not all incoming links give you an increase in PageRank. An anchor tag can have a `rel="nofollow"` attribute, which tells search engines to ignore the link entirely. Some places where "nofollow" tags are used are Wikipedia pages, blog comments, and Facebook profiles. If you have an incoming link from Wikipedia, the link will not help your PageRank because Wikipedia adds "nofollow" tags to all of their outgoing links. The "nofollow" tags are primarily in place to hinder spammers. For example, if Wikipedia didn't add "nofollow" tags, then spammers would have a huge incentive to edit Wikipedia by adding useless links to their web sites. These useless links would pollute Wikipedia, making it less useful, while improving SEO for malicious web sites. Generally speaking, incoming links are good, but it's important to realize that not all incoming links help SEO.

Services exist that claim they can increase your search engine performance as long as you pay them a certain price. Some of these services legitimately improve your ranking by the techniques described in this section, and other services are considered malicious and can possibly lower your SEO. It's generally a good idea to not invest money in services that claim to increase your SEO. Instead, pay attention to the techniques described in this section and grow your search ranking for free.

This section has discussed search engine optimization in great detail. SEO should always be in mind when building your web site, because decisions you make can make your web site perform much better in search engines. Just always remember that search engines try to give their users the best results they can, so if you have a good web site, you will probably perform well in search engines. However, following the advice given in this section will only help your search ranking. Always strive for a good ranking, because an unbelievable amount of your traffic can come from search engines. A good tool for evaluating your SEO is Google Webmaster tools; Webmaster tools offers information about your web site ranging from your PageRank to the number of incoming links your web site has, etc. Use the following SEO checklist as reference when building and improving your web site:

- Have a descriptive `<title>` and `<h1>`
- At least use the `<meta>` description tag
- The other `<meta>` tags are useful, but not as important as the description tag
- Make your content available to search engines
- Don't embed content in flash or images
- Be sure that at least some of your content is accessible by users that aren't logged in
- Be careful when using Ajax, Flash, etc.; make sure at least some of your content is loaded on the page load in plain HTML
- Always think about PageRank
- Always think about the anchor text other web sites are using to link to you
- Choose your link anchor text wisely
- Understand "nofollow" tags

At the time we were creating Cellarspot, we didn't know much about SEO. However, as we improved the site, we learned more about it. Later web sites that we built after Cellarspot used these techniques right off the bat, allowing them to grow in traffic much more rapidly than Cellarspot did.

Nearly half of Cellarspot's new visitors came from a search engine. This amazed us and made us realize how important SEO really is. SEO can literally make or break a web site, so thinking about SEO is absolutely essential when you are building a new site. The mechanism we used to measure how many users visited us from search engines will be discussed later in this chapter.

## 13.3.5   Google Analytics

Once you've explored ways to design and drive traffic to your web site, you'll want a way to evaluate your design and understand more about the traffic you're receiving. Being a web site owner and designer, you want to be able to measure traffic in an accurate way to see what features are helping, where users are coming from, and how users are using your web site. Fortunately for web site owners, an unbelievable, free tool is offered by Google called Google Analytics.

> **Google Analytics**
>
> A tool that provides traffic and usage statistics for web sites that have signed up and installed a JavaScript.

*Google Analytics* (GA) is a web site that allows you to track your user's behavior while they are using your web site. GA allows you to understand your user by providing a dashboard of useful statistics, graphs, and data points. GA records usage information about your web site only under two conditions: first, you must sign up for a GA account at http://www.google.com/analytics/, and second, you must insert a small JavaScript at the bottom of every page of your web site. Upon signing up for a GA account, you'll be given the specific JavaScript to include on every page. With an account created and the JavaScript installed, Google manages to generate an incredibly verbose report of your web site. GA gives you the following statistics:

- Number of unique visits per day
- Number of total page views per day
- Breakdown of how users came to your web site (direct, referrals, or search engines)
- Search keywords users searched for when they researched your web site
- Most visited pages
- Average time spent on your web site
- Screen resolutions
- Browsers used
- Operating systems used
- Geographical location, broken down by city, of your users
- Much more

GA allows you to look at the above statistics for any time period. That is, you can look at any of these statistics over any timeframe, such as a single day or a span of many years. Not only does GA give you numerical figures for these metrics, but they also provide attractive, comprehensive graphs. Take a look at the following screen shots of GA for Cellarspot.

Figure 13.6 shows the opening Cellarspot GA dashboard. The large graph you see shows how the number of unique visitors has varied from the time of April 1, 2007 through May 31, 2007. The information below the graph shows high-level, aggregate information about the total site. *Bounce rate* is the percentage of visitors that leave immediately after viewing the first page they see. If a user lands on your web site and leaves immediately without looking at any other pages, they have "bounced."

Figure 13.7 shows the breakdown of visits and how visitors reached Cellarspot. Direct Traffic is traffic that came from users typing "cellarspot.com" into their web browser's address bar. Search Engine traffic is traffic that came from search engines like Google or Yahoo. Referring Sites traffic is traffic that came from other web sites via a link.

Figure 13.8 shows the search keywords that users typed to lead themselves to Cellarspot. This information can be extremely helpful in determining what users were actually interested in that brought them to a site, or what they perceived as being the content of the site.

Figure 13.6 Google Analytics dashboard for Cellarspot

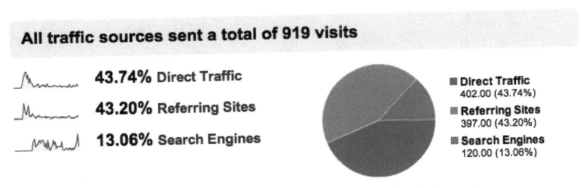

Figure 13.7 Google Analytics traffic sources for Cellarspot

| Dimension: Keyword ⌄ | Visits ↓ | Pages/Visit | Avg. Time on Site | % New Visits | Bounce Rate |
|---|---|---|---|---|---|
| 1.  cellarspot | 84 | 8.31 | 00:04:06 | 13.10% | 9.52% |
| 2.  bossi siena | 9 | 5.78 | 00:04:18 | 11.11% | 33.33% |
| 3.  cuvee napoleon | 7 | 2.71 | 00:04:43 | 14.29% | 57.14% |
| 4.  les charmes chardonnay | 4 | 1.50 | 00:00:59 | 25.00% | 25.00% |
| 5.  "alex loddengaard" | 1 | 3.00 | 00:00:47 | 100.00% | 0.00% |

Figure 13.8 Keywords used to search for Cellarspot

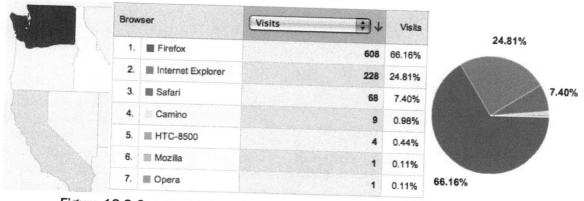

**Figure 13.9 Geographic location and browsers used by Cellarspot visitors**

The power that Google Analytics provides is impressive, especially because it's a completely free service.  GA can be used to greatly refine your web site idea or focus.  For example, you may find that your users spend most of their time on Feature A and very little of their time on Feature B.  With this information, you can focus more of your time on improving Feature A.  Or perhaps you would rather change your web site's design to put more focus on Feature B and less on Feature A.  GA lets you understand your users to a point where you can see what pages they are visiting, how they are finding your web site, and what browsers they are using most.

Google doesn't charge any money for GA because they use its data to better understand the internet and its usage.  Though Google doesn't allow others to see your web site's usage statistics, Google does use the data for internal purposes.  The information is mutually beneficial: both you and Google can learn a lot about how your users use your web site.  Without offering GA for free, Google wouldn't have access to all of this data about internet usage.

Google Analytics can help you understand how effective improvements to your web site are.  You can measure the increase in traffic to your web site both before and after you launch a new feature.  Similarly, you can measure the number of visitors who found your web site from a search engine before you implement a new SEO feature such as an embedded feature.  You can then wait a few weeks and re-measure the number of visitors coming from search engines to see how that feature affected your SEO.  Similar before and after tests can be performed on any metric that may be interesting to you: geographic visits, total visits, visits from a specific keyword, etc.  GA is a perfect medium for understanding the impact certain parts of your web site have on your web site as a whole.

Google Analytics, given that it gives you specific keywords people searched for when they clicked on your web site, can also give you a good understanding of the keywords users are visiting your web site with.  This can be helpful when deciding what your `<title>`, `<h1>`, and any link anchor text should be.  Catering these elements to the keywords users search for to visit your site will only improve your web site's performance for these keywords, which will drive more traffic to your web site.

Google Analytics provided priceless information about Cellarspot.  We learned a number of things ranging from what browsers we needed to support to the types of pages that were most visited from search engines.  We also realized that users didn't often visit the Cellarspot front page first.  Instead, they often landed on pages about wine when they came from search engines.  This made us completely rethink the wine pages.  We needed to provide information about Cellarspot on these pages, otherwise new visitors would most likely leave Cellarspot after they read the information they wanted to read on the wine page.  Cellarspot was once linked to by a popular wine blog, which resulted in a huge traffic spike.  Without GA, we wouldn't have known that we got this link.

## 13.4    Making Money

This section will outline a few simple, common ways for a web site to make money, some of which are available to any web site owner and free to install and get running.

### 13.4.1    Google AdSense

> **Google AdSense**
>
> Google's advertising service that allows you to place ads on your web page and make profits when users click the ads.

*Google AdSense* is an advertising service that displays ads purchased by AdWords customers on your web site. AdWords lets customers buy words for advertising purposes, while AdSense decides which participating web sites should show the ads. AdSense is clever about the ads it displays, only displaying ads that are similar to the content on your web site, but not displaying competitors of your web site. You are paid according to the number of clicks made on the ads displayed on your web site; as mentioned in the AdSense section, this type of advertisement program is known as cost per click, or CPC. The amount each click is worth is dependent on the popularity of your web site and of the web site providing the advertisement. Perhaps you've never heard of AdSense, but you've most certainly seen AdSense ads. Figure 13.10 shows an example of an ad served by Google AdSense.

**Figure 13.10 AdSense advertisements**

AdSense, like Analytics, is free to sign up and easy to install. Upon creating an AdSense account, you design the look and feel of your ads and are given a JavaScript block to place in the page where you want the ads displayed. Once it is installed, you can view statistics about your ads on the AdSense web site such as click rates, dollars made, dollar amount made per month and per day, along with other statistics. To sign up and get started, visit http://www.google.com/adsense/.

The placement of AdSense ads is a key to their success. Ads placed in sections of a web site that users are most likely to notice have a higher chance of being clicked. For example, ads displayed at the top-left of a web site are much more likely to be noticed and clicked on than ads being displayed at the bottom of a page. However, ads that hinder the user's experience on your web site may result in those users becoming annoyed with your web site. There is a balance between placing ads to make money and placing ads not to be intrusive to the user. For this reason, AdSense ads are most commonly installed in the right sidebar of a web site, where users are likely to look but not be annoyed.

> Cellarspot ran several AdSense advertisements on a few different pages. We saw a 0.7% click-through rate (CTR), which means that 0.7% of our displayed ads were clicked on. That probably sounds pretty small, but that's not far off from average CTR on the web. Over the course of about 18 months, we saw 71 clicks and made a whopping profit of $35. The most significantly limiting factor of getting lots of clicks was our small amount of traffic. Generally speaking, with more traffic comes more advertisement clicks. However, having AdSense on Cellarspot was better than not having any ads at all. Installing AdSense was easy, and the ads were not annoying to the users.

## 13.4.2 Referral Programs

*Referral programs* are programs that let web site owners make money by directing users to other web sites. They work in the following way. First, a web site owner signs up to be a referrer for another web site, say Amazon.com. Next, the referred site (Amazon.com in this case) gives the web site owner a special URL that, when linked to, will track whether or not a user came from the web site owner's web site.

> **referral program**
>
> A program that lets web site owners gain a commission on sales that were sent to a given destination from their web site.

The special URL contains a series of query parameters (GET variables), which are what track where a user was referred from. If a referred user purchases something on Amazon.com, then the web site owner will receive a commission on the purchase, usually ranging between 5% and 10%. Many large web sites such as Best Buy, Amazon.com, and many others allow web site owners to sign up for a referral program.

Referral programs are often useful ways to make money. For example, if your web site is a book club social network, then providing a link that allowed your users to purchase the books being discussed would be a very useful service to your users; highly reviewed books will have a good probability of being purchased by your users. Referral programs let you provide a useful service to your users by giving them a clear path to purchasing something, while allowing you to gain a commission on sales. Your users usually won't even know that you're receiving a commission.

Signing up to be a referrer is free and easy, which makes it a low-risk program to be involved with. On the other hand, force-feeding your users links to purchase things can hinder their experience. You should use a referral program only when it's natural and useful for your users to be referred to a product on an e-commerce web site. Often referral programs may even provide the ability to embed product widgets on your web site, making purchasing even easier for your users. Amazon.com is particularly good at providing non-intrusive, useful embedded features to their referrers.

In order to sign up for a referral program, first you must find one that sells products that your users might be interested in. Once you have found a web site that you'd like to be a referrer for, take a look at the very bottom of their web site. Usually web sites offering referral programs will have a link that says something along the lines of, "Become a Referrer," or "Referral Program." For example, today, Amazon.com's referral link says, "Join Associates." Also note that simply having links to Amazon.com will not earn you a commission; you need to be sure to sign up with the referral program and use the special URL that they provide you.

> We signed up to be a referrer for wine.com through a third-party referral company called Link-Share. Our bottle information pages had a link to wine.com to purchase the described bottle. Over the course of 18 months, one of our users purchased a $130 bottle of wine, giving us a $13 sales commission. Friends of ours have done very well with Amazon.com's referral program, some making on the order of hundreds of dollars each month.

## 13.4.3 Banner Advertisements

*Banner advertisements* are images, or possibly animated flash videos, that are displayed on a web site. Banner ads are similar to AdSense ads in that they take real estate on a web site and in return pay to be displayed there. Banner ads differ from AdSense in the way deals are negotiated and in the way the web site owner is compensated. As learned previously, AdSense works on a pay-per-click basis, where the web site owner is paid each time a user clicks on an ad. Banner ads, however, are paid on a cost-per-thousand (*CPM*) basis. That is, advertisers pay a dollar amount for each set of 1000 impressions, or page loads, that their ad is displayed on. If you were wondering, the "M" in CPM comes from the Roman numeral M, for 1000.

> **banner advertisements**
>
> Image or flash-video ads that are displayed on a web site.

**CPM**

An advertisement pricing scheme based on thousands of impressions, or page loads.

CPMs can range anywhere from a few cents to tens or even hundreds of dollars, mostly depending on the popularity of the web site displaying the ads. For example, CNN.com's CPM will be significantly higher than a web site with significantly less reputation and traffic. CPMs also vary depending on the size and placement of the ad, along with the actions of the ads. Popup ads actually cost a lot of money; advertisers pay more for popups than they do for ads that show up in the web site. The reasoning behind having CPMs vary is because some actions grab the user's attention more, hindering their experience. Advertisers, by purchasing popup ads, are essentially paying for the derogated user experience they incur.

Banner ads are most commonly found on large popular web sites. The main reason for this has to do with the way banner ads are bought and sold. In the case of AdSense, Google does all the work to match advertisers with web sites. Banner ads, however, require the web site running the ads to have a sales team to negotiate with advertisers on price, duration, and availability. Banner ads often yield higher revenues, but they also incur an operational cost to sell, get them installed, provide statistics to advertisers, etc. Banner ads require a lot more work, work that should be spent elsewhere in a new, unproven web site. Also worth mentioning is that many people have banner advertisement blockers enabled in their browsers, which means that some users don't even see banner ads.

Cellarspot never ran any banner ads, because we never had the bandwidth to negotiate, install, and coordinate with advertisers. However, if Cellarspot had grown to be a large, popular web site, then we would have hired a sales staff to manage the selling of banner ads. Again, banner ads generally yield more money, mostly because of their pay structure.

I recommend that you start simple with AdSense, and once your web site has proven itself, invest time and money in a program for banner ads. This is the common pattern that most sites follow.

## 13.4.4   Other Options

Though selling ads and participating in referral programs are easy ways to make a web site profitable, there exist plenty of other ways to make money. Some web sites offer simple services for free and charge a fee for their more advanced features. Remember The Milk is structured in this way: users get basic to-do lists for free, but they have to pay a fee for the more advanced features.

Some web sites survive by accepting donations, either by PayPal or some other donations mechanism. The best example of a donations-driven web site is Wikipedia, which is entirely funded by charitable contributions. Lots of businesses also use their web site as a medium for selling a product or service. Netflix is a good example here; they have created a powerful, easy-to-use web site that serves as a portal to their core business, completely rethinking the way movie rentals works.

Though this chapter has made an attempt at offering means for web sites to make money, its recommendations are not comprehensive. There exist plenty of other ways for web sites to make money; the mechanisms discussed in this chapter are the mainstream approaches.

We considered creating a subscription service for Cellarspot. Many of Cellarspot's users are wealthy, older males, who are familiar with subscription services. That is, people who grew up as late as the 1970s have been paying subscriptions for many of their services: magazines, cable TV, stock market news letters, etc. A subscription-only web site wouldn't be too unfamiliar to these users; many of them would be willing to pay, as long as the service they were paying for was worth the fee.

Generation Y, the generation who is growing up in the 1990s and 2000s, will be much less open to paying a subscription fee, mostly because so few web sites these days cost any money to use. Regardless, some web sites make sense to charge a subscription fee. It's up to you as the web site owner to determine what the best approach to making money is.

## 13.4.5 Funding Your Web Site

With any good idea come individuals and organizations interested in investing in that good idea. Web sites are no different than good ideas in this case. Startup companies, some of whose products are web sites, often spend time at their early stages to raise money through a set of investors. Money can come from many different sources, mostly dependent on the type of entity that is receiving the money. In academia, most fundraising comes from research grants. In industry, most fundraising comes from venture capital firms and angel investors. Typically startups use investment money to pay salaries, rent an office, buy office supplies, and pay for infrastructure required to build a solid product. Typically personal project web sites don't need investments, because they can be built in one's free time and require little money to operate. Companies such as Facebook, YouTube, Google, and others received money from venture capitalists when they were first getting started.

> **venture capital (VC)**
>
> Investment money that comes from a venture capital firm, who invests in a company because they see a prominent future in it.

*Venture capital* firms are firms whose job is to determine which startups are probable to succeed, and then to invest large sums of money into that company to help bootstrap their success story. In return for a venture capital's grant of money, the firm receives a significant ownership stake in the company that is being invested in. *Angel investors* are similar to venture capital firms in that they provide money and receive an ownership stake. However, angel investors are wealthy individuals, or groups of wealthy individuals.

> **angel investor**
>
> A wealthy individual or small group of individuals who invest money in companies.

*Research grants* typically come from colleges, non-profit organizations, or other academic entities. They do not usually involve an ownership stake. Instead they are merited on the furthering of an academic area. Generally, angels and venture capital firms invest in companies, while research grants are given to students, research groups, professors, and scientists.

Receiving funding involves a thorough application process. With all three of these mediums, the web site owner must prepare a plan as to how their product will succeed, and why it is important in today's world. Next, a presentation will be given to those interested in investing: a sales pitch. Once a group has agreed to fundraise, terms are agreed upon, and the web site owner receives the money.

Typically investors won't invest money in a company until that company has a comprehensive idea of the business they want to run. Typically investors are interested in seeing a prototype web site as well. Unfortunately, given that so many individuals want to start internet companies, getting access to angels and venture capital firms typically requires that you know someone close to these investors.

You should only take fundraising if you absolutely need to do so. In personal projects, fundraising probably isn't necessary or desired. With fundraising and investing comes pressure and expectation from those who gave you the money. Often with personal projects you don't want obligations; you want fun. In a business, fundraising is necessary to put food on the employees' tables.

Investors, like the rest of the economy, are subject to ups and downs. For example, towards the end of 2008, when the financial crisis seemed to be at its lowest point, venture capital firms decreased the amount of money they were investing by a significant amount. Though some startups were getting funded, the number of funded startups greatly decreased compared to the previous year.

> Cellarspot didn't take any investing, because we always considered it more of a personal project than a business, at least while we were starting. We had hopes to one day become a business and at that time evaluate the need for investing, but our plan was to go as long as possible without looking for fundraising. We paid for our server and its hosting out of our pockets.
>
> Perhaps fundraising would have bettered the financial burden of buying a server and hosting it, but we just wanted to have fun and make something cool. Fundraising can often take the fun out of things with the obligations that come along with receiving someone else's money.

## 13.5 Legal Issues

As if going live with a web site wasn't complicated enough, a few risks, dangers, and obligations should be understood in order to avoid potential legal offenses while you launch and operate a site.

### 13.5.1 Intellectual Property

*Intellectual property (IP)* is thoughts and ideas that are owned by a company or individual. Three of the most common types of IP are copyright, trademarks, and patents.

| **copyright** |
| --- |
| The implicit right of ownership and distribution one gets when creating original content. |

*Copyright* allows the creator of a material entity to maintain ownership over the entity, prohibiting others from stealing or copying that entity. Trademarks allow companies and individuals to claim ownership of logos and phrases to prohibit others from using their branding. Copyright and trademarks are the most common forms of IP on the internet

Copyrights are the rights one has by being the creator of source code, images, or any other content. Copyrights are implicit, meaning that the creator of an entity naturally owns it, even without explicitly filing paperwork. This means that you cannot copy resources from other sites such as source code, images, or text. Doing so will be a violation of copyright law, and depending on the severity of your plagiarism, could result in serious legal action against you. On the other hand, you also do not need to do anything to establish ownership of your web site's source code.

Licenses can be created to accompany intellectual entities, which allow those entities to be used by other people. For example, the Prototype JavaScript framework comes with a license describing the terms under which anyone may use it. Along these same lines, many web sites provide free licensed downloadable icons and images known as *stock images* or stock icons. Examples of these stock icon and image web sites are istockphoto.com and iconbuffet.com. Make sure a license exists whenever you use an intellectual entity, such as source code or an icon, that you didn't create.

| **trademark** |
| --- |
| A legal record of owning a logo, name, or phrase. |

A *trademark* establishes legal ownership over a name, logo, or phrase. Trademarks are like copyrights, except that trademarks have more to do with branding. By registering a trademark on your web site name, no one else is allowed to ever use the same web site name as you. The same fact is true with logos and phrases. For example, T-Mobile has a trademark on the marketing phrase, "Stick Together." This implies that no other company is allowed to use this phrase in marketing a similar product. Trademarks are registered through the United States Patent and Trademarks Office.

Though copyrights and trademarks are significant legal formalities that can impact you as a web site owner, you do not need to worry about them much while you're getting started. Registering a domain name is a good way of protecting your web site's name. Only companies usually apply for trademarks, because trademarks are fairly expensive to apply for, and are overkill in the case of a small, new web site. In general, you should try to choose a name and logo that are unique, and just build a cool web site. You can worry about the copyright and trademark obligations later.

A *patent* allows a company or individual to claim ownership of an idea, where others cannot use their idea, or at least have to pay to use it. Patents will not be discussed in this section, because they are the most complicated of IP. Filing for patents usually costs thousands of dollars in legal fees.

We never registered any trademarks for Cellarspot, because they're neither affordable nor necessary for small web sites. We also created all of our source code, images, and content, so we didn't have to worry about copyrights and licenses. Had we written more JavaScript, we would have probably used either the Prototype or jQuery library, which would have been legal. Each of these libraries comes with a license that allows anyone to use them for free.

## 13.5.2 Legal Liabilities

Believe it or not, but being a web site owner could make you legally liable for illegal activity that occurs on your site, such as copyright violations. Examples of copyright violation are using images, source code, and any other content in your web site that you got from different web site. If you violate copyright in a serious way, such as by creating an identical clone of another web site or by running an illegal software piracy service, then the owner of the copyright you are violating can take you to court. If you are an individual and not a registered company, then your personal assets, such as your laptop, car, or kitchen table can be taken from you if you're not able to pay for the legal penalties that you have accrued by violating copyright. Another interesting example of liability involves users' personal information. If you store your users' personal information and a hacker breaks into your web site and publishes that private data, you'll have a lot of angry customers. Some of them may even attempt to sue you for fraudulent use of that information, such as misuse of credit card numbers.

In order for a web site owner's individual assets to be protected, one must register a company. By registering a company, an individual is essentially putting all obligations on the company instead of on the individual. There exist many different types of companies, such as *Limited Liability Corporations (LLCs)* and corporations, and each of these has different legal requirements. Companies are registered through the state where the business is being run. Typically the process entails lawyers and lots of paperwork.

> **Limited Liability Corporation (LLC)**
>
> A type of registered company that protects its owners' personal assets.

Don't worry; you're really not running a risk by operating a web site. The circumstances when a company would go after an individual's personal assets are very rare. In cases like these, typically the company would spend more money on legal and court fees than they would snagging an individual's assets. That is, a company will nearly always lose money if they go after an individual, depending on that individual's wealth and legal offenses. You, as a good, honest web site owner, are probably safe from legal persecution. In most cases you would get some sort of letter asking you to remove offending content before any legal action would be taken.

> Cellarspot was never registered as a company, because the risk of our personal assets being seized was practically zero. We ran an honest web site, one that didn't use someone else's copyrighted material. Also, none of us had enough assets to make a court battle worth it for anyone.

## 13.5.3 Security Issues

You have an obligation to your users to secure their data as best you can. For this reason, a few measures can be taken to help tighten your web site's security. First, user passwords should never be stored unencrypted in your database. Instead, encrypted hashes should be stored, MD5 hashes being the most popular. An *MD5 hash* is an encrypted version of a normal string that is very difficult to decrypt. Storing a MD5 hash instead of a plain-text password means that when you perform checks to see if a user's login and password match, you'll have to compute a MD5 hash of their password before doing the comparison. Most web languages such as PHP and Python have built-in functions for computing MD5 hashes. Other techniques such as "salting" the MD5 hash can strengthen encrypting even more.

> **MD5 hash**
>
> An encrypted version of a string that is hard to decrypt.

Wireless networks have grown to be very widespread these days, and most people don't realize how insecure they are. A malicious user can very easily see how other users on the same wireless network are accessing the internet. These malicious users can even see the form data that other wireless users submit to unencrypted web sites. For this reason, sensitive input fields in a form such as password fields should be encrypted on the client-side, in JavaScript, before they are submitted. In practice, this means using JavaScript to compute a MD5 hash of a user's password, and submitting the MD5 hash to the form, not the plain text password. Unfortunately, JavaScript does not have a built-in MD5 function. Fortunately, many JavaScript frameworks exist such as jQuery that do provide the MD5 function. Often web sites will use the Secure Sockets Layer (SSL) over HTTPS (Secure HTTP) to encrypt the entire communication between the client and the web site.

Security is a large and complicated topic, one that deserves its own book. You are encouraged to search Google and Wikipedia to learn more about securing a web site, because launching a web site is the real deal. Security issues with your web site can be a major deterrent for your users, making it important for you to do diligence on understanding how your web site may be vulnerable or insecure.

---

Cellarspot generated a plain MD5 hash of a user's password in JavaScript before any form was submitted. Then on the server side, we computed a second MD5 hash, first by "salting" the original hash, before storing the encrypted password in the database. We would perform the same operations when comparing emails and passwords for login purposes. We never had any issues with security, because we were careful to encrypt sensitive information.

Cellarspot, being a social network, also had to follow through in our promises to hide information according to a user's privacy settings. We conducted thorough testing to make sure that a user's privacy settings were accurately depicted in our web site.

Cellarspot was lucky for being a relatively low-traffic site or a small target for hackers. Small web sites often slip under the hacker radar. Hackers typically spend their time being malicious against big web sites such as Google, Amazon.com, etc. The reasoning behind hackers going after large web sites is that if they bring down a large web site, then they can brag that they did so. On the other hand, if a hacker hacked a small web site, then they wouldn't have much to brag about. With that said, we still took security very seriously with Cellarspot. Users trusted us with their data when they signed up, and we had all intentions of keeping our promise of security and privacy.

---

## 13.5.4  Conclusion

With the closing of this chapter, you're now ready to go live with your web site and show the world what you are capable of and what you worked so hard to build. You have learned about many things, ranging from maintaining a web site with log messages to building features that will improve your web site's search engine optimization. The road to learning doesn't end here, though; there is always more to learn, and always more to do.

Just always remember, the true beauty of the internet is its low entry point, the fact that the gap between a personal project and a thriving, widely used web site is smaller than you think. Even if your web site doesn't become one of the internet hotspots, you'll still have gone through an informative, useful process that you will benefit from greatly. Your "startup," if you will, can be put on your resume, used for job interviews, fundraising proposals, and much more. Go live!

---

I wouldn't trade my Cellarspot experience for anything. We didn't make a lot of money or attract a lot of users, but we enjoyed the journey that Cellarspot took us through. I have used Cellarspot as a focal point in many of my software interviews, and most employers are eager to hear more about the work I did. I measure Cellarspot's success on the ways in which it has made me a better programmer, a better project manager, and a better technical person altogether. In this regard, going live with Cellarspot was an invaluable experience, not to mention extremely fun and exciting.

I have told my story. Now it's time for you to tell yours!

# Chapter Summary

- The gap between being a hobbyist web programmer and running a full-fledged, real web site is very small. With the right knowledge, it is very doable to "go live" with your own site.
- Do research by talking to users and examining competitors to ensure your web site will solve a real problem.
- Be thoughtful when deciding on the technologies you use for your web site; some technologies such as Ruby on Rails or Django allow you to write significantly less code. Some web hosts only support certain technologies.
- With regard to hosting, start small and cheap and upgrade as your web site's traffic grows.
- Design your web site in a way that will allow you to more easily debug and test it once you launch it.
- Google AdWords, viral marketing features, and search engine optimization are all good ways to drive more traffic to your web site.
- Google Analytics is a great tool for measuring your web site's traffic and usage.
- Google AdSense, referral programs, and banner advertisements are just a few ways for web sites to make money.
- Fundraising, though not necessary, can help startup web sites get kick started.
- Creating a web site means you have to abide by intellectual property laws and watch out for various legal obligations related to your site's content.

# References

- Wikipedia – Use Case: http://en.wikipedia.org/wiki/Use_case
- Apache Web Server: http://httpd.apache.org/
- Google AdWords: https://adwords.google.com/
- Wikipedia – Search Engine Optimization:
  - http://en.wikipedia.org/wiki/Search_engine_optimization
- Wikipedia – PageRank: http://en.wikipedia.org/wiki/PageRank
- Wikipedia – nofollow: http://en.wikipedia.org/wiki/Nofollow
- Google Analytics: http://www.google.com/analytics/
- Google Webmaster Tools: https://www.google.com/webmasters/tools/
- Google AdSense: https://www.google.com/adsense/
- Wikipedia – Intellectual Property:
  - http://en.wikipedia.org/wiki/Intellectual_property
- Wikipedia – Copyright: http://en.wikipedia.org/wiki/Copyrights
- Wikipedia – Trademark: http://en.wikipedia.org/wiki/Trademark

# Appendix A   Database Design

## A.1  Database Design and Definition

Throughout the SQL chapter we connected to and queried the IMDB database. This database was set up by IMDB and available for us to use. But what if you want to set up your own web application needing an entirely different database – how do you create a database from scratch for your own website? This is what we are going to explore in this appendix.

> **database design**
>
> The process of deciding the structure of a database.

Designing an accurate and consistent relational database is probably the most difficult and important part of using a relational database management system. If you design a database poorly your application can be slow and prone to replicated data and many errors. If your website is slow because of the database or falls over because your database contains bad data, your users will get easily frustrated and stop using your web site. Luckily RDBMSs and relational database design are based on sound theory and there are many books that cover the topic quite thoroughly. This is simply an introduction to key concepts. For a more thorough and complete coverage of database design, please see the reference list at the end of this appendix.

The first step toward creating a database from scratch is to decide what information you actually need to store in your database and how different pieces of information relate to one another. Once you have done that, you then think about how to logically structure that information into tables and how those tables should relate. In other words, what the tables are, what the columns are, and what the keys are. Next you think about how to physically create the structure on your RDBMS or what data types you'll be using. This entire process is called *database design*.

> **data definition language (DDL)**
>
> SQL statements used to create, delete, and edit the structure (i.e. tables, and columns) of a database.

After deciding what data to store and how to structure that data in your database, you use the SQL *data definition language* to create the database and create the tables in the database.

### A.1.1  Relational Database Design

Our two main goals of database design will be to:
1. accurately represent information, and
2. design a database structure that avoids repetitive data and thus data inconsistency.

An additional goal of database designers is to ensure that the database can run queries FAST! We will leave this as an advanced topic and refer you again to the references provided at the end of the appendix to learn how to tune and optimize your database.

Our final product of our design will be a *database schema*. A relational database schema is a description of the tables in a database and how they relate to one another. Specifically, a final database schema will contain:

> **database schema**
>
> The description of the tables in a database along with the relationships between them.

- the name of all tables in a database
- the columns belonging to each table
- the data type of each column, and whether the column allows NULL values

- the primary keys of each table
- any foreign keys referencing other tables

To get a database schema, there are three phases of database design:

1. Conceptual design – the process of determining what information should be stored in the database and what the relationships and dependencies are between the types of information to be stored.
2. Logical design – the process of mapping the information we have identified in the first step to tables, columns, and primary and foreign keys and then checking to see how we are doing in avoiding redundant data and refining our tables from there.
3. Physical design – the process of specifying how the database will be physically created in the RDBMS by choosing appropriate data types for our columns.

## The world Database

We ground our discussion of database design in the following scenario. We have been hired by an international non-profit organization, Ayuda, to design a database schema that stores current information about different countries in the world. For each country, Ayuda wants to store the name of the country in English, the standard, unique three-letter country code (e.g., 'USA' for United States of America), the surface area of the country, as well as what continent the country is in. In order to make decisions on which countries to dedicate aid, Ayuda wants to be able to know if the country is considered developed or undeveloped. Common indicators for how developed a country is are population, average income, and life expectancy. Ayuda is able to provide each country's gross national product and population and those two pieces of data together can be used to calculate average income. Ayuda is additionally interested in storing information about each country's government such as the type of government and the leader of the country.

In order to train its volunteers appropriately, Ayuda needs to know the languages spoken in each country. Ayuda also needs to know whether or not the language is official and what percentage of the population is speaking the language.

Lastly, Ayuda wants to store information about major cities of each country. Specifically, they want be able to store the name of the city, if it is the capital of the country, in what region of the country it resides, and its population.

## Conceptual Design

When starting to design a database, you usually have a scenario like the above. You need to think through what you need to store and why. If you are working with a client, you will likely go back and forth many times to refine what is necessary to store and what isn't. What you store will be dependent on the application you are building so the database design process is very subjective and context dependent – there may be many good database designs for the same database.

Once you have a solid idea of what you need to store and why, you try to identify the entities, attributes, and relationships. An entity is a person, place, event, or concept. An attribute is a characteristic of an entity. Entities will eventually map to tables and attributes will eventually map to columns of the tables. A relationship is how two entities are connected. Depending on the type of relationship, it will be represented by a column in a table or a table itself.

This process of identifying entities, attributes, and relationships is much like designing classes for an object-oriented system – the key difference being that the emphasis is on the relationships between entities instead of the behavior of classes. As in object-oriented programming, you can begin by identifying what the nouns are and whether they are an entity unto themselves or if they are actually a characteristic (i.e. an attribute) of some other entity.

In the description of what is needed for Ayuda's world database we can identify lots of nouns including country, continent, government, leader, population, capital, language, and city. It is fairly obvious that country is an entity with population, gross national product, and life expectancy all being characteristics of the country. It may be a little more difficult to decide whether or not continent should be considered its own entity or an attribute of country. To determine if a piece of data should be stored as an attribute instead of an entity consider if the data: (1) has any characteristics of its own, and (2) can be stored as a single piece of data (e.g., even though addresses usually don't have any attributes of their own, they are frequently considered entities since an address has a house number, street name, city, state, zip code, etc.). Since Ayuda doesn't need to store continent-specific information and since a continent can be stored simply by its name, we consider continent an attribute. Table A.1 presents one way to break down our scenario into entities and attributes.

| Entity (real world object) | Attributes (characteristics of the object) |
|---|---|
| Countries | name, code, surface area, continent, gnp, population, life expectancy, government, leader |
| Languages | name |
| Cities | name, region, population |

**Table A.1 Entities and attributes in the world database**

Next we identify the relationships that connect the entities above. Here is a list of relationships we can identify between countries, languages and cities as given by our scenario:

- A language is spoken in one or more countries.
- A language is an official language of a country.
- A language is spoken by a percentage of the population of the country.
- A city is in one country.
- A capital of a country is a city.

## Logical Design

Our next step is to map entities, attributes, and relationships to tables and columns. As mentioned earlier, entities map to tables, attributes map to columns, and relationships map either to tables or columns depending on the type of relationship. Listing the tables and columns corresponding to our entities and attributes above, simply means changing the column headings of Table A.1 and renaming attributes such that they don't use spaces (column names cannot have spaces).

| Table | Columns |
|---|---|
| Countries | name, code, surface_area, continent, gnp, population, life_expectancy, government, leader |
| Languages | name |
| Cities | name, region, population |

**Table A.2 world database schema version 1**

The next step is to determine what the primary keys of each table will be. Remember that a primary key is an attribute that uniquely identifies each row in a table. The primary key for Countries can simply be its county code as that is unique for each country. Similarly, the primary key for

**Languages** can be its name as there are no two languages with the same name. The trickier table to pick a primary key for is **Cities**. There could be two cities with the same name (e.g., Paris, France and Paris, Texas). We decide on a composite primary key consisting of name and region as there are probably no two distinct cities with the same name in the same region. Table A.3 lists the tables and columns including the proposed primary keys as being underlined column names.

| Table | Columns (primary keys underlined) |
|-------|-----------------------------------|
| Countries | name, <u>code</u>, surface_area, continent, gnp, population, life_expectancy, government, leader |
| Languages | <u>name</u> |
| Cities | <u>name</u>, <u>region</u>, population |

Table A.3 **world** database schema version 2 (with keys)

Now to the trickiest part – mapping relationships. There are several kinds of relationships between entities. Relationships where an entity is only related to only one other entity are the easiest to map. For example, take the "A city is in a country" relationship. Since a city is associated with only one country, we can represent this relationship by simply adding a column to **Cities** that references the country in which the city resides. Similarly, a capital is a kind of city and a country can only have one capital, so we can add a column to **Countries** that references the City that is its capital.

Now to the relationships involving countries and languages. A country can speak many languages and a language can be spoken in many countries. Relationships like these where many of one entity can be associated with many of another entity are stored in a separate "mapping" table that associates the two entities. We create the **CountriesLanguages** table and in it store the attributes related to a language in a country (i.e. whether or not the language is officially recognized and the percentage of the population speaking the language). Table A.4 adds the relationships discussed.

| Table | Columns (primary keys underlined, foreign keys in bold) |
|-------|----------------------------------------------------------|
| Countries | name, <u>code</u>, surface_area, continent, gnp, population, life_expectancy, government, leader, **capital_name**, **capital_region** |
| Languages | <u>name</u> |
| Cities | <u>name</u>, <u>region</u>, population, **country_code** |

Table A.4 **world** database schema version 3 (with relationships)

We now have a proposed list of tables and columns that properly model the data that Ayuda needs to store, but there are two tweaks we can make that make it a better schema. The first is that any time there is a primary key that is made up of more than one column, every table that references that table must store all of those columns (e.g., **Countries** has to store both the name and region of its capital). If this entity is referenced many places in the database it is more space efficient to just propose what is called a surrogate key. This is an extra column that is used to uniquely identify the entity but stores no new information about the entity. For example, we'll introduce a column in **Cities** named **id** to identify a city.

Secondly, the only information stored in **Languages** is the name of the language. For Ayuda, information about a language is only needed if it is associated with a country, so there is no need for a one-column **Languages** table; all language names will already need to be stored in **CountriesLanguages**. Table A.5 includes these tweaks.

| Table | Columns (primary keys underlined, foreign keys in bold) |
|-------|--------------------------------------------------------|
| Countries | name, <u>code</u>, surface_area, continent, gnp, population, life_expectancy, government, head_of_state, **capital** |
| Cities | <u>id</u>, name, region, population, **country_code** |
| CountriesLanguages | **<u>country code</u>**, <u>language</u>, official, percentage |

Table A.5 **world** database schema version 4 (tweaks)

## Normalization

A common mistake many people make (including seasoned web developers) when creating a database is putting too much information in one big table. For example, for the **world** database, why not combine **Countries** and **CountriesLanguages** into a table like in Table A.6?

| name | code | sur-face_are a | conti-nent | gnp | popula-tion | life_expectancy | govern-ment | capi-tal | lan-guage | offi-cial | per-centage |
|------|------|--------|--------|-----|--------|-----------------|-------------|----------|-----------|-----------|-------------|
| Argen-tina | ARG | 2780400 | South America | 340238 | 37032000 | 75.1 | Federal Republic | 69 | Spanish | T | 96.8 |
| Argen-tina | ARG | 2780400 | South America | 340238 | 37032000 | 75.1 | Federal Republic | 69 | Italian | F | 1.7 |
| Argen-tina | ARG | 2780400 | South America | 340238 | 37032000 | 75.1 | Federal Republic | 69 | Indian | F | 0.3 |

Table A.6 **CountrySpeak** combined table (poor design)

This design is redundant. For every country that speaks many languages (and most do), you will be repeating the name, code, surface area, continent, GNP, population, life expectancy, government, head of state, and capital for the country for as many languages as the country speaks.

Repeating data is bad for two reasons. The first is quite obvious: space. The less you repeat the less space you take in the database. Well, these days large hard drives are pretty cheap so for small or mid-sized databases, maybe this isn't such a compelling argument.

A second reason repetition is bad that is slightly less obvious, but even more important: data consistency. When you have repeated data in a table it is very easy to have inconsistencies when you insert, update, and delete data. For example, you could easily mistype inserting 3703200 as the population for one of the rows above. The difference between 37032000 and 3703200 is huge. Now when an Ayuda user wants to know the population of Argentina, which value should they trust (both seem like viable populations for a country)? An update example: when Argentina elects a new president, an Ayuda user could easily forget to update all rows, again leaving the database in an inconsistent state. Lastly, a deletion example: Ayuda decides they no longer want to keep information about languages spoken in Argentina and so they delete all rows. Unintentionally, they have deleted all information about Argentina even though they meant only to delete information about languages spoken in Argentina. In a world where "Data is King", inconsistency is something to be avoided if at all possible.

How can we minimize data duplication and inconsistencies in our schema? The answer is a technique called normalization. There are various levels of normalization and the higher the level the higher the guarantee of consistency. We'll go through the first three levels of normalization; once you get to the third level you are guaranteed to be free of most update, insert, and deletion errors.

A table is at the first level of normalization, also called First Normal Form, if and only if there are no repeated rows (each row has some unique information) and there are no multi-valued columns. It is not uncommon for those who don't have much experience with relational databases to create a database that stores information like in Table A.7.

| name | code | sur-face_area | conti-nent | gnp | popula-tion | life_expectancy | gov-ernment | head_of_state | capi-tal | Languages |
|------|------|--------------|------------|-----|-------------|-----------------|-------------|---------------|----------|-----------|
| Argen-tina | ARG | 2780400 | South America | 340238 | 37032000 | 75.1 | Federal Republic | Christina Fernandez | 69 | Spanish (T, 96.8), Italian (F, 1.7), Indian Languages (F, 0.3) |

**Table A.7 Design for CountrySpeak that is not even in First Normal Form**

*Fields in tables are not meant to store lists.* They are meant to store information about a single, discrete piece of information. Here are a few of the downsides of storing lists in a multi-valued column:

- You might not have anticipated enough space if the list grows too large.
- The basic INSERT, UPDATE, and DELETE statements are not sufficient to manipulate multi-valued columns.
- Web programmers will have to do a lot of string parsing to get information that they need from the list.
- Table name, primary key, and column name do not map to a specific piece of data.

A table is at the second level of normalization, also called Second Normal Form, if and only if it is in First Normal form and the primary key determines all non-key column values. Table A.6 is in First Normal Form, but is not in Second Normal Form because the country code does not determine the value for language, official, or percentage. As discussed above, a table that is not in Second Normal Form is subject to errors on insert, update, and delete.

A table is at the third level of normalization, also called Third Normal Form, if it is in Second Normal Form and all columns are directly dependent on the primary key. A way to remember what Third Normal Form means was given by Bill Kent: every non-key attribute "must provide a fact about the key, the whole key, and nothing but the key so help me Codd" (Codd invented the theoretical basis for relational databases). All tables in the world database schema proposed in Table A.5 is in Third Normal Form as all non-key columns depend on the primary key.

An example of a table in Second Normal Form (but not in Third Normal Form) would be if we added the head of state's date of birth to the Countries table. This is because the date of birth of the head of state relies on the person that is head of state, not on the country. The scenario where this could result in a data inconsistency is if the same person happened to be head of state in two countries at the same time (sounds ridiculous but could be viable if one country invades another), there is nothing to stop the head of state to have two different dates of birth in the two rows. In order to store this additional piece of information and stay in Third Normal Form, we would make a HeadOfState table in which we would store the name and date of birth and then Countries would link to this table through a foreign key. Table A.8 summarizes the three levels of normalization.

| First Normal Form | No duplicate rows and no multi-valued columns (i.e. columns of lists) |
|-------------------|----------------------------------------------------------------------|
| Second Normal Form | In First Normal Form and primary key determines all non-key columns |
| Third Normal Form | In Second Normal Form and all columns are dependent on primary key |

**Table A.8 Three levels of normalization**

## Physical Design

At this stage of the database design process, you should have a good idea of what your tables, columns, and keys will be and that the structure of the database is safe from data duplication and inconsistencies. The last step in the design process is to figure out how the database will physically be configured for the hardware on which it runs. This includes choosing the data types of each table field and optimizing the database. Database tuning and optimization is an advanced topic and is out of the scope of this book, so in this section we will focus on choosing data types for fields.

The data types that are available to you to use are RDBMS-dependent, so we will focus on the data types that MySQL offers. Choosing the appropriate data type for each field in a database is important both in terms of correctness and speed. For example, if a field is always going to be a number, don't represent it as a string data type. MySQL offers a number of data types broken into three categories: numeric, date/time, and strings. Table A.9 lists a few of the most common types.

| MySQL Data Type | Description |
|---|---|
| **Numeric** (http://dev.mysql.com/doc/refman/6.0/en/numeric-types.html) | |
| INT | A 4-byte integer whose signed range is from -2147483648 to 2147483647. |
| BIGINT | An 8-byte integer whose signed range is from -9223372036854775808 to 9223372036854775807. |
| FLOAT(M, D) | A 4-byte floating-point number whose display length is defined by M (default 10) and number of decimals is defined by D (default 2). Decimal precision can go to 24 binary digits (roughly 7 decimal places) for a FLOAT. |
| **Date and Time** (http://dev.mysql.com/doc/refman/6.0/en/date-and-time-types.html) | |
| DATE | A date in YYYY-MM-DD format, between 1000-01-01 and 9999-12-31 |
| DATETIME | A date and time combination in YYYY-MM-DD HH:MM:SS format, between 1000-01-01 00:00:00 and 9999-12-31 23:59:59. |
| **String Types** (http://dev.mysql.com/doc/refman/6.0/en/string-types.html) | |
| CHAR(M) | A fixed-length string between 1 and 255 characters in length (for example CHAR(5)), right-padded with spaces to the specified length when stored. |
| VARCHAR(M) | A variable-length string between 1 and 255 characters in length. |
| BLOB or TEXT | A field with a maximum length of 65535 characters. BLOBs are "Binary Large Objects" and are used to store large amounts of binary data, such as images or other types of files. Fields defined as TEXT also hold large amounts of data; the difference is that sorts and comparisons on stored data are case sensitive on BLOBs and are not case sensitive in TEXT fields. |
| ENUM | A string object with a value chosen from a list of allowed values enumerated explicitly in the column specification at table creation time. |

**Table A.9 Common MySQL data types**

Let's look at a few of the fields in the `Countries` table of the `world` database to get an idea of how data types for fields should be chosen. A country's name is a string of various lengths so we choose `VARCHAR`. To determine the length of the field we ask Ayuda what is the longest name of a country name they want to store information on. Their answer is: South Georgia and the Sandwich Items. This name is 44 bytes long (each character is 1 byte). To be safe we make the data type of the country name `VARCHAR(52)`. The country code is also of string type and is guaranteed to be 3 letters long so we will make it of `CHAR(3)` type.

To determine the data type of the surface area we talk to Ayuda and find out that they want to store the surface area in squared kilometers and down to two decimal places. For this, the default `FLOAT` should suffice.

We know the value in the continent field should be restricted to a list of values for continents, but there are a couple of ways to classify continents. After speaking with Ayuda, they say they want the value of the continent field to be one of Asia, Europe, North America, Africa, Oceania, Antarctica, or South America. So the data type of `continent` will be `ENUM('Asia', 'Europe', 'North America', 'Africa', 'Oceania', 'Antarctica', 'South America')`.

Ayuda wants to store the GNP of a country in terms of millions of dollars. The maximum amount for a GNP can go into the trillions, so we can't use a regular `INT`. One option is to use the `BIGINT` data type which will definitely store the range of values needed for GNP, but is 8 bytes long. Since Ayuda will be storing GNP at the accuracy of millions of dollars, the last six digits of any GNP stored will be zeroes. This is sort of useless information, so instead, we can use the default `FLOAT` type and use only 4 bytes to store the GNP.

### Final World Schema

The final schema for the world database is shown in Table A.10 and Table A.11.

| Countries | |
| --- | --- |
| **Field** | **Type** |
| name | VARCHAR(52) |
| <u>code</u> | CHAR(3) |
| surface_area | FLOAT |
| gnp | FLOAT |
| population | INT |
| life_expectancy | FLOAT(3,1) |
| continent | ENUM('Asia','Europe','North America','Africa', 'Oceania','Antarctica','South America') |
| government | VARCHAR(45) |
| head_of_state | VARCHAR(60) |
| **capital** | INT |

**Table A.10 Final Countries table for world database**
**(primary keys underlined; foreign keys bolded)**

| Cities | |
|---|---|
| **Field** | **Type** |
| <u>id</u> | INT |
| name | VARCHAR(35) |
| region | VARCHAR(20) |
| population | INT |
| **country_code** | CHAR(3) |

| CountriesLanguages | |
|---|---|
| **Field** | **Type** |
| <u>**country_code**</u> | CHAR(3) |
| <u>language</u> | VARCHAR(30) |
| official | ENUM('T', 'F') |
| percentage | FLOAT(4,1) |

**Table A.11** Final `Cities` and `CountriesLanguages` tables for `world` database
(primary keys underlined; foreign keys bolded)

## A.1.2  Data Definition Language

Phew! After all that work figuring out what the columns and tables should be for the `world` database, we are finally ready to actually define them using SQL's Data Definition Language. In MySQL to create database objects you use the **CREATE** keyword and to delete database objects you use the **DROP** keyword. The use of these is normally only permitted for users with high access levels on MySQL server; you might not have permission to use them on your school's server. The syntax to create a new database is shown in Example A.1.

```
CREATE DATABASE databaseName
```

**Example A.1** Syntax for **CREATE  DATABASE** statement

Just as with deleting table rows, you want to be careful when deleting a database because all its information is lost when you delete it. The syntax to delete a database is shown in Example A.2.

```
DROP DATABASE databaseName
```

**Example A.2** Syntax for **DROP  DATABASE** statement

Example A.3 creates a database called `test` and then deletes it in a MySQL client window. The same statements could be performed through a PHP script using the **CREATE** and **DROP** statements as arguments to `mysql_query` just as you would any other SQL statement.

```
mysql> CREATE DATABASE test;
Query OK, 1 row affected (0.00 sec)

mysql> SHOW databases;
+--------------------+
| Database           |
+--------------------+
| imdb               |
| imdb_small         |
| test               |
+--------------------+
11 rows in set (0.00 sec)
```

```
mysql> DROP DATABASE test;
Query OK, 0 rows affected (0.00 sec)

mysql> SHOW databases;
+---------------------+
| Database            |
+---------------------+
| imdb                |
| imdb_small          |
+---------------------+
10 rows in set (0.00 sec)
```

**Example A.3 Using CREATE DATABASE and DROP DATABASE statements**

To create a table in a database, you should first select the database in which you want to create the table using the USE command in the client window or the `mysql_select_db` in a PHP script. The CREATE TABLE statement requires:

- The name of the table
- The names of the columns
- Definition columns for each column, including data type of the column and any optional column properties

The syntax to create a database table is shown in Example A.4.

```
CREATE TABLE tableName (
        column1Name column1Type [column1Properties],
        column2Name column2Type [column2Properties],

        ...,
        columnNName columnNType [columnNProperties],
        PRIMARY KEY (priKeyCol1, priKeyCol2, ..., priKeyColN),
        FOREIGN KEY (columnMName) REFERENCES otherTable (otherColumn))
```

**Example A.4 Syntax for CREATE TABLE Statement**

There are a number of column properties that you can use, but we'll only introduce you to a few. The first is PRIMARY KEY. If the primary key of a table only consists of one column you can use this column property to define a column as being the primary key. If you have a primary key that consists of more than one column you have to use the clause at the bottom. In Example A.5, we define the Countries and Cities tables using the PRIMARY KEY column property, but for the CountriesLanguages table we have to use the PRIMARY KEY clause.

Another frequently used column property is NOT NULL which tells the database that a user cannot insert a row into this table where the value for this column is NULL.

The AUTO_INCREMENT column property can be used with INT and FLOAT types. AUTO_INCREMENT values should not be designated on an INSERT – instead the database automatically assigns the field a value starting at 1 and increments the field by 1 for each additional row added to the table. AUTO_INCREMENT is typically used on surrogate keys.

Example A.5 shows how to create the world database and its tables in a MySQL client.

```
mysql> CREATE DATABASE world;
Query OK, 1 row affected (0.00 sec)

mysql> USE world;
Database changed

mysql> CREATE TABLE Countries (
    -> name VARCHAR(52) NOT NULL,
    -> code CHAR(3) PRIMARY KEY,
    -> surface_area FLOAT,
    -> gnp FLOAT,
    -> population INT,
    -> life_expectancy FLOAT(3, 1),
    -> continent  ENUM('Asia','Europe','North
America','Africa','Oceania','Antarctica','South America') NOT NULL,
    -> government VARCHAR(45),
    -> head_of_state VARCHAR(60),
    -> capital INT,
    -> FOREIGN KEY (capital) REFERENCES City(id));

mysql> CREATE TABLE Cities (
    -> id INT AUTO_INCREMENT PRIMARY KEY,
    -> name VARCHAR(35) NOT NULL,
    -> region VARCHAR(20),
    -> population INT,
    -> country_code CHAR(3) NOT NULL,
    -> FOREIGN KEY (country_code) REFERENCES Country(code));

mysql> CREATE TABLE CountriesLanguages (
    -> country_code CHAR(3),
    -> language VARCHAR(30),
    -> official ENUM('T', 'F'),
    -> percentage FLOAT(4, 1),
    -> PRIMARY KEY (country_code, language),
    -> FOREIGN KEY (country_code) REFERENCES Country(code));
Query OK, 0 rows affected (0.00 sec)
```

**Example A.5 Creating the world database**

There are many more useful statements and components of the MySQL Data Definition Language that is out of the scope of this book. To learn more visit the MySQL Documentation for Data Definition Statements at http://dev.mysql.com/doc/refman/6.0/en/sql-syntax-data-definition.html

## References

- Wikipedia - Database design:    http://en.wikipedia.org/wiki/Database_design
- Wikipedia - Data Definition Language:    http://en.wikipedia.org/wiki/Drop_(SQL)
- Database Design for Mere Mortals:
  - http://www.amazon.com/Database-Design-Mere-Mortals-Hands/dp/0201752840/
- Database Modeling and Design: Logical Design:
  - http://www.amazon.com/Database-Modeling-Design-Kaufmann-Management/dp/0126853525/

# Index